ETHICAL CHALLENGES

INVITATION TO INSIGHTS

SKILL BUILDERS

Looking Out/Looking In

INTERPERSONAL COMMUNICATION

EIGHTH EDITION

RONALD B. ADLER
Santa Barbara City College

NEIL TOWNE
Grossmont College

HARCOURT BRACE COLLEGE PUBLISHERS

FORT WORTH PHILADELPHIA SAN DIEGO NEW YORK ORLANDO AUSTIN SAN ANTONIO
TORONTO MONTREAL LONDON SYDNEY TOKYO

Publisher	Ted Buchholz
Editor in Chief	Christopher P. Klein
Senior Acquisitions Editor	Carol Wada
Developmental Editor	Laurie Runion
Project Editor	John Haakenson
Production Manager	Serena Manning
Art Director	Sue Hart
Text Designer and Photo Permissions	Janet Bollow

Cover Image: Photo illustration by Dan Bryant

ISBN: 0–15–501728–4

Library of Congress Catalog Card Number: 95–075226

Copyright © 1996 by Holt, Rinehart and Winston, Inc.

Requests for permission to make copies of any part of the work should be mailed to: Permissions Department, Harcourt Brace & Company, 6277 Sea Harbor Drive, Orlando, Florida 32887-6777.

Some material in this work previously appeared in *Looking Out, Looking In,* Seventh Edition, copyright © 1993, 1990, 1987, 1984, 1981, 1978, 1975 by Holt, Rinehart and Winston, Inc.

Address for Editorial Correspondence: Harcourt Brace College Publishers, 301 Commerce Street, Suite 3700, Fort Worth, TX 76102.

Address for Orders: Harcourt Brace & Company, 6277 Sea Harbor Drive, Orlando, FL 32887-6777. 1-800-782-4479, or 1-800-433-0001 (in Florida).

(Copyright Acknowledgments begin on page 469, which constitutes a continuation of this copyright page.)

Printed in the United States of America

5 6 7 8 9 0 1 2 3 4   048   0 9 8 7 6 5 4 3 2

$Preface$

Michael Schudson, writing in the *Journal of Communication*, said it well:

> The most obvious and most damning thing about textbooks is that they are boring. Really boring . . . I loved school as a child, but I never met a textbook I wanted to take home with me.[1]

As students we shared Schudson's opinion; and as professors and authors, we've dedicated ourselves to proving that a textbook—at least one about interpersonal communication—doesn't *have* to be boring. You, of course, are the best judge of how well we have succeeded with *Looking Out/Looking In*.

✛ WHAT'S FAMILIAR

Like its predecessors, this edition strives to provide an introduction to interpersonal communication that reflects the fascinating nature and important role of this topic. We have written in a voice that strives to be readable without compromising academic integrity. We've supplemented our words with the work of others—writers, photographers, poets, cartoonists, and artists—believing that their perspectives will support, clarify, and expand on the message contained in the text. We have worked hard to develop an inviting visual design—especially important in an age when the medium affects reception of the message more than ever.

Presenting an interesting, clear introduction to the academic study of interpersonal communication isn't the only goal of *Looking Out/Looking In*. The book also aims at helping readers improve their own communicative competence. Contrary to naive views of effectiveness that students may bring to the course, *Looking Out/Looking In* shows that successful communication does not come from learning a collection of "techniques" that can be used "on" others. Instead, it suggests that competence is a matter of developing a repertoire of skills and then learning to choose the ones that are most appropriate and effective in a given situation. Lest some readers think that communication is a panacea that will lead to living "happily ever after," the book makes it clear that even the most competent communication does not always aim at creating warm, fuzzy relationships. Nonetheless, *Looking Out/Looking In* suggests that even impersonal or adversarial interactions often have the best chance for success when they are handled in a constructive, respectful manner.

Long time users will recognize that this edition retains the basic structure that has served readers well in the past. The number of chapters has remained constant, to allow the book to work within the constraints of an academic term. The order of chapters has also been retained, since there was a wide range of opinions among reviewers about the ideal sequence. As in the past, Chapters 2–10 can be covered in whatever order works best for the individual user.

✛ WHAT'S NEW

Although the approach and structure of this edition resembles its immediate predecessors, it contains a variety of changes that should serve both professors and students. Along with an overall updating of scholarship in every chapter, several other important changes will be apparent.

- The coverage of both gender and cultural influences on communication has been expanded. Separate sections describe the influence of culture on the self-concept (Chapter 2), perception (Chapter 3), emotional expression (Chapter 4), language (Chapter 5), nonverbal rules (Chapter 6), notions of intimacy (Chapter 8), and conflict styles (Chapter 10). Gender differences receive special attention in sections on sex roles (Chapter 3), communication of emotions (Chapter 4), language use (Chapter 5), intimacy and self-disclosure (Chapter 8), and methods of dealing with conflict (Chapter 10). In addition to these textual changes, a new collection of "Looking at Diversity" profiles gives readers an array of interesting first-person accounts from people whose backgrounds show how communication is affected by environment and physical condition.
- The challenge of dealing with dialectical tensions among contradictory goals is introduced in Chapter 1 and addressed throughout the book; especially in Chapter 8, which discusses how communicators must struggle between the apparently incompatible needs for intimacy and distance.
- The discussion of language in Chapter 5 has been reorganized to clarify the many ways in which the symbols we use affect our interaction. A new section on "The Uses (and Abuses) of Language" goes beyond just discussing misunderstandings. It also highlights language that is unnecessarily disruptive, as well as discussing the pros and cons of strategies such as euphemism and equivocation. An expanded discussion of pragmatic rules avoids the simplistic notion that precision alone will promote understanding. Material on "The Language of Responsibility" shows several ways speakers can take responsibility for their thoughts and actions.
- Expanded coverage of topics such as the transactional nature of communication (Chapter 1), uncertainty reduction (Chapter 3), and the pros and cons of various listening styles (Chapter 7), joins new material on subjects such as physical appearance (Chapter 6) and the ethics of indirect communication to expand and clarify how communication operates in everyday life.

- Canadian readers will notice more examples from their country. They will also see that many passages have been rewritten to avoid an excessive focus on the U.S.A. to the exclusion of our neighbors north of the border.

❖ PEDAGOGICAL AIDS

A variety of in-text pedagogical devices should help students learn concepts and develop skill better than ever before.

- **Activities** throughout the book are now identified by their goal. *Invitations to Insight* help readers understand how theory and research conducted by communication scholars apply to their own lives. *Skill Builders* help them improve their communication competence by practicing skills introduced in the book. *Ethical Challenges* highlight some of the dilemmas communicators face as they pursue their own goals.
- **End-of-chapter Resources** have been expanded to help readers take a closer look at topics that seem especially interesting and important. Along with *Readings* (from both scholarly and popular sources), new *Film* suggestions show that art does imitate life, providing an array of engrossing illustrations of interpersonal effectiveness and incompetence.
- **Communication Transcripts** continue to help readers understand how skills introduced in various chapters sound in everyday life. New styles of communication can seem awkward and artificial when first practiced in the classroom: The transcripts show that they can sound both authentic and effective when used by skillful communicators.

❖ RESOURCES FOR INSTRUCTORS AND STUDENTS

Along with the text itself, *Looking Out/ Looking In* is accompanied by an impressive array of materials that help make the book more useful.

- The **Activity Manual and Study Guide** has been thoroughly overhauled by Mary Wiemann. Along with retaining the most successful user-tested activities for classroom and home, the *Guide* now contains materials to help students improve their academic success. Expanded chapter outlines help students relate textbook to class lectures; fill-in-the-blanks exercises review key terms; and self-tests allow students to check their understanding of each chapter before they take graded exams.
- **MicroStudy,** a computerized study program provides an interactive tool for students to test themselves on course material. The program (available in DOS, Windows, and Macintosh formats) contains questions from the Study Guide's self-tests. In addition, instructors may customize the application by adding questions of their own.
- **ExamMaster**, a computerized test generating program makes the task of constructing and printing examinations quicker and easier than ever before. The program contains over 1,200 class-tested questions, and allows instructors to add their own.
- Two **videotapes**, *Understanding Interpersonal Misunderstandings* and *Interpersonal Communication in Action* (prepared by Sharon Ratliffe and David Hudson), show how principles from the text operate in everyday life.
- A comprehensive **Instructor's Manual** offers a wide variety of instructional strategies, course plans, and exercises that are useful for both first-time and experienced instructors. The Manual also contains hard copy of over 1,200 exam questions, indexed by text page number and type of question.
- An extensive set of **color overhead transparencies** helps instructors present concepts from the text in class lectures.

A forthcoming film guide, *Communication in Film: Teaching Communication Courses Using Feature Films*, prepared by Russ Proctor, will describe how a wide array of movies can be used to illustrate how concepts from the text appear in realistic situations. This guide takes advantage of students' inherent interest in the medium of film, showing them how movies can be both entertaining and educational. Harcourt Brace also offers Microsoft® *Cinemania '95*. *Cinemania '95* is your personal guide to the world's films—complete with over 19,000 reviews, video and audio clips, biographies, and cinema insight. This CD ROM software for Macintosh or Windows operating systems can help you locate the movies that will best illustrate the interpersonal concepts you want to teach. This software is available free to adopters and at a significantly reduced price to students.

✛ ACKNOWLEDGMENTS

A project as extensive as *Looking Out/ Looking In* couldn't happen without the hard work and good ideas of many people. The thoughtful suggestions of colleagues helped us know what to keep and what to change in this edition. Thanks go to Dale Ash, Prince George's Community College; Jim Coffey, Monroe Community College; Jeanne Elmhorst, Albuquerque Technical-Vocational Institute; Ray Ewing, Southeast Missouri State University; Julie James, Spokane Community College; Marylin Kelly, McLennan Community College; Shirlee Levin, Charles County Community College; Earl Patterson, Nova University; Joel Reyes, University of Texas–Pan American; Beverly Byrum-Robinson, Wright State University.

We would like to especially thank our Canadian reviewers whose suggestions have helped broaden the scope of this edition of *Looking Out/Looking In:* W. Schultz, University of Manitoba; Janet Whittington, Fanshawe College; Jerry Dion, Mohawk College; Penny Heaslip, University College of the Cariboo; Fred McDonald, Vanier College; Philip Walsh, Algonquin College of Applied Arts; Laurie Papas, Kwantlen College; Barry Caswell, Confederation College; Karen Kemp, Confederation College; Pat Hebert, Fanshawe College; Pam Tobin, Camosun College; Mary-Anna Zelenka, St. Lawrence College; Carol Peters, Grant MacEwan

Community College; Clive Lilwall, Durham College; Betty Barton, Grande Prairie Regional College; Doreen Dotzler, Gardner College of Christian Studies; Michael Douglas, Okanagan University College; E. Simpson, Grant MacEwan Community College; Bill Goss, East Kootenay Community College; Gilles Bourgeois, Frontenac County School Board; J. Arbus, Sault College; Elizabeth Skitmore, Algonquin College; Star Mahara, University College of the Cariboo; C. Elliott, John Abbott College; Lois Rennie, Capilano College; Mary-Jane Brown, Durham College; Wendy Fletcher, Medicine Hut College; Pat Leblanc, Centennial College; Diana Denton, Ryerson Polytechnic University; Gary Anderson, Camosun College; Delsey Hill, Okanagan College; and Lance Moen, Kelsey Institute.

We are especially grateful for the detailed suggestions of Jeanne Elmhorst, Albuquerque Technical-Vocational Institute and Russ Proctor, Northern Kentucky University, whose availability and insights have helped shape our thinking in general, and this edition in particular.

We continue to appreciate the comments of reviewers from earlier editions, whose comments have paid dividends over the years: Ken Green, Kate Katims, Russ Proctor, Sandra Sudweeks, Sarah Trenholm, as well as Roberta Duncan, University of Wyoming; Char Berquist, Bellevue Community College; Robert Johnson, Pensicola Junior College; Miriam Zimmerman, University of San Francisco; Jeanne Elmhorst, Albuquerque Technical-Vocational Institute; Nan Peck, Northern Virginia Community College; Lynn Phelps, Ohio University; Deborah Pearce, Xavier University; Peter Bridge, Champlain College; Paul Aschenbrenner, Hartnell College; Diane M. Hill, University of Rhode Island; Joanne G. Clayton, Davenport College; Sherry J. Holmen, Albuquerque Technical-Vocational Institute; Stephen L. Coffman, Eastern Montana College; Joyce Taylor, City College of San Francisco; David H. W. Smith, Monroe Community College; Dick Stine, Johnson County Community College; Colan T. Hanson, North Dakota State University; David E. Axon, Johnson Community College; Ruth F. Eisenberg, Pace University; Vernon Gantt, Murray State University; M.

Nicholas Gilroy, Bronx Community College; Virginia Katz, University of Minnesota at Duluth; Nancy Lampen, Monroe Community College; Jim Mammarella, San Antonio College; Gerard F. McDade, Community College of Philadelphia; Patsy Meisel, Mankato State University; Ramona Parrish, Virginia Western Community College; Wesley L. Robertson, Jefferson College; and Katherine M. Stannard, Framingham State College.

Our thanks also go to the team of professionals at Harcourt Brace in Fort Worth and Toronto: Carol Wada, Laurie Runion, Pat Murphree, Helen Stimus, John Haakenson, Sue Hart, Serena Manning, and Chris Caperton.

We continue to stand in awe of Janet Bollow's design talents: She has shaped the "look and feel" of the book ever since the first edition, and we know that its success is due in great part to her contributions.

Finally, we gratefully acknowledge the communicators with whom we spend most of our time. Feedback from our students and colleagues has taught us about our own professional communicative competence (and incompetence). Our families have provided a communication laboratory and sanctuary, as well as a model and reminder of just how vitally important interpersonal communication is. We couldn't have written this book without their insights and encouragement.

R.B.A.
N.O.T.

We shall not cease from exploration
And the end of all our exploring
Will be to arrive where we started
And know the place for the first time

T.S. Eliot
Four Quartets
New York: Harcourt Brace, 1943, p. 39

[1]M. Schudson, "Textbook Politics." *Journal of Communication* 44 (Winter 1994): 43-51.

Introduction

Since this is a book about interpersonal communication, it seems important to begin with a personal note. The word "we" you'll be reading in the following pages isn't just an editorial advice: It refers to us; Ron Adler and Neil Towne.

Ron lives in Santa Barbara, California, with his wife, Sherri and their nine-year-old son, Daniel. Their oldest daughter, Robin, has just graduated from college in Oregon, and their other daughter, Rebecca, is a college student in California. Ron couldn't be happier or more proud of his family, and he is convinced that the communication skills and concepts outlined in this book have helped them all over the years.

Ron spends most of his professional time writing and teaching about communication. In addition to helping create *Looking Out/Looking In,* he has contributed to six other books about topics including business communication, public speaking, small group communication, assertiveness, and social skills. Besides writing and teaching, Ron helps professional and business people improve their communication on the job.

Ron enjoys trees, views, old houses, and traveling. He treasures the company of good friends. Running, cycling, collecting rubber stamps, and fiddling with his computer add variety to his life. Ron's biggest challenge is balancing the demands of his career with the other important things in life. His only regret is that there aren't more hours in the day.

Ron Adler

Presently Neil teaches communication classes at Grossmont College, but that is about to change. After nearly four decades in the classroom working, laughing and sometimes crying with his students, he is about to hang it up and move on to his next adventures. These will take him to Northern California where he and his wife Bobbi will build a new home on the shore of beautiful Clear Lake. Although the change will be significant, Neil and Bobbi will most likely continue to help others learn to be better communicators by conducting workshops and teaching the Couple Communication class they developed more than twenty years ago.

When asked if he will miss the teaching, Neil pauses a moment to think and then responds, "I'm sure I will. My students always have been more than generous in letting me know that working

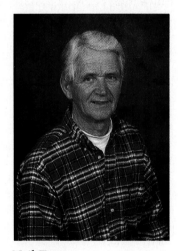

Neil Towne

through a communication course with me has been helpful to them. In recent years I can seldom go to a shopping center without being recognized by a former student who will identify herself or himself and want to reminisce of our time together in speech class. Yes, I'm sure I'll miss these close encounters of the student kind."

Neil is not shy in letting others know of the enjoyment he gets from his teaching, and he often shares his belief that his continual involvement with students keeps him involved and living in the present. Not only students, but also fellow faculty members have affirmed Neil's creditability as an instructor by voting him "distinguished teacher" of the year.

To be accurate, however, you need to know that Neil's greatest love is his family. Bobbi qualifies as his best friend, team communication teacher, accomplished homemaker, gourmet cook, terrific mom and, more recently, outstanding grandmother. Both she and Neil are completely captivated by their grandkids. Colin, Eric and Katie currently make up the crew, but by the time you read this there will be four. The "peace and quiet" that Neil and Bobbi thought they might enjoy when their six "kids" grew up, moved out and started families of their own has never quite materialized, but then they really wouldn't want it any other way. Although they may be exchanging the Pacific Ocean for Clear Lake it's still a given that their life will be awash with adventures, and these will include students, friends, family, writing, communication workshops, singing, church, board meetings, theater, walking and playing—every chance they get.

Brief Contents

Preface v
Introduction ix

Table of Contents

PART ONE

Looking In

C H A P T E R   1

A First Look at Interpersonal Relationships

THE SILENCING

As his name was called, James J. Pelosi, the 452nd West Point cadet of the class of '73, drew in his breath and went to the podium—steeling himself for one last moment of humiliation. The slender, bespectacled young man accepted his diploma, then turned to face the rows of starched white hats and—so he expected—a chorus of boos.

Instead, there was only silence. But when he returned to his classmates, the newly fledged lieutenant was treated to something new—a round of handshakes. "It was just as if I were a person again," he said. Thus ended one of the strangest and most brutal episodes in the long history of the corps.

Nineteen months ago, the Long Island cadet was hauled up before the West Point Honor Committee and charged with cheating on an engineering exam. In spite of conflicting testimony given at his trial and his own determined plea of innocence, the third-year cadet, one of the most respected in his company and himself a candidate for the Honor Committee, was convicted. Pelosi's case was thrown out by the Academy superintendent after his military lawyer proved there had been undue influence over the proceeding by the Honor Committee adviser, but that wasn't the end of it. The Academy honor code reserves a special fate for those thought by the majority to be guilty even when there is insufficient evidence to convict. It is called Silencing.

Pelosi's fellow cadets voted to support the Honor Committee sentence. And so for most of his third and all of his fourth year at West Point, Pelosi was ostracized. He was transferred by the Academy to what one friend called a "straight-strict" company—"one of the toughest in the corps." He ate alone each day at a table for ten; he lived by himself in a room meant for two or three; he endured insult and occasional brickbats tossed in his direction; he saw his mail mutilated and his locker vandalized. And hardly anyone, even a close friend who wept when he heard the Silencing decision, would talk to him in public. Under those conditions, most cadets resign. But even though he lost 26 pounds, Pelosi hung tough. "When you're right," he said later, "you have to prove yourself . . . I told myself I didn't care."

And in the end, James Pelosi survived—one of only a handful of Academy cadets in history to graduate after Silencing. He may even be the last, since six other cadets are now in the process of suing the Academy over its honor system. Now that he is out, and even though he faces the possibility of Silencing by some West Point graduates for the rest of his life if he stays in the Army, Lieutenant Pelosi is almost dispassionate in his criticism of the Academy and his fellow cadets. About as far as he will go is to say that "Silencing should be abolished. It . . . says cadets are above the law. This attitude of superiority bothers me." As for his own state of mind during the ordeal he told NEWSWEEK's Deborah Beers last week: "I've taken a psychology course and I know what isolation does to animals. No one at the Academy asks how it affects a person. Doesn't that seem strange?"

Newsweek Magazine

*P*erhaps you played this game as a child. The group chooses a victim—either as punishment for committing a real or imagined offense, or just for "fun." Then for a period of time, that victim is given the silent treatment. No one speaks to him or her, and no one responds to anything the victim says or does.

If you were the subject of this silent treatment, you probably experienced a range of emotions. At first you might have felt—or at least acted—indifferent. But after a while the strain of being treated as a nonperson probably began to grow. If the game went on long enough, it's likely you found yourself either retreating into a state of depression or lashing out with hostility: partly to show your anger and partly to get a response from the others.

Just like young schoolchildren, the West Point cadets described in "The Silencing" understood the importance of communication. They knew that the company of others is one of the most basic human needs, and that lack of contact is among the cruelest punishments a person can suffer. Besides being emotionally painful, the lack of contact and companionship is so serious that it can affect life itself.

Research demonstrating the importance of communication has existed for centuries. Fredrick II, emperor of Germany from 1196 to 1250, may have been the first social scientist to prove the point systematically. A medieval historian described one of his significant, if inhumane, experiments:

> He bade foster mothers and nurses to suckle the children, to bathe and wash them, but in no way to prattle with them, for he wanted to learn whether they would speak the Hebrew language, which was the oldest, or Greek, or Latin, or Arabic, or perhaps the language of their parents, of whom they had been born. But he labored in vain because all the children died. For they could not live without the petting and joyful faces and loving words of their foster mothers.[1]

Fortunately, contemporary researchers have found less dramatic ways to illustrate the importance of communication. In one study of isolation, subjects were paid to remain alone in a locked room. Of the five subjects, one lasted for eight days. Three held out for two days, one commenting, "Never again." The fifth subject lasted only two hours.[2]

The need for contact and companionship is just as strong outside the laboratory, as individuals who have led solitary lives by choice or necessity have discovered. W. Carl Jackson, an adventurer who sailed across the Atlantic Ocean alone in fifty-one days, summarized the feelings common to most loners:

> I found the loneliness of the second month almost excruciating. I always thought of myself as self-sufficient, but I found life without people had no meaning. I had a definite need for somebody to talk to, someone real, alive, and breathing.[3]

✤ WHY WE COMMUNICATE

You might object to stories like this, claiming that solitude would be a welcome relief from the irritations of everyday life. It's true that all of us need solitude, often more than we get. On the other hand, each of us has a point beyond which we do not *want* to be alone. Beyond this point solitude changes from a pleasurable to a painful condition. In other words, we all need people. We all need to communicate.

PHYSICAL NEEDS

We must love one another or die.

W. H. Auden

Communication is so important that its presence or absence affects physical health. In extreme cases communication can even become a matter of life or death. As a Navy pilot, Captain Eugene McDaniel was shot down over North Vietnam and held as a prisoner of war for six years, often in solitary confinement. In his book *Scars and Stripes*, he says POWs were likely to die much sooner if they couldn't communicate with one another. For this reason, McDaniel describes how he and other prisoners set up clandestine codes in which they sent messages by coughing, laughing, scratching, tapping on walls, and flapping laundry in code to spell out words. The inmates endured torture rather than give up these attempts to communicate. As McDaniel puts it:

> One thing I knew, I had to have communications with my own people here in this camp . . . Communication with each other was what the North Vietnamese captors took the greatest pains to prevent. They knew, as well as I and the others did, that a man could stand more pain if he is linked with others of his own kind in that suffering. The lone, isolated being becomes weak, vulnerable. I knew I had to make contact, no matter what the cost.[4]

The link between communication and physical well-being isn't restricted to prisoners. Medical researchers have identified a wide range of health threats that can result from a lack of close relationships. For instance:

- A lack of social relationships jeopardizes physical well-being to a degree that rivals dangers including cigarette smoking, high blood pressure, blood lipids, obesity, and lack of physical activity.[5]
- Socially isolated people are two to three times more likely to die prematurely than are those with strong social ties. The type of relationship doesn't seem to matter: Marriage, friendship, religious and community ties all seem to increase longevity.[6]
- Divorced men (before age seventy) die from heart disease, cancer, and strokes at double the rate of married men. Three times as many die from hypertension; five times as many commit suicide; seven times as many die from cirrhosis of the liver; and ten times as many die from tuberculosis.[7]
- The rate of all types of cancer is as much as five times higher for divorced men and women, compared to their married counterparts.[8]

■ Poor communication can contribute to coronary disease. One Swedish study examined thirty-two pairs of identical twins. One sibling in each pair had heart disease, whereas the other was healthy. The researchers found that the obesity, smoking habits, and cholesterol levels of the healthy and sick twins did not differ significantly. Among the significant differences, however, were "poor childhood and adult interpersonal relationships": the ability to resolve conflicts and the degree of emotional support given by others.[9]

■ The likelihood of death increases when a close relative dies. In one Welsh village, citizens who had lost a close relative died within one year at a rate more than five times greater than those who had not suffered from a relative's death.[10]

Research like this demonstrates the importance of satisfying personal relationships. Remember: Not everyone needs the same amount of contact, and the quality of communication is almost certainly as important as the quantity. The important point here is that personal communication is essential for our well-being. In other words, "people who need people" aren't "the luckiest people in the world" . . . they're the *only* people!

IDENTITY NEEDS

Communication does more than enable us to survive. It is the way—indeed, the *only* way—we learn who we are. As Chapter Two explains, our sense of identity comes from the way we interact with other people. Are we smart or stupid, attractive or ugly, skillful or inept? The answers to these questions don't come from looking in the mirror. We decide who we are based on how others react to us.

Deprived of communication with others, we would have no sense of identity. In his book *Bridges, Not Walls*, John Stewart dramatically illustrates this fact by citing the case of the famous "Wild Boy of Aveyron," who spent his early childhood without any apparent human contact. The boy was discovered in January 1800 digging for vegetables in a French village garden. He showed no behaviors one would expect in a social human. The boy could not speak but uttered only weird cries. More significant than this absence of social skills was his lack of any identity as a human being. As author Roger Shattuck put it, "The boy had no human sense of being in the world. He had no sense of himself as a person related to other persons."[11] Only with the influence of a loving "mother" did the boy begin to behave—and, we can imagine, think of himself—as a human.

Like the boy of Aveyron, each of us enters the world with little or no sense of identity. We gain an idea of who we are from the way others define us. As Chapter Two explains, the messages we receive in early childhood are the strongest, but the influence of others continues throughout life.

Some scholars have argued that we are most attracted to people who confirm our identity.[12] This confirmation can come in different

> *Whether the consequence of a mental attitude or a living condition, loneliness affects millions, usually for the worse. Death certificates read heart attack, cancer, or suicide; but coroners are missing the point. With no one to love or to love us, we tend to smoke, drink, brood, or simply cry ourselves into earlier graves.*
>
> Don E. Hamachek,
> *Encounters with Others*

forms, depending on the self-image of the communicator. People with relatively high self-esteem seek out others who confirm their value, and as much as possible avoid those who treat them poorly. Conversely, people who regard themselves as unworthy may look for relationships in which others treat them badly. This principle offers one explanation for why some people maintain damaging or unsuccessful relationships. If you view yourself as a loser, you may associate with others who will confirm that self-perception. Of course, relationships can change a communicator's identity as well as confirm it. Supportive relationships can transform feelings of inadequacy into self-respect, and damaging ones can lower self-esteem.

SOCIAL NEEDS

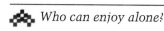

Who can enjoy alone?

John Milton,
Paradise Lost

Besides helping define who we are, communication provides a vital link with others. Researchers and theorists have identified a whole range of social needs we satisfy by communicating: *pleasure* (e.g., "because it's fun," "to have a good time"); **affection** (e.g., "to help others," "to let others know I care"); **inclusion** (e.g., "because I need someone to talk to or be with," "because it makes me less lonely"); *escape* (e.g., "to put off doing something I should be doing"); *relaxation* (e.g., "because it allows me to unwind"); and **control** ("because I want someone to do something for me," "to get something I don't have").[13]

As you look at this list of social motives for communicating, imagine how empty your life would be if these needs weren't satisfied. Then notice that it would be impossible to meet them without communicating with others. Because relationships with others are so vital, some theorists have gone as far as to argue that communication is the primary goal of human existence. Anthropologist Walter Goldschmidt terms the drive for meeting social needs the "human career."[14]

PRACTICAL GOALS

Besides satisfying social needs and shaping our identity, communication is the most widely used approach to satisfying what communication scholars call **instrumental goals:** getting others to behave in ways we want. Some instrumental needs are quite basic: Communication is the tool that lets you tell the hair stylist to take just a little off the sides, makes it possible to negotiate household duties, and enables you to convince the plumber that the broken pipe needs attention *now!*

Other instrumental goals are more important. Career success is the prime example. As Table 1–1 shows, communication skills—the ability to speak and listen effectively—are the top factors in helping college graduates find jobs in an increasingly competitive workplace. Good communication on the job is just as important. Jobs in the late 1990s emphasize service, and so depend heavily on the ability to work well with customers. Economist James Flanigan explains:

**TABLE 1–1 Factors Most Important in Helping
Graduating College Students Obtain Employment**

1. Oral (speaking) communication
2. Listening ability
3. Enthusiasm
4. Written skills
5. Technical competence
6. Appearance
7. Poise
8. Work experience
9. Resume
10. Specific degree held

D.B. Curtis, J.L. Winsor, and R.D. Stephens, "National Preferences in Business and
Communication Education," *Communication Education* 38 (1989): 6–14.

"Communication skills will fetch premium pay. The person who talks on the phone to mutual fund investors will have to be even more knowledgeable, efficient, and personable than the bank teller of old. Competition for such jobs won't be based on pay alone but on skills."[15] The same communication skills are increasingly important for getting along well with fellow workers. Harvard Business School Professor Rosabeth Moss Kanter shows that informal interpersonal relationships are the most dynamic sources of power in organizations today.[16] This means that good personal skills aren't just a social nicety: They can mean the difference between success and failure on the job.

Psychologist Abraham Maslow suggested that human needs such as the preceding fall into five hierarchical categories, each of which must be satisfied before we concern ourselves with the following ones.[17] As you read on, think about the ways in which communication is often necessary to satisfy each need. The most basic of these needs are physical: sufficient air, water, food, and rest, and the ability to reproduce as a species. The second of Maslow's needs involves safety: protection from threats to our well-being. Beyond physical and safety concerns are the social needs we have mentioned already. Even beyond these, Maslow suggests that each of us has **self-esteem** needs: the desire to believe that we are worthwhile, valuable people. The final category of needs described by Maslow involves **self-actualization:** the desire to develop our potential to the maximum, to become the best person we can be.

"If it weren't for the people, the goddamned people," said Finnerty, "always getting tangled up in the machinery. If it weren't for them, earth would be an engineer's paradise."

Kurt Vonnegut, Jr.,
Player Piano

ETHICAL CHALLENGE

ARE WE OUR BROTHER'S AND SISTER'S KEEPER?

As you read on pages 6–9, we communicate in an attempt to meet our own needs. Sometimes, however, our desires are incompatible with those of others.

Think of three situations from your personal experience where your success appears to be another person's loss. For each of these situations, consider your obligation to communicate in a way that helps the other person reach his or her goals. Is it possible to satisfy your own needs and those of others? If not, how do you reconcile conflicting needs?

✛ THE PROCESS OF COMMUNICATION

We've been talking about communication as though the actions described by this word were perfectly clear. Before going further we need to explain exactly what happens when people exchange messages with one another. Doing so will introduce you to a common working vocabulary and, at the same time, preview some of the topics we'll cover in later chapters.

A LINEAR VIEW

As recently as forty years ago, researchers viewed communication as something one person "does" to another.[18] In this **linear communication model,** communication is like giving an injection: a **sender encodes** ideas and feelings into some sort of **message** and then conveys them by means of a **channel** (speech, writing, and so on) into a **receiver,** who **decodes** the message (see Figure 1–1).

This perspective does provide some useful information. For instance, it highlights how different channels can affect the way a receiver responds to a message. Should you say "I love you" in person? Over the phone? By renting space on a billboard? By sending flowers and a card? With a singing telegram? Each channel has its differences.

FIGURE 1–1
Linear communication model

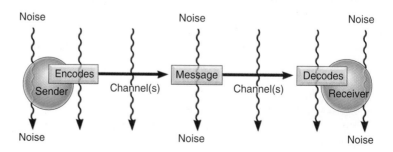

Computer-mediated communication (CMC) offers a good example of how channels affect the way in which people interact. At first, theorists predicted that CMC would be less personal than face-to-face communication. With no nonverbal cues, it seemed that CMC couldn't match the rich interaction that happens in person, or even over the phone. Recent studies, however, have shown that CMC can be just as deep and complex as personal contact.[19]

This research supports the suggestion of Steve Jobs, the co-founder of Apple Computer, that personal computers be renamed *"inter*-personal computers."[20] Sociolinguist Deborah Tannen describes how the computer-mediated channel of electronic mail (e-mail) transformed the quality of two relationships:

> E-mail deepened my friendship with Ralph. Though his office was next to mine, we rarely had extended conversations because he is shy. Face to face he mumbled so, I could barely tell he was speaking. But when we both got on e-mail, I started receiving long, self-revealing messages; we poured our hearts out to each other. A friend discovered that e-mail opened up that kind of communication with her father. He would never talk much on the phone (as her mother would), but they have become close since they both got on line.[21]

The linear model also introduces the concept of **noise**—a term used by social scientists to describe any forces that interfere with effective communication. Noise can occur at every stage of the communication process. Three types of noise can disrupt communication—external, physiological, and psychological. **External noise** (also called "**physical**") includes those factors outside the receiver that make it difficult to hear, as well as many other kinds of distractions. For instance, too much cigarette smoke in a crowded room might make it hard for you to pay attention to another person, and sitting in the rear of an auditorium might make a speaker's remarks unclear. External noise can disrupt communication almost anywhere in our model—in the sender, channel, message, or receiver. **Physiological noise** involves biological factors in the receiver or sender that interfere with accurate reception: illness, fatigue, and so on. **Psychological noise** refers to forces within a communicator that interfere with the ability to express or understand a message accurately. For instance, a fisherman might exaggerate the size and number of the fish he caught in order to convince himself and others of his talents. In the same way, a student might become so upset upon learning that she failed a test that she would be unable (perhaps unwilling is a better word) to understand clearly where she went wrong. Psychological noise is such an important communication problem that we have devoted much of Chapter Nine to investigating its most common form, defensiveness.

AN INTERACTIVE VIEW

Despite its simplicity, the linear view of communication isn't completely accurate. For one thing, it makes the questionable assumption that all communication involves encoding. We certainly do choose symbols to convey most verbal messages. But what about the many nonverbal cues that occur whether or not people speak: facial expressions, gestures, postures, vocal tones, and so on? Cues like these clearly do offer information about others, although they are often unconscious, and thus don't involve encoding. For this reason, it seems more accurate to replace the term *encoding* in our model with the broader label **behavior,** because it describes both deliberate and unintentional actions that can be observed and interpreted.[22]

A more obvious problem of the linear model is its suggestion that communication flows in one direction, from sender to receiver. Although some types of messages (printed and broadcast messages, for example) do flow in a one-way, linear manner, most types of communication—especially the interpersonal variety—are two-way exchanges. To put it differently, the linear view ignores the fact that receivers *react* to messages by sending other messages of their own.

Consider, for instance, the significance of a friend's yawn as you describe your romantic problems. Or imagine the blush you may see as you tell one of your raunchier jokes to a new acquaintance. Nonverbal behaviors like these show that most face-to-face communication is a two-way affair. The discernible response of a receiver to a sender's message is called **feedback.** Not all feedback is nonverbal, of course. Sometimes it is oral, as when you ask an instructor questions about an upcoming test or volunteer your opinion of a friend's new haircut. In other cases it is written, as when you answer the questions on a midterm exam or respond to a letter from a friend. Figure 1–2 makes the importance of feedback clear. It shows that most communication is, indeed, a two-way affair in which we both send and receive messages.

The **interactive communication model** in Figure 1–2 also identifies a clue to the cause of many misunderstandings. Although we naively assume that conversational give-and-take will help people understand one another, your personal experience shows that misunderstandings often occur.* Your constructive suggestion is taken as criticism; your friendly joke is taken as an insult; your hints are missed entirely. Such misunderstandings often arise because communicators often occupy different **environments**—fields of experience that help them understand others' behavior. In communication terminology, environment refers not only to a physical location but also to the personal experiences and cultural background that participants bring to a conversation.

Consider just some of the factors that might contribute to different environments:

A might belong to one ethnic group and B to another;

A might be rich and B poor;

A might be rushed and B have nowhere to go;

A might have lived a long, eventful life and B might be young and inexperienced;

A might be passionately concerned with the subject and B indifferent to it.

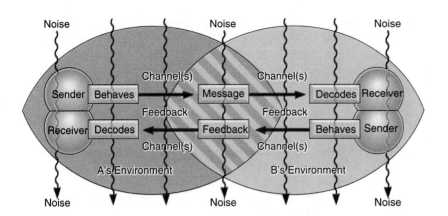

FIGURE 1–2
Interactive communication
model

Environments aren't always obvious. For example, a recent study revealed that college students who have been enrolled in debate classes become more argumentative and verbally aggressive than those who have not been exposed to this environment.[23]

Notice how the model in Figure 1–2 shows that the environments of A and B overlap. This interesting area represents the background that the communicators must have in common. As the shared environment becomes smaller, communication becomes more difficult. Consider a few examples in which different perspectives can make understanding difficult:

Parents (who have trouble recalling their youth) clash with their children (who have never known and cannot appreciate the responsibility that comes with parenting).

Members of a dominant culture (who have never experienced how it feels to be "different") fail to appreciate the concerns of people from nondominant co-cultures (whose own perspectives make it hard to understand the cultural blindness of the majority).

Professors (who have dedicated their professional lives to studying a topic) have a hard time sympathizing with the limited motivation and understanding of some students (whose personal lives and priorities make academic success a relatively low priority).

Differing environments make understanding difficult, but certainly not impossible. Hard work and many of the skills described in this book provide ways to bridge the gap that separates all of us to a greater or lesser degree. For now, recognizing the challenge that comes from dissimilar environments is a good start. You can't solve a problem until you recognize that it exists.

Even with the addition of feedback and environment, the model in Figure 1–2 isn't completely satisfactory. Notice that it portrays communication as a static activity, suggesting that there are discrete "acts" of communication beginning and ending at identifiable times,

---

*As you will learn in Chapters Five and Eight, clarity is not always the goal when people communicate. We often deliberately try to be vague in order to hide our real feelings and to save others from embarrassment.

and that a sender's message causes some effect in a receiver. Furthermore, it suggests that at any given moment a person is either sending or receiving.

A TRANSACTIONAL VIEW

Neither the linear nor the interactive models paints an accurate picture of most types of communication. The activity of communicating is best represented by a **transactional communication model.** There are several ways in which a transactional perspective differs from the more simplistic ones we've already discussed.

First, a transactional model reveals that we usually send and receive messages simultaneously, so that the images of sender and receiver in Figure 1–2 should not be separated as if a person were doing only one or the other, but rather superimposed and redefined as "communicators"[24] (see Figure 1–3). At a given moment we are capable of receiving, **decoding,** and responding to another person's behavior, while at the same time that other person is receiving and responding to ours. Consider, for example, what might occur when you and a housemate negotiate how to handle household chores. As soon as you begin to hear (receive) the words sent by your partner "I want to talk about cleaning the kitchen . . . ," you grimace and clench your jaw (sending a nonverbal message of your own while receiving the verbal one). This reaction leads your partner to interrupt himself, defensively sending a new message: "Now wait a minute. . . . "

Besides illustrating the simultaneous nature of face-to-face interaction, this example shows that it's difficult to isolate a single discrete "act" of communication from the events that precede and follow it. Your partner's comment about cleaning the kitchen (and the way it was presented) probably grew from exchanges you had in the past. Likewise, the way you'll act toward each other in the future depends on the outcome of this conversation. As communication researcher Steve Duck put it, "Relationships are best conceived . . . as unfinished business."[25]

What important truths does the transactional model reveal? Put simply, it shows that communication isn't something we do *to*

FIGURE 1–3
Transactional communication model

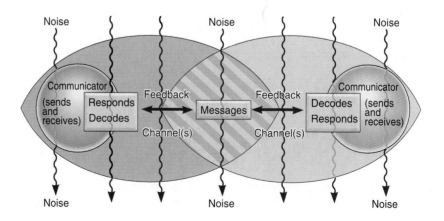

others; rather, it is an activity we do *with* them. In this sense, communication is rather like dancing—at least the kind of dancing we do with partners. Like dancing, communication depends on the involvement of a partner. And like good dancing, successful communication doesn't depend on the skills of just one person. A great dancer who doesn't consider and adapt to the skill level of his or her partner can make both people look bad. In communication and dancing, even two talented partners don't guarantee success. When two skilled dancers perform without coordinating their movements, the results feel bad to the dancers and look foolish to an audience. Finally, relational communication—like dancing—is a unique creation that arises out of the way in which the partners interact. The way you dance probably varies from one partner to another. Likewise, the way you communicate almost certainly varies with different partners.

Psychologist Kenneth Gergen captures the transactional nature of communication well when he points out how our success depends on interaction with others: "One cannot be 'attractive' without others who are attracted, a 'leader' without others willing to follow, or a 'loving person' without others to affirm with appreciation."[26]

The transactional nature of communication shows up dramatically in relationships between parents and their children. We normally think of "good parenting" as a skill that some people possess and others lack. We judge the ability of a mother and father in terms of how well their children turn out. In truth, the question of good parenting isn't quite so clear. Research suggests that the quality of interaction between parents and children is a two-way affair—that children influence parents just as much as the reverse.[27] For example, children who engage in what social scientists call "problematic behavior" evoke more high-control responses from their parents than do cooperative children. By contrast, youngsters with mild temperaments are less likely to provoke coercive reactions by their parents than more aggressive children. Parents with low self-esteem tend to send more messages that weaken the self-esteem of their children, who in turn are likely to act in ways that make the parents feel even worse about themselves. Thus, a mutually reinforcing cycle arises in which parents and children shape one another's feelings and behavior. In cases like this it's at least difficult and probably impossible to identify who is the "sender" and who is the "receiver" of messages. It's more accurate to acknowledge that parents and children—just like husbands and wives, bosses and employees, teachers and students, or any other people who communicate with one another—act in ways that mutually influence one another. The transactional nature of relationships is worth re-emphasizing: We don't communicate *to* others, we communicate *with* them.

By now you can see that a transactional model of communication should be more like a motion picture film than a gallery of still photographs. Although Figure 1–3 does a fair job of picturing the phenomenon we call communication, an animated version in which the environments, communicators, and messages constantly change would be an even better way of capturing the process. You can also

Sometimes she thought the trouble was, she and Leon were too well acquainted. The most innocent remark could call up such a string of associations, so many past slights and insults never quite settled or forgotten, merely smoothed over. They could no longer have a single uncomplicated feeling about one another.

Anne Tyler,
Morgan's Passing

see that communication is not something that people do *to* one another, but a process in which they create a relationship by interacting *with* each other.

Now we can summarize the definition of communication we have been developing. **Communication** is a *continuous, transactional process* involving participants who occupy different but overlapping *environments* and create a relationship by *simultaneously sending and receiving messages,* many of which are distorted by external, physiological, and psychological noise.

INVITATION TO INSIGHT

A MODEL MUDDLE

You can gain more appreciation for the value of communication models by using the one pictured in Figure 1–3 to analyze a communication problem you recently experienced. Which elements described in the model contributed to the problem? What steps might you and the other person or people involved have taken to overcome these difficulties?

✤ COMMUNICATION PRINCIPLES AND MISCONCEPTIONS

Before we look at the qualities that distinguish interpersonal communication, it's important to define what communication is and what it isn't, and to discuss what it can and can't accomplish.

COMMUNICATION PRINCIPLES

It's possible to draw several important conclusions about communication from what you have already learned in this chapter.

COMMUNICATION CAN BE INTENTIONAL OR UNINTENTIONAL People usually plan their words carefully before they ask the boss for a raise or offer a constructive criticism. Not all communication is so deliberate, however.[28] Sooner or later we all carelessly make a comment that would have gone better unsaid. Perhaps you lose your temper and blurt out a remark that you later regret, or maybe your private remarks are overheard by a bystander. In addition to these slips of the tongue, we unintentionally send many nonverbal messages. You might not be aware of your sour expression, impatient shifting, or sign of boredom, but others see them regardless.

IT'S IMPOSSIBLE NOT TO COMMUNICATE Because both deliberate and unintentional behaviors send a message, many theorists agree that it is impossible not to communicate. Whatever you do—whether you speak or remain silent, confront or avoid, act emotional or keep a poker face—you provide information to others about your thoughts and feelings.

Of course, the people who decode your message may not interpret it accurately. They might take your kidding seriously or underestimate your feelings, for example. The message that you intend to convey may not even resemble the one others infer from your actions. Thus, when we talk about "a communication breakdown" or "miscommunication," we rarely mean that communication has ended. Instead, we mean that it is inaccurate or unsatisfying.[29]

This explains why the best way to boost understanding is to discuss your intentions and your interpretations of the other person's behavior until you have negotiated a shared meaning. The perception-checking skills described in Chapter Three of *Looking Out/Looking In* and the listening skills introduced in Chapter Five will give you tools to make sure that the meanings of messages you send and receive are understandable to both you and others.

COMMUNICATION IS IRREVERSIBLE   We sometimes wish that we could back up in time, erasing words or acts and replacing them with better alternatives. Unfortunately, such reversal is impossible. There are occasions when further explanation can clear up another's confusion or when an apology can mollify another's hurt feelings; but in other cases no amount of explanation can erase the impression you have created. Despite the warnings judges issue in jury trials, it's impossible to "unreceive" a message. Words said and deeds done are irretrievable.

COMMUNICATION IS UNREPEATABLE   Because communication is an ongoing process, it is impossible to repeat the same event. The friendly smile that worked so well when meeting a stranger last week might not succeed with the person you encounter tomorrow: It might feel stale and artificial to you the second time around, or it might be wrong for the new person or occasion. Even with the same person, it's impossible to re-create an event. Why? Because neither you nor the other *is* the same person. You've both lived longer. The behavior isn't original. Your feelings about one another may have changed. You need not constantly invent new ways to act around familiar people, but you should realize that the "same" words and behavior are different each time they are spoken or performed. Chapter Eight will alert you to the stages through which a relationship progresses.

COMMUNICATION MISCONCEPTIONS

It's just as important to know what communication is not as to understand what it is.[30] Avoiding the following misconceptions can save you a great deal of personal trouble.

MEANINGS ARE NOT IN WORDS   The biggest mistake we can make is to assume that *saying* something is the same thing as *communicating* it. To use the terminology of our communication model, there's no

A word is not a bird: Once on the wing, it can never be caught again.

Russian proverb

guarantee that a receiver will decode a message in a way that matches the sender's intention. (If you doubt this proposition, list all the times you've been misunderstood in the past week.) Chapter Three outlines the many reasons why people can interpret a statement differently from the way you intended it, and Chapter Five describes the most common types of verbal misunderstandings and suggests ways to minimize them. Chapter Seven introduces listening skills that help ensure that the way you receive messages matches the ideas a speaker is trying to convey.

MORE COMMUNICATION IS NOT ALWAYS BETTER   Whereas not communicating enough can cause problems, there are also situations when *too much* talking is a mistake. Sometimes excessive communication is simply unproductive, as when two people "talk a problem to death," going over the same ground again and again without making progress. There are other times when talking too much actually aggravates a problem. We've all had the experience of "talking ourselves into a hole"—making a bad situation worse by pursuing it too far. As one communication book puts it, "More and more negative communication merely leads to more and more negative results."[31]

There are even times when *no* communication is the best course. Any good salesperson will testify that it's often best to stop talking and let the customer think about the product, and when two people are angry and hurt, they may say things they don't mean and will later regret. In such cases it's probably best to spend time cooling off, thinking about what to say and how to say it. Chapter Four will help you decide when and how to share feelings.

COMMUNICATION WILL NOT SOLVE ALL PROBLEMS   Sometimes even the best-planned, best-timed communication won't solve a problem. Imagine, for example, that you ask an instructor to explain why you received a poor grade on a project you believe deserved top marks. The professor clearly outlines the reasons why you received the low grade and sticks to that position after listening thoughtfully to your protests. Has communication solved the problem? Hardly.

Sometimes clear communication is even the *cause* of problems. Suppose, for example, that a friend asks you for an honest opinion of the $200 outfit he has just bought. Your clear and sincere answer, "I think it makes you look fat," might do more harm than good. Deciding when and how to self-disclose isn't always easy. See Chapter Eight for suggestions.

COMMUNICATION IS NOT A NATURAL ABILITY   Many people assume that communication is an aptitude that people develop without the need for training—rather like breathing. Although almost everyone does manage to function passably without much formal communication training, most people operate at a level of effectiveness far below their potential. In this sense, communication is rather like playing a sport—a skill that can be developed by training and practice.

✛ THE NATURE OF INTERPERSONAL COMMUNICATION

Now that you have a better understanding of the overall process of human communication, it's time to look at what makes some types uniquely interpersonal.

TWO VIEWS OF INTERPERSONAL COMMUNICATION

The most obvious way to define interpersonal communication is by the number of people involved. Indeed, a **contextual definition** of interpersonal communication includes any interaction between two people, usually face-to-face. Social scientists use the term **dyad** to describe two people interacting and they often use the adjective *dyadic* to describe this type of communication. In a contextual sense, the terms *dyadic communication* and *interpersonal communication* can be used interchangeably. Using a contextual definition, a sales-clerk and customer or a police officer ticketing a speeding driver would be examples of interpersonal acts, whereas a teacher and class or a performer and audience would not.

Dyadic communication *is* different from the kind of interaction that occurs in larger groups. For example, two-person exchanges are the earliest form of interaction we experience, and throughout life they are the most common type of communication. Unlike three-somes and other groups, dyads are complete and cannot be subdi-vided. If one person withdraws from the other, the relationship is finished. This indivisibility means that, unlike groups, the partners in a dyad can't form coalitions to get their needs met: They must work matters out with one another.

Despite the unique qualities of dyads, you might object to the contextual definition of interpersonal communication. Consider, for

Having just heard that his dear friend of 25 years had died of a heart attack, stockbroker Bernard Pechter was crying as he drove down Market St. at 6:15 a.m. on his way to work. A policewoman in a patrol car flashed her red lights and motioned him to pull over. She then ordered him out of the car, saying, "You look so sad I figured you need a hug." She held him for a few moments and drove off, leaving Bernard dumbfounded and also open-mouthed. But definitely feeling better.

Herb Caen,
San Francisco *Chronicle*

example, a routine transaction between a salesclerk and customer or the rushed exchange when you ask a stranger on the street for directions. Communication of this sort hardly seems interpersonal . . . or personal in any sense of the word. In fact, after transactions like this we commonly remark, "I might as well have been talking to a machine."

The impersonal nature of some two-person exchanges has led some scholars to argue that quality, not quantity, is what distinguishes interpersonal communication.[32] Using a **qualitative definition,** interpersonal communication occurs when people treat one another as unique individuals, regardless of the context in which the interaction occurs or the number of people involved. When quality of interaction is the criterion, the opposite of impersonal communication is *impersonal interaction,* not group, public, or mass communication.

Martin Buber captured the difference between personal and impersonal relationships in the title of his book *I and Thou.*[33] Buber wrote in German, where the word *Thou* translates into the intimate form of address, *du.* In French and Spanish, the word is *tu.* The familiar and formal ways of saying *you* capture the difference between qualitatively interpersonal and impersonal relationships.[34] In these languages the more intimate pronoun expresses a different kind of relationship—one that ideally possesses some qualities we will now discuss.

Several features distinguish qualitatively interpersonal communication from less personal exchanges.[35] The first is *uniqueness.* Whereas impersonal exchanges are governed by the social rules we learn from parents, teachers, and Miss Manners, the way we communicate in one truly personal relationship is unlike our behavior with anyone else. In one relationship you might exchange good-natured insults, while in another you are careful never to offend your partner. Likewise, you might handle conflicts with one friend or family member by expressing disagreements as soon as they arise, whereas the unwritten rule in another relationship is to withhold resentments until they build up and then clear the air periodically.

A second characteristic of qualitatively interpersonal relationships is *irreplaceability.* Because interpersonal relationships are unique, they can't be replaced. This explains why we usually feel so sad when a close friendship or love affair cools down. We know that no matter how many other relationships fill our lives, none of them will ever be quite like the one that just ended.

Interdependence is a third characteristic of qualitatively interpersonal relationships, where the fate of the partners is connected. You might be able to brush off the anger, affection, excitement, or depression of someone you're not involved with personally, but in an interpersonal relationship the other's life affects you. Sometimes interdependence is a pleasure, and at other times it is a burden. In either case, interdependence is a fact of life in qualitatively interpersonal relationships.

A fourth yardstick of interpersonal relationships is often (though not always) the amount of *disclosure* of personal information. In impersonal relationships we don't reveal much about ourselves, but in interpersonal ones we feel more comfortable sharing our thoughts and feelings. This doesn't mean that all interpersonal relationships are warm and caring, or that all self-disclosure is positive. It's possible to reveal negative, personal information: "I'm really mad at you . . ."

In impersonal communication we seek payoffs that have little to do with the people involved. You listen to professors in class or talk to potential buyers of your used car in order to reach goals that have little to do with developing personal relationships. By contrast, you spend time in qualitatively interpersonal relationships with friends, lovers, and others because of *intrinsic rewards* that come from your communication. It doesn't matter *what* you talk about: Developing the relationship is what's important.

Qualitatively interpersonal communication is relatively scarce. We chat pleasantly with shopkeepers or fellow passengers on the bus or plane; we discuss the weather or current events with most class-mates and neighbors; we deal with co-workers and teachers in a polite way, but considering the number of people with whom we communicate, personal relationships are by far in the minority.

The rarity of personal relationships isn't necessarily unfortunate. Most of us don't have the time or energy to create personal relationships with everyone we encounter. In fact, the scarcity of qualitatively interpersonal communication contributes to its value. Like precious jewels and one-of-a-kind artwork, interpersonal relationships are special because of their scarcity.

> *To know all your neighbors on the global level does not mean that you will automatically love them all; it does not, in and of itself, introduce a reign of peace and brotherhood. But to be potentially in touch with everybody at least makes fighting more uncomfortable. It becomes easier to argue instead.*
>
> Isaac Asimov,
> "The Fourth Revolution"

PERSONAL AND IMPERSONAL COMMUNICATION: A MATTER OF BALANCE

Now that you understand the differences between qualitatively inter-personal and impersonal communication, we need to ask some important questions. Is interpersonal communication better than the impersonal variety? Is more interpersonal communication the goal?

Most relationships aren't *either* interpersonal *or* impersonal. Rather, they fall somewhere on a continuum between these two extremes. Consider your own communication and you'll find that there is often a personal element in even the most impersonal situations. You might appreciate the unique sense of humor of a grocery checker or spend a few moments sharing private thoughts with the person cutting your hair. And even the most tyrannical, demanding, by-the-book boss might show an occasional flash of humanity.

Just as there's a personal element in many impersonal settings, there is also an impersonal side to our relationships with the people we care most about. There are occasions when we don't want to be personal: when we're distracted, tired, or busy, or just not interested. In fact, interpersonal communication is rather like rich food—it's fine in moderation, but too much can make you uncomfortable.

Along with the daily mix of personal and impersonal messages in our daily interaction with the people we are closest to, the nature of our relationships can change over time. The communication between young lovers who only talk about their feelings may change as their relationship develops, so that several years later their communication has become more routine and ritualized, and the percentage of time they spend on personal, relational issues drops and the conversation about less intimate topics increases. Chapter Eight discusses how communication changes as relationships pass through various stages, as well as describes the role of self-disclosure in keeping those relationships strong. As you read this information, you will see even more clearly that, while interpersonal communication can make life worth living, it isn't possible or desirable all the time.

It's clear that there is a place in our lives for both impersonal and interpersonal communication. Each type has its uses. The real challenge, then, is to find the right balance between the two types.

INVITATION TO INSIGHT

HOW PERSONAL ARE YOUR RELATIONSHIPS?

Use the characteristics of qualitatively interpersonal communication described on pages 20–21 to think about your own relationships. Make a list of several people who are "close" to you—family members, people you live with, friends, co-workers, and so on.

How would you rate these relationships on each of the scales below? After completing the exercise, ask yourself the important question: How satisfied are you with the answers you have found?

Uniqueness

1	2	3	4	5
Unique				Standardized, habitual

Replaceability

1	2	3	4	5
Replaceable				Irreplaceable

Dependence

1	2	3	4	5
Independent				Interdependent

Disclosure

1	2	3	4	5
Low disclosure				High disclosure

✦ COMMUNICATING ABOUT RELATIONSHIPS

By now you understand the characteristics that distinguish interpersonal relationships. But what kinds of messages do we exchange as we define our relationships?

CONTENT AND RELATIONAL MESSAGES

Virtually every verbal statement has a **content** dimension, containing the subject being discussed. The content of such statements as "It's your turn to do the dishes" or "I'm busy Saturday night" is obvious.

Content messages aren't the only thing being exchanged when two people communicate. In addition, almost every message—both verbal and nonverbal—also has a second, **relational** dimension, which makes statements about how the parties feel toward one another.[36] These relational messages deal with one or more social needs, most commonly control, affection, or respect. Consider the two examples we just mentioned:

■ Imagine two ways of saying "It's your turn to do the dishes": one that is demanding and another that is matter-of-fact. Notice how the different nonverbal messages make statements about how the sender views control in this part of the relationship. The demanding tone says, in effect, "I have a right to tell you what to do around the house," whereas the matter-of-fact one suggests, "I'm just reminding you of something you might have overlooked."
■ You can easily visualize two ways to deliver the statement "I'm busy Saturday night": one with little affection and the other with much liking.

Notice that in each of these examples the relational dimension of the message was never discussed. In fact, most of the time we aren't conscious of the many relational messages that bombard us every day. Sometimes we are unaware of relational messages because they match our belief about the amount of respect, control, and affection that is appropriate. For example, you probably won't be offended if your boss tells you to do a certain job because you agree that supervisors have the right to direct employees. In other cases, however, conflicts arise over relational messages even though content is not disputed. If your boss delivers the order in a condescending, sarcastic, or abusive tone of voice, you probably will be offended. Your complaint wouldn't be with the order itself but with the way it was delivered. "I may work for this company," you might think, "but I'm not a slave or an idiot. I deserve to be treated like a human being."

How are relational messages communicated? As the boss–employee example suggests, they are usually expressed nonverbally. To test this fact for yourself, imagine how you could act while saying,

"Can you help me for a minute?" in a way that communicates each of the following relationships:

| superiority | friendliness | sexual desire |
| helplessness | aloofness | irritation |

Although nonverbal behaviors are a good source of relational messages, they are ambiguous. The sharp tone you take as a personal insult might be due to fatigue, and the interruption you assume is an attempt to ignore your ideas might be a sign of pressure that has nothing to do with you. Before you jump to conclusions about relational clues, it's a good idea to check them out verbally. Chapter Three will introduce you to the skill of perception checking—a useful tool for verifying your hunches about nonverbal behavior.

METACOMMUNICATION

Not all relational messages are nonverbal. Social scientists use the term **metacommunication** to describe messages people exchange about their relationship. In other words, metacommunication is communication about communication. Whenever we discuss a relationship with others, we are metacommunicating: "I wish we could stop arguing so much" or "I appreciate how honest you've been with me." Verbal metacommunication is an essential ingredient in successful relationships. Sooner or later there are times when it becomes necessary to talk about what is going on between you and the other person. The ability to focus on the kinds of issues described in this chapter can be the tool for keeping the relationship on track.

Metacommunication is an important method for solving conflicts in a constructive manner. It provides a way to shift discussion from the content level to relational questions, where the problem often lies. For example, consider the conversation between Macon and Muriel in the Communication Transcript. Imagine how the discussion might have been more productive if they had focused on the relational issue of Macon's commitment to Muriel and her son. By sticking to the content level—the boy's math skill—Muriel avoided the kind of metacommunication that is often necessary to keep relationships healthy.

Metacommunication isn't just a tool for handling problems. It is also a way to reinforce the good aspects of a relationship: "I really appreciate it when you compliment me about my work in front of the boss." Comments like this serve two functions: First, they let others know that you value their behavior; second, they boost the odds that the other person will continue the behavior in the future.

Despite the benefits of metacommunication, bringing relational issues out in the open does have its risks. Discussing problems can be interpreted in two ways. On one hand, the other person might see it in a positive light—"Our relationship is working because we can still talk things out." On the other hand, your desire to focus on the relationship might look like a bad omen—"Our relationship isn't working if we have to keep talking it over."[37] Furthermore, metacommunication does involve a certain degree of analysis ("It seems

Communication Transcript

CONTENT AND RELATIONAL MESSAGES

Both content and relational communication are important. But when each person in a conversation focuses on a different level, problems are likely to arise. In this excerpt from Anne Tyler's novel The Accidental Tourist, *Muriel tries to turn Macon's content-related remark about her son into a discussion about the future of their relationship. Until Macon and Muriel agree about whether they will focus on content or relational issues, they are likely to remain at an uncomfortable impasse.*

"I don't think Alexander's getting a proper education," he said to her one evening.

"Oh, he's okay."

"I asked him to figure what change they'd give back when we bought the milk today, and he didn't have the faintest idea. He didn't even know he'd have to subtract."

"Well, he's only in second grade," Muriel said.

"I think he ought to switch to a private school."

"Private schools cost money."

"So? I'll pay."

She stopped flipping the bacon and looked over at him. "What are you saying?" she asked.

"Pardon?"

"What are you saying, Macon? Are you saying you're committed?"

Macon cleared his throat. He said, "Committed."

"Alexander's got ten more years of school ahead of him. Are you saying you'll be around for all ten years?"

"Um . . . "

"I can't just put him in a school and take him out again with every passing whim of yours."

He was silent.

"Just tell me this much," she said. "Do you picture us getting married sometime? I mean when your divorce comes through?"

He said, "Oh, well, marriage, Muriel . . . "

"You don't, do you. You don't know *what* you want. One minute you like me and the next you don't. One minute you're ashamed to be seen with me and the next you think I'm the best thing that ever happened to you."

He stared at her. He had never guessed that she read him so clearly.

"You think you can just drift along like this, day by day, no plans," she said. "Maybe tomorrow you'll be here, maybe you won't. Maybe you'll just go on back to Sarah. Oh yes! I saw you at Rose's wedding. Don't think I didn't see how you and Sarah looked at each other."

Macon said, "All I'm saying is—"

"All *I'm* saying," Muriel told him, "is take care what you promise my son. Don't go making him promises you don't intend to keep."

"But I just want him to learn to subtract!" he said.

Anne Tyler,
The Accidental Tourist

like you're angry with me"), and some people resent being analyzed. These cautions don't mean verbal metacommunication is a bad idea. They do suggest, though, that it's a tool that needs to be used carefully.

TYPES OF RELATIONAL MESSAGES

The number and variety of content messages is almost infinite, ranging from black holes to doughnut holes, from rock-and-roll to the Rock of Ages. But unlike the range of content messages, there are surprisingly few kinds of relational messages. Virtually all of them fit into one of three categories.

AFFINITY   An important kind of relational communication involves **affinity**—the degree to which people like or appreciate one another. Not all affinity messages are positive: A glare or an angry word shows the level of liking just as clearly as a smile or profession of love. The range of affinity messages shows that interpersonal relationships aren't always friendly. Friends who disagree or lovers who argue are still partners. As long as these relationships possess all the characteristics that distinguish them as interpersonal—uniqueness, irreplaceability, interdependence, and so on—we can say they are interpersonal. In this sense, liking and disliking (both signs that we *care* about the other person) are much more closely related to one another than either is to indifference.

RESPECT   At first glance respect might seem identical to affinity, but the two attitudes are different.[38] It's possible to like others without respecting them. For instance, you might like—or even probably love—your two-year-old cousin without respecting her. In the same way, you might have a great deal of affection for some friends, yet not respect the way they behave. The reverse is also true: It's possible to respect people we don't like. You might hold an acquaintance in high esteem for being a hard worker, honest, talented, or clever—yet not particularly enjoy that person's company.

Sometimes being respected is more important than being liked. Think about occasions in school when you were offended because an instructor or fellow students didn't seem to take your comments or questions seriously. The same principle holds on the job, where having your opinions count often means more than being popular. Even in more personal relationships, conflicts often focus on the issue of respect. Being taken seriously is a vital ingredient of self-esteem.

"You say, 'off with her head,' but what I'm hearing is, 'I feel neglected.'"
Drawing by Mike Ewers. Reprinted by permission

CONTROL   A final way to look at relationships involves he question of control—the degree to which the parties in a relationship have the power to influence one another.

Types of Control   Communication researchers have commonly identified the balance of relational control in two ways. **Decision control** revolves around who has the power to determine what will happen in the relationship. What will we do Saturday night? Shall we use our savings to fix up the house or to take a vacation? How much time should we spend together and how much should we spend apart? As these examples suggest, some decisions are small, whereas others are major. It's important to realize that even the smallest decisions reveal something about the balance of power in the relationship.

A very different way to see how partners influence one another is to examine **conversational control.** Some common indicators of conversational control include who talks the most, who interrupts whom, and who changes the topic most often.[39] The person who exercises the greatest amount of conversational control doesn't always make decisions. A roommate who chatters constantly might not persuade you to accept his beliefs. Nonetheless, the ability to determine who talks about what does constitute one type of influence.

Distribution of Control   Control can be distributed in three ways within a relationship.[40] As you read each of these ways, decide which pattern describes each of your relationships.

A **complementary relationship** exists when the distribution of power is unequal. One partner says, "Let's go dancing tonight," and the other says, "Fine." The boss asks several employees to work late, and they all agree. You know your friend has been feeling low lately,

and so you're willing to listen to her problems—even though you have other things to do.

In complementary situations like these, one party exercises control and the other is willing to go along. This structure explains why the controller is often labeled in communication jargon as "one up," whereas the party who is being controlled is termed "one down." As long as both parties are comfortable with their roles, a complementary relationship can be stable. On the other hand, relational problems are guaranteed if both parties struggle to occupy one-up positions.

Whereas power is unequal in complementary relationships, in a **symmetrical relationship** the partners seek an equal amount of control. There are three types of symmetry.[41] The first is **competitive symmetry,** where both parties strive to gain control—to be in a one-up position. You can probably recall many situations where you and another person struggled for this sort of control. By contrast, in a relationship characterized by **submissive symmetry,** the participants are both trying to be one-down and not dominate the other person. At first the idea of two partners striving to give up control may seem odd, but it is really quite common. Consider, for example, a couple discussing what to do during their evening out. "I don't care," one says, "whatever you want." The other replies, "I don't care either. Anything is fine with me." It's easy to imagine how this sort of conversation could go on for some time—and how it could characterize some relationships. **Neutralized symmetry** is quite different from the competitive and submissive varieties. In this sort of relationship, there are no clear one-up and one-down messages. Both parties agree on the desirability of being equal. Although neutralized symmetry sounds like the best approach, it isn't always practical or necessary. On trivial issues (what to eat for dinner, whether to buy green or yellow tennis balls) equal decision making often isn't worth the effort. On major issues (whether to move to a new city, how many children to have) it may not be possible. Despite these difficulties, the shared power of a symmetrical relationship is a goal in many relationships, especially for "modern" couples who object to the unequal, complementary power structure of traditional marriages.

Unlike the lopsidedness of complementary relationships and the total equality of symmetrical ones, **parallel relationships** handle power in a much more fluid way. Partners shift between one-up controlling positions and one-down roles, so that each person leads in some areas and shares power equally in many situations. John may handle the decisions about car repairs and menu planning, as well as taking the spotlight at parties with their friends. Mary manages the finances and makes most of the decisions about child care, as well as controlling the conversation when she and John are alone. When a decision is very important to one partner, the other willingly gives in, knowing that the favor will be returned later. When issues are important to both partners, they try to share power equally. But when an impasse occurs, each will make concessions in a way that keeps the overall balance of power equal.

CONTENT AND RELATIONSHIP, CULTURE AND GENDER

Many Americans, especially (but not only) American men, place more emphasis on their need for independence and less on their need for social involvement. This often entails paying less attention to the metamessage level of talk—the level that comments on relationships—focusing instead on the information level. The attitude may go as far as the conviction that only the information level really counts—or is really there. It is then a logical conclusion that talk not rich in information should be dispensed with. Thus, many daughters and sons of all ages, calling their parents, find that their fathers want to exchange whatever information is needed and then hang up, but their mothers want to chat, to "keep in touch."

American men's information-focused approach to talk has shaped the American way of doing business. Most Americans think it's best to "get down to brass tacks" as soon as possible, and not "waste time" in small talk (social talk) or "beating around the bush." But this doesn't work very well in business dealings with Greek, Japanese, or Arab counterparts for whom "small talk" is necessary to establish the social relationship that must provide the foundation for conducting business.

Another expression of this difference—one that costs American tourists huge amounts of money—is our inability to understand the logic behind bargaining. If the African, Indian, Arab, South American, or Mediterranean seller wants to sell a product, and the tourist wants to buy it, why not set a fair price and let the sale proceed? Because the sale is only one part of the interaction. Just as important, if not more so, is the interaction that goes on during bargaining: an artful way for buyer and seller to reaffirm their recognition that they're dealing with—and that they are—humans, not machines.

Deborah Tannen,
That's Not What I Meant!

INVITATION TO INSIGHT

MEASURING YOUR RELATIONSHIPS

What kinds of relational messages do you communicate? What do they say about your relationship with others? You can find out by following these steps.

1. Choose an important interpersonal relationship.

2. Place your initials on each of the scales below to represent the kinds of relational messages you communicate to the other person. Be prepared to offer specific examples of situations that illustrate this type of relational communication.

3. Place your partner's initials on each scale representing your perception of his or her relational messages, and be prepared to offer examples to back up your choices.

4. Invite your partner to complete steps 2 and 3, using a different color ink to distinguish his or her responses from yours.

5. Now compare your answers with your partner's, and answer the following questions:

   a. Are your responses similar or different? If they differ, whose perception is more accurate?

   b. Are you satisfied with the relationship as it is described here? If not, what can you do to improve it?

Low		High
	AFFINITY	
Low		**High**
	RESPECT	
Complementary	**Parallel**	**Symmetrical***
	CONTROL	

*Specify whether the relationship is characterized by competitive, submissive, or neutralized symmetry. If the relationship is neutrally symmetrical or parallel, describe the areas in which each has primary control.

✤ COMMUNICATION COMPETENCE: WHAT MAKES AN EFFECTIVE COMMUNICATOR?

It's easy to recognize good communicators, and even easier to spot poor ones. But what are the characteristics that distinguish effective communicators from their less successful counterparts? Answering this question has been one of the leading challenges for communication scholars.[42] Although all the answers aren't yet in, research has identified a great deal of important and useful information about communication competence.

COMMUNICATION COMPETENCE DEFINED

Defining **communication competence** isn't as easy as it might seem. Although scholars are still struggling to agree on a precise definition, most would agree that it involves achieving one's goals in a manner that is personally acceptable and, ideally, acceptable to others as well. This definition may seem vague on one hand and wordy on the other, but a closer look shows that it suggests several important characteristics of communication competence.

THERE IS NO "IDEAL" WAY TO COMMUNICATE   Your own experience shows that a variety of communication styles can be effective. Some very successful communicators are serious, while others use humor; some are gregarious, while others are more quiet; and some are more straightforward, while others hint diplomatically. Just as there are many kinds of beautiful music or art, there are many kinds of competent communication.

The number of forms that successful relationships can take is illustrated by research showing that there are three basic types of marriages: traditionals (who emphasize interdependence and harmony), independents (who value the relationship but emphasize individual differences between the partners), and separates (who view the marriage primarily as a matter of convenience).[43] In addition, the two partners in a marriage may have different orientations, such as separate/traditional or traditional/independent. While not all these types are equally successful, this typology shows that there is more than one way to have a successful marriage. For instance, the traditional arrangement that works so well for one couple might not suit another, whose independent lifestyle works just fine for them.

Along with the wide range of possible relationship types, the specific communication that is competent in one setting might be a colossal blunder in another. The joking insults you routinely trade with one friend might offend a sensitive family member, and last Saturday night's romantic approach would probably be out of place at work on Monday morning. This means that there can be no sure-fire list of rules or tips that will guarantee your success as a communicator.

COMPETENCE IS SITUATIONAL   Because competent behavior varies so much from one situation and person to another, it's a mistake to think that communication competence is a trait that a person either possesses or lacks. It's more accurate to talk about *degrees* or *areas* of competence.[44] You and the people you know are probably quite competent in some areas and less so in others. You might deal quite skillfully with peers, for example, while feeling clumsy interacting with people much older or younger, wealthier or poorer, more or less attractive than yourself. In fact, your competence with one person may vary from situation to situation. This means that it's an overgeneralization to say in a moment of distress, "I'm a terrible communicator!" when it's more accurate to say, "I didn't handle this situation very well, even though I'm better in others."

What qualifies as competent behavior in one culture might be completely inept, or even offensive in another.[45] On an obvious level, customs like belching after a meal or appearing nude in public that might be appropriate in some parts of the world would be considered outrageous in others. But there are more subtle differences in competent communication. For example, qualities like self-disclosure and speaking clearly that are valued in the United States are likely to be considered overly aggressive and insensitive in many Asian cultures, where subtlety and indirectness are considered important.

COMPETENCE REQUIRES JUGGLING CONFLICTING GOALS   Communicating competently would be challenging enough if all we had to do was satisfy our own physical, identity, social, and practical needs. But sometimes these goals conflict with one another, and with others' goals. Consider one simple example: You want to meet the social and identity needs of maintaining a friendly relationship with your long-winded neighbor, but if you spend the morning chatting you'll be late for work, frustrating the practical need of keeping your job. Another example offers more evidence of conflicting goals: In an argument with someone important to you, the desire to win (satisfying the identity need of being "right") clashes with the social need of keeping the relationship on an even keel.

Conflicts like these hint at the dialectical tensions that exist between various communication goals. **Dialectical tensions** arise when two opposing or incompatible forces exist simultaneously. In recent years, communication scholars have recognized the dialectical forces that make successful communication challenging.[46] Listing some of those tensions shows why communicating isn't as simple or straightforward as it might first seem.

Approval versus Personal Effectiveness   Approval is an important social need, but sometimes the only way to achieve your personal goals is to behave in ways that risk the disapproval of others. Suppose a fellow worker—or even worse, your boss—makes sexist or racist remarks you find offensive. You may be faced with the tough choice of keeping quiet and sacrificing your principles or speaking up and losing social approval . . . or even your job. In personal relationships, "blowing your top" may irritate your partner, but this sort of explosion might be the only way to get what you want when less aggressive tactics haven't worked.

Intimacy versus Distance   It's hard to imagine a more fundamental need than closeness. Yet along with the drive for intimacy, we have an equally important need to maintain some space between ourselves and others. On one hand, we know that sharing personal information is one way to build a strong relationship. On the other hand, we need to keep at least some information hidden. What, then, do you do in an intimate relationship when your partner asks an important question that you don't want to answer? The competing drives for intimacy and distance are so significant that Chapter Eight focuses exclusively on them.

Looking at Diversity

A MULTICULTURAL COMMUNICATION ODYSSEY

Ruth Martinez was born on a Navajo reservation in Arizona, where she spent her early childhood. At age five she began attending a boarding school run by the U.S. Bureau of Indian Affairs, where she lived for thirteen years. After earning her high school diploma, Ruth enlisted in the U.S. Army, where she served as a medic. When her tour of active duty ended, Ruth moved to Albuquerque, where she began attending college and working at Albuquerque Technical-Vocational Institute. She now is a single parent with four children.

The first time I realized there was more than one way to communicate was when I left home to live in boarding school. The students there came from three Indian nations: Navajo, Hopi, and Pueblo. Most of us spoke our own languages, but the administrators of the school insisted that we all use English. I think they were trying to make us give up some of our own heritage and join the mainstream American culture, and to a great degree they succeeded. I still can speak Navajo, but living away from home for many years made me less familiar with Navajo ways of communicating than with other lifestyles.

My time in the Army really changed the way I communicate. Native Americans aren't taught to be very talkative, so being quiet at boarding school was normal; but being silent in the military didn't work too well. I was a medic, and I had to speak up to do my job, both with patients and with the officers and enlisted people with whom I worked. Life in the Army also exposed me to people from many different backgrounds, and it challenged me to think about new styles of communicating. Almost everybody was much more open than I was as a Native American. They were very frank about their personal lives and comfortable discussing topics that would have been embarrassing back home. Although I'm still on the quiet side, I learned in the Army to make friends by changing my communication style, by opening up. When I moved to Albuquerque and got a job, I found that the same open, talkative style that I discovered in the Army was important in civilian life.

The biggest cultural lesson in this part of my life came while I was married to my former husband, Edward Earl Purvis, Jr. He is an African American, and that culture has a communication style that's as different from the Native American one as you can get. Edward helped me develop a

sense of humor—which isn't a big part of Navajo communication. He encouraged me to speak up and stand up for myself in ways I never did before. For example, I could joke and argue with my mother–in–law in ways I would never do with my own mom.

Just because I've developed new ways of communicating out in the wider world doesn't mean I've rejected my Navajo culture. I still can speak the language, and when I go home I revert to the more quiet, respectful style of interacting used by my family. I feel like my years away from the reservation have cost me a lot of knowledge about my native culture, and I regret that. At the same time, I'm grateful that I have learned how to get along with people from other backgrounds. I know people who have left the reservations as adults, and communicating with non–Navajos has been much harder for them.

I think a big part of communicating well is adjusting. Every culture has its own qualities, and to communicate in each one takes a different approach.

Autonomy versus Connection   As you read a few pages ago, interdependence is one characteristic of a qualitatively interpersonal relationship. At the same time, few people are willing to submerge all their identity or sacrifice all their independence. Some researchers have identified the inevitable tensions between the freedom and identity of being "me" and the rewards of being part of a "we" as the most powerful dialectic in interpersonal relationships.

Predictability versus Novelty, Consistency versus Flexibility   Predictability is an important need in relationships. In fact, some scholars have developed theories that characterize the reduction of uncertainty as a major goal of communication. It would be impractical and annoying—even disturbing—to have relationships where your partner was completely unpredictable. At the same time, too much predictability can be stifling.

Short-term versus Long-term Objectives   Sometimes it is impossible to achieve a short-term goal and work toward a longer-term one at the same time. Everyone who has worked for a boss recognizes this dilemma. Do you work late at the boss's request to boost your chances for promotion at the cost of sacrificing the evening's plans, or do you leave work on time and risk your career? You can't have it both ways. Do you let a co-worker's sarcastic remark slide to avoid a conflict, or do you stand up for yourself in order to prevent future problems? Again, each decision has its costs and benefits.

Own versus Other's Needs   We often have to decide how to reconcile our own needs with the conflicting ones that others bring to a relationship. Do you put aside the assignment that is due today to listen to a friend's problem, or do you stay on task? What do you do if you want to seek help from a professor who is obviously busy: Do you persist or back off? As with other dialectical tensions, there's no clear answer to the question of whose needs to put first. Achieving one goal may require abandoning or downplaying another, equally important one.

Conflicting Needs in Different Relationships   Even when the motives that shape communication with one person present no problems, contradictory desires for different relationships can create tensions. Consider a few examples: What do you do when the people at work are counting on you and the people at home are too? What does a young couple do when they want to spend time together but their families—each of which lives in a different town—want them home for the holidays? How do working parents juggle the demands of spending time with one another, their children, other family members, friends, and at work?

Dialectical tensions among conflicting goals are a fact of life. Completely satisfying the kinds of conflicting needs described here is impossible. When faced with dialectically opposed needs, competent communicators choose the approach that appears to work best under the difficult circumstances, and act in ways that make that approach succeed.

CHARACTERISTICS OF COMPETENT COMMUNICATORS

Despite the fact that competent communication varies from one situation to another, scholars have identified several common denominators that characterize effective communication in most contexts.

A WIDE RANGE OF BEHAVIORS   Effective communicators are able to choose their actions from a wide range of behaviors. To understand the importance of having a large communication repertoire, imagine that someone you know repeatedly tells jokes—perhaps racist or sexist ones—that you find offensive. You could respond to these jokes in a number of ways:

You could decide to say nothing, figuring that the risks of bringing the subject up would be greater than the benefits.

You could ask a third party to say something to the joke teller about the offensiveness of the stories.

You could hint at your discomfort, hoping that your friend would get the point.

You could joke about your friend's insensitivity, counting on humor to soften the blow of your criticism.

You could express your discomfort in a straightforward way, asking your companion to stop telling the offensive stories, at least around you.

You could even demand that the other person stop.

With this choice of responses at your disposal (and you can probably think of others as well), you could pick the one that had the best chance of success. But if you were able to use only one or two of these responses when raising a delicate issue—always keeping quiet or always hinting, for example—your chances of success would be much smaller. Indeed, many poor communicators are easy to spot by their limited range of responses. Some are chronic jokers. Others are always belligerent. Still others are quiet in almost every situation. Like a piano player who only knows one tune or a chef who can only prepare a few dishes, these people are forced to rely on a small range of responses again and again, whether or not they are successful.

ABILITY TO CHOOSE THE MOST APPROPRIATE BEHAVIOR   Simply possessing a large array of communication skills isn't a guarantee of effectiveness. It's also necessary to know which of these behaviors will work best in a particular situation. Choosing the best way to send a message is rather like choosing a gift: What is appropriate for one person won't suit another one at all. This ability to choose the best approach is essential, because a response that works well in one setting would flop miserably in another one.

Although it's impossible to say precisely how to act in every situation, there are at least three factors to consider when you are deciding which response to choose: context, your goal, and the other person.

Context   The time and place will almost always influence how you act. Asking your boss for a raise or your lover for a kiss might produce good results if the time is right, but the identical request might backfire if your timing is poor. Likewise, the joke that would be ideal at a bachelor party would probably flop at a funeral.

Your Goal   The way you should communicate depends on the results you are seeking. Inviting a new neighbor over for a cup of coffee or dinner could be just the right approach if you want to encourage a friendship; but if you want to maintain your privacy it might be wiser to be polite but cool. Likewise, your goal will determine your approach in situations in which you want to help another person. As you will learn in Chapter Seven, there are times when offering advice is just what is needed. But when you want to help others develop the ability to solve problems on their own, it's better to withhold your own ideas and function as a sounding board to let them consider alternatives and choose their solutions.

The Other Person   Your knowledge of the other party should also shape the approach you take. If you're dealing with someone who is very sensitive or insecure, your response might be supportive and cautious. With an old and trusted friend you might be blunt. In fact, understanding the other person is so important that researchers have labeled *empathy* the most important aspect of communication competence.[47] For this reason a major part of Chapter Three is devoted to developing your ability to empathize.

The social niche of the other party will often influence how you communicate. For instance, you would probably act differently toward an eighty-year-old person than you would toward a teenager. You would probably behave differently toward the president of your institution than you would toward a classmate, even in identical circumstances. Likewise, there are times when it's appropriate to treat a man differently than a woman, even in this age of gender equity.

SKILL AT PERFORMING BEHAVIORS   Once you have chosen the most appropriate way to communicate, it's still necessary to perform the required skills effectively. There is a big difference between knowing *about* a skill and being able to put it into practice. Simply being aware of alternatives isn't much help, unless you can skillfully put these alternatives to work.

Just reading about communication skills in the following chapters won't guarantee that you can start using them flawlessly. Like any other skills—playing a musical instrument or learning a sport, for example—the road to competence in communication is not a short one. As you learn and practice the communication skills in the following pages, you can expect to pass through several stages,[48] shown in Figure 1–4.

Beginning Awareness   The first step in learning any new skill is a beginning awareness. This is the point at which you first learn that there is a new and better way of behaving. If you play tennis, for example, awareness might grow when you learn about a new way of serving that can improve your power and accuracy. In the area of communication, *Looking Out/Looking In* should bring this sort of awareness to you.

Awkwardness   Just as you were clumsy when you first tried to ride a bicycle or drive a car, your initial attempts at communicating in new ways may also be awkward. This doesn't mean that there's anything wrong with these methods, but rather that you need more experience with them. After all, if it's reasonable to expect difficulty learning other skills, you ought to expect the same fumbling with the concepts in this book. As Ringo Starr put it when talking about music, "If you want to play the blues, you gotta pay your dues. . . . It don't come easy."

Skillfulness   If you are willing to keep working at overcoming the awkwardness of your initial attempts, you will arrive at the third learning

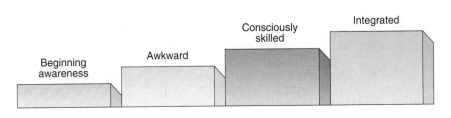

FIGURE 1–4
Stages in learning communication skills

stage, which is one of skillfulness. At this point you'll be able to handle yourself well, although you will still need to think about what you're doing. As in learning a new language, this is the time when you're able to speak grammatically and use the correct words, even though you still need to think hard to express yourself well. As an interpersonal communicator, you can expect the stage of skillfulness to be marked by a great deal of thinking and planning and also by good results.

Integration   Finally, after a period of time in the skillful phase, you'll find yourself at the final level of integration. This occurs when you're able to perform well without thinking about it. The behavior becomes automatic, a part of you. Integrated speakers of a foreign language converse without translating mentally from their native tongue. Integrated cyclists ride skillfully and comfortably, almost as if the bike were an extension of each cyclist's own body. And integrated communicators express themselves in skillful ways, not as a self-conscious act but because that is who they have become.

It's important to keep these stages in mind as you try out the ideas in this book. Prepare yourself for the inevitable awkwardness, knowing that if you're willing to keep practicing the new skills you will become more and more comfortable and successful with them. Realize that the effort is worth it, for once you have learned new methods of communicating you'll be rewarded with far more satisfying relationships.

EMPATHY/PERSPECTIVE TAKING   People have the best chance of developing an effective message when they understand the other person's point of view. And since others aren't always good at expressing their thoughts and feelings clearly, the ability to imagine how an issue might look from the other's point of view is an important skill. The value of taking the other's perspective suggests one reason why listening is so important. Not only does it help us understand others, it gives us information to develop strategies about how to best influence them. Because empathy is such an important element of communicative competence, much of Chapter Three is devoted to this topic.

COGNITIVE COMPLEXITY   **Cognitive complexity** is the ability to construct a variety of different frameworks for viewing an issue. Cognitive complexity is an ingredient of communication competence because it allows us to make sense of people using a variety of perspectives. For instance, imagine that a long-time friend seems to be angry with you. One possible explanation is that your friend is offended by something you've done. Another possibility is that something has happened in another part of your friend's life that is upsetting. Or perhaps nothing at all is wrong and you're just being overly sensitive. Researchers have found that the ability to analyze the behavior of others in a variety of ways leads to greater "conversational sensitivity," increasing the chances of acting in ways that will produce satisfying results.[49]

SELF-MONITORING   Psychologists use the term **self-monitoring** to describe the process of paying close attention to one's behavior and using these observations to shape the way one behaves. Self-monitors are able to separate a part of their consciousness and observe their behavior from a detached viewpoint, making observations like

"I'm making a fool out of myself."
"I'd better speak up now."
"This approach is working well. I'll keep it up."

Self-monitors are more skillful communicators than people who are less aware of their behavior.[50] For example, they are more accurate in judging others' emotional states, better at remembering information about others, less shy, and more assertive. Whereas low self-monitors may blunder through life, succeeding or failing without understanding why, high self-monitors have the detachment to ask themselves the question "How am I doing?" and to change their behavior if the answer isn't positive.

COMMITMENT TO THE RELATIONSHIP   One feature that distinguishes effective communication—at least in qualitatively interpersonal relationships—is commitment. In other words, people who seem to care about the relationship communicate better than those who don't.[51] This concern shows up in several kinds of commitment:

Commitment to the Other Person   Concern for the other person is revealed in a variety of ways: a desire to spend time with him or her instead of rushing, willingness to listen carefully instead of doing all the talking, the use of language that makes sense to the other person, and openness to change after hearing the other person's ideas.

Commitment to the Message   Effective communicators also care about what they have to say. They appear sincere, seem to know what they are talking about, and demonstrate through words and deeds that their ideas matter. Phony communication is a turnoff. So are wishy-washy positions and uninformed, ignorant statements.

Calvin and Hobbes   by Bill Watterson

A Desire for Mutual Benefit   The best communication leaves both parties as winners, each gaining from an exchange. In contrast, when communicators appear to be self-centered or manipulative, the relationship suffers. In fact, Chapter Ten shows how both parties can wind up losers when they care only about their own welfare.

A Desire to Interact and to Continue the Relationship   Communication is most effective when people care about one another. This doesn't mean it's necessary for gas station attendants and telephone operators to establish a deep relationship with every customer. Even these sorts of business transactions, however, are more satisfying when the implicit message is "I sincerely want to help you and hope you'll be a satisfied customer."

While commitment is an important ingredient of competence in many situations, there are times when the best approach may be to reduce involvement in a relationship. If the other person is physically or psychologically abusive, for example, disengaging can be the best way to protect yourself. Even in less extreme circumstances it may be competent to reduce your level of commitment. You might be satisfied with a relatively superficial relationship and choose not to grow closer, even if the other person is looking for more intimacy. Even though total commitment isn't always desirable, there's no question that when the relationship *does* matter, effort is just as important as skill in making it succeed.

How do you measure up as a competent communicator? Competence isn't a trait that people either possess or lack. Rather, it's a state that we achieve more or less frequently. A realistic goal, then, is not to become perfect but to boost the percentage of time when you communicate in ways outlined in this section.

SKILL BUILDER
CHECK YOUR COMPETENCE

Other people are often the best judges of your competence as a communicator. They can also offer useful information about how to improve your communication skill. Find out for yourself by following these steps:

1. Choose a person with whom you have an important relationship.

2. In cooperation with this person, identify several contexts in which you communicate. For example, you might choose different situations such as "handling conflicts," "lending support to friends," or "expressing feelings."

3. For each situation, have your friend rate your competence by answering the following questions:
   a. Do you have a wide repertoire of response styles in this situation, or do you always respond in the same way?
   b. Are you able to choose the most effective way of behaving for the situation at hand?

c. Are you skillful at performing behaviors? (Note that knowing how you *want* to behave isn't the same as being *able* to perform.)

    d. Do you communicate in a way that leaves others satisfied?

4. After reviewing your partner's answers, identify the situations in which your communication is most competent.

5. Choose a situation in which you would like to communicate more competently, and with the help of your partner

    a. Determine whether your repertoire of behaviors needs to be expanded.

    b. Identify the ways in which you need to communicate more skillfully.

    c. Develop ways to monitor your behavior in the key situation to get feedback on your effectiveness.

✤ SUMMARY

Communication is essential on many levels. Besides satisfying practical needs, effective communication can enhance physical health and emotional well-being. As children, we learn about our identity via the messages sent by others, and as adults our self-concept is shaped and refined through social interaction. Communication also satisfies social needs: involvement with others, control over the environment, and giving and receiving affection.

The process of communication is not a linear one that people "do" to one another, nor is it an interactive one in which people exchange messages in a kind of verbal and nonverbal tennis game. Rather, communication is a transactional process in which participants create a relationship by simultaneously sending and receiving messages, many of which are distorted by various types of noise.

Interpersonal communication can be defined contextually by the number of people involved, or qualitatively by the nature of interaction between them. In a qualitative sense, interpersonal relationships are unique, irreplaceable, interdependent, and intrinsically rewarding. Qualitatively interpersonal communication is relatively infrequent, even in the

strongest relationships. Both personal and impersonal communication are useful, and most relationships have both personal and impersonal elements.

Communication occurs on two levels: content and relational. Relational communication can be both verbal and nonverbal. Metacommunication consists of messages that refer to the relationship between the communicators. Relational messages usually refer to one of three dimensions of a relationship: affinity, respect, and control.

All communication, whether personal or impersonal, content or relational, follows the same basic principles. Messages can be intentional or unintentional. It is impossible not to communicate. Communication is irreversible and unrepeatable. Some common misconceptions should be avoided when thinking about communication: Meanings are not in words, but in people. More communication does not always make matters better. Communication will not solve all problems. Finally, communication—at least effective communication—is not a natural ability.

Communication competence is the ability to get what you are seeking from others in a manner that maintains the relationship on terms that are acceptable to all parties. Competence doesn't mean behaving the same way in all settings and with all people; rather, competence varies from one situation to another. The most competent communicators have a wide repertoire of behaviors, and they are able to choose the best behavior for a given situation and perform it skillfully. They are able to take others' points of view and analyze a situation in a variety of ways. They also monitor their own behavior and are committed to communicating successfully.

✚ KEY TERMS

affection
affinity
behavior
channel
cognitive complexity
communication
communication competence
competitive symmetry
complementary relationship
content message
control
conversational control
decision control
decoding
dialectical tension
dyad

encoding
environment
external noise
feedback
impersonal communication
  (contextual and qualitative)
inclusion
instrumental goals
interactive communication
  model
interpersonal communication
linear communication model
message
metacommunication
neutralized symmetry

noise
parallel relationship
physiological noise
psychological noise
receiver
relational message
respect
self-actualization
self-esteem
self-monitoring
sender
submissive symmetry
symmetrical relationship
transactional communication
  model

✚ MORE RESOURCES ON INTERPERSONAL RELATIONSHIPS

READINGS

Cialdini, Robert B. *Influence: Science and Practice*, 3rd ed. New York: HarperCollins, 1993.

Creating and maintaining positive relationships aren't the only goals of communication. This highly readable digest of social science research captures the range of instrumental goals communicators try to attain, and the ways they do so. Cialdini shows how interpersonal influence operates in a wide range of settings, including business transactions, medicine, religion, politics, and romance.

Daly, John A., and John M. Wiemann, eds. *Strategic Interpersonal Communication*. Hillsdale, N.J.: Erlbaum, 1994.

The authors detail some of the many ways people communicate strategically to accomplish their goals. Chapters focus on a wide range of strategic tactics and objectives, including seeking control and gaining compliance, comforting others, developing social bonds, and managing conflict.

Knapp, Mark L., Gerald R. Miller, and Kelly Fudge. "Background and Current Trends in the Study of Interpersonal Communication." In *Handbook of Interpersonal Communication*, 2d ed. Newbury Park, Calif.: Sage, 1994.

This chapter offers a broad discussion of the history, present status, and future potential of the scholarly study of interpersonal communication.

Littlejohn, Stephen W. *Theories of Human Communication*, 4th ed. Belmont, Calif.: Wadsworth, 1992.

This thorough book surveys the status of theories and research in human communication. Chapter 12 focuses on interpersonal communication and on several topics introduced in Looking Out/Looking In, *including perception, self-disclosure, interpersonal attraction, and conflict.*

Lynch, James J. *The Broken Heart: The Medical Consequences of Loneliness*. New York: Basic Books, 1977.

Lynch is the former director of the Psychosomatic Clinics at the University of Maryland's School of Medicine. He documents the strong link between poor physical health and inadequate interpersonal relationships.

Petronio, Sandra, Jess K. Alberts, Michael L. Hecht, and Jerry Buley, eds. *Contemporary Perspectives on Interpersonal Communication.* Madison, Wis.: Brown and Benchmark, 1993.

In this collection of scholarly writings, serious students will find some of the most influential work of social scientists who have studied interpersonal communication in the last decades of the 20th century. Topics include theoretical approaches to the subject, influence, bonding, relational development and maintenance, conversation management, and interpersonal competence.

Rubin, Lilian. *Just Friends: The Role of Friendship in Our Lives.* New York: Harper & Row, 1985.

An examination of the ambiguous yet vital relationship we call friendship. Based on interviews with three hundred men and women, this book explores the many varieties of friendship: casual versus "best friends," same- and opposite-sex friendships, marriage and friendship, and friendship and kinship.

Rubin, Zick. *Liking and Loving.* New York: Holt, Rinehart and Winston, 1973.

A thorough, readable treatment of the subject by a noted social psychologist.

Stewart, John. "Interpersonal Communication: Contact between Persons." In *Bridges, Not Walls: A Book about Interpersonal Communication,* 6th ed. New York: McGraw-Hill, 1995.

This introductory essay in Stewart's excellent reader elaborates on the differences between interpersonal and impersonal communication. In addition, it comments on the basic needs that communication fills.

FILMS

COMMUNICATION AS A TRANSACTIONAL PROCESS
Ordinary People (1980) Rated R

Conrad (Timothy Hutton) is recovering from a suicide attempt triggered by guilt over surviving the accident in which his brother died. His low self-esteem is also shaped by the (correct) perception that his mother, Beth (Mary Tyler Moore), doesn't seem to love him—that she only loved her dead brother. The well-intentioned father, Calvin (Donald Sutherland),

is ready to get on with his life, but he is caught in the middle between his wife and son. Conrad seeks help from a psychiatrist named Berger (Judd Hirsch), and after a difficult beginning he manages to get in touch with the source of his guilt. Despite the breakthrough, the film does not have a neat, happy ending: Calvin confronts his mother about her emotional sterility and she leaves home. In the final scene, Conrad and Calvin affirm their love for one another.

Ordinary People vividly illustrates the transactional nature of relationships. Virtually every interaction between the three members of the family is affected by the history of their relationship: the brother's death, Conrad's suicide attempt and hospitalization, and the resentment and hurt between Conrad and Beth.

DIMENSIONS OF RELATIONAL COMMUNICATION
The African Queen (1951) Not rated

Humphrey Bogart is the skipper of a tramp steamer. He is goaded into becoming involved in World War I's African theater by the prim, spinster missionary played by Katharine Hepburn. This is a gentle romance with a happy Hollywood ending, but Bogart and Hepburn engage in a contest of wills before they recognize their love for one another. The film provides an entertaining illustration of how content issues (in this case, centering on the boat's course) can be manifestations of relational issues, such as control, respect, and affection.

COMMUNICATION COMPETENCE
The Great Santini (1980) Rated PG

Bull Meechum (Robert Duvall) is an ace Marine fighter pilot who views himself as an all-around man: warrior, husband, father, and friend. He expects his family to go along with this image as they move to yet another duty station, this time at a South Carolina Marine air station. Meechum is a stereotype of the aggressive, insensitive male, and his wife, Lillian, is the classic devoted, uncritically supportive Southern wife. On the simplest level, the Meechums can be viewed as a dysfunctional family controlled by an insensitive self-centered male who makes life miserable for his wife and children. But despite Bull's many shortcomings, the Meechum family is basically a solid, functional one in which the members genuinely love—and even like—one another. Because this non-textbook set of relationships does work reasonably well, the film illustrates that communication competence varies from one relationship to another.

Communication and the Self

ho are you? Take a moment now to answer this question. How did you define yourself? As a student? A man or woman? By your age? Your religion? Your occupation? Of course, there are many ways of identifying yourself. List as many ways as you can to identify who you are. You'll need this list as you read the rest of this chapter, so be sure to complete it now. Try to include all the characteristics that describe you:

> your moods or feelings (e.g., happy, sad)
>
> your appearance (e.g., good-looking, unattractive)
>
> your social traits (e.g., friendly, shy)
>
> talents you possess or lack (e.g., musical, tone-deaf)
>
> your intellectual capacity (e.g., smart, stupid)
>
> your strong beliefs (e.g., religious, environmentalist)
>
> your social roles (e.g., parent, spouse)
>
> your physical condition (e.g., healthy, overweight)

Now take a look at what you've written. You'll probably see that the words you've chosen represent a profile of what you view as your most important characteristics. In other words, if you were required to describe the "real you," this list ought to be a good summary.

✣ COMMUNICATION AND THE SELF-CONCEPT

What you've done in developing this list is to give a partial description of your **self-concept:** the relatively stable set of perceptions you hold of yourself. If a special mirror existed that not only reflected your physical features but also allowed you to view other aspects of yourself—emotional states, talents, likes, dislikes, values, roles, and so on—the reflection you'd see would be your self-concept.

You probably recognize that the self-concept list you recorded earlier is only a partial one. To make the description complete, you'd have to keep adding items until your list ran into hundreds of words.

Take a moment now to demonstrate the many parts of your self-concept by simply responding to the question "Who am I?" over and over again. Add these responses to the list you started earlier.

Of course, not every item on your self-concept list is equally important. For example, the most significant part of one person's self-concept might consist of social roles, and for another it might be physical appearance, health, friendships, accomplishments, or skills.

You can discover how much you value each part of your self-concept by rank-ordering the items on the list you've compiled. Try it now: Place 1 next to the most fundamental thing about you, 2 next to the second most important term, and continue in this manner until you've completed your list.

This self-concept you've just described is extremely important. To see just how fundamental it is, try the following exercise.

INVITATION TO INSIGHT

TAKE AWAY

1. Look over the list of words you've just used to describe yourself. If you haven't already done so, pick the ten items that describe the most fundamental aspects of who you are. Be sure you've organized these items so that the most fundamental one is in first place and the one that is least central to your identity is number 10, arranging the words or phrases in between in their proper order.

2. Now find a comfortable spot where you can think without being interrupted. You can complete this exercise in a group with the leader giving instructions, or you can do it alone by reading the directions yourself when necessary.

3. Close your eyes and get a mental picture of yourself. Besides visualizing your appearance, you should also include in your image your less observable features: your disposition, your hopes, your concerns . . . of course including all the items you described in step 1.

4. Keep this picture in mind, but now imagine what would happen if the tenth item on your list disappeared from your makeup. How would you be different? Does the idea of giving up that item leave you feeling better or worse? How hard was it to let go of that item?

5. Now, without taking back the item you just abandoned, give up the ninth item on your list, and see what difference this makes to you. After pausing to experience your thoughts and feelings, give up each succeeding item on your list one by one.

6. After you've abandoned the number-one feature of who you are, take a few minutes to regather the parts of yourself that you abandoned, and then read on.

For most people this exercise dramatically illustrates just how fundamental the concept of self is. Even when the item being abandoned is an unpleasant one, it's often hard to give it up. And when asked to let go of their most central feelings or thoughts, most people balk. "I wouldn't be *me* without that," they insist. Of course, this proves our point: The concept of self is perhaps our most fundamental possession. Knowing who we are is essential, for without a self-concept it would be impossible to relate to the world.

HOW THE SELF-CONCEPT DEVELOPS

Most researchers agree that we are not born with a self-concept.[1] An infant lying in a crib has no notion of self, no notion—even if the ability to speak were miraculously made available—of how to answer the question "Who am I?" Consider what it would be like to have no idea of your characteristic moods, physical appearance, social traits, tal-

In order to get at any truth about myself, I must have contact with another person. The other is indispensable to my own existence, as well as to my knowledge about myself.

Jean-Paul Sartre

ents, intellectual capacity, beliefs, or important roles. If you can imagine this experience—*blankness*—you can start to understand how the world appears to someone with no sense of self. Of course, you have to take it one step further and *not know* you do not have any notion of self.

Soon after birth the infant begins to differentiate among the stimuli in the environment: familiar and unfamiliar faces, the sounds that mean food, the noises that frighten, the cat that jumps in the crib, the sister who tickles—each becomes a separate part of the world. Recognition of distinctions in the environment probably precedes recognition of the self.

During the first year of life the child begins to recognize "self" as distinct from surroundings. If you've ever watched children at this age you've probably marveled at how they can stare with great fascination at a foot, hand, and other body parts that float into view, almost as if they were strange objects belonging to someone else. Then the connection is made, almost as if the child were realizing "The hand is *me*," "The foot is *me*." These first revelations form the child's earliest concept of self. At this early stage, the self-concept is almost exclusively physical, involving the child's basic realization of existing and of possessing certain body parts over which some control is exerted. This limited self-concept barely resembles the more fully developed self-concepts older children hold.

Although children may behave more or less sociably, they don't automatically view themselves in a way that reflects their actual communication behavior. In fact, the opposite is closer to the truth: The self-concept is extremely subjective, being almost totally a product of interaction with others. You can begin to get a sense of how your self-concept has developed by trying the following exercise. Be sure to complete it before reading on.

INVITATION TO INSIGHT

"EGO BOOSTERS" AND "EGO BUSTERS"

1. Either by yourself or with a partner, recall someone you know or once knew who was an "ego booster"—who helped enhance your self-esteem by acting in a way that made you feel accepted, competent, worthwhile, important, appreciated, or loved.

   This person needn't have played a crucial role in your life as long as the role was positive. Often your self-concept is shaped by many tiny nudges as well as by a few giant events. A family member with whom you've spent most of your life can be an "ego booster," but so can the stranger on the street who spontaneously smiles and strikes up a friendly conversation.

2. Now recall an "ego buster" from your life—someone who acted in a large or small way to reduce your self-esteem. As with ego booster, ego buster

INVITATION TO INSIGHT

(continued)

messages aren't always intentional. The acquaintance who forgets your name after you've been introduced or the friend who yawns while you're describing an important problem can diminish your feelings of self-worth.

3. Now that you've thought about how others shape your self-concept, recall a time when you were an ego booster to someone else—when you deliberately or unintentionally boosted another's self-esteem. Don't merely settle for an instance in which you were nice: Look for a time when your actions left another person feeling valued, loved, needed, and so on. You may have to ask the help of others to answer this question.

4. Finally, recall a recent instance in which you were an ego buster for someone else. What did you do to diminish another's self-esteem? Were you aware of the effect of your behavior at the time?

   Your answer might show that some events we intend as boosters have the effect of busters. For example, you might joke with a friend in what you mean as a friendly gesture, only to discover that your remarks are received as criticism.

After completing the exercise (you *did* complete it, didn't you?), you should begin to see that your self-concept is shaped by those around you. This process of shaping occurs in two ways: reflected appraisal and social comparison.

REFLECTED APPRAISAL: THE LOOKING-GLASS SELF   As early as 1912, sociologist Charles Cooley used the image of a mirror to identify the process of **reflected appraisal:** the fact that each of us develops a self-concept that matches the way we believe others see us.[2] In other words, we are likely to feel less valuable, lovable, and capable to the degree that others have communicated ego busting signals; and we will probably feel good about ourselves to the extent that others seem to feel good about us. The validity of the principle of reflected appraisal will become clear when you realize that the self-concept you described in the list at the beginning of this chapter is a product of the positive and negative messages you have received throughout your life.

To illustrate this point further, let's start at the beginning. Newborn children aren't born with any sense of identity: They learn to judge themselves only through the way others treat them. At first the evaluations aren't linguistic. Nonetheless, even the earliest days of life are full of messages that constitute the first boosters and busters that start to shape the child's self-concept. The amount of time parents allow their baby to cry before attending to its needs nonverbally communicates over a period of time how important it is to them. Their method of handling the child also speaks volumes: Do they affectionately toy with it, or do they treat it like so much baggage,

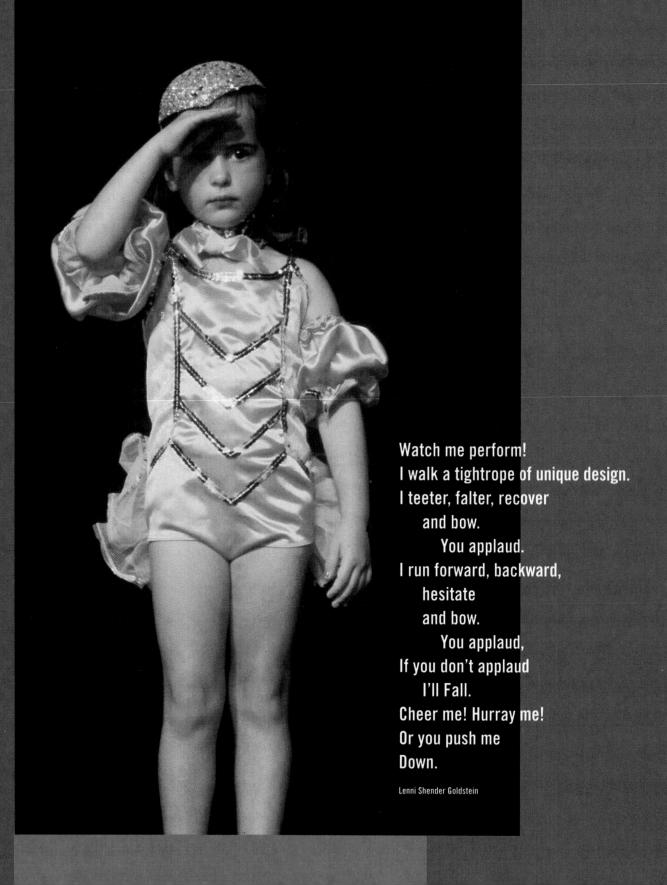

Watch me perform!
I walk a tightrope of unique design.
I teeter, falter, recover
    and bow.
        You applaud.
I run forward, backward,
        hesitate
        and bow.
        You applaud,
If you don't applaud
        I'll Fall.
Cheer me! Hurray me!
Or you push me
Down.

Lenni Shender Goldstein

changing diapers, feeding, and bathing it in a brusque, businesslike manner? Does the tone of voice with which they speak express love and enjoyment or disappointment and irritation?

Of course, many of these messages are not intentional ones. It is rare when a parent will deliberately try to tell a child it's not lovable; but whether they're intentional or not doesn't matter—nonverbal statements play a big role in shaping a youngster's feelings of being "OK" or "not OK."

As the child learns to speak and understand language, verbal messages also contribute to a developing self-concept. Every day a child is bombarded with scores of messages about him- or herself. Some of these are positive: "You're so cute!" "I love you." "What a big girl." Other messages are more discouraging: "What's the matter with you? Can't you do anything right?" "You're a bad boy." "Leave me alone. You're driving me crazy!"

Evaluations like these are the mirror by which we know ourselves; and since children are trusting souls who have no other way of viewing themselves, they accept at face value both the positive and negative evaluations of the apparently all-knowing and all-powerful adults around them.

These same principles in the formation of the self-concept continue in later life, especially when messages come from what sociologists term a **significant other**—a person whose opinions we especially value. A look at the ego boosters and ego busters you described in the previous exercise (as well as others you can remember) will show that the evaluations of a few especially important people can have long-range effects. A teacher from long ago, a special friend or relative, or perhaps a barely known acquaintance whom you respected can all leave an imprint on how you view yourself. To see the importance of significant others, ask yourself how you arrived at your opinion of yourself as a student . . . as a person attractive to others . . . as a competent worker . . . and you'll see that these self-evaluations were probably influenced by the way others regarded you.

Although messages from others have a powerful impact on shaping our identity, it is an exaggeration to suggest that feedback is *always* responsible for modifying the self-concept.[3] There are cases where a person's actual abilities play a larger role in shaping both self-evaluations and the perceptions of others. For example, if you are an outstanding athlete or a computer whiz, your accomplishments will probably boost your self-esteem, even if others don't give you much praise. Furthermore, the influence of significant others becomes less powerful as we grow older.[4] The critical comment that might devastate a child or adolescent would probably have less effect on an adult.

*If a child lives with criticism
  he learns to condemn.
If a child lives with hostility
  he learns to fight.
If a child lives with ridicule
  he learns to be shy.
If a child lives with shame
  he learns to feel guilty.
If a child lives with tolerance
  he learns to be patient.
If a child lives with
  encouragement
  he learns confidence.
If a child lives with praise
  he learns to appreciate.
If a child lives with fairness
  he learns justice.
If a child lives with security
  he learns to have faith.
If a child lives with approval
  he leans to like himself.
If a child lives with acceptance and friendship
  he learns to find love in
  the world.*

Dorothy Law Nolte,
Children Learn What They Live

We are not only our brother's keeper; in countless large and small ways, we are our brother's maker.

Bonaro Overstreet

ETHICAL CHALLENGE

HOW RESPONSIBLE ARE YOU?

What is your responsibility for creating and preserving others' self-esteem? Explore this question by following these steps.

1. Choose someone with whom you have an important relationship. Interview that person to discover how your words and deeds influence his or her self-concept. Pay special attention to identifying incidents when you have unknowingly said or done something that weakened your partner's self-esteem.

2. Once you recognize the power you have to shape another's self-concept, ask yourself what responsibility you have to treat the other person in a way that does not negatively affect his or her self-concept. Pay special attention to cases in which the choice seems to be either communicating honestly and diminishing the other person's self-esteem or downplaying your needs in order to protect your partner.

It is thus with most of us; we are what other people say we are. We know ourselves chiefly by hearsay.

Eric Hoffer

SOCIAL COMPARISON   So far we have looked at the way others' messages shape your self-concept. In addition to these messages, each of us forms our self-image by the process of **social comparison:** evaluating ourselves in terms of how we compare with others.

Two types of social comparison need highlighting. In the first, we decide whether we are *superior or inferior* by comparing ourselves to others. Are we attractive or ugly? A success or failure? Intelligent or stupid? It depends on those against whom we measure ourselves.[5]

You might feel just ordinary or inferior in terms of talent, friendships, or attractiveness if you compare yourself with an inappropriate reference group. You might never be as beautiful as a Hollywood star, as agile as a professional athlete, or as wealthy as a millionaire. When you consider the matter logically, these facts don't mean you're worthless. Nonetheless, many people judge themselves against unreasonable standards and suffer accordingly.

This principle is especially powerful when we compare ourselves to images in the media. In one study, young women's perceptions of their bodies changed for the worse after watching just thirty minutes of televised images of the "ideal" female form.[6] Furthermore, these distorted self-images can lead to serious behavioral disorders such as depression, anorexia nervosa, bulimia, and other eating disorders.

In addition to feelings of superiority and inferiority, social comparison also provides a way to decide if we are the *same as* or *different from* others. A child who is interested in ballet and who lives in a setting where such preferences are regarded as weird will start to accept this label if there is no support from others. Likewise, adults who want to improve the quality of their relationships but are surrounded by friends and family who don't recognize or acknowledge the importance of these matters may think of themselves as oddballs. Thus, it's easy to recognize that the **reference groups** against which we compare ourselves play an important role in shaping our view of ourselves.

You might argue that not every part of one's self-concept is shaped by others, insisting there are certain objective facts that are recognizable by self-observation. After all, nobody needs to tell a person that he is taller than others, speaks with an accent, has acne, and so on. These facts are obvious.

Though it's true that some features of the self are immediately apparent, the *significance* we attach to them—the rank we assign them in the hierarchy of our list and the interpretation we give them—depends greatly on the opinions of others. After all, there are many of your features that are readily observable, yet you don't find them important at all because nobody has regarded them as significant.

Recently, we heard a woman in her eighties describing her youth. "When I was a girl," she declared, "we didn't worry about weight. Some people were skinny and others were plump, and we pretty much accepted the bodies God gave us." In those days it was unlikely that weight would have found its way onto the self-concept list you constructed because it wasn't considered significant. Compare this attitude with what you find today: It's seldom that you pick up a popular magazine or visit a bookstore without reading about the latest diet fads, and television ads are filled with scenes of slender, happy people. As a result you'll rarely find a person who doesn't complain about the need to "lose a few pounds." Obviously, the reason for such concern has more to do with the attention paid to slimness these days than with any increase in the number of people in the population who are overweight. Furthermore, the interpretation of characteristics such as weight depends on the way people important to us regard them. We generally see fat as undesirable because others tell us it is. In a society where obesity is the ideal (and there are such societies), a person who regards herself as extremely heavy would be a beauty. In the same way, the fact that one is single or married, solitary or sociable, aggressive or passive takes on meaning depending on the interpretation society attaches to those traits. Thus, the importance of a given characteristic in your self-concept has as much to do with the significance you and others attach to it as with the existence of the characteristic.

By now you might be thinking, "It's not my fault that I've always been shy or unconfident. Since I developed a picture of myself as a result of the way others have treated me, I can't help being what I am." Though it's true that to a great extent you are a product of your environment, to believe you are forever doomed to a poor self-concept would be a big mistake. Having held a poor self-image in the past is no reason for continuing to do so in the future. You *can* change your attitudes and behaviors, as you'll soon read. So don't despair, and most of all don't use the fact that others have shaped your self-concept as an excuse for self-pity or for acting helpless. Now that you know the effect overly negative evaluations have had on you in the past, you'll be in a better position to revise your perception of yourself more favorably in the future.

I have found the secret for eternal optimism. It's called The Power of Negative Thinking. All my life I've suffered from periods of depression because I got thinking about how much better a lot of people do things than I do. That's behind me now. Today I'm concentrating on the negative. When I do something badly, all I'm going to think about is the great number of people who probably would have done it even worse.

Andy Rooney

ZIGGY®

i've GOT A REALLY iMPORTANT PATieNT COMING IN ANY MiNUTe NOW... CAN We WORK ON YOUR SeLF-esTeeM SOMe OTHeR TiMe ?...

2-10   © 1986 Universal Press Syndicate

It started with tragedy on a biting cold February morning. I was driving behind the Milford Corners bus as I did most snowy mornings on my way to school. It veered and stopped short at the hotel, which it had no business doing, and I was annoyed as I had to come to an unexpected stop. A boy lurched out of the bus, reeled, stumbled, and collapsed on the snowbank at the curb. The bus driver and I reached him at the same moment. His thin, hollow face was white even against the snow.

"He's dead," the driver whispered.

It didn't register for a minute. I glanced quickly at the scared young faces staring down at us from the school bus. "A doctor! Quick! I'll phone from the hotel. . . . "

"No use, I tell you he's dead." The driver looked down at the boy's still form. "He never even said he felt bad," he muttered. "Just tapped me on the shoulder and said, real quiet, 'I'm sorry. I have to get off at the hotel.' That's all. Polite and apologizing like."

At school, the giggling, shuffling morning noise quieted as the news went down the halls. I passed a huddle of girls. "Who was it? Who dropped dead on the way to school?" I heard one of them half-whisper.

"Don't know his name; some kid from Milford Corners" was the reply.

It was like that in the faculty room and the principal's office. "I'd appreciate your going out to tell the parents," the principal told me.

"They haven't a phone and, anyway, somebody from school should go there in person. I'll cover your classes."

"Why me?" I asked. "Wouldn't it be better if you did it?"

"I didn't know the boy," the principal admitted levelly. "And, in last year's sophomore personalities column I note that you were listed as his favorite teacher."

I drove through the snow and cold down the bad canyon road to the Evans place and thought about the boy, Cliff Evans. His favorite teacher! I thought. He hasn't spoken two words to me in two years! I could see him in my mind's eye all right, sitting back there in the last seat in my afternoon literature class. He came in the room by himself and left by himself. "Cliff Evans," I muttered to myself, "a boy who never talked." I thought a minute. "A boy who never smiled. I never saw him smile once."

The big ranch kitchen was clean and warm. I blurted out my news somehow. Mrs. Evans reached blindly toward a chair. "He never said anything about bein' ailing."

His stepfather snorted. "He ain't said nothin' about anything since I moved in here."

Mrs. Evans pushed a pan to the back of the stove and began to untie her apron. "Now hold on," her husband snapped. "I got to have breakfast before I go to town. Nothin' we can do now anyway. If Cliff hadn't been so dumb, he'd have told us he didn't feel good."

After school I sat in the office and stared blankly at the records spread out before me. I was to close the file and write the obituary for the school paper. The almost bare sheets mocked the effort. Cliff Evans, white, never legally adopted by stepfather, five young half-brothers and sisters. These meager strands of information and the list of D grades were all the records had to offer.

Cliff Evans had silently come in the school door in the mornings and gone out the school door in the evenings, and that was all. He had never belonged to a club. He had never played on a team. He had never held an office. As far as I could tell he had never done one happy, noisy kid thing. He had never been anybody at all.

How do you go about making a boy into a zero? The grade-school records showed me. The first and second grade teachers' annotations read "sweet, shy child," "timid but eager." Then the third grade note had opened the attack. Some teacher had written in a good, firm hand, "Cliff won't talk. Uncooperative. Slow learner." The other academic sheep had followed with "dull"; "slow-witted"; "low I.Q." They became correct. The boy's I.Q. score in the ninth grade was listed as 83. But his I.Q. in the third grade had been 106. The score didn't go under 100 until the seventh grade. Even shy, timid, sweet children have resilience. It takes time to break them.

I stomped to the typewriter and wrote a savage report pointing out what education had done to Cliff Evans. I slapped a copy on the principal's desk and another in the sad, dog-eared file. I banged the typewriter and slammed the file and crashed the door shut, but I didn't feel much better. A little boy kept walking after me, a little boy with a peaked, pale face; a skinny body in faded jeans; and big eyes that had looked and searched for a long time and then had become veiled.

I could guess how many times he'd been chosen last to play sides in a game, how many whispered child conversations had excluded him, how many times he hadn't been asked. I could see and hear the faces and voices that said over and over, "You're a nothing, Cliff Evans."

A child is a believing creature. Cliff undoubtedly believed them. Suddenly it seemed clear to me: When finally there was nothing left at all for Cliff Evans, he collapsed on a snowbank and went away. The doctor might list "heart failure" as the cause of death, but that wouldn't change my mind.

We couldn't find ten students in the school who had known Cliff well enough to attend the funeral as his friends. So the student body officers and a committee from the junior class went as a group to the church, being politely sad. I attended the services with them, and sat through it with a lump of cold lead in my chest and a big resolve growing through me.

I've never forgotten Cliff Evans nor that resolve. He has been my challenge year after year, class after class. I look for veiled eyes or bodies scrouged into a seat in an alien world. "Look, kids," I say silently, "I may not do anything else for you this year, but not one of you is going to come out of here a nobody. I'll work or fight to the bitter end doing battle with society and the school board, but I won't have one of you coming out of here thinking himself a zero."

Most of the time—not always, but most of the time—I've succeeded.

Jean Mizer

CHARACTERISTICS OF THE SELF-CONCEPT

Now that you have a better idea of how your self-concept has developed, we can take a closer look at some of its characteristics.

THE SELF-CONCEPT IS SUBJECTIVE Although we may believe that our self-concept is accurate, in truth it may well be distorted. Some people view themselves much more harshly than the objective facts warrant. We have all experienced a temporary case of the "uglies," convinced that we look much worse than others assure us we really appear. Research confirms what common sense suggests: that people are more critical of themselves when they are experiencing these negative moods than when they are feeling more positive.[7] Although we all suffer occasional bouts of self-doubt that affect our communication, some people suffer from long-term or even permanent states of excessive self-doubt and criticism.[8] It's easy to understand how this chronic condition can influence the way they approach and respond to others.

Distorted self-evaluations like these can occur for several reasons. One source is *obsolete information*. The effects of past failures in school or social relations can linger long after they have occurred, even though such events don't predict failure in the future. Likewise, your past successes don't guarantee future success. Perhaps your jokes used to be well received or your work was superior, but now the facts have changed.

"Oh, thank you, I only wish I felt as good as I look."

DRAWING BY SCHOENBAUM, COPYRIGHT © 1990 THE NEW YORKER MAGAZINE, INC.

Distorted feedback can also create a self-image that is worse or better than the factors warrant. Overly critical parents are one of the most common causes of a negative self-image. In other cases the remarks of cruel friends, uncaring teachers, excessively demanding employers, or even memorable strangers can have a lasting effect. Other distorted messages are unrealistically positive. A boss may think of herself as an excellent manager because her assistants shower her with false praise in order to keep their jobs or gain promotions. Likewise, a child's inflated ego may be based on the praise of doting parents.

Once communicators fasten onto a self-concept—whether it is positive or negative—the tendency is to seek out people who confirm it. Recent studies show that both college students and married couples with high self-esteem seek out partners who view them favorably, while those with negative self-concepts are more inclined to interact with people who view them unfavorably.[9] The tendency to look for people who confirm our self-concept has been called *self-verification*. It suggests that we are less concerned with learning the "truth" about ourselves than with reinforcing a familiar self-concept.

Along with obsolete information and distorted feedback, another cause for a strongly negative self-concept is the emphasis on *perfection*, which is common in our society. From the time most of us learn to understand language we are exposed to models who appear to be perfect. Children's stories and advertisements imply that the way to be a hero, the way to be liked and admired, is to show no flaws. Unfortunately, many parents perpetuate the myth of perfection by refusing to admit that they are ever mistaken or unfair. Children, of course, accept this perfectionist façade for a long time, not being in any position to dispute the wisdom of such powerful beings. And from the behavior of the adults around them comes a clear message: "A well-adjusted, successful person has no faults." Thus, children learn that, in order to gain acceptance, it's necessary to pretend to "have it all together," even though they know this isn't the case. Given this naive belief that everyone else is perfect and the knowledge that one isn't, it's easy to see how one's self-concept would suffer.

Don't misunderstand: It's not wrong to aim at perfection as an *ideal*. We're only suggesting that achieving this state is usually not possible, and to expect that you should do so is a sure ticket to an inaccurate and unnecessarily low self-concept.

A final reason people often sell themselves short is also connected to *social expectations*. Curiously the perfectionistic society to which we belong rewards those people who downplay the strengths we demand they possess (or pretend to possess). We term these people "modest" and find their behavior agreeable. On the other hand, we consider those who honestly appreciate their strengths to be "braggarts" or "egotists," confusing them with the people who boast about accomplishments they do not possess.[10] This convention leads most of us to talk freely about our shortcomings while downplaying our accomplishments. It's all right to proclaim that you're miserable if

I am not what I think I am. I am not what you think I am. I am what I think you think I am.

Aaron Bleiberg and Harry Leubling

TABLE 2–1   **Differences Between Communicators With High and Low Self-Esteem**

PERSONS WITH HIGH SELF-ESTEEM	PERSONS WITH LOW SELF-ESTEEM
1. Likely to think well of others.	1. Likely to disapprove of others.
2. Expect to be accepted by others.	2. Expect to be rejected by others.
3. Evaluate their own performance more favorably than people with low self-esteem.	3. Evaluate their own performance less favorably than people with high self-esteem.
4. Perform well when being watched: not afraid of others' reactions.	4. Perform poorly when being watched: sensitive to possible negative reaction.
5. Work harder for people who demand high standards of performance.	5. Work harder for undemanding, less critical people.
6. Inclined to feel comfortable with others they view as superior in some way.	6. Feel threatened by people they view as superior in some way.
7. Able to defend themselves against negative comments of others.	7. Have difficulty defending themselves against others' negative comments; more easily influenced.

Summarized by Don E. Hamachek, *Encounters with the Self* (2d ed.). New York: Holt, Rinehart and Winston, 1982, pp. 3–5.

I celebrate myself and sing myself.

Walt Whitman

you have failed to do well on a project; but it's considered boastful to express your pride at a job well done. It's fine to remark that you feel unattractive but egocentric to say that you think you look good.

After a while we begin to believe the types of statements we repeatedly make. The disparaging remarks are viewed as modesty and become part of our self-concept, and the strengths and accomplishments go unmentioned and are thus forgotten. And in the end we see ourselves as much worse than we are.

Self-esteem may be based on inaccurate thinking, but it still has a powerful effect on the way we relate to others. Table 2–1 summarizes some important differences between communicators with high and low self-esteem. Differences like these make sense when you realize that people who dislike themselves are likely to believe that others won't like them either. Realistically or not, they imagine that others are constantly viewing them critically, and they accept these imagined or real criticisms as more proof that they are indeed unlikable people. To use the well-known terminology of psychiatrist Eric Berne, they adopt an "I'm not OK—you're OK" orientation to life. Sometimes this low self-esteem is manifested in hostility toward others, since the communicator takes the approach that the only way to look good is to put others down.

One way to avoid falling into the trap of becoming overly critical is to recognize your strengths. The following exercise will give you a chance to suspend the ordinary rules of modesty and appreciate yourself publicly for a change.

INVITATION TO INSIGHT

RECOGNIZING YOUR STRENGTHS

1. This exercise can be done either alone or with a group. If you are with others, sit in a circle so that everyone can see one another.

2. Each person should share three personal strengths or accomplishments. These needn't feature areas in which you are an expert, and they don't have to be concerned with momentous feats. On the contrary, it's perfectly acceptable to talk about some part of yourself that leaves you feeling pleased or proud. For instance, you might say that, instead of procrastinating you completed a school assignment before the last minute, that you spoke up to a friend even though you were afraid of disapproval, that you bake a fantastic chocolate cake, or that you frequently drive hitchhikers to their destinations although it's out of your way.

3. If you're at a loss for items, ask yourself
   a. What are some ways in which you've grown in the past year? How are you more skillful, wise, or a better person than you previously were?
   b. Why do certain friends or family members care about you? What features do you possess that make them appreciate you?

4. After you've finished, consider the experience. Did you have a hard time thinking of things to share? Would it have been easier to list the things that are *wrong* with you? If so, is this because you are truly a wretched person or because you are in the habit of stressing your defects and ignoring your strengths? Consider the impact of such a habit on your self-concept, and ask yourself whether it wouldn't be wiser to strike a better balance distinguishing between your strengths and shortcomings.

THE SELF-CONCEPT RESISTS CHANGE   Despite the fact that we all change, there is a tendency to cling to an existing self-concept, even when evidence shows that it is obsolete. This tendency to seek and attend to information that conforms to an existing self-concept has been labeled **cognitive conservatism.**

It's understandable why we're reluctant to revise a previously favorable self-concept. As we write these words, we recall how some professional athletes doggedly insist that they can be of value to the team when they are clearly past their prime. It must be tremendously difficult to give up the life of excitement, recognition, and financial rewards that comes with such a talent. Faced with such a tremendous loss, the athlete might well try to play one more season, insisting that the old skills are still there. In the same way, a student who did well in earlier years but now has failed to study might be unwilling to admit that the label "good scholar" no longer applies; and a previously industrious worker, pointing to past commendations in a per-

Self-love, my liege, is not so vile a sin as self-neglecting.

Shakespeare,
King Henry V

It has become something of a cliché to observe that if we do not love ourselves, we cannot love anyone else. This is true enough, but it is only part of the picture. If we do not love ourselves, it is almost impossible to believe fully that we are loved by someone else. It is almost impossible to accept love. It is almost impossible to receive love. No matter what our partner does to show that he or she cares, we do not experience the devotion as convincing because we do not feel lovable to ourselves.

Nathaniel Branden,
The Psychology of Romantic Love

sonnel file and insisting that she is a top-notch employee, might resent a supervisor's mentioning increased absences and low productivity. (Remember that the people in these and other examples aren't *lying* when they insist that they're doing well in spite of the facts to the contrary; they honestly believe that the old truths still hold precisely because their self-concepts have been so resistant to change.)

Curiously, the tendency to cling to an outmoded self-perception also holds when the new image would be more favorable than the old one. We recall a former student whom almost anyone would have regarded as beautiful, with physical features attractive enough to appear in any glamour magazine. In spite of her appearance, in a class exercise this woman characterized herself as "ordinary" and "unattractive." When questioned by her classmates, she described how as a child her teeth were extremely crooked and how she had worn braces for several years in her teens to correct this problem. During this time she was often kidded by her friends, who never let her forget her "metal mouth," as she put it. Even though the braces had been off for two years, our student reported that she still saw herself as ugly and brushed aside our compliments by insisting that we were just saying these things to be nice—she knew how she *really* looked.

Examples like this show one problem that occurs when we resist changing an inaccurate self-concept. Our student denied herself a much happier life by clinging to an obsolete picture of herself. In the same way some communicators insist that they are less talented or worthy of friendship than others would suggest, thus creating their own miserable world when it needn't exist. These unfortunate souls probably resist changing because they aren't willing to go through the disorientation that comes from redefining themselves, correctly anticipating that it *is* an effort to think of oneself in a new way. Whatever their reasons, it's sad to see people in such an unnecessary state.

A second problem arising from the persistence of an inaccurate self-concept is self-delusion and lack of growth. If you hold an unrealistically favorable picture of yourself, you won't see the real need for change that may exist. Instead of learning new talents, working to change a relationship, or improving your physical condition, you'll stay with the familiar and comfortable delusion that everything is all right. As time goes by, this delusion becomes more and more difficult to maintain, leading to a third type of problem: defensiveness.

To understand this problem, you need to remember that communicators who are presented with information that contradicts their self-perception have two choices: They can either accept the new data and change their perception accordingly, or they can keep their original viewpoint and in some way refute the new information. Since most communicators are reluctant to downgrade a favorable image of themselves, their tendency is to opt for refutation, either by discounting the information and rationalizing it away or by counterattacking the person who transmitted it. The problem of defensiveness is so great that we will examine it in Chapter Nine.

CULTURE AND THE SELF-CONCEPT

In the relatively enlightened 1990s, the challenges and opportunities that come from cultural diversity are becoming more apparent. But the power of culture is far more basic and powerful than most people realize. Although we seldom recognize the fact, our whole notion of the self is shaped by the culture in which we have been reared.

The most obvious feature of a culture is the language members use. If you live in an environment where everyone speaks the same tongue, then language will seem to have little impact. But when your primary language is not the majority one, or when it is not prestigious, the sense of being a member of what social scientists call the "outgroup" is strong. At this point the speaker of a nondominant tongue can react in one of two ways: either to feel pressured to assimilate by speaking the "better" language, or to refuse to accommodate to the majority language and maintain loyalty to the ethnic tongue.[11] In either case, the impact of language on the self-concept is powerful. On one hand the feeling is likely to be "I'm not as good as speakers of the native language," and on the other the belief is "there's something unique and worth preserving in my language." A case study of

In Japan, in fact, everything had been made level and uniform—even humanity. By one official count, 90 percent of the population regarded themselves as middle-class; in schools, it was not the outcasts who beat up the conformists, but vice versa. Every Japanese individual seemed to have the same goal as every other—to become like every other Japanese individual. The word for "different," I was told, was the same as the word for "wrong." And again and again in Japan, in contexts varying from the baseball stadium to the watercolor canvas, I heard the same unswerving, even maxim: "The nail that sticks out must be hammered down."

Pico Iyer,
Video Night in Katmandu

Hispanic managers illustrates the dilemma of speaking a nondominant language.[12] The managers, employees in an Anglo-American organization, felt their sense of Mexican identity threatened when they found that the road to advancement would be smoother if they de-emphasized their Spanish and adopted a more colloquial English style of speaking.

Cultures affect the self-concept in more subtle ways, too. Most Western cultures are highly individualistic, whereas traditional other cultures—most Asian ones, for example—are much more collective. When asked to identify themselves, Americans, Canadians, Australians, and Europeans would probably respond by giving their first name, surname, street, town, and country. Many Asians do it the other way around.[13] If you ask Hindus for their identity, they will give you their caste and village as well as their name. The Sanskrit formula for identifying one's self begins with lineage and goes on to state family, house, and ends with one's personal name.[14]

These conventions for naming aren't just cultural curiosities: They reflect a very different way of viewing one's self. In collective cultures a person gains identity by belonging to a group. This means that the degree of interdependence among members of the society and its subgroups is much higher. Feelings of pride and self-worth are likely to be shaped not only by what the individual does, but by behavior of other members of the community. This linkage to others explains the traditional Asian denial of self-importance—a strong contrast to the self-promotion that is common in individualistic Western cultures.[15] In Chinese written language, for example, the pronoun "I" looks very similar to the word for selfish.[16] Table 2–2 sum-

T A B L E   2 – 2   The Self in Individualistic and Collectivistic Cultures

INDIVIDUALISTIC CULTURES	COLLECTIVISTIC CULTURES
Self is separate, unique individual; should be independent, self-sufficient	People belong to extended families or ingroups; "we" or group orientation
Individual should take care of him/herself and immediate family	Person should take care of extended family before self
Many flexible group memberships; friends based on shared interests and activities	Emphasis on belonging to a very few permanent ingroups which have a strong influence over the person
Reward for individual achievement and initiative; individual decisions encouraged; individual credit and blame assigned	Reward for contribution to group goals and well-being; cooperation with ingroup members; group decisions valued; credit and blame shared
High value on autonomy, change, youth, individual security, equality	High value on duty, order, tradition, age, group security, status, and hierarchy

Adapted by Sandra Sudweeks from material in H.C. Triandis, "Cross-Cultural Studies of Individualism and Collectivism" in J. Berman (ed.), *Nebraska Symposium on Motivation* 37 (Lincoln, Neb.: University of Nebraska Press, 1990), pp. 41–133.

TABLE 2 – 3 Individualism Index of Several Countries

U.S.A.	91	India	48
Australia	90	Japan	46
Great Britain	89	Argentina	46
Canada	80	Iran	41
Netherlands	80	Brazil	38
New Zealand	79	Turkey	37
Italy	76	Greece	35
Belgium	75	Philippines	32
Denmark	74	Mexico	30
Sweden	71	Portugal	27
France	71	Hong Kong	25
Ireland	70	Chile	23
Norway	69	Singapore	20
Switzerland	68	Thailand	20
Germany	67	Taiwan	17
South Africa	65	Peru	16
Finland	63	Pakistan	14
Austria	55	Colombia	13
Israel	54	Venezuela	12
Spain	51	Mean of 39 countries	51

Adapted from Geert Hofstede, *Culture's Consequences* (Newbury Park, Calif.: Sage, 1984), p. 158.

marizes some differences between individualistic cultures and more collective ones, and Table 2–3 shows where several countries fall on the individualism–collectivism spectrum.

This sort of cultural difference isn't just a matter of interest to anthropologists. It shows up in the level of comfort or anxiety people feel when communicating. In collective societies, there is a higher degree of communication apprehension. For example, as a group, residents of China, Korea, and Japan exhibit a significantly higher degree of anxiety about speaking out than do members of individualistic cultures such as the United States and Australia.[17] It's important to realize that different levels of communication apprehension don't mean that shyness is a "problem" in some cultures. In fact, just the opposite is true: In these societies reticence is valued. When the goal is to *avoid* being the nail that sticks out, it's logical to feel nervous when you make yourself appear different by calling attention to yourself. A self-concept that includes "assertive" might make a Westerner feel proud, but in much of Asia it would more likely be cause for shame.

The difference between individualism and collectivism shows up in everyday interaction. Communication researcher Stella Ting-Toomey has developed a theory that explains cultural differences in important norms, such as honesty and directness.[18] She suggests that

There is an old joke about a man who was asked if he could play a violin and answered, "I don't know. I've never tried." This is psychologically a very wise reply. Those who have never tried to play a violin really do not know whether they can or not. Those who say too early in life and too firmly, "No, I'm not at all musical," shut themselves off prematurely from whole areas of life that might have proved rewarding. In each of us there are unknown possibilities, undiscovered potentialities—and one big advantage of having an open self-concept rather than a rigid one is that we shall continue to expose ourselves to new experiences and therefore we shall continue to discover more and more about ourselves as we grow older.

S.I. Hayakawa

in individualistic Western cultures where there is a strong "I" orientation, the norm of speaking directly is honored; whereas in collectivistic cultures, where the main desire is to build connections between the self and others, indirect approaches that maintain harmony are considered more desirable. "I gotta be me" could be the motto of a Westerner, but "If I hurt you, I hurt myself" is closer to the Asian way of thinking.

THE SELF-FULFILLING PROPHECY AND COMMUNICATION

The self-concept is such a powerful force on the personality that it not only determines how you see yourself in the present but also can actually influence your future behavior and that of others. Such occurrences come about through a phenomenon called the self-fulfilling prophecy.

A **self-fulfilling prophecy** occurs when a person's expectations of an event make the outcome more likely to occur than would otherwise have been true. Self-fulfilling prophecies occur all the time although you might never have given them that label. For example, think of some instances you may have known.

You expected to become nervous and botch a job interview and later did so.

You anticipated having a good (or terrible) time at a social affair and found your expectations being met.

A teacher or boss explained a new task to you, saying that you probably wouldn't do well at first. You did not do well.

A friend described someone you were about to meet, saying that you wouldn't like the person. The prediction turned out to be correct—you didn't like the new acquaintance.

In each of these cases there is a good chance that the event occurred because it was predicted to occur. You needn't have botched the interview, the party might have been boring only because you helped make it so, you might have done better on the job if your boss hadn't spoken up, and you might have liked the new acquaintance if your friend hadn't given you preconceptions. In other words, what helped make each event occur was the expectation of it.

TYPES OF SELF-FULFILLING PROPHECIES   There are two types of self-fulfilling prophecies. *Self-imposed prophecies* occur when your own expectations influence your behavior. In sports you've probably "psyched" yourself into playing either better or worse than usual, so that the only explanation for your unusual performance was your attitude. Similarly, you've probably faced an audience at one time or another with a fearful attitude and forgotten your remarks, not because you were unprepared, but because you said to yourself, "I know I'll blow it." Research has demonstrated the power of self-imposed prophecies. In one study, communicators who believed they were incompetent proved less likely than others to pursue rewarding relationships and more likely to sabotage their existing relationships than did people who were less critical of themselves.[19]

Certainly you've had the experience of waking up in a cross mood and saying to yourself, "This will be a 'bad day.'" Once you made such a decision, you may have acted in ways that made it come true. If you approached a class expecting to be bored, you most probably did lose interest, owing partly to a lack of attention on your part. If you avoided the company of others because you expected they had nothing to offer, your suspicions would have been confirmed—nothing exciting or new did happen to you. On the other hand, if you approached the same day with the idea that it could be a good one, this expectation probably would have been met also. Smile at people, and they'll probably smile back. Enter a class determined to learn something, and you probably will—even if it's how not to instruct students! Approach many people with the idea that some of them will be good to know, and you'll most likely make some new friends. In these cases and ones like them, your attitude has a great deal to do with how you see yourself and how others will see you.

A second category of self-fulfilling prophecies is imposed by one person on another, so that the expectations of one person govern another's actions. The classic example was demonstrated by Robert Rosenthal and Lenore Jacobson in a study they described in their book *Pygmalion in the Classroom.*[20] The experimenters told teachers that 20 percent of the children in a certain elementary school showed unusual potential for intellectual growth. The names of these 20 percent were drawn by means of a table of random numbers, which is to say that the names were drawn out of a hat. Eight months later these unusual or "magic" children showed significantly greater gains in IQ than did the remaining children, who had not been singled out for the teachers' attention. The change in the teachers' expectations regarding the intellectual performance of these allegedly "special" children

cathy®   by Cathy Guisewite

The difference between a lady and a flower girl is not how she behaves, but how she's treated. I shall always be a flower girl to Professor Higgins, because he always treats me as a flower girl, and always will; but I know I can be a lady to you, because you always treat me as a lady, and always will.

G.B. Shaw
Pygmalion

had led to an actual change in the intellectual performance of these randomly selected children. In other words, the children did better, not because they were any more intelligent than their classmates, but because they learned that their teachers—significant others—believed they could.

To put this phenomenon in context with the self-concept, we can say that when a teacher communicates to a child the message "I think you're bright," the child accepts that evaluation and changes her self-concept to include it. Unfortunately, we can assume that the same principle holds for students whose teachers send the message "I think you're stupid."

This type of self-fulfilling prophecy has been shown to be a powerful force for shaping the self-concept and thus the behavior of people in a wide range of settings outside the schools. In medicine, patients who unknowingly use placebos—substances such as injections of sterile water or doses of sugar pills that have no curative value—often respond just as favorably to treatment as those who actually received a drug. The patients believe they have taken a substance that will help them feel better, and this belief actually brings about a "cure." In psychotherapy Rosenthal and Jacobson describe several studies suggesting that patients who believe they will benefit from treatment do so regardless of the type of treatment they receive. In the same vein, when a doctor believes a patient will improve, the patient may do so precisely because of this expectation, whereas another person for whom the physician has little hope often fails to recover. Apparently the patient's self-concept as sick or well—as shaped by the doctor—plays an important role in determining the actual state of health.

INFLUENCE OF SELF-FULFILLING PROPHECIES   The influence of self-fulfilling prophecies on communication can be strong, acting either to improve or harm relationships. If, for instance, you assume that another person is unlikable, then you'll probably act in ways that communicate your feelings. In such a case, the other person's behavior will probably match your expectations: We usually don't go out of our way to be nice to people who aren't nice to us. If, on the other hand, you treat the other person as likable, the results are likely to be more positive.

In business, the power of the self-fulfilling prophecy was proved as early as 1890. A new tabulating machine had just been installed at the U.S. Census Bureau in Washington, D.C. In order to use the machine, the bureau's staff had to learn a new set of skills that the machine's inventor believed to be quite difficult. He told the clerks that after some practice they could expect to punch about 550 cards per day; to process any more would jeopardize their psychological well-being. Sure enough, after two weeks the clerks were processing the anticipated number of cards and reported feelings of stress if they attempted to move any faster.

Later an additional group of clerks was hired to operate the same machines. These workers knew nothing of the devices, and no one

There is a joke which goes right to the heart of this matter. It is about a man whose tire goes flat on a dark and lonely country road. When he discovers that he doesn't have a jack, he recalls seeing a farm house about a mile back. And so he starts to walk there in the hopes of borrowing one. While he is walking, he talks to himself about his situation: "Wow, I'm really stranded here. The guy will probably want a few dollars to lend me his jack. Why should he do it for nothing? Everyone wants to make a few bucks. A few bucks! If I don't get the jack, I'll never get out of here. He'll realize that, and probably want fifteen dollars, maybe twenty-five dollars. Twenty-five dollars? This guy's really got me by the old cashews. He'll ask fifty dollars, for sure— maybe a hundred."

Well, he goes on in this way until he reaches the farm house. He knocks at the door. An elderly farmer answers and with a cheerful smile asks, "Is there something I can do for you, young man?" "Do for me? Do for me?" says the man, "I'll tell you what you can do, you can take your goddamn jack and shove it!"

. . . If, as in this case, you predict that you will not be lent a jack in a spirit of gracious cooperation, you prepare yourself for the confrontation in such a way that you guarantee the jack will not be lent in a spirit of gracious cooperation. Your prediction is transformed into a fact, which then becomes the reality.

Neil Postman,
Crazy Talk, Stupid Talk

---

had told them about the upper limit of production. After only three days, the new employees were each punching over 2,000 cards per day with no ill effects. Again, the self-fulfilling prophecy seemed to be in operation. The original workers believed themselves capable of punching only 550 cards and so behaved accordingly, whereas the new clerks had no limiting expectations as part of their self-concepts and so behaved more productively.[21]

The self-fulfilling prophecy operates in families as well. If parents tell a child long enough that he can't do anything right, his self-concept will soon incorporate this idea, and he will fail at many or most of the tasks he attempts. On the other hand, if a child is told she is a capable or lovable or kind person, there is a much greater chance of her behaving accordingly.

The self-fulfilling prophecy is an important force in interpersonal communication, but it doesn't explain behavior. There are certainly times when the expectation of an event's outcome won't bring it about. Your hope of drawing an ace in a card game won't in any way affect the chance of that card turning up in an already shuffled deck, and your belief that good weather is coming won't stop the rain from falling. In the same way, believing you'll do well in a job interview when you're clearly not qualified for the position is unrealistic. Similarly, there will probably be people you don't like and occasions you won't enjoy, no matter what your attitude. To connect the self-fulfilling prophecy with the "power of positive thinking" is an over-simplification.

In other cases your expectations will be borne out because you're a good predictor and not because of the self-fulfilling prophecy. For example, some children are not well equipped to do well in school; in such cases it would be wrong to say that the child's performance was shaped by a parent or teacher, even though the behavior did match that which was expected. In the same way, some workers excel and others fail, some patients recover and others don't, in agreement with or contrary to our predictions, but not because of them.

Keeping these qualifications in mind, you will find it important to recognize the tremendous influence that self-fulfilling prophecies play in our lives. To a great extent we are what we believe we are. In this sense we and those around us constantly create our self-concepts and thus ourselves.

CHANGING YOUR SELF-CONCEPT

After reading this far, you know more clearly just what the self-concept is, how it is formed, and how it affects communication. But we still haven't focused directly on perhaps the most important question of all: How can you change the parts of your self-concept with which you aren't happy? There's certainly no quick method for becoming the person you'd like to be: Personal growth and self-improvement are a lifetime process. But we can offer several suggestions that will help you move closer to your goals.

HAVE REALISTIC EXPECTATIONS   It's extremely important to realize that some of your dissatisfaction might come from expecting too much of yourself. If you demand that you handle every act of communication perfectly, you're bound to be disappointed. Nobody is able to handle every conflict productively, to be totally relaxed and skillful in conversations, always to ask perceptive questions, or to be 100 percent helpful when others have problems. Expecting yourself to reach such unrealistic goals is to doom yourself to unhappiness at the start.

Sometimes it's easy to be hard on yourself because everyone around you seems to be handling themselves so much better than you. It's important to realize that much of what seems like confidence and skill in others is a front to hide uncertainty. They may be suffering from the same self-imposed demands of perfection that you place on yourself.

Even in cases where others definitely seem more competent than you, it's important to judge yourself in terms of your own growth and not against the behavior of others. Rather than feel miserable because you're not as talented as an expert, realize that you probably are a better, wiser, or more skillful person than you used to be, and that this is a legitimate source of satisfaction. Perfection is fine as an ideal, but you're being unfair to yourself if you expect actually to reach it.

HAVE A REALISTIC PERCEPTION OF YOURSELF   One source of a poor self-concept is an inaccurate self-perception. As you've already read, such unrealistic pictures sometimes come from being overly harsh on yourself, believing that you're worse than the facts indicate. By showing the self-concept list you developed on pages 46–47 to others who know you, it will be possible to see whether you have been selling yourself short. Of course, it would be foolish to deny that you could be a better person than you are, but it's also important to recognize your strengths. A periodic session of recognizing your strengths such as you tried earlier in this chapter is often a good way to put your strengths and shortcomings into perspective.

An unrealistically poor self-concept can also arise from the inaccurate feedback of others. Perhaps you are in an environment where you receive an excessive number of prickly messages, many of which are undeserved, and a minimum of fuzzy messages. We've known many homemakers, for example, who have returned to college after many years spent in homemaking, where they received virtually no recognition for their intellectual strengths. It's amazing that these women have the courage to come to college at all, so low are their self-concepts; but come they do, and most are thrilled to find that they are much brighter and more competent intellectually than they suspected. In the same way, workers with overly critical supervisors, children with cruel "friends," and students with unsupportive teachers all are prone to low self-concepts owing to excessively negative feedback.

If you fall into this category, it's important to put the unrealistic evaluations you receive into perspective and then to seek out more supportive people who will acknowledge your assets as well as point out your shortcomings. Doing so is often a quick and sure boost.

HAVE THE WILL TO CHANGE   Often we say we want to change, but we aren't willing to do the necessary work. In such cases it's clear that the responsibility for growing rests squarely on your shoulders, as the example following the exercise shows.

"YOU'RE A VERY FINE FELLOW!"

ECHO POINT

© GAHAN WILSON.

SKILL BUILDER

RE-EVALUATING YOUR "CAN'TS"

1. Choose a partner and for five minutes or so take turns making and listing statements that begin with "I can't. . . ." Try to focus your statements on your relationships with family, friends, co-workers, students, and even strangers: anyone with whom you have a hard time communicating. Sample statements:
   "I can't be myself with strangers I'd like to get to know at parties."
   "I can't tell a friend how much I care about her."
   "I can't bring myself to ask my supervisor for the raise I think I deserve."
   "I can't ask questions in class."

2. Notice your feelings as you make each statement: self-pity, regret, concern, frustration, and so on, and reveal these to your partner.

3. Now repeat aloud each statement you've just made, except this time change each "can't" to a "won't." After each sentence, tell your partner whatever thoughts you have about what you've just said.

4. After you've finished, decide whether "can't" or "won't" is more appropriate for each item, and explain your choice to your partner.

5. Are there any instances of the self-fulfilling prophecy in your list—times when your decision that you "couldn't" do something was the only force keeping you from doing it?

We hope the point of this exercise is clear. Often we maintain an unrealistic self-concept by claiming that we "can't" be the person we'd like to be when in fact we're simply not willing to do what's required. You *can* change in many ways, if only you are willing to make the effort.

You might, for instance, decide that you'd like to become a better conversationalist. Seeking the advice of your instructor or some other communication adviser, you receive two pieces of advice. First, you're instructed to spend the next three weeks observing people who handle themselves well in conversations and to record exactly what they do that makes them so skillful. Second, your adviser suggests that you read several books on the subject of conversational skills. You begin these tasks with the best intentions, but after a few days the task of recording conversations becomes a burden—it would be so much easier just to listen to others talk. And your diligent reading program becomes bogged down as the press of other work fills up your time. In other words, you find you just "can't" fit the self-improvement plan into your busy schedule.

Let's be realistic. Becoming a better communicator is probably one of many goals in your life. It's possible that other needs are more pressing, which is completely reasonable. However, you should realize that changing your self-concept often requires a good deal of commitment, and without that effort your good intentions alone probably won't get you much closer to this goal. In communication, as in most other aspects of life, "there's no such thing as a free lunch."

HAVE THE SKILL TO CHANGE Often trying isn't enough. In some instances you would change if you knew of a way to do so. To see if this is the case for you, go back to your list of *can'ts* and *won'ts*, and see if any items there are more appropriately "don't know how." If so, then the way to change is to learn how. You can do so in two ways.

First, you can seek advice—from books such as this one, the references listed at the end of each chapter, and other printed sources. You can also get advice from instructors, counselors, and other experts, as well as friends. Of course, not all the advice you receive will be useful, but if you read widely and talk to enough people, you have a good chance of learning the things you want to know.

A second method of learning how to change is to observe models—people who handle themselves in the ways you would like to master. It's often been said that people learn more from models than in any other way, and by taking advantage of this principle you will find that the world is full of teachers who can show you how to communicate more successfully. Become a careful observer. Watch what people you admire do and say, not so that you can copy them, but so that you can adapt their behavior to fit your own personal style.

At this point, you might be overwhelmed at the difficulty of changing the way you think about yourself and the way you act. Remember, we never said that this process would be an easy one (although it sometimes is). But even when change is difficult, you know that it's possible if you are serious. You don't need to be perfect, but you can improve your self-concept if you choose.

✛ PRESENTING THE SELF: COMMUNICATION AS IMPRESSION MANAGEMENT

So far we have described how communication shapes the way communicators view themselves. In the remainder of this chapter we will turn the tables and focus on the topic of **impression management**— the communication strategies people use to influence how others view them. In the following pages you will see that many of our messages aim at creating desired impressions.

PUBLIC AND PRIVATE SELVES

To understand why impression management exists, we have to discuss the notion of self in more detail. So far we have referred to the "self" as if each of us had only one identity. In truth, each of us possesses several selves, some private and others public. Often these selves are quite different.

The **perceived self** is a reflection of the self-concept. Your perceived self is the person you believe yourself to be in moments of honest self-examination. We can call the perceived self "private" because you are unlikely to reveal all of it to another person. You can verify the private nature of the perceived self by reviewing the self-concept list you developed while reading pages 46–47. You'll probably find some elements of yourself there that you would not disclose to many people, and some that you would not share with anyone. You might, for example, be reluctant to share some feelings about your appearance ("I think I'm rather unattractive"), your intelligence ("I'm not as smart as I wish I were"), your goals ("The most important thing to me is becoming rich"), or your motives ("I care more about myself than about others").

In contrast to the perceived self, the **presenting self** is a public image—the way we want to appear to others . . . not too different from what has been termed the **ideal self.** In most cases the presenting self we seek to create is a socially approved image: diligent student, loving partner, conscientious worker, loyal friend, and so on. Sociologist Erving Goffman used the word **face** to describe this socially approved identity, and he coined the term **facework** to describe the verbal and nonverbal ways we act to maintain our own presenting image and the images of others.[22] He argued that each of us can be viewed as a kind of playwright who creates roles that we want others to believe, as well as the performer who acts out those roles. Goffman suggested that each of us maintains face by putting on a **front** when we are around others whom we want to impress. By contrast, behavior in the **back** region when we are alone may be quite different. You can recognize the difference between front- and backstage behavior by recalling a time when you observed a driver, alone in his or her car, behaving in ways that would never be acceptable in public. All of us engage in backstage ways of acting that we would never do in public. Just recall how you behave in front of the bathroom mirror when the door is locked, and you will appreciate the difference between public and private behavior. If you knew someone were watching, would you behave differently?

It is an oversimplification to suggest that each of us uses impression management strategies to create just one front. In the course of even a single day, most people perform a variety of roles: "respectful student," "joking friend," "friendly neighbor," and "helpful worker," to suggest just a few. We even play a variety of roles with the same person. As you grew up you almost certainly

"Hah! This is the Old King Cole nobody ever sees."

Looking at Diversity

IMPRESSION MANAGEMENT ON CAMPUS AND IN THE INNER CITY

In this profile **Daria Muse** *describes how impression management* *made it possible for her to communicate successfully in two strikingly different environments: her home neighborhood of South-Central Los Angeles and her school in the suburban San Fernando Valley.*

During my elementary and middle-school years, I was a well-behaved, friendly student at school and a tough, hard-nosed "bad girl" in my neighborhood. This contrast in behavior was a survival tool, for I lived in a part of South-Central Los Angeles where "goody-goodies" aren't tolerated, and I attended school in Northridge, where trouble-makers aren't tolerated.

Beckford Ave. Elementary School was in the heart of a middle-class suburbia, and I, coming from what has been described as the "urban jungle," was bused there every day for six years.

In a roundabout way, I was told from the first day of school that if I wanted to continue my privileged attendance in the hallowed classrooms of Beckford, I would have to conform and adapt to their standards. I guess I began to believe all that they said because slowly I began to conform.

Instead of wearing the tight jeans and T-shirt which were the style in South-Central at the time, I wore schoolgirl dresses like those of my female classmates. I even changed my language. When asking a question, instead of saying, "Boy! Gimme those scissors before I knock you up you head!" in school, I asked, "Excuse me, would you please hand me the scissors?" When giving a compliment in school I'd say, "You look very nice today," instead of "Girl, who do you think you are, dressin' so fine, Miss Thang."

This conformation of my appearance and speech won me the acceptance of my proper classmates at Beckford Elementary School, but after getting out of the school bus and stepping onto the sidewalks of South-Central, my appearance quit being an asset and became a dangerous liability.

One day, when I got off the school bus, a group of tough girls who looked as though they were part of a gang approached me, looked at my pink and white lace dress, and accused me of trying to "look white." They surrounded me and demanded a response that would prove to them that I was still loyal to my black heritage. I screamed, "Lay off me, girl, or I'll bust you in the eyes so bad that you'll need a telescope just to see!" The girls walked away without causing any more trouble.

From then on, two personalities emerged. I began living a double life. At school I was prim and proper in appearance and in speech, but during the drive on the school bus from Northridge to South-Central, my other personality emerged. Once I got off the bus I put a black jacket over my dress, I hardened my face, and roughened my speech to show everyone who looked my way that I was not a girl to be messed with. I led this double life throughout my six years of elementary school.

Now that I am older and can look back at that time objectively, I don't regret displaying contrasting behavior in the two different environments. It was for my survival. Daria, the hard-nosed bad girl, survived in the urban jungle and Daria, the well-behaved student, survived in the suburbs.

As a teen-ager in high school I still display different personalities: I act one way in school, which is different from the way I act with my parents, which is different from the way I act with my friends, which is different from the way I act in religious services. But don't we all? We all put on character masks for our different roles in life. All people are guilty of acting differently at work than at play and differently with co-workers than with the boss. There's nothing wrong with having different personalities to fit different situations; the trick is knowing the real you from the characters.

changed characters as you interacted with your parents. In one context you acted as responsible adult ("You can trust me with the car!) and at another time you were the helpless child ("I can't find my socks!"). At some times—perhaps on birthdays or holidays—you were a dedicated family member, and at other times you may have played the role of rebel. Likewise, in romantic relationships we switch among many ways of behaving, depending on the context: friend, lover, business partner, scolding critic, apologetic child, and so on.

INVITATION TO INSIGHT

YOUR MANY ROLES

You can get a sense of the many fronts you create by keeping a record of the situations in which you communicate over a one- or two-day period. For each situation, identify a dramatic title to represent the image you try to create. A few examples might be "party animal," "helpful housekeeper," "wise older sibling," and "sophisticated film critic."

The degree to which we act as impression managers is surprising. Some behaviors that hardly seem deliberate are really small public performances. For example, experimental subjects expressed facial disgust in reaction to eating sandwiches laced with a supersaturated salt-water solution only when there was another person present: When they were alone, they made no faces on eating the same snack.[23] Another study showed that communicators only engage in facial mimicry (such as smiling or looking sympathetic in response to another's message) in face-to-face settings when their expressions can be seen by the other person. When they are speaking over the phone and their reactions cannot be seen, they do not make the same expressions.[24] Studies like these suggest that most of our behavior is aimed at sending messages to others—in other words, impression management.

You can see by now that much impression management is unconscious. The experimental subjects described in the preceding paragraph didn't consciously think "Somebody is watching me eat this salty sandwich so I'll make a face" or "Since I'm in a face-to-face conversation, I'll show I'm sympathetic by mimicking the facial expressions of my conversational partner." Decisions like these are often instantaneous and outside of our conscious awareness.

Despite the claims of some theorists, it seems like an exaggeration to suggest that *all* behavior is aimed at making impressions. Young children certainly aren't strategic communicators. A baby spontaneously laughs when pleased and cries when sad or uncomfortable without any notion of creating an impression in others. Likewise, there are times when we, as adults, act spontaneously. But when a significant other questions our presenting self, the likelihood of acting to prop it up increases. This process isn't always conscious: At a nonconscious level of awareness we monitor others' reactions, and swing into action when our face is threatened—especially by significant others.[25]

Research shows that some people are much more aware of their impression management behavior than others. These high self-monitors have the ability to pay attention to their own behavior and others' reactions, adjusting their communication to create the desired impression. By contrast, low self-monitors express what they are thinking and feeling without much attention to the impression their behavior creates.[26] You can get an idea of whether you are a high or a low self-monitor by answering the following questions.

INVITATION TO INSIGHT

SELF-MONITORING INVENTORY

These statements concern personal reactions to a number of different situations. No two statements are exactly alike, so consider each statement carefully before answering. If a statement is true, or mostly true, as applied to you, circle the T. If a statement is false, or not usually true, as applied to you, circle the F.

1. I find it hard to imitate the behavior of other people.   T   F
2. I guess I put on a show to impress or entertain people.   T   F
3. I would probably make a good actor.   T   F
4. I sometimes appear to others to be experiencing deeper emotions than I actually am.   T   F
5. In a group of people I am rarely the center of attention.   T   F
6. In different situations and with different people, I often act like very different persons.   T   F
7. I can only argue for ideas I already believe.   T   F
8. In order to get along and be liked, I tend to be what people expect me to be rather than anything else.   T   F
9. I may deceive people by being friendly when I really dislike them.   T   F
10. I'm not always the person I appear to be.   T   F

SCORING: Give yourself one point for each of questions 1, 5, and 7 that you answered F. Give yourself one point for each of the remaining questions that you answered T. Add up your points. If you are a good judge of yourself and scored 7 or above, you are probably a high self-monitoring individual; 3 or below, you are probably a low self-monitoring individual.

Source: Mark Snyder, "The Many Me's of the Self-Monitor," *Psychology Today,* March, 1983, p. 34. Reprinted with permission.

What is the ideal score for this self-quiz? There are certainly advantages to being a high self-monitor.[27] People who pay attention to themselves are generally good actors who can create the impression they want, acting interested when bored or friendly when they really feel quite the opposite. This allows them to handle social situations smoothly, often putting others at ease. They are also good "people-readers" who can adjust their behavior to get the desired reaction from others. Along with these advantages, there are some potential drawbacks to being an extremely high self-monitor. Their analytical nature may prevent them from experiencing events completely, since a portion of their attention will always be viewing the situation from a detached position. High self-monitors' ability to act means that it is difficult to tell how they are really feeling. In fact, because high self-monitors change roles often, they may have a hard time knowing *themselves* how they really feel.

People who score low on the self-monitoring scale live life quite differently from their more self-conscious counterparts. They have a more simple, focused idea of who they are and who they want to be. Low self-monitors are likely to have a more narrow repertoire of behaviors, so that they can be expected to act in more or less the same way regardless of the situation. This means that low self-monitors are easy to read. "What you see is what you get" might be their motto. While this lack of flexibility may make their social interaction less smooth in many situations, low self-monitors can be counted on to be straightforward communicators.

By now it should be clear that neither extremely high nor low self-monitoring is the ideal. There are some situations when paying attention to yourself and adapting your behavior can be useful, and other times when reacting without considering the effect on others is a better approach. This need for a range of behaviors demonstrates again the notion of communicative competence outlined in Chapter One: Flexibility is the key to successful relationships. In the reading on page 77, titled "Will the Real Me Please Stand Up?" writer Barry Stevens describes the challenges of managing impressions while being true to oneself.

WILL THE REAL ME PLEASE STAND UP?

n the beginning, I was one person, knowing nothing but my own experience.

Then I was told things, and I became two people: the little girl who said how terrible it was that the boys had a fire going in the lot next door where they were roasting apples (which was what the woman said)—and the little girl who, when the boys were called by their mothers to go to the store, ran out and tended the fire and the apples because she loved doing it.

So then there were two of I. One I always doing something that the other I disapproved of. Or other I said what I disapproved of. All this argument in me so much.

In the beginning was I, and I was good.

Then came in other I. Outside authority. This was confusing. And then other I became very confused because there were so many different outside authorities.

Sit nicely. Leave the room to blow your nose. Don't do that, that's silly. Why, the poor child doesn't even know how to pick a bone! Flush the toilet at night because if you don't it makes it harder to clean. DON'T FLUSH THE TOILET AT NIGHT—you wake people up! Always be nice to people. Even if you don't like them, you mustn't hurt their feelings. Be frank and honest. If you don't tell people what you think of them, that's cowardly. Butter knives. It is important to use butter knives.

Butter knives? What foolishness! Speak nicely. Sissy! Kipling is wonderful! Ugh! Kipling (turning away).

The most important thing is to have a career. The most important thing is to get married. The hell with everyone. Be nice to everyone. The most important thing is sex. The most important thing is to have everyone like you. The most important thing is to be sophisticated and say what you don't mean and don't let anyone know what you feel. The most important thing is a black seal coat and china and silver. The most important thing is to be clean. The most important thing is to always pay your debts. The most important thing is not to be taken in by anyone else. The most important thing is to love your parents. The most important thing is to work. The most important thing is to be independent. The most important thing is to speak correct English. The most important thing is to go to the right plays and read the right books. The most important thing is to do what others say. And others say all these things.

All the time, I is saying, live with life. That is what is important.

But when I lives with life, other I says no, that's bad. All the different other I's say this. It's dangerous. It isn't practical. You'll come to a bad end. Of course . . . everyone felt that way once, the way you do, but *you'll learn.*

Out of all the other I's some are chosen as a pattern that is me. But there are all the other possibilities of patterns within what all the others say which come into me and become other I which is not myself, and sometimes these take over. Then who am I?

I does not bother about who am I. I is, and is happy being. But when I is happy being, other I says get to work, do something worthwhile! I is happy doing dishes. "You're weird!" I is happy being with people saying nothing. Other I says talk. Talk, talk, talk. I gets lost.

I know that things are to be played with, not possessed. I likes putting things together, lightly. Taking things apart, lightly. "You'll never have anything!" Making things of

things in a way that the things themselves take part in, putting themselves together with surprise and delight to I. "There's no money in that!"

I is human. If someone needs, I gives. "You can't do that! You'll never have anything for yourself! We'll have to support you!"

I loves. I loves in a way that other I does not know. I loves. "That's too warm for friends!" "That's too cool for lovers!" "Don't feel so bad, he's just a friend. It's not as though you loved him." "How can you let him go? I thought you loved him." So cool the warm for friends and hot up the love for lovers, and I gets lost.

So both I's have a house and a husband and children and all that, but both I's are confused because other I says, "You see? You're lucky," while I goes on crying. "What are you crying about? Why are you so ungrateful?" I doesn't know gratitude or ingratitude, and cannot argue. I goes on crying. Other I pushes it out, says, "I am happy! I am very lucky to have such a fine family and a nice house and good neighbors and lots of friends who want me to do this, do that." I is not reasonable either. I goes on crying.

Other I gets tired, and goes on smiling because that is the thing to do. Smile, and you will be rewarded. Like the seal who gets tossed a piece of fish. Be nice to everyone and you will be rewarded. People will be nice to you, and you can be happy with that. You know they like you. Like a dog who gets patted on the head for good behavior. Tell funny stories. Be gay. Smile, smile, smile. . . . I is crying. . . . "Don't be sorry for yourself! Go out and do things for people!" "Go out and be

with people!" I is still crying, but now, that is not heard and felt so much.

Suddenly: "What am I doing?" "Am I to go through life playing the clown?" "What am I doing, going to parties that I do not enjoy?" "What am I doing, being with people who bore me?" "Why am I so hollow and the hollowness filled with emptiness?" A shell. How has this shell grown around me? Why am I proud of my children and unhappy about their lives which are not good enough? Why am I disappointed? Why do I feel so much waste?

I comes through, a little. In moments. And gets pushed back by other I.

I refuses to play the clown any more. Which I is that? "She used to be fun, but now she thinks too much about herself." I lets friends drop away. Which I is that? "She's being too much by herself. That's bad. She's losing her mind." Which mind?

Barry Stevens,
Person to Person

WHY MANAGE IMPRESSIONS?

Why bother trying to shape others' opinions? Sometimes we create and maintain a front to follow social rules. As children we learn to act polite, even when bored. Likewise, part of growing up consists of developing a set of manners for various occasions: meeting strangers, attending school, going to church, and so on. Young children who haven't learned all the do's and don'ts of polite society often embarrass their parents by behaving inappropriately ("Mommy, why is that man so fat?"); but, by the time they enter school, behavior that might have been excusable or even amusing just isn't acceptable. Good manners are often aimed at making others more comfortable. For example, able-bodied people often mask their discomfort upon encountering someone who is disabled by acting nonchalant or stressing similarities between themselves and the disabled person.[28]

Social rules govern our behavior in a variety of settings. It would be impossible to keep a job, for example, without meeting certain expectations. Salespeople are obliged to treat customers with courtesy. Employees need to appear reasonably respectful when talking to the boss. Some forms of clothing would be considered outrageous at work. By agreeing to take on a job, you are signing an unwritten contract that you will present a certain face at work, whether or not that face reflects the way you might be feeling at a particular moment.

Even when social roles don't dictate the proper way to behave, we often manage impressions for a second reason: to accomplish personal goals. You might, for example, dress up for a visit to traffic court in hope that your front (responsible citizen) will convince the judge to treat you sympathetically. You might act sociable to your neighbors so they will agree to your request that they keep their dog off your lawn.

Sometimes impression management aims at achieving one or more of the relational goals we discussed in Chapter One: affiliation,

We may be born naked, but we waste little time correcting the oversight. Almost from the moment we wriggle into the world, we start getting dressed. Conventional wisdom claims that clothing is simply a means of survival, but clearly there's more to it. Whether it's a couple of strategically placed shells or a suit of armor, a G-string or a caribou parka, clothing is a set of signals to all we meet. And though clothes may indeed protect us from the elements, their real job is to protect us from social opprobrium, or to make a statement—to a potential boss, a potential bride, or a very real enemy.

Banana Republic Catalog

control, or respect. For instance, you might act more friendly and lively than you feel upon meeting a new person, so that you will appear likable. You could sigh and roll your eyes when arguing politics with a classmate to gain an advantage in an argument. You might smile and preen to show the attractive stranger at a party that you would like to get better acquainted. In situations like these you aren't being deceptive as much as putting "your best foot forward."

All these examples show that it is difficult—even impossible— *not* to create impressions. After all, you have to send some sort of message. If you don't act friendly when meeting a stranger, you have to act aloof, indifferent, hostile, or in some other manner. If you don't act businesslike, you have to behave in an alternative way: casual, goofy, or whatever. Often the question isn't whether or not to present a face to others; it's only which face to present.

HOW DO WE MANAGE IMPRESSIONS?

How do we create a public face? There are three different types of communication that help create a front: manner, appearance, and setting.[29] *Manner* consists of a communicator's words and nonverbal actions. Physicians, for example, display a wide variety of manners as they conduct physical examinations. Some are friendly and conversational, while others adopt a brusque and impersonal approach. Still others are polite but businesslike. Much of a communicator's manner comes from what he or she says. A doctor who remembers details about your interests and hobbies is quite different from one who sticks to clinical questions. One who explains a medical procedure creates a different impression than another who reveals little to the patient. Along with the content of speech, nonverbal behaviors play a big role in creating impressions. A doctor who greets you with a friendly smile and a handshake comes across quite differently from one who gives nothing more than a curt nod. Manner varies widely in other professional and personal settings—professors, salespeople, hair stylists, and so on—and the impressions they create differ accordingly. The same principle holds in personal relationships. Your manner plays a major role in shaping how others view you. Chapters Five and Six will describe in detail how your words and nonverbal behaviors create impressions. Since you *have* to speak and act, the question isn't whether your manner sends a message; rather, it's whether these messages will be intentional.

Along with manner, a second dimension of impression management is *appearance*—the personal items people use to shape an image. Sometimes appearance is part of creating a professional image. A physician's white lab coat and a police officer's uniform both set the wearer apart as someone special. A tailored suit or a rumpled outfit create very different impressions in the business world. Off the job, clothing is just as important. We choose clothing that sends a message about ourselves, sometimes trendy and sometimes traditional. Some people dress in ways that accent their sexuality, while others hide it. Clothing can say "I'm an athlete," "I'm wealthy," or "I'm an environmentalist." Along with dress, other aspects of appearance play a strong role in impression management. Are you suntanned or pale? What is your hairstyle?

A final way to manage impressions is through the choice of *setting*—physical items we use to influence how others view us. In modern western society the automobile is a major part of impression management. This explains why many people lust after cars that are far more expensive and powerful than they really need. A sporty convertible or fancy imported sedan doesn't just get drivers from one place to another: It also makes statements about the kind of people they are. The physical setting we choose and the way we arrange it is another important way to manage impressions. What colors do you choose for the place you live? What artwork? What music do you play? Of course we choose a setting that we enjoy; but in many cases we create an environment that will present the desired front to others. If you doubt this fact, just recall the last time you straightened up the house before important guests arrived. Backstage you might be comfortable with a messy place, but your public front—at least to some people—is quite different.

IMPRESSION MANAGEMENT AND HONESTY

After reading this far, impression management might sound like an academic label for manipulation or phoniness. If the perceived self is the "real" you, it might seem that any behavior that contradicts it would be dishonest.

There certainly are situations where impression management is dishonest. A manipulative date who pretends to be affectionate in order to gain sexual favors is clearly unethical and deceitful. So are job applicants who lie about academic records to get hired or salespeople who pretend to be dedicated to customer service when their real goal is to make a quick buck. But managing impressions doesn't necessarily make you a liar. In fact, it is almost impossible to imagine how we could communicate effectively without making decisions about which front to present in one situation or another. It would be ludicrous for you to act the same way with strangers as you do with close friends, and nobody would show the same face to a two-year-old as they would to an adult.

Each of us has a repertoire of faces—a cast of characters—and part of being a competent communicator is choosing the best role for the situation. Consider a few examples:

- You offer to teach a friend a new skill: playing the guitar, operating a computer program, or sharpening up a tennis backhand. Your friend is making slow progress with the skill, and you find yourself growing impatient.
- At a party you meet someone whom you find very attractive, and you are pretty sure that the feeling is mutual. On one hand you feel an obligation to spend most of your time with the person whom you came with, but the opportunity here is very appealing.

- At work you face a belligerent customer. You don't believe that anyone has the right to treat you this way.
- A friend or family member makes a joke about your appearance that hurts your feelings. You aren't sure whether to make an issue of the remark or pretend that it doesn't bother you.

In each of these situations—and in countless others every day—you have a choice about how to act. It is an oversimplification to say that there is only one honest way to behave in each circumstance and that every other response would be insincere and dishonest. Instead, impression management involves deciding which face—which part of yourself—to reveal. For example, when teaching a new skill, you choose to display the "patient" instead of the "impatient" side of yourself. In the same way, at work you have the option of acting hostile or nondefensive in difficult situations. With strangers, friends, or family you can choose whether to disclose your feelings. Which face to show to others is an important decision, but in any case you are sharing a real part of yourself. You may not be revealing *everything*—but as you will learn in Chapter Eight, complete self-disclosure is rarely appropriate.

ETHICAL CHALLENGE

THE MANY YOU'S

1. Make a list of the different presenting selves you try to communicate at school, to different family members, to friends, and to various types of strangers.
2. Which of these selves are honest and which are deceptive?
3. Are any deceptive impressions you try to create justified? What would be the consequences of being completely candid in the situations you have described?
4. Based on your answers to these questions, develop a set of guidelines to distinguish ethical from unethical impression management.

✚ SUMMARY

The self-concept is a relatively stable set of perceptions individuals hold about themselves. It begins to develop soon after birth, being shaped by both verbal and nonverbal messages from significant others and from reflected appraisal based on comparison with reference groups. The self-concept is subjective, and can vary in important ways from the way a person is perceived by others. Although the self may evolve over time, the self-concept resists change.

A self-fulfilling prophecy occurs when a person's expectations of an event influence the outcome. One type of prophecy consists of predictions by others, while another category is self-imposed. Self-fulfilling prophecies can be both positive and negative.

It is possible to change one's self-concept in ways that lead to more effective communication. It is necessary to have realistic expectations about how much change is possible, and to begin with a realistic assessment of oneself. Willingness to exert the effort to change is important, and in some cases change requires new information or skill.

Impression management consists of strategic communication designed to influence others' perceptions of an individual. Impression management aims at presenting one or more faces to others, which may be different from private, spontaneous behavior that occurs outside of others' presence. Some communicators are high self-monitors who are highly conscious of their own behavior, while others are less aware of how their words and actions affect others.

Impression management occurs for two reasons. In many cases it is based on following social rules and conventions. At other times it aims at achieving a variety of content and relational goals. In either case, communicators engage in creating impressions by managing their manner, appearance, and the settings in which they interact with others. Although impression management might seem manipulative, it can be an authentic form of communication. Since each person has a variety of faces that he or she can reveal, choosing which one to present need not be dishonest.

✦ KEY TERMS

back
cognitive conservatism
face
facework
front

ideal self
impression management
perceived self
presenting self
reference groups

reflected appraisal
self-concept
self-fulfilling prophecy
significant other
social comparison

✦ MORE RESOURCES ON COMMUNICATION AND THE SELF

READINGS

Curtis, Rebecca C., ed. *Self-Defeating Behaviors: Experimental Research, Clinical Impressions, and Practical Implications.* New York: Plenum, 1989.
Curtis describes how some people insist on disparaging themselves. She describes the extent to which communicators will go to maintain an unfavorable self-concept.

Cushman, Donald P., and Dudley D. Cahn, Jr. *Communication in Interpersonal Relationships.* Albany: State University of New York Press, 1985.
Several parts of this challenging book detail the theory and research that explain the role the self-concept plays in interpersonal communication. See especially Chapters 2 and 3.

Duck, Steve, ed. *Learning About Relationships.* Newbury Park, Calif.: Sage, 1993.
This book describes the lasting effects of early life experiences on later relationships. Most chapters describe the many ways parents influence their children's self-concept and social skills.

Gergen, Kenneth, J. "Multiple Identity: The Healthy, Happy Human Being Wears Many Masks." *Psychology Today* 5 (May 1972): 31–35, 64–66.
This article suggests that we wear a series of masks; instead of a single identity there is a whole series of "you's" that emerge in various situations.

Giacalone, Robert A., and Paul Rosenfeld. *Applied Impression Management: How Image-Making Affects Managerial Decisions.* Newbury Park, Calif.: Sage, 1992.
It's no surprise that impression management plays a major role in success on the job. This book offers a practical look at how impression management operates in contexts including negotiation, conflict, career advancement, performance appraisals, gender differences, and cultural diversity.

Goffman, Erving. *The Presentation of Self in Everyday Life.* New York: Doubleday Anchor, 1959; *Interaction Ritual: Essays on Face-to-Face Behavior.* New York: Doubleday Anchor, 1967.

These books provide a thorough introduction to the topic of impression management, written by the most influential theorist on the subject. Goffman introduces the notion of face, and discusses how individuals communicate in a manner to create and preserve various social fronts.

Hamachek, Don E. *Encounters with the Self* (3rd ed.). Fort Worth, Tex.: Harcourt Brace Jovanovich, 1992.

This is a thorough, readable introduction to the self. Hamachek describes how communication shapes the self-concept, the accuracy and inaccuracy of self-perceptions, and how to change the self-concept. Individual chapters describe influences on formation of the self: developmental stages, parent-child relationships, and academic experiences.

Hayakawa, S. I. *Symbol, Status and Personality.* New York: Harcourt Brace Jovanovich, 1953.

After more than forty years, Hayakawa's description of the self-concept (in Chapter 4) is still one of the clearest and most interesting ones around.

McCroskey, James C., and John A. Daly. *Personality and Interpersonal Communication.* Newbury Park, Calif.: Sage, 1987.

This collection of scholarly articles describes the concept of personality and examines its relationship to interpersonal communication. It explores such questions as "What kind of communication is exhibited by people with various personalities?" and "How does the self-concept affect communication behavior?"

Rosenthal, Robert, and Lenore Jacobson. *Pygmalion in the Classroom.* New York: Irvington, 1992.

This book contains a fascinating description of how self-fulfilling prophecies operate in education, social science research, medicine, and everyday life.

Snyder, Mark. "Self-Fulfilling Stereotypes." *Psychology Today* 16 (July 1982): 60–68.

Snyder demonstrates how stereotyped expectations about others can actually create behavior that confirms prejudicial attitudes. This article illustrates the harmful consequences of some self-fulfilling prophecies.

Wilmot, William W. *Dyadic Communication* (3d ed.). New York: Random House, 1987.

Wilmot's second chapter, "Perception of Self," expands several concepts introduced in the pages you have just read. The discussion of multiple selves provides an especially valuable explanation of the nature of self-esteem.

FILMS

THE INFLUENCE OF SIGNIFICANT OTHERS
The Color Purple (1985) Rated PG-13

In the rural South in the early 1900s, Celie (Whoopi Goldberg) is abused sexually and emotionally by her father and then by her husband, "Mister" (Danny Glover). Mister compounds his cruelty by openly flaunting his love for juke joint singer Shug Avery (Margaret Avery), whom he eventually invites to move in. The turning point in the film comes when Shug begins to recognize and acknowledge the beauty in Celie, who flourishes in Shug's love. This film is a graphic illustration of the power of others to shape an individual's self-concept. It is also a tribute to the human spirit, as Celie manages to retain enough self-esteem to accept Shug's belief that she is, indeed, a loveable person.

IMPRESSION MANAGEMENT
Breaking Away (1979) Rated PG

Nineteen-year-old Dave Stoller (Dennis Christopher) has grown up in Bloomington, Indiana, the son of a stonecutter. Dave and his friends feel intimidated by the Indiana University students who arrive in town each year; they seem rich, smart, and superior. They call Dave and his buddies "Cutters"—a derogatory reference to their fathers' profession.

Dave is ambivalent about his identity. Although he is proud of his Cutter friends and family, he thinks they hold him back from attending college and pursuing "a better life." Dave finds a unique way to deal with being caught between cultures: He forges an altogether different identity by spinning an elaborate fantasy about being an Italian bicycle racer. He convinces a college co-ed that he is a foreign exchange student, and he sweeps her off her feet with flowers, stories, and Italian serenades.

Maintaining this fake Italian identity requires energy, juggling and deceit. Dave's act comes crashing down when a touring Italian cycling team breaks his spokes and leaves him in a ditch. The event is a wake-up call for Dave. He confesses the Italian ruse to his university girlfriend, who is devastated that she has been fooled. Dave then takes a walk through campus with his father (Paul Dooley), who has mixed feelings about Dave's identity, too. Although he wants his son to go to college, he is afraid that Dave will "thumb the diploma in his face." When Dad finally says to Dave, "You're not a Cutter; I'm a Cutter," he gives Dave permission to make a better life for himself.

In the end, Dave finds he can manage two identities at the same time. He decides it's okay to be both a Cutter and a college student. What isn't okay is to be something he's not—an Italian. That is simply too hard for a young man from Indiana to manage.

SELF-FULFILLING PROPHECY
Stand and Deliver (1988) Rated PG–13

Jaime Escalante (Edward James Olmos) is a mild-mannered math teacher who is commissioned to the tough classrooms of Garfield High. He is soft-spoken, cerebral, and demanding—in other words, the kind of teacher that street-hardened students would normally despise and ignore. While the students do, in fact, regard him suspiciously at first, by the story's end they adore him. Perhaps more important, they achieve top-flight scores on their advance placement calculus exam, which is their ticket to a college education.

How can we account for the students' success? The film suggests that the primary factor is not Escalante's knowledge of math, his lecture techniques, or his classroom charisma. The key is that he believes in his students, who hadn't been believed in before. Because he believes in them, they stop thinking of themselves as losers. Escalante helps them master a subject they thought was impossible, and in so doing radically changes their self-concepts. This is a powerful story that offers contemporary support for the "Pygmalion" theory of the self-fulfilling prophecy.

CHAPTER 3

Perception: What You See Is What You Get

tudy M.C. Escher's drawing "Relativity" on the opposite page. It pictures a strange universe in which the inhabitants of each world exist at right angles, using the same staircase but oblivious to each other's existence. Each has his or her own conception of up and down, right and left. If these characters were introduced to the residents of other worlds, they would find them odd, defying the rule of gravity.

This surreal vision provides a useful metaphor for problems we encounter every day. Each of us experiences a different reality, and failing to understand other people's point of view can lead to problems on both practical and relational levels. But perceptual differences can enhance as well as interfere with relationships. By seeing the world through others' eyes you can gain insights that are different—and often more valuable—than those arising out of your own experiences.

This chapter will help you deal with the problem of perceptual differences. We will begin by looking at some of the reasons the world appears different to each of us. In our survey we'll explore several areas: how our psychological makeup, personal needs, interests, and biases shape our perceptions; the physiological factors that influence our view of the world; the social roles that affect our image of events; and finally the role culture plays in creating our ideas of what behavior is proper. In doing so, we'll cover many of the types of physiological and psychological noise that were described in the communication model in Chapter One. After examining the perceptual factors that can drive us apart, we will look at two useful skills for bridging the perceptual gap.

THE PERCEPTION PROCESS

We need to begin our discussion of perception by examining the gap between "what is" and what we know. At one time or another you've probably seen photos of sights invisible to the unaided eye: perhaps an infrared photo of a familiar area or the vastly enlarged image of a minute object taken by an electron microscope. You've also noticed how certain animals are able to hear sounds and smell odors that are not apparent to humans. Experiences like these remind us that there is much more going on in the world than we are able to experience with our limited senses, that our idea of reality is in fact only a partial one.

Even within the realm of our senses we're only aware of a small part of what is going on around us. For instance, most people who live in large cities find that the noises of traffic, people, and construction soon fade out of their awareness. Others can take a walk through the forest without distinguishing one bird's call from another or noticing the differences between various types of vegetation. On a personal level, we've all had the experience of failing to notice something

I've always admired those reporters who can descend on an area, talk to key people, ask key questions, take samplings of opinions, and then set down an orderly report very much like a road map. I envy this technique and at the same time do not trust it as a mirror of reality. I feel that there are too many realities. What I set down here is true until someone else passes that way and rearranges the world in his own style. In literary criticism the critic has no choice but to make over the victim of his attention into something the size and shape of himself. . . .

So much there is to see, but our morning eyes describe a different world than do our afternoon eyes, and surely our wearied evening eyes can only report a weary evening world.

John Steinbeck,
Travels with Charley

unusual about a friend—perhaps a new hairstyle or a sad expression—until it's called to our attention.

Sometimes our failure to recognize some events while noticing others comes from not paying attention to important information. But in other cases it's simply impossible to be aware of everything, no matter how attentive we might be: There is just too much going on.

William James said that "to the infant the world is just a big blooming, buzzing confusion." One reason for this is the fact that infants are not yet able to sort out the myriad impressions with which we're all bombarded. As we grow, we learn to manage all this data, and as we do so, we begin to make sense out of the world.

Because this ability to organize our perceptions in a useful way is such a critical factor in our ability to function, we need to begin our study of perception by taking a closer look at this process. We can do so by examining the three steps by which we attach meaning to our experiences: selection, organization, and interpretation.

SELECTION

We usually see only the things we are looking for—so much that we sometimes see them where they are not.

Eric Hoffer

Because we're exposed to more input than we can possibly manage, the first step in perception is the **selection** of which data we will attend to. There are several factors that cause us to notice some messages and ignore others.

Stimuli that are *intense* often attract our attention. Something that is louder, larger, or brighter stands out. This explains why—other things being equal—we're more likely to remember extremely tall or short people and why someone who laughs or talks loudly at a party attracts more attention (not always favorable) than do quiet guests.

Repetitious stimuli, repetitious stimuli, repetitious stimuli, repetitious stimuli, repetitious stimuli, repetitious stimuli also attract attention.[1] Just as a quiet but steadily dripping faucet can come to dominate our awareness, people to whom we're frequently exposed become noticeable.

cathy®   **by Cathy Guisewite**

ATTENTION IS ALSO FREQUENTLY RELATED TO contrast OR change IN STIMULATION. Put differently, unchanging people or things become less noticeable. This principle gives an explanation (excuse?) for why we take wonderful people for granted when we interact with them frequently. It's only when they stop being so wonderful or go away that we appreciate them.

Motives also determine what information we select from our environment. If you're anxious about being late for a date, you'll notice whatever clocks may be around you; and if you're hungry, you'll become aware of any restaurants, markets, and billboards advertising food in your path. Motives also determine how we perceive people. For example, someone on the lookout for a romantic adventure will be especially aware of attractive potential partners, whereas the same person at a different time might be oblivious to anyone but police or medical personnel in an emergency.

Selection isn't an objective process: Paying attention to some things and ignoring others invariably distorts our observations. Some of these distortions are due to *omission*. Consider, for example, the times a friend has asked you to describe "what happened" at a party or some other event. We've already suggested that it would be impossible to describe everything that occurred: the clothes everyone wore, the number and type of drinks each person had, the sequence of musical numbers played, every word spoken by every guest, and so on.

As these examples show, many of the details we omit are trivial. In other cases, however, we leave out important information. This kind of omission results in *oversimplification*. A long, thoughtful explanation winds up being described simply as "he said, 'no.'" "What's she like?" you might ask and get the answer "She's from England and she's beautiful." Although this description may be true, it ignores the fact that the person being described may also be a single parent, a genius, a neurotic, a top-notch skier, along with a host of other significant characteristics. The tendency to oversimplify when selecting information to notice reminds us of the person who, when asked to describe the novel *War and Peace,* replied, "It's about Russia."

ORGANIZATION

Along with selecting information from the environment, we must arrange it in some meaningful way. You can see how the principle of **organization** works by looking at Figure 3–1. You can view the picture either as one of a vase or as one of two twins, depending on whether you focus on the light or the dark areas. In instances such as this we make sense of stimuli by noticing some data that stand out as a *figure* against a less striking *ground.* The "vase–face" drawing is interesting because it allows us to choose between two sets of figure–ground relationships.

This principle of figure–ground organization operates in nonvisual ways, too. Recall, for instance, how certain speech can suddenly stand out from a babble of voices. Sometimes the words are noticeable

FIGURE 3-1

FIGURE 3–2

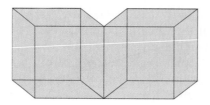

because they include your name, whereas at other times they might be spoken by a familiar voice.

In examples like the ones just mentioned, the process of organization is relatively simple. But there are other cases in which messages are ambiguous, having more than one possible way of being organized. You can see a visual example of such an ambiguous stimulus in Figure 3–2. How many ways can you view the boxes? One? Two? Three? Keep looking. If you're stumped, Figure 3–3 will help.

Just as you were inclined to view these boxes in one way, each of us uses a particular organizing scheme to make sense of the information about others. We do this by using **perceptual schema**—cognitive frameworks that allow us to organize the raw data we have selected. Five types of schema help us classify others. **Physical constructs** classify people according to their appearance: male or female, beautiful or ugly, fat or thin, young or old, and so on. **Role constructs** use social position: student, attorney, wife, and so on. **Interaction constructs** focus on social behavior: friendly, helpful, aloof, and sarcastic are examples. The fourth organizing scheme uses **psychological constructs:** curious, nervous, insecure, and so on. Finally, **membership constructs** help us identify others according to the group in which they belong: Republican, immigrant, and so on.

These schema affect communication in two ways. First, they allow us to form impressions of others. Imagine that you've just met a new person in class or at a party. Without these constructs, you would have no way to answer the question "What's this person like?" Once you have used various perceptual constructs to classify others, they become a useful way to predict future behavior. If you've classified a professor, for example, as "friendly," you'll handle questions or

FIGURE 3–3

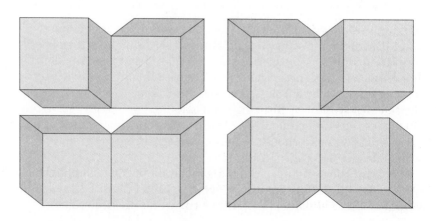

problems one way; if your analysis is "mean," your behavior will probably be quite different. Note that there's an element of selection in the constructs we use: Choosing some constructs means that you ignore others. If you categorize people by their age or style of clothing, for example, you are likely to ignore other characteristics such as their friendliness or intelligence.

The constructs we use strongly affect the way we relate to others. Young children usually don't classify people according to their skin color. They are just as likely to identify an Anglo, Black, or Asian by age, size, or personality. As they become more socialized, however, they learn that one common organizing principle in today's society is ethnicity, and their perceptions of others change. What constructs do you use to classify the people you encounter in your life? Consider how your relationship might change if you used different schema.

INVITATION TO INSIGHT

YOUR PERCEPTUAL SCHEMA

1. Identify the constructs described in the preceding section that you would use to categorize people in each of the following contexts. Describe both the *general type of construct* (e.g., "physical," "membership") and the *specific category* within each type (e.g., "attractive," "roughly the same age as me").
   a. Spending time with new acquaintances at a party
   b. Socializing with fellow workers on the job
   c. Choosing teammates for an important class project
   d. Offering help to a stranded motorist
2. Consider how valid the constructs you use are in making decisions about the type of communication in which you engage.
   a. Explain which of your constructs are valid.
   b. Explain which constructs are not valid, and suggest better alternatives.
   c. Describe how your relationships might change if you used different constructs.

Once we have selected an organizing scheme to classify people, we use that scheme to make generalizations about members of the groups who fit the categories we use. For example, if you were especially aware of gender you might be alert to the differences between the way men and women behave or the way they are treated. If religion played an important part in your life, you might think of members of your faith differently from others. If ethnicity was an important issue for you, you would probably tune into the differences between members of various ethnic groups. There's nothing wrong with generalizations as long as they are accurate. In fact, it would be impossible to get through life without them.

But when generalizations lose touch with reality, they lead to **stereotyping**—exaggerated generalizations associated with a categorizing system.[2] Stereotypes may be based on a kernel of truth, but they go beyond the facts at hand and make claims that usually have no valid basis.

You can begin to get a sense of your tendency to make generalizations and stereotype by completing the following sentences:

1. Women are _____
2. Men are _____
3. Hispanics _____
4. Anglos _____
5. Blacks _____
6. Older people _____

It's likely that you were able to complete each sentence without much hesitation. Does this mean you were stereotyping? You can answer this question by deciding whether your generalizations fit the three characteristics of stereotypes:

- You often categorize people on the basis of this easily recognized characteristic. For example, the first thing you notice about a person is his or her skin color.
- You ascribe a set of characteristics to most or all members of this category. For example, you assume that all older people are doddering or all men are insensitive to women's concerns.
- You apply the set of characteristics to any member of the group. For example, when you meet an older person, you expect him or her to be senile.[3]

By themselves, stereotypes don't lead to communication problems. If the person with whom you are interacting happens to fit the pattern in your mind, there may be no difficulties. But if your mental image does not happen to match the characteristics of the other person, the potential for misunderstandings and defensiveness is high. One way to avoid the kinds of communication problems that come from excessive stereotyping is to "decategorize" others, giving yourself a chance to treat them as individuals instead of assuming that they possess the same characteristics as every other member of the group to which you assign them.

The process of organizing goes beyond our generalized perceptions of people. We also can organize our interactions with others in different ways; and these differing organizational schemes can have a powerful effect on our relationships with them. Communication theorists have used the term **punctuation** to describe the determination of causes and effects in a series of interactions.[4] You can begin to understand how the punctuation operates by visualizing a running quarrel between a husband and wife. The husband accuses the wife of being too critical, while she complains that he is withdrawing from her. Notice that the order in which each partner punctuates this cycle affects how the dispute looks. The husband begins by blaming the wife: "I withdraw because you're so critical." The wife organizes the

Farcus

by David Waisglass
Gordon Coulthart

WAISGLASS/COULTHART

"Kid, there are two types of
people in this world . . . those
who generalize, and those
who don't."

situation differently, starting with the husband: "I criticize because you withdraw." Once the cycle gets rolling, it is impossible to say which accusation is accurate. The answer depends on how the sentence is punctuated. Figure 3–4 illustrates how this process operates in a variety of relationships.

Anyone who has seen two children argue about "who started it" can understand that haggling over causes and effects isn't likely to solve a conflict. In fact, the kind of finger pointing that goes along with assigning blame will probably make matters worse. Rather than argue about whose punctuation of an event is correct, it's far more productive to recognize that a dispute can look different to each party, and then move on to the more important question of "What can we do to make things better?"

FIGURE 3–4

SKILL BUILDER

PUNCTUATION PRACTICE

You can appreciate how different punctuation patterns can influence attitudes and behavior by following these directions.

1. Use the format pictured in Figure 3–4 to diagram the following situations:
   a. A father and daughter are growing more and more distant. The daughter withdraws because she interprets her father's coolness as rejection. The father views his daughter's aloofness as a rebuff and withdraws further.
   b. The relationship between two friends is becoming strained. One jokes to lighten up the tension, and the other becomes more tense.
   c. A dating couple is on the verge of breaking up. One partner frequently asks the other to show more affection. The other withdraws physical contact.

2. Identify two punctuating schemes for each of the situations described in step 1. Consider how the differing schemes would affect the way the two people in that situation respond to one another.

3. Now identify a difficult communication issue in your own life. Punctuate it in two ways: your own and the way it might be viewed by the other person. Discuss how seeing the issue from the other person's point of view might change the way you communicate as you discuss the issue.

INTERPRETATION

Once we have selected and organized our perceptions, we interpret them in a way that makes some sort of sense. **Interpretation** plays a role in virtually every interpersonal act. Is the person who smiles at you across a crowded room interested in romance or simply being polite? Is a friend's kidding a sign of affection or irritation? Should you take an invitation to "drop by any time" literally or not?

Several factors cause us to interpret an event in one way or another:

Relational satisfaction. The behavior that seems positive when you are happy with a partner might seem completely different when the relationship isn't satisfying. For example, couples in unsatisfying relationships are more likely than satisfied partners to blame one another when things go wrong.[5] They are also more likely to believe that their partners are selfish and have negative intentions. Unhappy spouses are more likely than happy ones to make negative interpretations of their mate's behavior. To see how this principle operates, recall the husband–wife quarrel we discussed earlier. Suppose the wife suggests that they get away for a weekend vacation. If the marriage has been troubled, the husband might interpret his wife's idea as more criticism ("You never pay attention to me") and the fight will continue. If the relationship is solid, he is more likely to view the suggestion as a bid for a romantic getaway. It wasn't the event that shaped the reaction, but the way the husband interpreted the event.

Degree of involvement with the other person. We sometimes view people with whom we have or seek a relationship more favorably than those whom we observe from a detached perspective.[6] One recent study revealed how this principle operates in everyday life. A group of male subjects was asked to critique presentations by women who allegedly owned restaurants. Half of these presentations were designed to be competent and half incompetent. The men who were told they would be having a casual date with the female speakers judged their presentations—whether competent or not—more highly than those who didn't expect any involvement with the speakers.[7]

Past experience. What meaning have similar events held? If, for example, you've been gouged by landlords in the past, you might be skeptical about an apartment manager's assurances that careful housekeeping will assure the refund of your cleaning deposit.

Assumptions about human behavior. "People generally do as little work as possible to get by." "In spite of their mistakes, people are doing the best they can." Beliefs like these will shape the way we interpret another's actions.

Expectations. Anticipation shapes interpretations. If you imagine that your boss is unhappy with your work, you'll probably feel threatened by a request to "see me in my office first thing Monday morning." On the other hand, if you imagine that your work will be rewarded, your weekend will probably be pleasant.

Knowledge. If you know that a friend has just been jilted by a lover or been fired from a job, you'll interpret his aloof behavior differently from your interpretation if you were unaware of what had happened. If you know that an instructor speaks sarcastically to all students, you won't be as likely to take her remarks personally.

Personal moods. When you're feeling insecure, the world is a very different place from the world you experience when you're confident. The same goes for happiness and sadness or any other opposing emotions. The way we feel determines how we interpret events.

Although we have talked about selection, organization, and interpretation separately, the three phases of perception can occur in differing sequences. For example, a parent or baby-sitter's past interpretations (such as "Jason is a troublemaker") can influence future selections (his behavior becomes especially noticeable) and the organization of events (when there's a fight, the assumption is that Jason started it). As with all communication, perception is an ongoing process in which it is hard to pin down beginnings and endings.

❖ INFLUENCES ON PERCEPTION

Now that we've explored the psychological processes by which we perceive, it's time to look at some of the influences that cause us to select, organize, and interpret information.

PHYSIOLOGICAL INFLUENCES

The first set of influences we need to examine involves our physical makeup. Within the wide range of human similarities, each of us perceives the world in a unique way because of physiological factors. In other words, although the same events exist "out there," each of us receives a different image because of our perceptual hardware. Consider the long list of factors that shape our views of the world:

THE SENSES   The differences in how each of us sees, hears, tastes, touches, and smells stimuli can affect interpersonal relationships. Consider the following everyday situations:

"Turn down that radio! It's going to make me go deaf."

"It's not too loud. If I turn it down, it will be impossible to hear it."

"It's freezing in here."

"Are you kidding? We'll suffocate if you turn up the heat!"

"Why don't you pass that truck? The highway is clear for a mile."

"I can't see that far, and I'm not going to get us killed."

These disputes aren't just over matters of opinion. The sensory data we receive are different. Differences in vision and hearing are the easiest to recognize, but other gaps exist as well. There is evidence that identical foods taste differently to various individuals.[8] Odors that please some people repel others. Likewise, temperature variations that leave some of us uncomfortable are inconsequential to

> To a Laplander, a temperature of fifty-eight degrees may be "hot," to a South African it may be "cold." The statement "It is hot (or cold)" is a statement about what is going on inside one's body. The statement "The temperature is now ninety degrees (or fifty-eight degrees)" is a statement about what is going on outside one's body. . . .
>
> This distinction is by no means trivial. . . . I can never prove to a Laplander that fifty-eight degrees is "cool," but I can prove to him that it is fifty-eight degrees. In other words, there is no paradox in two different people's concluding that the weather is both "hot" and "cold" at the same time. As long as they both know that each of them is talking about a different reality, their conversation can proceed in a fairly orderly way.
>
> Neil Postman, *Crazy Talk, Stupid Talk*

others. Remembering these differences won't eliminate them, but it will make it easier to remember that the other person's preferences aren't crazy, just different.

AGE   Older people often view the world differently from younger ones because they have a greater scope and number of experiences. There are also developmental differences that shape perceptions. Swiss psychologist Jean Piaget described a series of stages that children pass through on their way to adulthood.[9] According to Piaget, younger children are incapable of performing mental feats that are natural to the rest of us. Until they approach the age of seven, for example, they aren't able to take another person's point of view. This fact helps explain why children often seem egocentric, selfish, and uncooperative. A parent's exasperated plea, "Can't you see I'm too tired to play?" just won't make sense to a four-year-old full of energy, who imagines that everyone else must feel the same.

HEALTH   Recall the last time you came down with a cold, flu, or some other ailment. Do you remember how different you felt? You probably had much less energy. It's likely that you felt less sociable, and that your thinking was slower than usual. These kinds of changes have a strong impact on how you relate to others. It's good to realize that someone else may be behaving differently because of illness. In the same way, it's important to let others know when you feel ill, so they can give you the understanding you need.

FATIGUE   Just as being ill can affect your relationships, so can being overly tired. Again it's important to recognize the fact that you or someone else may behave differently when fatigued. Trying to deal with important issues at such a time can get you into trouble.

HUNGER   People often get grumpy when they haven't eaten and sleepy after stuffing themselves. A number of physiological changes occur as we eat and become hungry again. Trying to conduct important business at the wrong time in this cycle can lead to problems.

BIOLOGICAL CYCLES   Are you a "morning person" or a "night person"? Most of us can answer this question pretty easily, and there's a good physiological reason behind our answer. Each of us is in a daily cycle in which all sorts of changes constantly occur, including body temperature, sexual drive, alertness, tolerance to stress, and mood.[10] Most of these changes are due to hormonal cycles. For instance, adrenal hormones, which affect feelings of stress, are secreted at

🔹 TRYING ON OLD AGE

How would you like to travel through time? That is, how would you like a glimpse into your golden years? That's the opportunity students are getting in psychologist Randall Wright's class on aging and human development.

Wright asked students at Ouachita Baptist University to put together a costume that would make them look like senior citizens to casual observers. To create the illusion of age, Wright suggested wearing earplugs to reduce hearing, wrapping joints with elastic bandages to create stiffness and using or discarding glasses to impair eyesight.

The students put in five hours of role-playing as older versions of themselves. They also submitted descriptions and ratings of the exercise as well as photographs of how they looked before and after donning their costumes.

Most of the students gained valuable insights during their sojourn in old age. Even such mundane activities as walking across the street took on new meanings, as one student observed: "With our legs wrapped, we walked consid-

erably slower than most people. Inevitably, cars had to wait on us . . . not only do you feel a bother to other people, you worry about your life."

One student described how it felt to be ignored, while another was accosted by a group of boys in a passing car who screamed insults and demanded money.

Not all the experiences were frightening, however. One student was asked when he had last eaten and was offered $10 as he pretended to rummage in a garbage can for food. Another male student said that "the highlight of my experiment came when a little old lady on the opposite bench winked at me."

Being old for a few hours was an eye-opening exercise, the students overwhelmingly agreed. "Most felt that the simulation increased their knowledge and understanding of the elderly," says Wright. "In this case, living the lesson was better than learning it from a textbook."

Holly Hall

---

higher rates during some hours. In the same manner, the male and female sex hormones enter our systems at variable rates. We often aren't conscious of these changes, but they surely influence the way we relate to each other. Once we're aware that our own daily cycles and those of others govern our feelings and behavior, it becomes possible to manage our lives so that we deal with important issues at the most effective times.

For some women, the menstrual cycle plays an important role in shaping feelings and thus affects communication. Women aren't the only ones whose communication is affected by periodic changes in mood. Men, too, go through recognizable mood cycles, even though they aren't marked by obvious physical changes. Although they may

SALLY FORTH   by Greg Howard

©1982. Reprinted with special permission of North American Syndicate, Inc.

not be aware of it, many men seem to go through biologically regulated periods of good spirits followed by equally predictable times of depression.[11] The average length of this cycle is about five weeks, although in some cases it's as short as sixteen days or as long as two months. However long it may be, this cycle of ups and downs is quite regular.

Although neither men nor women can change these emotional cycles, simply learning to expect them can be a big help in improving communication. When you understand that a bad mood is predictable from physiological causes, you can plan for it. You'll know that every few weeks your patience will be shorter, and you'll be less likely to blame your bad moods on innocent bystanders. The people around you can also learn to expect your periodic lows. If they can attribute them to biology, maybe they will show you some understanding.

 INVITATION TO INSIGHT

NEW BODY, NEW PERSPECTIVE

You can get a clearer idea of how physiology influences perception by trying the following exercise.

1. Choose one of the following situations:
   An evening in a singles' bar
   A volleyball game
   A doctor's physical examination

2. How would the event you chose seem different if
   Your eyesight were much worse (or better).
   You had a hearing loss.
   You were eight inches taller (or shorter).
   You were coming down with a serious cold.
   You were a member of the opposite sex.
   You were ten years older (or younger).

CULTURAL DIFFERENCES

So far you have seen how physical factors can make the world a different place for each of us. But there's another kind of perceptual gap that often blocks communication—the gap between people from different backgrounds. Every culture has its own world view, its own way of looking at the world. Remembering these differing cultural perspectives can be a good way of learning more about both ourselves and others. But at times it's easy to forget that people everywhere don't see things the way we do.

The power of culture to shape perceptions was demonstrated in studies over thirty years ago exploring the domination of vision in one eye over the other.[12] Researchers used a binocular-like device that projects different images to each eye. The subjects were twelve natives of the United States and twelve Mexicans. Each was presented with ten pairs of photographs, each pair containing one picture from U.S. culture (e.g., a baseball game) and one from Mexican culture (e.g., a bullfight). After viewing each pair of images, the subjects reported what they saw. The results clearly indicated the power of culture to influence perceptions: Subjects had a strong tendency to see the image from their own background.

Not all perceptual differences are so subtle. The most obvious cross-cultural problems arise out of poor translation from one language to another:

- Chevrolet was baffled when its Nova model did not sell well in Latin American countries. Officials from General Motors finally realized the problem: In Spanish, *no va* means "does not go."
- One airline lost customers when it promoted the "rendezvous lounges" on its planes flying Brazilian routes. In Portuguese, *rendezvous* is a place to have sex.
- McDonald's Corporation was chagrined to learn that in French-Canadian slang "big macs" are large breasts.[13]

Nonverbal behaviors, too, differ from one part of the world to another. In many cultures, the American "OK" sign, made by touching the thumb and forefinger, is an obscene gesture representing the female genitalia. To a woman, it is a proposition for sex, and to a man it is an accusation of homosexuality.[14] It's easy to imagine the problems that could result in an unsuspecting American's innocent gesture.

The range of cultural differences is wide. In Middle Eastern countries, personal odors play an important role in interpersonal relationships. Arabs consistently breathe on people when they talk. As anthropologist Edward Hall explains:

> To smell one's friend is not only nice, but desirable, for to deny him your breath is to act ashamed. Americans, on the other hand, trained as they are not to breathe in people's faces, automatically communicate shame in trying to be polite. Who would expect that when our highest diplomats are putting on their best manners they are also communicating shame? Yet this is what occurs constantly, because diplomacy is not only "eyeball to eyeball" but breath to breath.[15]

A woman from Texas went to Washington, D.C. for a job in dormitory administration. When the dorm staff got together for meetings, she kept searching for the right time to break in—and never found it. Although back home she was considered outgoing and confident, in Washington she was perceived as shy and retiring. When she was evaluated at the end of a year, she was told to take an assertiveness-training course because of her inability to speak up.

That's why slight differences in conversational style—tiny little things like microseconds of a pause—can have enormous impact on your life. These little signals make up the mechanics of conversation, and when they're even slightly off, conversation is thrown off—or even cut off. The result in this case was a judgment of psychological problems—even in the mind of the woman herself, who really wondered what was wrong with her and signed up for assertiveness training.

Deborah Tannen,
That's Not What I Meant!

Looking at Diversity

ANCESTRY VS. ENVIRONMENT: A JAPANESE-CANADIAN PERSPECTIVE

David Suzuki

My genes can be traced in a direct line to Japan. I am a pure-blooded member of the Japanese race. And whenever I go there, I am always astonished to see the power of that biological connection. In subways in Tokyo, I catch familiar glimpses of the eyes, hairline or smile of my Japanese relatives. Yet when those same people open their mouths to communicate, the vast cultural gulf that separates them from me becomes obvious: English is my language, Shakespeare is my literature, British history is what I learned and Beethoven is my music.

For those who believe that in people, just as in animals, genes are the primary determinant of behaviour, a look at second- and third-generation immigrants to Canada gives powerful evidence to the contrary. The overriding influence is environmental. We make a great mistake by associating the inheritance of physical characteristics with far more complex traits of human personality and behaviour.

Each time I visit Japan, I am reminded of how Canadian I am and how little the racial connection matters. I first visited Japan in 1968 to attend the International Congress of Genetics in Tokyo. For the first time in my life, I was surrounded by people who all looked like me. While sitting in a train and looking at the reflections in the window, I found that it was hard to pick out my own image in the crowd. I had grown up in a Caucasian society in which I was a minority member. My whole sense of self had developed with that perspective of looking different. All my life I had wanted large eyes and brown hair so I could be like everyone else. Yet on that train, where I did fit in, I didn't like it.

On this first visit to Japan I had asked my grandparents to contact relatives and let them know I was coming. I was the first in the Suzuki clan in Canada to visit them. The closest relative on my father's side was my grandmother's younger brother, and we arranged to meet in a seaside resort near his home. He came to my hotel room with two of his daughters. None of them spoke any English, while my Japanese was so primitive as to be useless. In typical Japanese fashion, they showered me with gifts, the most important being a package of what looked like wood carved in the shape of bananas! I had no idea what it was. (Later I learned the package contained dried tuna fish from which slivers are shaved off to flavour soup. This is considered a highly prized gift.) We sat in stiff silence and embarrassment, each of us struggling to dredge up a common word or two to break the quiet. It was excruciating! My great uncle later wrote my grandmother to tell her how painful it had been to sit with her grandson and yet be unable to communicate a word.

To people in Japan, all non-Japanese—black, white or yellow—are *gaijin* or foreigners. While *gaijin* is not derogatory, I find that its use is harsh because I sense doors clanging shut on me when I'm called one. The Japanese do have a hell of a time with me because I look like them and can say in perfect Japanese, "I'm a foreigner and I can't speak Japanese." Their reactions are usually complete incomprehension followed by a sputtering, "What do you mean? You're speaking Japanese." And finally a pejorative, "Oh, a *gaijin!*"

Even beliefs about the very value of talk differ from one culture to another.[16] Western cultures view talk as desirable and use it for social purposes as well as task performance. Silence has a negative value in these cultures. It is likely to be interpreted as lack of interest, unwillingness to communicate, hostility, anxiety, shyness, or a sign of interpersonal incompatibility. Westerners are uncomfortable with silence, which they find embarrassing and awkward.

On the other hand, Asian cultures perceive talk quite differently. For thousands of years, Asian cultures have discouraged the expression of thoughts and feelings. Silence is valued, as Taoist sayings indicate: "In much talk there is great weariness," or "One who speaks does not know; one who knows does not speak." Unlike Westerners who are uncomfortable with silence, Japanese and Chinese believe that remaining quiet is the proper state when there is nothing to be said. To Easterners a talkative person is often considered a show-off or insincere.

It's easy to see how these different views of speech and silence can lead to communication problems when people from different cultures meet. Both the talkative Westerner and the silent Asian are behaving in ways they believe are proper; yet each views the other with disapproval and mistrust. Only when they recognize the different standards of behavior can they adapt to one another, or at least understand and respect their differences.

It isn't necessary to travel overseas to encounter differing cultural perspectives. Within this country there are many subcultures, and the members of each one have backgrounds that cause them to see things in unique ways. Failure to recognize these differences can lead to unfortunate and unnecessary misunderstandings. For example, an uninformed Anglo teacher or police officer might interpret the downcast expression of a Latino female as a sign of avoidance, or even dishonesty, when in fact this is the proper behavior in her culture for a female being addressed by an older man. To make direct eye contact in such a case would be considered undue brashness or even a sexual come-on.

Eye contact also differs in traditional black and white cultures. Whereas whites tend to look away from a conversational partner while speaking and at the other person when listening, blacks do just the opposite, looking at their companion more when talking and less when listening.[17] This difference can cause communication problems without either person's realizing the cause. For instance, whites are likely to use eye contact as a measure of how closely the other person is listening: The more others look, the more they seem to be paying attention. A white speaker, therefore, might interpret a black partner's lack of eye contact as a sign of inattention or rudeness when quite the opposite could be true. Since this sort of interpretation is usually unconscious, the speaker wouldn't even con-

Father, Mother, and Me,
  Sister and Auntie say
All the people like us are We,
  And everyone else is They.
And They live over the sea
  While we live over the way,
But—would you believe it?—
  They look upon We
As only a sort of They!

We eat pork and beef
  With cow-horn-handled knives.
They who gobble Their rice off a
    leaf
  Are horrified out of Their lives;
While They who live up a tree,
  Feast on grubs and clay,
(Isn't it scandalous?) look upon
    We
  As a simply disgusting They!

We eat kitcheny food.
  We have doors that latch.
They drink milk and blood
  Under an open thatch. We have
    doctors to fee.
  They have wizards to pay.
And (impudent heathen!) They
  look upon We
As a quite impossible They!

All good people agree,
  And all good people say,
All nice people, like us, are We
  And everyone else is They:
But if you cross over the sea,
  Instead of over the way,
You may end by (think of it!)
  looking on We
As only a sort of They!

Rudyard Kipling,
"We and They"

sider the possibility of testing her assumptions with the kind of perception check you will learn later in this chapter.

Along with ethnicity, geography also can influence perception. A
fascinating series of studies revealed that climate and geographic latitude were remarkably accurate predictors of communication predispositions.[18] People living in southern latitudes of the United States
are more socially isolated, less tolerant of ambiguity, higher in self-
esteem, more likely to touch others, and more likely to verbalize
their thoughts and feelings. This sort of finding helps explain why
communicators who travel from one part of a country to another find
that their old patterns of communicating don't work as well in their
new location. A Southerner whose relatively talkative, high-touch
style seemed completely normal at home might be viewed as pushy
and aggressive in a new northern home.

SOCIAL ROLES

So far you have seen how cultural and physiological variations can
block communication. Along with these differences, another set of
perceptual factors can lead to communication breakdowns. From
almost the time we're born, each of us is indirectly taught a whole set
of roles that we'll be expected to play. In one sense this collection of
prescribed parts is necessary because it enables a society to function
smoothly and provides the security that comes from knowing what's
expected of you. But in another way, having roles defined in advance

can lead to wide gaps in understanding. When roles become unquestioned and rigid, people tend to see the world from their own viewpoint, having no experiences that show them how other people view it. Naturally, in such a situation communication suffers.

GENDER ROLES   In every society gender is one of the most important factors in determining how people perceive one another. Children learn the importance of sex-typed behavior by watching other people and being exposed to media as well as by reinforcement.[19] Once members of a society learn customary sex roles, they tend to regard violations of those roles as unusual—or even undesirable.

Some theorists have suggested that stereotypical masculine and feminine behaviors are not opposite poles of a single continuum, but rather two separate sets of behavior.[20] With this view, an individual can act in a masculine manner or a feminine manner, or exhibit both types of characteristics. The male-female dichotomy, then, is replaced with four psychological sex types, including masculine, feminine, **androgynous** (combining masculine and feminine traits), and undifferentiated (neither masculine nor feminine). Combining the four psychological sex types with the traditional physiological sex types produces the eight categories listed in Table 3–1.

Each of these eight psychological sex types perceives interpersonal relationships differently. For example, masculine males probably see their interpersonal relationships as opportunities for competitive interaction, as opportunities to win something. Feminine females probably see their interpersonal relationships as opportunities to be nurturing, to express their feelings and emotions. Androgynous males and females, on the other hand, probably differ little in their perceptions of their interpersonal relationships.

Androgynous individuals probably see their relationships as opportunities to behave in a variety of ways, depending on the nature of the relationships themselves, the context in which a particular relationship takes place, and the myriad other variables affecting what might constitute appropriate behavior. These variables are usually ignored by the sex-typed masculine males and feminine females, who have a smaller repertoire of behavior.

T A B L E   3 – 1   Psychological Sex Types

	MALE	FEMALE
Masculine	Masculine males	Masculine females
Feminine	Feminine males	Feminine females
Androgynous	Androgynous males	Androgynous females
Undifferentiated	Undifferentiated males	Undifferentiated females

OCCUPATIONAL ROLES   The kind of work we do often influences our view of the world. Imagine five people taking a walk through the park. One, a botanist, is fascinated by the variety of trees and plants. The zoologist is looking for interesting animals. The third, a meteorologist, keeps an eye on the sky, noticing changes in the weather. The fourth companion, a psychologist, is totally unaware of nature, instead concentrating on the interaction among the people in the park. The fifth person, being a pickpocket, quickly takes advantage of the others' absorption to make some money. There are two lessons in this little story. The first, of course, is to watch your wallet carefully. The second is that our occupational roles shape our perceptions.

Even within the same occupational setting, the different roles that participants have can affect their perceptions. Consider a typical college classroom, for example: The experiences of the instructor and students often are quite dissimilar. Having dedicated a large part of their lives to their work, most professors see their subject matter—whether French literature, physics, or speech communication—as vitally important. Students who are taking the course to satisfy a general education requirement may view the subject quite differently: maybe as one of many obstacles that stand between them and a degree, maybe as a chance to meet new people. Another difference centers on the amount of knowledge possessed by the parties. To an instructor who has taught the course many times, the material probably seems extremely simple; but to students encountering it for the first time, it may seem strange and confusing. Toward the end of a semester or quarter the instructor might be pressing onward hurriedly to cover all the material in the course, whereas the students are fatigued from their studies and ready to move more slowly. We don't

THE INVESTIGATION

need to spell out the interpersonal strains and stresses that come from such differing perceptions.

Perhaps the most dramatic illustration of how occupational roles shape perception occurred in 1971.[21] Stanford psychologist Philip Zimbardo recruited a group of middle-class, well-educated young men. He randomly chose eleven to serve as "guards" in a mock prison set up in the basement of Stanford's psychology building. He issued the guards uniforms, handcuffs, whistles, and billy clubs. The remaining ten subjects became "prisoners" and were placed in rooms with metal bars, bucket toilets, and cots.

Zimbardo let the guards establish their own rules for the experiment. The rules were tough: No talking during meals, rest periods, and after lights out. Head counts at 2:30 A.M. Troublemakers received short rations.

Faced with these conditions, the prisoners began to resist. Some barricaded their doors with beds. Others went on hunger strikes. Several ripped off their identifying number tags. The guards reacted to the rebellion by clamping down hard on protesters. Some turned sadistic, physically and verbally abusing the prisoners. They threw prisoners into solitary confinement. Others forced prisoners to call each other names and clean out toilets with their bare hands.

Within a short time the experiment had become reality for both prisoners and guards. Several inmates had stomach cramps and lapsed into uncontrollable weeping. Others suffered from headaches, and one broke out in a head-to-toe rash after his request for early "parole" was denied by the guards.

The experiment was scheduled to go on for two weeks, but after six days Zimbardo realized that what had started as a simulation had become too intense. "I knew by then that they were thinking like prisoners and not like people," he said. "If we were able to demonstrate that pathological behavior could be produced in so short a time, think of what damage is being done in 'real' prisons. . . . "

This dramatic exercise in which twenty-one well-educated, middle-class citizens turned almost overnight into sadistic bullies and demoralized victims tells us that *how* we think is a function of our roles in society. It seems that *what* we are is determined largely by society's designation of *who* we are. Fortunately, many officials in the field of law enforcement are aware of the perceptual blindness that can come with one's job. These professionals have developed programs that help to overcome the problem, as the following reading illustrates.

 INVITATION TO INSIGHT

ROLE REVERSAL

Walk a mile in another person's shoes. Find a group that is foreign to you, and try to become a member of it for awhile.

If you're down on the police, see if your local department has a ride-along program where you can spend several hours on patrol with one or two officers.

If you think the present state of education is a mess, become a teacher yourself. Maybe an instructor will give you the chance to plan one or more classes.

If you're adventuresome, follow the example of the police officers in the article on pages 109–110 and become a homeless person for a day. See how you're treated.

If you're a political conservative, try getting involved in a radical organization; if you're a radical, check out the conservatives.

Whatever group you join, try to become part of it as best you can. Don't just observe. Get into the philosophy of your new role and see how it feels. You may find that all those weird people aren't so strange after all.

FIELD EXPERIMENTS:
PREPARATION FOR THE CHANGING POLICE ROLE

We are all aware that it is extremely difficult to immerse the average policeman into situations that will reveal the feelings of the down-and-outer, the social outcast, the have-nots, and show us their perspective of normal law-enforcement procedures. Obviously the officer, in his police role, would not fit into a ghetto of any kind. But suppose he were a man with a great deal of courage, willing for the sake of experimentation to become a bum, a skid row habitant.

Our Covina officers who were willing to become skid row habitants were carefully selected and conditioned for the role they were about to play. Each man was given three dollars with which to purchase a complete outfit of pawn shop clothing. The only new article of attire he was allowed was footwear—reject tennis shoes purchased for a few small coins. Among his other props were such items as a shopping bag filled with collected junk, and a wine bottle camouflaged with a brown paper sack.

Conditioned and ready, our men, assigned in pairs, moved into the Los Angeles skid row district. They soon discovered that when they tried to leave the area, walking a few blocks into the legitimate retail sections, they were told, "Go back where you belong!" Our men knew in reality they were not "bums," but they found that other citizens quickly categorized them and treated them accordingly.

(continued on next page)

Some women, when approached on the sidewalk and asked for a match, stepped out into the street rather than offer a reply, much less a light for a smoke.

During the skid row experiment, our men ate in the rescue missions, and sat through the prayer services with other outcasts and derelicts. They roamed the streets and the alleys, and discovered many leveling experiences. Some were anticipated, others were not. Perhaps the most meaningful experience of the skid row exercise occurred to Tom Courtney, a young juvenile officer with five years' police service.

It was dusk, and Tom and his partner were sauntering back to a prearranged gathering place. Feeling a little sporty, the pair decided to "polish off" the bottle of wine. They paused in a convenient parking lot and Tom tipped the bottle up. As if from nowhere, two uniformed policemen materialized before the surprised pair. Tom and his partner were spread-eagled against a building and searched. Forgetting the admonishment not to reveal identities and purpose unless absolutely necessary, Tom panicked and identified himself.

Later, Tom found it difficult to explain why he was so quick in his revelation. "You wouldn't understand," he told me; then blurted he "thought he might get shot."

I found it difficult to receive this as a rational explanation, especially since Tom stated that the officers, while firm, were courteous at all times. With some additional prodding, Tom admitted that as he was being searched, he suddenly thought of every negative thing he had ever heard about a policeman. He even perceived a mental flash of a newspaper headline: "Police Officer Erroneously Shot While on Field Experiment."

"I know better now," Tom continued, "but when you feel that way about yourself, you believe—you believe."

I attempted to rationalize with Tom his reason for fear. I asked if he was certain that the officers were courteous. He replied in the affirmative, but added, "They didn't smile, or tell me what they were going to do next." Tom had discovered a new emotional reaction within his own personal makeup, and it left a telling impression.

Today, Tom Courtney is still telling our department personnel, "For God's sake, smile when you can. And above all, tell the man you're shaking down what you are going to do. Take the personal threat out of the encounter, if you can."

Equally important as Tom's experience, I believe, is the lesson we learned about personal judgments. Our men in the "Operation Empathy" experiment found they were adjudged by the so-called normal population as "being like" all the other inmates of skid row, simply because their appearance was representative.

Perhaps we would all do well to heed the lesson, for now, more than at any other time in our history, policemen must guard against the natural tendency to lump people into categories simply because they look alike.

The invisible barrier that stands between the law enforcer and the law breaker is being bridged through experimentation. Human beings are dealing with human beings, and successful field experiments, conducted by law enforcement, have shown that empathy, understanding another's emotions and feelings, can, in some potentially volatile situations, play an important role toward nonviolence in police-involved situations.

R. Fred Ferguson, *Chief of Police, Riverside Police Department, Riverside, California. Formerly Chief, Covina Police Department, Covina, California.*

SELF-CONCEPT

A final factor that influences how we think of ourselves and interact with others is the self-concept. Extensive research shows that a person with high self-esteem is more likely to think well of others whereas someone with low self-esteem is likely to have a poor opinion of others.[22] Your own experience may bear this out: Persons with low self-esteem are often cynical and quick to ascribe the worst possible motives to others, whereas those who feel good about themselves are disposed to think favorably about the people they encounter. As one writer put it, "What we find 'out there' is what we put there with our unconscious projections. When we think we are looking out a window, it may be, more often than we realize, that we are really gazing into a looking glass."[23]

Besides distorting the facts about others, our self-concepts also lead us to have distorted views of ourselves. We already hinted at this fact when we explained in Chapter Two that the self-concept is not objective. "It wasn't my fault," you might be tempted to say, knowing deep inside that you were responsible. "I look horrible," you might think as you look into the mirror, despite the fact that everyone around you sincerely insists you look terrific.

✣ THE ACCURACY—AND INACCURACY— OF PERCEPTION

By now it's obvious that many factors distort the way we interpret the world. Social scientists use the term **attribution** to describe the process of attaching meaning to behavior. We attribute meaning both to our own actions and to the actions of others, but we often use different yardsticks. Research has uncovered several perceptual errors that lead to inaccurate attributions.[24]

WE OFTEN JUDGE OURSELVES MORE CHARITABLY THAN OTHERS

In an attempt to convince ourselves and others that the positive face we show to the world is true, we tend to judge ourselves in the most generous terms possible. Social scientists have labeled this tendency the **self-serving bias.**[25] When others suffer, we often blame the problem on their personal qualities. On the other hand, when we're the victims, we find explanations outside ourselves. Consider a few examples:

- When *they* botch a job, we might think they weren't listening well or trying hard enough; when *we* make the mistake, the problem was unclear directions or not enough time.
- When *he* lashes out angrily, we say he's being moody or too sensitive; when *we* blow off steam, it's because of the pressure we've been under.

I have heard students say things like, "It was John's fault, his speech was so confusing nobody could have understood it." Then, two minutes later, the same student remarked, "It wasn't my fault, what I said could not have been clearer. John must be stupid." Poor John! He was blamed when he was the sender and when he was the receiver. John's problem was that he was the other person, and that's who is always at fault.

Stephen W. King

■ When *she* gets caught speeding, we say she should have been more careful; when *we* get the ticket, we deny we were driving too fast or say, "Everybody does it."

The egocentric tendency to rate ourselves more favorably than others see us has been demonstrated experimentally.[26] In one study, a random sample of men were asked to rank themselves on their ability to get along with others.[27] Defying mathematical laws, all subjects— every last one—put themselves in the top half of the population. Sixty percent rated themselves in the top 10 percent of the population, and an amazing 25 percent believed they were in the top 1 percent. In the same study, 70 percent of the men ranked their leadership in the top quarter of the population, whereas only 2 percent thought they were below average. Sixty percent said they were in the top quarter in athletic abilities, whereas only 6 percent viewed themselves as below average.

Distortions like these usually revolve around the desire to maintain a presenting self-concept that has been threatened. The desire to maintain face is often strong. If you want to present yourself as a good student or musician, for example, an instructor who gives you a poor grade or a critic who doesn't appreciate your music *must* be wrong, and you'll find evidence to show it. If you want to think of yourself as a good worker or parent, you'll find explanations for the problems in your job or family that shift the responsibility away from you. Of course, the same principle works for people with excessively negative self-images: They'll go out of the way to explain any information that's favorable to them in terms that show they really are incompetent or undesirable. The list of defense mechanisms in Chapter Nine shows how inventive people can be when a threatened presenting image is at stake.

WE ARE INFLUENCED BY WHAT IS MOST OBVIOUS

The error of being influenced by what is most obvious is understandable. As you read at the beginning of this chapter, we select stimuli from our environment that are noticeable: intense, repetitious, unusual, or otherwise attention-grabbing. The problem is that the most obvious factor is not necessarily the only cause—or the most significant one for an event. For example,

■ When two children (or adults, for that matter) fight, it may be a mistake to blame the one who lashes out first. Perhaps the other one was at least equally responsible, teasing or refusing to cooperate.
■ You might complain about an acquaintance whose malicious gossiping or arguing has become a bother, forgetting that by putting up with such behavior in the past you have been at least partially responsible.
■ You might blame an unhappy working situation on the boss, overlooking other factors beyond her control such as a change in the economy, the policy of higher management, or demands of customers or other workers.

"The truth is, Cauldwell, we never see ourselves as others see us."

THE SATURDAY EVENING POST

WE CLING TO FIRST IMPRESSIONS

Labeling people according to our first impressions is an inevitable part of the perception process. These labels are a way of making interpretations. "She seems cheerful." "He seems sincere." "They sound awfully conceited."

If they're accurate, impressions like these can be useful ways of deciding how to respond best to people in the future. Problems arise, however, when the labels we attach are inaccurate; once we form an opinion of someone, we tend to hang onto it and make any conflicting information fit our image.

Suppose, for instance, you mention the name of your new neighbor to a friend. "Oh, I know him," your friend replies. "He seems nice at first, but it's all an act." Perhaps this appraisal is off-base. The neighbor may have changed since your friend knew him, or perhaps your friend's judgment is simply unfair. Whether the judgment is accurate or not, once you accept your friend's evaluation, it will probably influence the way you respond to the neighbor. You'll look for examples of the insincerity you've heard about . . . and you'll probably find them. Even if the neighbor were a saint, you would be likely to interpret his behavior in ways that fit your expectations. "Sure he *seems* nice," you might think, "but it's probably just a front." Of course, this sort of suspicion can create a self-fulfilling prophecy, transforming a genuinely nice person into someone who truly becomes an undesirable neighbor.

Given the almost unavoidable tendency to form first impressions, the best advice we can give is to keep an open mind and to be willing to change your opinion as events prove it mistaken.

WE TEND TO ASSUME OTHERS ARE SIMILAR TO US

In Chapter Two you read one example of this principle: that people with low self-esteem imagine others view them unfavorably, whereas people who like themselves imagine that others like them, too. The frequently mistaken assumption that others' views are similar to our own applies in a wide range of situations:

- You've heard a slightly raunchy joke that you think is pretty funny. You might assume that it won't offend a somewhat strait-laced friend. It does.
- You've been bothered by an instructor's tendency to get off the subject during lectures. If you were a professor, you'd want to know if anything you were doing was creating problems for your students, so you decide that your instructor will probably be grateful for some constructive criticism. Unfortunately, you're wrong.
- You lost your temper with a friend a week ago and said some things you regret. In fact, if someone said those things to you, you'd consider the relationship was finished. Imagining that your friend feels the same way, you avoid making contact. In fact, your friend feels that she was partly responsible and has avoided you because she thinks you're the one who wants to end things.

Examples like these show that others don't always think or feel the way we do and that assuming similarities exist can lead to problems. How can you find out the other person's real position? Sometimes by asking directly, sometimes by checking with others, and sometimes by making an educated guess after you've thought the matter out. All these alternatives are better than simply assuming everyone would react as you do.

❖ PERCEPTION CHECKING TO PREVENT MISUNDERSTANDINGS

Serious problems can arise when people treat interpretations as if they were matters of fact. Like most people, you probably resent others jumping to conclusions about the reasons for your behavior.

"Why are you mad at me?" (Who said you were?)

"What's the matter with you?" (Who said anything was the matter?)

"Come on now. Tell the truth." (Who said you were lying?)

As you'll learn in Chapter Nine, even if your interpretation is correct, a dogmatic, mind-reading statement is likely to generate defensiveness. The skill of **perception checking** provides a better way to handle your interpretations.

ELEMENTS OF PERCEPTION CHECKING

A complete perception check has three parts:

- A description of the behavior you noticed
- At least two possible interpretations of the behavior
- A request for clarification about how to interpret the behavior.

Perception checks for the preceding three examples would look like this:

"When you stomped out of the room and slammed the door," (*Behavior*) "I wasn't sure whether you were mad at me" (*First interpretation*) "or just in a hurry." (*Second interpretation*) "How *did* you feel?" (*Request for clarification*)

"You haven't laughed much in the last couple of days." (*Behavior*) "It makes me wonder whether something's bothering you" (*First interpretation*) "or whether you're just feeling quiet." (*Second interpretation*) "What's up?" (*Request for clarification*)

"You said you really liked the job I did," (*Behavior*) "but there was something about your voice that made me think you may not like it." (*First interpretation*) "Maybe it's just my imagination, though." (*Second interpretation*) "How do you really feel?" (*Request for clarification*)

Perception checking is a tool for helping you understand others accurately instead of assuming that your first interpretation is correct. Because its goal is mutual understanding, perception checking is a cooperative approach to communication. Besides leading to more accurate perceptions, it minimizes defensiveness by preserving the other person's face. Instead of saying in effect "I know what you're thinking . . . " a perception check takes the more respectful approach that states or implies "I know I'm not qualified to judge you without some help."

PERCEPTION-CHECKING CONSIDERATIONS

Like every communication skill outlined in *Looking Out/Looking In*, perception checking isn't a mechanical formula that will work in every situation. As you develop the ability to check your perceptions fully, consider the following factors in deciding when and how to use this approach.

COMPLETENESS   Sometimes an effective perception check won't need all the parts listed earlier to be effective:

> "You haven't dropped by lately. Is anything the matter?" (*Single interpretation combined with request for clarification*)

> "I can't tell whether you're kidding me about being cheap or if you're serious." (*Behavior combined with interpretations*) "Are you mad at me?"

> "Are you *sure* you don't mind driving? I can use a ride if it's no trouble, but I don't want to take you out of your way." (*No need to describe behavior*)

Sometimes even the most skimpy perception check—a simple question like "What's going on?"—will do the job. You might also rely on other people to help you make sense of confusing behavior: "Rachelle has been awfully quiet lately. Do you know what's up?" A complete perception check is most necessary when the risk of sounding judgmental is highest.

NONVERBAL CONGRUENCY   A perception check can only succeed if your nonverbal behavior reflects the open-mindedness of your words. An accusing tone of voice or a hostile glare will contradict the sincerely worded request for clarification, suggesting that you have already made up your mind about the other person's intentions.

CULTURAL RULES   The straightforward approach of perception checking has the best chance of working in what Chapter Five identifies as *low-context cultures:* ones in which members use language as clearly and logically as possible. The dominant cultures of North America and Western Europe fit into this category, and members of these groups are most likely to appreciate the kind of straight talking that perception checking embodies. On the other hand, members of *high-context cultures* (more common in Latin America and Asia) value social harmony over clarity. Low-context communicators are more likely to regard candid approaches like perception checking as potentially embarrassing, preferring instead less direct ways of understanding one another. Thus, a "let's get this straight" perception check that might work well with a EuroAmerican manager who was raised to value clarity could be a serious mistake with a Mexican-American or Asian-American boss who has spent most of his or her life in a high-context culture.

SKILL BUILDER

PERCEPTION CHECKING PRACTICE

Practice your perception checking ability by developing three-part verifications for the following situations:

1. You made what you thought was an excellent suggestion to an instructor. The professor looked uninterested but said she would check on the matter right away. Three weeks have passed and nothing has changed.

2. A neighbor and good friend has not responded to your "Good morning" for three days in a row. This person is usually friendly.

3. You haven't received the usual weekly phone call from the folks back home in over a month. The last time you spoke, you had an argument about where to spend the holidays.

4. An old friend with whom you have shared the problems of your love life for years has recently changed when around you: The formerly casual hugs and kisses have become longer and stronger, and the occasions where you "accidentally" brush up against one another have become more frequent.

❖ EMPATHY AND COMMUNICATION

Perception checking is a valuable tool for clarifying ambiguous messages. But ambiguity isn't the only cause of perceptual problems. Sometimes we understand *what* people mean without understanding *why* they believe as they do. At times like this we are short on the vital ability to empathize.

EMPATHY DEFINED

Empathy is the ability to re-create another person's perspective; to experience the world from the other's point of view. As we'll use the term here, **empathy** involves three dimensions.[28] On one level, empathy involves *perspective taking*—the ability to take on the viewpoint of another person. This understanding requires a suspension of judgment, so that for the moment you set aside your own opinions and take on those of the other person. Besides cognitive understanding, empathy also has an *emotional* dimension that allows us to experience the feelings that others have. We know their fear, joy, sadness, and so on. When we combine the perspective-taking and emotional dimensions, we see that empathizing allows you to experience the other's perception—in effect, to become that person temporarily. A third ingredient of empathy is a genuine *concern* for the welfare of the other person. When we empathize we go beyond just thinking and feeling as others do and genuinely care about their well-being.

⬖ SIBLING RIVALRY: A NEW PERSPECTIVE

Empathizing with another person can be extremely difficult, especially when the other occupies a very different position. Authors Adele Faber and Elaine Mazlish help mothers find a way to understand how the arrival of a new brother or sister might seem to a preschool child.

Imagine that your spouse puts an arm around you and says, "Honey, I love you so much, and you're so wonderful that I've decided to have another wife just like you."

When the new wife finally arrives, you see that she's very young and kind of cute. When the three of you are out together, people say hello to you politely, but exclaim ecstatically over the newcomer. "Isn't she adorable! Hello sweetheart . . . You are precious!" Then they turn to you and ask, "How do you like the new wife?"

The new wife needs clothing. Your husband goes into your closet, takes some of your sweaters and pants and gives them to her. When you protest, he points out that since you've put on a little weight, your clothes are too
tight on you and they'll fit her perfectly.

The new wife is maturing rapidly. Every day she seems smarter and more competent. One afternoon as you're struggling to figure out the directions on the new computer . . . she bursts into the room and says, "Oooh, can I use it? I know how."

When you tell her she can't use it, she runs crying to your husband. Moments later she returns with him. Her face is tear-stained and he has his arm around her. He says to you, "What would be the harm in letting her have a turn? Why can't you share?"

One day you find your husband and the new wife lying on the bed together. He's tickling her and she's giggling. Suddenly the phone rings and he answers it. Afterwards he tells you that something important has come up and he must leave immediately. He asks you to stay home with the new wife, and make sure she's all right.

Adele Faber and Elaine Mazlish,
Siblings without Rivalry

It is easy to confuse empathy with **sympathy,** but the concepts are different in two important ways. First, sympathy means you feel compassion *for* another person's predicament, whereas empathy means you have a personal sense of what that predicament is like. Consider the difference between sympathizing with an unwed mother or a homeless person and empathizing with them—imagining what it would be like to be in their position. Despite your concern, sympathy lacks the degree of identification that empathy entails. When you sympathize, it is the other's confusion, joy, or pain. When you empathize, the experience becomes your own, at least for the moment.

Both perspectives are important ones, but empathy is clearly the more complete of the two.

Empathy is different from sympathy in another way. We only sympathize when we accept the reasons for another's pain as valid, whereas it's possible to empathize without feeling sympathy. You can empathize with a difficult relative, a rude stranger, or even a criminal without feeling much sympathy for them. Empathizing allows you to understand another person's motives without requiring you to agree with them. After empathizing you will almost certainly understand them better, but sympathy won't always follow.

There is no consistent evidence that suggests the ability to empathize is better for one sex or the other.[29] Some people, however, seem to have a hereditary capacity for greater empathizing than do others.[30] Studies of identical and fraternal twins indicate that identical female twins are more similar to one another in their ability to empathize than are fraternal twins. Interestingly, there seems to be no difference between males. Although empathy may have a biological basis, the role of environment can still play an important role. For example, parents who are sensitive to their children's feelings tend to have children who also reach out to others.[31]

Total empathy is impossible to achieve. Completely understanding another person's point of view is simply too difficult a task for humans with different backgrounds and limited communication skills. Nonetheless, it is possible to get a strong sense of what the world looks like through another person's eyes. The following method will help you become more empathic.

Apart from abstract propositions of comparison (such as two and two make four), propositions which tell us nothing by themselves about concrete reality, we find no proposition ever regarded by any one as evidently certain that has not either been called a falsehood, or at least had its truth sincerely questioned by someone else.

William James,
The Will to Believe

Calvin and Hobbes by Watterson. ©1994 by Watterson. Dist. by Universal Press Syndicate. Reprinted with permission. All rights reserved.

It was six men of Indostan
　　To learning much inclined,
Who went to see the elephant
　　Though all of them were
　　　blind

That each by observation
　　Might satisfy his mind.

The first approached the elephant
　　And, happening to fall
Against the broad and sturdy
　　side,
　　At once began to bawl:
"Why, bless me! But the elephant
　　Is very much like a wall!"

The second, feeling of the tusk,
　　Cried: "Ho! What have we
　　　here
So very round and smooth and
　　sharp?
　　To me, 'tis very clear,
This wonder of an elephant
　　Is very like a spear!"

The third approached the animal,
　　And, happening to take
The squirming trunk within his
　　hands
　　Thus boldly up he spake:
"I see," quoth he, "the elephant
　　Is very like a snake!"

The fourth reached out his eager
    hand
    And felt about the knee:
"What most this wondrous beast
    is like
    Is very plain," quoth he:
"'Tis clear enough the elephant
    Is very like a tree!"

The fifth who chanced to touch
    the ear
    Said: "E'en the blindest
    man
Can tell what this resembles
    most—
    Deny the fact who can:
This marvel of an elephant
    Is very like a fan!"

The sixth no sooner had begun
    About the beast to grope
Than, seizing on the swinging
    tail
    That fell within his scope,
"I see," quoth he, "the elephant
    Is very like a rope!"

And so these men of Indostan
    Disputed loud and long,
Each in his own opinion
    Exceeding stiff and strong;
Though each was partly in the
    right,
    And all were in the
    wrong.

John G. Saxe

THE "PILLOW METHOD": A TOOL FOR BUILDING EMPATHY

Perception checking is a relatively quick, easy tool for clarifying potential misunderstandings. But some issues are too complex and serious to be handled with this approach. Writer Paul Reps describes a tool for boosting empathy when it seems impossible to find merit in another's position.[32]

Developed by a group of Japanese schoolchildren, the **pillow method** gets its name from the fact that a problem has four sides and a middle, just like a pillow (see Figure 3–5). As the examples on pages 124–125 show, viewing the issue from each of these perspectives almost always leads to valuable insights.

POSITION 1: I'M RIGHT, YOU'RE WRONG   This is the perspective we usually take when viewing an issue. We immediately see the virtues in our position and find fault with anyone that happens to disagree with us. Detailing this position takes little effort, and provides little new information.

POSITION 2: YOU'RE RIGHT, I'M WRONG   At this point you switch perspectives and build the strongest possible arguments to explain how others can view the issue differently from you. Besides identifying the strengths in the other's position, this is the time to play the devil's advocate and find flaws in yours.

Finding fault with your viewpoint and trying to support the other's position requires discipline and a certain amount of courage, even though this is only an exercise and you will soon be able to retreat to position 1 if you choose. But most people learn that switching perspectives shows that there is some merit to the other person's side of the controversy.

There are some issues where it seems impossible to call the other position "right." Criminal behavior, deceit, and disloyalty often seem

FIGURE 3–5
The pillow method

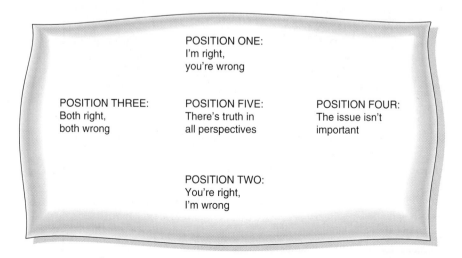

POSITION ONE:
I'm right,
you're wrong

POSITION THREE:
Both right,
both wrong

POSITION FIVE:
There's truth in
all perspectives

POSITION FOUR:
The issue isn't
important

POSITION TWO:
You're right,
I'm wrong

beyond justification. At times like these it is possible to arrive at position 2 by realizing that the other person's behavior is understandable. For example, without approving you may be able to understand how someone would resort to violence, tell lies, or cheat. Whatever the particulars, the goal of position 2 is to find some way of comprehending how anyone could behave in a way that you originally found impossible to defend.

The belief that one's own view of reality is the only reality is the most dangerous of all delusions.

Paul Watzlawick

POSITION 3: BOTH RIGHT, BOTH WRONG   From this position you acknowledge the strengths and weaknesses of each person's arguments. If you have done a good job with position 2, it should be clear that there is some merit in both points of view, and that each side has its flaws. Taking a more evenhanded look at the issue can lead you to be less critical and more understanding of another's point of view.

Position 3 can also help you find the commonalities between your position and the other's. Perhaps you've both been right to care so much about the issue, but both wrong in failing to recognize the other person's concerns. Perhaps there are underlying values that you both share, and similar mistakes that you've both made. In any case, the perspective of position 3 should help you see that the issue isn't as much a matter of complete right and wrong as it first appeared to be.

POSITION 4: THE ISSUE ISN'T AS IMPORTANT AS IT SEEMS   This perspective will help you realize that the controversy isn't as critical as you thought. Although it is hard to think of some issues as unimportant, a little thought will show that most concerns aren't as vital as we make them out to be. The impact of even the most traumatic events—the death of a loved one or the breakup of a relationship, for example—usually fades over time. The effects may not disappear, but we learn to accept them and get on with life. The importance of a dispute can also fade when you realize you've let it overshadow other equally important parts of your relationship. It's easy to become so wrapped up over a dispute about one subject that you forget about the other ways in which you are close to the other person.

CONCLUSION: THERE IS TRUTH IN ALL FOUR PERSPECTIVES   After completing the first four positions, a final step is to recognize that each of them has some merit. While logic might suggest that it's impossible for a position to be both right and wrong, both important and unimportant, your own experience will show that there is some truth in each of the positions you have explored. This fifth is very different from the "I'm right and you're wrong" attitude that most people bring to an issue. Once you have looked at an issue from these five perspectives, it is almost certain that you will gain new insights. These insights may not cause you to change your mind, or even solve the problem at hand. Nonetheless, the new understanding can increase your tolerance for the other person's position, and thus improve the communication climate.

The test of a first-rate intelligence is the ability to hold two opposed ideas in mind at the same time and still retain the ability to function.

F. Scott Fitzgerald

Communication Transcript

THE PILLOW METHOD IN ACTION

Background

My almost-eighteen-year-old daughter wants to move away from home and live with a friend in an apartment in town. My wife and I wish she'd continue to live at home for another year, until she moves away to attend an out-of-town university.

Our daughter is an adventurous, mature, responsible person. She found the social and academic atmosphere in high school tedious and discouraging. Late in her sophomore year she passed the high school proficiency exam and enrolled in the local community college. She's done well academically, and likes the more adult atmosphere. She spent last semester overseas in the college's international education abroad program where she studied and traveled throughout Europe. She has one more year in the community college, before transferring to the university several hundred miles away.

Position One:
We are right and she is wrong.

We don't see why our daughter needs to leave home. Our relationship is terrific. We like one another, and have fun together when she's around. We trust and respect her, and we don't try to control her movements or friendships. We ask her about her plans and tell her about ours, just like roommates

would do, but she comes and goes as she sees fit.

In terms of money, moving to an apartment in town when she can live at home would be a waste. We figure that the cost of a year's extra rent, utilities, and food is about $5,000. That money could be better spent in many ways: for her university studies out of town, for a new car, or as a nest egg after graduation. Sure, she would have fun living independently, but waiting a year makes sense.

Position Two:
Our daughter is right and we're wrong.

After being on her own overseas and attending college for almost two years, our daughter is right when she says she is capable of living on her own. Although her chronological age is only eighteen, she is mature beyond her years. We would be making a mistake if we compared her to kids her age instead of to people who are at the same level of maturity.

Our daughter is also right when she says that our different lifestyles make it time for a move. She stays up late at night and sleeps in mornings when there's no work or school, while we are early risers. She doesn't mind letting clutter build up for several days before cleaning, and we like the place always to be

neat. She likes to play music loud, and we like it more quiet. Living together creates friction over lifestyles that wouldn't exist if we had our separate territory.

Concerning money, our daughter is right to say that we would be spending the same amount for an apartment if she had gone away to college instead of having spent her first two years living at home. In fact, those semesters at the community college have actually *saved* us money, compared to the cost if she'd spent four years at the university. So, in one sense we're wrong to say that her move is costing us anything we weren't always prepared to spend.

Position Three:
Both of us are right and both are wrong.

We're right to say that our daughter's staying at home one more year would save thousands of dollars for other uses. We're wrong to dismiss or downplay her need to live independently and only measure the move in terms of money.

She's right to say that it's time to live independently. I remember how much I wanted to live on my own in my late teens, so I can appreciate her feelings by recalling mine. She's probably mistaken to assume that living on her own will make as much of a difference in her life as she expects it will.

Position Four:
The issue isn't important.

In another year our daughter will have her own place, no matter what. If she moves before then, we and she will find the money somehow. If she stays home, we will manage to accommodate to one another's habits. Both approaches have their advantages and both have drawbacks. There's no perfect solution.

No matter how this turns out, we are all handling the issue in a respectful way that keeps our relationship strong, and that's the most important thing.

Conclusion

Before using the pillow method to think through all sides of this issue, the parental perspective seemed like the stronger one. Now I can understand better how important the issue is to my daughter. I can also see that, in some ways, her position is more defensible than mine. My wife and I have decided to sit down with our daughter and lay out the amount of money in her "college fund." We will explain that spending the money on an apartment now will leave her less in the future and let her decide on the best way to spend the money.

No matter which way the decision goes, the pillow method helped me handle this issue with our daughter in a way that is far more respectful and less contentious than it otherwise would have been. Our relationship is stronger and happier, and that's far more important than the amount in a bank account or where any of us lives.

SKILL BUILDER

PILLOW TALK

Try using the pillow method in your life. It isn't easy, but once you begin to understand it, the payoff in increased understanding is great.

1. Choose a person or viewpoint with whom or which you strongly disagree. If you've chosen a person, it's best to have him or her there with you; but if that's not possible, you can do it alone.

2. What disagreement should you choose? No doubt there are many in your life:
   parent–child
   teacher–student
   employer–employee
   brother–sister
   friend–friend
   nation–nation
   Republican–Democrat

3. For each problem you choose, really place yourself in each position on the pillow as you encounter it:
   a. Your position is correct, and your opponent's is wrong.
   b. Your opponent's position is correct, and yours is wrong.
   c. Both your positions are correct, and both are wrong.
   d. It isn't important which side is right or wrong.
   Finally, affirm the fact that all four positions are true.

4. The more important the problem is to you, the harder it will be to accept positions 2, 3, and 4 as valid. But the exercise will work only if you can suspend your present position and imagine how it would feel to hold the other ones.

5. How can you tell if you've been successful with the pillow method? The answer is simple: If after going over all of the steps you can understand—not necessarily accept but just understand—the other person's position, you've done it. After you've reached this understanding, do you notice any change in how you feel about the other person?

✤ SUMMARY

There is more to the world "out there" than any person is capable of understanding. We make sense of our environment by the three-step process of selecting certain stimuli from the environment, organizing them into meaningful patterns, and interpreting them in a manner that is shaped by past experience, assumptions about human behavior, expectations, knowledge, and personal moods.

A number of factors affect the way we select, organize, and interpret information. Physiological influences such as the five senses, age, and health play an important role. Cultural background also shapes the way we view the world, as do social roles and self-concept. In addition to these factors, we commonly make a number of perceptual errors when attributing meaning to others' behavior.

Perception checking can be a useful tool for verifying interpretations of others' behavior instead of assuming that the first hunch is correct. A complete perception check includes a description of the other's behavior, at least two plausible interpretations of its meaning, and a request for clarification about what the behavior does signify.

Empathy is the ability to experience another person's point of view. Empathy differs from sympathy because it more closely matches the other's experience, and because it does not necessarily require agreement or pity. One means for boosting empathy is the pillow method, which involves viewing an issue from five different perspectives.

✛ KEY TERMS

androgynous
attribution
empathy
interaction constructs
interpretation
membership constructs

organization
perception checking
perceptual schema
physical constructs
pillow method
psychological constructs

punctuation
role constructs
selection
self-serving bias
stereotyping
sympathy

✛ MORE RESOURCES IN PERCEPTION

READINGS

Bartley, S. Howard. *Perception in Everyday Life.* New York: Harper & Row, 1972.

This interesting introduction to the field of psychobiology covers a wide-ranging discussion of the physiological influences on perception. Anecdotes and informal discussion by the author make a potentially intimidating subject interesting and understandable.

Cox, Maureen V. *The Child's Point of View,* 2d ed. New York: Guilford Press, 1991.

A useful survey for readers who want to understand children's perceptions of the world.

Eisenberg, Nancy, and Janet Strayer, eds. *Empathy and Its Development.* Cambridge, U.K.: Cambridge University Press, 1987.

This collection of scholarly writings provides a thorough review of the research and theory regarding empathy. Topics include the development of empathy in children and adults, gender and age differences in empathy and sympathy, the affective and cognitive dimensions of empathy, and the relationship between parental empathy and child adjustment.

Gudykunst, William B. *Bridging Differences: Effective Intergroup Communication.* Newbury Park, Calif.: Sage, 1991.

Gudykunst offers a broad look at the challenges of communicating with what he terms "strangers": people from groups different from our own. He summarizes many of the biases that distort our perceptions of others from unfamiliar backgrounds and offers methods for better understanding and communicating with others.

Harrington, Walt. *Crossings: A White Man's Journey into Black America.* New York: HarperCollins, 1993.

In his 1961 classic, Black Like Me, *white author John Howard Griffin chronicled the experience of chemically altering his skin color and becoming an African American in others' eyes. Thirty years later, Walt Harrington's marriage to a black woman allowed him to explore the world of black-white relationships "by proxy," as he puts it. Because immutable custom marks the offspring of such unions as members of the nondominant race, Harrington became the parent of black children. This experience sensitized him to an array of* racial issues that he otherwise would have never recognized.

Harrington never claims to have shared the direct experience of being an African American. But his perspective, with one foot in each world, makes him an effective interpreter of the black point of view to white Americans. The book uncovers some prevailing attitudes that blacks and whites hold about each other. In doing so it reaffirms the simple but important point that, underneath the skin, people are much more similar than different.

Hastrof, Albert H., and Hadley Cantril. "They Saw a Game: A Case Study." *Journal of Abnormal and Social Psychology* 49 (January 1954).

This study clearly illustrates how selective perception operates by showing how football fans view their home team as saints and the opposition as monsters.

Kincaid, D. Lawrence, ed. *Communication Theory: Eastern and Western Perspectives.* San Diego, Calif.: Academic Press, 1987.

A collection of scholars review the difference between Eastern and Western viewpoints on a variety of issues, including business communication, interpersonal relationships, and political communication.

Peters, William. *A Class Divided: Then and Now.* New Haven, Conn.: Yale University Press, 1986.

This is the fascinating story of Jane Elliott, an Iowa third-grade teacher who taught her students through a powerful experiment in empathy by discriminating against some according to the color of their eyes. The experience first brought pain, then lifelong insights.

Samovar, Larry A., and Richard E. Porter. *Intercultural Communication: A Reader,* 7th ed. Belmont, Calif.: Wadsworth, 1994.

This collection of readings offers many insights into how cultural background affects communication.

Schneider, David J., Albert H. Hastrof, and Phoebe C. Ellsworth. *Person Perception,* 2d ed. Reading, Mass.: Addison-Wesley, 1979.

Probably the best introduction to the subject available. The book covers such matters as snap judgments, perceptual accuracy, bias, and self-perception.

Snyder, Mark. "Self-Fulfilling Stereotypes." *Psychology Today* 16 (July 1982): 60–68.

Snyder illustrates the power of perception by citing research that describes how expecting others to behave in stereotypical ways actually increases the likelihood that they will act according to the predictions.

FILMS

PERCEPTUAL DISTORTION
Being There (1980) Rated PG

Chance (Peter Sellers) is a mentally retarded gardener who has lived and worked his entire life inside the walls of an elegant Washington town house. His only exposure to the world is television. When the owner of the house dies, Chance is expelled into a society he does not understand. Through a fluke, Chance is adopted by Ben Rand (Melvyn Douglas), a dying millionaire industrialist, and his wife, Eve (Shirley MacLaine), who introduce him to the elite of Washington's social and political world, including the president of the United States.

Although Chance the gardener (his hosts mistakenly call him Chauncey Gardner) knows nothing about anything, his hosts, the president, and eventually the nation misinterpret his simple, abstract statements about his trade (for example, "Spring is a time for planting") as profound observations about society and human nature. He becomes a national sensation, and as the film ends he appears to be destined to succeed his millionaire host as husband to Eve and head of an industrial empire.

The film serves as an entertaining allegory for the perceptual error of seeing what one wants to see. Viewers who are willing to go beyond the amusing story line can recall personal experiences in which they may have distorted others' behavior to fit their preexisting beliefs.

MULTIPLE PERSPECTIVES
Rashomon (1950) Not rated

Set in eighth-century Japan, this is the story of a samurai and his wife, who are ambushed by a bandit who kills the man and rapes the woman. At the bandit's trial, the story of the incident is told from four points of view: the bandit's, the wife's, the dead man's (speaking through a medium), and a woodcutter's (who has stolen the dead man's knife, and so has his own self-interest to protect). The event seems radically different from each perspective. Despite the English subtitles, director Akira Kurosawa's first film is an outstanding illustration of how the same event can be perceived in many different ways.

He Said/She Said (1991) Rated PG–13

Dan (Kevin Bacon) and Lorie (Elizabeth Perkins) are journalists who work for the same newspaper. They compete with one another—and predictably, they also fall in love. This is their story, told in turn from each person's point of view. The first half of the film is Dan's version of the relationship (written by Ken Kwapis). The second half (written by Marisa Silver) tells Lorie's side of the story.

The dual-perspective approach works well here because the romantic relationship is a familiar one, and because the two points of view aren't dramatically different. The subtle variations show how even small differences in perception can affect a relationship.

DEVELOPING EMPATHY

The Doctor (1991) Rated PG–13

Jack McKee (William Hurt) is an ace surgeon and a first-class egotist. He treats his patients with a breezy self-assurance, brushing aside their concerns with jokes and indifference. It's not that McKee is mean-spirited: He just views his patients as objects upon which he can practice his skill, and not as human beings with feelings.

McKee receives a major attitude adjustment when his nagging cough is diagnosed as throat cancer, and his surgeon treats him with the same mechanical indifference that he had bestowed on his patients. As McKee suffers the indignities of a hospital patient and confronts his mortality, his attitude toward the human side of medical care predictably changes.

The film should become a part of the medical school curriculum, but it also shows other viewers how walking a mile in another person's shoes can lead to greater tolerance and understanding

Emotions: Thinking, Feeling, and Acting

*I*t's impossible to talk about communication without acknowledging the importance of emotions. Think about it: Feeling confident can make the difference between success and failure in everything from giving a speech to asking for a date, whereas insecurity can ruin your chances. Being angry or defensive can spoil your time with others, whereas feeling and acting calm will help prevent or solve problems. The way you share or withhold your feelings of affection can affect the future of your relationships. On and on the list of feelings goes: appreciation, loneliness, joy, insecurity, curiosity, irritation. The point is clear: Communication shapes our feelings, and feelings influence our communication.

Because this subject of emotions is so important, we'll spend this chapter taking a closer look. Just what are feelings, and how can we recognize them? How are feelings caused, and how can we control them, increasing the positive ones and decreasing the negative? When and how can we best share our feelings with others?

✥ WHAT ARE EMOTIONS?

Suppose an extraterrestrial visitor asked you to explain emotions. How would you answer? You might start by saying that emotions are things that we feel. But this doesn't say much, for in turn you would probably describe feelings as synonymous with emotions. Social scientists generally agree that there are several components to the phenomena we label as feelings.

PHYSIOLOGICAL CHANGES

When a person has strong emotions, many bodily changes occur. For example, the physical components of fear include an increased heartbeat, a rise in blood pressure, an increase in adrenaline secretions, an elevated blood sugar level, a slowing of digestion, and a dilation of pupils. Some of these changes are recognizable to the person having them. These sensations are termed **proprioceptive stimuli,** meaning that they are activated by the movement of internal tissues. Proprioceptive messages can offer a significant clue to your emotions once you become aware of them. A churning stomach or tense jaw can be a signal that something is wrong. You can get a sense of your own proprioceptive messages by trying the following exercise.

NONVERBAL REACTIONS

Not all physical changes that accompany emotions are internal. Feelings are often apparent by observable changes. Some of these changes involve a person's appearance: blushing, sweating, and so on. Other changes involve behavior: a distinctive facial expression, posture, gestures, different vocal tone and rate, and so on.

INVITATION TO INSIGHT

HOW DOES IT FEEL?

Here's a way to learn more about yourself from your body. You can do this exercise with a group or individually outside the classroom. If you do it alone, read all the steps ahead of time so that you can work through the whole experience without interrupting yourself. However, the exercise will have more impact if you do it for the first time in a group because in this way your facilitator can read the instructions for you. Also, in a group your feelings can be shared and compared.

The ellipses (. . .) in the instructions indicate points where you should pause for a moment and examine what you're feeling.

1. Wherever you are, find yourself a comfortable position, either lying or sitting. You'll need to find a quiet place with no distractions. You'll find that the exercise works better if you dim the lights.

2. Close your eyes. The visual sense is so dominant that it's easy to neglect your other senses.

3. Now that your eyes are closed and you're comfortable, take a trip through your body and visit its various parts. As you focus on each part, don't try to change what you find . . . just notice how you are, how you feel.

4. Now let's begin. Start with your feet. How do they feel? Are they comfortable, or do they hurt? Are your toes cold? Do your shoes fit well, or are they too tight?

Now move your attention to your legs. . . . Is there any tension in them, or are they relaxed? . . . Can you feel each muscle? . . . Are your legs crossed? Is there pressure where one presses against the other? . . . Are they comfortable?

Now pay attention to your hips and pelvis . . . the area where your legs and backbone join. Do you feel comfortable here, or are you not as relaxed as you'd like to be? If you're seated, direct your attention to your buttocks. . . . Can you feel your body's weight pressing against the surface you're sitting on?

Now move on to the trunk of your body. How does your abdomen feel? . . . What are the sensations you can detect there? . . . Is anything moving? . . . Focus on your breathing. . . . Do you breathe off the top of your lungs, or are you taking deep, relaxed breaths? . . . Does the air move in and out through your nose or your mouth? Is your chest tight, or is it comfortable?

Checking your breathing has probably led you to your throat and neck. Is your throat comfortable, or do you feel a lump there you need to keep swallowing? . . . How about your neck? . . . Can you feel it holding your head in its present position? . . . Perhaps moving your head slowly from side to side will help you feel these muscles doing their work. . . . Is there tension in your neck or shoulders?

Every thought, gesture, muscle tension, feeling, stomach gurgle, nose scratch, fart, hummed tune, slip of the tongue, illness—everything is significant and meaningful and related to the now. It is possible to know and understand oneself on all these levels, and the more one knows the more he is free to determine his own life.

If I know what my body tells me, I know my deepest feelings and I can choose what to do. . . . Given a complete knowledge of myself, I can determine my life; lacking that mastery, I am controlled in ways that are often undesirable, unproductive, worrisome, and confusing.

William Schutz,
Here Comes Everybody

INVITATION TO INSIGHT

(continued)

Now let's move to your face. . . . What expression are you wearing? . . . Are the muscles of your face tense or relaxed? Which ones? Your mouth . . . brow . . . jaw . . . temples? Take a few moments and see. . . .

Finally, go inside your head and see what's happening there. . . . Is it quiet and dark, or are things happening there? . . . What are they? Does it feel good inside your head, or is there some pressure or aching? . . .

You've made a trip from bottom to top. Try feeling your whole body now. . . . See what new awareness of it you've gained. . . . Are there any special parts of your body that attract your attention now? . . . What are they telling you?

Now there's another very important part of your body to focus on. It's the part of you where you *feel* when you're happy or sad or afraid. Take a moment and find that spot. . . . See how you are now in there. . . . See what happens when you ask yourself, "How am I now? How do I feel?" . . . See what happens in that place when you think of a personal problem that's been bothering you lately. . . . Be sure it's something that's important to your life now. . . . Now see if you can get the feel of this problem there in the place where you feel things. . . . Let yourself feel all of it. . . . If the feeling changes as you focus on it, that's OK. Just stay with the feeling wherever it goes and see how it is. . . . If what you feel now makes a difference to you, see what that difference is. . . . Now, take a few minutes to use it in whatever way you like, and then slowly open your eyes.

5. Now think about the following questions. If you're with a group, you may want to discuss them there.

   a. Did you find out things about your body that you hadn't noticed before? Did you discover some tensions that you'd been carrying around? How long do you think you've been this way? Did recognizing them make any difference to you?

   b. Could you find the part of yourself where you usually feel things? Where was it? Or are there different spots for different feelings? Did focusing on your problem make some kind of difference to you?

Although it's reasonably easy to tell when someone is feeling a strong emotion, it's more difficult to be certain exactly what that emotion might be. A slumped posture and sigh may be a sign of sadness, or it may signal fatigue. Likewise, trembling hands might indicate excitement, or they may be an outward sign of fear. As you'll learn in Chapter Six, nonverbal behavior is usually ambiguous; and it's dangerous to assume that it can be "read" with much accuracy.

Although we usually think of nonverbal behavior as the reaction to an emotional state, there may be times when the reverse is true—when nonverbal behavior actually *causes* emotions. Research by Paul Ekman uncovered instances when experimental subjects were able to create various emotional states by altering their facial expressions.[1] When volunteers were coached to move their facial muscles in ways that appeared afraid, angry, disgusted, amused, sad, surprised, and contemptuous, the subjects' bodies responded as if they were having these feelings. Interestingly, the link between smiling and happiness was not as strong because, Ekman speculates, smiles can represent so many different emotions: happiness, anger, sadness, and so on.

COGNITIVE INTERPRETATIONS

Although there may be cases in which there is a direct connection between physical behavior and emotional states, in most situations the mind plays an important role in determining how we feel. On page 132 you read that some physiological components of fear are a racing heart, perspiration, tense muscles, and elevated blood pressure. Interestingly enough, these symptoms are similar to the physical changes that accompany excitement, joy, and other emotions. In other words, if we were to measure the physical condition of some-one having a strong emotion, we would have a hard time knowing whether that person was trembling with fear or quivering with excite-ment. The recognition that the bodily components of most emotions are similar led some psychologists to conclude that the experience of fright, joy, or anger comes primarily from the *label* we give to the

DRAWING BY WEBER © 1981 THE NEW YORKER MAGAZINE, INC.

"What the hell was that? Something just swept over me—like contentment or something."

same physical symptoms at a given time.[2] Psychologist Philip Zimbardo offers a good example of this principle:

> I notice I'm perspiring while lecturing. From that I infer I am nervous. If it occurs often, I might even label myself a "nervous person." Once I have the label, the next question I must answer is "Why am I nervous?" Then I start to search for an appropriate explanation. I might notice some students leaving the room, or being inattentive. I am nervous because I'm not giving a good lecture. That makes me nervous. How do I know it's not good? Because I'm boring my audience. I am nervous because I am a boring lecturer and I want to be a good lecturer. I feel inadequate. Maybe I should open a delicatessen instead. Just then a student says, "It's hot in here, I'm perspiring and it makes it tough to concentrate on your lecture." Instantly, I'm no longer "nervous" or "boring."[3]

In his book *Shyness*, Zimbardo discusses the consequences of making inaccurate or exaggerated attributions. In a survey of more than 5,000 subjects, over 80 percent described themselves as having been shy at some time in their lives, whereas more than 40 percent considered themselves presently shy. Most significantly, those who labeled themselves "not shy" behaved in virtually the *same way* as their shy counterparts. They would blush, perspire, and feel their hearts pounding in certain social situations. The biggest difference between the two groups seemed to be the label with which they described themselves.[4] This is a significant difference. Someone who notices the symptoms we've described and thinks, "I'm such a shy person!" will most likely feel more uncomfortable and communicate less effectively than another person with the same symptoms who thinks, "Well, I'm a bit shaky (or excited) here, but that's to be expected."

We'll take a closer look at ways to reduce unpleasant emotions through cognitive processes later in this chapter.

✥ TYPES OF EMOTIONS

So far our discussion has implied that although emotions may differ in tone, they are similar in most other ways. In truth, emotions vary in many respects.

PRIMARY AND MIXED EMOTIONS

Emotions are rather like colors: Some are simple, whereas others are blends. Robert Plutchik's "emotion wheel" (see Figure 4–1) illustrates the difference.[5] For example, jealousy can be viewed as a combination of several different emotions: distress, anger, disgust, contempt, fear, and even shame.[6] Likewise, loneliness can include feelings of anger toward self and others, estrangement, and depression.[7] Plutchik has identified eight **primary emotions,** which are inside the perimeter of the wheel. He suggests that these primary feelings can combine to

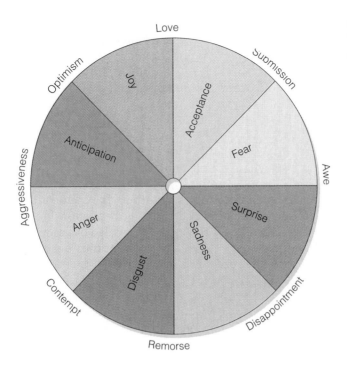

FIGURE 4-1
The emotion wheel: Primary and mixed emotions

form other, **mixed emotions,** some of which are listed outside the circle.

   Whether or not you agree with the specific emotions Plutchik identifies as primary and secondary, the wheel suggests that many feelings need to be described in more than a single term. To understand why, consider the following examples. For each one, ask yourself two questions: How would I feel? What feelings might I express?

   An out-of-town friend has promised to arrive at your house at six o'clock. When he hasn't arrived by nine, you are convinced that a terrible accident has occurred. Just as you pick up the phone to call the police and local hospitals, your friend breezes in the door with an offhand remark about getting a late start.

   You and your companion have a fight just before leaving for a party. Deep inside, you know you were mostly to blame, even though you aren't willing to admit it. When you arrive at the party, your companion leaves you to flirt with several other attractive guests.

   In situations like these you would probably feel mixed emotions. Consider the case of the overdue friend. Your first reaction to his arrival would probably be relief—"Thank goodness, he's safe!" But you would also be likely to feel anger—"Why didn't he phone to tell me he'd be late?" The second example would probably leave you with an even greater number of mixed emotions: guilt at contributing to the fight, hurt and perhaps embarrassment at your friend's flirtations, and anger at this sort of vengefulness.

Despite the commonness of mixed emotions, we often communicate only one feeling . . . usually the most negative one. In both the preceding examples you might show only your anger, leaving the other person with little idea of the full range of your feelings. Consider the different reaction you would get by showing *all* your emotions in these cases, and others.

INTENSE AND MILD EMOTIONS

Another way emotions are like colors is in their intensity. Figure 4–2 illustrates this point clearly.[8] Each vertical slice represents the range of a primary emotion from its mildest to its most intense state. This model shows the importance not only of choosing the right emotional family when expressing yourself but also of describing the strength of the feeling. Some people fail to communicate clearly because they understate their emotions, failing to let others know how strongly they feel. To say you're "annoyed" when a friend breaks an important promise, for example, would probably be an understatement. In other cases, people chronically overstate the strength of their feelings. To them, everything is "wonderful" or "terrible." The problem with this sort of exaggeration is that when a truly intense emotion comes

FIGURE 4–2
Intensity of emotions

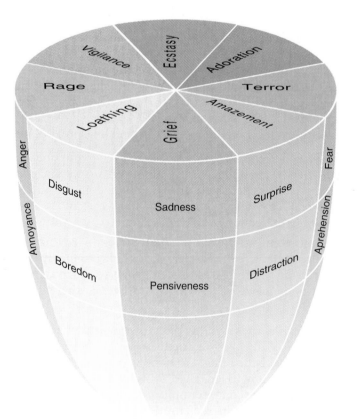

INVITATION TO INSIGHT

RECOGNIZING YOUR EMOTIONS

Keep a three-day record of your feelings. You can do this by spending a few minutes each evening recalling what emotions you felt during the day, what other people were involved, and the circumstances in which the emotion occurred.

At the end of the three-day period you can understand the role emotions play in your communication by answering the following questions:

1. How did you recognize the emotions you felt: through proprioceptive stimuli, nonverbal behaviors, or cognitive processes?

2. Did you have any difficulty deciding which emotion you were feeling?

3. What emotions do you have most often? Are they primary or mixed? Mild or intense?

4. In what circumstances do you or don't you express your feelings? What factors influence your decision to show or not show your feelings? The type of emotion? The person or persons involved? The situation (time, place)? The subject that the emotion involves (money, sex, and so on)?

5. What are the consequences of the type of communicating you just described in step 4? Are you satisfied with these consequences? If not, what can you do to become more satisfied?

along, they have no words left to describe it adequately. If chocolate chip cookies from the local bakery are "fantastic," how does it feel to fall in love?

✛ INFLUENCES ON EMOTIONAL EXPRESSION

Most people rarely express their emotions, at least verbally. People are generally comfortable making statements of fact and often delight in expressing their opinion, but they rarely disclose how they feel. Why is it that people fail to express their feelings? Let's take a look at several reasons.

CULTURE

Over 100 years of research has confirmed the fact that certain basic emotions are experienced by people around the world.[9] No matter where a person is born and regardless of his or her background, the ability to feel happiness, sadness, surprise, anger, disgust, and fear seems to be universal. People from all cultures also express these emotions in the same way, at least in their facial expressions. A smile or scowl, for example, is understood everywhere.

Looking at Diversity

A NATIVE AMERICAN PERSPECTIVE ON EMOTIONAL EXPRESSION

Todd Epaloose *was raised on the Zuñi Pueblo, New Mexico. He spent part of his childhood on the reservation and part attending school in the city. He now lives in Albuquerque, where he studies environmental protection technology and works in a medical lab. As an urbanite who still spends time with his family on the reservation, Todd alternates between two worlds. On the reservation he is surrounded by his Native American culture, while in the city he has developed the skills necessary to succeed in a technological society. In this profile, Todd reflects on the differences between the ways Zuñi and Anglo cultures deal with emotional expression.*

Zuñi and Anglo cultures are as different as night and day in the ways they treat communication about emotions. In mainstream U.S. culture speaking up is accepted, or even approved. This is true from the time you are a child. Parents are proud when their child speaks up—whether that means showing affection, being curious, or even expressing unhappiness in a way that the parents approve. Being quiet gets a child labeled as "shy," and is considered a problem. Assertiveness is just as important in school, at work, and in adult relationships.

In Zuñi culture, emotions are much less public. We are a private people, who consider a public display of feelings embarrassing. Self-control is considered a virtue. I think a lot of our emotional reticence comes from a respect for privacy. Your feelings are your own, and showing them to others is just as wrong as taking off your clothes in public. It's not that traditional Zuñis have fewer or less intense feelings than people in the city: it's just that there is less value placed on showing them in obvious ways.

The way we express affection is a good example of Zuñi attitudes and rules for sharing emotions. Our families are full of love—at least as much as families in mainstream American culture. But someone from the city might not recognize this love, since it isn't displayed very much. There isn't a lot of hugging and kissing, even between children and parents. Also, there isn't a lot of verbal expression: People don't say "I love you" to one another very much. The feeling is there, but it's *understood* without being mentioned. We show our emotions by our actions: by helping one another, by caring for the people we love when they need us. That's enough to keep us happy.

I think that one source of the difference between Anglo and Zuñi communication styles comes from the way each culture treats time. In the city, time is precious. There's never enough of it, so people try to do things as quickly as possible. This means that it's important to get your feelings across *now*. Waiting is uncomfortable, and "wastes" time. In traditional Zuñi culture, time is not such a scarce commodity. There's less of a hurry. This means that getting a message (like how you feel) expressed quickly isn't so important. There's plenty of time to figure out how someone feels, and if the matter is important enough, it will become clear sooner or later.

Looking at Diversity continued

One way to summarize the difference between the two cultures has to do with talking and listening. Anglo culture places an emphasis on talking—on expressing yourself clearly and completely. Zuñis aren't such great talkers, but that helps make us better listeners. Because we don't speak so much, we have both the need and the time to be better at paying attention to what other people *say* and what they *do* to show their emotions. This listening can be helpful in school, where we care less about competing for a teacher's recognition than in understanding what we are supposed to learn. It also makes us good, steady workers who learn our jobs, concentrate on our duties, and work extremely hard to perfect our efficiency. We may not get the recognition that comes from being good talkers, but in the long run I am confident that our restraint will be rewarded. As the saying goes, "what goes around comes around."

Which approach is best? I think both cultures have strengths. Many Zuñis and other Native Americans who want to join mainstream culture are at a disadvantage. They aren't very good at standing up for their rights, and so they get taken advantage of. Even at home, there are probably times when it's important to express feelings to prevent misunderstandings. On the other hand, I think some Native American emotional restraint might be helpful for people who are used to Anglo communication styles. Respecting others' privacy can be important: Some feelings are nobody else's business, and prying or demanding that they open up seems pushy and rude. Native American self-control can also add some civility to personal relationships. I'm not sure that "letting it all hang out" is always the best way.

One final word: I believe that in order to really understand the differences between emotional expression in Native American and Anglo cultures you have to live in both. If that isn't possible, at least realize that the familiar one isn't the only good approach. Try to respect what you don't understand.

Of course, this doesn't mean that the same events generate an emotion in all cultures. The notion of eating snails might bring a smile of delight to some residents of France, though it would cause many North Americans to grimace in disgust. More to the point of this book, research has shown that fear of strangers and risky situations is more likely to frighten people living in the United States and Europe than those in Japan, while Japanese are more apprehensive about relational communication than Americans and Europeans.[10]

There are also differences in the degree to which people in various cultures display their feelings. One of the most significant factors that influences emotional expression is the position of a culture on the individualism–collectivism spectrum. Members of collectivistic cultures (such as Japan and India) prize harmony among members of their "in-group," and discourage expression of any negative emotions that might upset relationships among people who belong to it. By contrast, members of highly individualistic cultures like the United States and Canada feel comfortable revealing their feelings to people with whom they are close.[11] Individualists and collectivists also handle emotional expression with members of out-groups differently: Whereas collectivists are quite frank about expressing negative emotions toward outsiders, individualists are more likely to hide such emotions as dislike.[12] It's easy to see how differences in display rules can lead to communication problems. For example, individualistic North Americans might view collectivistic Asians as less than candid, whereas a person raised in Asia could easily regard North Americans as overly demonstrative.

GENDER

Even within our culture, the ways in which men and women have expressed their emotions vary in some significant areas.[13] Research on emotional expression suggests that there is at least some truth in the cultural stereotype of the unexpressive male and the more demonstrative female. As a group, women are more likely than men to express feelings of vulnerability, including fear, sadness, loneliness, and embarrassment. Men rarely express these sentiments, especially to their male friends, although they may open up to the woman they love. On the other hand, men are less bashful about revealing their strengths and positive emotions. As Chapter Eight explains, neither stereotypical male nor female notions of emotional expressiveness are superior. Because the styles can be quite different, the challenge communicators face is how to coordinate their own style with others whose notions of appropriate emotional expressiveness are different.

Differences between the sexes also exist in the sensitivity to others' emotions. Psychologist Robert Rosenthal and his colleagues developed the Profile of Nonverbal Sensitivity (PONS) test to measure the ability to recognize emotions that are expressed in the facial expressions, movements, and vocal cues of others. Women consistently score slightly higher on this test than men.[14]

Of course, these gender differences are statistical averages, and many men and women don't fit these profiles. Furthermore, gender isn't the *only* variable that affects emotional sensitivity. Another factor is whether the other person is of the same or opposite sex: People generally are better at recognizing emotions of members of the same sex. Familiarity with the other person also leads to greater sensitivity. For example, dating and married couples are significantly better at recognizing each other's emotional cues than are strangers. A third factor is the difference in power between the two parties. People who are less powerful learn—probably from necessity—to read the more powerful person's signals. One experiment revealed that "women's intuition" should be relabeled "subordinate's intuition." In opposite-sex twosomes, the person with less control—regardless of sex—was better at interpreting the leader's nonverbal signals than vice versa.[15]

SOCIAL CONVENTIONS

In mainstream U.S. society the unwritten rules of communication discourage the direct expression of most emotions.[16] Count the number of genuine emotional expressions you hear over a two- or three-day period and you'll discover that emotional expressions are rare. People are generally comfortable making statements of fact and often delight in expressing their opinions, but they rarely disclose how they feel.

Not surprisingly, the emotions that people *do* share directly are usually positive. Communicators are reluctant to send messages that embarrass or threaten the "face" of others.[17] Historians offer a detailed description of the ways contemporary society discourages expressions of anger.[18] When compared to past centuries, Americans today strive to suppress this "unpleasant" emotion in almost every context, including child-raising, the workplace, and personal relationships. Research supports this analysis. One study of married couples revealed that the partners shared complimentary feelings ("I love you") or face-saving ones ("I'm sorry I yelled at you"). They also willingly disclosed both positive and negative feelings about absent third parties ("I like Fred," "I'm uncomfortable around Gloria"). On the other hand, the husbands and wives rarely verbalized face-threatening feelings ("I'm disappointed in you") or hostility ("I'm mad at you").[19]

Surprisingly, social rules even discourage too much expression of positive feelings.[20] A hug and kiss for Mother is all right, though a young man should shake hands with Dad. Affection toward friends becomes less and less frequent as we grow older, so that even a simple statement such as "I like you" is seldom heard between adults.

SOCIAL ROLES

Expression of emotions is also limited by the requirements of many social roles. Salespeople are taught always to smile at customers, no matter how obnoxious. Teachers are portrayed as paragons of rationality, supposedly representing their field of expertise and instructing their students with total impartiality. Students are rewarded for asking "acceptable" questions and otherwise being submissive creatures.

INABILITY TO RECOGNIZE EMOTIONS

The result of all these restrictions is that many of us lose the ability to feel deeply. Just as a muscle withers away when it is unused, our capacity to recognize and act on certain emotions decreases without practice. It's hard to cry after spending most of one's life fulfilling the role society expects of a man even when the tears are inside. After years of denying your anger, the ability to recognize that feeling takes real effort. For someone who has never acknowledged love for one's friends, accepting that emotion can be difficult indeed.

FEAR OF SELF-DISCLOSURE

In a society that discourages the expression of feelings, emotional self-disclosure can seem risky.[21] For a parent, boss, or teacher whose life has been built on the image of confidence and certainty, it may be frightening to say, "I'm sorry. I was wrong." A person who has made a life's work out of not relying on others has a hard time saying, "I'm lonesome. I want your friendship."

Moreover, someone who musters up the courage to share feelings such as these still risks unpleasant consequences. Others might misunderstand: An expression of affection might be construed as a romantic invitation, and a confession of uncertainty might appear to be a sign of weakness. Another risk is that emotional honesty might make others feel uncomfortable. Finally, there's always a chance that emotional honesty could be used against you, either out of cruelty or thoughtlessness. Chapter Eight discusses alternatives to complete disclosure and suggests circumstances when it can be both wise and ethical to keep your feelings to yourself.

✚ GUIDELINES FOR EXPRESSING EMOTIONS

Emotions are a fact of life. Nonetheless, communicating them effectively isn't a simple matter. It's obvious that showing every feeling of boredom, fear, anger, or frustration would get you in trouble. Even the indiscriminate sharing of positive feelings—love, affection, and so on—isn't always wise. On the other hand, withholding emotions can be personally frustrating and can keep relationships from growing and prospering.

The following suggestions can help you decide when and how to express your emotions. Combined with the guidelines for self-disclosure in Chapter Nine, they can improve the effectiveness of your emotional expression.

RECOGNIZE YOUR FEELINGS

Answering the question "How do you feel?" isn't always easy. As you've already read, there are a number of ways in which feelings become recognizable. Physiological changes can be a clear sign of your emotional state. Monitoring nonverbal behaviors is another excellent way to keep in touch with your feelings. You can also recognize your emotions by monitoring your thoughts, as well as the verbal messages you send to others. It's not far from the verbal statement "I hate this!" to the realization that you're angry (or bored, nervous, or embarrassed).

CHOOSE THE BEST LANGUAGE

Most people suffer from impoverished emotional vocabularies. Ask them how they're feeling and the response will almost always include the same terms: *good* or *bad, terrible* or *great,* and so on. Take a moment now and see how many feelings you can write down. After you've done your best, look at Table 4–1 and see which ones you've missed.

Relying on a small vocabulary of feelings is as limiting as using only a few terms to describe colors. To say that the ocean in all its moods, the sky as it varies from day to day, and the color of your true love's eyes are all "blue" only tells a fraction of the story. Likewise, it's overly broad to use a term like *good* or *great* to describe how you feel in situations as different as earning a high grade, finishing a marathon, and hearing the words "I love you" from a special person.

An emotion without social rules of containment and expression is like an egg without a shell: a gooey mess.

Carol Tavris

There are several ways to express a feeling verbally:

- Through *single words:* "I'm angry" (or "excited," "depressed," "curious," and so on).
- By describing *what's happening to you:* "My stomach is tied in knots," "I'm on top of the world."
- By describing *what you'd like to do:* "I feel like running away," "I'd like to give you a hug," "I feel like giving up."

Many communicators think they are expressing feelings when, in fact, their statements are emotionally counterfeit. For example, it sounds emotionally revealing to say, "I feel like going to a show" or "I feel we've been seeing too much of each other." But in fact, neither of these statements has any emotional content. In the first sentence the word *feel* really stands for an intention: "I *want* to go to a show." In the second sentence the "feeling" is really a thought: "I *think* we've been seeing too much of each other." You can recognize the absence of emotion in each case by adding a genuine word of feeling to it. For instance, "I'm *bored* and I want to go to a show" or "I think we've been seeing too much of each other and I feel *confined.*"

SHARE MIXED FEELINGS

Many times the feeling you express isn't the only one you're experiencing. For example, you might often express your anger but overlook the confusion, disappointment, frustration, sadness, or embarrassment that preceded it.

RECOGNIZE THE DIFFERENCE BETWEEN FEELING AND ACTING

Just because you feel a certain way doesn't mean you must always act on it. This distinction is important because it can liberate you from the fear that acknowledging and showing a feeling will commit you to some disastrous course of action. If, for instance, you say to a friend, "I feel so angry that I could punch you in the nose," it becomes possible to explore exactly why you feel so furious and then to resolve the problem that led to your anger. Pretending that nothing is the matter, on the other hand, will do nothing to diminish your resentful feelings, which can then go on to contaminate the relationship.

ACCEPT RESPONSIBILITY FOR YOUR FEELINGS

It's important to make sure that your language reflects the fact that you're responsible for your feelings. Instead of "You're making me angry," say, "I'm getting angry." Instead of "You hurt my feelings," say, "I feel hurt when you do that." As you'll soon read, people don't make us like or dislike them, and believing that they do denies the responsibility each of us has for our own emotions.

CHOOSE THE BEST TIME AND PLACE TO EXPRESS YOUR FEELINGS

Often the first flush of a strong feeling is not the best time to speak out. If you're awakened by the racket caused by a noisy neighbor, storming over to complain might result in your saying things you'll regret later. In such a case, it's probably wiser to wait until you have thought out carefully how you might express your feelings in a way that would be most likely to be heard.

Even after you've waited for the first flush of feeling to subside, it's still important to choose the time that's best suited to the message. Being rushed or tired or disturbed by some other matter is probably a good reason for postponing the expression of your feeling. Often dealing with your emotions can take a great amount of time and effort, and fatigue or distraction will make it difficult to follow through on the matter you've started. In the same manner you ought to be sure that the recipient of your message is ready to hear you out before you begin.

EXPRESS YOUR FEELINGS CLEARLY

Either out of confusion or discomfort, we sometimes express our emotions in an unclear way. One key to making your emotions clear is to realize that you most often can summarize them in a few words—*hurt, glad, confused, excited, resentful,* and so on. In the same way, with a little thought you can probably describe very briefly any reasons you have for feeling a certain way.

In addition to avoiding excessive length, a second way to prevent confusion is to avoid overqualifying or downplaying your emotions— "I'm a *little* unhappy" or "I'm *pretty* excited" or "I'm *sort of* confused." Of course, not all emotions are strong ones. We do feel degrees of sadness and joy, for example, but some communicators have a tendency to discount almost every feeling. Do you?

A third danger to avoid is expressing feelings in a coded manner. This happens most often when the sender is uncomfortable about revealing the feeling in question. Some codes are verbal ones, as when the sender hints more or less subtly at the message. For example, an indirect way to say, "I'm lonesome" might be "I guess there isn't much happening this weekend, so if you're not busy, why don't you drop by?" Such a message is so indirect that the chances that your real feeling will be recognized are slim. For this reason, people who send coded messages stand less of a chance of having their emotions understood—and their needs met.

TABLE 4 – 1   Some Feelings

afraid	concerned	exhausted	hurried	nervous	sexy
aggravated	confident	fearful	hurt	numb	shaky
amazed	confused	fed up	hysterical	optimistic	shocked
ambivalent	content	fidgety	impatient	paranoid	shy
angry	crazy	flattered	impressed	passionate	sorry
annoyed	defeated	foolish	inhibited	peaceful	strong
anxious	defensive	forlorn	insecure	pessimistic	subdued
apathetic	delighted	free	interested	playful	surprised
ashamed	depressed	friendly	intimidated	pleased	suspicious
bashful	detached	frustrated	irritable	possessive	tender
bewildered	devastated	furious	jealous	pressured	tense
bitchy	disappointed	glad	joyful	protective	terrified
bitter	disgusted	glum	lazy	puzzled	tired
bored	disturbed	grateful	lonely	refreshed	trapped
brave	ecstatic	happy	loving	regretful	ugly
calm	edgy	harassed	lukewarm	relieved	uneasy
cantankerous	elated	helpless	mad	resentful	vulnerable
carefree	embarrassed	high	mean	restless	warm
cheerful	empty	hopeful	miserable	ridiculous	weak
cocky	enthusiastic	horrible	mixed up	romantic	wonderful
cold	envious	hostile	mortified	sad	worried
comfortable	excited	humiliated	neglected	sentimental	

Finally, you can express yourself clearly by making sure that both you and your partner understand that your feeling is centered on a specific set of circumstances rather than being indicative of the whole relationship. Instead of saying, "I resent you," say, "I resent you when you don't keep your promises." Rather than "I'm bored with you," say "I'm bored when you talk about your money."

SKILL BUILDER

FEELINGS AND PHRASES

You can try this exercise alone or with a group.

1. Choose a situation from Column A and a receiver from Column B.

2. Create a statement that would most effectively express your feeling for this combination.

3. Now create statements of feeling for the same situation with other receivers from Column B. How are the statements different?

4. Repeat the process with various combinations, using other situations from Column A.

Column A. Situations	*Column B: Receivers*
a. You have been stood up for a date or appointment.	a. An instructor
b. The other person pokes fun at your schoolwork.	b. A family member (you decide which one)
c. The other person compliments you on your appearance, then says, "I hope I haven't embarrassed you."	c. A classmate you don't know well
d. The other person gives you a hug and says, "It's good to see you."	d. Your best friend

---

✤ MANAGING DIFFICULT EMOTIONS

Although feeling and expressing many emotions add to the quality of interpersonal relationships, not all feelings are beneficial. For instance, rage, depression, terror, and jealousy do little to help you feel better or improve your relationships. The following pages will give you tools to minimize these unproductive emotions.

FACILITATIVE AND DEBILITATIVE EMOTIONS

We need to make a distinction between **facilitative emotions,** which contribute to effective functioning, and **debilitative emotions,** which keep us from feeling and relating effectively.

There is nothing good or bad but thinking makes it so.

Shakespeare,
Hamlet

One big difference between the two types is their *intensity.* For instance, a certain amount of anger or irritation can be constructive because it often provides the stimulus that leads you to improve the unsatisfying conditions. Rage, on the other hand, will usually make matters worse. The same holds true for fear. A little bit of nervousness before an important athletic contest or job interview might give you the boost that will improve your performance. (Mellow athletes or employees usually don't do well.) But total terror is something else. Even a little suspicion can make people more effective communicators. One study revealed that couples who doubted that their relational partners were telling the truth were better at detecting deception than were trusting mates.[22] Of course, an extreme case of paranoia would have the opposite and debilitative effect, reducing the ability to interpret the partner's behavior accurately.

A second characteristic that distinguishes debilitative feelings from facilitative ones is their extended *duration.* Feeling depressed for a while after the breakup of a relationship or the loss of a job is natural. But spending the rest of your life grieving over your loss would accomplish nothing. In the same way, staying angry at someone for a wrong inflicted long ago can be just as punishing to you as to the wrongdoer. Our goal, then, is to find a method for getting rid of debilitative feelings while remaining sensitive to your more facilitative emotions, which can improve your relationships. Fortunately, there is such a method. It is based on the idea that one way to change feelings is to change unproductive thinking.

THOUGHTS CAUSE FEELINGS

For most people, emotions seem to have a life of their own. You wish you could feel calm when approaching strangers, yet your voice quivers. You try to appear confident when asking for a raise, yet your eye twitches nervously.

At times like these it's common to say that strangers or your boss *make* you feel nervous just as you would say that a bee sting causes you to feel pain. The apparent similarities between physical and emotional discomfort become clear if you look at them in the following way:

Event	*Feeling*
Bee sting ⟶	physical pain
Meeting strangers ⟶	nervous feelings

When looking at your emotions in this way, you seem to have little control over how you feel. However, this apparent similarity between physical pain and emotional discomfort (or pleasure) isn't as great as it seems to be. Cognitive psychologists argue that it is not *events* such as meeting strangers or being jilted by a lover that cause people to feel bad, but rather the *beliefs they hold* about these events.

Albert Ellis, who developed the cognitive approach called *rational-emotive therapy,* tells a story that makes this point clear. Imagine yourself walking by a friend's house and seeing your friend stick his head out of a window and call you a string of vile names. (You supply the friend and the names.) Under these circumstances it's likely that you would feel hurt and upset. Now imagine that instead of walking by the house you were passing a mental institution when the same friend, who was obviously a patient there, shouted the same offensive names at you. In this case, your feelings would probably be quite different—most likely sadness and pity. You can see that in this story the activating event of being called names was the same in both cases, yet the emotional consequences were very different. The reason for your different feelings has to do with your thinking in each case. In the first instance, you would most likely think that your friend was very angry with you; further, you might imagine that you must have done something terrible to deserve such a response. In the second case, you would probably assume that your friend had some psychological difficulty, and most likely you would feel sympathetic.

From this example you can start to see that it's the *interpretations* people make of an event, during the process of self-talk, that determine their feelings.* Thus, the model for emotions looks like this:

Event   *Thought*   *Feeling*

Being called names → "I've done something wrong." → hurt, upset

Being called names → "My friend must be sick."   → concern, sympathy

The same principle applies in more common situations. For example, the words "I love you" can be interpreted in a variety of ways. They could be taken at face value as a genuine expression of deep affection. They might also be decoded in a variety of other ways; for example, as an attempt at manipulation, a sincere but mistaken declaration uttered in a moment of passion, or an attempt to make the recipient feel better. One study revealed that women are more likely than men to regard expressions of love as genuine statements, instead of attributing them to some other cause.[23] It's easy to imagine how different interpretations of a statement like "I love you" can lead to different emotional reactions:

Event   *Thought*   *Feeling*

Hearing "I love you" → "This is a genuine → delight (perhaps)
                              statement."

Hearing "I love you" → "S/he's just saying this → anger
                              to manipulate me."

GUINDON 3-12   © 1980 Los Angeles Times Syndicate

©1990. Used Courtesy of Richard Guindon.

---

*There are two other ways emotions are caused that do not involve self-talk. The first involves a conditioned response, in which a stimulus that was originally paired with an emotion-arousing event triggers the same emotion in future instances. You might, for instance, feel a wave of sadness when you catch a whiff of the perfume a former lover wore at the time of your breakup. The other cause of emotions that does not involve self-talk occurs when a person has learned that a certain feeling (or more correctly, behaviors that reflect that feeling) results in a desirable response from others. For example, some people cry or mope because doing so gets them a sympathetic response.

I never was what you would call a fancy skater— and while I seldom actually fell, it might have been more impressive if I had. A good resounding fall is no disgrace. It is the fantastic writhing to avoid a fall which destroys any illusion of being a gentleman. How like life that is, after all!

Robert Benchley

INVITATION TO INSIGHT

TALKING TO YOURSELF

You can become better at understanding how your thoughts shape your feelings by completing the following steps.

1. Take a few minutes to listen to the inner voice you use when thinking. Close your eyes now and listen to it. . . . Did you hear the voice? Perhaps it was saying, "What voice? I don't have any voice. . . ." Try again, and pay attention to what the voice is saying.

2. Now think about the following situations, and imagine how you would react in each. How would you interpret them with your inner voice? What feelings would follow from each interpretation?
   a. While sitting on a bus, in class, or on the street, you notice an attractive person sneaking glances at you.
   b. During a lecture your professor asks the class, "What do you think about this?" and looks toward you.
   c. You are telling friends about your vacation, and one yawns.
   d. You run into a friend on the street and ask how things are going. "Fine," she replies and rushes off.

3. Now recall three recent times when you felt a strong emotion. For each one, recall the activating event and then the interpretation that led to your emotional reaction.

IRRATIONAL THINKING AND DEBILITATIVE EMOTIONS

Focusing on the self-talk that we use to think is the key to understanding debilitative feelings. Many debilitative feelings come from accepting a number of irrational thoughts—we'll call them *fallacies* here—which lead to illogical conclusions and in turn to debilitating feelings. We usually aren't aware of these thoughts, which makes them especially powerful.[24]

1. The Fallacy of Perfection People who accept the **fallacy of perfection** believe that a worthwhile communicator should be able to handle every situation with complete confidence and skill.

Once you accept the belief that it's desirable and possible to be a perfect communicator, the next step is to assume that people won't appreciate you if you are imperfect. Admitting your mistakes, saying, "I don't know," or sharing feelings of uncertainty seem like social defects when viewed in this manner. Given the desire to be valued and appreciated, it's tempting to try to *appear* perfect, but the costs of such deception are high. If others ever find you out, they'll see you as a phony. Even when your act isn't uncovered, such a performance uses up a great deal of psychological energy and thus makes the rewards of approval less enjoyable.

The mind is its own place,
and in itself can make a
Heav'n of Hell, a Hell of
Heav'n.

John Milton,
Paradise Lost

A man said to the universe:
"Sir, I exist!"
"However," replied the universe,
"The fact has not created in me
A sense of obligation."

Stephen Crane

Subscribing to the myth of perfection not only can keep others from liking you, but also can act as a force to diminish your own self-esteem. How can you like yourself when you don't measure up to the way you ought to be? How liberated you become when you can comfortably accept the idea that you are not perfect! That

Like everyone else, you sometimes have a hard time expressing yourself.

Like everyone else, you make mistakes from time to time, and there is no reason to hide this.

You are honestly doing the best you can to realize your potential, to become the best person you can be.

2. The Fallacy of Approval   The mistaken belief known as the **fallacy of approval** is based on the idea that it is not just desirable but *vital* to get the approval of virtually every person. People who accept this belief go to incredible lengths to seek acceptance from others even when they have to sacrifice their own principles and happiness to do so. Accepting this irrational myth can lead to some ludicrous situations:

Feeling nervous because people you really don't like seem to disapprove of you

Feeling apologetic when others are at fault

Feeling embarrassed after behaving unnaturally to gain another's approval

In addition to the obvious discomfort that arises from denying your own principles and needs, the myth of approval is irrational because it implies that others will respect and like you more if you go out of your way to please them. Often this simply isn't true. How is it possible to respect people who have compromised important values just to gain acceptance? How is it possible to think highly of people who repeatedly deny their own needs as a means of buying approval? Though others may find it tempting to use these individuals to suit their ends or amusing to be around them, they hardly deserve genuine affection and respect.

Striving for universal acceptance is irrational because it's simply not possible. Sooner or later a conflict of expectations is bound to occur; one person will approve if you behave only in a certain way, but another will only accept the opposite course of action. What are you to do then?

Don't misunderstand: Abandoning the fallacy of approval doesn't mean living a life of selfishness. It's still important to consider the needs of others, and to meet them whenever possible. It's also pleasant—we might even say necessary—to strive for the respect of those people you value. The point here is that when you must abandon your own needs and principles in order to seek these goals, the price is too high.

3. The Fallacy of Shoulds   One huge source of unhappiness is the **fallacy of shoulds,** the inability to distinguish between what *is* and what *should be.* You can see the difference by imagining a person who is full of complaints about the world:

"There should be no rain on weekends."

"People ought to live forever."

"Money should grow on trees."

"We should all be able to fly."

Beliefs like these are obviously foolish. However pleasant wishing may be, insisting that the unchangeable should be changed won't affect reality one bit. And yet many people torture themselves by engaging in this sort of irrational thinking when they confuse *is* with *ought.* They say and think things like this:

"My friend should be more understanding."

"She shouldn't be so inconsiderate."

"They ought to be more friendly."

"You should work harder."

The message in each of these cases is that you would *prefer* people to behave differently. Wishing that things were better is perfectly legitimate, and trying to change them is, of course, a good idea; but it's unreasonable to *insist* that the world operate just as you want it to or to feel cheated when things aren't ideal.

Becoming obsessed with shoulds has three troublesome consequences. First, it leads to unnecessary unhappiness, for people who are constantly dreaming about the ideal are seldom satisfied with what they have. A second drawback is that merely complaining without acting can keep you from doing anything to change unsatisfying conditions. A third problem with shoulds is that this sort of complaining can build a defensive climate with others, who will resent being nagged. It's much more effective to tell people about what you'd like than to preach: Say, "I wish you'd be more punctual" instead of "You should be on time." We'll discuss ways of avoiding defensive climates in Chapter Nine.

4. The Fallacy of Overgeneralization   The **fallacy of overgeneralization** comprises two types. The first occurs when we base a belief on a *limited* amount of *evidence*. For instance, how many times have you found yourself saying something like

> "I'm so stupid! I can't even understand how to do my income tax."

> "Some friend I am! I forgot my best friend's birthday."

In cases like these, we focus on a limited type of shortcoming as if it represented everything about us. We forget that along with our difficulties we also have solved tough problems, and that though we're sometimes forgetful, at other times we're caring and thoughtful.

A second related category of overgeneralization occurs when we *exaggerate* shortcomings:

> "You *never* listen to me."

> "You're *always* late."

> "I can't think of *anything.*"

On closer examination, absolute statements like these are almost always false and usually lead to discouragement or anger. You'll feel far better when you replace overgeneralizations with more accurate messages to yourself and others:

> "You often don't listen to me."

> "You've been late three times this week."

> "I haven't had any ideas I like today."

Many overgeneralizations are based on abuse of the verb *to be.* For example, unqualified thoughts such as "He *is* an idiot [all the time?]" and "I *am* a failure [in everything?]" will make you see yourself and others in an unrealistically negative way, thus contributing to debilitative feelings.

5. The Fallacy of Causation   The **fallacy of causation** is based on the irrational belief that emotions are caused by others rather than by one's own self-talk.

This fallacy causes trouble in two ways. The first plagues people who become overly cautious about communicating because they don't want to "cause" any pain or inconvenience for others. This attitude occurs in cases such as:

Visiting friends or family out of a sense of obligation rather than a genuine desire to see them;

Keeping quiet when another person's behavior is bothering you;

Pretending to be attentive to a speaker when you are already late for an appointment or feeling ill;

Praising and reassuring others who ask for your opinion even when your honest response would be negative.

There's certainly no excuse for going out of your way to say things that will result in pain for others, and there will be times when you choose to inconvenience yourself to make life easier for those you care about. It's essential to realize, however, that it's an overstatement to say that you are the one who causes others' feelings. It's more accurate to say that they *respond* to your behavior with feelings of their own. For example, consider how strange it sounds to suggest that you make others fall in love with you. Such a statement simply doesn't make sense. It would be closer to the truth to say that you act in one way or another, and some people might fall in love with you as a result of these actions, whereas others wouldn't. In the same way, it's incorrect to say that you *make* others angry, upset—or happy, for that matter. It's better to say that others create their own responses to your behavior.

Restricting your communication because of the fallacy of causation can result in three types of damaging consequences. First, as a result of your caution you often will fail to have your own needs met. There's little likelihood that others will change their behavior unless they know that it's affecting you in a negative way. A second consequence is that you're likely to begin resenting the person whose behavior you find bothersome. Obviously, this reaction is illogical because you have never made your feelings known, but logic doesn't change the fact that burying your problem usually leads to a buildup of hostility.

Even when withholding feelings is based on the best intentions, it often damages relationships in a third way—once others find out about your deceptive nature, they will find it difficult ever to know when you are really upset with them. Even your most fervent assurances that everything is fine sound suspicious because there's always the chance that you may be covering up resentments you're unwilling to express. Thus, in many respects taking responsibility for others' feelings is not only irrational but also counterproductive.

The fallacy of causation also operates when we believe that others cause *our* emotions. Sometimes it certainly seems as if they do, either raising or lowering our spirits by their actions. But think about it for a moment: The same actions that will cause you happiness or pain one day have little effect at other times. The insult or compliment that affected your mood strongly yesterday leaves you unaffected today. Why? Because in the latter case you attached less importance to either. You certainly wouldn't feel some emotions without others' behavior; but it's your thinking, not their actions, that determines how you feel.

6. The Fallacy of Helplessness   The irrational idea of the **fallacy of helplessness** suggests that satisfaction in life is determined by forces beyond your control. People who continuously see themselves as victims make such statements as:

> "There's no way a woman can get ahead in this society. It's a man's world, and the best thing I can do is to accept it."

> "I was born with a shy personality. I'd like to be more outgoing, but there's nothing I can do about that."

> "I can't tell my boss that she is putting too many demands on me. If I did, I might lose my job."

The mistake in statements like these becomes apparent once you realize that there are many things you can do if you really want to. As you read in Chapter Two, most "can't" statements can be more correctly rephrased either as *"won't"* ("I can't tell him what I think" becomes "I won't be honest with him") or as *"don't know how"* ("I can't carry on an interesting conversation" becomes "I don't know what to say"). Once you've rephrased these inaccurate "can'ts," it becomes clear that they're either a matter of choice or an area that calls for your action—both quite different from saying that you're helpless.

When viewed in this light, it's apparent that many "can'ts" are really rationalizations to justify not wanting to change. Lonely people, for example, tend to attribute their poor interpersonal relationships to uncontrollable causes. "It's beyond my control," they think. Also, they expect their relational partners to reject them. Notice the self-fulfilling prophecy in this attitude: Believing that your relational prospects are dim can lead you to act in ways that make you an unattractive prospect. Once you persuade yourself that there's no hope, it's easy to give up trying. On the other hand, acknowledging that there is a way to change—even though it may be difficult—puts the responsibility for your predicament on your shoulders. You *can* become a better communicator—this book is one step in your movement toward that goal. Don't give up or sell yourself short!

7. The Fallacy of Catastrophic Expectations   Fearful communicators who subscribe to the irrational **fallacy of catastrophic expectations** operate on the assumption that if something bad can possibly happen, it will. Typical catastrophic fantasies include:

> "If I invite them to the party, they probably won't want to come."
>
> "If I speak up in order to try to resolve a conflict, things will probably get worse."
>
> "If I apply for the job I want, I probably won't be hired."
>
> "If I tell them how I really feel, they'll probably laugh at me."

Once you start expecting terrible consequences, a self-fulfilling prophecy can begin to build. One study revealed that people who believed that their romantic partners would not change for the better were likely to behave in ways that contributed to the breakup of the relationship.[25]

Although it's naive to think that all your interactions with others will meet with success, it's just as damaging to assume that you'll fail. One way to escape from the fallacy of catastrophic expectations is to think about the consequences that would follow even if you don't communicate successfully. Keeping in mind the folly of trying to be perfect and of living only for the approval of others, realize that failing in a given instance usually isn't as bad as it might seem. What if people do laugh at you? Suppose you don't get the job? What if others do get angry at your remarks? Are these matters really *that* serious?

Before moving on, we need to add a few thoughts about thinking and feeling. First, you should realize that thinking rationally won't completely eliminate debilitative feelings. Some debilitative feelings, after all, are very rational: grief over the death of someone you love, euphoria over getting a new job, and apprehension about the future of an important relationship after a serious fight, for example. Thinking rationally can eliminate many debilitative feelings from your life, but not all of them.

"So the prince and the princess lowered their expectations and lived reasonably contentedly forever after."

INVITATION TO INSIGHT

HOW IRRATIONAL ARE YOU?

1. Return to the situations described in the exercise Talking to Yourself on page 152. Examine each one to see whether your self-talk contains any irrational thoughts.

2. Keep a two- or three-day record of your debilitative feelings. Are any of them based on irrational thinking? Examine your conclusions, and see if you repeatedly use any of the fallacies described in the "preceding" section.

3. Take a class poll to see which irrational fallacies are most "popular." Also, discuss what subjects seem to stimulate most of this irrational thinking (for example, schoolwork, dating, jobs, family).

MINIMIZING DEBILITATIVE EMOTIONS

How can you overcome such irrational thinking? Social scientists have developed a simple yet effective approach.[26] When practiced conscientiously, it can help you cut down on the self-defeating thinking that leads to many debilitative emotions.

1. *Monitor your emotional reactions.* The first step is to recognize when you're having debilitative emotions. (Of course, it's also nice to be aware of pleasant feelings when they occur!) As we suggested earlier, one way to notice feelings is through proprioceptive stimuli: butterflies in the stomach, racing heart, hot flashes, and so on. Although such reactions might be symptoms of food poisoning, more often they reflect a strong emotion. You can also recognize certain ways of behaving that suggest your feelings: stomping instead of walking normally, being unusually quiet, or speaking in a sarcastic tone of voice are some examples.

   It may seem strange to suggest that it's necessary to look for emotions—they ought to be immediately apparent. The fact is, however, that we often suffer from debilitating feelings for some time without noticing them. For example, at the end of a trying day you've probably caught yourself frowning and realized that you've been wearing that mask for some time without realizing it.

2. *Note the activating event.* Once you're aware of how you're feeling, the next step is to figure out what activating event triggered your response. Sometimes it is obvious. For instance, a common source of anger is being accused unfairly (or fairly) of foolish behavior; being rejected by somebody important to you is clearly a source of hurt, too. In other cases, however, the activating event isn't so apparent.

   Sometimes there isn't a single activating event but rather a series of small incidents that finally build toward a critical mass and trigger a debilitative feeling. This sort of thing happens when you're trying to work or sleep and are continually interrupted by a string of interruptions, or when you suffer a series of small disappointments.

The best way to begin tracking down activating events is to notice the circumstances in which you have debilitative feelings. Perhaps they occur when you're around *specific* people. In other cases, you might be bothered by certain *types of individuals* owing to their age, role, background, or some other factor. Or perhaps certain *settings* stimulate unpleasant emotions: parties, work, school. Sometimes the *topic* of conversation is the factor that sets you off, whether it be politics, religion, sex, or some other subject.

3. *Record your self-talk.* This is the point at which you analyze the thoughts that are the link between the activating event and your feeling. If you're serious about getting rid of debilitative emotions, it's important actually to write down your **self-talk** when first learning to use this method. Putting your thoughts on paper will help you see whether they actually make any sense.

Monitoring your self-talk might be difficult at first. This is a new skill, and any new activity seems awkward. If you persevere, however, you'll find you will be able to identify the thoughts that lead to your debilitative feelings. Once you get in the habit of recognizing this internal monolog, you'll be able to identify your thoughts quickly and easily.

4. *Dispute your irrational beliefs.* Disputing your irrational beliefs is the key to success in the rational-emotive approach. Use the list of irrational fallacies on pages 152–59 to discover which of your internal statements are based on mistaken thinking.

You can do this most effectively by following three steps. First, decide whether each belief you've recorded is rational or irrational. Next, explain why the belief does or doesn't make sense. Finally, if the belief is irrational, you should write down an alternative way of thinking that is more sensible and that can leave you feeling better when faced with the same activating event in the future.

After reading about this method for dealing with unpleasant emotions, some readers have objections.

"This rational-emotive approach sounds like nothing more than trying to talk yourself out of feeling bad." This accusation is totally correct. After all, since we talk ourselves *into* feeling bad, what's wrong with talking ourselves *out* of bad feelings, especially when they are based on irrational thoughts? Rationalizing may be an excuse and a self-deception, but there's nothing wrong with being rational.

"The kind of disputing we just read sounds phony and unnatural. I don't talk to myself in sentences and paragraphs." There's no need to dispute your irrational beliefs in any special literary style. You can be just as colloquial as you want. The important thing is to clearly understand what thoughts led you into your debilitative feeling so you can clearly dispute them. When the technique is new to you, it's a good idea to write or talk out your thoughts in order to make them clear. After you've had some practice, you'll be able to do these steps in a quicker, less formal way.

No one can make you feel inferior unless you agree to it.

Eleanor Roosevelt

I believe that courage is all too often mistakenly seen as the absence of fear. If you descend by rope from a cliff and are not fearful to some degree, you are either crazy or unaware. Courage is seeing your fear in a realistic perspective, defining it, considering the alternatives and choosing to function in spite of risk.

Leonard Zunin

"This approach is too cold and impersonal. It seems to aim at turning people into cold-blooded, calculating, emotionless machines." This is simply not true. A rational thinker can still dream, hope, and love: There's nothing necessarily irrational about feelings like these. Basically rational people even indulge in a bit of irrational thinking once in a while. But they usually know what they're doing. Like healthy eaters who occasionally treat themselves to a snack of junk food, rational thinkers occasionally indulge themselves in irrational thoughts, knowing that they'll return to their healthy lifestyle soon with no real damage done.

"This technique promises too much. There's no chance I could rid myself of all unpleasant feelings, however nice that might be." We can answer this by assuring you that rational-emotive thinking probably won't totally solve your emotional problems. What it can do is to reduce their number, intensity, and duration. This method is not the answer to all your problems, but it can make a significant difference—which is not a bad accomplishment.

SKILL BUILDER

RATIONAL THINKING

1. Return to the diary of irrational thoughts you recorded on page 160. Dispute the self-talk in each case, and write a more rational interpretation of the event.

2. Now try out your ability to think rationally on the spot. You can do this by acting out the scenes listed in step 4. You'll need three players for each one: a subject, the subject's "little voice"—his or her thoughts—and a second party.

3. Play out each scene by having the subject and second party interact while the "little voice" stands just behind the subject and says what the subject is probably thinking. For example, in a scene where the subject is asking an instructor to reconsider a low grade, the voice might say, "I hope I haven't made things worse by bringing this up. Maybe he'll lower the grade after rereading the test. I'm such an idiot! Why didn't I keep quiet?"

4. Whenever the voice expresses an irrational thought, the observers who are watching the skit should call out, "Foul." At this point the action should stop while the group discusses the irrational thought and suggests a more rational line of self-talk. The players should then replay the scene with the voice speaking in a more rational way.

   Here are some scenes. Of course, you can invent others as well.
   a. A couple is just beginning their first date.
   b. A potential employee has just begun a job interview.
   c. A teacher or boss is criticizing the subject for showing up late.
   d. A student and instructor run across each other in the market.

Communication Transcript

RATIONAL THINKING IN ACTION

The following scenarios demonstrate how the rational thinking method described on pages 160–61 apply in everyday challenges. Notice that thinking rationally doesn't eliminate debilitative feelings. Instead, it helps keep them in control, making effective communication more possible.

Situation 1: Dealing with Annoying Customers

Activating Event

I work in a shopping mall that swarms with tourists and locals. Our company's reputation is based on service, but lately I've been losing my patience with the customers. The store is busy from the second we open until we close. Many of the customers are rude, pushy, and demanding. Others expect me to be a tour guide, restaurant reviewer, medical consultant, and even a baby-sitter. I feel like I'm ready to explode.

Beliefs and Self-Talk

1. I'm sick of working with the public. People are really obnoxious!
2. The customers should be more patient and polite instead of treating me like a servant.
3. This work is driving me crazy! If I keep working here, I'm going to become as rude as the customers.
4. I can't quit: I could never find another job that pays this well.

Disputing Irrational Beliefs

1. It's an overgeneralization to say that *all* people are obnoxious. Actually, most of the customers are fine. Some are even very nice. About 10 percent of them cause most of the trouble. Recognizing that most people are okay leaves me feeling less bitter.
2. It's true that obnoxious customers *should* be more polite, but it's unrealistic to expect that everybody will behave the way they ought to. After all, it's not a perfect world.
3. By saying that the customers are driving me crazy I suggest that I have no control over the situation. I'm an adult, and I am able to keep a grip on myself. I may not like the way some people behave, but it's my choice how to respond to them.
4. I'm not helpless. If the job is too unpleasant, I can quit. I probably wouldn't find another job that pays as well as this one, so I have to choose which is more important: money or peace of mind. It's my choice.

Situation 2: Meeting My Girlfriend's Family

Activating Event

Tracy and I are talking about marriage—maybe not soon, but eventually. Her family is very close, and they want to meet me. I'm sure I'll like them, but I am not sure what they think about me. I was married once before, at a young age. It was a big mistake, and it didn't last. Furthermore, I was laid off two months ago, and I'm between jobs. The family is coming to town next week, and I am very nervous about what they will think of me.

Beliefs and Self-Talk

1. They've got to like me! This is a close family, and I'm doomed if they think I'm not right for Tracy.
2. No matter how sensibly I act, all they'll think of is my divorce and unemployment.
3. Maybe the family is right. Tracy deserves the best, and I'm certainly not that!

Disputing Irrational Beliefs

1. The family's approval is definitely important. Still, my relationship with Tracy doesn't depend on it. She's already said that she's committed to me, no matter what they think. The sensible approach is to say I *want* their approval, but I don't *need* it.
2. I'm expecting the absolute worse if I think that I'm doomed no matter what happens when we meet. There is a chance that they will dislike me, but there's also a chance that things will work out fine. There's no point in dwelling on catastrophes.
3. Just because I've had an imperfect past doesn't mean I'm wrong for Tracy. I've learned from my past mistakes, and I am committed to living a good life. I know I can be the kind of husband she deserves, even though I'm not perfect.

✦ SUMMARY

Emotions have several dimensions. They are signalled by internal physiological changes, manifested by nonverbal reactions, and defined in most cases by cognitive interpretations. Some emotions are primary, while others are combinations of two or more emotions. Some are intense, while others are relatively mild.

There are several reasons why people do not verbalize many of the emotions they feel. Social rules discourage the expression of some feelings, particularly negative ones. Many social roles do not allow expression of certain feelings. Some people express emotions so rarely that they lose the ability to recognize when they are feeling them. Finally, fear of the consequences of disclosing some emotions leads people to withhold expression of them.

Since total expression of feelings is not appropriate for adults, several guidelines help define when and how to share emotions effectively. Self-awareness, clear language, and expression of mixed feelings are important. Willingness to accept responsibility for feelings instead of blaming them on others leads to better reactions. Choosing the proper time and place to share feelings is also important.

Although some emotions are facilitative, other debilitative feelings inhibit effective functioning. Many of these debilitative emotions are caused by various types of irrational thinking. It is often possible to communicate more confidently and effectively by identifying troublesome emotions, identifying the activating event and self-talk that triggered them, and replacing any irrational thoughts with a more logical analysis of the situation.

✦ KEY TERMS

debilitative emotions
facilitative emotions
fallacy of approval
fallacy of catastrophic expecta-
    tions

fallacy of causation
fallacy of helplessness
fallacy of overgeneralization
fallacy of perfection
fallacy of shoulds

mixed emotions
primary emotions
proprioceptive stimuli
self-talk

✦ MORE RESOURCES ON EMOTIONS

READINGS

Brody, Leslie R., and Judith A. Hall, "Gender and Emotion." In Michael Lewis and Jeanette M. Haviland, eds. *Handbook of Emotions.* New York: Guilford, 1993.

This chapter outlines the similarities and differences in how men and women experience and express emotions. It also offers explanations of gender differences, focusing on the role of socialization.

Duck, Steve. "Social Emotions: Showing Our Feelings about Other People." In *Human Relationships.* Newbury Park, Calif.: Sage, 1992.

This chapter describes the thoughts and communication behaviors that center on a variety of emotions, including love, jealousy, embarrassment and shyness, and loneliness.

Ellis, Albert. *A New Guide to Rational Living.* North Hollywood, Calif.: Wilshire Books, 1977.

Ellis is probably the best-known advocate of changing feelings by thinking rationally, and this is his most widely read book.

Lazarus, Arnold, and Allen Fay. *I Can If I Want To.* New York: Morrow, 1975.

The authors expand on the list of irrational fallacies described in this chapter, providing real-life examples of each and then suggesting corrective behavior. A useful book.

Metts, Sandra, and John W. Bowers, "Emotion in Interpersonal Communication." In Mark L. Knapp and Gerald R. Miller, *Handbook of Interpersonal Communication,* 2d ed. Newbury Park, Calif.: Sage, 1994.

Drawing from the work of a wide range of scholars, Metts and Bowers provide an overview of various theories of emotion, expanding on the information in this chapter of Looking Out/Looking In.

Tavris, Carol. *Anger: The Misunderstood Emotion.* New York: Simon and Schuster, 1982.

Tavris cites many studies to show that the "let it all hang out" approach to anger does little good for either sender or receiver. This doesn't mean that unassertiveness is desirable either. The most effective way to deal with anger in interpersonal disputes, Tavris argues, is to express feelings clearly and politely.

FILMS

THE CONSEQUENCES OF UNEXPRESSED FEELINGS

I Never Sang for My Father (1971) Rated PG

When death ends a relationship, those who live on may be left with more regrets about what was not expressed than about anything they may have said. This is certainly true in *I Never Sang for My Father,* the story of Tom (Melvyn Douglas), an 81-year-old patriarch who is left alone after the death of his wife, and his middle-aged son Gene (Gene Hackman), who has found a new love after the death of his own wife a year earlier. Tom is a man of few personal words: He won't acknowledge that his life is ending, and he certainly won't admit that he loves and needs his son. Gene is no more forthcoming. He won't reveal his marriage plans and his intentions to move thousands of miles away to California, leaving his father behind.

In an intensely emotional scene the father finally does break down and acknowledge his grief, and Gene invites him to come to California with him and his new wife. But the film, like many lives, doesn't have a guaranteed happily-ever-after ending. Tom and his son have lived too many years emotionally isolated to make up for lost time. We see that relationships, like trees, grow and are shaped gradually over the years. Once they have established their form, they are not easily or quickly reformed.

PART TWO ✚

Looking Out

CHAPTER 5

JEANNE
ITS A MAD MAD WORLD AND YOU LIVE HERE.
ROCCO
MARKAS
ONLY YOU
ANTHONYS

Language: Barrier and Bridge

And the whole earth was of one language and one speech. And it came to pass, as they journeyed from the East, that they found a plain in the land of Shinar; and they dwelt there.

2And they said to one another, go to, let us make brick, and burn them thoroughly. And they had brick for stone, and slime had they for mortar.

3And they said, go to, let us build us a city and a tower, whose top may reach unto Heaven; and let us make us a name, lest we be scattered abroad upon the face of the whole earth.

4And the Lord came down to see the city and the tower, which the children of men builded.

5And the Lord said, behold, the people is one, and they have all one language; and this they began to do: and now nothing will be restrained from them, which they have imagined to do.

6Go to, let us go down, and there confound their language, that they may not understand one another's speech.

7So the Lord scattered them abroad from thence upon the face of all the earth; and they left off to build the city.

8Therefore is the name of it called Babel; because the Lord did there confound the language of all the earth; and from thence did the Lord scatter them abroad upon the face of all the earth.

Genesis 11:1–9

*T*he problems that began with Babel live on today. Sometimes it seems as if none of us speaks the same language. We misunderstand others, and they don't understand us. Yet despite its frustrations and challenges, there is no question that language is a marvelous tool. It is the gift that allows us to communicate in a way that no other animals appear to match. Without language we would be more ignorant, ineffectual, and isolated.

In this chapter we will explore the nature of language, taking a look at how to take best advantage of its strengths and minimize its limitations. After an overview of how language operates, we will focus on how to overcome some common barriers to understanding that arise when people encounter one another. We will then move beyond the challenges of simply understanding one another and explore how the language we use affects the climate of interpersonal relationships. Finally, we will broaden our focus even more to look at how linguistic practices shape the attitudes of entire cultures.

✢ THE NATURE OF LANGUAGE

We will begin our survey by looking at some features that characterize all languages. These features explain both why language is such a useful tool and why it can be so troublesome.

LANGUAGE IS SYMBOLIC

Words are arbitrary symbols that don't have any meaning in themselves. The word *five*, for example, is a kind of code that represents the number of fingers on your hand only because we agree that it does. As communication theorists have pointed out, there is nothing particularly five-like in the number "five." To a speaker of French, the symbol "cinq" would convey the same meaning; to a computer programmer, the same value would be represented by the electronically coded symbol "00110101."

Calvin and **Hobbes**   by **Bill Watterson**

Even sign language, as "spoken" by most deaf people, is symbolic in nature and not the pantomime it might seem. Because this form of communication is symbolic and not literal, there are literally hundreds of different sign languages spoken around the world that have evolved independently whenever significant numbers of deaf people are in contact.[1] These distinct languages include American Sign Language, British Sign Language, French Sign Language, Danish Sign Language, Chinese Sign Language . . . even Australian Aboriginal and Mayan Sign Languages.

Despite the fact that symbols are arbitrary, people often act as if they had some meaning in themselves. S.I. Hayakawa points out the vague sense we often have that foreign languages are rather odd, and that the speakers really ought to call things by their "right" names. To illustrate the mistaken belief that words are inherently connected to the things they label, Hayakawa describes the little boy who was reported to have said, "Pigs are called pigs because they are such dirty animals."[2]

LANGUAGE IS SUBJECTIVE

Show a dozen people the same symbol and ask them what it means, and you're likely to get twelve different answers. Does the national flag bring up associations of soldiers giving their lives for their country? Parades? Institutionalized bigotry? Mom's apple pie? What about a cross: What does it represent? The gentleness and wisdom of Jesus Christ? Hate-filled Ku Klux Klan rallies? Your childhood Sunday school? The necklace your sister always wears?

Like these symbols, words can be interpreted in many different ways. And, of course, this is the basis for many misunderstandings. It's possible to have an argument about feminism without ever realizing that you and the other person are using the word to represent entirely different ideas. The same goes for *socialism, Republicans, health food,* and thousands on thousands of other symbols. Words don't have meaning; people do—and often in widely different ways.

Despite the potential for linguistic problems, the situation isn't hopeless. We do, after all, communicate with one another reasonably well most of the time. And with enough effort, we can clear up most of the misunderstandings that do occur. One key to more accurate use of language is to avoid assuming that others interpret words the same way we do. In truth, the chances for successful communication increase when we *negotiate* the meaning of a statement. By working to clarify the way language is used, we move closer to a shared understanding.

The need to negotiate meanings highlights both the shortcomings and strengths of language. On one hand, it is an imprecise tool for communicating. In any interchange we are likely to be misunderstood, and the odds are great that our understanding of others is flawed. On the other hand, the same language that works so imperfectly allows us to discover and clarify problems of understanding when they occur.

"I don't know what you mean by 'glory,'" Alice said.

Humpty Dumpty smiled contemptuously. "Of course you don't—till I tell you. I meant 'there's a nice knock-down argument for you!'"

"But 'glory' doesn't mean 'a nice knock-down argument,'" Alice objected.

"When I use a word," Humpty Dumpty said, in a rather scornful tone, "it means just what I choose it to mean—neither more nor less."

"The question is," said Alice, "whether you can make words mean so many different things."

"The question is," said Humpty Dumpty, "which is to be master—that's all."

Lewis Carroll,
Through the Looking Glass

LANGUAGE IS RULE-GOVERNED

The only reason symbol-laden languages work at all is that people agree on how to use them. The linguistic agreements that make communication possible can be codified in rules. Languages contain several types of rules. **Phonological rules** govern how sounds are combined to form words. For instance, the words *champagne, double,* and *occasion* have the same meaning in French and English, but are pronounced differently.

Whereas phonological rules determine how spoken language sounds, **syntactic rules** govern the way symbols can be arranged. For example, in English, syntactic rules require every word to contain at least one vowel and prohibit sentences such as "Have you the cookies brought?" which would be a perfectly acceptable arrangement in German.

Although most of us aren't able to describe the syntactic rules that govern our language, it's easy to recognize their existence by noticing how odd a statement that violates them appears. Sometimes, however, apparently ungrammatical speech is simply following a different set of syntactic rules. For example, "Black English," which is spoken by some members of the African-American community, treats forms of the verb *to be* differently than does standard English.[3] An expression like "I be angry" that would be ungrammatical in standard English is perfectly correct in Black English, where it would be equivalent to the standard expression "I've been angry for a while."

Sign languages spoken by the deaf demonstrate the importance of syntactic rules. True sign languages have their own syntax and grammar, which have a completely different character from any spoken or written language. It is not possible to transliterate a spoken tongue into Sign word by word or phrase by phrase as we often can do when switching between two spoken languages—their structures are just too different. Most uninformed people believe that sign language is unspoken English or French, but in truth it is nothing of the sort.

Semantic rules also govern our use of the language. But where syntax deals with structure, semantics governs meaning. Semantic rules reflect the ways in which speakers of a language respond to a particular symbol. Semantic rules are what make it possible for us to agree that "bikes" are for riding and "books" are for reading, and they help us know whom we will and won't encounter when we use rooms marked "men" or "women." Without semantic rules, communication would be impossible, for each of us would use symbols in unique ways, unintelligible to one another.

Semantic rules help us understand the meaning of individual words, but they often don't explain how language operates in everyday life. Consider the statement "let's get together tomorrow." The semantic meaning of the words in this sentence is clear enough, yet the statement could be taken in several ways. We learn to make sense of speech acts like this through **pragmatic rules,** which help us decide what interpretation of a message is appropriate in a given context.

PENN DEBATES THE MEANING OF WATER BUFFALO

PHILADELPHIA—In the midst of final exams at the University of Pennsylvania last week, students at this Ivy League campus were spending much of their time discussing, of all things, the water buffalo.

But it was not a required course in undergraduate zoology that was absorbing so much of their attention. It was another academic matter entirely, the boundary between free speech and racial insults.

It all began near midnight on Jan. 13, when Jacobowitz, an 18-year-old from Long Island, N.Y., was working late, typing a paper.

That evening, a dozen members of a black sorority were out celebrating Founders' Day, singing songs and having fun, they said.

The noise reverberated into Jacobowitz's open window, and he leaned out to complain.

"Shut up, you water buffalo!" he shouted. "If you're looking for a party, there's a zoo a mile from here."

Jacobowitz was easy enough to find. He readily admitted to the "water buffalo" comment.

"I volunteered to talk because I didn't do anything wrong," said Jacobowitz.

Then why use the phrase *water buffalo?*

"I don't know why it popped into my head. They were stomping and making a 'woo, woo' noise. It seemed to describe what they were doing," he said.

His defenders have also noted that Jacobowitz attended a Jewish day school where the Hebrew word for water oxen, *behameh,* was sometimes tossed around as a mild insult.

"It is said Jew to Jew. Nobody takes any offense," Jacobowitz said. In that context, the word means "a thoughtless person" or a "fool."

But none of these explanations impressed the campus official assigned to enforce Penn's code of conduct on racial harassment.

After being interviewed twice by campus police, Jacobowitz was summoned in January to meet with Robin Read, an official who investigates allegations of racial harassment. She asked Jacobowitz whether he had "racist thoughts" when he made his water buffalo comment. He firmly denied having such thoughts and gave his explanation. She also allegedly told him that his comment seemed to be a racial insult because water buffalo are "big, black animals that live in Africa."

David G. Savage
Los Angeles *Times*

175

The best way to appreciate how regulative rules work is to think of communication as a kind of cooperative game. Like all games, success depends on all the players understanding and following the same set of rules. The statement "let's get together tomorrow" illustrates this point. These words are likely to mean one thing when uttered by your boss and another entirely when spoken by your lover; one thing when uttered at the office and something quite different when whispered at a cocktail party. As long as everyone involved uses the same set of pragmatic rules to make sense of statements like this, understanding occurs. Problems arise, though, when communicators use different pragmatic rules to interpret a statement. For example, the inter-racial conflict arising out of the "water buffalo" incident described on page 175 can be explained in terms of the students involved using different sets of pragmatic rules to explain a shouted complaint.

Pragmatic rules can be quite complex. Consider the use of humor: One study identified twenty-four different functions humor can serve in conversations.[4] These include showing the speaker's sense of humor, entertaining others, decreasing another person's aggressive

T A B L E 5 – 1 Pragmatic Rules Govern the Use and Meaning of a Statement.

Notice how the same message ("You look very pretty today") takes on different meaning depending on which of a variety of rules are used to formulate and interpret it.

	BOSS'S PERSPECTIVE	EMPLOYEE'S PERSPECTIVE
Content Actual words and behaviors	"You look very pretty today."	
Speech act The intent of a statement	Compliment an employee	Unknown
Relational contract The perceived relationship between communicators	Boss who treats employees like family members	Subordinate employee, dependent on boss's approval for advancement
Episode Situation in which the interaction occurs	Casual conversation	Possible come-on by boss?
Life script Self-concept of each communicator	Friendly guy	Woman determined to succeed on own merits
Cultural archetype Cultural norms that shape member's perceptions and actions	Middle-class American	Middle-class American

Adapted from W.B. Pearce and V. Cronen, *Communication, Action, and Meaning.* New York: Praeger, 1980.

behavior, easing the disclosure of difficult information, expressing feelings, protecting the speaker's ego from attack, avoiding self-disclosure, and expressing aggression. It's easy to imagine how a joke aimed at serving one of these functions—reducing boredom, for example— might be interpreted by the recipient as an attack.

Coordinated management of meaning (CMM) theory describes some types of pragmatic rules that operate in everyday conversations. It suggests that we use rules at several levels to create our own messages and interpret others' statements.[5] Table 5–1 uses a CMM framework to illustrate how a sexual harassment claim might arise when two communicators use different rules to make sense of a statement. In situations like this, it's important to make sure that the other person's use of language matches yours before jumping to conclusions about the meaning of his or her statements. The skill of perception checking described in Chapter Three can be a useful tool at times like this.

INVITATION TO INSIGHT

YOUR LINGUISTIC RULES

To what extent do linguistic rules affect your understanding of and relationships with others? Explore this question by following these steps:

1. Recall a time when you encountered someone whose speech violated the system of phonological and/or syntactic rules that you are used to. What was your impression of this person? To what degree was this impression influenced by her or his failure to follow familiar linguistic rules? Consider whether this impression was or was not valid.

2. Recall at least one misunderstanding that arose when you and another person followed different semantic rules. Use hindsight to consider whether this misunderstanding (and others like it) could be avoided. If semantic misunderstandings can be minimized, explain what approaches might be useful.

3. Use the discussion of coordinated management of meaning theory in the preceding pages to identify at least two pragmatic rules that govern the use of language in one of your relationships. Share these rules with other students. Do they use language in the same way as you and your relational partner?

After reading this far, you should be aware that language isn't as simple as it first seems. You have already seen that failure to use language with the care and caution it deserves can lead to problems. Sometimes these problems are relatively minor, but in other cases they can be disastrous, as the following account shows.

THE GREAT MOKUSATSU MISTAKE:
WAS THIS THE DEADLIEST ERROR OF OUR TIME?

For many months after the Japanese collapse in 1945, people wondered whether it was the atomic bomb or Russia's entry into the war that had brought to an end the fighting in the Pacific. But it gradually became clear that the importance of these two events in persuading Japan to surrender had been overrated; that Japan had been a defeated nation long before August 1945.

"The Japanese had, in fact, already sued for peace before the Atomic Age was announced to the world with the destruction of Hiroshima, and before the Russian entry into the war," Fleet Admiral Chester W. Nimitz told Congress; and other American military leaders confirmed this report.

Why, then, did not Japan accept the Potsdam Declaration, which called upon Japan to surrender, when it was issued in late July of 1945, instead of waiting until the second week in August, after Hiroshima and Nagasaki had been blasted into radioactive rubble and the Russians had begun their drive into Manchuria? That question has never been satisfactorily answered.

The true story of Japan's rejection of the Potsdam Declaration *may* be the story of an incredible mistake—a mistake which so altered the course of history in the Far East that we shall never be able to estimate its full effect on our nation—a mistake which, ironically, was made by a Japanese and involved just one Japanese word.

I say that it "may be" because part of the actual truth lies buried in human motivations which will probably always puzzle historians. But another part of it is clearly demonstrable. Let me tell the story; then you can judge for yourself what really happened.

By the spring of 1945 there was no question in the minds of Japan's leaders that their nation had been badly beaten.

The plight of the nation was so desperate that the actual figures were kept secret even from some of the cabinet ministers. Japan's industrial complex had crumbled under the aerial assault. Steel production was down 79 percent, aircraft production down 64 percent. By September a lack of aluminum would halt the building of planes entirely.

Allied air attacks were destroying railroads, highways, and bridges faster than they could be replaced. Hundreds of thousands of bodies were buried in the smoking ruins of cities and towns. Millions were homeless. In Tokyo alone, almost half of the homes had been leveled. People were fleeing the cities. A combination of American surface, air, and undersea attack had cut off shipments from the occupied regions on which Japan depended for her life. Food was running out.

American planes destroyed the last of Japan's fleet in a battle off Kyushu on the very day in April when Suzuki took office. The aged Premier was an admiral without a navy.

"We must stop the war at the earliest opportunity," he said when he learned the true condition of his nation's war potential. The *jushin,* the senior statesmen, had advised the Emperor in February of 1945 that surrender was necessary *no matter what the cost.*

The Potsdam Declaration was issued on July 26, 1945. It was signed by the United States, Great Britain, and (to the surprise of the Japanese) China. The reaction among Japanese leaders was one of exultation. The terms were far more lenient than expected. The Japanese were quick to note that instead of demanding unconditional surrender from the *government,* the last item of the proclamation called upon the government to proclaim the unconditional surrender of the *armed forces.*

The document also promised that Japan would not be destroyed as a nation, that the Japanese

(continued)

(continued from page 179)

would be free to choose their own form of government, that sovereignty over the home islands would be returned to them after occupation, that they would be allowed access to raw materials for industry, and that Japanese forces would be allowed to return home.

Most important of all, the phrasing of the proclamation hinted strongly that the Emperor would be left on the throne, the one point which had been of most concern to the cabinet in all its discussions of surrender. The Japanese were expected to read between the lines, which they very quickly did.

Upon receiving the text of the proclamation, the Emperor told Foreign Minister Togo without hesitation that he deemed it acceptable. The full cabinet then met to discuss the Allied ultimatum.

Despite the fact that the cabinet members were considering acceptance of the Potsdam terms, they could not at first decide whether the news of the Allied proclamation should be released to the Japanese public. Foreign Minister Togo, anxious to prepare the people for the surrender, argued for four hours for its prompt release to the press. At six in the evening he won his point over strong army objections and late that night the declaration was released to the newspapers.

But there was another factor which the cabinet also was forced to consider. As yet the Japanese had received news of the statement of Allied policy at Potsdam only through their radio listening posts. It was not addressed to their government and the ultimatum had not yet gone through official channels. Could the cabinet act on the basis of such unofficial information?

"After mature deliberation the hastily convened cabinet decided to keep silence for a while about the Potsdam proclamation pending further developments," says Kase.

The delay in announcing acceptance of the Allied terms was not expected to be long, but Prime Minister Suzuki was to meet the very next day with the press. The Japanese newsmen undoubtedly would question him about the proclamation. What should he say?

Hiroshi Shimomura, president of the powerful Board of Information—counterpart of Germany's propaganda ministry—and a member of the cabinet, recalls in his account of this fateful session that it was decided that the prime minister, if asked, should treat the subject lightly.

"This was to be done in order not to upset the surrender negotiations then under way through Russia," says Shimomura.

Premier Suzuki was to say merely that the cabinet had reached no decision on the Allied demands and that the discussion was continuing. Although the policy was to be one of silence, the very fact that the cabinet did not reject the ultimatum at once would make it clear to the Japanese people what was in the wind.

When Premier Suzuki confronted the press on July 28, he said that the cabinet was holding to a policy of *mokusatsu*. The word *mokusatsu* not only has no exact counterpart in English but it is ambiguous even in Japanese. Suzuki, as we know, meant that the cabinet had decided to make no comment on the Potsdam proclamation, with the implication that something significant was impending. But the Japanese were tricked by their own language. For in addition to meaning "to withhold comment," *mokusatsu* may also be translated as "to ignore."

The word has two characters in Japanese. *Moku* means "silence" and *satsu* means "kill," thus implying in an absolutely literal sense "to kill with silence." This can mean—to a Japanese—either to ignore or to refrain from comment.

Unfortunately the translators at the Domei News Agency could not know what Suzuki had in mind. As they hastily translated the prime minister's statement into English, they chose the wrong meaning. From the towers of Radio Tokyo the news crackled to the Allied world that the Suzuki cabinet had decided to "ignore" the Potsdam ultimatum.

The cabinet was furious at Suzuki's choice of words and the subsequent error by Domei. The reaction of Kase, who had fought long and hard for peace, was one of dismay.

"This was a piece of foolhardiness," he says. "When I heard of this I strongly remonstrated with the cabinet chief secretary, but it was too late. . . . Tokyo radio flashed it—to America! The punishment came swiftly. An atomic bomb was dropped on Hiroshima on August 6 by the Allies, who were led by Suzuki's outrageous statement into the belief that our government had refused to accept the Potsdam proclamation."

But for this tragic mistake, Kase laments, Japan might have been spared the atomic attack and the Russian declaration of war.

William J. Coughlin

❖ THE IMPACT OF LANGUAGE

So far, we have focused on language only as a medium for helping communicators understand one another. But along with this important function, the words we use can shape our perceptions of the world around us and reflect the attitudes we hold toward one another.

On the broadest level, the language that communicators use can affect the way they view one another and the world around them. This chapter describes how language can shape an entire culture's world view and how problems can arise when speakers of different languages encounter one another. But even among communicators who speak the same language, the labels we use to describe people, things, events, and ideas can affect our perceptions in a variety of ways.

NAMING AND IDENTITY

"What's in a name?" Romeo asked rhetorically. If Juliet had been a social scientist, she would have answered "A great deal." Research has demonstrated that names are more than just a simple means of identification: They shape the way others think of us, the way we view ourselves, and the way we act.

Different names have different connotations. In one study, psychologists asked college students to rate over a thousand names according to their likability, how active or passive they seemed, and their masculinity or femininity. In spite of the large number of subjects, the responses were quite similar.[6] Michael, John, and Wendy were likable and active and were rated as possessing the masculine or feminine traits of their sex. Percival, Isadore, and Alfreda were less likable, and their sexual identity was less clear. Other research also suggests that names have strong connotative meanings. More common names are generally viewed as being more active, stronger, and better than unusual ones.[7] The impact of names does affect first impressions, but the effect doesn't seem so powerful once communicators become more familiar with one another.[8]

By the middle of childhood, we are able to start controlling the names by which we want to be called. The labels we choose for ourselves and encourage others to use says a great deal about who we think we are and how we want others to view us. For many people, changes in age lead to changes in names. The diminutive that seemed to fit as a child doesn't fit as well in adolescence or adulthood. Thus, Vinnie may become Vince, and Danny may insist on being called Dan or Daniel. It still may be fine for close friends to use diminutives, but not others. The shift to more formal, adult names may not be as pronounced for some women: It's not uncommon to meet an adult Betsy or Susie. But when being taken seriously is the goal in a world where women are all too often treated with less respect than they deserve, having a serious name can be an asset. A male president of the United

States may have been elected without changing his name from Bill to William, but it's hard to imagine a female public figure who would risk being called Cindy or Babs. Contemporary female officeholders prove the point: Names like Patty Schroeder or Sandy O'Connor just don't sound right.

Many women in Western society, aware of the power of names to influence identity, are aware that choosing how to identify themselves after marriage can be a significant decision. They may follow the tradition of taking their husband's last name, hyphenate their own name and their husband's, or keep their birth name. A fascinating study by Karen Foss and Belle Edson revealed that a woman's choice is likely to reveal a great deal about herself and her relationship with her husband.[9] Surveys revealed that women who took their husband's name placed the most importance on relationships, with social expectations of how they should behave rated second and issues of self coming last. On the other hand, women who kept their birth names put their personal concerns ahead of relationships and social expectations. Women with hyphenated names fell somewhere between the other groups, valuing self and relationships equally.

Female forms of address influence others' perceptions as well as shape the self-concept and behavior of the women who choose them. Research conducted in the late 1980s showed that women who choose the title "Ms." give the impression of being more achievement oriented, socially assertive, and dynamic—but less interpersonally warm than counterparts who prefer more traditional forms of "Miss" or "Mrs."[10]

AFFILIATION, ATTRACTION, AND INTEREST

Besides shaping an individual's identity, speech can also be a way of building and demonstrating solidarity with others. Research has demonstrated that communicators are attracted to others whose style of speaking is similar to theirs.[11] Likewise, communicators who want to show affiliation with one another adapt their speech in a variety of ways, including their choice of vocabulary, rate of talking, number and placement of pauses, and level of politeness.[12] Adolescents who all adopt the same vocabulary of slang words and speech mannerisms illustrate the principle of linguistic solidarity. The same process works among members of other groups, ranging from street gangs to military personnel. Communication researchers call the process of adapting one's speech style to match that of others with whom the communicator wants to identify **convergence.**

When two or more people feel equally positive about one another, their linguistic convergence will be mutual. But when communicators want or need approval they often adapt their speech to accommodate the other person's style, trying to say the "right thing" or speak in a way that will help them fit in. We see this process when immigrants who want to gain the rewards of material success in a new culture strive to master the host language. Likewise, employees who seek advancement tend to speak more like their superiors, supervisors adopt the speech style of managers, and managers converge toward their bosses.

The principle of speech accommodation works in reverse, too. Communicators who want to set themselves apart from others adopt the strategy of **divergence,** speaking in a way that emphasizes their differences from others. For example, members of an ethnic group, even though fluent in the dominant language, might use their own dialect as a way of showing solidarity with one another—a sort of "us against them" strategy. Divergence also operates in other settings. A physician or an attorney, for example, who wants to establish credibility with his or her client, might speak formally and use professional jargon to create a sense of distance. The implicit message here is, "I'm different (and more knowledgeable) than you."

Along with convergence and divergence, an individual's choice of words can reflect his or her liking and interest. Social customs discourage us from expressing like or dislike in an overt way. Only a clod would say, "I don't like you" in most situations. Likewise, bashful or cautious suitors might not admit their attraction to a potential partner. Even when people are reluctant to speak candidly, the language they use can suggest their degree of interest and attraction toward a person, an object, or an idea. Morton Weiner and Albert Mehrabian outline several linguistic clues that can reveal these attitudes.[13]

- *Demonstrative pronoun choice:*
  "*These* people want our help" indicates greater affinity than "*Those* people want our help."
- *Sequential placement:*
  "Jack and Jill are my friends" may suggest a different level of liking than "Jill and Jack are my friends."
- Negation:
  For the question "What do you think of it?", the response "It's not bad" is less positive than "It's good."
- *Duration*
  The length of time spent discussing a person or subject also can be a strong indicator of attraction to the subject or the person with whom the speaker is talking.

POWER

Communication researchers have identified a number of language patterns that add to or detract from a speaker's power to influence others. Notice the difference between these two statements:

"Excuse me, sir. I hate to say this, but I . . . uh . . . I guess I won't be able to turn in the assignment on time. I had a personal emergency and . . . well . . . it was just impossible to finish it by today. I'll have it on your desk on Monday, O.K.?"

"I won't be able to turn in the assignment on time. I had a personal emergency and it was impossible to finish it by today. I'll have it on your desk Monday."

Whether or not the professor finds the excuse acceptable, it's clear that the second one sounds more confident, whereas the tone of the first is apologetic and uncertain. Table 5–2 identifies several **powerless speech mannerisms** illustrated in the statements you just read. A number of studies have shown that speakers whose talk is free of these mannerisms are rated as more competent, dynamic, and attractive than speakers who sound powerless.[14] One study revealed that even a single type of powerless speech mannerism can make a person appear less authoritative or socially attractive.[15]

Despite its apparent advantages, a consistently powerful style of speaking isn't always the best approach. In some cultures politeness is valued more highly than directness. In China or Japan, for example, a powerful approach would be highly offensive. Even in more direct Western cultures, language that is *too* powerful may intimidate or annoy others. Consider these two different approaches to handle a common situation:

> "Excuse me. My baby is having a little trouble getting to sleep. Would you mind turning down the music just a little?"

> "My baby can't sleep because your music is too loud. Please turn it down."

The more polite, if less powerful, approach would probably produce better results than the stronger statement. How can this fact be reconciled with the research on powerful language? The answer lies in the tension between the potentially opposing goals of getting immediate results and developing positive relationships. If you come across as too powerful, you may get what you're seeking in the short term but alienate the other person in ways that will make your relation-

TABLE 5 – 2   **Examples of Powerless Language**

Hedges	"I'm *kinda* disappointed . . . " "I *think* we should . . . " "I *guess* I'd like to . . . "
Hesitations	"*Uh*, can I have a minute of your time?" "*Well*, we could try this idea . . . " "I wish you would—*er*—try to be on time."
Intensifiers	"*So* that's how I feel . . . " "I'm not *very* hungry."
Polite forms	"Excuse me, *sir* . . . "
Tag questions	"It's about time we got started, *isn't it?*" "*Don't you think* we should give it another try?"
Disclaimers	"*I probably shouldn't say this but* . . . " "*I'm not really sure but* . . . "

❧ WHAT'S IN A FIRST NAME?

Solidarity reigns when two people call each other by first name. Power reigns when one calls the other by first name but it's not reciprocal. If a man tells his servant, "When the guests arrive, show them into the drawing room, Steven," can Steven reply, "I'd be glad to, Ronald"? If a teacher calls on Johnny to read the lesson aloud, can Johnny ask, "Which page, Margaret?" If the doctor or dentist or psychotherapist calls the secretary or client "Mary," can Mary respond in kind?

Age, gender, and status all play roles here. In a sense the age relationship is a model for power and solidarity. Any adult can call any child by first name, but children must call at least some adults by title–last name (Mr., Ms., Miss, Mrs., Dr.). Ways of talking to children—calling them by first name, patting and caressing them, asking them personal questions—show affection. But they also reflect a difference in status because the right to show affection in that way is not reciprocal.

Women are often caught in the grip of this paradox. They are far more often called by their first names and touched than are men. Talk-show hosts, panel moderators, students, and others far more often address men with Ph.D.s as "Doctor" than they do women with Ph.D.s. It's common for strangers—travel agents, salespeople, telephone-order clerks—to use the first names of all women customers. In one sense, this shows condescension: lack of respect. Just as people feel free to touch, pat, and first-name children, they feel freer to use these friendly signs with women.

But the fact remains that people who treat women in this way are doing it to be friendly; using "Miss" or "Mrs." (let alone "Ms."!) would feel awkward, like anything that goes against habit. Many women prefer to be called by first name because it's distancing to be addressed by title–last name. And women are more likely than men to be troubled by distancing.

Deborah Tannen

---

ship more difficult in the long run. Furthermore, a statement that is *too* powerful can convey relational messages of disrespect and superiority—just as likely to antagonize others as to gain their compliance.

In some situations polite, less apparently powerful forms of speech can even enhance a speaker's effectiveness.[16] For example, a boss might say to a secretary, "Would you mind retyping this letter?" In truth, both the boss and secretary know this is an order and not a request, but the questioning form is more considerate, and leaves the secretary feeling better about the boss.[17] The importance of achieving both content and relational goals helps explain why a mixture of powerful and polite speech is usually most effective.[18]

✚ THE USES (AND ABUSES) OF LANGUAGE

By now it's apparent that language can shape the way we perceive and understand the world. Next we will look at some specific types of usage and explore both the value and potential problems they generate.

PRECISION AND VAGUENESS

Most people assume that the goal of language is to make our ideas clear to one another. When clarity *is* the goal, we need language skills to make our ideas understandable to others. Sometimes, however, we want to be less than perfectly clear. The following pages will point out some cases where ambiguity and vagueness serve useful purposes as well as cases where perfect understanding is the goal.

EQUIVOCATION **Equivocal language** consists of words that have more than one commonly accepted definition. Some equivocal misunderstandings are amusing, as the following newspaper headlines illustrate:

> Family Catches Fire Just in Time
>
> Man Stuck on Toilet; Stool Suspected
>
> 20-Year Friendship Ends at the Altar
>
> Trees Can Break Wind

Some equivocal misunderstandings are trivial. We recall dining at a Mexican restaurant and ordering a "tostada with beans." Instead of being served a beef tostada with beans on the side, we were sur-

"Let me get this straight now. Is what you want to build a jean factory or a gene factory?"

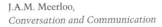

THE MANY MEANINGS OF "I LOVE YOU"

"I love you" [is] a statement that can be expressed in so many varied ways. It may be a stage song, repeated daily without any meaning, or a barely audible murmur, full of surrender. Sometimes it means: I desire you or I want you sexually. It may mean: I hope you love me or I hope that I will be able to love you. Often it means: It may be that a love relationship can develop between us or even I hate you. Often it is a wish for emotional exchange: I want your admiration in exchange for mine or I give my love in exchange for some passion or I want to feel cozy and at home with you or I admire some of your qualities. A declaration of love is mostly a request: I desire you or I want you to gratify me, or I want your protection or I want to be intimate with you or I want to exploit your loveliness.

Sometimes it is the need for security and tenderness, for parental treatment. It may mean: My self-love goes out to you. But it may also express submissiveness: Please take me as I am, or I feel guilty about you, I want, through you, to correct the mistakes I have made in human relations. It may be self-sacrifice and a masochistic wish for dependency. However, it may also be a full affirmation of the other, taking the responsibility for mutual exchange of feelings. It may be a weak feeling of friendliness, it may be the scarcely even whispered expression of ecstasy. "I love you,"—wish, desire, submission, conquest; it is never the word itself that tells the real meaning here.

J.A.M. Meerloo,
Conversation and Communication

prised to see the waiter bring us a plate containing a tostada *filled* with beans. As with most equivocal misunderstandings, hindsight showed that the phrase "tostada with beans" has two equally correct meanings.

Other equivocal misunderstandings can be more serious. A nurse gave one of her patients a scare when she told him that he "wouldn't be needing" his robe, books, and shaving materials anymore. The patient became quiet and moody. When the nurse inquired about the odd behavior, she discovered that the poor man had interpreted her statement to mean he was going to die soon. In fact, the nurse meant he would be going home shortly.

It's difficult to catch every equivocal statement and clarify it while speaking. For this reason, the responsibility for interpreting statements accurately rests in large part with the receiver. Feedback of one sort or another—for example, the kind of perception checking introduced in Chapter Three and the paraphrasing described in Chapter Seven can help clear up misunderstandings.

Despite its obvious problems, equivocal language has its uses. As Chapter Eight describes in detail, there are times when using language that is open to several interpretations can be useful. It helps people get along by avoiding the kind of honesty and clarity that can embarrass both the speaker and listener. For example, if a friend proudly shows you a newly completed painting and asks your opinion about it, you might respond equivocally by saying, "Gee, it's really unusual. I've never seen anything like it" instead of giving a less ambiguous but more hurtful response such as "This may be the ugliest thing I've ever seen!"

ABSTRACTION   High-level abstractions are convenient ways of generalizing about similarities between several objects, people, ideas, or events. Figure 5–1 is an **abstraction ladder** that shows how to describe the same phenomenon at various levels of abstraction.

We use higher-level abstractions all the time. For instance, rather than saying, "Thanks for washing the dishes," "Thanks for vacuuming the rug," "Thanks for making the bed," it's easier to say, "Thanks for cleaning up." In such everyday situations, abstractions are a useful kind of verbal shorthand.

At other times the vagueness of abstractions allows us to avoid confrontations by deliberately being unclear.[19] Suppose, for example, your boss is enthusiastic about a new approach to doing business that you think is a terrible idea. Telling the truth might seem too risky; but lying—saying, "I think it's a great idea"—wouldn't feel right either. In situations like this an abstract answer can hint at your true belief without a direct confrontation: "I don't know . . . It's sure unusual . . . It *might* work." The same sort of abstract language can help you avoid embarrassing friends who ask for your opinion with questions like "What do you think of my new haircut?" An abstract response like "It's really different!" may be easier for you to deliver—and for your friend to receive—than the clear, brutal truth: "It's really

FIGURE 5–1

Abstraction Ladder   A boss gives feedback to an employee about career advancement at various levels of specificity.

cathy

by Cathy Guisewite

Panel 1: OKAY, I'LL SEE YOU LATER, CATHY. / "LATER" AS IN "TONIGHT," OR "LATER" AS IN, "SOMETIME IN THIS LIFETIME"?

Panel 2: OH, HA, HA. GIVE ME A CALL SOMETIME. / "GIVE YOU A CALL" AS IN, "YOU RESPECT MY RIGHT TO TAKE THE INITIATIVE" OR, "GIVE YOU A CALL" AS IN "CALL ONLY WHEN YOU SPECIFICALLY ASK"?

Panel 3: YOU'RE A RIOT, CATHY. WELL, I'VE GOT TO GO. / "I'M A RIOT" AS IN, "YOU LOVE ME" OR "I'M A RIOT" AS IN, "WE JUST BROKE UP"?

Panel 4: MEN SHOULD COME WITH INSTRUCTION BOOKLETS.

ugly!" Chapter Nine will have more to say about abstract equivocations as an alternative to complete self-disclosure on the one hand and lies on the other.

Although vagueness does have its uses, highly abstract language can cause four types of problems. The first is stereotyping. Imagine someone who has had one bad experience and, as a result, blames an entire group: "Marriage counselors are worthless," "Californians are all flaky," or "Men are no good." Overly abstract expressions like these can cause people to *think* in generalities, ignoring uniqueness. As you learned in Chapter Two, expecting people to act a certain way can become a self-fulfilling prophecy. If you expect the worst of people, you have a good chance of getting it.

Besides narrowing your own options, excessively abstract language can also confuse others. Telling the hair stylist, "not too short" or "more casual" might produce the look you want, or it might lead to an unpleasant surprise. The following conversation illustrates the kind of frustration and confusion that can arise from overly abstract descriptions.

A: We never do anything that's fun anymore.

B: What do you mean?

A: We used to do lots of unusual things, but now it's the same old stuff, over and over.

B: But last week we went on that camping trip, and tomorrow we're going to that party where we'll meet all sorts of new people. Those are new things.

A: That's not what I mean. I'm talking about *really* unusual stuff.

B: (*Becoming confused and a little impatient*) Like what? Taking hard drugs or going over Niagara Falls in a barrel?

A: Don't be stupid. All I'm saying is that we're in a rut. We should be living more exciting lives.

B: Well, I don't know what you want.

Overly abstract language also leads to confusing directions:

Professor: I hope you'll do a thorough job on this paper.
Student: When you say thorough, how long should it be?
Professor: Long enough to cover the topic thoroughly.
Student: How many sources should I look at when I'm researching it?
Professor: You should use several—enough to show me that you've really explored the subject.
Student: And what style should I use to write it?
Professor: One that's scholarly but not too formal.
Student: Arrgh!!!

Even appreciation can suffer from being expressed in overly abstract terms. Psychologists have established that behaviors that are reinforced will recur with increased frequency. Your statements of appreciation will encourage others to keep acting in ways you like; but if they don't know just what it is that you appreciate, the chances of their repeating that behavior are lessened. There's a big difference between "I appreciate your being so nice" and "I appreciate the way you spent time talking to me when I was upset."

Overly abstract language can leave you unclear even about your own thoughts. At one time or another we've all felt dissatisfied with ourselves and others. Often these dissatisfactions show up as thoughts such as "I've got to get better organized" or "She's been acting strangely lately." Sometimes abstract statements such as these are shorthand for specific behaviors that we can identify easily; but in other cases we'd have a hard time explaining what we'd have to do to get organized or what the strange behavior is. Without clear ideas of these concepts, it's hard to begin changing matters. Instead, we tend to go around in mental circles, feeling vaguely dissatisfied without knowing exactly what is wrong or how to improve it.

Overly abstract language can lead to problems of a more serious nature. For instance, accusations of sexual assault can arise because one person claims to have said "no" when the other person insists no such refusal was ever conveyed. In response to this sort of disagreement, specific rules of sexual conduct have become more common in work and educational settings. Perhaps the best known code of this type is the one developed at Ohio's Antioch College. The policy uses low-level abstractions to minimize the chances of anyone claiming confusion about a partner's willingness. For example, the code states

> To knowingly take advantage of someone who is under the influence of alcohol, drugs, and/or prescribed medication is not acceptable behavior in the Antioch community.
>
> If sexual contact and/or conduct is not mutually and simultaneously initiated, then the person who initiates sexual contact/conduct is responsible for getting verbal consent of the other individual(s) involved.
>
> If one person wants to initiate moving to a higher level of sexual intimacy . . . that person is responsible for getting verbal consent of the other person(s) involved before moving to that level.

If someone has initially consented but then stops consenting during a sexual interaction, she/he should communicate withdrawal verbally and/or through physical resistance. The other individual(s) must stop immediately.[20]

Some critics have ridiculed rules like these as being unrealistically legalistic and chillingly inappropriate for romantic relationships.[21] Whatever its weaknesses, the Antioch code illustrates how low-level abstractions can reduce the chance of a serious misunderstanding. Specific language may not be desirable or necessary in many situations, but in an era when misinterpretations can lead to accusations of physical assault, it does seem to have a useful place.

Research shows that low-level descriptions can help improve the quality of relationships, even when conflicts arise. One study found that well-adjusted couples had just as many conflicts as poorly adjusted couples, but the way adjusted pairs handled their problems was significantly different. Instead of blaming one another by using evaluative language, the well-adjusted couples expressed their complaints in behavioral terms.[22]

It's hard to overestimate the value of specific, behavioral language because speaking in this way vastly increases the chance not only of thinking clearly about what's on your mind but also of others understanding you. A behavioral description should include three elements: the participants, the circumstances, and the behavior itself.

Who Is Involved?   At first the answer to this question might seem simple. If you're thinking about a personal problem or goal, you might reply, "I am"; if you're expressing appreciation, complaining, or making a request of another person, he or she would be the one who is involved. Although the question of involvement may be easy, it often calls for more detail. Ask yourself whether the problem or goal you're thinking about involves an entire category of people (women, salespeople, strangers), a subclass of the group (attractive women, rude salespeople, strangers you'd like to meet), or a specific person (Jane Doe, the salesclerk at a particular store, a new person in your neighborhood). If you're talking to another person, consider whether your appreciation, complaint, or request is directly solely at him or her or whether it also involves others.

In What Circumstances Does the Behavior Occur?   You can identify the circumstances by answering several questions. In what places does the behavior occur? Does it occur at any particular times? When you are discussing particular subjects? Is there anything special about you when it occurs: Are you tired, embarrassed, busy? Is there any common trait shared by the other person or people involved? Are they friendly or hostile, straightforward or manipulative, nervous or confident? In other words, if the behavior you're describing doesn't occur all the time (and few behaviors do), you need to pin down what circumstances set this situation apart from other ones.

In many situations it's important to be specific but I can't think of any examples offhand.

Ashleigh Brilliant

What Behaviors Are Involved?   Although such terms as *more cooperative* and *helpful* might sound as if they're concrete descriptions of behavior, they are usually too vague to explain clearly what's on your mind. Behaviors must be *observable,* ideally both to you and to others. For instance, moving down the abstraction ladder from the relatively vague term *helpful,* you might arrive at "does the dishes every other day," "volunteers to help me with my studies," or "fixes dinner once or twice a week without being asked." It's easy to see that terms like these are easier for both you and others to understand than are more vague abstractions.

There is one exception to the rule that behaviors should be observable, and that involves the internal processes of thoughts and emotions. For instance, in describing what happens to you when a friend has kept you waiting for a long time, you might say, "My stomach felt as if it were in knots—I was really worried. I kept thinking that you had forgotten and that I wasn't important enough to you for you to remember our date." What you're doing when offering such a description is to make unobservable events clear.

You can better understand the value of behavioral descriptions by looking at the examples in Table 5–3. Notice how much more clearly they explain the speaker's thought than do the more vague terms.

SKILL BUILDER
DOWN-TO-EARTH LANGUAGE

You can appreciate the value of non-abstract language by translating the following into behavioral terms:

a. An abstract goal for improving your interpersonal communication (for example, "be more assertive" or "stop being so sarcastic")

b. A complaint you have about another person (for instance, that he or she is "selfish" or "insensitive")

c. A request for someone to change (as "I wish you'd be more punctual" or "Try to be more positive")

d. An appreciation you could share with another person (such as "Thanks for being so helpful" or "I appreciate your patience")

In each case, describe the person or people involved, the circumstances in which the behavior occurs, and the precise behaviors involved. What difference will using behavioral descriptions such as the ones you have created here be likely to make?

EUPHEMISM   **Euphemisms** (from the Greek word meaning "to use words of good omen") are pleasant terms substituted for blunt ones. Euphemisms soften the impact of information that might be unpleasant. Unfortunately, this pulling of linguistic punches often obscures the accuracy of a message.

T A B L E   5 – 3   Abstract Vs. Behavioral Descriptions

	Abstract Description	Behavioral Description			Remarks
		Who is Involved	In What Circumstances	Specific Behaviors	
Problem	I'm no good at meeting strangers.	People I'd like to date.	When I meet them at parties or at school.	Think of myself, "They'd never want to date me." Also, I don't originate conversations.	Behavioral description more clearly identifies thoughts and behaviors to change.
Goal	I'd like to be more assertive.	Telephone and door-to-door solicitors.	When I don't want the product or can't afford it.	Instead of apologizing or explaining, say, "I'm not interested" and keep repeating this until they go away.	Behavioral description clearly outlines how to act; abstract description doesn't.
Appreciation	"You've been a great boss."	(No clarification necessary)	When I've needed to change my schedule because of school exams or assignments.	"You've rearranged my hours cheerfully."	Give both abstract and behavioral descriptions for best results.
Complaint	"I don't like some of the instructors around here."	Professors A and B	In class when students ask questions the professors think are stupid.	Either answer in a sarcastic voice (you might demonstrate) or accuse us of not studying hard enough.	If talking to A or B, use only behavioral description. With others, use both abstract and behavioral descriptions.
Request	"Quit bothering me!"	You and your friends X and Y.	When I'm studying for exams.	Instead of asking me over and over to party with you, I wish you'd accept my comment that I need to study and leave me to do it.	Behavioral description will reduce defensiveness and make it clear that you don't *always* want to be left alone.

There are certainly cases where tactless honesty can be brutal: "What do I think of your new hairstyle? I think it's ugly!" or "How do I feel about the relationship? I can hardly wait to get away from you!" At the same time, being too indirect can leave others wondering where you stand: "What an original haircut," or "We could grow closer than we are now." When choosing how to broach difficult subjects, the challenge is to be as kind as possible without sacrificing either your integrity or the clarity of your message. (The guidelines for self-disclosure outlined in Chapter Eight will help you.)

RELATIVE LANGUAGE   **Relative words** gain their meaning by comparison. For example, do you attend a large or small school? This depends on what you compare it to. Alongside a campus such as the University of Michigan, with over 30,000 students, your school may look small; but compared with a smaller institution, it may seem quite large. Relative words such as "fast" and "slow," "smart" and "stupid," "short" and "long," are clearly defined only through comparison.

Some relative terms are so common that we mistakenly assume that they have a clear meaning. In one study, graduate students were asked to assign numerical values to such terms as "doubtful," "toss-up," "likely," "probable," "good chance," and "unlikely."[23] There was a tremendous variation in the meaning of most of these terms. For example, the responses for "possible" ranged from 0 to 99 percent. "Good chance" meant between 35 and 90 percent, while "unlikely" fell between 0 and 40 percent.

Using relative terms without explaining them can lead to communication problems. Have you ever responded to someone's question about the weather by saying it was warm, only to find out the person thought it was cold? Have you followed a friend's advice and gone to a "cheap" restaurant, only to find that it was twice as expensive as you expected? Have classes you heard were "easy" turned out to be hard? The problem in each case resulted from failing to link the relative word to a more measurable term.

STATIC EVALUATION   "Mark is a nervous guy." "Karen is short-tempered." "You can always count on Wes." Statements that contain or imply the word "is" lead to the mistaken assumption that people are consistent and unchanging—clearly an incorrect belief. Instead of labeling Mark as permanently and totally nervous, it would probably be more accurate to outline the situations in which he behaves nervously. The same goes for Karen, Wes, and the rest of us: We are more changeable than the way static, everyday language describes us.

Describing John as "boring" (you can substitute "friendly," "immature," or many other adjectives) is less correct than saying, "The John I encountered yesterday seemed to me to be. . . ." The second type of statement describes the way someone behaved at one point; the first categorizes him as if he had always been that way.

Subscripting is one linguistic device of dating to reduce **static evaluation.** Adding a subscript whenever appropriate will show the

The Husbands In My Life

A Greek named Heraclitus claimed that you never see the same river twice because the water that was there one minute is not there the next. In this respect, it seems to me, husbands are like rivers. For example, my husband Tom.

Tom$_1$ is of course the lover; Tom$_2$, the man of business. Both these Toms are substantially the same today as when we were married in 1948.

Tom$_3$, the father, is different. He wasn't born until 1950. I watched his birth with some pity, a little resentment, and a strong upsurge of motherly feeling toward him. He was almost as bewildered as was Tom, Jr. But, whereas the baby took strong hold in his new world, Tom$_3$ stood at the edge of fatherhood for a while, until I felt like taking him by the ear with an old-fashioned motherly grip and leading him to his son. Today, though, Tom$_3$ bears little resemblance to Tom$_{3\,(1950)}$. Actually, I feel a little shut out now when Tom$_3$ and Tom, Jr., are especially close, as when they're planning a fishing trip.

Tom$_4$, the fisherman, is a loathsome person—an adolescent, self-centered, unpredictable, thoughtless, utterly selfish braggart. Yesterday, he bought Junior a fishing rod.

"Pampering him," I said. "He needs other things so much more—his teeth straightened, summer camp."

"He needs a fishing rod," Tom$_4$ said.

"You're teaching him to become a thoughtless husband," I charged.

"Oh, I don't know," Tom$_4$ said. "Maybe he'll marry a girl who likes to fish."

That stopped me for a minute. I'd never thought of there being such girls. Perhaps Tom$_4$ was disappointed in me. I was just wondering what I could wear on a fishing trip when Tom$_4$ shattered my good intentions by saying, "A fishing trip for Junior is a good deal more important than a permanent for Nancy."

This came as a surprise. Tom$_{3b}$ as father of Nancy was not the Tom$_{3a}$ father of Junior. Usually Nancy could get away with anything. At five, she had known better than to cut up the evening paper before her father had seen it, but Tom$_{3b}$ had just laughed. He was certainly no relation to the husband-at-breakfast Tom who would scream if his wife got the pages of the morning paper out of place. He'd always been a little too indulgent with Nancy and too severe with Junior, but now he was begrudging Nancy a permanent.

"Do you want to have an unattractive daughter?" I asked, but Tom$_{3b}$ wasn't there. Tom$_5$, the amateur plumber and ardent do-it-yourselfer, had taken over. He was at the sink fussing with the garbage disposer, promising to fix it Saturday.

"Why don't you buy Nancy a fishing rod?" I suggested.

And who looked back at me? Tom$_6$ the bewildered husband. "Are you joking?" he asked.

"Certainly not," I said indignantly. "You should train her to make a good wife."

Tom$_6$ laughed. Then Tom$_7$ took over. Tom$_7$ is the appreciative husband. He's a very determined fellow. He laughs loud and long.

"Very funny," he said. "I always appreciate your sense of humor. I always tell my—"

"Don't overdo it," I snarled. "I'm not being funny. Maybe she should have a fishing rod."

"She has her permanent," Tom$_8$ said with a laugh. "When she gets a little older she can fish with that." Tom$_8$ is a clown, the life of the party. Some day I may murder him.

I poured the coffee and resisted the temptation to drip a little on Tom$_8$'s balding head. "Polygamy's wonderful," I murmured with a sigh, as I set the coffee pot down.

Tom$_7$ looked at me with concern. "Have you seen your doctor lately?" he asked.

"No, there are enough men in my life," I answered. But Tom$_2$ was looking at his watch. I realized that my remark had been wasted. Not one of my husbands was listening.

Mary Graham Lund

transitory nature of many objects and behaviors. For example, a teacher might write as an evaluation of a student: "Susan $_{MAY 12}$ had difficulty cooperating with her classmates." Although the actual device of subscripting is awkward in writing and impractical in conversation, the idea it represents can still be used. Instead of saying, "I'm shy," a more accurate statement might be "I haven't approached any new people since I moved here." The first statement implies that your shyness is an unchangeable trait, rather like your height, while the second one suggests that you are capable of changing.

THE LANGUAGE OF RESPONSIBILITY

Besides providing a way to make the content of a message clear or obscure, language reflects the speaker's willingness to take responsibility for his or her beliefs and feelings. This acceptance or rejection of responsibility says a great deal about the speaker, and can shape the tone of a relationship. To see how, read on.

"IT" STATEMENTS   Notice the difference between the sentences of each set:

"It bothers me when you're late."
"I'm worried when you're late.

"It's nice to see you."
"I'm glad to see you."

"It's a boring class."
"I'm bored in the class."

As their name implies, **"it" statements** replace the personal pronoun "I" with the less immediate word "it." By contrast, **"I" language** clearly identifies the speaker as the source of a message. Communicators who use "it" statements avoid responsibility for ownership of a message, instead attributing it to some unidentified source. This habit isn't just imprecise; more important, it is an unconscious way to avoid taking a position. You can begin to appreciate the increased directness of "I" language by trying to use it instead of the less direct and more evasive "it" statements in your own conversations.

"BUT" STATEMENTS   Statements that take the form "X-but-Y" can be confusing. A closer look at the **"but" statement** explains why. In each sentence, the word "but" cancels the thought that precedes it:

"You're really a great person, but I think we ought to stop seeing each other."

"You've done good work for us, but we're going to have to let you go."

"This paper has some good ideas, but I'm giving it a D grade because it's late."

"My hand is doing this movement . . ."

"Is it *doing the movement?"*

"I am moving my hand like this . . . and now the thought comes to me that . . ."

"The thought 'comes' to you?"

"I have the thought."

"You have *it?"*

"I think. Yes. I think that I use 'it' very much, and I am glad that by noticing it I can bring it all back to me."

"Bring it back?"

"Bring myself back. I feel thankful for this."

"This?"

"Your idea about the 'it.'"

"My idea?"

"I feel thankful towards you."

Claudio Naranjo

These "buts" often are a strategy for wrapping the speaker's real but unpleasant message between more palatable ideas in a "psychological sandwich." This approach can be a face-saving strategy worth using at times. When the goal is to be absolutely clear, however, the most responsible approach can be to deliver the central idea without the distractions that can come with "but" statements.

QUESTIONS   Some questions are sincere requests for information. At other times, though, questions are a linguistic way to avoid making a declaration. "What are we having for dinner?" may hide the statement "I want to eat out" or "I want to get a pizza."

"How many textbooks are assigned in that class?" may hide the statement "I'm afraid to get into a class with too much reading."

"Are you doing anything tonight?" can be a less risky way of saying "I want to go out with you tonight."

"Do you love me?" safely replaces the statement "I love you," which may be too embarrassing, too intimate, or too threatening to say directly.

Sometimes being indirect can be a tactful way to approach a topic that would be difficult to address head on. When used unnecessarily, though, it can be a way to avoid speaking for yourself.

"I" AND "YOU" LANGUAGE   We've already seen that "I" language is a way of accepting responsibility for a message. **"You" language** is quite different. It expresses a judgment of the other person. Notice how each of the following statements implies that the subject of the complaint is doing something wrong:

"You left this place a mess!"

"You didn't keep your promise!"

"You're really crude sometimes!"

Despite its name, "you" language doesn't have to contain the pronoun "you," which is often implied rather than stated outright:

"That was a stupid joke!" ["Your jokes are stupid."]

"Don't be so critical!" ["You're too negative."]

"Mind your own business!" ["You're too nosy."]

Whether the judgment is stated outright or implied, it's easy to see why "you" language can arouse defensiveness. A "you" statement implies that the speaker is qualified to judge the target—not an idea that most listeners are willing to accept, even when the evaluation is correct.

Fortunately, "I" language provides a more accurate and less provocative way to express a complaint.[24] "I" language shows that the speaker takes responsibility for the gripe by describing his or her reaction to the other's behavior without making any judgments about its worth. A complete "I" statement has three parts: It describes (1) the other person's behavior, (2) your feelings, and (3) the consequences the other's behavior has for you:

When you point one accusing finger at someone, three of your own fingers point back at you.

Lous Nizer

"I get embarrassed [Feeling] when you talk about my bad grades in front of our friends [Behavior]. I'm afraid they'll think I'm stupid [Consequence]."

"When you didn't pick me up on time this morning [Behavior] I was late for class and I wound up getting chewed out by the professor [Consequences]. That's why I got so mad [Feeling]."

"I haven't been very affectionate [Consequence] because you've hardly spent any time with me in the past few weeks [Behavior]. I'm confused [Feeling] about how you feel about me."

When the chances of being misunderstood or getting a defensive reaction are high, it's a good idea to include all three elements in your "I" message. In some cases, however, only one or two of them will get the job done:

"I went to a lot of trouble fixing this dinner, and now it's cold. Of course I'm mad!" [The behavior is obvious.]

"I'm worried because you haven't called me up." ["Worried" is both a feeling and a consequence.]

Even the best "I" statement won't work unless it's delivered in the right way. If your words are nonjudgmental but your tone of voice, facial expression, and posture all send "you" messages, a defensive response is likely to follow. The best way to make sure your actions match your words is to remind yourself before speaking that your goal is to explain how the other's behavior affects you—not to act like a judge and jury.

Advantages of "I" Language   Using "I" language has several benefits, both for you and for the recipients: reducing defensiveness, and increasing honesty and information.

1. *Defense Reduction* Others are more likely to accept your message when it's delivered in "I" language than when you make judgmental "you" statements. Even accurate "you" statements ("you're late," "you broke your promise") are hard to take. By contrast, "I" statements aren't a direct attack on the recipient. Since they describe how the speaker feels, they are easier to accept without justification. This doesn't mean using "I" language will *eliminate* defensiveness, but it will almost certainly *reduce* it.

2. *Honesty* Even though they are kinder than "you" language, "I" statements are just as honest. They let you speak your mind, sharing what bothers you. They aren't artificially "nice" or watered down to avoid displeasing the other person. In fact, because "I" statements are easier on the recipient, you are more likely to use them when you might be reluctant to blurt out an accusing "you" message.

3. *Completeness* "I" statements deliver more information than "you" messages. Instead of making the other person guess about what's bothering you, they describe the other person's behavior. "I" statements also describe how the other's behavior affects you and how you are feeling—much more information than most "you" messages.

Problems with "I" Language   Some readers have reservations about using "I" language, despite its theoretical appeal. The best way to overcome questions about this communication skill is to answer them.

1. *"I get too angry to use 'I' language."* It's true that when you're angry the most likely reaction is to lash out with a judgmental "you" message. But it's probably smarter to keep quiet until you've thought about the consequences of what you might say than to blurt out something you'll regret later. It's also important to note that there's plenty of room for expressing anger with "I" language. It's just that you own the feeling as yours ("You bet I'm mad at you!") instead of distorting it into an attack ("That was a stupid thing to do!").

2. *"Even with 'I' language, the other person gets defensive."* Like every communication tool described in this book, "I" language won't always work. You may be so upset or irritated that your judgmental feelings contradict your words. Even if you deliver a perfectly worded "I" statement with total sincerity, the other person might be so defensive or uncooperative that nothing you say will make matters better. But using "I" language will almost certainly *improve* your chances for success, with little risk that this approach will make matters worse.

3. *"'I' language sounds artificial."* "That's not the way I talk," some people object. Much of the awkwardness that comes with first

Communication Transcript

"I" AND "YOU" LANGUAGE ON THE JOB

For some time, Rebecca has been frustrated by her fellow worker Tom's frequent absences from the job. She hasn't spoken up because she likes Tom, and also because she doesn't want to sound like a complainer. Lately, though, Tom's absences have become longer and more frequent. Today he extended his half-hour lunch an extra forty-five minutes. When he returns to the office, Rebecca confronts him with her gripe using "you" language.

Rebecca Where have you been? You were due back at 12:30, and it's almost 1:30 now.

Tom *(Surprised by Rebecca's angry tone, which she has never used before with him)* I had a few errands to run. What's the problem?

Rebecca We all have errands to run, Tom. But it's not fair for you to do yours on company time.

Tom *(Feeling defensive after hearing Rebecca's accusation)* I don't see why you have to worry about how I do my job. Beth *(their boss)* hasn't complained, so why should you worry?

Rebecca Beth hasn't complained because all of us have been covering for you. You should appreciate what a tight spot we're in, making excuses every time you come in late or leave early. *(Again, Rebecca uses "you" language to tell Tom how he should*

think and act.)

Tom *(Now too defensive to consider Rebecca's concerns)* Hey, I thought we all covered for one another here. What about the time last year when I worked late for a week so you could go to your cousin's wedding in San Antonio?

Rebecca That's different! Nobody was lying then. When you take off, I have to make up stories about where you are. You're putting me in a very difficult spot, Tom, and it's not fair. You can't count on me to keep covering for you.

Tom *(Feeling guilty, but too angry from Rebecca's judgments and threat to acknowledge his mistakes)* Fine. I'll never ask you for a favor again. Sorry to put you out.

Rebecca may have succeeded in reducing Tom's lateness, but her choice of "you" language left him feeling defensive and angry. The climate in the office is likely to be more strained—hardly the outcome Rebecca was seeking. Notice how she could have handled the same issue using "I" language to describe her problem instead of blaming Tom.

Rebecca Tom, I need to talk to you about a problem. *Notice how Rebecca identifies the problem as hers, instead of attacking Tom.)*

Tom What's up?

Rebecca You know how you come in late to work sometimes or take long lunch hours?

Tom *(Sensing trouble ahead, and sounding wary)* Yeah?

Rebecca Well, I need to tell you that it's putting me in a tight spot. *(Rebecca describes the problem in behavioral terms, and then goes on to express her feeling.)* When Beth asks where you are, I don't want to say you're not here because that might get you in trouble. So sometimes I make excuses or even lie. But Beth is sounding suspicious of my excuses, and I'm worried about that.

Tom *Feeling defensive because he knows he's guilty, but also sympathetic to Rebecca's position)* I don't want you to get in trouble. It's just that I've got to take care of a lot of personal business.

Rebecca I know, Tom. I just want you to understand that it's getting impossible for me to cover for you.

Tom Yeah, okay. Thanks for helping out.

Notice how "I" language made it possible for Rebecca to confront Tom honestly, but without blaming or attacking him personally. Even if Tom doesn't change, Rebecca has gotten the problem off her chest, and she can feel proud that she did so in a way that didn't sound ugly or annoying.

using "I" language is due to its unfamiliarity. As you become more comfortable making "I" statements they will sound more and more natural—and become more and more effective.

One of the best ways to overcome your initial awkwardness is to practice making "I" statements in a safe way: by trying them out in a class, writing them in letters, and delivering them to receptive people on relatively minor issues. After your skill and confidence have grown, you will be ready to tackle really challenging situations in a way that sounds natural and sincere.

SKILL BUILDER

PRACTICING "I" LANGUAGE

You can develop your skill at delivering "I" messages by following these steps:

1. Visualize situations in your life when you might have sent each of the following messages:

   You're not telling me the truth!
   You only think of yourself!
   Don't be so touchy!
   Quit fooling around!
   You don't understand a word I'm saying!

2. Write alternatives to each statement using "I" language.

3. Think of three "you" statements you could make to people in your life. Transform each of these statements into "I" language and rehearse them with a classmate.

"WE" LANGUAGE   Despite its obvious advantages, even the best constructed and delivered "I" messages won't always succeed. As author Thomas Gordon points out, "Nobody welcomes hearing that his behavior is causing someone a problem, no matter how the message is phrased."[25] For this reason, Gordon points out that "I" statements can leave the recipient feeling "hurt, sorry, surprised, embarrassed, defensive, argumentative, or even tearful." Furthermore, "I" language in large doses can start to sound egotistical. Research shows that self-absorbed people, also known as "conversational narcissists," can be identified by their constant use of first-person singular pronouns.[26] For this reason, "I" language works best in moderation.

One way to avoid overuse of "I" statements is to consider the pronoun "we." **"We" statements** imply that the issue is the concern and responsibility of both the speaker and receiver of a message. Consider a few examples:

"We need to figure out a budget that doesn't bankrupt us."

"I think we have a problem. We can't seem to talk about money without fighting."

"We aren't doing a very good job of keeping the place clean, are we?"

It's easy to see how "we" language can help build a constructive climate. Besides being immediate, it suggests a kind of "we're in this together" orientation. People who use first-person-plural pronouns signal their closeness, commonality, and cohesiveness with others.[27] On the other hand, "we" statements aren't always appropriate. Sometimes using this pronoun sounds presumptuous, because it suggests you are speaking for the other person as well as yourself. It's easy to imagine someone responding to your statement "We have a problem . . . " by saying "Maybe *you* have a problem, but don't tell me *I* do!"

Given the pros and cons of both "I" and "we" language, what advice can we give about the most effective pronouns to use in interpersonal communication? Researchers have found that I/We combinations (for example, "I think that we . . . " or "I would like to see us . . . ") have a good chance of being received favorably.[28] Because too much of any pronoun comes across as inappropriate, combining pronouns is generally a good idea. If your "I" language reflects your position without being overly self-absorbed, your "you" language shows concern for others without judging them, and your "we" language includes others without speaking for them, you will probably come as close as possible to the ideal use of pronouns. Table 5–4 summarizes the advantages and drawbacks of each type of speech, and offers suggestions for approaches that have a good chance of success.

DISRUPTIVE LANGUAGE

Not all linguistic problems come from misunderstandings. Sometimes people understand one another perfectly and still wind up in a conflict. Of course, not all disagreements can, or should be, avoided. But eliminating three bad linguistic habits from your communication repertoire can minimize the kind of clashes that don't need to happen, allowing you to save your energy for the unavoidable and important struggles.

FACT-OPINION CONFUSION   Factual statements are claims that can be verified as true or false. By contrast, opinion statements are based on the speaker's beliefs. Unlike matters of fact, they can never be proved or disproved. Consider a few examples of the difference between factual and opinion statements:

Fact	*Opinion*
It rains more in Seattle than in Portland.	The climate in Portland is better than in Seattle.
Kareem Abdul-Jabbar is the all-time leading scorer in the National Basketball Association.	Kareem is the greatest basketball player in the history of the game.
Per-capita income in the United States is lower than in several other countries.	The United States is not the best model of economic success in the world.

T A B L E 5 – 4   Pronoun Use and Its Effects

PRONOUN	PROS	CONS	RECOMMENDATIONS
"I" language	Takes responsibility for personal thoughts, feelings, and wants. Less defense-provoking than "you" language.	Can be perceived as egotistical, narcissistic, and self-absorbed.	Use "I" messages when other person doesn't perceive a problem. Combine "I" with "we" language.
"We" language	Signals inclusion, immediacy, cohesiveness, and commitment.	Can speak improperly for others.	Combine with "I" language. Use in group settings to enhance unity. Avoid when expressing personal thoughts, feelings and wants.
"You" language		Can sound evaluative and judgmental.	Use "I" language during - confrontations.

When factual and opinion statements are set side by side like this, the difference between them is clear. In everyday conversation, however, we often present our opinions as if they were facts, and in doing so we invite an unnecessary argument. For example:

- "That was a dumb thing to say!"
- "Spending that much on _____ is a waste of money!"
- "You can't get a fair shake in this country unless you're a white male."

Notice how much less antagonistic each statement would be if it were prefaced by a qualifier such as "In my opinion . . . " or "It seems to me. . . . "

FACT-INFERENCE CONFUSION   Labeling your opinions can go a long way toward relational harmony, but developing this habit won't solve all linguistic problems. Difficulties also arise when we confuse factual statements with inferential statements—conclusions arrived at from an interpretation of evidence.

Arguments often result when we label our inferences as facts:

A: Why are you mad at me?

B: I'm not mad at you. Why have you been so insecure lately?

A: I'm not insecure. It's just that you've been so critical.

B: What do you mean, "critical"? I haven't been critical. . . .

Instead of trying to read the other person's mind, a far better course is to identify the observable behaviors (facts) that have caught your attention and to describe the interpretations (inferences) that you have drawn from them. After describing this train of thought, ask the other person to comment on the accuracy of your interpretation.

"When you didn't return my phone call (fact), I got the idea that you're mad at me (inference). Are you?" (question)

"You've been asking me whether I still love you a lot lately (fact), and that makes me think you're feeling insecure (inference). Is that right?" (question)

EMOTIVE LANGUAGE   **Emotive language** seems to describe something, but really announces the speaker's attitude toward it. If you approve of a friend's round-about approach to a difficult subject, you might call her "tactful"; if you don't like it, you might accuse her of "beating around the bush." Whether the approach is good or bad is more a matter of opinion than of fact, although this difference is obscured by emotive language.

You can appreciate how emotive words are really editorial statements when you consider these examples:

If you approve, say	*If you disapprove, say*
thrifty	cheap
traditional	old-fashioned
extrovert	loudmouth
cautious	coward
progressive	radical
information	propaganda
military victory	massacre
eccentric	crazy

Using emotive labels can have ugly consequences. Although experimental subjects who heard a derogatory label used against a member of a minority group expressed annoyance at this sort of slur, the negative emotional terms did have an impact.[29] Not only did the unwitting subjects rate the minority individual's competence lower when that person performed poorly, they also found fault with others who associated socially with that minority person—even members of the subject's own ethnic group.

The best way to avoid arguments involving emotive words is to describe the person, thing, or idea you are discussing in neutral terms,

"Sorry, Chief, but of course I didn't mean 'bimbo' in the pejorative sense."

DRAWING BY LORENZ; ©1987 THE NEW YORKER MAGAZINE, INC.

and to label your opinions as such. Instead of saying "I wish you'd quit making those sexist remarks" say, "I really don't like it when you call us 'girls' instead of 'women.'" Not only are nonemotive statements more accurate, they have a much better chance of being well received by others.

INVITATION TO INSIGHT

CONJUGATING "IRREGULAR VERBS"

Here's a way to see how emotive words work. According to S.I. Hayakawa, the idea of "conjugating irregular verbs" this way originated with Bertrand Russell. The technique is simple: Just take an action or personality trait, and show how it can be viewed either favorably or unfavorably, according to the label we give it. For example:

    I'm casual.
    You're a little careless.
    He's a slob.
Or try this one:
    I'm thrifty.
    You're money conscious.
    He's a tightwad.

1. Now try a few conjugations yourself, using the following statements:

   a. I'm tactful.　　　　　　d. I'm relaxed.
   b. I'm conservative.　　　 e. My child is high-spirited.
   c. I'm quiet.　　　　　　　f. I have a lot of self-pride.

2. Now recall at least two situations in which you used an emotive word as if it were a description of fact and not an opinion. A good way to remember these situations is to think of a recent argument you had and imagine how the other people involved might have described it. How would their words differ from yours?

✤ GENDER AND LANGUAGE

So far we have discussed language as if it were identical for both sexes. In many cases, however, there are significant differences between the way men and women speak.

CONTENT

Although there is a great deal of variation within each gender, on the average men and women discuss a surprisingly different range of topics. The first research on conversational topics was conducted over seventy years ago. Despite the changes in male and female roles since then, the results of several studies are remarkably similar.[30] In these surveys, women and men ranging in age from seventeen to eighty described the range of topics each discussed with friends of the same sex. Certain subjects were common to both men and women: work, movies, and television proved to be frequent topics for both groups. Both men and women reserved discussions of sex and sexuality for members of the same sex. The differences between men and women were more striking than the similarities. Female friends spent much more time discussing personal and domestic subjects, relationship problems, family, health and reproductive matters, weight, food and clothing, men, and other women. Men, on the other hand, were more likely to discuss music, current events, sports, business, and other men. Both men and women were equally likely to discuss personal

© David Sipress from The Cartoon Bank

appearance, sex, and dating in same-sex conversations. True to one common stereotype, women are more likely to gossip about close friends and family. By contrast, men spent more time gossiping about sports figures and media personalities. Women's gossip was no more derogatory than men's.

These differences can lead to frustration when men and women try to converse with one another. Researchers report that "trivial" is the word often used by both men and women to describe topics discussed by the opposite sex. "I want to talk about important things," a woman might say, "like how we're getting along. All he wants to do is talk about the news or what we'll do this weekend."

REASONS FOR COMMUNICATING

Men and women, at least in the dominant cultures of the United States and Canada, often use language in different ways for different purposes. As a group, women are more inclined than men to use conversation to establish and maintain relationships with others. In fact, communication researcher Julia Wood flatly states that "for women, talk *is* the essence of relationships."[31] When a group of women were surveyed to find out what kinds of satisfaction they gained from talking with their friends, the most common theme mentioned was a feeling of empathy—"To know you're not alone," as some put it.[32] Whereas men commonly described same-sex conversations as something they *liked*, females characterized their woman-to-woman talks as a kind of contact they *needed*.

Because they use conversation to pursue social needs, women typically use statements showing support for the other person, demonstrations of equality, and efforts to keep the conversation going. With these goals, it's not surprising that traditionally female speech often contains statements of sympathy and empathy: "I've felt just like that myself," "The same thing happened to me!" Women are also inclined to ask lots of questions that invite the other person to share information: "How did you feel about that?" "What did you do next?" The importance of nurturing a relationship also explains why female speech is often somewhat powerless and tentative. Saying "This is just my opinion . . . " is less likely to put off a conversational partner than a more definite "Here's what I think . . . "

The greater frequency of female conversations reflects their importance. Nearly 50 percent of the women surveyed said they called friends at least once a week just to talk, whereas less than half as many men did so. In fact, 40 percent of the men surveyed reported that they never called another man just to chat.

Men's speech is often driven by quite different goals than women's speech. Men are more likely to use language to accomplish the job at hand than to nourish relationships. This explains why men are less likely than women to disclose their vulnerabilities, which would be a sign of weakness. When someone is sharing a problem, instead of empathizing men are prone to offer advice: "That's nothing to worry about . . . " "Here's what you need to do. . . . " Besides taking care of business, men are more likely than women to use conversations to exert control, preserve their independence, and enhance their status. This explains why men are more prone to dominate conversations and one-up their partners. Men interrupt their conversational partners to assert their own experiences or point of view. (Women interrupt too, but they usually do so to offer support: quite a different goal.) Just because male talk is competitive doesn't mean it's not enjoyable. Men often regard talk as a kind of game: When researchers asked men what they liked best about their all-male talk, the most frequent answer was its ease.[33] Another common theme was appreciation of the practical value of conversation: new ways to solve problems. Men also mentioned enjoying the humor and rapid pace that characterized their all-male conversations.

Differences like these begin early in childhood. Sociolinguist Deborah Tannen summarizes a variety of studies showing that boys use talk to assert control over one another, while girls' conversations are aimed at maintaining harmony.[34] Transcripts of conversations between preschoolers aged two to five showed that girls are far more cooperative than boys.[35] They preceded their proposals for action by saying "let's," as in "Let's go find some" or "Let's turn back." By contrast, boys gave orders like "Lie down" or "Gimme your arm."

CONVERSATIONAL STYLE

Women behave differently in conversations than do men.[36] For example, although both men and women use expletives, men swear more than women.[37] Women ask more questions in mixed-sex conversations than do men—nearly three times as many, according to one study. Other research has revealed that in mixed-sex conversations, men interrupt women far more than the other way around. Some theorists have argued that differences like these result in women's speech that is less powerful and more emotional than men's. Research has supported these theories—at least in some cases. Even when clues about the speakers' sex were edited out, raters found clear differences between transcripts of male and female speech. In one study women's talk was judged more aesthetic, while men were seen as more dynamic, aggressive, and strong. In another, male job applicants were rated more fluent, active, confident, and effective than females.

Other studies have revealed that men and women behave differently in certain conversational settings. For example, in mixed-sex dyads men talk longer than women, while in same-sex situations women speak for a longer time. In larger groups, men talk more, while in smaller settings women do more of the speaking. In same-sex conversations there are other differences between men and women: Females use more questions, justifiers, intensive adverbs, personal pronouns, and adverbials. Men use more directives, interruptions, and filler words to begin sentences.[38]

Consider the marriage of a man who has had most of his conversations with other men, to a woman who has had most of hers with other women. . . . He is used to fast-paced conversations that typically stay on the surface with respect to emotions, that often enable him to get practical tips or offer them to others and that are usually pragmatic or fun. She is used to conversations that, while practical and fun too, are also a major source of emotional support, self-understanding and the understanding of others. Becoming intimate with a man, the woman may finally start expressing her concerns to him as she might to a close friend. But she may find, to her dismay, that his responses are all wrong. Instead of making her feel better, he makes her feel worse. The problem is that he tends to be direct and practical, whereas what she wants more than anything else is an empathetic listener. Used to years of such responses from close friends, a woman is likely to be surprised and angered by her husband's immediate "Here's what ya do. . . ."

Mark Sherman and Adelaide Haas

Given these differences, it's easy to wonder how men and women manage to communicate with one another at all. One reason cross-sex conversations do run smoothly is because women accommodate to the topics men raise. Both men and women regard topics introduced by women as tentative, whereas topics that men bring up are more likely to be pursued. Thus, women seem to grease the wheels of conversation by doing more work than men in maintaining conversations. A complementary difference between men and women also promotes cross-sex conversations: Men are more likely to talk about themselves with women than with other men; and since women are willing to adapt to this topic, conversations are likely to run smoothly, if one-sidedly.

An accommodating style isn't always a disadvantage for women. One study revealed that females who spoke tentatively were actually more influential with men than those who used more powerful speech.[39] On the other hand, this tentative style was less effective in persuading women. (Language use had no effect on men's persuasiveness.) This research suggests that women who are willing and able to be flexible in their approach can persuade both other women and men . . . as long as they are not dealing with a mixed-sex audience.

NONGENDER VARIABLES

Despite the differences in the way men and women speak, the link between gender and language use isn't as clear-cut as it might seem. A large number of studies have found no significant difference between male and female speech in areas such as use of profanity, use of qualifiers such as "I guess" or "This is just my opinion," tag questions, and vocal fluency. Some on-the-job research shows that male and female supervisors in similar positions behave the same way and are equally effective. Other studies, however, have found differences between the style of men and women. Female managers were rated as providing more information, putting more emphasis on happy interpersonal relationships, and being more encouraging, receptive to new ideas, concerned, and attentive. Male managers were rated as being more dominant, direct, and quick to challenge. The researchers concluded that "male and female managers [exerted] leadership in their own distinct fashions." They also argued that females may be superior managers because their verbal communication promotes more job satisfaction.

A growing body of research explains some of the apparent contradictions between the similarities and differences between male and female speech. Research has revealed other factors that influence language use as much or more than sex.[40] For example, social philosophy plays a role. Feminist wives talk longer than their partners, while nonfeminist wives speak less than their husbands. Orientation toward problem-solving also plays a role in conversational style. The cooperative or competitive orientations of speakers has more influence on how they interacted than does their gender.

The speaker's occupation also influences speaking style. For example, male day-care teachers' speech to their students resembles the language of female teachers more closely than it resembles the language of fathers at home. Overall, doctors interrupt their patients more often than the reverse, although male patients do interrupt female physicians more often than their male counterparts. A close study of trial transcripts showed that the speaker's experience on the witness stand and occupation had more to do with language use than did gender. If women generally use "powerless" language, this fact probably reflects their historical social role in society at large.

SEX ROLES

Why is the research on sex differences so confusing? In some cases male and female speech seems identical, while other studies reveal important differences. As we've already said, one reason for the confusion is that other factors besides biological sex influence the way people speak: the setting in which conversation takes place, the expertise of the speakers, their social roles (husband/wife, boss/employee, and so on). Also, female roles are changing so rapidly that many women simply don't use the conversational styles that characterized their older sisters and mothers. But in addition to these factors, another powerful force that influences the way individual men and women speak is their **sex role**—the social orientation that governs behavior, rather than the biological gender. Researchers have identified three sex roles: masculine, feminine, and androgynous. These sex types don't always line up neatly with biological differ-

"Talk to me, Alice. I speak woman."

DRAWING BY M. STEVENS. ©1992 THE NEW YORKER MAGAZINE, INC.

ences. There are "masculine" females, "feminine" males, and androgynous communicators who combine traditionally masculine and feminine characteristics.

Research shows that linguistic differences are often a function of these sex roles more than the speaker's biological sex. Masculine sex-type communicators—whether male or female—use more dominant language than either feminine or androgynous speakers. Feminine communicators have the most submissive speaking style, while androgynous speakers fall between these extremes. When two masculine communicators are in a conversation, they often engage in a one-up battle for dominance, responding to the other's bid for control with a counterattempt to dominate the relationship. Feminine sex-type speakers are less predictable. They use dominance, submission, and equivalent behavior in an almost random fashion. Androgynous individuals are more predictable: They most frequently meet another's bid for dominance with a symmetrical attempt at control, but then move quickly toward an equivalent relationship.

All this information suggests that, when it comes to communicating, "masculinity" and "femininity" are culturally recognized sex roles, and not biological traits. Research certainly suggests that neither a stereotypically male or female style is the best choice. For example, one study showed that a "mixed gender strategy" that balanced the traditionally male, task-oriented approach with the stereotypically feminine, relationship-oriented approach received the highest marks by both male and female respondents.[41] As opportunities for men and women become more equable, we can expect that the differences between male and female use of language will become smaller.

On the television screen, a teacher of first-graders who has just won a national award is describing her way of teaching. "You take each child where you find him," she says. "You watch to see what he's interested in, and then you build on his interests."

A five-year-old looking at the program asks her mother, "Do only boys go to that school?"

"No," her mother begins, "she's talking about girls too, but—"

But what? The teacher being interviewed on television is speaking correct English. What can the mother tell her daughter about why a child, in any generalization, is always *he* rather than *she?* How does a five-year-old comprehend the generic personal pronoun?

The effect on personality development of this one part of speech was recognized by thoughtful people long before the present assault on the English language by the forces of Women's Liberation. Fifteen years ago, Lynn T. White, then president of Mills College, wrote:

The grammar of English dictates that when a referent is either of indeterminate sex or both sexes, it shall be considered masculine. The penetration of this habit of language into the minds of little girls as they grow up to be women is more profound than most people, including most women, have recognized: for it implies that personality is really a male attribute, and that women are a human sub-species. . . . It would be a miracle if a girl-baby, learning to use the symbols of

our tongue, could escape some wound to her self-respect: whereas a boy-baby's ego is bolstered by the pattern of our language.

Now that our language has begun to respond to the justice of Women's Liberation, a lot of people apparently are trying to kick the habit of using *he* when they mean anyone, male or female. In fact, there is mounting evidence that a major renovation of the language is in progress with respect to this pronoun. It is especially noticeable in the speeches of politicians up for election: "And as for every citizen who pays taxes, I say that he or she deserves an accounting!" A variation of the tandem form is also cropping up in print, like the copy on a coupon that offers the bearer a 20 percent saving on "the cost of his/her meal." A writer in the New York newspaper *The Village Voice* adopts the same form to comment "that every artist of major stature is actually a school in him/herself."

Adding the feminine pronoun to the masculine whenever the generic form is called for may be politically smart and morally right, but the result is often awkward.

Some of the devices used to get around the problem are even less acceptable, at least to grammarians. It is one thing for a student to announce in assembly that "Anybody can join the Glee Club as long as they can carry a tune," but when this patchwork solution begins to appear in print, the language is in trouble. In blatant defiance of every teacher of freshman English, a full-page advertisement in *The New York Times* for its college and school subscription service begins with this headline: "If someone you know is attending one of these colleges, here's something they should know that can save them money." Although the grammatical inconsistency of the *Times*'s claim offends the ear—especially since "they" in the headline can refer only to "colleges"—the alternatives would present insurmountable problems for the writer. For example, the sentence might read, "If someone you know . . . etc., here's something he or she should know that can save

him/her money." Or, in order to keep the plural subject in the second clause, the writer might have begun, "If several people you know are attending one or more of these colleges. . . . " But by that time will the reader still care?

In the long run, the problem of the generic personal pronoun is a problem of the status of women. But it is more immediately a matter of common sense and clear communication. Absurd examples of the burdens now placed upon masculine pronouns pop up everywhere. "The next time you meet a handicapped person, don't make up your mind about him in advance," admonishes a radio public service announcement. A medical school bulletin, apparently caught by surprise, reports that a certain scholarship given annually "to a student of unquestioned ability and character who has completed his first year" was awarded to one Barbara Kinder.

Since there is no way in English to solve problems like these with felicity and grace, it is becoming obvious that what we need is a new singular personal pronoun that is truly generic: a common-gender pronoun. Several have been proposed, but so far none appears to have the transparently logical relationship to existing pronouns that is necessary if a new word is to gain wide acceptance. Perhaps a clue to the solution is to be found in people's persistent use of *they* as a singular pronoun.

In the plural forms, both genders are included in one word: *They* can refer to males or females or a mixed group. So why not derive the needed singular common-gender pronouns from the plural? *They, their,* and *them* suggest *tey, ter,* and *tem*. With its inflected forms pronounced to rhyme with the existing plural forms, the new word would join the family of third person pronouns as shown in the box. . . .

Someone will probably object to the idea of a common-gender pronoun in the mistaken belief that it is a neuter form and therefore underrates sexual differences. The opposite is true. Once *tey* or a similar word is adopted, *he* can become exclusively masculine, just as *she* is now exclusively feminine. The new pronoun will thus accentuate the significant and valuable differences between females and males—those of reproductive function and form—while affirming the essential unity and equality of the two sexes within the species.

Language constantly evolves in response to need. It is groping today for ways to accommodate the new recognition of women as full-fledged members of the human race. If the new pronoun helps anyone toward that end, *tey* should be free to adopt it.

If anyone objects, it is certainly *ter* right—but in that case let *tem* come up with a better solution.

Casey Miller and Kate Swift

SINGULAR	PLURAL	
Distinct Gender	*Common Gender*	*Common Gender*
Nominative *he* and *she*	*tey*	*they*
Possessive *his* and *her* (or *hers*)	*ter* (or *ters*)	*their* (or *theirs*)
Objective *him* and *her*	*tem*	*them*

✜ LANGUAGE AND CULTURE

Anyone who has tried to translate ideas from one language to another knows that conveying the same meaning isn't always easy.[42] Sometimes the results of a bungled translation can be amusing. For example, the American manufacturers of Pet milk unknowingly introduced their product in French-speaking markets without realizing that the word *pet* in French means "to break wind."[43] Likewise, the English-speaking representative of a U.S. soft drink manufacturer naively drew laughs from Mexican customers when she offered free samples of Fresca soda pop. In Mexican slang the word *fresca* means "lesbian."

Even choosing the right words during translation won't guarantee that non-native speakers will use an unfamiliar language correctly. For example, Japanese insurance companies warn their policy holders who are visiting the United States to avoid their cultural tendency to say "excuse me" or "I'm sorry" if they are involved in a traffic accident.[44] In Japan, apologizing is a traditional way to express goodwill and maintain social harmony, even if the person offering the apology is not at fault. But in the United States an apology can be taken as an admission of guilt, and result in Japanese tourists being held accountable for accidents in which they may not be responsible.

Difficult as it may be, translation is only a small part of the differences in communication between members of different cultures. Differences in the way language is used and the very world view that a language creates make communicating across cultures a challenging task.

VERBAL COMMUNICATION STYLES

Using language is more than just choosing a particular group of words to convey an idea. Each language has its own unique style that distinguishes it from others. Matters like the amount of formality or informality, precision or vagueness, and brevity or detail are major ingredients in speaking competently. And when a communicator tries to use the verbal style from one culture in a different one, problems are likely to arise.[45]

One way in which verbal styles vary is in their *directness.* Anthropologist Edward Hall identified two distinct cultural ways of using language.[46] **Low-context cultures** use language primarily to express thoughts, feelings, and ideas as clearly and logically as possible. Low-context communicators look for the meaning of a statement in the words spoken. By contrast, **high-context cultures** value language as a way to maintain social harmony. Rather than upset others by speaking clearly, communicators in these societies learn to discover meaning from the context in which a message is delivered: the nonverbal behaviors of the speaker, the history of the relationship, and the general social rules that govern interaction between people. Table 5–5 summarizes some key differences between the way low- and high-context cultures use language.

North American culture falls toward the low-context end of the scale. Residents of the United States and Canada value straight talk and grow impatient with "beating around the bush." By contrast, most Asian and Middle-Eastern cultures fit the high-context pattern. In many Asian cultures, for example, maintaining harmony is important, and so communicators will avoid speaking clearly if that would threaten another person's face. For this reason, Japanese or Koreans are less likely than Americans to offer a clear "no" to an undesirable request. Instead they would probably use roundabout expressions like "I agree with you in principle, but . . . " or "I sympathize with you. . . . "

The same sort of clash between directness and indirectness can aggravate problems between straight-talking, low-context Israelis who value speaking clearly and Arabs, whose high-context culture stresses smooth interaction. It's easy to imagine how the clash of cultural styles could lead to misunderstandings and conflicts between Israelis and their Palestinian neighbors. Israelis could view their Arab counterparts as evasive, while the Palestinians could perceive the Israelis as insensitive and blunt.

Even within a single country, subcultures can have different notions about the value of direct speech. For example, Puerto Rican language style resembles high-context Japanese or Korean more than low-context English.[47] As a group, Puerto Ricans value social harmony and avoid confrontation, which leads them to systematically speak in an indirect way to avoid giving offense.

TABLE 5 – 5   Low- and High-Context Communication Styles

LOW CONTEXT	HIGH CONTEXT
Majority of information carried in explicit verbal messages, with less focus on the situational context.	Important information carried in contextual cues (time, place, relationship, situation). Less reliance on explicit verbal messages.
Self-expression valued. Communicators state opinions and desires directly and strive to persuade others to accept their own viewpoint.	Relational harmony valued and maintained by indirect expression of opinions. Communicators abstain from saying "no" directly.
Clear, eloquent speech considered praiseworthy. Verbal fluency admired.	Communicators talk "around" the point, allowing the other to fill in the missing pieces. Ambiguity and use of silence admired.

Another way in which language styles can vary across cultures is whether they are *elaborate* or *succinct*. Speakers of Arabic, for instance, commonly use language that is much more rich and expressive than most communicators who use English. Strong assertions and exaggerations that would sound ridiculous in English are a common feature of Arabic. This contrast in linguistic style can lead to misunderstandings between people from different backgrounds. As one observer put it,

> First, an Arab feels compelled to overassert in almost all types of communication because others expect him [or her] to. If an Arab says exactly what he [or she] means without the expected assertion, other Arabs may still think that he [or she] means the opposite. For example, a simple "no" by a guest to the host's requests to eat more or drink more will not suffice. To convey the meaning that he [or she] is actually full, the guest must keep repeating "no" several times, coupling it with an oath such as "By God" or "I swear to God." Second, an Arab often fails to realize that others, particularly foreigners, may mean exactly what they say even though their language is simple. To the Arabs, a simple "no" may mean the indirectly expressed consent and encouragement of a coquettish woman. On the other hand, a simple consent may mean the rejection of a hypocritical politician.[48]

Succinctness is most extreme in cultures where silence is valued. In many native American cultures, for example, the favored way to handle ambiguous social situations is to remain quiet.[49] When you contrast this silent style to the talkativeness that is common in mainstream American cultures when people first meet, it's easy to imagine how the first encounter between an Apache or Navajo and an Anglo might feel uncomfortable to both people.

Along with differences such as directness and indirectness and elaborate and succinct styles, a third way languages differ from one culture to another involves *formality* and *informality*. The informal approach that characterizes relationships in countries like the United States, Canada, and Australia and the Scandinavian countries is quite different from the great concern for using proper speech in many parts of Asia and Africa. Formality isn't so much a matter of using correct grammar as of defining social position. In Korea, for example, the language reflects the Confucian system of relational hierarchies.[50] It has special vocabularies for different sexes, for different levels of social status, for different degrees of intimacy, and for different types of social occasions. For example, there are different degrees of formality for speaking with old friends, nonacquaintances whose background one knows, and complete strangers. One sign of being a learned person in Korea is the ability to use language that recognizes these relational distinctions. When you contrast these sorts of distinctions with the casual friendliness many North Americans use even when talking with complete strangers, it's easy to see how a Korean might view communicators in the United States as boorish, and how an American might see Koreans as stiff and unfriendly.

LANGUAGE AND WORLD VIEW

Different linguistic styles are important, but there may be even more fundamental differences that separate speakers of various languages. For almost 150 years, some theorists have put forth the notion of **linguistic determinism:** that the world view of a culture is unavoidably shaped and reflected by the language its members speak. The best-known example of linguistic determinism is the notion that Eskimos have a large number of words (estimated at everything from 17 to 100) for what we simply call "snow." Different terms are used to describe conditions like a driving blizzard, crusty ice, and light powder. This example suggests how linguistic determinism operates. The need to survive in an Arctic environment led Eskimos to make distinctions that would be unimportant to residents of warmer environments, and once the language makes these distinctions, speakers are more likely to see the world in ways that match the broader vocabulary.

Even though there is some doubt that Eskimos really have so many words for snow,[51] other examples do seem to support the principle of linguistic determinism.[52] For instance, bilingual speakers seem to think differently when they change languages. In one study, French-Americans were asked to interpret a series of pictures. When they spoke in French, their descriptions were far more romantic and emotional than when they used English to describe the same kinds of images. Likewise, when students in Hong Kong were asked to complete a values test, they expressed more traditional Chinese values when they answered in Cantonese than when they spoke English. In Israel, both Arab and Jewish students saw bigger distinctions between their group and "outsiders" when using their native language than when they spoke in English, a neutral tongue. Examples like these show the power of language to shape cultural identity . . . sometimes for better, and sometimes for worse.

Linguistic influences start early in life. English-speaking parents often label the mischievous pranks of their children as "bad," implying that there is something immoral about acting wild. "Be good!" they are inclined to say. On the other hand, French adults are more likely to say *"Sois sage!"*—"Be wise." The linguistic implication is that misbehaving is an act of foolishness. Swedes would correct the same action with the words *"Var snall!"*—"Be friendly," "Be kind." By contrast, German adults use the command *"Sei artig!"*—literally "Be of your own kind"—in other words, get back in step, conform to your role as a child.[53]

The best-known declaration of linguistic determinism is the **Sapir–Whorf hypothesis,** formulated by Edward Sapir and Benjamin Whorf.[54] Following Sapir's theory, Whorf observed that the language spoken by Hopi Native Americans represents a view of reality that is dramatically different from more familiar tongues. For example, the Hopi language makes no distinction between nouns and verbs. Therefore the people who speak it describe the entire world as being constantly in process. Whereas we use nouns to characterize people or

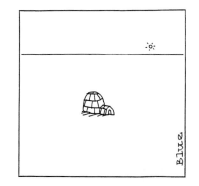

"Yeah . . . I'm bored, too. Let's think up another couple hundred words for snow."

objects as being fixed or constant, Hopi view them more as verbs, constantly changing. In this sense our language represents much of the world rather like a snapshot camera, whereas Hopi reflects a world view more like a motion picture.

Although there is little support for the extreme linguistically deterministic viewpoint that it is *impossible* for speakers of different languages to view the world identically, the more moderate notion of **linguistic relativism**—that language exerts a strong influence on perceptions—does seem valid. As one scholar put it, "The differences between languages are not so much in what *can* be said, but in what it is *relatively easy* to say."[55] Some languages contain terms that have no English equivalents.[56] for example, consider a few words in other languages that have no English equivalents:

Nemawashi (Japanese): The process of informally feeling out all the people involved with an issue before making a decision

Lagniappe (French/Creole): An extra gift given in a transaction that wasn't expected by the terms of a contract

Lao (Mandarin): A respectful term used for older people, showing their importance in the family and in society

Dharma (Sanskrit): Each person's unique, ideal path in life, and knowledge of how to find it

Koyaanisquatsi (Hopi): Nature out of balance; a way of life so crazy it calls for a new way of living

Once words like these exist and become a part of everyday life, the ideas that they represent are easier to recognize. But even without such terms, each of the concepts above is still possible to imagine. Thus, speakers of a language that includes the notion of *lao* would probably treat its older members respectfully and those who are familiar with *lagniappe* might be more generous. Despite these differences, the words aren't essential to follow these principles. Although language may shape thoughts and behavior, it doesn't dominate them absolutely.

The importance of language as a reflection of world view isn't just a matter of interest for anthropologists and linguists. The labels we use in everyday conversation both reflect and shape the way we view ourselves and others. This explains why businesses often give employees impressive titles, and why a woman's choice of the label "Ms." or "Mrs." can be a statement about her identity.

Relational titles aren't the only linguistic elements that may shape attitudes about men and women. The reading on pages 212–13 suggests that language reforms like avoiding "he" as a gender-neutral pronoun can lead to less discriminatory thinking. A recent study examined precisely this question.[57] Students were corrected every time they used "he" as a generic pronoun in their writing. At the end of a semester, results showed that the corrections did reduce the use of gender-biased language. However, students did not change their mental images or their attitudes toward language reforms.

Looking at Diversity

THE BILINGUAL WORLD OF THE DEAF

Larry Littleton *lost his hearing at age seven after contracting spinal meningitis. He spent the next eight years relying exclusively on lip reading to understand others' speech and using his own voice to express ideas. At age fifteen he learned American Sign Language and finger spelling. Larry has worked for Southern California Edison conducting energy audits, and he volunteers his time speaking to students and community groups.*

Most people don't realize that American Sign Language (ASL) is a complete language with its own vocabulary. Some of the symbols we use even have different meanings in ASL than they do in other sign languages. For example, I just came back from Australia where the sign that we use to mean "sex" means "fun," and the one that means "socks" to us means "learn" to them. You can imagine how confused I was when an Australian used his sign language to ask me, "Are you having fun learning while you're here?" and I thought he was asking, "Are you having sex in socks while you're here?"

Being a bilingual speaker who understands both ASL and English helps me appreciate how different the two languages are. For one thing, I think ASL is a more expressive language. English speakers depend on words to get ideas

across. In ASL, a lot more of the meaning comes from how you act out a sign. For example, in ASL the difference between "I'm a little sorry," "I'm sorry" and "I'm terribly sorry" come from your facial expression, your posture, and the way you gesture as you make the sign. I guess you could say that being expressive may be *useful* in spoken language, but it's *essential* in ASL.

Besides being more expressive than English, ASL is more concise. I just read about a study of one elementary school classroom with a hearing teacher and an ASL interpreter. In one week the speaking teacher used almost 86,000 words; but the interpreter only used 43,000 words to get across the same message to the deaf students. Maybe the interpreter missed some ideas, but I also think the difference came because sign language is so concise and expressive. Let me show you an example. In speaking I could tell you "Sorry, I've lost my train of thought." In ASL, the whole idea gets communicated almost instantly, in one sign [he demonstrates]. Here's another example: I can make one sign [he gestures] that means the same as the seven words: "Don't worry: It's not a big deal."

ASL is good at communicating concepts, but it doesn't work as well when the message contains specific details. When people who are deaf need to get across a precise message—a phone number or somebody's name, for example, they usually fingerspell. Fingerspelling has its own set of symbols for each

letter of the alphabet, and you communicate by spelling the word out one letter at a time. Fingerspelling isn't really a different language from English: it's just a different way of "writing."

I think ASL and spoken languages both have strengths. Because they're precise, spoken languages are useful when you need to get across specific details. But when you want to be expressive, I think ASL works much better. I know one ASL interpreter whose translations are beautiful: Almost everything she says comes across like poetry or music. I also think sign languages are more universal. A while ago I was traveling in Europe with a bunch of hearing people. When we got to countries where nobody could speak the local language, my signing got us through a lot of tough situations. I think that's because using sign language develops a communicator's creativity and expressiveness. The same thing happened when I was in Thailand last year. Almost nobody spoke English in the village where I lived, but I got along pretty well because I have had so much practice expressing my ideas with my face and gestures, and also because I spend so much time and energy observing how others act.

I think everybody can benefit from being bilingual, and ASL is a wonderful second language to learn. Besides developing your expressiveness, it can help you appreciate that people who are deaf have the same ideas and feelings that hearing people do.

Along with gender, labeling can both affect and reflect the way members of an ethnic group define themselves. Over the years labels of racial identification have gone through cycles of popularity. In North America, the first freed slaves preferred to be called "Africans." In the late nineteenth and early twentieth centuries "colored" was the term of choice, but later "Negro" became the respectable word. Then, in the sixties, the term "Black" grew increasingly popular—first as a label for militants, and later as a term preferred by more moderate citizens of all colors. More recently "African American" has gained popularity. Recent surveys have found that between 60 and 72 percent of Blacks surveyed prefer the term "Black," while between 15 and 25 percent prefer African American. (The rest either had no opinion or chose other labels.)[58]

Decisions about which name to use reflect a person's attitude. For example, one recent survey revealed that individuals who prefer the label "Black" choose it because it is "acceptable" and "based on consensus" of the larger culture.[59] They describe themselves as patriotic, accepting of the status quo, and attempting to assimilate into the larger culture. By contrast, people who choose the term "Afro-American" derive their identity from their ethnicity and do not want to assimilate into the larger culture, only succeed in it.

✛ SUMMARY

Language is both a marvelous communication tool and the source of many interpersonal problems. Every language is a collection of symbols, governed by a variety of rules. Because of its symbolic nature, language is not a precise vehicle: Meanings rest in people, not in words themselves.

Besides conveying meanings about the content of a specific message, language both reflects and shapes the perceptions of its users. Terms used to name people influence the way they are regarded. The terms used to label speakers and the language they use reflects the level of affiliation, attraction, and interest of a speaker toward a subject. Language patterns also reflect and shape a speaker's perceived power.

When used carelessly, language can lead to a variety of interpersonal problems. The level of precision or vagueness of messages can affect a receiver's understanding of them. Both precise messages and vague, evasive ones have their uses in interpersonal relationships, and a competent communicator has the ability to choose the optimal level of precision for the situation at hand. Language also acknowledges or avoids the speaker's acceptance of responsibility for his or her positions, and competent communicators know how to use "I" and "we" statements to accept the optimal level of responsibility and relational harmony. Some language habits—confusing facts with opinions or inferences and using emotive terms—can lead to unnecessary disharmony in interpersonal relationships.

The relationship between gender and language is a confusing one. There are many differences in the ways men and women speak: The content of their conversations varies, as do their reasons for communicating and their conversational style. However, not all differences in language use can be accounted for by the speaker's gender. Occupation, social philosophy, and orientation toward problem solving also influence the use of language, and psychological sex role can be more of an influence than biological sex.

Different languages often shape and reflect the views of a culture. Low-context cultures like the United States use language primarily to express feelings and ideas as clearly and unambiguously as possible. High-context cultures such as Japan and Saudi Arabia, however, avoid specificity in order to promote social harmony. Some cultures value brevity and the succinct use of language, while others have high regard for elaborate forms of speech. In some societies formality is important, while others value informality. Beyond these differences, there is evidence to support linguistic relativism—the notion that language exerts a strong influence on the world view of the people who speak it.

✤ KEY TERMS

abstraction ladder
"but" statement
convergence
divergence
emotive language
equivocal language
euphemisms
high-context cultures

"I" language
"it" statements
linguistic relativism
low-context cultures
phonological rules
powerless speech mannerisms
Relative words

Sapir–Whorf hypothesis
semantic rules
sex roles
static evaluation
syntactic rules
"we" statements
"you" language

✤ MORE RESOURCES ON LANGUAGE

READINGS

Ellis, Andrew, and Geoffrey Beattie. *The Psychology of Language and Communication.* New York: Guilford Press, 1986.

An encyclopedic, multidisciplinary look at a wide array of linguistic topics: the relationship between verbal and nonverbal channels, the structure and management of conversations, the perception and comprehension of language, and the development of linguistic skill.

Henley, Nancy M., and Cheris Kramarae. "Gender, Power, and Miscommunication." In Nikolas Coupland, Howard Giles, and John M. Wiemann, eds., *"Miscommunication" and Problematic Talk.* Newbury Park, Calif.: Sage, 1991.

The authors explore several explanations for differences and problems that arise when men and women communicate across the gender barrier. After considering the "female deficit" notion (that women need to gain skill in stereotypical male speech) and the "two cultures" theory (that men

and women operate side-by-side in significantly different cultures), the authors argue that a study of the relationship between gender and communication involves other issues such as failure to recognize similarities between the sexes, an excessive focus on white, North American behavior to the exclusion of other cultures, and social biases against women.

Ng, Sik Hung, and James J. Bradac. *Power in Language: Verbal Communication and Social Influence.* Newbury Park, Calif.: Sage, 1993.

This is a thorough look at research on how power is communicated through speech to impress and influence others. The authors also discuss how speakers at times avoid direct, powerful speech to pursue other relational goals. The book offers a good look at how social scientists strive to understand human behavior, and how the principles that govern the effects of speech involve far more than "common sense."

Pearson, Judy C., Lynn H. Turner, and William Todd-Mancillas. *Gender and Communication* (3d ed.). Dubuque, Iowa: W.C. Brown, 1994.

Chapter 5, "Language Usage of Women and Men," compares stereotyped perceptions of male–female language differences with the actual differences as revealed by social scientists. The authors also offer explanations about why these differences exist, and suggest some corrective actions.

Rheingold, Howard, *They Have a Word for It.* Los Angeles: Jeremy P. Tarcher, 1988.

Rheingold has collected a lexicon of words and phrases from languages around the world that lend support to the Sapir–Whorf hypothesis. This entertaining 200-page compendium of "untranslatable phrases" illustrates that speaking a new language does, indeed, prompt a different world view. Imagine how life might be different to speakers of Bantu, whose word mbuki-mvuki *means "to shuck off clothes in order to dance." Entertainment aside, the bibliography at the end of this book contains a valuable list of sources for exploring the notion of linguistic relativism.*

Rothwell, J. Dan. *Telling It Like It Isn't: Language Misuse and Malpractice/What We Can Do About It.* Englewood Cliffs, N.J.: Prentice-Hall, 1982.

An interesting, readable catalog of the semantic abuses that interfere with satisfying personal relationships. Rothwell cites such diverse sources as The Anatomy of Swearing, *Sartre's* Being and Nothingness, *and advertisements for Perrier mineral water to illustrate the many ways language affects perception.*

Tannen, Deborah. *That's Not What I Meant! How Conversational Style Makes or Breaks Your Relations with Others.* New York: Morrow, 1986.

Tannen offers an explanation of how conversational style leads to misunderstandings and relational struggles. Highly entertaining and readable, this book provides a good introduction to the field of conversational analysis.

———. *You Just Don't Understand: Women and Men in Conversation.* New York: Morrow, 1990.

Although Tannen's first book took a general look at various conversational styles as influenced by geography, ethnicity, and class backgrounds, this time she focuses exclusively on how gender affects communication. The book summarizes a large amount of research in a readable manner, concluding that, from early childhood, there are some fundamental differences in male and female communication styles.

Wood, Julia T. *Gendered Lives: Communication, Gender, and Culture.* Belmont, Calif.: Wadsworth, 1994.

Chapter 5, "Gendered Verbal Communication," describes the many ways in which gender and language affect one another. Besides describing the differences between male and female speech, Wood argues that speech and writing create an unequal balance between men and women.

FILMS

THE IMPORTANCE OF LANGUAGE

The Miracle Worker (1962) Not rated

Many scholars claim that language is *the* feature that defines humans. This Academy Award–winning film lends support to that position. It chronicles the story of Helen Keller (Patty Duke), who, deaf and mute from an early age, is an enigmatic terror to her loving family until a new teacher, Annie Sullivan (Ann Bancroft), enters their lives. For a month Keller and Sullivan struggle in a battle of wills. The teacher struggles to break through Helen's walls of darkness and silence, and Helen fights her every step of the way. One evening Keller disrupts a family dinner by deliberately knocking over a water pitcher. In one of the most memorable scenes of stage and film, Sullivan drags her rebellious pupil and the empty pitcher outside to the water pump, where Helen suddenly learns the relationship between the liquid and the fingerspelled symbols W–A–T–E–R. Helen's discovery of the relationship between symbols and the physical world illustrates the miraculous nature of language, and the world that it makes possible.

Although the pivotal water scene is worth viewing alone, the entire film drives home the fundamental difference language makes in human consciousness and communication. Keller's life clearly falls into two chapters: before and after the acquisition of language. Seeing the difference, it is impossible to ignore or fail to appreciate the miracle we so often take for granted.

LANGUAGE AND SOCIAL STATUS

My Fair Lady (1964), Rated G

Linguistics professor Henry Higgins (Rex Harrison) takes on the professional challenge of his life: teaching cockney flower girl Eliza Doolittle (Audrey Hepburn) to masquerade as royalty by learning proper elocution. (A nonmusical, *Pygmalion*, was made in

1938.) The film illustrates—albeit in a romanticized manner—the importance of language as a marker of social status.

POWERFUL AND POWERLESS SPEECH

Wall Street (1987) Rated R, and *Baby Boom* (1987) Rated PG

Social critics have pigeonholed the 1980s as a decade of greed and corporate gamesmanship. These two films capture the communication style (and personal costs) that come with a rise to the top of the organizational heap. In profiling the ups and downs of young adults who play the corporate game, the films offer a picture of the relationship between power and language.

Baby Boom tells the story of J.C. Wyatt (Diane Keaton), a fast-track yuppie executive who decides to raise a baby girl whom she unexpectedly inherits. Due to the demands of parenting, J.C. loses her job and moves to rural Vermont. At first she is lost, but she soon invents a gourmet baby food company that is worth millions and is invited back into the corporate fold. In *Wall Street*, Bud Fox (Charlie Sheen) is an ambitious young broker for a Wall Street firm who wants to become a big-time financial "player." Through persistence he gets an audience with corporate raider Gordon Gekko (Michael Douglas). Impressed by Fox's determination and his willingness to break securities laws, Gekko adopts the younger man as a protégé, a decision both the mentor and pupil later regret.

Both films profile the rise and fall in the fortunes of their protagonists. From a linguistic perspective, it is interesting to note that the speech styles of both J.C. and Bud change along with their situations. When they are near the pinnacle of their corporate careers, both characters' speech exhibits all the characteristics associated with power in their culture.

But when they are uncomfortable or out of favor, they sound like different people. As you watch the films, consider the degree to which powerful (and powerless) speech reflects a communicator's relationship to others and the degree to which speech style *shapes* the attitudes of those around them.

GENDER DIFFERENCES IN LANGUAGE

Tootsie (1982), Rated PG

Michael Dorsey (Dustin Hoffman) is an aspiring New York actor who can't get any roles . . . at least as a man. But, in a flash of inspiration, he transforms himself into Dorothy Michaels, a middle-aged woman, and wins a part as a hospital administrator in a daytime soap opera. The contrast between Hoffman's use of language as Michael and Dorothy provides an excellent illustration of some differences between stereotypically male and female language use.

LANGUAGE AND CULTURE

Children of a Lesser God (1986) Rated R

John Leeds (William Hurt) takes a job at a residential school for deaf children, where he meets Sarah (Marlee Matlin). John is both attracted to and frustrated by Sarah's passionate refusal to learn lip reading, which she views as a concession to the hearing world and a compromise of the integrity and value of sign language. The film profiles Leeds's changes in attitudes about the relationship of deaf and hearing people as well as the development of his relationship with Sarah. The film introduces viewers to the linguistic and cultural world of the deaf. Through it we learn some fundamental differences between sign and spoken language as well as more about how the deaf suffer from many misunderstandings and stereotypes.

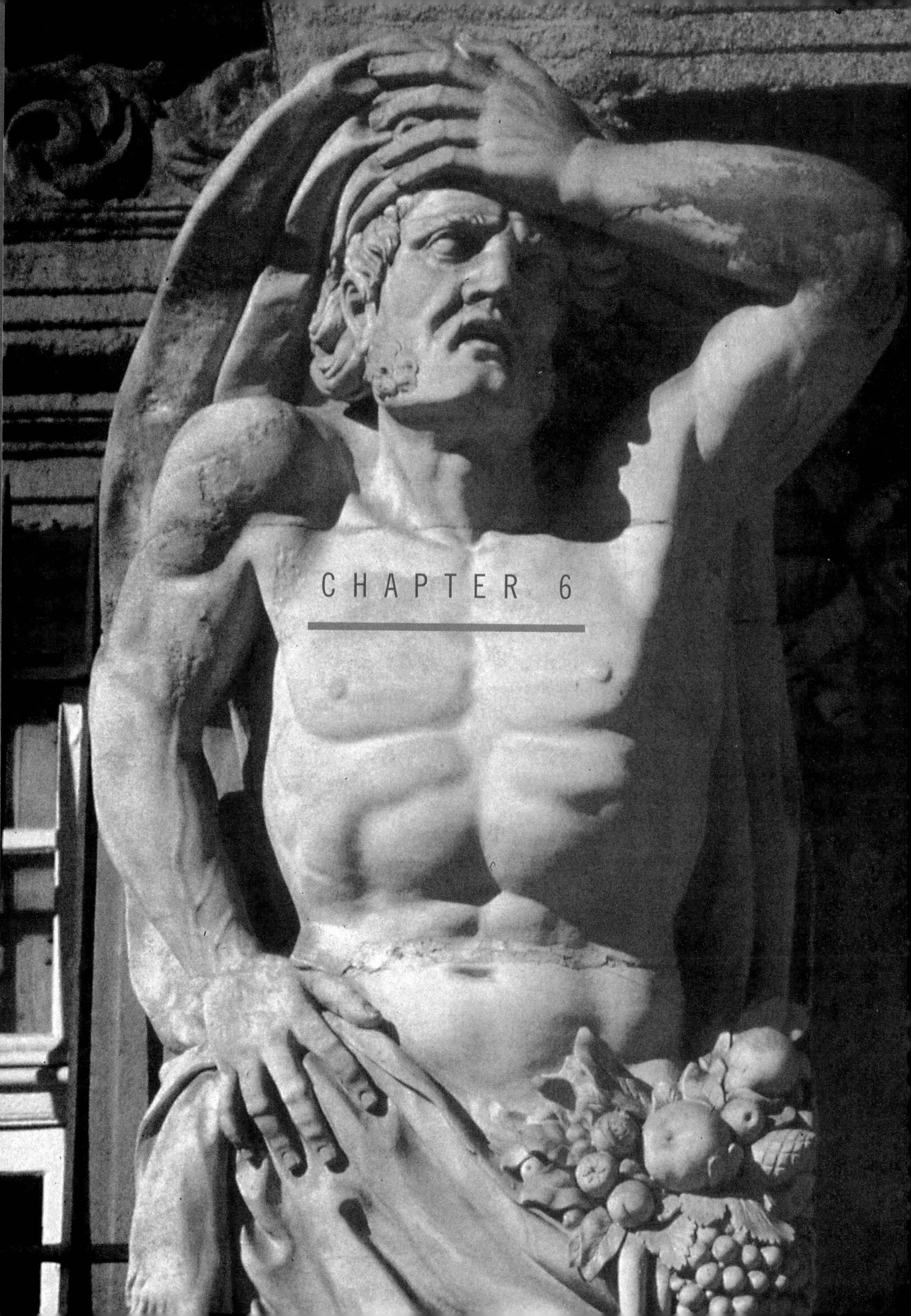

CHAPTER 6

Nonverbal Communication: Messages without Words

THE ADVENTURES OF SHERLOCK HOLMES

I was seized with a keen desire to see Holmes again, and to know how he was employing his extraordinary powers. His rooms were brilliantly lit, and, even as I looked up, I saw his tall, spare figure pass twice in a dark silhouette against the blind. He was pacing the room swiftly, eagerly, with his head sunk upon his chest and his hands clasped behind him. To me, who knew his every mood and habit, his attitude and manner told their own story. He was at work again. He had risen out of his drug-created dreams and was hot upon the scent of some new problem. I rang the bell and was shown up to the chamber which had formerly been in part my own.

His manner was not effusive. It seldom was; but he was glad, I think, to see me. With hardly a word spoken, but with kindly eye, he waved me to an armchair, threw across his case of cigars, and indicated a spirit case and a gasogene in the corner. Then he stood before the fire and looked me over in his singular introspective fashion.

"Wedlock suits you," he remarked. "I think, Watson, that you have put on seven and a half pounds since I saw you."

"Seven!" I answered.

"Indeed, I should have thought a little more. Just a trifle more, I fancy, Watson. And in practice again, I observe. You did not tell me that you intended to go into harness."

"Then, how do you know?"

"I see it, I deduce it. How do I know that you have been getting yourself very wet lately, and that you have a most clumsy and careless servant girl?"

"My dear Holmes," said I, "this is too much. You would certainly have been burned, had you lived a few centuries ago. It is true that I had a country walk on Thursday and came home in a dreadful mess, but as I have changed my clothes I can't imagine how you deduce it. As to Mary Jane, she is incorrigible, and my wife has given her notice; but there, again, I fail to see how you work it out."

He chuckled to himself and rubbed his long, nervous hands together.

"It is simplicity itself," said he; "my eyes tell me that on the inside of your left shoe, just where the firelight strikes it, the leather is scored by six almost parallel cuts. Obviously they have been caused by someone who has very carefully scraped round the edges of the sole in order to remove crusted mud

from it. Hence, you see, my double deduction that you had been out in vile weather, and that you had a particularly malignant boot-slitting specimen of the London slavey. As to your practice, if a gentleman walks into my rooms smelling of iodoform, with a black mark of nitrate of silver upon his right forefinger, and a bulge on the right side of his top hat to show where he has secreted his stethoscope, I must be dull, indeed, if I do not pronounce him to be an active member of the medical profession."

I could not help laughing at the ease with which he explained his process of deduction. "When I hear you give your reasons," I remarked, "the thing always appears to me to be so ridiculously simple that I could easily do it myself, though at each successive instance of your reasoning I am baffled until you explain your process. And yet I believe that my eyes are as good as yours."

"Quite so," he answered, lighting a cigarette, and throwing himself down into an armchair. "You see, but you do not observe."

Sir Arthur Conan Doyle,
A Scandal in Bohemia

ometimes it's difficult to know how other people really feel. Often they don't know for sure themselves, and other times they have some reason for not wanting to tell you. In either case, there are times when you can't find out what is going on inside another's mind simply by asking.

What should you do in these cases? They happen every day and often in the most important situations. Sherlock Holmes said the way to understand people was to watch them—not only to see, but to observe.

Observing yourself and others is what this chapter is about. In the following pages you'll become acquainted with the field of nonverbal communication—the way we express ourselves, not by what we say but by what we *do*. Some social scientists have argued that 93 percent of the emotional impact of a message comes from nonverbal sources. Others have reasoned more convincingly that the figure is closer to 65 percent.[1] Whatever the precise figure, the point remains: Nonverbal communication contributes a great deal to conveying meanings. It stands to reason, then, that the ability to understand nonverbal messages is an important part of communicative competence.

We need to begin our study of nonverbal communication by defining that term. At first this might seem like a simple task: If *non* means "not" and *verbal* means "words," *nonverbal communication* means "communicating without words." In fact, this literal definition isn't completely accurate. For instance, most communication scholars don't define American Sign Language (used by many people with hearing impairments) as nonverbal even though the messages are unspoken. On the other hand, you'll soon read that certain aspects of the voice aren't really verbal. (Can you think of any? Table 6–1 will help you.)

This isn't the place to explore the rather complex debate about exactly what is and what isn't nonverbal. Interesting as that subject may be, we can move along in this introduction by defining **nonverbal communication** as "those messages expressed by other than lin-

NONVERBAL COMMUNICATION MEANS:

smiling, frowning
laughing, crying, sighing
standing close to others
being standoffish
the way you look:
your hair, your clothing
your face, your body

your handshake (sweaty palms?)
your postures
your gestures
your mannerisms

your voice:
soft-loud
fast-slow
smooth-jerky

the environment you create:
your home, your room
your office, your desk
your kitchen
your car

TABLE 6 – 1   Types of Communication

	VOCAL COMMUNICATION	NONVOCAL COMMUNICATION
VERBAL COMMUNICATION	Spoken words	Written words
NONVERBAL COMMUNICATION	Tone of voice, sighs, screams, vocal qualities (loudness, pitch, and so on)	Gestures, movement, appearance, facial expression, and so on

Adapted from John Stewart and Gary D'Angelo, *Together: Communicating Interpersonally* (2d ed.). (Reading, Mass.: Addison-Wesley, 1980): 22.

guistic means." This rules out not only sign languages but written words as well, but it includes messages transmitted by vocal means that don't involve language—the sighs, laughs, and other assorted noises we alluded to a moment ago. In addition, our definition allows us to explore the nonlinguistic dimensions of the spoken word—volume, rate, pitch, and so on.

Our brief definition only hints at the richness of nonverbal messages. You can begin to understand their prevalence by trying a simple experiment.

 INVITATION TO INSIGHT

VERBAL AND NONVERBAL COMMUNICATION

Here's an experiment you can try either at home or in class. It will help you begin learning how nonverbal communication works.

1. Pick a partner, and find a place where you have some space to yourselves.

2. Now sit back-to-back with your partner, making sure that no parts of your bodies are touching. You should be seated so that you can talk easily without seeing each other.

3. Once you're seated, take two minutes to carry on a conversation about whatever subject you like. The only requirement is that you not look at or touch each other. Communicate by using words only.

4. Next, turn around so that you're facing your partner, seated at a comfortable distance. Now that you can both see and hear each other, carry on your conversation for another two minutes.

5. Continue to face each other, but for the next two minutes don't speak. Instead, join hands with your partner and communicate whatever messages you want to through sight and touch. Try to be aware of how you feel as you go through this step. There isn't any right or wrong way to behave here—there's nothing wrong with feeling embarrassed, silly, or any other way. The only requirement is to *remain silent.*

After you've finished the experiment, take some time to talk it over with your partner. Start by sharing how you felt in each part of the experience. Were you comfortable, nervous, playful, affectionate? Did your feelings change from one step to another? Could your partner tell these feelings without your expressing them? If so, how? Did your partner communicate his or her feelings too?

✚ CHARACTERISTICS OF NONVERBAL COMMUNICATION

If this experiment seemed strange to you, we hope you still went through with it because it points out several things about nonverbal communication.

NONVERBAL COMMUNICATION EXISTS

Even when you were in the nontalking stage, you probably could pick up some of your partner's feelings by touching hands and noting posture and expressions—maybe more than you could during your conversation. We hope that this exercise showed you that there are other languages besides words that carry messages about your relationships.

The point isn't so much *how* you or your partner behaved during the exercises—whether you were tense or relaxed, friendly or distant. We wanted to show you that even without any formal experience you can recognize and to some degree interpret messages that other people send nonverbally. In this chapter we want to sharpen the skills you already have, to give you a better grasp of the vocabulary of nonverbal language and to show you how this knowledge can help you understand yourself and others better.

ALL NONVERBAL BEHAVIOR HAS COMMUNICATIVE VALUE

The fact that communication without words took place between you and your partner brings us to this second important feature of nonverbal communication. To understand what we mean here, think about the exercise you just finished. Suppose we'd asked you not to communicate any messages at all while with your partner. What would you have done? Closed your eyes? Withdrawn into a ball? Left the room? You can probably see that even these behaviors communicate messages—that you're avoiding contact.

Take a minute now to try *not* communicating. Join a partner, and spend some time trying not to reveal any messages to one another. What happens?

This impossibility of not communicating is extremely important to understand because it means that each of us is a kind of transmitter that cannot be shut off. No matter what we do, we give off information about ourselves.[2]

Stop for a moment, and examine yourself as you read this. If someone were observing you now, what nonverbal clues would that person get about how you're feeling? Are you sitting forward or reclining back? Is your posture tense or relaxed? Are your eyes wide open, or do they keep closing? What does your facial expression communicate? Can you make your face expressionless? Don't people with expressionless faces communicate something to you?

Of course, we don't always intend to send nonverbal messages. Unintentional nonverbal behaviors differ from deliberate ones.[3] For example, we often stammer, blush, frown, and sweat without meaning to do so. Whether or not our nonverbal behavior is intentional, others recognize it and make interpretations about us based on their observations. Some theorists argue that unintentional behavior may provide information, but it shouldn't count as communication. We draw the boundaries of nonverbal communication more broadly, suggesting that even unconscious and unintentional behavior conveys messages, and thus is worth studying as communication.

What you are speaks so loudly I cannot hear what you say.

Ralph Waldo Emerson

Writer [to movie producer Sam Goldwyn]: Mr. Goldwyn, I'm telling you a sensational story. I'm only asking for your opinion, and you fall asleep.

Goldwyn: Isn't sleeping an opinion?

"I tell you, Mr. Arthur, this survey has no way of registering a non-verbal response."

Visitors to other countries may learn some words in their hosts' language in an effort at courtesy, and then unwittingly offend them by making the wrong gesture. The sign of the University of Texas football team, the Longhorns, is to extend the second finger and the pinkie. In Italy this gesture means a man's wife has been unfaithful to him—a very serious insult! Similarly, the cheerful V-for-Victory sign in the United States conveys an angry vulgarity in England. (Richard Nixon's two-handed victory salute produced no end of merriment among the British.)

Carole Wade and Carol Tavris

The fact that you and everyone around you is constantly sending nonverbal clues *is* important because it means that you have a constant source of information available about yourself and others. If you can tune into these signals, you'll be more aware of how those around you are feeling and thinking, and you'll be better able to respond to their behavior.

NONVERBAL COMMUNICATION IS CULTURE-BOUND

Cultures have different nonverbal languages as well as verbal ones. Fiorello LaGuardia, legendary Mayor of New York from 1933–1945, was fluent in English, Italian, and Yiddish. Researchers who watched films of his campaign speeches found that they could tell with the sound turned off which language he was speaking by noticing the changes in his nonverbal behavior.[4]

Some nonverbal behaviors have different meanings from culture to culture. The "okay" gesture made by joining thumb and forefinger to form a circle is a cheery affirmation to most Americans, but it has less positive meanings in other parts of the world.[5] In France and Belgium it means "You're worth zero." In Greece and Turkey it is a vulgar sexual invitation, usually meant as an insult. Given this sort of cross-cultural ambiguity, it's easy to imagine how an innocent tourist might wind up in serious trouble.

Less obvious cross-cultural differences can damage relationships without the parties ever recognizing exactly what has gone wrong. As you read in Chapter Five, Edward Hall points out that, whereas Americans are comfortable conducting business at a distance of roughly four feet, people from the Middle East stand much closer.[6] It is easy to visualize the awkward advance and retreat pattern that might occur when two diplomats or businesspeople from these cultures meet. The Middle Easterner would probably keep moving forward to close the gap that feels so wide, whereas the American would continually back away. Both would feel uncomfortable, probably without knowing why.

Communicators become more tolerant of others once they understand that unusual nonverbal behaviors are the result of cultural differences. In one study, American adults were presented with videotapes of speakers from the United States, France, and Germany.[7] When the sound was eliminated, viewers judged foreigners more negatively than their fellow citizens. But when the speakers' voices were added (allowing viewers to recognize that they were from a different country), the critical ratings dropped.

Like distance, patterns of eye contact vary around the world.[8] A direct gaze is considered appropriate for speakers in Latin America, the Arab world, and southern Europe. On the other hand, Asians, Indians, Pakistanis, and northern Europeans gaze at a listener peripherally or not at all. In either case, deviations from the norm are likely to make a listener uncomfortable.

Differing cultural norms for nonverbal behavior make the potential for cross-cultural misunderstandings great. For example, many

Anglo schoolteachers use quasi-questions that hint at the information they are seeking: "Does the name 'Hamilton' ring a bell?" An elementary-school instructor might encourage the class to speak up by making an incorrect statement that demands refutation: "So twelve divided by four is six, right?" Most Anglo students would recognize this behavior as a way of testing their understanding. But this style of questioning is unfamiliar to many students raised in traditional black cultures, who aren't likely to respond until they are directly questioned by the instructor.[9] Given this difference, it is easy to imagine how some teachers might view minority children as unresponsive or slow, when in fact they are simply playing by a different set of rules.

Despite differences like these, many nonverbal behaviors are universal. Certain expressions have the same meanings around the world. Smiles and laughter are universal signals of positive emotions, for example, while sour expressions convey displeasure in every culture.[10] Charles Darwin believed that expressions like these are the result of evolution, functioning as survival mechanisms that allowed early humans to convey emotional states before the development of language. The innateness of some facial expressions becomes even more clear when we examine the behavior of children born deaf and blind.[11] Despite a lack of social learning, these children display a broad range of expression. They smile, laugh, and cry in ways virtually identical to normal infants.

Although nonverbal expressions like these may be universal, the way they are used varies widely around the world. Some cultures discourage the overt demonstration of feelings like happiness or anger. In other cultures the same feelings are perfectly appropriate. Thus, a Japanese might appear much more controlled and placid than an Arab, when in fact their feelings might be identical.

The same principle operates closer to home among subcultures. For example, observations have shown that black women in all-black groups are nonverbally more expressive and interrupt each other more than white women in all-white groups.[12] This doesn't mean that black women always feel more intensely than their white counterparts. A more likely explanation is that the two groups follow different cultural rules. The researchers found that in racially mixed groups both black and white women moved closer to each others' style. This nonverbal convergence shows that skilled communicators can adapt their behavior when interacting with members of other cultures or subcultures in order to make the exchange more smooth and effective.

The men walked hand-in-hand, laughing sleepily together under blinding vertical glare. Sometimes they put their arms round each other's necks; they seemed to like to touch each other, as if it made them feel good to know the other man was there. It wasn't love; it didn't mean anything we could understand.

Graham Greene,
Journey without Maps

NONVERBAL COMMUNICATION IS PRIMARILY RELATIONAL

Some nonverbal messages serve utilitarian functions. For example, a police officer directs the flow of traffic and a team of street surveyors uses hand motions to coordinate their work. But nonverbal communication also conveys a more common (and more interesting) variety of *social* messages.[13]

One important category of social messages conveyed by nonverbal communication involves *identity management*. Chapter Two discussed how we strive to create an image of ourselves as we want others to view us. Nonverbal communication plays an important role in this process—in many cases more important than verbal messages. Consider, for example, what happens when you attend a party where you are likely to meet strangers you would like to get to know better. Instead of projecting your image verbally ("Hi! I'm attractive, friendly, and easygoing"), you behave in ways that will present this identity. You might smile a lot, and perhaps try to strike a relaxed pose. It's also likely that you dress carefully—even if the image involves looking as though you hadn't given a lot of attention to your appearance.

Along with identity management, nonverbal communication allows us to *define the kinds of relationships we want to have with others*. Think about the wide range of ways you could behave when greeting another person. You could wave, shake hands, nod, smile, clap the other person on the back, give a hug, or avoid all contact. Each one of these decisions would send a message about the nature of your relationship with the other person.

Nonverbal behavior can be more powerful than words in defining the kind of relationship you are seeking. Recall all the times and ways you have learned that someone you know is upset with you. Most often the first clues don't come from direct statements but from nonverbal clues. Perhaps the message is conveyed through a lack of eye contact, different facial expressions, an increase in distance, or decreased touch. In any case, the change in behavior clearly proves the power of nonverbal communication to define the status of a relationship.

Nonverbal messages perform a third valuable social function: *conveying emotions* that we may be unwilling or unable to express... or ones we may not even be aware of. In fact, nonverbal communication is much better suited to expressing attitudes and feelings than ideas. You can prove this for yourself by imagining how you could express each item on the following list nonverbally:

You're tired.

You're in favor of capital punishment.

You're attracted to another person in the group.

You think prayer in the schools should be allowed.

You're angry at someone in the room.

This experiment shows that, short of charades, ideas don't lend themselves to nonverbal expressions nearly as well as attitudes. Sometimes the attitudinal message relates to the content of the conversation going on at the time ("I think that's a great idea!") and sometimes they reflect a relational message ("I'm bored talking to you").

NONVERBAL COMMUNICATION SERVES MANY FUNCTIONS

Just because this chapter deals with nonverbal communication, don't get the idea that our words and our actions are unrelated. Quite the opposite is true: Verbal and nonverbal communication are interconnected elements in every act of communication. Nonverbal behaviors can operate in several relationships with verbal messages.

1. **Repeating** If someone asked you for directions to the nearest drugstore, you could say, "North of here about two blocks," **repeating** your instructions nonverbally by pointing north. Pointing is an example of what social scientists call **emblems**—deliberate nonverbal behaviors that have a very precise meaning, known to virtually everyone within a cultural group. For example, we all know that a head nod means "yes," a head shake means "no," a wave means "hello" or "goodbye," and a hand to the ear means "I can't hear you."

2. **Substituting** Emblems also can replace a verbal message. When a friend asks, "What's up?" you might shrug your shoulders instead of answering in words. Not all **substituting** consists of emblems, however. Sometimes substituting responses are more ambiguous and less intentional. Many facial expressions operate primarily like verbal interjections such as "gosh," "really?", "oh, please!" and so on.[14] In other cases, nonverbal substituting can be useful when communicators are reluctant to express their feelings in words.

TABLE 6–2 Flirting Behaviors (Listed in decreasing order of occurrence)

FACIAL/HEAD PATTERNS	POSTURE PATTERNS	
Smile	Solitary dance	Thigh touch
Room-encompassing glance	Lean	Placement
	Point	Approach
Laugh	Dance (acceptance)	Foot to foot
Short, darting glance	Parade	Request dance
Fixed gaze	Aid solicitation	Hug
Hair flip	Play	Frontal body contact
Head toss	Brush	Breast touch
Head nod	Knee touch	Hang
Giggle	Shoulder hug	Lateral body contact
Whisper	**GESTURES**	
Neck presentation		
Lip lick	Gesticulation	Caress (back)
Pout	Caress (object)	Arm flexion
Coy smile	Primp	Caress (torso)
Face to face	Caress (leg)	Buttock pat
Kiss	Caress (arm)	Tap
Eyebrow flash	Hand hold	Caress (face/hair)
Lipstick application	Palm	Hike skirt

M. Moore, "Nonverbal Courtship Patterns in Women: Context and Consequences," *Ethology and Sociobiology* 6 (1985): 237–247.

Faced with a message you find disagreeable, you might sigh, roll your eyes, or yawn when speaking out would not be appropriate.

Courtship is another situation in which nonverbal gestures can signal "I'm interested" when the same message would be awkward to express verbally. Psychologist Monica Moore and a team of graduate students spent hundreds of hours observing women and men courting one another, recording every nonverbal step of the process.[15] Moore discovered that the woman most commonly makes the initial decision about whether to encourage contact by nonverbally signaling her interest to a man. Table 6–2 lists the variety of behaviors used to send this sort of signal. Most terms are self-explanatory. A "solitary dance" consists of moving one's body in time to the music.

3. **Complementing** If you saw a student talking to a teacher, and the student's head was bowed slightly, his voice was low and hesitating, and he shuffled slowly from foot to foot, you might conclude that he felt inferior to the teacher, possibly embarrassed about something he did. The nonverbal behaviors you observed provided the context for the verbal behaviors—they conveyed the relationship between the teacher and student. **Complementing** nonverbal behaviors signal the attitudes the interactants have for one another.

Much complementing behavior consists of **illustrators**—nonverbal behaviors that accompany and support spoken words.

Scratching your head when searching for an idea and snapping your fingers when it occurs are examples of illustrators that complement verbal messages. Research shows that North Americans use illustrators more often when they are emotionally aroused—trying to explain ideas that are difficult to put into words when they are furious, horrified, very agitated, distressed, or excited.[16]

4. **Accenting** Just as we use italics to highlight an idea in print, we use nonverbal devices to emphasize oral messages. Pointing an accusing finger adds emphasis to criticism (as well as probably creating defensiveness in the receiver). **Accenting** certain words with the voice ("It was *your* idea!") is another way to add nonverbal emphasis.

5. **Regulating** Nonverbal behaviors can serve a **regulating** function by controlling the flow of verbal communication. For example, parties in a conversation often unconsciously send and receive turn-taking cues.[17] When you are ready to yield the floor, the unstated rule is this: Create a rising vocal intonation pattern, then use a falling intonation pattern or draw out the final syllable of the clause at the end of your statement. Finally, stop speaking. If you want to maintain your turn when another speaker seems ready to cut you off, you can suppress the attempt by taking an audible breath, using a sustained intonation pattern (since rising and falling patterns suggest the end of a statement), and avoid any pauses in your speech. There are other nonverbal cues for gaining the floor and for signaling that you do not want to speak.

6. **Contradicting** People often simultaneously express different and even **contradicting** messages in their verbal and nonverbal behaviors. A common example of this sort of "double message" is the experience we've all had of hearing someone with a red face and bulging veins yelling, "Angry? No, *I'm not angry!*"

Usually, however, the contradiction between words and nonverbal clues isn't this obvious. At times we all try to seem different from what we are. There are many reasons for this contradictory behavior: to cover nervousness when giving a speech or in a job interview, to keep someone from worrying about us, or to appear more attractive than we believe we really are.

Even though some of the ways in which people contradict themselves are subtle, **double messages** have a strong impact. As we grow older we become better at interpreting these contradictory messages. Children between the ages of six and twelve use a speaker's words to make sense of a message. But as adults, we rely more on nonverbal cues to form many impressions. For example, audiences put more emphasis on nonverbal cues than on words to decide whether speakers are honest.[18] They also use nonver-

Beware of the man whose belly does not move when he laughs.

Chinese Proverb

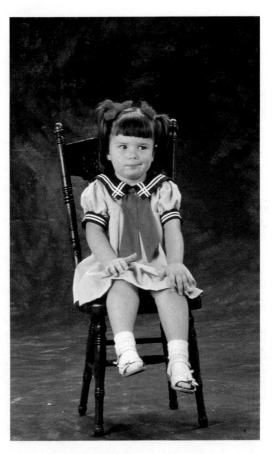

bal behaviors to judge the character of speakers as well as their competence and composure; and differences in nonverbal behavior influence how much listeners are persuaded by a speaker.[19]

Deception is perhaps the most interesting type of double message. Signals of deception—often called **leakage**—can occur in every type of nonverbal behavior. Some nonverbal channels are more revealing than others, however. Facial expressions are less revealing than body clues, probably because deceivers pay more attention to controlling their faces. Even more useful is the voice, which offers a rich variety of leakage clues.[20] In one experiment, subjects who were encouraged to be deceitful made more speech errors, spoke for shorter periods of time, and had a lower rate of speech than others who were encouraged to express themselves honestly. Another study revealed that the vocal frequency of a liar's voice tends to be higher than that of a truth teller. Research also shows that deceivers delivering a prepared lie responded more quickly than truth tellers, mainly because there was less thinking involved. When unprepared, however, deceivers generally took longer than both prepared deceivers and truth tellers.

As this research shows, deceivers don't always broadcast cues that reveal their lies. Nonverbal evidence of lying is most likely to occur when deceivers haven't had a chance to rehearse, when they feel strongly about the information being hidden, or when they feel anxious or guilty about their lies. Even when **deception cues** are abundant, they aren't necessarily direct signals of lying itself; rather, they may reflect the anxiety that some liars feel. Table 6–3

T A B L E   6 – 3   Leakage of Nonverbal Cues to Deception

DECEPTION CUES ARE MOST LIKELY WHEN THE DECEIVER	DECEPTION CUES ARE LEAST LIKELY WHEN THE DECEIVER
Wants to hide emotions being felt at the moment.	Wants to hide information unrelated to his or her emotions.
Feels strongly about the information being hidden.	Has no strong feelings about the information being hidden.
Feels apprehensive about the deception.	Feels confident about the deception.
Feels guilty about being deceptive.	Experiences little guilt about the deception.
Gets little enjoyment from being deceptive.	Enjoys the deception.
Needs to construct the message carefully while delivering it.	Knows the deceptive message well and has rehearsed it.

Based on material from "Mistakes When Deceiving" by Paul Ekman, in *The Clever Hans Phenomenon: Communication with Horses, Whales, Apes, and People,* ed. Thomas A. Sebeok and Robert Rosenthal (New York: New York Academy of Sciences, 1981), pp. 269–278.

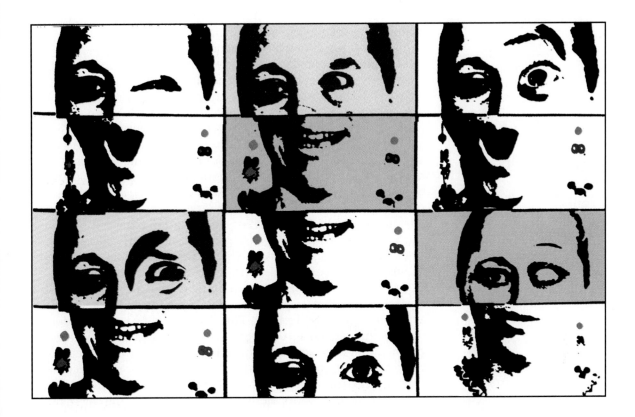

she dresses in flags
comes on
like a mack truck
she paints
her eyelids green
and her mouth
is a loud speaker
rasping out
profanity

at cocktail parties
she is everywhere
like a sheep dog
working a flock
nipping at your sleeve
spilling your drink
bestowing
wet sloppy kisses

but i
have received
secret messages
carefully written
from the shy
quiet woman
who hides
in this
bizarre
gaudy castle

Ric Masten

outlines some conditions under which liars are likely to betray themselves through nonverbal leakage.

Despite the abundance of nonverbal deception cues, it isn't always easy to detect deception. The range of effectiveness in uncovering deceptive messages is broad, ranging from 45 percent to 70 percent.[21] Sometimes the very suspicion that someone is lying can improve the deceiver's attempts to hide the truth. Research shows that communicators who probe the messages of deceptive communicators are no better at detecting lies than those who don't investigate the truth of a message.[22] One explanation for this surprising finding is that deceivers who are questioned become more vigilant about revealing the truth, and that their greater caution results in a better coverup of deception cues.

Some people are better than others at uncovering deception. For example, younger people are better than older ones at uncovering lies.[23] Women are consistently more accurate than men at detecting lying and what the underlying truth really is.[24] The same research shows that, as people become more intimate, their accuracy in detecting lies declines. This is a surprising fact: Intuition suggests that we ought to be better at judging honesty as we become more familiar with others. Despite their overall accuracy at detecting lies, women are more inclined to fall for the deception of intimate partners than are men. No matter how skillful or inept we may be at interpreting nonverbal behavior, training can make us better.[25]

Before we finish considering how nonverbal behaviors can deceive, it is important to realize that not all deceptive communication is aimed at taking advantage of the recipient. Some are a polite way to express an idea that would be difficult to handle if expressed in words. For example, recall a time when you became bored with a conversation while your companion kept rambling on. At such a time the most straightforward statement would be, "I'm tired of talking to you and want to get away." It's obvious that the less direct nonverbal signal—glancing at your watch, for example—is a kinder way to express yourself. In this sense, the ability to deliberately send nonverbal messages that contradict your words can be a kind of communication competence.

NONVERBAL COMMUNICATION IS AMBIGUOUS

You learned in Chapter Five that verbal messages are easily misunderstood; but nonverbal messages are even more ambiguous. Imagine two possible meanings of silence from your companion after a fun-filled evening. Or suppose that a much admired person with whom you've worked suddenly begins paying more attention to you than ever before. What could some possible meanings of this behavior be? Although nonverbal behavior can be very revealing, it can have so many possible meanings that it's impossible to be certain which interpretation is correct.

Not all nonverbal behavior is equally ambiguous. In laboratory settings, subjects are better at identifying positive facial expressions such as happiness, love, surprise, and interest than negative ones like fear, sadness, anger, and disgust.[26] In real life, however, spontaneous nonverbal expressions are so ambiguous that observers are unable to identify the emotions they convey with accuracy any better than blind guessing.[27]

Despite the ambiguity of nonverbal messages, some people are more skillful decoders than others.[28] Those who are better senders of nonverbal messages are also better receivers. Decoding ability also increases with age and training, though there are still differences in ability because of personality and occupation. For instance, extroverts are relatively accurate judges of nonverbal behavior, whereas dogmatists are not. Women seem to be better than men at decoding nonverbal messages. Over 95 percent of the studies examined in one analysis showed that women are more accurate at interpreting nonverbal signals.[29] Despite these differences, even the best nonverbal decoders do not approach 100 percent accuracy.

This exercise should have shown you the difference between merely observing somebody's behavior and actually interpreting it. Noticing someone's shaky hands or smile is one thing, but deciding what such behaviors mean is quite another. If you're like most people, you probably found that a lot of your guesses were incorrect. Now, if that was true here, it may also be true in your daily life. Being a sharp nonverbal observer can give you some good hunches about how people are feeling, but the only way you can find out if these hunches are correct is to *check them out* verbally, using the skill of perception checking you learned in Chapter Three.

"That was unkind, darling. When their mouths turn up at the corners they want to be friends."

INVITATION TO INSIGHT

READING "BODY LANGUAGE"

In your journey through the supermarket checkout stand or while waiting for a plane, you've probably noticed books that promise to teach you how to read "body language." These books claim that you can become a kind of mind reader, learning the deepest secrets of everyone around you. But it's not quite as simple as it sounds. Here's an exercise that will both increase your skill in observing nonverbal behavior and show you the dangers of being too sure that you're a perfect reader of body language. You can try the exercise either in or out of class, and the period of time over which you do it is flexible, from a single class period to several days. In any case, begin by choosing a partner, and then follow these directions:

1. For the first period of time (however long you decide to make it), observe the way your partner behaves. Notice movements, mannerisms, postures, style of dress, and so on. To remember your observations, jot them down. If you're doing this exercise out of class over an extended period of time, there's no need to let your observations interfere with whatever you'd normally be doing: Your only job here is to compile a list of your partner's behaviors. In this step you should be careful *not to interpret* your partner's actions; just record what you see.

2. At the end of the time period, share what you've seen with your partner, who should do the same with you.

3. For the next period of time your job is not only to observe your partner's behavior but also to *interpret* it. This time in your conference you should tell your partner what you thought his or her actions revealed. For example, does careless dressing suggest oversleeping, loss of interest in appearance, or the desire to feel more comfortable? If you noticed frequent yawning, did you think this meant boredom, fatigue after a late night, or sleepiness after a big meal? Don't feel bad if your guesses weren't all correct. Remember, nonverbal clues tend to be ambiguous. You may be surprised how checking out the nonverbal clues you observe can help build a relationship with another person.

✤ DIFFERENCES BETWEEN VERBAL AND NONVERBAL COMMUNICATION

Nonverbal and verbal messages are both indispensable: It's hard to imagine how we could function without either one. Much of the value of these two ways of communicating come from their differences.

SINGLE VS. MULTIPLE CHANNELS

Most verbal messages—words, sentences, and paragraphs—reach us one at a time, rather like pearls on a string. In fact, it's physically impossible for a person to speak more than one word at a time. Unlike the spoken word, however, nonverbal messages don't arrive in such an orderly, sequential manner. Instead, they bombard us simultaneously from a multitude of channels. Consider the everyday act of meeting a stranger for the first time. On a verbal level there's relatively little information exchanged in the clichés that occupy the first few minutes of most conversations ("How's it going . . . " "Great weather we've been having . . . " "What's your major?"). But at the same moment the number of nonverbal messages available to you is overwhelming: the other people's facial expressions, postures, gestures, the clothing they wear, the distance they stand from you, and so on. In one way this multichannel onslaught of nonverbal messages is a boon, since it provides so many ways of learning about others. In another sense, however, the number of simultaneous messages is a problem, for it's difficult to recognize the overwhelming amount of nonverbal information we receive from others every moment.

DISCRETE VS. CONTINUOUS

Verbal messages—words, sentences, and paragraphs—form messages with clear beginnings and endings. In this sense we can judge whether others are communicating verbally by observing whether they are speaking or writing. Unlike the written and spoken word, however, nonverbal communication is continuous and never ending. As we've already said, nonverbal communication is a constant, unstoppable process. The postures, gestures, and other types of messages described in the following pages provide a constant flow of messages. Even the absence of a message (an unanswered letter or an unreturned phone call) is a message. As one communication expert said when referring to nonverbal communication, "Nothing never happens."

CLEAR VS. AMBIGUOUS

Although verbal communication can be confusing, we have already seen that most nonverbal cues are even more vague. Nonverbal messages aren't completely ambiguous, of course: It's probably accurate to guess that a frown signifies some sort of negative feeling and that a smile indicates a positive emotion. But we often need language to tell us *why* others feel as they do. Is the boss smiling because she likes your idea or because she finds it amusing, although completely impractical? Does your instructor's frown indicate confusion with your remarks or disagreement? The best way to find out is to ask for a verbal clarification, not to depend on your reading of the nonverbal cues.

VERBAL VS. NONVERBAL IMPACT

When we are exposed to both verbal and nonverbal messages, research shows that we find the nonverbal signals much more powerful.[30] In a variety of settings (including job interviews, therapy sessions, first meetings), adults rely more on nonverbal messages than on words when interpreting the messages of others. Nonverbal cues are especially likely to carry weight when they contradict a speaker's words. In one series of experiments, friendly, neutral, and unfriendly verbal messages were paired with parallel nonverbal behaviors. Raters who judged the verbal and nonverbal messages separately found them equal in strength. But when the two messages were combined, the nonverbal ones accounted for as much as 12.5 times as much power as the verbal statements.

DELIBERATE VS. UNCONSCIOUS

Although we usually think about what we want to say before speaking or writing, most nonverbal messages aren't deliberate. Of course we do pay attention to some of our nonverbal behavior: smiling when we want to convince others we're happy, or making sure our handshake is firm to show that we're straightforward and decisive. But there are so many nonverbal channels that it's impossible to think about and to control all of them. Thus, our slumping shoulders might contradict our smiles, and our sweating palms might cancel out all the self-confidence of our firm handshakes. The unconscious nature of most nonverbal behavior explains why it offers so many useful cues about how others are feeling.

✤ TYPES OF NONVERBAL COMMUNICATION

Keeping the five characteristics of nonverbal communication in mind, let's take a look at some of the ways we communicate in addition to words.

The first area of nonverbal communication we'll discuss is the broad field of **kinesics,** or body position and motion. In this section we'll explore the role that posture, gestures, body orientation, facial expressions, and eye behaviors play in our relationships with each other.

BODY ORIENTATION

We'll start with **body orientation**—the degree to which we face toward or away from someone with our body, feet, and head. To understand how this kind of physical positioning communicates nonverbal messages, you might try an experiment. You'll need two friends to help you. Imagine that two of you are in the middle of a personal conversation when a third person approaches and wants to join you. You're not especially glad to see this person, but you don't want to sound rude by asking him to leave. Your task is to signal to the intruder that you'd rather be alone, using only the position of

your bodies. You can talk to the third person if you wish, but you can't verbally tell him that you want privacy.

When you've tried this experiment or if you've ever been in a real situation similar to it, you know that by turning your body slightly away from an intruder you can make your feelings very clear. An intruder finds himself in the difficult position of trying to talk over your shoulder, and it isn't long before he gets the message and goes away. The nonverbal message here is "We're interested in each other right now and don't want to include you in our conversation." The general rule this situation describes is that facing someone directly signals your interest, and facing away signals a desire to avoid involvement. This explains how we can pack ourselves into intimate distance with total strangers in places like a crowded elevator without offending others. Because there's a very indirect orientation here (everyone is usually standing shoulder to shoulder, facing in the same direction), we understand that despite the close quarters everyone wants to avoid personal contact.

By observing the way people position themselves you can learn a good deal about how they feel. Next time you're in a crowded place where people can choose whom to face directly, try observing who seems to be included in the action and who is being subtly shut out. And in the same way, pay attention to your own body orientation. You may be surprised to discover that you're avoiding a certain person without being conscious of it or that at times you're "turning your back" on people altogether. If this is the case, it may be helpful to figure out why. Are you avoiding an unpleasant situation that needs clearing up, communicating your annoyance or dislike for the other, or sending some other message?

I don't want to disgrace you—

*I've shined up my bones and
smoothed my skin in quiet folds
around me, arranged my limbs
tastefully in elegant lines that
none may see elbow or knee,
I've instructed my jaw not to
rin nor gape, my lips to stay
firmly in place:*

*I shall not blink nor stare nor
will a hair upon my head move,
and I can hold my feet still,
that not a toe will tumble:*

I don't want to disgrace you—

*but my hands have their own
history and instinctively at
your entrance*

rise to your face

Gerald Huckaby

POSTURE

Another way we communicate nonverbally is through our **posture.** To see if this is true, stop reading for a moment, and notice how you're sitting. What does your position say nonverbally about how you feel? Are there any other people near you now? What messages do you get from their present posture? By paying attention to the postures of those around you, as well as your own, you'll find another channel of nonverbal communication that can furnish information about how people feel about themselves and each other.

An indication of how much posture communicates is shown by our language. It's full of expressions that link emotional states with body postures:

I won't take this lying down!
He can stand on his own
   two feet.
She has to carry a heavy burden.

Take a load off your back.
He's all wrapped up in
   himself.
Don't be so nervous.

Such phrases show that an awareness of posture exists for us even if it's often unconscious. The main reason we miss most posture messages is that they aren't very obvious. It's seldom that a person who feels weighted down by a problem hunches over so much that she stands out in a crowd, and when we're bored, we usually don't lean back and slump enough to embarrass the other person. In the reading of posture, then, the key is to look for small changes that might be shadows of the way people feel.

For example, a teacher who has a reputation for interesting classes told us how he uses his understanding of postures to do a better job. "Because of my large classes I have to lecture a lot," he said. "And that's an easy way to turn students off. I work hard to make my talks entertaining, but you know that nobody's perfect, and I do have my off days. I can tell when I'm not doing a good job of communicat-

ing by picking out three or four students before I start my talk and watching how they sit throughout the class period. As long as they're leaning forward in their seats, I know I'm doing OK, but if I look up and see them starting to slump back, I know I'd better change my approach."

Psychologist Albert Mehrabian has found that other postural keys to feelings are tension and relaxation. He says that we take relaxed postures in nonthreatening situations and tighten up when threatened.[31] Based on this observation, he says we can tell a good deal about how others feel simply by watching how tense or loose they seem to be. For example, he suggests that watching tenseness is a way of detecting status differences: The lower-status person is generally the more rigid, tense-appearing one, whereas the one with higher status is more relaxed. This is the kind of situation that often happens when an employee sits ramrod straight while the boss leans back in her chair. The same principle applies to social situations, where it's often possible to tell who's uncomfortable by looking at pictures. Often you'll see someone laughing and talking as if he were perfectly at home, but his posture almost shouts nervousness. Some people never relax, and their posture shows it.

Sometimes posture communicates vulnerability in situations far more serious than mere social or business ones. One study revealed that rapists sometimes use postural clues to select victims they believe are easy to intimidate.[32] Easy targets are more likely to walk slowly and tentatively, stare at the ground, and move their arms and legs in short, jerky motions.

> *Fie, fie upon her! There's language in her eyes, her cheek, her lip. Nay, her foot speaks; her wanton spirits look out at every joint and motive in her body.*
>
> William Shakespeare,
> *Troilus and Cressida*

INVITATION TO INSIGHT

POSTURE'S MEANING

Try spending an hour or so observing the posture of those around you. See if you can get some idea of how they're feeling by the way they carry themselves. Also, pay attention to your own posture. In what situations do you tense up? Is this a sign of anger, aggressiveness, excitement, fear? Do you ever find yourself signaling boredom, interest, attraction, or other emotions by your posture? Do the feelings you find yourself expressing posturally ever surprise you?

GESTURES

We have already discussed how emblems and illustrators convey messages. Sometimes **gestures** like these are intentional—a cheery wave or thumbs up, for example. In other cases, however, our gestures are unconscious. Occasionally an unconscious gesture will consist of an unambiguous emblem, such as a shrug that clearly means "I don't know." Another revealing set of gestures is what psychiatrist Albert Scheflen calls *preening behaviors*—stroking or combing one's hair,

THE LOOK OF A VICTIM

Little Red Riding Hood set herself up to be mugged. Her first mistake was skipping through the forest to grandma's house. Her second mistake was stopping to pick flowers. At this point, as you might remember in the story, the mean, heavy wolf comes along and begins to check her out. He observes, quite perceptively, that she is happy, outgoing, and basically unaware of any dangers in her surrounding environment. The big bad wolf catches these nonverbal clues and splits to grandma's house. He knows that Red is an easy mark. From this point we all know what happens.

Body movements and gestures reveal a lot of information about a person. Like Little Red Riding Hood, pedestrians may signal to criminals that they are easy targets for mug-

ging by the way they walk. When was the last time you assessed your "muggability rating"? In a recent study two psychologists set out to identify those body movements that characterized easy victims. They assembled "muggability ratings" of sixty New York pedestrians from the people who may have been the most qualified to judge— prison inmates who had been convicted of assault.

The researchers unobtrusively videotaped pedestrians on weekdays between 10:00 A.M. and 12:00 P.M. Each pedestrian was taped for six to eight seconds, the approximate time it takes for a mugger to size up an approaching person. The judges (prison inmates) rated the "assault potential" of the sixty pedestrians on a ten-point scale. A rating of one indicated someone was "a very easy rip-off," of two, "an easy dude to corner." Toward the other end of the scale, nine meant a per-

son "would be heavy; would give you a hard time," and ten indicated that the mugger "would avoid it, too big a situation, too heavy." The results revealed several body movements that characterized easy victims: "Their strides were either very long or very short; they moved awkwardly, raising their left legs with their left arms (instead of alternating them); on each step they tended to lift their whole foot up and then place it down (less muggable sorts took steps in which their feet rocked from heel to toe). Overall, the people rated most muggable walked as if they were in conflict with themselves; they seemed to make each move in the most difficult way possible."

Loretta Malandro and Larry Barker

glancing in a mirror, and rearranging one's clothing. Scheflen suggests that these behaviors signal some sort of interest in the other party: perhaps an unconscious sexual come-on or perhaps a sign of less intimate interest.[33] More often, however, gestures are ambiguous. In addition to illustrators, another group of ambiguous gestures consists of what we usually call *fidgeting*—movements in which one part of the body grooms, massages, rubs, holds, fidgets, pinches, picks, or otherwise manipulates another part. Social scientists call these behaviors **manipulators.**[34] Social rules may discourage us from performing most manipulators in public, but people still do so without noticing.

Research reveals what common sense suggests—that increased use of manipulators is often a sign of discomfort.[35] But not *all* fidgeting signals uneasiness. People also are likely to use manipulators when relaxed. When they let their guard down (either alone or with friends), they will be more likely to fiddle with an earlobe, twirl a strand of hair, or clean their fingernails. Whether or not the fidgeter is hiding something, observers are likely to interpret manipulators as a signal of dishonesty. Since not all fidgeters are liars, it's important not to jump to conclusions about the meaning of manipulations.

Actually, *too few* gestures may be as significant an indicator of double messages as *too many.*[36] Lack of gesturing may signal a lack of interest, sadness, boredom, or low enthusiasm. Illustrators also decrease whenever someone is cautious about speaking. For these reasons, a careful observer will look for either an increase or a decrease in the usual level of gestures.

FACE AND EYES

The face and eyes are probably the most noticed parts of the body, but this doesn't mean that their nonverbal messages are the easiest to read. The face is a tremendously complicated channel of expression for several reasons.

First, it's hard even to describe the number and kind of expressions we commonly produce with our face and eyes. For example, researchers have found that there are at least eight distinguishable positions of the eyebrows and forehead, eight more of the eyes and lids, and ten for the lower face.[37] When you multiply this complexity by the number of emotions we feel, you can see why it would be almost impossible to compile a dictionary of facial expressions and their corresponding emotions.

Another reason for the difficulty in understanding facial expressions is the speed with which they can change. For example, slow-motion films show expressions fleeting across a subject's face in as short a time as it takes to blink an eye.[38] Also, it seems that different emotions show most clearly in different parts of the face: happiness and surprise in the eyes and lower face; anger in the lower face, brows, and forehead; fear and sadness in the eyes; and disgust in the lower face.

Ekman and Friesen have identified six basic emotions that facial expressions reflect—surprise, fear, anger, disgust, happiness, and sad-

Communication Transcript

ON BEING BLACK: THE BURDEN OF NONVERBAL IMPRESSION MANAGEMENT

My first victim was a woman—white, well dressed, probably in her early twenties. I came upon her late one evening on a deserted street in Hyde Park, a relatively affluent neighborhood in an otherwise mean, impoverished section of Chicago. As I swung onto the avenue behind her, there seemed to be a discreet, uninflammatory distance between us. Not so. She cast back a worried glance. To her, the youngish black man—a broad six feet two inches with a beard and billowing hair, both hands shoved into the pockets of a bulky military jacket—seemed menacingly close. After a few more quick glimpses, she picked up her pace and was soon running in earnest. Within seconds she disappeared into a cross street. As a softy who is scarcely able to take a knife to a raw chicken—let alone hold on to a person's throat—I was surprised, embarrassed, and dismayed all at once.

That first encounter, and those that followed, signified that a vast, unnerving gulf lay between nighttime pedestrians—particularly women—and me.

After dark, on the warrenlike streets of Brooklyn where I live, I often see women who fear the worst from me. They seem to have set their faces on neutral, and with their purse straps strung across their chests bandolier-style, they forge ahead as though bracing themselves against being tackled. I understand, of course, that the danger they perceive is not a hallucination. Women are particularly vulnerable to street violence, and young black males are drastically overrepresented among the perpetrators of that violence. Yet these truths are no solace against the kind of alienation that comes of being ever the suspect, a fearsome entity with whom pedestrians avoid making eye contact.

Over the years, I learned to smother the rage I felt at so often being taken for a criminal. Not to do so would surely have led to madness. I now take precautions to make myself less threatening. I move about with care, particularly late in the evening. I give a wide berth to nervous people on subway platforms during the wee hours, particularly when I have exchanged business clothes for jeans. If I happen to be entering a building behind some people who appear skittish, I may walk by, letting them clear the lobby before I return, so as not to seem to be following them. I have been calm and extremely congenial on those rare occasions when I've been pulled over by the police.

And on late-evening constitutionals I employ what has proved to be an excellent tension-reducing measure: I whistle melodies from Beethoven and Vivaldi and the more popular classical composers. Even steely New Yorkers hunching toward nighttime destinations seem to relax, and occasionally they even join in the tune. Virtually everybody seems to sense that a mugger wouldn't be warbling bright, sunny selections from Vivaldi's *Four Seasons*. It is my equivalent of the cowbell that hikers wear when they know they are in bear country.

Brent Staples

"Black Men and Public Space"

Knowing that race can undermine status, African-Americans frequently take aggressive countermeasures in order to avoid embarrassment. One woman, a Harvard-educated lawyer, carries a Bally bag when going to certain exclusive shops. Like a sorceress warding off evil with a wand, she holds the bag in front of her to rebuff racial assumptions, in the hope that the clerk will take it as proof that she is fit to enter.

Ellis Cose,
The Rage of a Privileged Class

ness. Expressions reflecting these feelings seem to be recognizable in and between members of all cultures. Of course, *affect blends*—the combination of two or more expressions in different parts of the face—are possible. For instance, it's easy to imagine how someone would look who is fearful and surprised or disgusted and angry.

People are quite accurate at judging facial expressions for these emotions. Accuracy increases when judges know the target or the context in which the expression occurs, or when they have seen several samples of the target's expressions.

In spite of the complex way in which the face shows emotions, you can still pick up messages by watching it. One of the easiest ways is to look for expressions that seem to be overdone. Often when someone is trying to fool himself or another, he'll emphasize his mask to a point where it seems too exaggerated to be true. Another way to detect a person's feelings is by watching her expression at moments when she isn't likely to be thinking about her appearance. We've all had the experience of glancing into another car while stopped in a traffic jam, or of looking around at a sporting event and seeing expressions that the wearer would probably never show in more guarded moments. At other times, it's possible to watch a **microexpression** as it flashes across a person's face. For just a moment we see a flash of emotion quite different from the one a speaker is trying to convey. Finally, you may be able to spot contradictory expressions on different parts of someone's face: The eyes say one thing, but the expression of the mouth or eyebrows might be sending quite a different message.

The eyes themselves can send several kinds of messages. Meeting someone's glance with your eyes is usually a sign of involvement, whereas looking away often signals a desire to avoid contact. As we mentioned earlier, this is why solicitors on the street—panhandlers, salespeople, petitioners—try to catch our eye. Once they've managed to establish contact with a glance, it becomes harder for the approached person to draw away.

Another kind of message the eyes communicate is a positive or negative attitude. When someone glances toward us with the proper facial expression, we get a clear message that the looker is interested in us—hence the expression "making eyes." At the same time, when our long glances toward someone else are avoided by her, we can be pretty sure that the other person isn't as interested in us as we are in her. (Of course, there are all sorts of courtship games in which the receiver of a glance pretends not to notice any message by glancing away, yet signals interest with some other part of the body.)

The eyes communicate both dominance and submission. We've all played the game of trying to stare down somebody, and in real life there are also times when downcast eyes are a sign of giving in. In some religious orders, for example, subordinate members are expected to keep their eyes downcast when addressing a superior.

Even the pupils of our eyes communicate. E. H. Hess and J. M. Polt of the University of Chicago measured the amount of pupil dilation while showing men and women various types of pictures.[39] The results of the experiment were interesting: A person's eyes grow larger in proportion to the degree of interest in an object. For example, men's pupils grew about 18 percent larger when looking at pictures of a naked woman, and the degree of dilation for women looking at a naked man's picture was 20 percent. Interestingly enough, the greatest increase in pupil size occurred when women looked at a picture of a mother and an infant. A good salesperson can increase profits by being aware of pupil dilation, as Edward Hall describes. He was once in a Middle Eastern bazaar, where an Arab merchant insisted that a customer looking at his jewelry buy a certain piece that the shopper had been ignoring. But the vendor had been watching the pupils of the buyer's eyes and had known what the buyer really wanted.[40]

INVITATION TO INSIGHT

THE EYES HAVE IT

Prove for yourself the role eye contact plays in social influence by trying a simple experiment.

1. Choose a situation in which you can make simple requests from a series of strangers. You might, for example, ask to cut in line to use a photocopying machine, or you could ask passersby for a small amount of change to make an important phone call.

2. Make similar requests to at least twenty different people. Use the same words for each request, but alternate your nonverbal behavior. Half the time make direct eye contact, and the other half of the time avoid looking directly at the other person when you make your request.

3. Record your results, and see if your eye behavior played any role in generating compliance to your request.

4. If eye contact does make a difference, describe how you could apply your findings to real-life situations.

It was terribly dangerous to let your thoughts wander when you were in any public place or within range of a telescreen. The smallest thing could give you away. A nervous tic, an unconscious look of anxiety, a habit of muttering to yourself—anything that carried with it the suggestion of abnormality, of having something to hide. In any case, to wear an improper expression on your face (to look incredulous when a victory was announced, for example) was itself a punishable offense. There was even a word for it in Newspeak: *facecrime*, it was called.

George Orwell,
1984

VOICE

The voice itself is another channel of nonverbal communication. Social scientists use the term **paralanguage** to describe nonverbal, vocal messages. The way a message is spoken can give the same word or words many meanings. For example, note how many meanings come from a single sentence just by shifting the emphasis from one word to another:

This is a fantastic communication book.
   (Not just any book, but *this* one in particular.)
This is a *fantastic* communication book.
   (This book is superior, exciting.)
This is a fantastic *communication* book.
   (The book is good as far as communication goes; it may not be so great as literature or drama.)
This is a fantastic communication *book.*
   (It's not a play or record; it's a book.)

There are many other ways our voice communicates—through its tone, speed, pitch, volume, number and length of pauses, and **disfluencies** (such as stammering, use of "uh," "um," "er," and so on). All these factors can do a great deal to reinforce or contradict the message our words convey.

Researchers have identified the power of paralanguage through the use of content-free speech—ordinary speech that has been electronically manipulated so that the words are unintelligible, but the paralanguage remains unaffected. (Hearing a foreign language that you don't understand has the same effect.) Subjects who hear content-free speech can consistently recognize the emotion being expressed, as well as identify its strength.[41]

The impact of paralinguistic cues is strong. In fact, when asked to determine a speaker's attitudes, listeners pay more attention to paralanguage than to the content of the words. Furthermore, when vocal factors contradict a verbal message (as when a speaker shouts, "I am

cathy®   **by Cathy Guisewite**

not angry!"), listeners judge the speaker's intention from the para-language, not the words themselves.[42]

Paralanguage can affect behavior in many ways, some of which are rather surprising. Researchers have discovered that communicators are most likely to comply with requests delivered by speakers whose rate was similar to their own: People who spoke rapidly responded most favorably to fast talkers, while slow speakers preferred others whose rate was also slow.[43] Besides complying with same-rate speakers, listeners also feel more positively about people who seem to talk at their own rate.

Vocal changes that contradict spoken words are not easy to conceal. If the speaker is trying to hide fear or anger, the voice will probably sound higher and louder, and the rate of talk may be faster than normal. Sadness produces the opposite vocal pattern: quieter, lower-pitched speech delivered at a slower rate.[44]

Sarcasm is one instance in which we use both emphasis and tone of voice to change a statement's meaning to the opposite of its verbal message. Experience this reversal yourself with the following three statements. First say them literally, and then say them sarcastically.

"Thanks a lot!"

"I really had a wonderful time on my blind date."

"There's nothing I like better than lima beans."

As with other nonverbal messages, people often ignore or misinterpret the vocal nuances of sarcasm. Members of certain groups—children, people with weak intellectual skills, and poor listeners—are more likely to misunderstand sarcastic messages than others.[45]

Communication through paralanguage isn't always intentional. Often our voices give us away when we're trying to create an impression different from our actual feelings. For example, you've probably had experiences of trying to sound calm and serene when you were really seething with inner nervousness. Maybe your deception went along perfectly for a while—just the right smile, no telltale fidgeting of the hands, posture appearing relaxed—and then, without being able to do a thing about it, right in the middle of your relaxed comments, your voice squeaked! The charade was over.

Besides reinforcing or contradicting messages, some vocal factors influence the way a speaker is perceived by others. For example, communicators who speak loudly and without hesitations are viewed as more confident than those who pause and speak quietly.[46] People with more attractive voices are rated more highly than those whose speech sounds less attractive.[47] Just what makes a voice attractive can vary. As Figure 6–1 shows, culture can make a difference. Surveys show that there are both similarities and differences between what Mexicans and Americans view as the "ideal" voice. Accent plays an important role in shaping perceptions. Generally speaking, accents that identify a speaker's membership in a group lead to more positive evaluations (if the group is a prestigious one) or negative ratings (if the group is low status).[48] Other factors combine with accent to shape

A pause in the wrong place, an intonation misunderstood, and a whole conversation went awry.

E.M. Forster,
A Passage to India

MEXICAN IDEAL SPEAKER'S VOICE

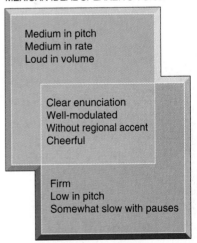

Medium in pitch
Medium in rate
Loud in volume

Clear enunciation
Well-modulated
Without regional accent
Cheerful

Firm
Low in pitch
Somewhat slow with pauses

U.S. IDEAL SPEAKER'S VOICE

FIGURE 6–1
A Comparison of the Ideal Speakers' Voice Types in Mexico and the United States

THE WAY YOU TALK CAN HURT YOU?

W omen also have a distinctive style of speaking: "I was shopping last night? And I saw this wonderful dress? It was so black and slinky?" It's hard to convey intonation in print, but the question marks indicate a rise in pitch at the end of the sentence, as in a question. Many women, especially younger women, use this intonation in declarative sentences: "This is Sally Jones? I have an appointment with Dr. Smith? And I'd like to change it to another day?"

I cringe when I hear this. The rising intonation sounds timid and lacking in self-confidence; the speaker seems to be asking for approval or permission to speak when there's no need to. She should make her point straightforwardly, in an assertion that drops in pitch as it ends.

And I worry that rising intonation harms women. It gets them taken less seriously than they should be in public debates; it encourages salesmen and car mechanics to cheat them when they wouldn't try cheating a man.

A woman friend who studies languages says I've got it wrong. Unlike men, who use conversation to fight for status, she tells me, women see it as co-operative. And they use rising pitch to convey this to their audience. Their tone encourages the supportive interjections, such as "Uh huh," "Exactly," and "I know what you mean," with which women far more than men interlard each other's speech. And it asks listeners to contribute their ideas on the speaker's topic.

At the very least, women's use of rising intonation involves an ambiguity. It uses a sound that in other contexts conveys timidity, for a very different purpose. Given this ambiguity, we shouldn't be surprised if female speakers who are trying to be co-operative are often heard as hesitant.

It's clearly idiotic to treat conversation as a contest, as so many men do. We'd all benefit from a more co-operative approach. But we need a new symbol to express this, one with no connotations of weakness.

If we find this symbol, we can all, men and women, speak in friendly but firm tones. We can tell anecdotes without lecturing but also without seeming to kowtow. When we call the doctor's, we can say: "This is Sally (or Sam) Jones." (No question about it.) "I have an appointment with Dr. Smith." (I'm reminding you of a fact.) "And I'd like to change it to another day." (Now: Can you help me?)

Thomas Hurka,
Essays on Ethics

perceptions. For instance, the apparent age reflected by a speaker's voice affects the preferences of listeners.[49] Older-sounding communicators whose language was accent-free were rated as most competent, while older-sounding speech by people who did not speak in a culturally standard way were judged least competent.

SKILL BUILDER

BUILDING VOCAL FLUENCY

You can become more adept at both conveying and interpreting vocal messages by following these directions.

1. Join a partner and designate one person *A* and the other *B.*

2. Partner *A* should choose twenty-five to fifty items from the telephone directory, using his or her voice to convey one of the following attitudes:
   a. egotism
   b. friendliness
   c. insecurity
   d. irritation
   e. confidence

3. Partner *B* should try to detect the emotion being conveyed.

4. Switch roles and repeat the process. Continue alternating roles until each of you has both conveyed and tried to interpret at least four emotions.

5. After completing the preceding steps, discuss the following questions:
   a. What vocal cues did you use to make your guesses?
   b. Were some emotions easier to guess than others?
   c. Given the accuracy of your guesses, how would you assess your ability to interpret vocal cues?
   d. How can you use your increased sensitivity to vocal cues to improve your everyday communication competence?

TOUCH

Touch can communicate many messages and signal a variety of relationships.[50]

functional/professional (dental exam, haircut)

social/polite (handshake)

friendship/warmth (clap on back, Spanish *abrazo*)

sexual arousal (some kisses, strokes)

aggression (shoves, slaps)

You might object to the examples following each of these categories, saying that some nonverbal behaviors occur in several types of relationships. A kiss, for example, can mean anything from a polite but superficial greeting to the most intense arousal. What makes a

 *The unconscious parental feelings communicated through touch or lack of touch can lead to feelings of confusion and conflict in a child. Sometimes a "modern" parent will say all the right things but not want to touch his child very much. The child's confusion comes from the inconsistency of levels: If they really approve of me so much like they say they do, why won't they touch me?*

William Schutz

given touch more or less intense? Researchers have suggested a number of factors:

What part of the body does the touching

What part of the body is touched

How long the touch lasts

How much pressure is used

Whether there is movement after contact is made

Whether anyone else is present

The situation in which the touch occurs

The relationship between the persons involved[51]

From this list you can see that there is, indeed, a complex language of touch. Since nonverbal messages are inherently ambiguous, it's no surprise that this language can often be misunderstood. Is a hug playful or suggestive of stronger feelings? Is a touch on the shoulder a friendly gesture or an attempt at domination? The ambiguity of nonverbal behavior often leads to serious problems. In one highly publicized date-rape trial, William Kennedy Smith described Patricia Bowman as "brushing up against" him, whereas she described having "bumped into" him. He interpreted her touch as sexually suggestive. From her perspective, the touch had no such meaning—it was an accident, and nothing more.[52] This sort of ambiguity shows the value of perception-checking skills you learned in Chapter Three to clarify the accuracy of your interpretations.

Touch plays a powerful role in shaping how we respond to others.[53] For instance, in a laboratory task, subjects evaluated partners more positively when they were touched (appropriately, of course) by them.[54] Besides increasing liking, touch also boosts compliance. In one study, subjects were approached by a female confederate who requested that they return a dime left in the phone booth from which they had just emerged. When the request was accompanied by a light touch on the subject's arm, the probability that the subject would return the dime increased significantly.[55] In a similar experiment, subjects were asked by a male or female confederate to sign a petition or complete a rating scale. Again, subjects were more likely to cooperate when they were touched lightly on the arm. In the rating-scale variation of the study, the results were especially dramatic: 70 percent of those who were touched complied, whereas only 40 percent of the untouched subjects were willing to cooperate (indicating a predisposition not to comply).[56] An additional power of touch is its on-the-job utility. One study showed that a restaurant waiter's fleeting touches on the hand and shoulder resulted in larger tips.[57]

Besides being the earliest means we have of making contact with others, touching is essential to our healthy development. During the nineteenth and early twentieth centuries a large percentage of children born every year died. In some orphanages the mortality rate was nearly 100 percent, but even children in the most "progressive" homes, hospitals, and other institutions died regularly. When researchers finally tracked down the causes of this disease, they found that the infants suffered from lack of physical contact with parents or nurses, rather than lack of nutrition, medical care, or other factors. They hadn't been touched enough, and as a result they died. From this knowledge came the practice of "mothering" children in institutions—picking the baby up, carrying it around, and handling it several times each day. At one hospital that began this practice, the death rate for infants fell from between 30 and 35 percent to below 10 percent.[58]

Contemporary research confirms the relationship between touch and health. Studies at the University of Miami's School of Medicine's Touch Research Institute have shown that premature babies grow faster and gain more weight when massaged.[59] The same institute's researchers demonstrated that massage can help premature children gain weight, aid colicky children to sleep better, improve the mood of depressed adolescents, and boost the immune function of cancer and HIV patients. Research shows that touch between therapists and clients has the potential to encourage a variety of beneficial changes: more self-disclosure, client self-acceptance, and more positive client-therapist relationships.[60]

In traditional U.S. culture touching is generally more appropriate for women than for men.[61] Males touch their male friends less than they touch their female friends, and also less than females touch their female friends. Fear of homosexuality seems to be a strong reason why men are reluctant to touch one another. Although females are more comfortable about touching than men, gender isn't the only factor that shapes contact. In general, the degree of touch comfort goes along with openness to expressing intimate feelings, an active interpersonal style, and satisfactory relationships.[62]

> *In our now more than slightly cockeyed world, there seems to be little provision for someone to get touched without having to go to bed with whoever does the touching. And that's something to think about. We have mixed up simple healing, warm touching with sexual advances. So much so, that it often seems as if there is no middle way between "Don't you dare touch me!" and "Okay, you touched me, so now we should make love!" A nation which is able to distinguish the fine points between offensive and defensive pass interference, bogies, birdies, and par, a schuss and a slalom, a technical, a personal, and a player-control foul should certainly be able to make some far more obvious distinctions between various sorts of body contact.*
>
> Sidney Simon,
> *Caring, Feeling, Touching*

INVITATION TO INSIGHT

THE RULES OF TOUCH

Like most types of nonverbal behavior, touching is governed by cultural and social rules. Imagine you are writing a guidebook for visitors from another culture. Describe the rules that govern touching in the following relationships. In each case, describe how the gender of the participants affects the rules.

   a. An adult and a five-year-old child
   b. An adult and a twelve-year-old
   c. Two good friends
   d. Boss and employee

PHYSICAL ATTRACTIVENESS

The importance of beauty has been emphasized in the arts for centuries. More recently, social scientists have begun to measure the degree to which physical attractiveness affects interaction between people.[63] For example, women who are perceived as attractive have more dates, receive higher grades in college, persuade males with greater ease, and receive lighter court sentences. Both men and women whom others view as attractive are rated as being more sensitive, kind, strong, sociable, and interesting than their less fortunate brothers and sisters. Who is most likely to succeed in business? Place your bet on the attractive job applicant. For example, shorter men have more difficulty finding jobs in the first place, and men over six feet two inches receive starting salaries that average 12.4 percent higher than comparable applicants under six feet.

The influence of attractiveness begins early in life. Preschoolers were shown photographs of children their own age and asked to choose potential friends and enemies. The researchers found that children as young as three agreed as to who was attractive ("cute") and unattractive ("homely"). Furthermore, the children valued their attractive counterparts—both of the same and the opposite sex—more highly. Also, preschool children rated by their peers as pretty were most liked, and those identified as least pretty were least liked. Children who were interviewed rated good-looking children as having positive social characteristics ("He's friendly to other children") and unattractive children negatively ("He hits other children without reason").

Teachers also are affected by students' attractiveness. Physically attractive students are usually judged more favorably—more intelligent, friendly, popular than their less attractive counterparts.[64] Fortunately, attractiveness is something we can control without having to call a plastic surgeon. We view others as beautiful or ugly, not just on the basis of the "original equipment" they come with, but also on how they use that equipment. Posture, gestures, facial expressions, and other behaviors can increase the attractiveness of an otherwise unremarkable person. Exercise can improve the way each of us looks. Finally, the way we dress can make a significant difference in the way others perceive us, as you'll now see.

CLOTHING

Besides protecting us from the elements, clothing is a means of nonverbal communication. One writer has suggested that clothing conveys at least ten types of messages to others:[65]

1. Economic level
2. Educational level
3. Trustworthiness
4. Social position
5. Level of sophistication

6. Economic background
7. Social background
8. Educational background
9. Level of success
10. Moral character

Research shows that we do make assumptions about people based on their attire. Communicators who wear special clothing often gain persuasiveness. For example, experimenters dressed in uniforms resembling police officers were more successful than those dressed in civilian clothing in requesting pedestrians to pick up litter, and in persuading them to lend a dime to an overparked motorist.[66] Like-

*"Tell me about yourself, Kugelman—your hopes, dreams, career path,
and what that damn earring means."*

wise, solicitors wearing sheriff's and nurse's uniforms increased the
level of contributions to law enforcement and health care cam-
paigns.[67] Uniforms aren't the only kind of clothing that carries influence. In one study, a male and female were stationed in a hallway so
that anyone who wished to go by had to avoid them or pass between
them. In one condition the conversationalists wore "formal daytime
dress"; in the other, they wore "casual attire." Passersby behaved differently toward the couple, depending on the style of clothing: They
responded positively with the well-dressed couple and negatively
when the same people were casually dressed.[68] Similar results in
other situations show the influence of clothing. We are more likely to
obey people dressed in a high-status manner. Pedestrians were more
likely to return lost coins to well-dressed people than to those dressed
in low-status clothing.[69] We are also more likely to follow the lead of
high-status dressers, even when it comes to violating social rules.
Eighty-three percent of the pedestrians in one study followed a well-
dressed jaywalker who violated a "wait" crossing signal, whereas only
48 percent followed a confederate dressed in lower-status clothing.[70]
Women who are wearing a jacket are rated as being more powerful
than those wearing only a dress or skirt and blouse.[71]

Despite the frequency with which we make them, our clothing-
based assumptions aren't always accurate. The stranger wearing wrin-
kled, ill-fitting old clothes might be a manager on vacation, a
normally stylish person on the way to clean a fireplace, or even an
eccentric millionaire. As we get to know others better, the importance of clothing shrinks.[72] This fact suggests that clothing is especially important in the early stages of a relationship, when making a
positive first impression is necessary to encourage others to know us
better. This advice is equally important in personal situations and in

employment interviews. In both cases, our style of dress (and personal grooming) can make all the difference between the chance to progress further and outright rejection.

ETHICAL CHALLENGE
CLOTHING AND IMPRESSION MANAGEMENT

Using clothing as a method of creating impressions is a fact of life. Discover for yourself how dressing can be a type of deception.

1. Identify three examples from your experience when someone dressed in a manner that disguised or misrepresented their true status or personal attributes. What were the consequences of this misrepresentation for you or others?

2. Now identify three occasions in which you successfully used clothing to create a favorable but inaccurate impression. What were the consequences of this deception for others?

3. Based on your conclusions, define any situations when clothing may be used as an unethical means of impression management. List both "misdemeanors," in which the consequences are not likely to cause serious harm, and "felonies," in which the deception has the potential to cause serious harm.

PROXEMICS

Proxemics is the study of the way people and animals use space. As you'll see by the end of this chapter, you can sometimes tell how people feel toward each other simply by noting the distance between them. To begin to understand how this is so, try this exercise:

INVITATION TO INSIGHT
DISTANCE MAKES A DIFFERENCE

1. Choose a partner, and go to opposite sides of the room and face each other.

2. Very slowly begin walking toward each other while carrying on a conversation. You might simply talk about how you feel as you follow the activity. As you move closer, try to be aware of any change in your feelings. Continue moving slowly toward each other until you are only an inch or so apart. Remember how you feel at this point.

3. Now, while still facing each other, back up until you're at a comfortable distance for carrying on your conversation.

4. Share your feelings with each other and/or the whole group.

During this experiment your feelings probably changed at least three times. During the first phase, when you were across the room from your partner, you probably felt unnaturally far away. Then as you neared a point about three feet from him or her, you probably felt like stopping; this is the distance at which two people in our culture normally stand while conversing socially. If your partner wasn't someone you're emotionally close to, you probably began to feel quite uncomfortable as you moved through this normal range and came closer; it's possible that you had to force yourself not to move back. Some people find this phase so uncomfortable that they can't get closer than twenty inches or so to their partner.

What was happening here? Each of us carries around a sort of invisible bubble of personal space wherever we go. We think of the area inside this bubble as our private territory—almost as much a part of us as our own bodies. As you moved closer to your partner, the distance between your bubbles narrowed and at a certain point disappeared altogether: Your space had been invaded, and this is the point at which you probably felt uncomfortable. As you moved away again, your partner retreated out of your bubble, and you felt more relaxed.

Of course, if you were to try this experiment with someone very close to you—your mate, for example—you might not have felt any discomfort at all, even while touching. The reason is that our willingness to get close to others—physically as well as emotionally—varies according to the person we're with and the situation we're in. And it's precisely the distance that we voluntarily put between ourselves and others that gives a nonverbal clue about our feelings and the nature of the relationship.

Anthropologist Edward T. Hall has defined four distances that we use in our everyday lives.[73] He says that we choose a particular one depending on how we feel toward the other person at a given time, the context of the conversation, and our interpersonal goals.

INTIMATE DISTANCE   The first of Hall's zones begins with skin contact and ranges out to about eighteen inches. We usually use **intimate distance** with people who are emotionally very close to us, and then mostly in private situations—making love, caressing, comforting, protecting. By allowing someone to move into our intimate distance we're letting them enter our territory. When we do this voluntarily, it's usually a sign of trust: We've willingly lowered our defenses. On the other hand, when someone invades this most personal area without our consent, we usually feel threatened. This explains the discomfort we sometimes feel when forced into crowded places like buses or elevators with strangers. At times like these the standard behavior in our society is to draw away or tense our muscles and avoid eye contact. This is a nonverbal way of signaling, "I'm sorry for invading your territory, but the situation forced it." Invasions of intimate distance can be taken as a form of sexual harassment, even if the invader has no malicious intentions. For this reason, it's important to honor the cultural rules of spatial integrity.

Once I heard a hospital nurse describing doctors. She said there were beside-the-bed doctors, who were interested in the patient, and foot-of-the-bed doctors, who were interested in the patient's condition. They unconsciously expressed their emotional involvement—or lack of it—by where they stood.

Edward T. Hall

PERSONAL DISTANCE   The second spatial zone, **personal distance,** ranges from eighteen inches at its closest point to four feet at its farthest. Its closer phase is the distance at which most couples stand in public. But if someone of the opposite sex stands this near one partner at a party, the other partner is likely to feel uncomfortable. This "moving in" often is taken to mean that something more than casual conversation is taking place. The far range of personal distance runs from about two and a half to four feet. It's the zone just beyond the other person's reach. As Hall puts it, at this distance we can keep someone "at arm's length." This choice of words suggests the type of communication that goes on at this range: The contacts are still reasonably close, but they're much less personal than the ones that occur a foot or so closer.

SOCIAL DISTANCE   **Social distance** ranges from four to about twelve feet. Within it are the kinds of communication that usually occur in business. Its closer phase, from four to seven feet, is the distance at which conversations usually occur between salespeople and customers and between people who work together. Most people feel uncomfortable when a salesclerk comes as close as three feet, whereas four or five feet nonverbally signals "I'm here to help you, but I don't mean to be too personal or pushy."

We use the far range of social distance—seven to twelve feet—for more formal and impersonal situations. This is the distance at which we sit from our boss (or other authority figure) as she stares across her desk at us. Sitting at this distance signals a far different and less relaxed type of conversation than if we were to pull a chair around to the boss's side of the desk and sit only three or so feet away.

Choosing the optimal distance can have a powerful affect on how we regard others and how we respond to them. For example, students are more satisfied with teachers who reduce the distance between themselves and their classes. They also are more satisfied with the course itself, and they are more likely to follow the teacher's instructions.[74] Likewise, medical patients are more satisfied with physicians who are not standoffish.[75]

PUBLIC DISTANCE   **Public distance** is Hall's term for the farthest zone, running outward from twelve feet. The closer range of public distance is the one that most teachers use in the classroom. In the farther reaches of public space—twenty-five feet and beyond—two-way communication is almost impossible. In some cases, it's necessary for speakers to use public distance because of the size of their audience, but we can assume that anyone who voluntarily chooses to use it when he or she could be closer is not interested in having a dialogue.

TERRITORIALITY

Whereas personal space is the invisible bubble we carry around as an extension of our physical being, **territory** remains stationary. Any geographical area such as a room, house, neighborhood, or country to

Some thirty inches from my nose
The frontier of my Person goes,
And all the untilled air between
Is private *pagus* or demesne.

Stranger, unless with bedroom eyes
I beckon you to fraternize,
Beware of rudely crossing it:
I have no gun, but I can spit.

W.H. Auden

which we assume some kind of "rights" is our territory. What's interesting about territoriality is that there is no real basis for the assumption of proprietary rights of "owning" some area, but the feeling of "owning" exists nonetheless. Your room in the house is *your* room whether you're there or not (unlike personal space, which is carried around with you), and it's your room because you say it is. Although you could probably make a case for your room's *really* being your room (and not the family's or that of the mortgage holder on the house), what about the desk you sit at in each class? You feel the same way about the desk, that it's yours even though it's certain that the desk is owned by the school and is in no way really yours.

The way people use space can communicate a good deal about power and status. Generally we grant people with higher status more personal territory and greater privacy. We knock before entering our boss's office, whereas she can usually walk into our work area without hesitating. In traditional schools professors have offices, dining rooms, and even toilets that are private, whereas the students, who are presumably less important, have no such sanctuaries. Among the military greater space and privacy usually come with rank: Privates sleep forty to a barrack, sergeants have their own private rooms, and generals have government-provided houses.

INVITATION TO INSIGHT

DISTANCE VIOLATIONS

You can test the importance of distance for yourself by violating the cultural rules for use of the proxemic zones outlined on pages 260–62.

1. Join a partner. Choose which one of you will be the experimenter and which will be the observer.

2. In three separate situations, the experimenter should deliberately use the "wrong" amount of space for the context. Make the violations as subtle as possible. You might, for instance, gradually move into another person's intimate zone when personal distance would be more appropriate. (Be careful not to make the violations too offensive!)

3. The observer should record the verbal and nonverbal reactions of others when the distance zones are violated. After each experiment, inform the people involved about your motives and ask whether they were consciously aware of the reason for any discomfort they experienced.

PHYSICAL ENVIRONMENT

In this section, we want to emphasize the ways in which physical settings, architecture, and interior design affect our communication. Begin by recalling for a moment the different homes you've visited lately. Were some of these homes more comfortable to be in than others? Certainly a lot of these kinds of feelings are shaped by the people you were with, but there are some houses where it seems impossible to relax, no matter how friendly the hosts are. We've spent what seemed like endless evenings in what Mark Knapp calls "unliving rooms," where the spotless ashtrays, furniture coverings, and plastic lamp covers seem to send nonverbal messages telling us not to touch anything, not to put our feet up, and not to be comfortable. People who live in houses like this probably wonder why nobody ever seems to relax and enjoy themselves at their parties. One thing is quite certain: They don't understand that this environment they have created can communicate discomfort to their guests.

The impressions that home designs communicate can be remarkably accurate. Researchers showed 99 students slides of the insides or outsides of twelve upper-middle-class homes and then asked them to infer the personality of the owners from their impressions.[76] The students were especially accurate after glancing at interior photos. The decorating schemes communicated accurate information about the homeowners' intellectualism, politeness, maturity, optimism, tenseness, willingness to take adventures, family orientations, and reservedness. The home exteriors also gave viewers accurate perceptions of the owners' artistic interests, graciousness, privacy, and quietness.

Besides communicating information about the designer, an environment can shape the kind of interaction that takes place in it. In one experiment at Brandeis University, Maslow and Mintz found that the attractiveness of a room influenced the happiness and energy of people working in it.[77] The experimenters set up three rooms: an "ugly" one, which resembled a janitor's closet in the basement of a campus building; an "average" room, which was a professor's office; and a "beautiful" room, which was furnished with carpeting, drapes, and comfortable furniture. The subjects in the experiment were asked to rate a series of pictures as a way of measuring their energy and feelings of well-being while at work. Results of the experiment showed that while in the ugly room, the subjects became tired and bored more quickly and took longer to complete their task. When they moved to the beautiful room, however, they rated the faces they were judging higher, showed a greater desire to work, and expressed feelings of importance, comfort, and enjoyment. The results teach a lesson that isn't surprising: Workers generally feel better and do a better job when they're in an attractive environment.

TIME

Social scientists use the term **chronemics** to describe the study of how humans use and structure time. The way we handle time can express both intentional and unintentional messages.[78] For instance, in a culture like ours that values time highly, waiting can be an indicator of status. "Important" people (whose time is supposedly more valuable than others) may be seen by appointment only, while it is acceptable to intrude without notice on lesser beings. To see how this rule operates, consider how natural it is for a boss to drop into a subordinate's office unannounced, while the employee would never

A good house is planned from the inside out. First, you decide what it has to do for its occupants. Then, you let the functions determine the form. The more numerous and various those functions, the more responsive and interesting the house should be. And it may not look at all like you expect.

Dan MacMasters,
Los Angeles Times

intrude into the boss's office without an appointment. A related rule is that low-status people must never make more important people wait. It would be a serious mistake to show up late for a job interview, although the interviewer might keep you cooling your heels in the lobby. Important people are often whisked to the head of a restaurant or airport line, while presumably less exalted masses are forced to wait their turn.

The use of time depends greatly on culture. In some cultures, punctuality is critically important, while in others it is barely considered. Punctual mainlanders often report welcoming the laid-back Hawaiian approach toward time. One psychologist discovered the difference between North and South American attitudes when teaching at a university in Brazil.[79] He found that some students arrived halfway through a two-hour class, and that most of them stayed put and kept asking questions when the class was scheduled to end. A half hour after the official end of the period, the professor finally closed off discussion, since there was no indication that the students intended to leave. This flexibility of time is quite different from what is common in most North American colleges and universities!

Even within a culture, rules of time vary. Sometimes the differences are geographic. In New York City, the party invitation may say 9:00, but nobody would think of showing up before 9:30. In Salt Lake City, guests are expected to show up on time, or perhaps even a bit early. Even within the same geographic area, different groups establish their own rules about the use of time. Consider your own experience. In school, some instructors begin and end class punctually, while others are more casual. With some people you feel comfortable talking for hours in person or on the phone, while with others time seems to be precious and not "wasted."

✤ SUMMARY

Nonverbal communication consists of messages expressed by nonlinguistic means such as distance, touch, body posture and orientation, expressions of the face and eyes, movement, vocal characteristics, clothing, physical environment, and time.

Nonverbal communication is pervasive; in fact, it is impossible to not send nonverbal messages. Most nonverbal communication reveals attitudes and feelings, in contrast to verbal messages which are better suited to expressing ideas. Although many nonverbal behaviors are universal, their use and significance varies from one culture to another. Nonverbal communication serves many functions. It can repeat, substitute for, complement, accent, regulate, and contradict verbal messages.

Nonverbal messages differ from verbal ones in several ways. They involve multiple channels, are continuous instead of discrete, are usually more ambiguous, and are more likely to be unconscious. When presented with conflicting verbal and nonverbal messages, communicators are more likely to rely on the nonverbal ones.

✤ KEY TERMS

accenting
body orientation
chronemics
complementing
contradicting
deception cues
disfluencies
double messages
emblems

gestures
illustrators
intimate distance
kinesics
leakage
manipulators
microexpression
nonverbal communication
paralanguage

personal distance
posture
proxemics
public distance
regulating
repeating
social distance
substituting
territory

✤ MORE RESOURCES ON NONVERBAL COMMUNICATION

READINGS

Buller, David B. "Deception." In *Strategic Interpersonal Communication.* John A. Daly and John M. Wiemann, eds. Hillsdale, N.J.: Erlbaum, 1994.

This article summarizes the nonverbal and verbal behaviors that characterize both deliberate and unintentional deception, as well as discusses the role of deception in interpersonal relationships.

Burgoon, Judee K. "Nonverbal Signals." In *Handbook of Interpersonal Communication.* Mark L. Knapp and Gerald R. Miller, eds. Newbury Park, Calif.: Sage, 1994.

Burgoon offers a definition of nonverbal communication that is more restricted than the one in this chapter. She focuses on the ways communicators produce and process nonverbal messages as well as describes the functions nonverbal communica- *tion performs. The chapter also describes how culture and gender influence the production and interpretation of nonverbal messages.*

Ekman, Paul. *Telling Lies: Clues to Deceit in the Marketplace, Politics, and Marriage.* New York: Norton, 1985.

Ekman summarizes hundreds of research studies examining the role of nonverbal communication in deception. The focus is on detecting others' lies rather than becoming a more effective liar oneself.

Hall, Edward T. *The Hidden Dimension.* Garden City, N.Y.: Anchor Books, Doubleday, 1969.

Hall has probably done more work on proxemics than anyone else, and this book gives you a good survey of the field, including the research with animals that led to our knowledge about how humans use space. It also contains chapters on how different cultures handle space.

———. *The Silent Language.* New York: Fawcett Books, 1959.

A good blend of theory and anecdotes, this book introduces several kinds of nonverbal communication and their cultural implications. As a quote on the cover says, "Diplomats could study this book with profit."

Hickson, Mark L., and Don W. Stacks. *NVC: Nonverbal Communication: Studies and Applications,* second edition. Dubuque, Iowa: W.C. Brown, 1989.

In addition to surveying the various nonverbal channels, Hickson and Stacks examine the role of nonverbal communication in same-sex and opposite-sex relationships, in the family, and on the job. A final chapter also discusses research methodology.

Knapp, Mark L., and Judy Hall, *Nonverbal Communication in Human Interaction,* third edition. Fort Worth, Tex.: Harcourt Brace Jovanovich, 1992.

This comprehensive survey of the field discusses various types of nonverbal communication, and then concludes with chapters that describe how various nonverbal signals combine in everyday life and how nonverbal behavior is acquired.

Matsumoto, Michihiro. *The Unspoken Way: Haragei.* New York: Kodansha International, 1988.

A discussion of the rules of nonverbal behavior in Japanese business and society. This book illustrates how nonverbal customs vary from one culture to another.

Montagu, Ashley. *Touching: The Human Significance of the Skin,* third edition. New York: Harper & Row, 1986.

Montagu has written 335 fascinating pages about skin and the importance it has in our development. It's a book you'll probably want to read before you plan to have children.

FILMS

THE POWER AND LIMITATIONS OF NONVERBAL COMMUNICATION

Quest for Fire (1982) Rated R

This story takes place at the dawn of humanity, before speech has developed. It follows the adventures of three men who seek fire for their tribe. As critics have pointed out, this film can easily be regarded as a laughable Alley Oop caveman picture. Anthropologists can certainly find fault with the many inaccuracies of Neolithic life. Nonetheless, viewers who are willing to accept these flaws may find a moving account of how Neolithic people began to acquire the qualities of civilization. From a communication perspective, the way a lack of language limits the characters reinforces both the power and limitations of nonverbal communication.

MASCULINE AND FEMININE NONVERBAL BEHAVIOR

Tootsie (1982) Rated PG, *Victor/Victoria* (1982) Rated R, *Yentl* (1983) Rated PG, and *Some Like It Hot* (1959) Not Rated

One way to recognize the difference between male and female styles of nonverbal communication is to observe the same person playing both roles. Filmmakers have found this notion intriguing enough to produce several movies in which characters disguise themselves as members of the opposite sex.

Some Like It Hot is Billy Wilder's outrageous farce about two jazz musicians. The Mob has put out a contract on the lives of Joe (Tony Curtis) and Jerry (Jack Lemmon), who hide from their pursuers by donning female clothes and joining an all-woman band. Complications arise when both develop a crush on the group's singer, Sugar Kane Kowalyn Monroe).

In *Tootsie,* Michael Dorsey (Dustin Hoffman) is an aspiring New York actor who can't get any roles . . . at least as a man. In a flash of inspiration he transforms himself into Dorothy Michaels, a middle-aged woman, and wins a part in a daytime soap opera. The film chronicles the misunderstandings that occur between Michael/Dorothy and his friend Sandy (Teri Garr), his fellow actor Julie (Jessica Lange), and her father, Les (Charles Durning).

Yentl (Barbra Streisand) is a young Jewish girl who wants more than anything to be a scholar. But in her central European culture, studying is for men only. She successfully disguises herself as a boy, and happily pursues the academic life she has dreamed of. The plot thickens when she falls in love with another student who, of course, thinks she is a man. Life becomes even more complicated for Yentl when s/he chooses through a string of circumstances to marry a local girl. The plot sounds far-fetched, but the drama is compelling.

Victor/Victoria takes the concept of sex impersonation to new extremes by portraying a woman acting as a man acting as a woman. Julie Andrews plays a starving singer desperate for work. Although there is no market for female singers, audiences love female impersonators. She assumes this role and is a smash success. The plot becomes much more complicated when a Chicago nightclub owner falls in love with Victor/Victoria, refusing to believe the love of his life is a man. He's right of course, but if the truth comes out he/she will lose his/her job.

The plots and acting in all four films are entertaining and compelling, but for observers of communication, the transformations that accompany each character's sex change provide outstanding examples of the ways in which many of the dimensions of nonverbal communication described in this chapter vary between men and women.

Listening: More Than Meets the Ear

i have just
wandered back
into our conversation
and find
that you
are still
rattling on
about something
or other
i think i must
have been gone
at least
twenty minutes
and you
never missed me
now this might say
something

about my acting ability
or it might say
something about
your sensitivity
one thing
troubles me tho
when it
is my turn
to rattle on
for twenty minutes
which i
have been known to do
have you
been missing too

Ric Masten

s Ric Masten's poem on the opposite page shows, there's more to listening than gazing politely at a speaker and nodding your head every so often. As you will soon learn, listening is a demanding and complex activity—and just as important as speaking in the communication process.

If frequency is a measure of importance, then listening easily qualifies as the most prominent kind of communication. We spend more time listening to others than in any other type of communication. One study (summarized in Figure 7–1) revealed that college students spent an average of 14 percent of their communicating time writing, 16 percent speaking, 17 percent reading, and a whopping 53 percent listening. Listening was broken down further into listening to mass communication media, such as radio and television, and listening to face-to-face messages. The former category accounted for 21 percent of the students' communication time, and the latter accounted for 32 percent—more than any other type of communication.[1] On the job, listening is just as important. Studies show that most employees of major corporations in North America spend about 60 percent of each workday listening to others.[2]

Besides being the most frequent form of communication, listening is arguably just as important as speaking in terms of making relationships work. In one survey, marital counselors identified "failing to take the other's perspective when listening" as one of the most frequent communication problems in the couples with whom they work.[3] When a group of adults was asked what communication skills were most important in family and social settings, listening was ranked first.[4] When the same group was asked to identify the most important on-the-job communication skills, listening again ranked at the top of the list. A study examining the link between listening and career success revealed that better listeners rose to higher levels in their organizations.[5] The ability to listen well was linked to persuasive skills, showing that good listeners are also good speakers.

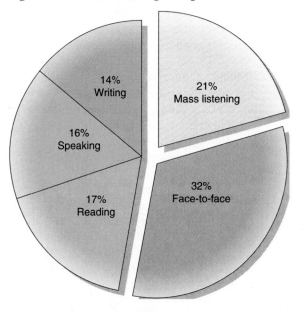

FIGURE 7–1
Types of communication activities

This chapter will explore the nature of listening. After looking at all the elements that make up the process of listening, we will take a look at a variety of poor listening habits and their causes. After reviewing this gloomy picture, you will learn some ways to improve your listening skills, so that your chances of understanding others are better. Finally we'll explore listening and responding skills that can help others solve their problems.

✛ ELEMENTS IN THE LISTENING PROCESS

Before we go any further, it is important to offer a clear definition of listening. There's more to this activity than passively absorbing a speaker's words. In truth, **listening** is a process that consists of five elements: hearing, attending, understanding, responding, and remembering.

HEARING   **Hearing** is the physiological dimension of listening. It occurs when sound waves strike the ear at a certain frequency and loudness. Hearing is also influenced by background noise. If there are other loud noises, especially at the same frequency as the message we are trying to hear, it becomes difficult to sort out the important signals from the background. Hearing is also influenced by auditory fatigue, a temporary loss of hearing caused by continuous exposure to the same tone or loudness. If you spend an evening at a loud party, you may have trouble hearing well, even after getting away from the crowd. If you are exposed to loud noise often enough, permanent hearing loss can result.

ATTENDING   **Attending** is the process of filtering out some messages and focusing on others. As you read in Chapter Three, we attend to messages that stand out from background noise in some way: by being more intense, repetitious, different, and so on. Not surprisingly, research shows that we also attend most carefully to messages when we perceive that there is a payoff for doing so.

UNDERSTANDING   **Understanding** occurs when we make sense of a message. It is possible to hear and attend to a message without understanding it at all. And, of course, it's possible to *misunderstand* a message. This chapter describes the many reasons why we misunderstand others—and why they misunderstand us. It also outlines skills that will help you improve your own understanding of others.

RESPONDING   **Responding** to a message consists of giving observable feedback to the speaker. Listeners don't always respond visibly to a speaker . . . but research suggests that they should. One study of 195 critical incidents in banking and medical settings showed that a major difference between effective and ineffective listening was the kind of feedback offered.[6] Good listeners showed that they were attentive by nonverbal behaviors such as keeping eye contact and reacting with appropriate facial expressions. Their verbal behavior—answering questions and exchanging ideas, for example—also demonstrated their attention. It's easy to imagine how other responses would signal less effective listening. A slumped posture, bored expression, and yawning send a clear message that you are not tuned in to the speaker.

Adding responsiveness to our listening model demonstrates the fact we discussed in Chapter One that communication is *transactional* in nature. Listening isn't just a passive activity. As listeners we are active participants in a communication transaction. At the same time that we receive messages we also send them.

REMEMBERING **Remembering** is the ability to recall information. Research suggests that people remember only about half of what they hear *immediately* after hearing it. They forget half even if they work hard at listening. This situation would probably not be too bad if the half remembered right after were retained, but it isn't. Within two months, half of the half is forgotten, bringing what we remember down to about 25 percent of the original message. This loss, however, doesn't take two months: People start forgetting immediately (within eight hours the 50 percent remembered drops to about 35 percent). Given the amount of information we process every day—from teachers, friends, the radio, TV, and other sources—the *residual message* (what we remember) is a small fraction of what we hear.

This high rate of forgetfulness isn't as depressing as it might seem. Although most people recall very few details of their conversations, they do retain an overall impression about the speaker, especially in important relationships.[7]

By now you can see that listening isn't as simple as it might seem. The challenges of attending to, understanding, responding, and remembering all the messages we hear are tremendous. You can begin to get a sense of how tough it is to listen effectively by trying this exercise.

> *We should all know this: that listening, not talking, is the gifted and great role, and the imaginative role. And the true listener is much more beloved, magnetic, than the talker, and he is more effective, and learns more and does more good. And so try listening. Listen to your wife, your husband, your father, your mother, your children, your friends; to those who love you and those who don't, to those who bore you, to your enemies. It will work a small miracle. And perhaps a great one.*
>
> Brenda Ueland

INVITATION TO INSIGHT

LISTENING BREAKDOWNS

You can overcome believing in some common myths about listening by recalling specific instances when

a. you heard another person's message but did not attend to it.

b. you attended to a message but forgot it almost immediately.

c. you attended to and remembered a message but did not understand it accurately.

d. you understood a message but did not respond sufficiently to convey your understanding to the sender.

e. you failed to remember some or all of an important message.

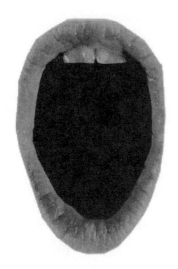

Everybody's talkin' at me

I don't hear a word they're sayin'

Only the echoes of my mind.

Fred Neil,
Everybody's Talkin'

As friends, we don't see eye to eye. But then, we don't hear ear to ear either.

Buster Keaton

✦ TYPES OF NONLISTENING

The preceding exercise demonstrated some of the most common types of poor listening. As you read on, you'll begin to recognize them as behaviors that you and those around you probably use quite often. Although you'll soon learn that a certain amount of inaccurate listening is understandable and sometimes even desirable, it's important to be aware of these types so that you can avoid them when understanding others is important to you.

PSEUDOLISTENING   **Pseudolistening** is an imitation of the real thing. Good pseudolisteners give the appearance of being attentive: They look you in the eye, nod and smile at the right times, and may even answer you occasionally. Behind that appearance of interest, however, something entirely different is going on, for pseudolisteners use a polite façade to mask thoughts that have nothing to do with what the speaker is saying. Often pseudolisteners ignore you because of something on their minds that's more important to them than your remarks. Other times they may simply be bored or think that they've heard what you have to say before and so tune out your remarks. Whatever the reasons, the significant fact is that pseudolistening is really counterfeit communication.

STAGE-HOGGING   **Stage-hogs** (sometimes called "conversational narcissists") try to turn the topic of conversations to themselves instead of showing interest in the speaker.[8] One stage-hogging strategy is a "shift-response"—changing the focus of the conversation from the speaker to the narcissist:

A: "I had a great time mountain-biking last weekend!"
B: "Mountain biking's okay, but I'd rather go running."
C: "My math class is really tough."
D: "You think math is tough? You ought to try my physics class!"

Interruptions are another hallmark of stage-hogging in mainstream North American culture. Besides preventing the listener from learning potentially valuable information, they can damage the relationship between the interrupter and the speaker. For example, applicants who interrupt the questions of employment interviewers are likely to be rated less favorably than job seekers who wait until the interviewer has finished speaking before they respond.[9]

When confronted with stage-hogs, people respond in one of two ways. Sometimes the reaction is passive: talking less, tuning out the speaker, showing disinterest nonverbally, and leaving the conversation. Other strategies are more active: trying to recapture the floor, hinting about the stage-hog's dominance, or confronting the speaker about his or her narcissism. Reactions like these give stage-hogs a taste of their own medicine, turning the conversation into a verbal tug-of-war.

AT A LECTURE—ONLY 12% LISTEN

Bright-eyed college students in lecture halls aren't necessarily listening to the professor, the American Psychological Association was told yesterday.

If you shot off a gun at sporadic intervals and asked the students to encode their thoughts and moods at that moment, you would discover that:

- *About 20 percent of the students, men and women, are pursuing erotic thoughts.*
- *Another 20 percent are reminiscing about something.*
- *Only 20 percent are actually paying attention to the lecture; 12 percent actively listen.*
- *The others are worrying, daydreaming, thinking about lunch or—surprise—religion (8 percent).*

This confirmation of the lecturer's worst fears was reported by Paul Cameron, 28, an assistant professor at Wayne State University in Detroit. The annual convention, which ends Tuesday, includes about 2,000 such reports to 10,000 psychologists in a variety of meetings.

Cameron's results were based on a nine-week course in introductory psychology for 85 college sophomores. A gun was fired 21 times at random intervals, usually when Cameron was in the middle of a sentence.

San Francisco Sunday
Examiner and Chronicle

Not all interruptions are attempts at stage-hogging. One study revealed a difference between male and female interrupters.[10] Men typically interrupted conversations far more often than women. Their goals were usually to control the discussion. Women interrupted for very different reasons: to communicate agreement, to elaborate on the speaker's idea, or to participate in the topic of conversation. These sorts of responses are more likely to be welcomed as a contribution to the discussion, and not as attempts to grab the stage.

SELECTIVE LISTENING   Selective listeners respond only to the parts of your remarks that interest them, rejecting everything else. All of us are selective listeners from time to time, as, for instance, when we screen out radio commercials and music and keep an ear cocked for a weather report or an announcement of the time. In other cases, selective listening occurs in conversations with people who expect a thorough hearing but only pay attention to their partner when the subject turns to their favorite topic—perhaps money, sex, a hobby, or some particular person. Unless and until you bring up one of these pet subjects, you might as well talk to a tree.

INSULATED LISTENING   Insulated listeners are almost the opposite of their selective cousins just mentioned. Instead of looking for something, these people avoid it. Whenever a topic arises that they'd rather not

When we speak we do not listen, my son and I. I complain of slights, hurts inflicted on me. He sings a counterpoint, but not in harmony. Asking a question, he doesn't wait to hear. Trying to answer, I interrupt his refrain. This comic opera excels in disharmony only.

Duet
Lenni Shender Goldstein

A father once told me, "I can't understand my kid. He just won't listen to me at all."

"Let me restate what you just said," I replied. "You don't understand your son because he won't listen to you?"

"That's right," he replied.

"Let me try again," I said. "You don't understand your son because he won't listen to you?"

"That's what I said," he impatiently replied.

"I thought that to understand another person, you needed to listen to him," I suggested.

Stephen Covey

deal with, insulated listeners simply fail to hear or acknowledge it. You remind them about a problem, perhaps an unfinished job, poor grades, or the like, and they'll nod or answer you and then promptly forget what you've just said.

DEFENSIVE LISTENING   Defensive listeners take things you intended as innocent comments as personal attacks. The teenager who perceives her parents' questions about her friends and activities as distrustful snooping is a defensive listener, as is the insecure breadwinner who explodes any time his mate mentions money, or the touchy parent who views any questioning by her children as a threat to her authority and parental wisdom. As your reading in Chapter Nine will suggest, it's fair to assume that many defensive listeners are suffering from shaky presenting images and avoid admitting it by projecting their own insecurities onto others.

AMBUSHING   Ambushers listen carefully to you, but only because they're collecting information they'll use to attack what you say. The cross-examining prosecution attorney is a good example of an ambusher. Needless to say, using this kind of strategy will justifiably initiate defensiveness in the other person.

INSENSITIVE LISTENING   Insensitive listeners offer the final example of people who don't receive another person's messages clearly. As we've said before, people often don't express their thoughts or feelings openly but instead communicate them through a subtle and unconscious choice of words or nonverbal clues or both. Insensitive listeners aren't able to look beyond the words and behavior to understand their hidden meanings. Instead, they take a speaker's remarks at face value. The kind of companions Ralph Schoenstein describes on page 279 are insensitive listeners.

Calvin and Hobbes   by Bill Watterson

IS ANYONE LISTENING?

America has better means of communication than any nation on earth. We are constantly developing splendid new techniques for the dissemination of sound, pictures, and print. The only problem is that on the most basic level of communication—person-to-person, live, mouth-to-ear, low-frequency conversation—we're still in the dark ages; for everyone sends well enough, but very few of us are receiving.

Last week in the elevator of my mother's apartment house, a man asked her, "How are you?"

Since Mother had just spent three hours with a tax collector, she smiled graciously and said, "Lousy, thank you."

The man returned the smile and said, "That's nice."

Mother suspected that he either had misunderstood her or was simply a sadist. However, later the same day, she passed a woman who said, "How are you?"

"Suicidally distraught," said Mother.

"Fine," said the woman. "Hope the family's well, too."

This second exchange gave Mother the kind of revelation that only scientists have known when discovering great truths. Because that man and woman weren't people who would have wanted to see Mother out of the way (neither is in her will), she reached a profound conclusion: If you are well enough to be talking, people consider your condition superb, even if you colorfully describe an internal hemorrhage.

Mother's pioneering experimentation in the amenities has so inspired me that I have dedicated myself to continuing her work. Yesterday, I made real progress.

"How are you?" asked a man in front of my house.

"I'll be dead in a week," I said.

"Glad to hear it. Take care now."

There is no known way to shake the composure of the man who makes a perfunctory inquiry about your health; he loves his lines so well that the grimmest truth can't make him revise them. Never is human communication so defeated as when someone asks casually about your condition.

Some day, perhaps when I'm under a bus getting the last rites, I expect such a man to throw me a breezy, "How are you?"

"As well as can be expected," I'll say.

"Good. And the kids?"

"The older one goes to the chair tomorrow. The little one was lost on a Scout hike."

"Swell. The wife okay?"

"She just ran off with the milkman."

"Glad to hear it. You'll have to bring the whole family over one night soon."

Ralph Schoenstein,
Time Lurches On

❖ WHY WE DON'T LISTEN

After thinking about the styles of nonlistening described in the previous pages, most people begin to see that they listen carefully only a small percentage of the time. It's pretty discouraging to realize that much of the time you aren't hearing others and they aren't getting your messages, but this is a fact of life. Sad as it may be, it's impossible to listen *all* the time, for several reasons.

MESSAGE OVERLOAD   The amount of speech most of us encounter every day makes careful listening to everything we hear impossible. As you have already read, many of us spend almost half the time we're awake listening to verbal messages—from teachers, co-workers, friends, family, salespeople, and total strangers, not to mention radio and television. This means that we often spend five hours or more a day listening to people talk. It's impossible to keep our attention totally focused for this amount of time. Therefore, at times we have to let our attention wander. Given the onslaught of messages, it's understandable—perhaps even justifiable—to use pseudolistening and other nonlistening responses. You can explore the moral obligation to listen carefully by completing the Ethical Challenge on page 282.

PREOCCUPATION   Another reason we don't always listen carefully is that we're often wrapped up in personal concerns that are of more immediate importance to us than the messages others are sending. It's hard to pay attention to someone else when you're anticipating an upcoming test or thinking about the wonderful time you had last night with good friends. Yet we still feel we have to "listen" politely to others, and so we continue with our charade.

RAPID THOUGHT   Listening carefully is also difficult for a physiological reason. Although we're capable of understanding speech at rates up to 600 words per minute, the average person speaks between 100 and 150 words per minute.[11] Thus, we have a lot of "spare time" to spend with our minds while someone is talking. And the temptation is to use this time in ways that don't relate to the speaker's ideas, such as thinking about personal interests, daydreaming, planning a rebuttal, and so on. The trick is to use this spare time to understand the speaker's ideas better rather than let your attention wander.

EFFORT   Listening effectively is hard work. The physical changes that occur during careful listening show the effort it takes: The heart rate quickens, respiration increases, and body temperature rises.[12] Notice that these changes are similar to the body's reaction to physical effort. This is no coincidence, for listening carefully to a speaker can be just as taxing as more obvious efforts.

EXTERNAL NOISE   The physical world in which we live often presents distractions that make it hard to pay attention to others. The sound of traffic, music, others' speech, and so on, interferes with our ability to hear well. Consider, for example, how the efficiency of your listening decreases when you are seated in a crowded, hot, stuffy room that is surrounded by traffic and other noises. In such circumstances even the best intentions aren't enough to ensure clear understanding.

HEARING PROBLEMS   Sometimes a person's listening ability suffers from a physiological hearing problem. Once a hearing problem has been diagnosed, it's often possible to treat it. The real tragedy occurs when a hearing loss goes undetected. In such cases both the person with the defect and others can become frustrated and annoyed at the ineffective communication that results. If you suspect that you or someone you know suffers from a hearing loss, it's wise to have a physician or audiologist perform an examination.

FAULTY ASSUMPTIONS   We often make incorrect assumptions that lead us to believe we're listening attentively when quite the opposite is true. When the subject is a familiar one, it's easy to think that you've "heard it all before" although in fact the speaker is offering new information. A related problem arises when you assume that a speaker's thoughts are too simple or too obvious to deserve careful attention, when the truth is that you ought to be listening carefully. At other times just the opposite occurs: You think that another's comments are too complex to be able to understand (as in some lectures), and so you give up trying to make sense of them. A final mistake people often make is to assume that a subject is unimportant, and to stop paying attention when they ought to be listening carefully.

LACK OF APPARENT ADVANTAGES   It often appears that we have more to gain by speaking than by listening. One big advantage of speaking is that it gives you a chance to control others' thoughts and actions. Whatever your goal—to be hired by a prospective boss, to convince others to vote for the candidate of your choice, or to describe the way you want your hair cut—the key to success seems to be the ability to speak well.

Another apparent advantage of speaking is the chance it provides to gain the admiration, respect, or liking of others. Tell jokes, and everyone will think you're a real wit. Offer advice, and they'll be grateful for your help. Tell them all you know, and they'll be impressed by your wisdom. But keep quiet . . . and you think you'll look like a worthless nobody.

Finally, talking gives you the chance to release energy in a way that listening can't. When you're frustrated, the chance to talk about your problems can often help you feel better. In the same way, you can often lessen your anger by letting it out verbally. It is also helpful to share your excitement with others by talking about it, for keeping it inside often makes you feel as if you might burst.

 AT THE PARTY

Unrhymed, unrhythmical,
the chatter goes:

Yet no one hears his own
remarks as prose.

Beneath each topic
tunelessly discussed

The ground-bass is
reciprocal mistrust.

The names in fashion
shuttling to and fro

Yield, when deciphered,
messages of woe.

You cannot read me like
an open book.

I'm more myself than you
will ever look.

Will no one listen to my
little song?

Perhaps I shan't be with
you very long.

A howl for recognition,
shrill with fear,

Shakes the jam-packed
apartment, but each ear

Is listening to its hearing,
so none hear.

W.H. Auden

TABLE 7-1   Comparison of Communication Activities

	LISTENING	SPEAKING	READING	WRITING
LEARNED	First	Second	Third	Fourth
USED	Most	Next to most	Next to least	Least
TAUGHT	Least	Next to least	Next to most	Most

Although it's true that talking does have many advantages, it's important to realize that listening can pay dividends, too. As you'll soon read, being a good listener is one good way to help others with their problems; and what better way is there to have others appreciate you? As for controlling others, it may be true that it's hard to be persuasive while you're listening, but your willingness to hear others out will often encourage them to think about your ideas in return. Like defensiveness, listening is often reciprocal: You get what you give.

LACK OF TRAINING   Even if we want to listen well, we're often hampered by a lack of skill. A common but mistaken belief is that listening is like breathing—an activity that people do well naturally. "After all," the common belief goes, "I've been listening since I was a child. I don't need to study the subject in school."

The truth is that listening is a skill much like speaking: Virtually everybody does it, though few people do it well. One study illustrates this point. In the study, 144 managers were asked to rate their listening skills. Astonishingly, not one of the managers described himself or herself as a "poor" or "very poor" listener, while 94 percent rated themselves as "good" or "very good."[13] The favorable self-ratings contrasted sharply with the perceptions of the managers' subordinates, many of whom said their boss's listening skills were weak. As we have already discussed, some poor listening is inevitable. The good news is that listening can be improved through instruction and training.[14] Despite this fact, the amount of time spent teaching listening is far less than that devoted to other types of communication. Table 7-1 reflects this upside-down arrangement.

ETHICAL CHALLENGE

IS NONLISTENING EVER ACCEPTABLE?

What responsibility do you have to listen as carefully and thoughtfully as possible to other speakers? Are there ever cases where the poor listening habits listed on pages 276–78 (for example, pseudolistening, stage-hogging, defensive listening) are justified? Are there any situations where you would feel allright knowing that others weren't listening carefully to you?

✜ INFORMATIONAL LISTENING

After reading the last few pages, you might decide that listening well is impossible. Fortunately, with the right combination of attitude and skill, you can do a reasonably good job. The first step is to realize that different types of listening are suited for different purposes. With informational listening the goal is to make sure you are accurately receiving the same thoughts the other person is trying to convey—not always an easy feat when you consider the forces that interfere with understanding.

The situations that call for informational listening are endless and varied: following the directions of an instructor or boss, listening to a friend's account of a vacation, learning about your family history from a relative's tales, swapping ideas in a discussion about religion or politics . . . the list goes on and on. You can become a more effective informational listener by following several guidelines.

TALK LESS   Zeno of Citium put it most succinctly: "We have been given two ears and but a single mouth, in order that we may hear more and talk less." If your true goal is to understand the speaker, avoid the tendency to hog the stage and shift the conversation to your ideas. Talking less doesn't mean you should remain completely silent. As you'll soon read, feedback that clarifies your understanding and seeks new information is an important way to understand a speaker. Nonetheless, most of us talk too much when we're claiming to understand others. You can appreciate this point by trying the following exercise.

> So the first simple feeling I want to share with you is my enjoyment when I can really hear someone. I think perhaps this has been a long-standing characteristic of mine. I can remember this in my early grammar school days. A child would ask the teacher a question and the teacher would give a perfectly good answer to a completely different question. A feeling of pain and distress would always strike me. My reaction was, "But you didn't hear him!" I felt a sort of childish despair at the lack of communication which was (and is) so common.
>
> Carl R. Rogers

INVITATION TO INSIGHT

SPEAKING AND LISTENING WITH A "TALKING STICK"

Explore the benefits of talking less and listening more by using a "Talking Stick." This exercise is based on the Native American tradition of "council." Gather a group of people in a circle and designate a particular item as the talking stick. (Almost any manageable object will do.) Participants then pass the object around the circle. Each person may speak

a. when holding the stick;

b. for as long as he or she holds the stick; and

c. without interruption from anyone else in the circle.

When a member is through speaking, the stick passes to the left, and the speaker surrendering the stick must wait until it has made its way around the circle before speaking again.

After each member of the group has had the chance to speak, discuss how this experience differed from more common approaches to listening. Decide how the desirable parts of this method could be introduced into everyday conversations.

FIGURE 7-2

GET RID OF DISTRACTIONS   Some distractions are external: ringing telephones, radio or television programs, friends dropping in, and so on. Other diversions are internal: preoccupation with your own problems, an empty stomach, and so on. If the information you're seeking is really important, do everything possible to eliminate the internal and external noise that interferes with careful listening.

DON'T JUDGE PREMATURELY   Most people would agree with the principle that it's essential to understand a speaker's ideas before judging them. Despite this commonsense fact, all of us are guilty of forming snap judgments, evaluating others before hearing them out. This tendency is greatest when the speaker's ideas conflict with our own. Conversations that ought to be exchanges of ideas turn into verbal battles, with the "opponents" trying to ambush one another in order to win a victory. Disagreements aren't the only kind of conversation in which the tendency to judge others is strong: It's also tempting to counterattack when others criticize you, even when those criticisms may contain valuable truths and when understanding them may lead to a change for the better. Even if there is no criticism or disagreement, we tend to evaluate others based on sketchy first impressions, forming snap judgments that aren't at all valid. Not all premature judgments are negative. It's also possible to jump to overly favorable conclusions about the quality of a speaker's remarks when we like that person or agree with the ideas being expressed. The lesson contained in these negative examples is clear: Listen first. Make sure you understand. *Then* evaluate.

LOOK FOR KEY IDEAS   It's easy to lose patience with long-winded speakers who never seem to get to the point—or *have* a point, for that matter. Nonetheless, most people do have a central idea. By using your ability to think more quickly than the speaker can talk, you may be able to extract the central idea from the surrounding mass of words you're hearing. If you can't figure out what the speaker is driving at, you can always ask in a tactful way by using the skills of questioning and paraphrasing, which we'll examine now.

ASK QUESTIONS   So far we have been discussing listening methods basically passive in nature; that is, those that can be carried out silently. It's also possible to verify or increase your understanding in a more active way by asking questions to be sure you are receiving the speaker's thoughts and feelings accurately.

   Despite their apparent benefits, not all questions are equally helpful. Whereas **sincere questions** are aimed at understanding others, **counterfeit questions** are really disguised attempts to send a message, not receive one. Counterfeit questions come in several varieties:

- *Questions that trap the speaker.* When your friend says, "You didn't like that movie, did you?", you're being backed into a corner. It's clear that your friend disapproves, so the question leaves you with two choices: You can disagree and defend your position, or you can devalue your reaction by lying or equivocating—"I guess it wasn't

> *The greatest compliment that was ever paid me was when one asked me what I thought, and attended to my answer.*
>
> Henry David Thoreau

FIGURE 7–3

The Chinese characters that make up the verb "to listen" tell us something significant about this skill.

EAR

EYES

UNDIVIDED ATTENTION

HEART

Calligraphy by Angie Au.

perfect." Consider how much easier it would be to respond to the sincere question, "What did you think of the movie?"

A tag question like "did you?" or "isn't that right?" at the end of a question can be a tip-off that the asker is looking for agreement, not information. Although some tag questions are genuine requests for confirmation, counterfeit ones are used to coerce agreement: "You said you'd call at 5 o'clock, but you forgot, didn't you?" Similarly, leading questions that begin with "Don't you" (such as, "Don't you think he would make a good boss?") direct others toward a desired response. As a simple solution, changing "Don't you?" to "Do you?" makes the question less leading.

■ *Questions that make statements.* "Are you finally off the phone?" is more of a statement than a question—a fact unlikely to be lost on the targeted person. Emphasizing certain words can also turn a question into a statement: "You lent money to *Tony?*" We also use questions to offer advice. The person who responds with "Are you going to stand up to him and give him what he deserves?" clearly has stated an opinion about what should be done.

■ *Questions that carry hidden agendas.* "Are you busy Friday night?" is a dangerous question to answer. If you say "No," thinking the person has something fun in mind, you won't like hearing, "Good, because I need some help moving my piano." Obviously, such questions are not designed to enhance understanding: They are setups for the proposal that follows. Other examples include, "Will you do me a favor?" and "If I tell you what happened, will you promise not to get mad?" Wise communicators answer questions that mask hidden agendas cautiously, with responses like "It depends" or "Let me hear what you have in mind before I answer."

- *Questions that seek "correct" answers.* Most of us have been victims of questioners who only want to hear a particular response. "Which shoes do you think I should wear?" can be a sincere question—unless the asker has a predetermined preference. When this happens, the asker isn't interested in listening to contrary opinions, and "incorrect" responses get shot down. Some of these questions may venture into delicate territory. "Honey, do you think I look ugly?" can be a request for a "correct" answer.
- *Questions based on unchecked assumptions.* "Why aren't you listening to me?" assumes the other person isn't paying attention. "What's the matter?" assumes that something is wrong. As Chapter Three explains, perception checking is a much better way of checking out assumptions. As you recall, a perception check offers a description and interpretations, followed by a sincere request for clarification: "When you kept looking over at the TV I thought you weren't listening to me, but maybe I was wrong. *Were* you paying attention?"

Unlike the counterfeit questions we've just examined, sincere questions are genuine requests for new information that clarifies a speaker's thoughts or feelings. Although the value of sincere questioning might seem obvious, there are two reasons why people often don't use this information-seeking approach. First, communicators are often reluctant to show their ignorance by asking for explanation of what seems to be an obvious point. At times like this it's a good idea to recall a quote attributed to Confucius: "He who asks a question is a fool for five minutes. He who does not ask is a fool for life."

A second reason people are often disinclined to ask questions is that they think they already understand a speaker; but do we in fact understand others as often or as well as we think? You can best answer by thinking about how often people misunderstand *you* while feeling certain that they know what you've meant. If you are aware that others should ask questions of you more often, then it's logical to assume that the same principle holds true in reverse.

 So the first simple feeling I want to share with you is my enjoyment when I can really hear someone. I think perhaps this has been a long-standing characteristic of mine. I can remember this in my early grammar school days. A child would ask the teacher a question and the teacher would give a perfectly good answer to a completely different question. A feeling of pain and distress would always strike me. My reaction was, "But you didn't hear him!" I felt a sort of childish despair at the lack of communication which was (and is) so common.

Carl R. Rogers

INVITATION TO INSIGHT

COUNTERFEIT QUESTIONS

Check your understanding of counterfeit questions by looking at Jill and Mark's conversation on page 305. Create examples of poor responses that Mark could have given Jill by showing how and where he could have:

a. Asked a question that was really a statement.

b. Asked a question with a hidden agenda.

c. Asked a question that begged for a "correct" answer.

INVITATION TO INSIGHT

continued

d. Asked a question based on an unchecked assumption.

e. Denied Jill the right to her feelings.

f. Minimized the significance of the situation.

g. Focused on "then and there" rather than "here and now."

h. Cast judgment on Jill.

In each case, speculate how Jill might have reacted to Mark's poor response.

PARAPHRASE Questioning is often a valuable tool for increasing understanding. Sometimes, however, it won't help you receive a speaker's ideas any more clearly, and it can even lead to further communication breakdown. To see how, consider the common example of asking directions to a friend's home. Suppose you've received these instructions: "Drive about a mile and then turn left at the traffic signal." Now imagine that a few common problems exist in this simple message. First, suppose that your friend's idea of a mile differs from yours: Your mental picture of the distance is actually closer to two miles, whereas your friend's is closer to 300 yards. Next, consider that "traffic signal" really means "stop sign"; after all, it's common for us to think one thing and say another. Keeping these problems in mind, suppose you tried to verify your understanding of the directions by asking, "After I turn at the light, how far should I go?" to which your friend replied that the house is the third from the corner. Clearly, if you parted after this exchange, you would encounter a lot of frustration before finding the elusive residence.

What was the problem here? It's easy to see that questioning might not have helped you, for your original idea of how far to drive and where to turn were mistaken. Such mistakes exemplify the biggest problem with questioning: Your inquiries don't tell you whether you have accurately received information that has *already* been sent.

The need to understand others is even more important in a variety of everyday situations: making sure you know just what the boss wants, clarifying a school assignment before leaving class, knowing exactly what's behind critical comments others might direct at you, and understanding what others mean when they offer advice.

Since questioning doesn't always provide the information you need, consider another kind of feedback—one that would tell you whether you understood what had already been said before you asked additional questions. Such feedback involves restating in your own words the message you thought the speaker had just sent, without adding anything new:

(To a direction-giver) "You're telling me to drive down to the traffic light by the high school and turn toward the mountains, is that it?"

(To the boss) "So you need me both this Saturday *and* next Saturday—right?"

(To a professor) "When you said 'Don't worry about the low grade on the quiz,' did you mean it won't count against my grade?"

Statements like these that reword the listener's interpretation of a message are commonly termed **paraphrasing** or **active listening.** Like all complete paraphrasing statements, each of the examples above consists of two parts: First, a restatement of what the listener thought the speaker meant; and second, a request for clarification. The preceding examples focused on understanding a speaker's *thoughts.* In other cases a paraphrasing statement will focus on clarifying the *feelings* behind a speaker's words:

"You said you understand, but you look confused. Are you?"

"You seem to be in a hurry. I get the idea you don't want to talk now. Is that right?"

"You said 'Forget it,' but you still sound mad. Are you?"

All the examples we have examined so far show how paraphrasing can clarify the words a speaker has just uttered. When you want to summarize the *theme* that seems to have run through another person's conversation, a complete or partial perception check is appropriate:

"You keep reminding me to be careful. Are you worried about something, or is it just my imagination?"

"Every time I bring up the idea of going camping you change the subject. What's going on?"

Whether your paraphrasing reflects a speaker's thoughts or feelings, and whether it focuses on a specific comment or a general theme, the key to success is to restate the other person's comments in your own words as a way of cross-checking the information. If you simply repeat the speaker's comments verbatim, you will sound foolish . . . and you still might well be misunderstanding what has been said. Notice the difference between simply parroting a statement and true paraphrasing:

Speaker: "I'd like to go, but I can't afford it."
Parroting: "You'd like to go, but you can't afford it."
Paraphrasing: "So if we could find a way to pay for you, you'd be willing to come. Is that right?"

Speaker: "Gawd, do you look awful!"
Parroting: "You think I look terrible."
Paraphrasing: "You think I've put on too much weight?"

Paraphrasing won't always be accurate. But even if your restatement is off-base, your response gives the other person a chance to make a correction. Besides increasing the chance of understanding others, paraphrasing is an excellent way to keep the tone of a confrontation positive. When you are sincerely trying to understand the other person, you are less likely to engage in the kind of hostile behavior that can lead to a destructive battle. For this reason, some communication experts suggest that the ratio of active listening to confronting should be at least 5:1, if not more.[15]

Because it's an unfamiliar way of responding, paraphrasing may feel awkward at first; but if you start by paraphrasing occasionally and then gradually increase the frequency of such responses, you can begin to learn the benefits of this method.

SKILL BUILDER

PARAPHRASING PRACTICE

This exercise will help you see that it is possible to understand someone who disagrees with you, without arguing or sacrificing your point of view.

1. Find a partner, then move to a place where you can talk comfortably. Designate one person as A and the other B.

2. Find a subject on which you and your partner apparently disagree—a current-events topic, a philosophical or moral issue, or perhaps simply a matter of personal taste.

3. Person A begins by making a statement on the subject. Person B's job is then to paraphrase the idea back, beginning by saying something like "What I hear you saying is. . . ." It is very important that in this step B feeds back only what she heard A say without adding any judgment or interpretation. B's job is simply to understand here, and doing so in no way should signify agreement or disagreement with A's remarks.

4. A then responds by telling B whether her response was accurate. If there was some misunderstanding, A should make the correction, and B should feed back her new understanding of the statement. Continue this process until you're both sure that B understands A's statement.

5. Now it's B's turn to respond to A's statement and for A to help the process of understanding by correcting B.

6. Continue this process until each partner is satisfied that she has explained herself fully and has been understood by the other person.

7. Now discuss the following questions:
   a. As a listener, how accurate was your first understanding of the speaker's statements?
   b. How did your understanding of the speaker's position change after you used active listening?
   c. Did you find that the gap between your position and that of your partner narrowed as a result of active listening?
   d. How did you feel at the end of your conversation? How does this feeling compare to your usual emotional state after discussing controversial issues?
   e. How might your life change if you used active listening at home? At work? With friends?

Finding Common Ground through Listening

*t*he reports from the front-lines of the abortion wars are as dispiriting as ever. Hostilities have only escalated and opponents have now become enemies.

But in a vine-covered building behind a wooden fence in suburban Boston, a small group of family therapists is trying to establish a demilitarized zone. The Public Conversations Project they have created is on a leading edge of the nascent movement struggling to defuse the civil wars.

Their project grew out of a question that director Laura Chasin asked herself and her colleagues in 1990: "Do we as family therapists have skills that can be helpfully applied 'out there'?"

Over the past year and a half, they invited groups of people to join a different sort of conversation. Some of their names were provided by Planned Parenthood and Massachusetts Citizens for Life; all identified themselves as pro-choice or pro-life.

Under the ground rules, people were not allowed to try to persuade each other. Instead, over three hours and under the guidance of a project member, they talked and listened. They explored stereotypes of each other, acknowledged ambivalence and watched what emerged from this process.

Some questions indeed led down hopeless, dead ends. When does life begin? Is the fetus a person? Who should decide? But of the 50 people who went through the process, only two were totally unable to find new ways of talking.

"The main thing that happened was the way these people perceived each other," says Chasin. "They came in thinking, oh my God, I'm going to be meeting with *them.* They went out thinking these people are compassionate, principled and share concerns that I have."

Indeed at moments in the video-taped conversations, it is impossible to know the opponents without a label. Which side said, for example, "How do we get people who are in the business of making laws to start thinking about a world in which there would be no need for abortion?"

"These people were in such pitched battles," said another project member, "they didn't have a clue what they had in common." But gradually they uncovered a shared concern about the well-being of children and mothers. Both sides agreed that using abortion as a form of birth control was wrong. They agreed as well about the importance of preventing unintended pregnancy and about the need for sex education.

Chasin and her colleagues harbor no grand illusions that this process will forge A Great Compromise on abortion—take your placards and go home.

But, once a pattern has been "busted," once people are no longer defined as demons, they hope that the public, like the family, may be able to come up with some solutions. Indeed, there are hints of this success in other parts of this movement.

In Missouri, Wisconsin, Texas and California, pro-life and pro-choice people are meeting and talking—carefully.

Ellen Goodman

✤ LISTENING TO HELP

We listen for information out of self-interest. Another reason for listening, however, is to help others with their problems. Sometimes the dilemma is a major one: "I don't know whether we should stay together or split up"; or "I keep getting turned down for jobs I want." At other times the problem is less profound. A friend might be trying to decide what birthday gift to buy or how to spend the weekend.

There's no question about the value of receiving help with personal problems. One survey showed that "comforting ability" was among the most important communication skills a friend could have.[16] The value of personal support is clear when big problems arise, but research shows that the smaller, everyday distresses and upsets can actually take a bigger toll on mental health and physical well-being.[17]

Whether the problem is large or small, knowing how to help is a valuable skill. To understand your present style of helping, try the following exercise before reading on.

INVITATION TO INSIGHT

WHAT WOULD YOU DO?

1. In a moment you'll read a list of situations in which someone tells you of a problem. In each case, write out the words you'd use in responding to this person.

2. Here are the statements:
    a. I don't know what to do about my parents. It seems as if they just don't understand me. Everything I like seems to go against their values, and they just won't accept my feelings as being right for me. It's not that they don't love me—they do. But they don't accept me.
    b. I've been pretty discouraged lately. I just can't get a good relationship going with any guys. . . . I mean a romantic relationship . . . you know. I have plenty of men whom I'm good friends with, but that's always as far as it goes. I'm tired of being just a pal. . . . I want to be more than that.
    c. *(Child to parents)* I hate you guys! You always go out and leave me with some stupid sitter. Why don't you like me?
    d. I'm really bummed out. I don't know what I want to do with my life. I'm pretty tired of school, but there aren't any good jobs around, and I sure don't want to join the service. I could just drop out for a while, but that doesn't really sound very good either.
    e. Things really seem to be kind of lousy in my marriage lately. It's not that we fight too much or anything, but all the excitement seems to be gone. It's like we're in a rut, and it keeps getting worse. . . .
    f. I keep getting the idea that my boss is angry at me. It seems as if lately he hasn't been joking around very much, and he hasn't said anything at all about my work for about three weeks now. I wonder what I should do.

INVITATION TO INSIGHT

continued

3. Once you've written your response to each of these messages, imagine the probable outcome of the conversation that would have followed. If you've tried this exercise in class, you might have two group members role-play each statement. Based on your idea of how the conversation might have gone, decide which responses were helpful and which were unproductive.

Most of the responses you made probably fell into one of several categories. None of these ways of responding is good or bad in itself, but there's a proper time and place for each kind of response. The problem usually occurs, however, when we use them in the wrong situations or depend on one of two styles or responses for all situations.

As you read the following descriptions of these ways of responding, see which ones you used most frequently in the previous exercise, and think about the results that probably would have occurred from your response.

ADVISING   When approached with another's problem, the most common tendency is an **advising response:** to help by offering a solution.[18] Although such a response is sometimes valuable, often it isn't as helpful as you might think.

Often your suggestion may not offer the best course to follow, in which case it can even be harmful. There's often a temptation to tell others how we would behave in their place, but it's important to realize that what's right for one person may not be right for another. A related consequence of advising is that it often allows others to avoid responsibility for their decisions. A partner who follows a suggestion of yours that doesn't work out can always pin the blame on you. Finally, often people simply don't want advice: They may not be ready to accept it, needing instead simply to talk out their thoughts and feelings.

Before offering advice, then, you need to be sure that three conditions are present:

1. Be confident that the advice is correct. You may be certain about some matters of fact, such as the proper way to solve a school problem or the cost of a piece of merchandise, but resist the temptation to act like an authority on matters you know little about. Furthermore, it is both unfair and risky to make suggestions when you aren't positive that they are the best choice. Realize that just because a course of action worked for you doesn't guarantee that it will be correct for everybody.

2. Ask yourself whether the person seeking your advice seems willing to accept it. In this way you can avoid the frustration of making good suggestions, only to find that the person with the problem had another solution in mind all the time.

3. Be certain that the receiver won't blame you if the advice doesn't work out. You may be offering the suggestions, but the choice and responsibility for accepting them are up to the recipient of your advice.

JUDGING   A **judging response** evaluates the sender's thoughts or behaviors in some way. The judgment may be favorable—"That's a good idea" or "You're on the right track now"—or unfavorable—"An attitude like that won't get you anywhere." But in either case it implies that the person doing the judging is in some way qualified to pass judgment on the speaker's thoughts or actions.

Sometimes negative judgments are purely critical. How many times have you heard such responses as "Well, you asked for it!" or "I *told* you so!" or "You're just feeling sorry for yourself"? Although comments like these can sometimes serve as a verbal slap that brings problem-holders to their senses, they usually make matters worse.

In other cases negative judgments are less critical. These involve what we usually call *constructive criticism,* which is intended to help the problem-holder improve in the future. This is the sort of response given by friends about everything from the choice of clothing to jobs to friends. Another common setting for constructive criticism occurs in school, where instructors evaluate students' work to help them master concepts and skills. But whether it's justified or not, even constructive criticism runs the risk of arousing defensiveness since it may threaten the self-concept of the person at whom it is directed.

Judgments have the best chance of being received when two conditions exist.

1. The person with the problem should have requested an evaluation of you. Occasionally an unsolicited judgment may bring someone to his or her senses, but more often this sort of uninvited evaluation will trigger a defensive response.
2. Your judgment should be genuinely constructive and not designed as putdowns. If you are tempted to use judgments as a weapon, don't fool yourself into thinking that you are being helpful. Often the statement "I'm telling you this for your own good . . . " simply isn't true.

If you can remember to follow these two guidelines, your judgments will probably be less frequent and better received.

ANALYZING   In an **analyzing statement,** the listener offers an interpretation of a speaker's message. Analyses like these are probably familiar to you:

"I think what's really bothering you is. . . . "

"She's doing it because. . . . "

"I don't think you really meant that."

"Maybe the problem started when she. . . . "

Interpretations are often effective ways to help people with problems consider alternative meanings—ways they would have never thought of without your help. Sometimes a clear analysis will make a confusing problem suddenly clear, either suggesting a solution or at least providing an understanding of what is occurring.

In other cases, an analysis can create more problems than it solves. There are two problems with analyzing. First, your interpretation may not be correct, in which case the speaker may become even more confused by accepting it. Second, even if your analysis is accurate, telling it to the problem-holder might not be useful. There's a chance that it will arouse defensiveness (since analysis implies superiority and evaluativeness), and even if it doesn't, the person may not be able to understand your view of the problem without working it out personally.

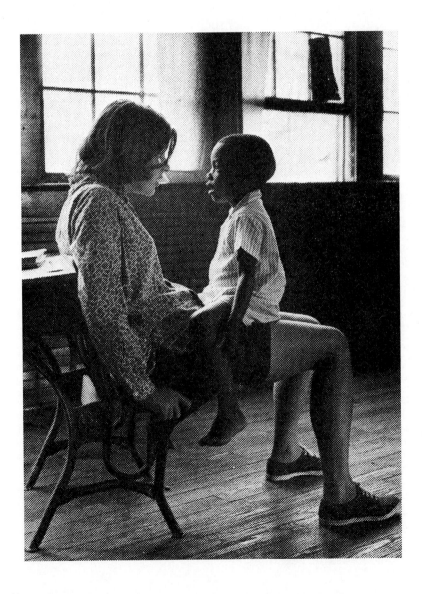

How can you know when it's helpful to offer an analysis? There are several guidelines to follow:

1. Offer your interpretation in a tentative way rather than as absolute fact. There's a big difference between saying "Maybe the reason is . . . " or "the way it looks to me . . . " and insisting, "This is the truth."
2. Your analysis ought to have a reasonable chance of being correct. An inaccurate interpretation—especially one that sounds plausible—can leave a person more confused than before.
3. You ought to be sure that the other person will be receptive to your analysis. Even if you're completely accurate, your thoughts won't help if the problem-holder isn't ready to consider them.
4. Be sure that your motive for offering an analysis is truly to help the other person. It can be tempting to offer an analysis to show how brilliant you are or even to make the other person feel bad for not having thought of the right answer in the first place. Needless to say, an analysis offered under such conditions isn't helpful.

QUESTIONING   A few pages ago we talked about questioning as one way for you to understand others better. A **questioning response** can also be a way to help others think about their problems and understand them more clearly. For example, questioning can help a problem-holder define vague ideas more precisely. You might respond to a friend with a line of questioning: "You said Greg has been acting 'differently' toward you lately. What has he been doing?" Another example of a question that helps clarify is: "You told your roommates that you wanted them to be more helpful in keeping the place clean. What would you like them to do?"

Questions can also encourage a problem-holder to examine a situation in more detail by talking either about what happened or about personal feelings—for example, "How did you feel when they turned you down? What did you do then?" This type of questioning is particularly helpful when you are dealing with someone who is quiet or is unwilling under the circumstances to talk about the problem very much.

Although questions have the potential to be helpful, they also run the risk of confusing or distracting the person with the problem. The best questioning follows these principles:

1. Don't ask questions just to satisfy your own curiosity. You might become so interested in the other person's story that you will want to hear more. "What did he say then?" you might be tempted to ask. "What happened next?" Responding to questions like these might confuse the person with the problem, or even leave him or her more agitated than before.
2. Be sure your questions won't confuse or distract the person you're trying to help. For instance, asking someone, "When did the problem begin?" might provide some clue about how to solve it—but it could also lead to a long digression that would only confuse matters. As with advice, it's important to be sure you're on the right track before asking questions.

🐾 SO PENSEROSO

Come, megrims, mollygrubs and collywobbles!
Come, gloom that limps and misery that hobbles!
Come also, most exquisite melancholiage,
As dank and decadent as November foliage!
I crave to shudder in your moist embrace,
To feel your oystery fingers on my face.
This is my hour of sadness and of soulfulness,
And cursed be he who dissipates my dolefulness.
I do not desire to be cheered,
I desire to retire, I am thinking of growing a beard,
A sorrowful beard, with a mournful, a dolorous hue in it,
With ashes and glue in it.
I want to be drunk with despair,
I want to caress my care,
I do not wish to be blithe,
I wish to recoil and writhe,
I will revel in cosmic woe,
And I want my woe to show.
This is the morbid moment,
This is the ebony hour.
Aroint thee, sweetness and light!
I want to be dark and sour!
Away with the bird that twitters!
All that glitters is jitters!
Roses, roses are gray,
Violets cry Boo! and frighten me.
Sugar is stimulating,
And people conspire to brighten me.
Go hence, people, go hence!
Go sit on a picket fence!
Go gargle with mineral oil,
Go out and develop a boil!
Melancholy is what I brag and boast of,
Melancholy I mean to make the most of,
You beaming optimists shall not destroy it.
But while I am at it, I intend to enjoy it.
Go, people, stuff your mouths with soap,
And remember, please, that when I mope, I mope!

Ogden Nash

3. Don't use questions to disguise your suggestions or criticism. We've all been questioned by parents, teachers, or other figures who seemed to be trying to trap us or indirectly to guide us. In this way, questioning becomes a strategy that can imply that the questioner already has some idea of what direction the discussion should take, but isn't willing to tell you directly.

SUPPORTING   There are times when other people want to hear more than a reflection of how *they* feel: They would like to know how *you* feel about them. **Supportive responses** reveal a listener's solidarity with the speaker's situation.

There are several types of support:

Agreement	"You're right—the landlord is being unfair." "Yeah, that class was tough for me too."
Offers to help	"I'm here if you need me." "Let me try to straighten him out. Maybe he'll listen to me."
Praise	"I don't care what the boss said: I think you did a great job!" "You're a terrific person, and if she doesn't recognize it, that's her problem!"
Reassurance	"The worst part is over. It will get easier from here." "I know you'll do a great job."
Diversion	"Let's catch a movie and get your mind off this." "That reminds me of the time we . . . "

Despite their apparent value, supporting responses may not be helpful. In fact, they can even make things worse. Telling a person who is obviously upset that everything is fine or joking about what seems like a serious problem can leave others thinking that you don't regard their problems as very significant. They might interpret your comments as put-downs, leaving them feeling worse than before.

It's easy to identify what effective support *doesn't* sound like. There are certain phrases that usually indicate a lack of empathy on the part of a listener. You're probably not being supportive if you:

- *Deny others the right to their feelings.* Many nonempathic responses imply that certain emotions are wrong or should be stifled. Consider the stock phrase "Don't worry about it." Although the remark may be intended as a reassuring comment, the underlying message is that the speaker wants the person to feel differently. The irony is that the direction probably won't work—after all, it's unlikely that people can or will stop worrying just because you tell them to do so. Other examples of denying feelings include "It's nothing to get so upset about" and "That's a silly way to feel." Research about such responses is clear: "Messages that explicitly acknowledge, elaborate, and legitimize the feelings and perspective of a distressed person are perceived as more helpful messages than those which only implicitly recognize or deny the feelings and perspective of the other."[19]

- *Minimize the significance of the situation.* Consider the times you've been told, "Hey, it's only_____." You can probably fill in the blank in a variety of ways: "a job," "her opinion," "a test," "puppy love," "a party." How did you react when you were told this? You probably thought the person who said it "just didn't understand." To someone who has been the victim of verbal abuse, the hurtful message isn't "just words"; to a child who didn't get an invitation, it isn't "just a party"; to a worker who has been chewed out by the boss, it isn't "just a job." When you minimize the significance of someone else's experience, you aren't responding empathically. Instead, you are interpreting the event from your perspective and rendering judgment—rarely a helpful response.

- *Focus on "then and there" rather than "here and now."* Although it is sometimes true that "you'll feel better tomorrow," it sometimes isn't. You can probably remember times when you felt *worse* the next day. More important, focusing on the future avoids empathizing in the present. Even if the prediction that "ten years from now you won't remember her name" proves correct, it provides little comfort to someone experiencing heartbreak today. "Everything is going to turn out fine" and "There are lots of other

THE FAR SIDE   By GARY LARSON

Looking at Diversity

AN HIV PERSPECTIVE ON HELPFUL LISTENING

Michael Broomhall *has been infected with the HIV virus for nine years. He spends much of his time attending college, volunteering at the local AIDS project, and educating community members about AIDS and HIV.*

Many people who learn I'm HIV positive say, "I wish I could help." Actually, I can help or hurt myself much more than anybody else. I could choose to see myself as a victim and sit around watching television and waiting to die; but I've decided to get the most out of every day of my life. A positive attitude has worked for most of the past nine years, and I think it's one reason why I'm still relatively healthy.

Even though my own attitude is the most important thing, the way others treat me does make a difference. It isn't so much their specific words as some of their attitudes. Let me give you some examples.

Judgmental people aren't helpful at all. I can tell by the way some people look at me that they think, "If you're HIV positive, you probably deserve it." *Nobody* deserves to get this disease! Even if I did some foolish things in my past, most of them were out of ignorance. Anyhow, judgments won't do me much good now.

Another very unhelpful attitude is pity. There's a kind of condescension that some people get. It's like, "I'm healthy and you're sick, you poor guy." Pity may not be helpful, but genuine sympathy can be a real comfort. I think the difference is that sympathetic friends try to understand what it's like for me, and they appreciate the tough things I'm going through. They feel sorry *with* me, not *for* me.

People who ask personal questions just to satisfy their morbid curiosity really put me off. "What does your family think?" That's none of their business. Neither is, "What's it like?" if the only reason for asking is to poke around for something interesting. I don't mind it at all when people ask me questions that will keep them healthy. I do a lot of speaking to students, and I'll tell them anything that might save their lives. I should say that some people with HIV or AIDS are more private than I am, and they don't want to talk about the disease at all. I think you have to respect each person's own feelings on this one.

I really appreciate people who are available to give practical or emotional support. I appreciate it when friends or medical people ask, "What do you want?" or, "Is there anything you need?" and then respect my answer. People who get pushy about helping when I don't want it can be annoying. I remember one nurse who I'm sure had good intentions asking how I was doing. When I answered "Okay," she replied, "Just okay?" Even if I *wasn't* okay, I didn't need somebody else to decide whether I needed their help.

Finally, I really appreciate people who are available for me as friends, and not just helpers. I'm not only a walking virus: I'm a regular person with the same kinds of feelings and quirks that anybody else would have. Nobody can make me forget that I have this virus, but they can help me do good work and enjoy life.

fish in the sea—you'll land one soon" are variations on the same theme. They are platitudes, because everything may not "turn out fine" and the person might not "land one soon." There are times when "the bigger picture" offers reassurance (see *Analyzing*), but most "then and there" clichés suggest that the listener is uncomfortable dealing with the present.

- *Cast judgment.* It usually isn't encouraging to hear "You know, it's your own fault—you really shouldn't have done that" after you've confessed to making a poor decision. This response suggests the listener is playing judge rather than walking in your shoes. As we'll discuss in Chapter Nine, evaluative and condescending statements are more likely to engender defensiveness than to help people change for the better.

- *Defend yourself.* When your response to others' concerns is to defend yourself ("Don't blame me; I've done my part"), it's clear you are more concerned with yourself than with the other person. Chapter Nine offers detailed advice for responding nondefensively to criticism. Until then, realize that justifying yourself isn't compatible with understanding or helping others.

- *Rain on the speaker's parade.* Most of the preceding examples deal with difficult situations or messages about pain. Empathizing, however, involves identifying with others' joys as well as their sorrows. Many of us can recall coming home with exciting news, only to be told: "A 5 percent raise? That isn't so great"; "An A-minus? Why didn't you get an A?"; or "Big deal—I got one of those years ago." Taking the wind out of someone's sails is the opposite of empathizing.

Despite the potential drawbacks, supporting responses *can* be helpful. Guidelines for effective supporting include:

1. Recognize that you can support another person's struggles without approving of their decisions. Suppose, for instance, that a friend has decided to quit a job that you think she should keep. You could still be supportive by saying "I know you've given this a lot of thought, and that you're doing what you think is best." Responses like this can provide support without compromising your principles.
2. Monitor the other person's reaction to your support. If it doesn't seem to help, consider other types of responses that let him or her explore the issue.

Even if your advice, judgments, and analysis are correct and your questions are sincere, and even if your support comes from the best motives, these responses often fail to help. One survey demonstrated how poorly such traditional responses work.[20] Mourners who had recently suffered from the death of a loved one reported that 80 percent of the statements made to them were unhelpful. Nearly half of the "helpful" statements were advice: "You've got to get out more." "Don't question God's will." Despite their frequency, these suggestions were helpful only 3 percent of the time. The next most frequent

If you think communication is all talk, you haven't been listening.

Ashleigh Brilliant

All speech . . . is a dead language until it finds a willing and prepared hearer.

Robert Louis Stevenson

response was reassurance, such as "She's out of pain now." Like advice, this kind of support was helpful only 3 percent of the time. Far more helpful were expressions that acknowledged the mourner's feelings. The remainder of this chapter will explore two kinds of responses that make just this sort of acknowledgment possible: prompting and paraphrasing.

PROMPTING   Advising, judging, analyzing, questioning, and supporting are all active styles of helping that call for a great deal of input from the respondent. Another approach to problem solving is more passive. **Prompting** involves using silences and brief statements of encouragement to draw others out, and in so doing help them solve their own problems. Consider this example:

Pablo: Julie's dad is selling a complete computer system for only $1,200, but if I want it I have to buy it now. He's got another interested buyer. It's a great deal. But buying it would wipe out my savings. At the rate I spend money, it would take me a year to save up this much again.

Tim: Uh huh.

Pablo: I wouldn't be able to take that ski trip over winter break . . . but I sure could save time with my schoolwork . . . and do a better job too.

Tim: That's for sure.

Pablo: Do you think I should buy it?

Tim: I don't know. What do *you* think?

Pablo: I just can't decide.

Tim: (*silence*)

Pablo: I'm going to do it. I'll never get a deal like this again.

Prompting works especially well when you can't help others make a decision. At times like this your presence can act like a catalyst to help others find their own answers. Prompting will work best when it's done sincerely. Your nonverbal behaviors—eye contact, posture, facial expression, tone of voice—have to show that you are concerned with the other person's problem. Mechanical prompting is likely to irritate instead of help.

PARAPHRASING   A few pages ago you read about the value of paraphrasing to understand others. The same skill can be used as a helping tool. When you use this approach, be sure to reflect both the *thoughts* and the *feelings* you hear being expressed. This conversation between two friends shows how reflecting can offer support and help a person find the answer to her own problem:

The Communication Transcript on page 305 suggests several reasons why paraphrasing can be so helpful.[21] First, listeners who reflect the speaker's thoughts and feelings (instead of judging or analyzing, for example) show their involvement and concern. The nonevaluative nature of reflecting encourages the problem-holder to discuss the matter further. Reflecting feelings as well as thoughts allows the problem-holder to unload more of the concerns he or she has been carrying around, often leading to the relief that comes from catharsis. Finally, paraphrasing helps the problem-holder to sort out the problem. The clarity that comes from this sort of perspective can make it possible to find solutions that weren't apparent before.

Although the immediate goal of reflective listening is to help the other person, an additional payoff is that the relationship between speaker and listener improves. For example, couples who communicate in ways that show they understand one another's feelings and ideas are more satisfied with their marriages than couples who express less understanding.[22] The opposite is also true: In marriages where husbands do not give emotional responses to their wives, the stress level grows.

Because empathy is the ingredient that makes paraphrasing thoughts and feelings helpful, it's a mistake to think of reflective listening as a technique that you can use mechanically.[23] It's essential to realize that empathy is a relational matter and not something that can be created just by paraphrasing, or by any other kind of behavior. Carl Rogers, the psychologist generally considered the foremost advocate of active listening, made the case against mechanical paraphrasing strongly: "I am *not* trying to 'reflect feelings.' I am trying to determine whether my understanding of the client's inner world is correct—whether I am seeing it as he or she is experiencing it at this moment."[24] In other words, reflecting is not an end in itself; rather, it is one way to help others by understanding them better.

There are several factors to consider before you decide to paraphrase:

1. *Is the problem complex enough?* Sometimes people are simply looking for information and not trying to work out their feelings. At times like this, paraphrasing would be out of place. If someone asks you for the time of day, you'd do better simply to give her the information than to respond by saying, "You want to know what time it is." If you're fixing dinner and someone wants to know when it will be ready, it would be exasperating to reply "You're interested in knowing when we'll be eating."
2. *Do you have the necessary time and concern?* The kind of paraphrasing we've been discussing here takes a good deal of time. Therefore, if you're in a hurry to do something besides listen, it's wise to avoid starting a conversation you won't be able to finish. Even more important than time is concern. It's not necessarily wrong to be too preoccupied to help or even to be unwilling to exert the considerable effort that active listening requires: You can't help everyone with every problem. It's far better to state honestly that you're unable or unwilling to help than to pretend to care when you really don't.
3. *Are you genuinely interested in helping the other person?* Sometimes as you listen to others, it's easy to relate their thoughts to

Most conversations seem to be carried out on two levels, the verbal level and the emotional level. The verbal level contains those things which are socially acceptable to say, but it is used as a means of satisfying emotional needs. Yesterday a friend related something that someone had done to her. I told her why I thought the person acted the way he had and she became very upset and started arguing with me. Now, the reason is clear. I had been listening to her words and had paid no attention to her feelings. Her words had described how terribly this other person had treated her, but her emotions had been saying, "Please understand how I felt. Please accept my feeling the way I did." The last thing she wanted to hear from me was an explanation of the other person's behavior.

Hugh Prather

your own life or to seek more information just to satisfy your own curiosity. Remember that paraphrasing is a form of helping someone else. The general obligation to reciprocate the other person's self-disclosure with information of your own isn't necessary when the goal is to solve a problem. Research shows that speakers who reveal highly intimate personal information don't expect, or even appreciate, the same kind of disclosure from a conversational partner.[25] Rather, the most competent and socially attractive response is one that sticks to the same topic but is lower in intimacy. In other words, when we are opening up to others, we don't appreciate their pulling a conversational take-away such as "You're worried? So am I! Let me tell you about how I feel . . . "

4. *Can you withhold judgment?* You've already seen that paraphrasing allows other people to find their own answers. You should only use this style if you can comfortably paraphrase without injecting your own judgments. It's sometimes tempting to rephrase others' comments in a way that leads them toward the solution you think is best without ever clearly stating your intentions. As you will read in Chapter Nine, this kind of strategy is likely to backfire by causing defensiveness if it's discovered. If you think the situation meets the criteria for advice described earlier in this chapter, you should offer your suggestions openly.

5. *Is your paraphrasing in proportion to other responses?* Although active listening can be a very helpful way of responding to others' problems, it can become artificial and annoying when it's overused. This is especially true if you suddenly begin to use it as a major response. Even if such responses are potentially helpful, this sudden switch in your behavior will be so out of character that others might find it distracting. A far better way to use paraphrasing is gradually to introduce it into your repertoire of helpfulness, so that you can become comfortable with it without appearing too awkward. Another way to become more comfortable with this style is to start using it on real but relatively minor problems, so that you'll be more adept at knowing how and when to use it when a big crisis does occur.

By now it's clear that there are many ways to help others—probably more than you use. You can also see that each helping style has its advantages and drawbacks. This leads us to the important question of which style or styles are most helpful. There isn't a simple answer to this question.

WHICH STYLE TO USE?

Research shows that *all* styles can help others accept their situation, feel better, and have a sense of control over their problems.[26] Furthermore, communicators who are able to use a wide variety of helping styles are usually more effective than those who rely on just one or two approaches.[27]

Communication Transcript

PARAPHRASING ON THE JOB

The following conversation between two co-workers shows how paraphrasing can help listeners find solutions to their problems. Notice how Jill comes to a conclusion about her problem without advice from Mark. Notice also how the paraphrasing sounds natural when combined with occasional sincere questions and other helping styles.

Jill I've had the strangest feeling about John (*their boss*) lately.

Mark What's that? (*A simple question invites Jill to go on.*)

Jill I'm starting to think maybe he has this thing about women—or maybe it's just about me.

Mark You mean he's coming on to you? (*Mark paraphrases what he thinks Jill has said.*)

Jill Oh no, not at all! But it seems like he doesn't take women—or at least me—seriously. (*Jill corrects Mark's misunderstanding and explains herself.*)

Mark What do you mean? (*Mark asks another simple question to get more information.*)

Jill Well, whenever we're in a meeting or just talking around the office and he asks for ideas, he always seems to pick men. He gives orders to women—men, too—but he never asks the women to say what *they* think.

Mark So you think maybe he doesn't take women seriously, is that it? (*Mark paraphrases Jill's last statement.*)

Jill Yeah. Well, he sure doesn't seem interested in their ideas. But that doesn't mean he's a total woman-hater or a male chauvinist pig. I know he counts on some women in the office. Teresa has been here forever, and he's always saying he couldn't live without her. And when Brenda got the new computer system up and running last month, I know he appreciated that. He gave her a day off and told everybody how she saved our lives.

Mark Now you sound confused. (*Reflects her apparent feeling.*)

Jill I *am* confused. I don't think it's just my imagination. I mean I'm a good producer, but he has never—not once—asked me for my ideas about how to improve sales or anything. And I can't remember a time when he's asked any other women. But maybe I'm over-reacting.

Mark You're not positive whether you're right, but I can tell that this has you concerned. (*Mark paraphrases both Jill's central theme and her feeling.*)

Jill Yes. But I don't know what to do about it.

Mark Maybe you should . . . (*Starts to offer advice, but catches himself and decides to ask a sincere question instead.*) So what are your choices?

Jill Well, I could just ask him if he's aware that he never asks women's opinions. But that might sound too aggressive and angry.

Mark And you're *not* angry? (*Tries to clarify how Jill is feeling.*)

Jill Not really. I don't know whether I *should* be angry because he's not taking ideas seriously, or whether he just doesn't take *my* ideas seriously, or whether it's nothing at all.

Mark So you're mostly confused. (*Reflects Jill's apparent feeling again.*)

Jill Yes! I don't know where I stand with John, and not being sure is starting to get to me. I wish I knew what he thinks of me. Maybe I could just tell him I'm confused about what is going on here and ask him to clear it up. But what if it's nothing? Then I'll look insecure.

Mark (*Mark thinks Jill should confront the boss, but he isn't positive that this is the best approach, so he paraphrases what Jill seems to be saying.*) And that would make you look bad.

Jill I'm afraid maybe it would. I wonder if I could talk it over with anybody else in the office and get their ideas . . .

Mark . . . see what they think . . .

Jill Yeah. Maybe I could ask Brenda. She's easy to talk to, and I do respect her judgment. Maybe she could give me some ideas about how to handle this.

Mark Sounds like you're comfortable with talking to Brenda first.

Jill (*Warming to the idea*) Yes! Then if it's nothing, I can calm down. But if I do need to talk to John, I'll know I'm doing the right thing.

Mark Great. Let me know how it goes.

THEY LEARN TO AID CUSTOMERS BY BECOMING GOOD LISTENERS

Do you need someone to listen to your troubles? Have your hair done. Beauty salon chairs may be to today's women what conversation-centered backyard fences were to their grandmothers and psychiatrists' couches are to their wealthier contemporaries.

"We are not as family-oriented as our ancestors were," says counselor-trainer Andy Thompson. "They listened to and helped each other. Now that we have become a society of individuals isolated from one another by cars, telephones, jobs and the like, we have had to find other listeners."

Community training program director for Crisis House, Thompson has designed and is conducting human relations training sessions for workers to whom customers tend to unburden their woes most frequently—cosmetologists, bartenders and cabdrivers.

"People can definitely help others just by letting them talk," he said. "Relatives, friends or spouses who listen do a lot to keep the mental health of this country at a reasonable rate. Workers in situations that encourage communications can make the same meaningful contribution."

Thompson explained that his training is not meant to replace, or be confused with, professional treatment or counseling. His students fill a gap between family and professionals.

"There are not enough psychiatrists or psychologists to go around," he said. "And some professionals become so technical that their help doesn't mean much to persons who just need a someone who will let them get problems and questions out in the open where they can look at them."

Thompson's first course of training, completed recently, was for cosmetologists.

The human relations training program attempts to make the most of these built-in assets by using a method Thompson calls "reflective listening."

"The purpose is to let the customer talk enough to clarify her own thinking," he said. "We are not interested in having cosmetologists tell women what to do, but to give them a chance to choose their own course of action.

"There is a tendency among listeners to try to rescue a person with problems and pull them out of negative situations. People don't really want that. They just want to discuss what is on their minds and reach their own conclusions."

Cosmetologists are taught to use phrases that aid customers in analyzing their thoughts. Some of the phrases are, "You seem to think . . . " "You sound like . . . " "You appear to be . . . " "As I get it, you . . . " and "It must seem to you that . . . "

There also are barriers to conversation that the cosmetologists are taught to avoid.

"A constant bombardment of questions can disrupt communications," Thompson said. "Commands will have the same effect. Many of them are impossible to follow anyway.

"How many can respond to orders to 'Stop feeling depressed,' 'Don't be so upset,' or 'Don't think about it.'

"The same applies to negative criticism, 'That's dumb,' for instance; and evaluations, such as 'Oh, you're just confused.'

"Comments that seem threatening—'You had better stop feeling sad,' as an example—will end a conversation as quickly as changing the subject or not paying attention."

San Diego Union

You can boost the odds of choosing the best helping style in each situation by considering three factors. First, think about the *situation* and match your response to the nature of the problem. Sometimes people need your advice. In other cases your encouragement and support will be most helpful, and in still other instances your analysis or judgment may be truly useful. And, as you have seen, there are times when your probes and paraphrasing can help others find their own answer.

Besides considering the situation, you should also think about the *other person* when deciding which approach to use. Some people are able to consider advice thoughtfully, while others use suggestions to avoid making their own decisions. Many communicators are extremely defensive, and aren't capable of receiving analysis or judgments without lashing out. Still others aren't equipped to think through problems clearly enough to profit from paraphrasing and probing. Sophisticated helpers choose a style that fits the person.

Finally, think about *yourself* when deciding how to respond. Most of us reflexively use one or two helping styles. You may be best at listening quietly, offering a prompt from time to time. Or perhaps you are especially insightful, and can offer a truly useful analysis of the problem. Of course, it's also possible to rely on a response style that is *unhelpful*. You may be overly judgmental or too eager to advise, even when your suggestions aren't invited or productive. As you think about how to respond to another's problems, consider both your strengths and weaknesses.

✤ SUMMARY

Listening is the most common—and perhaps the most overlooked form of communication. Listening consists of five elements: hearing, attending, understanding, responding, and remembering.

A number of responding styles masquerade as listening, but are only poor imitations of the real thing. We listen poorly for a variety of reasons. Some have to do with the tremendous number of messages that bombard us daily, and with the personal preoccupations and rapid thoughts that distract us from focusing on the information we are exposed to. Another set of reasons includes the considerable effort involved in listening carefully, and the mistaken belief that listening is a natural ability that doesn't require skill or work and which lacks the rewards that come from speaking. A

few listeners fail to receive messages due to physical hearing defects. One important type of listening involves seeking information from others. Some keys to success in this area are to talk less, reduce distractions, avoid making premature judgments, and seek the speaker's key ideas. Asking questions and paraphrasing are two important ways of seeking information.

A second type of listening focuses on helping others solve their problems. Some common helping styles are advising, judging, analyzing, questioning and supporting. Prompting and paraphrasing are less common but effective response styles. The most helpful communicators use a variety of these styles, choosing the one most appropriate for themselves, the situation at hand, and the person with the problem.

✤ KEY TERMS

active listening	insensitive listening	remembering
advising response	insulated listening	responding
ambushing	judging response	selective listening
analyzing statement	listening	sincere questions
attending	paraphrasing	stage-hogging
counterfeit questions	prompting	supporting response
defensive listening	pseudolistening	understanding
hearing	questioning response	

✤ MORE RESOURCES ON LISTENING

READINGS

Albrecht, Terence L., Brant R. Burleson, and Deana Goldsmith. "Supportive Communication." In *Handbook of Interpersonal Communication*, second edition, Mark L. Knapp and Gerald R. Miller, editors. Newbury Park, Calif.: Sage, 1994.

This chapter describes the damaging consequences of a lack of social support, and explains how communicators can provide support for one another in a variety of ways, including listening.

Burleson, Brant R. "Comforting Messages: Features, Functions, and Outcomes." In *Strategic Interpersonal Communication.* John A. Daly and John M. Wiemann, editors. Hillsdale, N.J.: Erlbaum, 1994.

Burleson is a leading researcher on comforting communication. This survey describes the nature and results of supportive responses.

Glatthorn, Allan A., and Herbert R. Adams. *Listen Your Way to Management Success.* Glenview, Ill.: Scott, Foresman, 1983.

As its title suggests, this book is written for current and would-be managers. There is less emphasis on research than in other listening surveys but more attention to communication in on-the-job settings. Glatthorn and Adams also discuss how listening operates in conflicts and in dealing with power in organizations.

Gordon, Thomas. *Parent Effectiveness Training.* New York: Wyden, 1970.

Although Gordon's method is aimed at parents, the principles of communication he discusses are equally appropriate for other types of relationships. His treatment of paraphrasing is clear and detailed.

Steil, Lyman K., Larry L. Barker, and Kittie W. Watson. *Effective Listening: Key to Your Success.* Reading, Mass.: Addison-Wesley, 1983.

Another book that emphasizes listening in business settings. Self-quizzes, quotations, and many examples make the book both informative and interesting.

Wolvin, Andrew W., and Carolyn G. Coakley. *Listening*, third edition. Dubuque, Iowa: W.C. Brown, 1988.

Wolvin and Coakley describe the process of listening and examine the functions it serves: for entertainment, understanding, criticism, and so on.

FILMS

NONLISTENING AND ITS ALTERNATIVES
Kramer vs. Kramer (1979) Rated PG

Ted Kramer (Dustin Hoffman) is an advertising executive whose involvement in his career excludes his wife, Joanna (Meryl Streep), driving her to leave him and their seven-year-old son, Billy (Justin Henry). The early scenes illustrate how Ted's failure to listen to Joanna has been the major cause of the breakup. As the film goes on, we discover that characters who truly listen to one another develop rewarding relationships, while those who don't live isolated lives.

LISTENING TO HELP
Ordinary People (1980) Rated R

Besides its value in illustrating the transactional nature of communication (as described in Chapter One), this film provides a useful look at listening behaviors. Teenaged Conrad (Timothy Hutton) seeks help from a psychiatrist named Berger (Judd Hirsch) to overcome the pain he feels after the death of his brother and the emotional fallout that has contaminated his family's relationships since that event.

After a difficult beginning, Conrad manages to get in touch with the source of his guilt. Berger's combination of acceptance and challenging illustrate the value of a wide range of listening styles.

PART THREE ✚

Looking at Relationships

Intimacy and Distance in Relationships

A relationship can be a push–pull affair. On one hand we hunger for contact. We want the support and release that come from opening up, from sharing our thoughts and feelings with others. But at the same time we seek contact, we also fear and avoid it. We are afraid to reveal ourselves for fear of looking foolish, of being hurt. We like the privacy that comes from keeping thoughts to ourselves and from not having to explain or justify our actions.

This chapter will help you strike a balance between the extremes of intimacy and distance. It will describe the forces that draw people together, and will outline the stages that relationships follow. You will read about self-disclosure: what it is, why we reveal ourselves to others, and how to disclose appropriately. Finally, we will also look at non-disclosing forms of communication and discuss the role they play in interpersonal relationships.

✛ INTIMACY, DISTANCE, AND RELATIONSHIPS

The Seventies' singing group Three Dog Night said it well: One *can* be the loneliest number. For most of us, the desire to connect with others is a powerful one. With the pressures of everyday life we often forget or ignore the pursuit and maintenance of close relationships, but, as Chapter One explained, strong attachments with others not only make us happier—they can also make us healthier and help us live longer.

In his book *Intimacy*, psychotherapist C. Edward Crowther offers a reminder of just how important close relationships can be.[1] As part of a study of people who were dying in hospices and hospitals in the United States and England, he asked each person individually what mattered most in life. Fully 90 percent of these terminally ill patients put intimate relationships at the top of the list. As a 50-year-old mother of three children who was dying of cancer put it, "You need not wait until you are in my condition to know nothing in life is as important as loving relationships."

What does it mean to be intimate? A scene from the Broadway musical *Fiddler on the Roof* raises this question:

Him: Do you love me?

Her: Do I love you? For twenty years I've cleaned the house, raised the kids, given your dinner parties, washed your clothes. After all these years, why ask?

Him: But do you love me?

Her: For twenty years I've lived with you, argued with you, worried with you, worried *about* you, fought with you, starved with you, slept with you! What do you think love is?

Him: Then do you love me?

This dialogue raises some good questions. Does intimacy mean spending time together? Sharing feelings? Having sex? Going through thick and thin? Are intimacy and love identical?

DIMENSIONS OF INTIMACY

The dictionary defines *intimacy* as arising from "close union, contact, association, or acquaintance." This definition suggests that the key element of intimacy is closeness, one element that "ordinary people" have reported as characterizing their intimate relationships.[2] However, it doesn't explain what *kinds* of closeness can create a state of intimacy. In truth, **intimacy** has several dimensions. The first form is *physical.* Even before birth, the developing fetus experiences a physical closeness with its mother that will never happen again, "floating in a warm fluid, curling inside a total embrace, swaying to the undulations of the moving body and hearing the beat of the pulsing heart.[3] As they grow up, fortunate children are continually nourished by physical intimacy: being rocked, fed, hugged, and held. As we grow older, the opportunities for physical intimacy are less regular, but still possible and important. Some physical intimacy is sexual, but this category also can include affectionate hugs, kisses, and even struggles. Companions who have endured physical challenges together—in athletics or emergencies, for example—form a bond that can last a lifetime.

In other cases intimacy comes from *intellectual* sharing. Not every exchange of ideas counts as intimacy, of course. Talking about next week's midterm with your professor or classmates isn't likely to forge strong relational bonds. But when you engage another person in an exchange of important ideas, a kind of closeness develops that can be powerful and exciting.

A third type of intimacy is *emotional:* exchanging important feelings. This chapter will offer several guidelines for disclosing your thoughts and feelings to others. If you follow these suggestions, you will probably recognize a qualitative change in your relationships.

If we define intimacy as being close to another person, then *shared activities* can provide another way to achieve this state. Shared activities can include everything from working side by side at a job to meeting regularly for exercise workouts. When partners spend time together, they can develop unique ways of relating that transform the relationship from an impersonal one to one with interpersonal qualities. For example, both friendships and romantic relationships are often characterized by several forms of play. Partners invent private codes, fool around by acting like other people, tease one another, and play games—everything from having punning contests to arm wrestling.[4]

Some intimate relationships exhibit all four qualities: physical intimacy, intellectual exchanges, emotional disclosure, and shared activities. Other intimate relationships exhibit only one or two. Some relationships, of course, aren't intimate in any way. Acquaintances, roommates, and co-workers may never become intimate. In some cases even family members develop smooth but relatively impersonal relationships.

Not even the closest relationships always operate at the highest level of intimacy. At times you might share all your thoughts or feel-

IF YOU CAN READ THIS, YOU'RE TOO CLOSE.

CARTOON BY PETER STEINER.
REPRINTED WITH PERMISSION.

ings with a friend, family member, or lover; at other times you might withdraw. You might freely share your feelings about one topic and stay more aloof about another one. The same principle holds for physical intimacy, which waxes and wanes in most relationships.

INTIMACY AND DISTANCE: STRIKING A BALANCE

Intimacy is certainly important, but so is distance. It's impossible to have a close relationship with everyone: There simply isn't enough time and energy. Even if we could seek intimacy with everyone we encountered, few of us would want that much closeness. Consider the range of everyday contacts that don't require any sort of intimacy. Some are based on economic exchange (for example, the people at work or the shopkeeper you visit several times a week); some are based on group membership (for example, church or school); some on physical proximity (for example, neighbors, carpooling); and some grow out of third-party connections (for example, mutual friends, child care). Simply engaging in conversational give-and-take can be a kind of enjoyable recreation, not too different from the impromptu "jamming" of musicians who gather together to create music without revealing any personal information.[5]

These examples suggest that intimacy isn't essential, even with people we encounter often. It's possible to have a very satisfying relationship with some friends, neighbors, fellow workers, or even some family members without a high amount of closeness. You can probably think of several quite satisfying relationships that have moderate or even low amounts of intimacy. If you recall the characteristics of interpersonal relationships described in Chapter One, you will see that just one—disclosure—involves intimacy. The other dimensions—uniqueness, irreplaceability, interdependence, intrinsic rewards, and scarcity—are all possible without a great amount of disclosure. This means that it is quite possible to have a wide range of satisfying relationships without having much intimacy at all. (This doesn't mean that intimacy is unimportant—just that it isn't the *only* measure of relational satisfaction.)

Some scholars have pointed out that an obsession with intimacy can lead to *less* satisfying relationships.[6] People who consider intimate communication as the only kind worth pursuing place little value on relationships that don't meet this standard. This can lead them to regard interaction with strangers and casual acquaintances as superficial, or at best as the groundwork for deeper relationships. When you consider the pleasure that can come from polite but distant communication, the limitations of this view become clear. Intimacy is definitely rewarding, but it isn't the only way of relating to others.

Even the kinds of social niceties that are often polite but insincere serve an important social function.[7] Behaving civilly to people you don't like provides the lubrication that keeps public life from degenerating into a series of nasty squabbles. You may not like your landlord, your boss, or a neighbor (and they may not like you!) but good manners can help you take care of necessary business. Even when no conflicts exist, social conventions provide a way to make contact with strangers and acquaintances without expending the energy required to build a personal relationship. Casual remarks about the weather or current events may not create deeply personal relationships, but they can provide a satisfying way of connecting with others.

Even the strongest interpersonal relationships require some distance. On a short-term basis, the desire for closeness waxes and wanes. Lovers may go through periods of much sharing and times of relative withdrawal. Likewise, they experience periods of passion and then times of little physical contact. Friends have times of high disclosure where they share almost every feeling and idea, and then disengage for days, months, or even longer. Figure 8–1 illustrates some

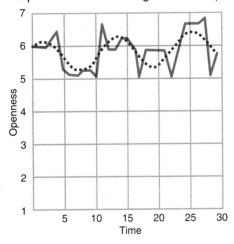

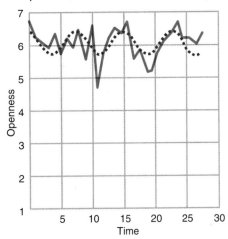

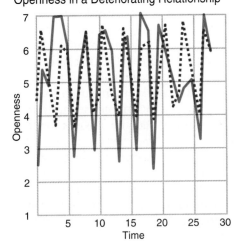

FIGURE 8–1
Cyclical Phases of Openness and Withdrawal in Relationships

From C.A. VanLear, "Testing a Cyclical Model of Communicative Openness in Relationship Development: Two Longitudinal Studies." *Communication Monographs* 58 (1991): 337–361. Copyright held by the Speech Communication Association. Reproduced by permission of the publisher.

patterns of variation in openness uncovered in a study of college students' communication patterns.[8] The students reported the degree of openness in one of their important relationships—a friendship, romantic relationship, or marriage—over a range of thirty conversations. The graphs show a definite pattern of fluctuation between disclosure and privacy in every stage of the relationships.

The desire for both intimacy and distance create what communication scholars have called **dialectical tension**—the state that exists when two opposing or incompatible forces occur simultaneously. The dialectical tension between intimacy and distance makes intuitive sense. Intimacy is rather like chocolate. We may enjoy, even crave it; but too much of a good thing can extinguish the desire for more. Despite this fact, the tension between the opposing drives of openness and closedness can be a dilemma for many friends, family members, and lovers. For example, many former couples report that the breakup of their relationships grew in great part from their difficulty in managing the contradictions between the desires for intimacy and distance.[9]

The opposing needs for openness and separateness operate not only within a relationship. The same conflicting drives also exist between the relational partners—a couple, family members, friends—and the social system in which they operate.[10] Imagine, for instance, the consequences a couple might face when they first tell their friends and families about their growing love, or a family might experience when a member's alcoholism becomes public knowledge. Revelations like these have several potential payoffs for the disclosers: Most noticeably, they can lead others to offer emotional or even material support. On the other hand, openness can lead to disapproval. Another reward of revealing the details of a relationship can be catharsis (no more secrets!), but disclosure can also lead to unwanted gossiping. Openness can sometimes create bonds between the confessors and the people to whom they disclose, but it also risks forcing a wedge between them. Research shows that, in at least some cases, marital adjustment is lower for couples who discuss their problems with outsiders.[11] Given the opposing risks and benefits of disclosure, it's no surprise that the decision to go public with the details of a relationship often isn't easy to make.

The level of intimacy that feels right can change over time. In his book *Intimate Behavior*, Desmond Morris suggests that each of us repeatedly goes through three stages: "Hold me tight," "Put me down," and "Leave me alone."[12] This cycle becomes apparent in the first years of life when children move from the "hold me tight" phase that characterizes infancy into a new "put me down" stage of exploring the world by crawling, walking, touching, and tasting. This move for independence isn't all in one direction: the same three-year-old who insists "I can do it myself" in August may cling to parents on the first day of preschool in September. As children grow into adolescents, the "leave me alone" orientation becomes apparent. Teenagers who used to happily spend time with their parents now may groan at

Love one another, but make not a bond of love:

Let it rather be a moving sea between the shores of your souls.

Fill each other's cup but drink not from one cup.

Give one another of your bread but eat not of the same loaf.

Sing and dance together and be joyous, but let each one of you
  be alone,

Even as the strings of a lute are alone though they quiver with
  the same music.

Kahlil Gibran, *The Prophet*

---

the thought of a family vacation, or even the notion of sitting down at the dinner table each evening. More time is spent with friends or alone. Although this time can be painful for parents, most developmental experts recognize it as a necessary phase in moving from childhood to adulthood.

As the need for independence from family grows, adolescents take care of their "hold me tight" needs by associating with their peers. Friendships during the teenage years are vital, and the level of closeness with contemporaries can be a barometer of happiness. This is the time when physical intimacy becomes an option, and sexual exploration may provide a new way of achieving closeness.

In adult relationships, the same cycle of intimacy and distance repeats itself. In marriages, for example, the "hold me tight" bonds of the first year are often followed by a desire for independence. This need for autonomy can manifest itself in a number of ways, such as the desire to make friends or engage in activities that don't include the spouse, or the need to make a career move that might disrupt the relationship. As the discussion of relational stages later in this chapter will explain, this movement from closeness to autonomy may lead to the breakup of relationships; but it can also be part of a cycle that redefines the relationship in a new form that can recapture or even surpass the intimacy that existed in the past.

Given the equally important needs for intimacy and distance, the challenge is to communicate in a manner that provides the best possible mix of intimate and nonintimate relationships. It's neither possible nor desirable to become intimate with everyone you encounter, and a life with no intimacy can be empty. The material in the rest of this chapter can help you find the optimal level of intimacy in your relationships.

INVITATION TO INSIGHT

YOUR IQ (INTIMACY QUOTIENT)

What is the level of intimacy in your important relationships? Find out by following these directions.

1. Identify the point on each scale below that best describes one of your important relationships.

   a. Your level of physical intimacy

1	2	3	4	5
low				high

   b. Your amount of emotional intimacy

1	2	3	4	5
low				high

   c. The extent of your intellectual intimacy

1	2	3	4	5
low				high

   d. The degree of shared activities in your relationship

1	2	3	4	5
low				high

2. Now answer the following questions:

   a. What responses to each dimension of intimacy seem most significant to you?

   b. Are you satisfied with the intimacy profile outlined by your responses?

   c. If you are not satisfied, what steps can you take to change your degree of intimacy?

MALE AND FEMALE INTIMACY STYLES

Until recently most social scientists believed that women were better than men at developing and maintaining intimate relationships.[13] This view grew from the assumption that the disclosure of personal information is the most important ingredient of intimacy. Most research *does* show that women (taken as a group, of course) are more willing than men to share their thoughts and feelings.[14] In terms of the amount and depth of information exchanged, female-female relationships are at the top of the disclosure list. Male-female relationships come in second, while relationships between men involve less disclosure than any other type. At every age, women disclose more than men, and the information they reveal is more personal and more likely to involve disclosure of feelings. Although both sexes are equally likely to reveal negative information, men are less likely to share positive feelings.

Through the mid-1980s many social scientists interpreted the relative lack of male self-disclosure as a sign that men were unwilling or even unable to develop close relationships. Some argued that the female trait of disclosing personal information and feelings made women more "emotionally mature" and "interpersonally competent" than men. Personal-growth programs and self-help books urged men to achieve closeness by learning to open up and share their feelings.

But scholarship conducted in the past decade has shown that emotional expression isn't the *only* way to develop close relationships. Unlike women who value personal talk, men grow close to one another by doing things. In one study more than 75 percent of the men surveyed said that their most meaningful experiences with friends came from activities other than talking.[15] They reported that, through shared activities, they "grew on one another," developed feelings of interdependence, showed appreciation for one another, and demonstrated mutual liking. Likewise, men regarded practical help as a measure of caring. Research like this shows that, for many men, closeness grows from activities that don't depend heavily on disclosure: A friend is a person who does things *for* you and *with* you.

The difference between male and female measures of intimacy help explain some of the stresses and misunderstandings that can arise between the sexes. For example, a woman who looks for emotional disclosure as a measure of affection may overlook an "inexpressive" man's efforts to show he cares by doing favors or spending time together. Fixing a leaky faucet or taking a hike may look like ways to avoid getting close, but to the man who proposes them, they may be measures of affection and bids for intimacy. Likewise, differing ideas about the timing and meaning of sex can lead to misunderstandings. Whereas many women think of sex as a way to express intimacy that has already developed, men are more likely to see it as a way to *create* that intimacy.[16] In this sense, the man who encourages sex early in a relationship or after a fight may not be just a testosterone-crazed lecher: He may view the shared activity as a way to build closeness. By contrast, the woman who views personal talk as the pathway to intimacy may resist the idea of physical closeness before the emotional side of the relationship has been discussed.

CULTURAL INFLUENCES ON INTIMACY

Historically, the notions of public and private behavior have changed dramatically.[17] What would be considered intimate behavior in modern terms was quite public at times in the past. For example, in sixteenth-century Germany, the new husband and wife were expected to consummate their marriage upon a bed carried among witnesses who would validate the marriage![18] Conversely, at the same time in England as well as in colonial America, the customary level of communication between spouses was rather formal: not much different from the way acquaintances or neighbors spoke to one another.

Even today, the notion of intimacy varies from one culture to another. In one study, researchers asked residents of Britain, Japan, Hong Kong, and Italy to describe their use of thirty-three rules that governed interaction in social relationships.[19] The rules governed a wide range of communication behaviors: everything from the use of humor to shaking hands to the management of money. The results

Looking at Diversity

ARRANGED MARRIAGE IN INDIA

Indira and Jit Pasrich met in Delhi, India, in 1970. They moved to California in 1980 where they raised two children. In this account, Indira shows how notions of marriage are different in collective societies, where the in-group extends beyond the couple alone to include the entire family.

Most people think of arranged marriages as something from another time and place, that would never happen today. Some arranged marriages in India *are* very different from anything you would find here. There are even cases where the bride and groom don't meet until just before their wedding ceremony!

On the surface, at least, arranged marriages between middle class Indians like Jit and me often aren't too different from what often happens in the U.S.A., Canada, or Europe. Our story is an example. I was working in Delhi. One afternoon a friend suggested we meet for tea after work, and Jit and his family just "happened" to drop by. It didn't take very long to realize that this casual encounter was really planned. That first meeting went well enough that we kept meeting until we gradually saw that our marriage would be a good match.

What makes Indian marriages like ours more "arranged" than most you find here is the influence of the husband's and wife's families. In India, people don't just think about their own wants and needs. They also consider how their actions will affect the other people who matter most to them, which usually means their families. So a successful marriage isn't just one in which the bride and groom are happy: both of their families must approve too. You could say that, in India, you don't just marry a husband or wife: You marry an entire family. The consequences of an unsuccessful marriage can affect everyone.

When a couple marries without involvement by their families, Indians call it a "love marriage." I think that term isn't a good one, since the partners in an arranged marriage can love each other just as much. It's just that they also love and care about their families enough to choose a partner who is right for everyone.

I think both the Indian and Western ideas of closeness have their good points. Western individualism helps people find their own path in life, and frees them from sacrificing what is personally important. On the other hand, I think the kind of commitment to others besides yourself that is common in India makes people less self-centered and more concerned about others. I just wish it was possible to combine the best features of both cultures!

showed that the greatest differences between Asian and European cultures focused on the rules for dealing with intimacy: showing emotions, expressing affection in public, sexual activity, respecting privacy, and so on.

Disclosure is especially high in mainstream North American society. In fact, natives of the United States are more disclosing than members of any culture studied.[20] They are likely to disclose more about themselves to acquaintances, and even strangers. By contrast, Germans and Japanese tend to disclose little about themselves except in personal relationships with a select few. Within American culture, intimacy varies from one group to another. For example, working-class black men are much more disclosing than their white counterparts.[21] By contrast, upwardly mobile black men communicate more like white men with the same social agenda, disclosing less with their male friends.

In some collectivist cultures such as Taiwan and Japan there is an especially great difference in the way people communicate with members of their "in-groups" (such as family and close friends) and with those they view as outsiders.[22] They generally do not reach out to strangers, often waiting until they are properly introduced before entering into a conversation. Once introduced, they address outsiders with a degree of formality. They go to extremes to hide unfavorable information about in-group members from outsiders, on the principle that one doesn't wash dirty laundry in public. By contrast, members of more individualistic cultures like the United States and Australia make less distinction between personal relationships and casual ones. They act more familiar with strangers and disclose more personal information, making them excellent "cocktail party conversationalists." Social psychologist Kurt Lewin captured the difference nicely when he noted that Americans were easy to meet but difficult to get to know, while Germans were difficult to meet, but then easy to know well.[23]

Differences like these mean that the level of self-disclosure appropriate in one culture may seem completely inappropriate in another one. If you were raised in the United States or Canada you might view people from other cultures as undisclosing, or even standoffish. But the amount of information that the nonnatives share might actually be quite personal and revealing according to the standards of their culture. The converse is also true: To members of other cultures, North Americans probably appear like exhibitionists who spew personal information to anyone within earshot.

✢ PRELUDE TO INTIMACY: INTERPERSONAL ATTRACTION

We can't be intimate with everyone. What makes us want to develop personal relationships with some people and not with others? What attracts us to one another? This is a question social scientists have studied extensively. Though it would take an entire book to describe their findings, we can summarize a number of explanations. As you read them, consider which ones fit you.

WE LIKE PEOPLE WHO ARE SIMILAR TO US—USUALLY   A large body of research confirms this fact.[24] One of the first steps in getting acquainted with a stranger is the search for common ground—interests, experiences, or

other factors you share. When we find similarities, we usually feel some kind of attraction toward the person who is like us.

This doesn't mean that the key to popularity is to agree with everyone about everything. Research shows that attraction is greatest when we are similar to others in a high percentage of important areas. For example, a couple who support each other's career goals, like the same friends, and have similar beliefs about human rights can tolerate trivial disagreements about the merits of sushi or Miles Davis. With enough similarity in key areas, they can even survive disputes about more important subjects, such as how much time to spend with their families or whether separate vacations are acceptable. But if the number and content of disagreements become too great, the relationship may be threatened.

Similarity turns from attraction to repulsion when we encounter people who are like us in many ways, but who behave in a strange or socially offensive manner. For instance, you have probably disliked people others have said were "just like you" but who talked too much, were complainers, or had some other unappealing characteristic. In fact, there is a tendency to have stronger dislike for similar but offensive people than for those who are offensive but different. One likely reason is that such people threaten our self-esteem, causing us to fear that we may be as unappealing as they are. In such circumstances, the reaction is often to put as much distance as possible between ourselves and this threat to our ideal self-image.

WE LIKE PEOPLE WHO ARE DIFFERENT FROM US—IN CERTAIN WAYS   The fact that "opposites attract" seems to contradict the principle of similarity we just described. In truth, though, both are valid. Differences strengthen a relationship when they are *complementary*—when each partner's characteristics satisfy the other's needs. Individuals, for instance, are often likely to be attracted to each other when one partner is dominant and the other passive. Relationships also work well when the partners agree that one will exercise control in certain areas ("You make the final decisions about money") and the other will take the lead in different ones ("I'll decide how we ought to decorate the place"). Strains occur when control issues are disputed.

Studies that have examined successful and unsuccessful couples over a twenty-year period show the interaction between similarities and differences. The research demonstrates that partners in successful marriages were similar enough to satisfy each other physically and mentally but were different enough to meet each other's needs and keep the relationship interesting. The successful couples found ways to keep a balance between their similarities and differences, adjusting to the changes that occurred over the years.

WE LIKE PEOPLE WHO LIKE US—USUALLY   This source of attraction is especially strong in the early stages of a relationship. At that time we are attracted to people who we believe are attracted to us. Conversely, we will probably not care for people who either attack or seem indifferent toward us. After we get to know others, their liking becomes less of a factor. By then we form our preferences more from the other reasons listed in this section.

*"It would work with us Francine. We share the same
narrow personal interests and concerns."*

DRAWING BY DANA FREDON. © 1979 *THE NEW YORKER MAGAZINE*, INC.

It's no mystery why reciprocal liking builds attractiveness. People who approve of us bolster our feelings of self-esteem. This approval is rewarding in its own right, and it can also confirm a presenting self-concept that says, "I'm a likable person."

However, you can probably think of cases where you haven't liked people who seemed to like you. These experiences usually fall into two categories. Sometimes we think the other person's supposed liking is counterfeit—an insincere device to get something from us. The acquaintance who becomes friendly whenever he needs to borrow your car or the employee who flatters the boss to get a raise are examples. This sort of behavior really isn't "liking" at all. The second category occurs when the other person's approval doesn't fit with our own self-concept. As you read in Chapter Two, we cling to an existing self-concept even when it is unrealistically unfavorable. When someone says you're good-looking, intelligent, and kind, but you believe you are ugly, stupid, and mean, you may choose to disregard the flattering information and remain in your familiar state of unhappiness. Groucho Marx summarized this attitude when he said he would never join any club that would consider having him as a member.

WE ARE ATTRACTED TO PEOPLE WHO CAN HELP US   Some relationships are based on a semieconomic model called **exchange theory.** It suggests that we often seek out people who can give us rewards—either physical or emotional—that are greater than or equal to the costs we encounter in dealing with them. When we operate on the basis of exchange, we decide (often unconsciously) whether dealing with another person is "a good deal" or "not worth the effort."

At its most blatant level, an exchange approach seems cold and calculating, but in some dimensions of a relationship it can be reasonable. A healthy business relationship is based on how well the parties help one another, and some friendships are based on an informal kind of barter: "I don't mind listening to the ups and down of your love life because you rescue me when the house needs repairs." Even close relationships have an element of exchange. Husbands and wives tolerate each other's quirks because the comfort and enjoyment they get make the unhappy times worth accepting. Most deeply satisfying relationships, however, are built on more than just the benefits that make them a good deal.

WE LIKE COMPETENT PEOPLE—PARTICULARLY WHEN THEY'RE "HUMAN"   We like to be around talented people, probably because we hope their skills and abilities will rub off on us. On the other hand, we are uncomfortable around those who are *too* competent—probably because we look bad by comparison.

Given these contrasting attitudes, it's no surprise that people are generally attracted to those who are talented, but who have visible flaws that show they are human, just like us. There are some qualifications to this principle. People with especially high or low self-esteem find "perfect" people more attractive than those who are competent but flawed, and some studies suggest that women tend to be more impressed by uniformly superior people of both sexes, whereas men find desirable but "human" subjects especially attractive. On the whole, though, the principle stands: The best way to gain the liking of others is to be good at what you do but to admit your mistakes.

The fact that a certain degree of imperfection is attractive drives another nail into the coffin of the perfectionistic myth described in Chapter Four. We mistakenly believe that we need to appear flawless in order to gain the respect and affection of others when, in fact, acting "perfect" may drive away the people we want to draw closer.

WE ARE ATTRACTED TO PEOPLE WHO DISCLOSE THEMSELVES TO US—APPROPRIATELY

Telling others important information about yourself can help build liking. Sometimes the basis of this attraction comes from learning about how we are similar, either in experiences ("I broke off an engagement myself") or in attitudes ("I feel nervous with strangers, too"). Another reason self-disclosure increases liking is because it is a sign of regard. When people share private information with you, it suggests they respect and trust you—a kind of liking that we've already seen increases attractiveness.

Not all disclosure leads to liking. People whose sharing is poorly timed often meet with bad results. It's probably unwise, for example, to talk about your sexual insecurities with a new acquaintance or to express your pet peeves to a friend at her birthday party. In addition to bad timing, opening up too much can also be a mistake. Research shows that people are judged as attractive when they match the amount and content of what they share with that of the other person in a relationship. See pages 357–359 for more guidelines about when and how to self-disclose.

WE FEEL STRONGLY ABOUT PEOPLE WE ENCOUNTER OFTEN   As common sense suggests, we are likely to develop relationships with people we interact with frequently. In many cases, proximity leads to liking. We're more likely to develop friendships with close neighbors than with distant ones, for instance; and several studies show that the chances are good that we'll choose a mate with whom we often cross paths. Facts like these are understandable when we consider that proximity allows us to get more information about other people and benefit from a relationship with them.

Familiarity, on the other hand, can also breed contempt. Evidence to support this fact comes from police blotters as well as university laboratories. Thieves frequently prey on nearby victims, even though the risk of being recognized is greater. Spouse and child abuse is distressingly common. Most aggravated assaults occur within the family or among close neighbors. Within the law, the same principle holds: You are likely to develop strong personal feelings of either like or dislike regarding others you encounter frequently.

INVITATION TO INSIGHT

ANALYZING INTERPERSONAL ATTRACTION

1. List the names of five people with whom you have strong positive personal relationships. Use the list that follows to identify the basis of your attraction.
   a. Are their interests, attitudes, values, beliefs, or backgrounds similar to yours?
   b. Do they fill a complementary need for you?
   c. Are they attracted to you?
   d. Is your relationship a fair exchange of rewards?
   e. Are they competent but human?
   f. Have they shared personal information with you?
   g. Do you encounter them frequently?
2. Now consider five people with whom you would like to build a stronger relationship. Use the same list to decide whether you are the kind of person they would be attracted to.

✛ DEVELOPMENTAL STAGES IN INTIMATE RELATIONSHIPS

The process of interpersonal attraction is only the beginning of a relationship. As attraction motivates us to seek intimacy with some people we encounter, communication passes through several stages that characterize different levels of intimacy.

STAGES OF RELATIONAL COMMUNICATION

One of the best-known models of relational stages was developed by Mark Knapp, who broke down the rise and fall of relationships into ten stages, contained in the two broad phases of "coming together" and "coming apart."[25] Other researchers have suggested that any model of relational communication ought to contain a third area of "relational maintenance"—the time when communicators act in ways that keep their relationship functioning.[26] Figure 8–2 shows how Knapp's ten stages fit into this three-part view of relational communication.

The following stages are especially descriptive of intimate, romantic relationships and close friendships. The pattern for other intimate relationships, such as families, would follow different paths. Some valuable associations don't require a high level of intimacy. They are based on other, equally important foundations: career activities, shared political interests, and religion, to mention just a few.[27]

INITIATING The goals in the first stage are to show that you are interested in making contact and to show that you are the kind of person worth talking to. Communication during this **initiating** stage is usually brief, and it generally follows conventional formulas: handshakes, remarks about innocuous subjects like the weather, and friendly expressions. These kinds of behavior may seem superficial and meaningless, but they are a way of signaling that we're interested in building some kind of relationship with the other person. They allow us to say without saying, "I'm a friendly person, and I'd like to get to know you."

EXPERIMENTING   Once we have made contact with a new person, the next step is to decide whether we are interested in pursuing the relationship further. This task involves **uncertainty reduction**—the process of getting to know others by gaining more information about them.[28] The need to reduce uncertainty is especially important when we first meet others. A usual part of uncertainty reduction is the search for common ground, and it involves the conversational basics such as "Where are you from?" "What's your major?" From there we look for other similarities: "You're a runner, too? How many miles do you do a week?"

The hallmark of the **experimenting** stage is small talk. As Mark Knapp says, this small talk is like Listerine: "We hate it, but we take large quantities every day."[29] We tolerate the ordeal of small talk because it serves several functions. First, it is a useful way to find out what interests we share with the other person. It also provides a way to "audition" the other person—to help us decide whether a relationship is worth pursuing. In addition, small talk is a safe way to ease into a relationship. You haven't risked much as you decide whether to proceed further. Finally, small talk *does* provide some kind of link to others. It's often better than being alone.

The willingness to pursue relationships with strangers is partly a matter of personal style. Some people are outgoing and others more

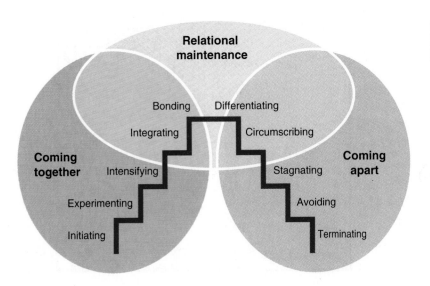

FIGURE 8–2
Stages of Relational
Development

shy, but culture also shapes behavior toward newcomers, especially ones from a different background. Research suggests that members of high-context cultures are more cautious in their first encounters with strangers, and make more assumptions about them based on their backgrounds than do members of low-context cultures.[30] This fact might explain why people from certain backgrounds appear unfriendly, when in fact they are simply operating by a set of rules different from those common in low-context North America.

The quality of communication changes after even a small amount of experimenting. In one study, strangers met with each other for two, four, or six minutes.[31] In every case, researchers found that, as the parties learned more about one another, they asked fewer questions and disclosed more personal information. In addition, as the amount of information the partners knew about one another increased, so did their attraction for one another.

INTENSIFYING   In the **intensifying** stage the kind of truly interpersonal relationship defined in Chapter One begins to develop. Several changes in communication patterns occur during intensifying. The expression of feelings toward the other becomes more common. Dating couples use a wide range of communication strategies to describe

THE FAR SIDE   By GARY LARSON

their feelings of attraction.[32] About a quarter of the time they express their feelings directly, using metacommunication to discuss the state of the relationship. More often they use less direct methods of communication: spending an increasing amount of time together, asking for support from one another, doing favors for the partner, giving tokens of affection, hinting and flirting, expressing feelings nonverbally, getting to know the partner's friends and family, and trying to look more physically attractive.

Other changes mark the intensifying stage. Forms of address become more familiar. The parties begin to see themselves as "we" instead of separate individuals. It is during the intensifying stage that we begin to express directly feelings of commitment to one another: "I'm sure glad we met." "You're the best thing that's happened to me in a long time."

Although commitment grows as a relationship intensifies, communication between partners shows that doubts can still remain. Romantic couples use a variety of strategies to test the commitment of one another.[33] These approaches include asking direct questions, "testing" the partner by presenting challenges that require proof of commitment, hinting in order to gain expressions of commitment, asking third parties for information, and attempting to make the partner jealous. Although these behaviors are frequent in the early stages of a relationship, they decline as the partners spend more time together.

INTEGRATING   As the relationship strengthens, the parties begin to take on an identity as a social unit. Invitations begin to come addressed to the couple. Social circles merge. The partners begin to take on each other's commitments: "Sure we'll spend Thanksgiving with your family." Common property may begin to be designated—our apartment, our car, our song.[34] Partners even begin to speak alike, using personal idioms and sentence patterns.[35] In this sense, the **integrating** stage is a time when we give up some characteristics of our old selves and become different people.

As we become more integrated with others, our sense of obligation to them grows.[36] We feel obliged to provide a variety of resources such as class notes and money, whether or not the other person asks for them. When intimates do make requests of one another, they are relatively straightforward. Gone are the elaborate explanations, inducements, and apologies. In short, partners in an integrated relationship expect more from one another than they do in less intimate associations.

BONDING   During the **bonding** stage, the parties make symbolic public gestures to show the world that their relationship exists. The most common form of bonding in romantic relationships is a wedding ceremony and the legal ties that come with it. Bonding generates social support for the relationship. Custom and law both impose certain obligations on partners who have officially bonded.

Gail and I had come up with something we called the "Weeja bug." Positioning myself directly behind her, I would clasp her around the waist, and then we would walk, sometimes down a busy street, as if we were this mythical four-legged Weeja bug. I don't know how it got started, but we came to associate it with silly high spirits and bursts of great affection.

Cut to a year later, and a woman named Jessica. Overcome with sudden high spirits and a burst of great affection, I clasp her on a busy corner, in the embrace of the Weeja bug and attempt to cross the street.

"What are you doing?" she screams, leaping away.

Robert Masello,
"The Private Language of Lovers"

Some Western cultures have rituals to mark the progress of a friendship and to give it public legitimacy and form. In Germany, for example, there's a small ceremony called Duzen, *the name itself signifying the transformation in the relationship. The ritual calls for the two friends, each holding a glass of wine or beer, to entwine arms, thus bringing each other physically close, and to drink up after making a promise of eternal brotherhood with the word* Bruderschaft. *When it's over, the friends will have passed from a relationship that requires the formal* Sie *mode of address to the familiar* du.

Lillian B. Rubin,
Just Friends: The Role of Friendship in Our Lives

Bonding marks a turning point in relationships. Up to now the relationship may have developed at a steady pace: Experimenting gradually moved into intensifying and then into integrating. Now, however, there is a spurt of commitment. The public display and declaration of exclusivity make this a critical period in the relationship.

DIFFERENTIATING   Now that the two people have formed this commonality, they need to re-establish individual identities. This **differentiating** stage is the point where the "hold me tight" orientation that has existed shifts, and "put me down" messages begin to occur. Partners use a variety of strategies to gain privacy from one another.[37] Sometimes they confront the other party directly, explaining that they don't want to continue a discussion. In other cases they are less direct, offering nonverbal cues, changing the topic, or leaving the room.

Differentiation is likely to occur when a relationship begins to experience the first, inevitable stress. This need for autonomy needn't be a negative experience, however. People need to be individuals as well as parts of a relationship, and differentiation is a necessary step toward autonomy. The key to successful differentiation is maintaining a commitment to the relationship, while creating the space for being an individual as well.

CIRCUMSCRIBING   So far we have been looking at the growth of relationships. Although some reach a plateau of development, going on successfully for as long as a lifetime, others pass through several stages of decline and dissolution. In the **circumscribing** stage communication between members decreases in quantity and quality. Restrictions and restraints characterize this stage, and dynamic communication

becomes static. Rather than discuss a disagreement (which requires some degree of energy on both parts), members opt for withdrawal: either mental (silence or daydreaming and fantasizing) or physical (where people spend less time together). Circumscribing doesn't involve total avoidance, which may come later. Rather, it entails a certain shrinking of interest and commitment.

STAGNATING   If circumscribing continues, the relationship enters the **stagnating** stage. Members behave toward each other in old, familiar ways without much feeling. No growth occurs. The relationship is a hollow shell of its former self. We see stagnation in many workers who have lost enthusiasm for their job yet continue to go through the motions for years. The same sad event occurs for some couples who unenthusiastically have the same conversations, see the same people, and follow the same routines without any sense of joy or novelty.

AVOIDING   When stagnation becomes too unpleasant, parties in a relationship begin to create distance between each other. This is the **avoiding** stage. Sometimes they do it under the guise of excuses ("I've been sick lately and can't see you") and sometimes directly ("Please don't call me; I don't want to see you now"). In either case, by this point the handwriting is on the wall about the relationship's future.

The deterioration of a relationship from bonding through circumscribing, stagnating, and avoiding isn't inevitable. One of the key differences between marriages that end in separation and those that are restored to their former intimacy is the communication that occurs when the partners are unsatisfied.[38] Unsuccessful couples deal with their problems by avoidance, indirectness, and less involvement with one another. By contrast, couples who "repair" their relationship communicate much more directly. They confront one another with their concerns, and spend time and effort negotiating solutions to their problems.

TERMINATING   Characteristics of this final **terminating** stage include summary dialogues of where the relationship has gone and the desire to dissociate. The relationship may end with a cordial dinner, a note left on the kitchen table, a phone call, or a legal document stating the dissolution. Depending on each person's feelings, this stage can be quite short, or it may be drawn out over time, with bitter jabs at each other. In either case, termination doesn't have to be totally negative. Understanding each other's investments in the relationship and needs for personal growth may dilute the hard feelings.

The best predictor of whether the parties will become friends is whether they were friends before their romantic involvement.[39] The way the couple split up also makes a difference. It's no surprise to find that friendships are most possible when communication during the breakup was positive: expressions that there were no regrets for time spent together and other attempts to minimize hard feelings. When communication during termination was negative (manipulative, complaining to third parties), friendships were less likely.

When he pictured their introduction . . . it seemed nothing more than the beginning of their parting. When she had looked up at him that first night and rattled the ice cubes in her paper cup, they were already moving toward their last edgy, miserable year together, towards those months when anything either of them said was wrong, toward that sense of narrowly missed connections. They were like people who run to meet, holding out their arms, but their aim is wrong; they pass each other and keep running. It had all amounted to nothing, in the end.

Anne Tyler,
The Accidental Tourist

INVITATION TO INSIGHT

YOUR RELATIONAL STAGE

You can gain a clearer appreciation of the accuracy and value of relational stages by answering the following questions.

1. Describe the present stage of your relationship and the behaviors that characterize your communication in this stage. Give specific examples to support your assessment.

2. Discuss the trend of the communication in terms of the stages described on pages 328–333. Are you likely to remain in the present stage, or do you anticipate movement to another stage? Which one? Explain your answer.

3. Describe your level of satisfaction with the answer to question 2. If you are satisfied, describe what you can do to increase the likelihood that the relationship will operate at the stage you described. If you are not satisfied, discuss what you can do to move the relationship toward a more satisfying stage.

4. Because both parties define a relationship, define your partner's perspective. Would she or he say that the relationship is at the same stage as you describe it? If not, explain how your partner would characterize it. What does your partner do to determine the stage at which your relationship operates? (Give specific examples.) How would you like your partner to behave in order to move the relationship to or maintain it at the stage you desire? What can you do to encourage your partner to behave in the way you desire?

CHARACTERISTICS OF RELATIONAL DEVELOPMENT AND MAINTENANCE

The ten stages we have just examined offer insights about relational development, but they need further explanation to paint an accurate picture of how communicators operate as they define and shape their relationship.

NOT ALL RELATIONSHIPS MOVE THROUGH ALL TEN STEPS   At first glance, Knapp's ten steps of relational communication seem to suggest that all relationships follow the same trajectory, from initiation through termination. Your own experience almost certainly shows that this isn't necessarily the case. Some never make it past the early stages of initiating and experimenting. Others (with fellow workers or neighbors, for example), develop as far as integrating or even intensifying without ever reaching the stage of bonding. The ten-step model illustrates the range of possibilities, but it doesn't describe a guaranteed pathway for every relationship.

INTIMACY IS NOT THE ONLY GOAL OF RELATIONSHIPS   Stages like intensifying and bonding can suggest that the high point of every relationship is intimacy. This certainly isn't the case. Many important and satisfying relationships are not interpersonal in the qualitative sense described in Chapter One. Fellow workers, neighbors, and community members often meet their needs without ever achieving any real degree of intimacy. Even some family members get along well by deliberately keeping their physical and emotional distance from one another. Relationships of this sort might achieve a modest degree of integration, but never go further.

MOVEMENT OCCURS WITHIN STAGES   According to Knapp, a relationship can exist in only one stage at a time. At any moment it will exhibit the most predominant traits of just one of the ten levels described on pages 328–333. Despite this fact, elements of other levels are usually present. For example, two lovers deep in the throes of integrating may still do their share of experimenting and have differentiating disagreements. Likewise, family members who spend most of their energy avoiding one another may have an occasional good spell in which their former closeness briefly intensifies. Even though there may be overtones of several stages, one will predominate.

No relationship is stable, so it is reasonable to expect that from day to day the interaction between people will change. Nonetheless, if you take a step back from any relationship, you will probably be able to recognize a common theme that characterizes one of the ten stages.

MOVEMENT BETWEEN STEPS IS GENERALLY SEQUENTIAL   Typically relationships move from one stage to another in a step-by-step manner as they develop and deteriorate. This doesn't mean that every relationship will move through all ten stages. Some reach a certain point and then go no further. When this occurs, movement is usually across the staircase to the corresponding point of deterioration. For example, two people who have just met at a party may move from initiating to avoiding, whereas a couple that has progressed to intensifying is likely to begin circumscribing their relationship before it decays into stagnation and avoidance.

There are exceptions to the rule of sequential development. Occasionally partners may skip a stage: Sudden elopements and desertions are an example. Nonetheless, most of the time sequential, one-step-at-a-time progression allows the relationship to unfold at a pace that is manageable for the partners.

RELATIONSHIPS ARE CONSTANTLY CHANGING   Relationships are certainly not doomed to deteriorate. But even the strongest ones are rarely stable for long periods of time. In fairy tales a couple may live "happily ever after," but in real life this sort of equilibrium is less common. Consider a husband and wife who have been married for some time. Although they have formally bonded, their relationship will probably shift forward and backward along the spectrum of stages. Sometimes the partners will feel the need to differentiate from one another. The relationship may become more circumscribed, or even stagnant. From

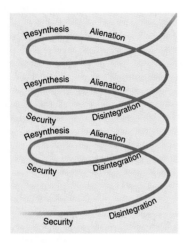

FIGURE 8–3
A Helical Model of Relational
Cycles

this point the marriage may fail, but this fate isn't certain. With effort, the partners may move across the staircase, from stagnating to experimenting or from circumscribing to intensifying.

Communication theorist Richard Conville describes the constantly changing, evolving nature of relationships as a cycle in which partners move through a series of stages, returning to ones they previously encountered . . . although at a new level[40] (see Figure 8–3). In this cycle, partners move from security (integration, in Knapp's terminology) to disintegration (differentiating) to alienation (circumscribing) to resynthesis (intensifying, integrating) to a new level of security. This process repeats itself again and again.

This back-and-forth movement reflects three dialectical tensions that tug at the parties in every relationship.[41] The first centers on the alternating desires for *connection and autonomy* that we discussed earlier in this chapter. Each of us wants—even needs—to have associations with others, yet we also begin to feel suffocated if we lose complete freedom to operate independently. Another pull is between the needs for both *openness and privacy*. Self-disclosure and mutual understanding are characteristics of interpersonal relationships, but too much openness leaves us feeling invaded. The third tug is between the desires for *predictability and novelty*. Too much predictability leaves us feeling bored, but too much novelty leaves us feeling uncertain about the relationship. Given these tensions, it's not surprising that relationships are constantly in flux.

MOVEMENT IS ALWAYS TO A NEW PLACE   Even though a relationship may move back to a stage it has experienced before, it will never be the same. For example, most healthy long-term relationships will go through several phases of experimenting, when the partners try out new ways of behaving with one another. Though each phase is characterized by the same general features, the specifics will feel different each time. As you learned in Chapter One, communication is irreversible. Partners can never go back to "the way things were." Sometimes this fact may lead to regrets: It's impossible to take back a cruel comment or forget a crisis. On the other hand, the irreversibility of communication can make relationships exciting, since it lessens the chance for boredom.

✜ SELF-DISCLOSURE IN RELATIONSHIPS

One way we judge the strength of relationships is by the amount of information we share with others. "We don't have any secrets," some people proudly claim. Opening up certainly is important. As Chapter One explained, one ingredient in qualitatively interpersonal relationships is disclosure. Chapter Seven showed that we find others more attractive when they share certain private information with us. Given the obvious importance of self-disclosure, we need to take a closer look at the subject. Just what is it? When is it desirable? How can it best be done?

The best place to begin is with a definition. **Self-disclosure** is the process of deliberately revealing information about oneself that is significant and that would not normally be known by others. Let's take a closer look at some parts of this definition. Self-disclosure must be *deliberate.* If you accidentally mention to a friend that you're thinking about quitting a job or proposing marriage, that information doesn't qualify as self-disclosure. Besides being intentional, the information must also be *significant.* Volunteering trivial facts, opinions, or feelings—that you like fudge, for example—hardly counts as disclosure. The third requirement is that the information being disclosed is *not known by others.* There's nothing noteworthy about telling others that you are depressed or elated if they already know that.

DEGREES OF SELF-DISCLOSURE

Although our definition of self-disclosure is helpful, it doesn't reveal the important fact that not all self-disclosure is equally revealing— that some disclosing messages tell more about us than others.

Social psychologists Irwin Altman and Dalmas Taylor describe two ways in which communication can be more or less disclosing.[42] Their model of **social penetration** is pictured in Figure 8–4. The first dimension of self-disclosure in this model involves the **breadth** of information volunteered—the range of subjects being discussed. For example, the breadth of disclosure in your relationship with a fellow worker will expand as you begin revealing information about your life away from the job as well as on-the-job details. The second dimension of disclosure is the **depth** of the information being volunteered, the shift from relatively nonrevealing messages to more personal ones.

Depending on the breadth and depth of information shared, a relationship can be defined as casual or intimate. In a casual relationship the breadth may be great, but not the depth. A more intimate relationship is likely to have high depth in at least one area. The most intimate relationships are those in which disclosure is great in both breadth and depth. Altman and Taylor see the development of a relationship as a progression from the periphery of their model to its center, a process that typically occurs over time. Each of your personal relationships probably has a different combination of breadth of subjects and depth of disclosure. Figure 8–5 pictures a student's self-disclosure in one relationship.

What makes the disclosure in some messages deeper than others? One way to measure depth is by how far it goes on two of the dimensions that define self-disclosure. Some revelations are certainly more *significant* than others. Consider the difference between saying, "I love my family" and "I love you." Other statements qualify as deep disclosure because they are *private.* Sharing a secret that you've only told a few close

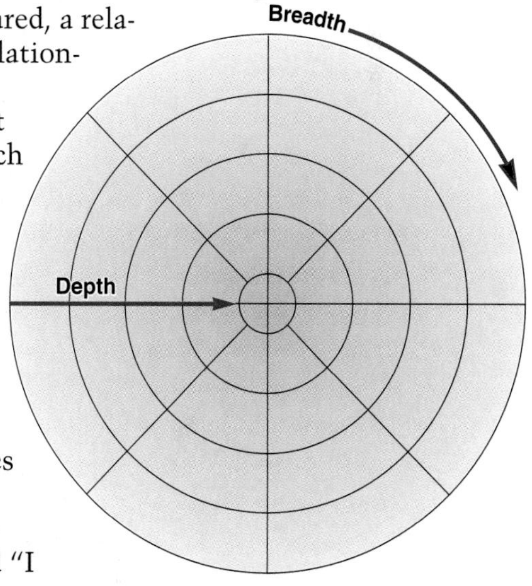

FIGURE 8–4
Social penetration model

FIGURE 8–5
Sample model of social penetration

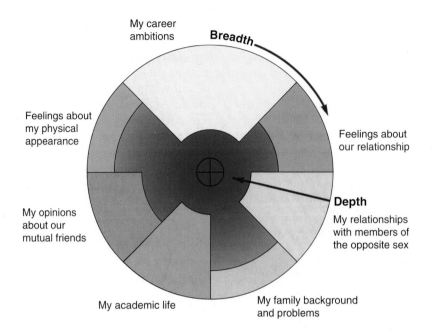

friends is certainly an act of self-disclosure, but it's even more revealing to divulge information that you've never told anyone.

Another way to classify the depth of disclosure is to look at the
types of information we share.

CLICHÉS   **Clichés** are ritualized, stock responses to social situations—
virtually the opposite of self-disclosure: "How are you doing? "Fine!"
"We'll have to get together soon."

Remarks such as these usually aren't meant to be taken literally;
in fact, the other person would be surprised if you responded to a
casual "How are you?" with a lengthy speech on your health, state of
mind, love life, or finances. Yet it's a mistake to consider clichés
meaningless, for they serve several useful functions. For instance,
they can give two speakers time to size each other up and decide
whether it's desirable to carry their conversation any further. Our first
impressions are generally based more on the nonverbal characteristics
of the other person than on the words we hear spoken. Things like
eye contact, vocal tone, facial expression, posture, and so on can often
tell us more about another person than can the initial sentences in a
conversation. Given the value of these nonverbal cues and the awkwardness of actually saying, "I want to take a few minutes to look
you over before I commit myself to getting acquainted," the exchange
of a few stock phrases can be just the thing to get you through this
initial period comfortably.

Clichés can also serve as codes for other messages we don't usually express directly, such as "I want to acknowledge your presence"
(for instance, when two acquaintances walk past each other). Addi-

tional unstated messages often contained in clichés are "I'm interested in talking if you feel like it" or "Let's keep the conversation light and impersonal; I don't feel like disclosing much about myself right now." Accompanied by a different set of nonverbal cues, a cliché can say, "I don't want to be impolite, but you'd better stay away from me for now." In all these cases clichés serve as a valuable kind of shorthand that makes it easy to keep the social wheels greased and indicates the potential for further, possibly more profound conversation.

FACTS   Not all factual statements qualify as self-disclosure: They must fit the criteria of being intentional, significant, and not otherwise known:

> "This isn't my first try at college. I dropped out a year ago with terrible grades."

> "I'm practically engaged." (On meeting a stranger while away from home.)

> "That idea that everyone thought was so clever wasn't really mine. I read it in a book last year."

Facts like these can be meaningful in themselves, but they also have a greater significance in a relationship. Disclosing important information suggests a level of trust and commitment to the other person that signals a desire to move the relationship to a new level.

OPINIONS   Still more revealing is the level of opinions:

> "I used to think abortion was no big deal, but lately I've changed my mind."

> "I really like Karen."

> "I don't think you're telling me what's on your mind."

Opinions like these usually reveal more about a person than facts alone. If you know where the speaker stands on a subject, you can get a clearer picture of how your relationship might develop. Likewise, every time you offer a personal opinion, you are giving others valuable information about yourself.

FEELINGS   The fourth level of self-disclosure—and usually most revealing one—is the realm of feelings. At first glance, feelings might appear to be the same as opinions, but there is a big difference. As we saw, "I don't think you're telling me what's on your mind" is an opinion. Now notice how much more we learn about the speaker by looking at three different feelings that might accompany this statement:

> "I don't think you're telling me what's on your mind, *and I'm suspicious.*"

*he stripped
the dark circles
of mystery off
revealed his eyes
and thus
he waited
exposed*

*and I
did sing the song
around
until I found
the chorus
that speaks
of windows*

*looking out
means looking in
my friend
and I'm all right
now
I'm fine
I have seen
the beauty
that is mine*

*you can
watch the sky
for signals
but look
to the eyes
for signs*

Ric Masten

"I don't think you're telling me what's on your mind, *and I'm angry.*"

"I don't think you're telling me what's on your mind, *and I'm hurt.*"

The difference between these four levels of communication suggests why relationships can be frustrating. One reason has to do with the depth of disclosure, which may not lead to the kind of relationship one or both parties are seeking. Sometimes the communicators might remain exclusively on the level of facts. This might be suitable for a business relationship but wouldn't be very likely in most other circumstances. Even worse, other communicators never get off the level of clichés. And just as a diet of rich foods can become unappealing if carried to excess, the overuse of feelings and opinions can also become disagreeable. In most cases the successful conversation is one in which the participants move from one level to another, depending on the circumstances.

Another common problem occurs when two communicators want to relate to each other on different levels. If one is willing to deal only with facts and perhaps an occasional opinion and the other insists on revealing personal feelings, the results are likely to be uncomfortable for both. Consider the following meeting between Jack and Roger at a party.

J: Hi. My name's Jack. I don't think we've met before. (*cliché*)

R: I'm Roger. Nice to meet you. (*cliché*)

J: Do you know anybody here? I've just moved in next door and don't know a soul except for the host. What's his name . . . Lou? (*fact*)

R: Lou's right. Well, I'm here with my wife—that's her over there— and we know a few other people. (*fact; both speakers are comfortable so far*)

J: Well, I used to have a wife, but she split. She really did me in. (*fact and opinion*)

R: Oh? (*cliché; he doesn't know how to reply to this comment*)

J: Yeah. Everything was going along great—I thought. Then one day she told me she was in love with her gynecologist and that she wanted a divorce. I still haven't gotten over it. (*feeling and fact*)

R: Well, uh, that's too bad. (*cliché; Roger is now very uncomfortable*)

J: I don't think I'll ever trust another woman. I'm still in love with my wife, and it's killing me. She really broke my heart. (*feeling and fact*)

R: I'm sorry. Listen, I've got to go. (*cliché*)

Clearly, Jack moved to the level of disclosing feelings long before Roger was prepared to accept this kind of communication. Though this type of discussion might have helped a friendship if it had come at a later time, Jack only succeeded in driving Roger away by coming on too fast. Remember the hazards of moving too quickly to a level your partner is likely to find uncomfortable.

INVITATION TO INSIGHT

EXAMINING YOUR SELF-DISCLOSURE

Here's a chance to explore the levels of self-disclosure you use with some important people in your life.

1. Choose a "significant other" as the subject of this exercise.

2. Spend a three-day period recording the number of statements you make in each category: clichés, facts, opinions, and feelings.

3. Try to be aware of the topics that you discuss on each level, along with the number of statements in each category.

4. Based on your findings, answer these questions:
   a. Which categories of self-disclosure do you engage in most frequently? Least often?
   b. What type of disclosure (fact, opinion, or feeling) do you use in each topic area?
   c. Explain the reason for omitting topical categories (for example, conflicts, the future) or levels of disclosure or both (for example, feelings).
   d. Explain the consequences of any omissions described in part c.

A MODEL OF SELF-DISCLOSURE

One way to look at the important part self-disclosure plays in inter-personal communication is by means of a device called the **Johari Window.**[43] (The window takes its name from the first names of its creators, Joseph Luft and Harry Ingham.) Imagine a frame like Figure 8–6 that contains everything there is to know about you: your likes and dislikes, your goals, your secrets, your needs—everything.

Of course, you aren't aware of everything about yourself. Like most people, you're probably discovering new things about yourself all the time. To represent this, we can divide the frame containing everything about you into two parts: the part you know about and the part you're not aware of, as in Figure 8–7.

We can also divide this frame containing everything about you in another way. In this division one part represents the things about you that others know, and the second part contains the things about you

FIGURE 8–6

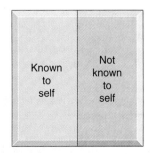

FIGURE 8–7

FIGURE 8-8

that you keep to yourself. Figure 8–8 represents this view.

When we impose these two divided frames one atop the other, we have a Johari Window. By looking at Figure 8–9 you can see the *everything about you* divided into four parts.

Part 1 represents the information of which both you and the other

FIGURE 8-9

person are aware. This part is your *open area.* Part 2 represents the *blind area:* information of which you are unaware but the other person knows. You learn about information in the blind area primarily through feedback. Part 3 represents your *hidden area:* information that you know but aren't willing to reveal to others. Items in this hidden area become public primarily through self-disclosure, which is the focus of this chapter. Part 4 represents information that is *unknown* to both you and others. At first the unknown area seems impossible to verify. After all, if neither you nor others know what it contains, how can you be sure it exists? We can deduce its existence because we are constantly discovering new things about ourselves. It is not unusual to discover, for example, that you have an unrecognized talent, strength, or weakness. Items move from the unknown area either directly into the open area when you disclose your insight or through one of the other areas first.

The relative size of each area in our personal Johari Windows changes from time to time, according to our moods, the subject we are discussing, and our relationship with the other person. Despite these changes, most people's overall style of disclosure could be represented by a single Johari Window. Figure 8–10 pictures windows representing four extreme interaction styles.

Style I depicts a person who is neither receptive to feedback nor willing to self-disclose. This person takes few risks and may appear

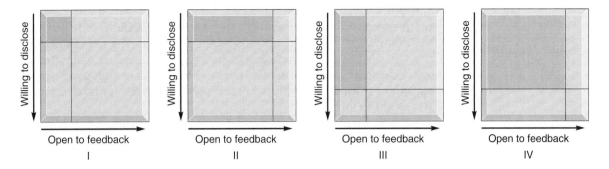

FIGURE 8-10

aloof and uncommunicative. The largest quadrant is the unknown area: Such people have a lot to learn about themselves, as do others. Style II depicts a person who is open to feedback from others but does not voluntarily self-disclose. This person may fear exposure, possibly because of not trusting others. People who fit this pattern may appear highly supportive at first. They want to hear *your* story and appear willing to deny themselves by remaining quiet. Then this first impression fades, and eventually you see them as distrustful and detached. A Johari Window describing such people has a large hidden area.

Style III in Figure 8–10 describes people who discourage feedback from others but disclose freely. Like the people pictured in diagram II, they may distrust others' opinions. They certainly seem self-centered. Their largest quadrant is the blind area: They do not encourage feedback, and so fail to learn much about how others view them.

Diagram IV depicts people who are both willing to disclose information about themselves and open to others' ideas. They are trusting enough to seek the opinions of others and disclose their own. In extreme, this communication style can be intimidating and overwhelming because it violates the usual expectations of how nonintimates ought to behave. In moderation, however, this open style provides the best chance for developing highly interpersonal relationships.

Interpersonal communication of any depth is virtually impossible if the individuals involved have little open area. Going a step further, you can see that a relationship is limited by the individual who is less open—that is, who possesses the smaller open area. Figure 8–11 illus-

FIGURE 8-11

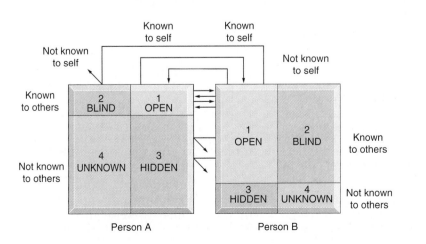

trates this situation with Johari Windows. Person A's window is set up in reverse so that A's and B's open areas are adjacent. Notice that the amount of communication (represented by the arrows connecting the two open areas) is dictated by the size of the smaller open area of A. The arrows originating from person B's open area and being turned aside by A's hidden and blind areas represent unsuccessful attempts to communicate.

You have probably found yourself in situations that resemble Figure 8–11. Perhaps you have felt the frustration of not being able to get to know someone who was too reserved. Perhaps you have blocked another person's attempts to build a relationship with you in the same way. Whether you picture yourself more like person A or person B, the fact is that self-disclosure on both sides is necessary for the development of any interpersonal relationship. This chapter will describe just how much self-disclosure is optimal and of what type.

INVITATION TO INSIGHT

BUILDING A JOHARI WINDOW

You can use the Johari Window model to examine the level of self-disclosure in your own relationships.

1. Use the format described in the preceding section to draw two Johari Windows representing the relationship between you and one other person. Remember to reverse one of the windows so that your open areas and those of the other person face each other.

2. Describe which parts of yourself you keep in the hidden area. Explain your reasons for doing so. Describe the costs or benefits or both of not disclosing these parts of yourself.

3. Look at the blind area of your model. Is this area large or small because of the amount of feedback (much or little) that you get from your partner or because of your willingness to receive the feedback that is offered?

4. Explain whether you are satisfied with the results illustrated by your answers. If you are not satisfied, explain what you can do to remedy the problem.

CHARACTERISTICS OF SELF-DISCLOSURE

By now it's clear that self-disclosure isn't a common type of communication, even in close relationships. The following characteristics show the place of self-disclosure in interpersonal affairs.

SELF-DISCLOSURE USUALLY OCCURS IN DYADS   Although it is possible for people to disclose a great deal about themselves in groups, such communication usually occurs in one-to-one settings. Since revealing significant information about yourself involves a certain amount of risk, limiting the disclosure to one person at a time minimizes the chance that your revelations will lead to unhappy consequences.

SELF-DISCLOSURE OCCURS INCREMENTALLY   Although occasions do occur in which partners start their relationship by telling everything about themselves to each other, such instances are rare. In most cases the amount of disclosure increases over time. We begin relationships by revealing relatively little about ourselves; then if our first bits of self-disclosure are well received and bring on similar responses from the other person, we're willing to reveal more. This principle is important to remember. It would usually be a mistake to assume that the way to build a strong relationship would be to reveal the most private details about yourself when first making contact with another person. Unless the circumstances are unique, such baring of your soul would be likely to scare potential partners away rather than bring them closer.

RELATIVELY FEW TRANSACTIONS INVOLVE HIGH LEVELS OF SELF-DISCLOSURE   Just as it's unwise to seek great self-disclosure too soon, it's also unproductive to reveal yourself too often. Except for unique settings—such as in therapy—there's usually no need to disclose frequently or steadily. When used properly, self-disclosure may strengthen relationships, but like most medicines, large amounts of disclosure are not necessary to produce good results.

SELF-DISCLOSURE IS RELATIVELY SCARCE   What is the optimal amount of self-disclosure? You might suspect that the correct answer is "the more the better," at least in personal relationships. Research has shown that the matter isn't this simple, however.[44] For example, there seems to be a curvilinear relationship between openness and satisfaction in marriage, so that a moderate amount of openness produces better results than either extreme disclosure or withholding. Most conversations—even among friends—focus on everyday, mundane topics and disclose little or no personal information.[45] Even partners in intimate relationships rarely talk about personal information.[46] One good mea-

"No, Thursday's out. How about never—is never good for you?"

sure of happiness is how well the level of disclosure matches the expectations of communicators: If we get what we believe is a reasonable amount of candor from others, we are happy. If they tell us too little—or too much—we become less satisfied.

SELF-DISCLOSURE USUALLY OCCURS IN THE CONTEXT OF POSITIVE RELATIONSHIPS

This principle makes sense. We're generally more willing to reveal information about ourselves when we feel accepted by the other person. This doesn't mean that you should avoid making disclosing statements that contain negative messages (for example, "I feel uncomfortable about what happened last night"). Such explanations are likely to be successful if they're designed to be constructive, to help your relationship grow. On the other hand, disclosure that has the effect of attacking the other person ("You sure aren't very bright") is almost guaranteed to be destructive. For this reason, it's especially important to phrase negative messages in the supportive, assertive ways described in Chapters Nine and Ten.

REASONS FOR SELF-DISCLOSURE

Self-disclosure has the potential to improve and expand interpersonal relationships, but it serves other functions as well.[47] As you read each of the following reasons why people reveal themselves, see which apply to you.

CATHARSIS   Sometimes you might disclose information in an effort to "get it off your chest." In a moment of candor you might, for instance, reveal your regrets about having behaved badly in the past.

"Bob, as a token of my appreciation for this wonderful lunch I would like to disclose to you my income-tax returns for the past four years."

SELF-CLARIFICATION   Sometimes you can clarify your beliefs, opinions, thoughts, attitudes, and feelings by talking about them with another person. This sort of "talking the problem out" occurs with psychotherapists, but it also goes on with others, all the way from good friends to bartenders or hairdressers.

SELF-VALIDATION   If you disclose information ("I think I did the right thing . . . ") with the hope of obtaining the listener's agreement, you are seeking validation of your behavior—confirmation of a belief you hold about yourself. On a deeper level, this sort of self-validating disclosure seeks confirmation of important parts of your self-concept.

RECIPROCITY   A well-documented conclusion from research is that one act of self-disclosure begets another.[48] Thus, in some situations you may choose to disclose information about yourself to encourage another person to do so also.

IMPRESSION FORMATION   Sometimes we reveal personal information to make ourselves more attractive. Some observers have made this point bluntly, asserting that self-disclosure has become another way of "marketing" ourselves.[49] Consider a couple on their first date. It's not hard to imagine how one or both partners might share personal information to appear more sincere, interesting, sensitive, or interested in the other person. The same principle applies in other situations. A salesperson might say "I'll be honest with you . . . " primarily to show that she is on your side, and a new acquaintance might talk about the details of his past to seem more friendly and likable.

RELATIONSHIP MAINTENANCE AND ENHANCEMENT   A large body of research supports the role of self-disclosure in relational success.[50] For example, there is a strong relationship between the quality of self-disclosure and marital satisfaction.[51] The same principle applies in other personal relationships. The bond between grandparents and grandchildren, for example, grows stronger when the honesty and depth of sharing between them is high.[52]

SOCIAL CONTROL   Revealing personal information may increase your control over the other person, and sometimes over the situation in which you and the other person find yourselves. For example, an employee who tells the boss that another firm has made overtures probably will have an increased chance of getting raises and improvements in working conditions.

MANIPULATION   Although most of the preceding reasons might strike you as being manipulative, they often aren't premeditated strategies. There are cases, however, when an act of self-disclosure is calculated in advance to achieve a desired result. Of course, if a disclosure's hidden motive ever becomes clear to the receiver, the results will most likely be quite unlike those intended.

The reasons for disclosing vary from one situation to another, depending on several factors. The strongest influence on why people disclose seems to be how well we know the other person.[53] When the target of disclosure is a friend, the most frequent reason people give for volunteering personal information is relationship maintenance and enhancement. In other words, we disclose to friends in order to strengthen the relationship. The second important reason is self-clarification—to sort out confusion to understand ourselves better.

With strangers, reciprocity becomes the most common reason for disclosing. We offer information about ourselves to strangers to learn more about them, so we can decide whether and how to continue the relationship. The second most important reason is impression formation. In other words, we often reveal information about ourselves to strangers to make ourselves look good. This information, of course, is usually positive—at least in the early stages of a friendship.

✛ ALTERNATIVES TO SELF-DISCLOSURE

Although self-disclosure plays an important role in interpersonal relationships, it isn't the only type of communication available. To understand why complete honesty isn't always an easy or ideal choice, consider some familiar dilemmas:

> A new acquaintance is much more interested in becoming friends than you are. She invites you to a party this weekend. You aren't busy, but you don't want to go. What would you say?

> Your boss asks you what you think of his new wardrobe. You think it's cheap and flashy. Would you tell him?

> You're attracted to your best friend's mate, who has confessed that he feels the same way about you. You both agreed that you won't act on your feelings, and that even bringing up the subject would make your friend feel terribly insecure. Now your friend has asked whether you're attracted at all to the mate. Would you tell the truth?

> You've just been given a large, extremely ugly painting as a gift by a relative who visits your home often. How would you respond to the question "Where will you hang it?"

Situations like these highlight some of the issues that surround deceptive communication. On one hand, our moral education and common sense lead us to abhor anything less than the truth. Ethicists point out that the very existence of a society seems based on a foundation of truthfulness.[54] Although isolated cultures do exist where deceit is a norm, they are dysfunctional and on the verge of breakdown.

Although honesty is desirable in principle, it often has risky, potentially unpleasant consequences. It's tempting to avoid situations where self-disclosure would be difficult, but examples like the ones you just read show that evasion isn't always possible. Research and personal experience show that communicators—even those with the best intentions—aren't always completely honest when they find themselves in situations in which honesty would be uncomfortable.[55] Three common alternatives to self-disclosure are lying, equivocating, and hinting. We will take a closer look at each one.

LYING

A **lie** is a deliberate attempt to hide or misrepresent the truth. To most of us, lying appears as a breach of ethics. At first glance it appears that the very possibility of a society depends on the acceptance of truthfulness as a social norm. Although lying to gain unfair advantage over an unknowing victim seems clearly wrong, another kind of mistruth—the "white lie"—isn't so easy to dismiss as completely unethical. Some are defined (at least by the people who tell them) as being unmalicious, or even helpful to the person to whom they are told. Whether or not they are innocent, white lies are certainly common. In one study, 130 subjects were asked to keep track of the truthfulness of their everyday conversational statements.[56] Only 38.5 percent of these statements—slightly more than a third— proved to be totally honest.

REASONS FOR LYING   What reasons do people give for being so deceitful? When subjects in the study were asked to give a lie-by-lie account of their motives for concealing or distorting the truth, five major reasons emerged.

1. *To save face.* Over half the lies were justified as a way to prevent embarrassment. Such lying is often given the approving label "tact," and is used "when it would be unkind to be honest, but dishonest to be kind."[57] Sometimes a face-saving lie saves face for the recipient, as when you pretend to remember someone at a party in order to save them from the embarrassment of being forgotten. In other cases a lie protects the teller from humiliation. You might, for instance, cover up your mistakes by blaming them on outside forces: "You didn't receive the check? It must have been delayed in the mail."
2. *To avoid tension or conflict.* Sometimes it seems worthwhile to tell a small lie to prevent a large conflict. You might, for example, say you're not upset at a friend's teasing in order to prevent the hassle that would result if you expressed your annoyance. It's often easier to explain your behavior in dishonest terms than to make matters worse. You might explain your apparent irritation by saying "I'm not mad at you; it's just been a tough day."
3. *To guide social interaction.* Sometimes we lie to make everyday relationships run smoothly. You might, for instance, pretend to be glad to see someone you actually dislike, or fake interest in a dinner companion's boring stories to make a social event pass quickly. Children who aren't skilled or interested in these social lies are often a source of embarrassment for their parents.

The injunction against bearing false witness, branded in stone and brought down by Moses from the mountaintop, has always provoked ambivalent, conflicting emotions. On the one hand, nearly everyone condemns lying. On the other, nearly everyone does it every day. How many of the Ten Commandments can be broken so easily and with so little risk of detection over the telephone?

Paul Gray,
"Lies, Lies, Lies" in *Time* 10/5/92, p. 35.

🔲 *Words, like Nature, half reveal and half conceal the Soul within.*

Alfred Tennyson

4. *To expand or reduce relationships.* Some lies are designed to make the relationship grow: "You're going downtown? I'm headed that way. Can I give you a ride?" "I like science fiction, too. What have you read lately?" Lies that make the teller look good also fit into this category. You might try to impress a potential employer by calling yourself a management student when you've only taken a course or two in business. Sometimes we tell untruths to reduce interaction with others. Lies in this category often allow the teller to escape unpleasant situations: "I really have to go. I should be studying for a test tomorrow." In other cases people lie to end a relationship entirely: "You're really great, but I'm just not ready to settle down yet."

5. *To gain power.* Sometimes we tell lies to show we're in control of a situation. Turning down a last-minute request for a date by claiming you're busy can be one way to put yourself in a one-up position, saying in effect, "Don't expect me to sit around waiting for you to call." Lying to get confidential information—even for a good cause—also falls into the category of achieving power.

This five-part scheme isn't the only way to categorize lies. The taxonomy outlined in Table 8–1 is more complicated than the five-part one above, and covers some types of lies that don't fit into the simpler scheme. Exaggerations, for example, are lies told to boost the effect of a story. In exaggerated tales the fish grow larger, hikes grow longer and more strenuous, and so on. The stories may be less truthful, but they become more interesting—at least to the teller.

Most people think white lies are told for the benefit of the recipient. In the study cited above, the majority of subjects claimed such lying was "the right thing to do." Other research paints a less flattering picture of who benefits most from lying. One study found that two out of every three lies are told for "selfish reasons."[58] A look at Table 8–1 seems to make this figure too conservative. Of the 322 lies recorded, 75.8 percent were for the benefit of the liar. Less than 22

MRS. LOOMIS DECIDED TO TELL HER HUSBAND HOW SHE REALLY FELT.

TABLE 8 – 1   TYPES OF WHITE LIES AND THEIR FREQUENCY

	BENEFIT SELF	BENEFIT OTHER	BENEFIT THIRD PARTY
Basic Needs	68	1	1
A. Acquire resources	29	0	0
B. Protect resources	39	1	1
Affiliation	128	1	6
A. Positive	65	0	0
1. Initiate interaction	8	0	0
2. Continue interaction	6	0	0
3. Avoid conflict	48	0	0
4. Obligatory acceptance	3	0	0
B. Negative	43	1	3
1. Avoid interaction	34	1	3
2. Leave-taking	9	0	0
C. Conversational control	20	0	3
1. Redirect conversation	3	0	0
2. Avoid self-disclosure	17	0	3
Self-Esteem	35	63	1
A. Competence	8	26	0
B. Taste	0	18	1
C. Social desirability	27	19	0
Other	13	5	0
A. Dissonance reduction	3	5	0
B. Practical joke	2	0	0
C. Exaggeration	8	0	0

From Camden, C., M.T. Motley, and A. Wilson, "White Lies in Interpersonal Communication: A Taxonomy and Preliminary Investigation of Social Motivations," *Western Journal of Speech Communication* 48 (1984): 315.

percent were for the benefit of the person hearing the lie, while a mere 2.5 percent were intended to aid a third party.

Before we become totally cynical, however, the researchers urge a charitable interpretation. After all, most intentional communication behavior—truthful or not—is designed to help the speaker achieve a goal. Therefore, it's unfair to judge white lies more harshly than other types of messages. If we define selfishness as the extent to which some desired resource or interaction is denied to the person hearing the lie or to a third party, then only 111 lies (34.5 percent) can be considered truly selfish. This figure may be no worse than the degree of selfishness in honest messages.

EFFECTS OF LIES   What are the consequences of learning that you've been lied to? In an interpersonal relationship, the discovery can be traumatic. As we grow closer to others, our expectations about their honesty grow stronger. After all, discovering that you've been deceived requires you to redefine not only the lie you just uncovered,

When their marriage of more than a decade ended in divorce, Anaheim banker Ronald Askew sued his ex-wife for fraud because she admittedly concealed the fact that she had never felt sexually attracted to him. On Wednesday, an Orange County jury agreed, and ordered Bonnette Askew to pay her ex-husband $242,000 in damages.

"I'm astonished by this verdict and I've looked at divorce in 62 societies," said Helen Fisher, an American Museum of Natural History anthropologist who authored the recent book "Anatomy of Love: The Natural History of Monogamy, Adultery and Divorce."

Bonnette Askew, 45, acknowledged in court that she had never been sexually attracted to her husband. But she said she always loved him and noted that their marriage was not sexless and that they had two children together.

She first admitted her lack of sexual desire for him during a joint therapy session in 1991. "I guess he confused sex with love," Bonnette Askew said, adding that she concealed her lack of desire because she "didn't want to hurt his male ego."

But Ronald Askew, 50, said his lawsuit had more to do with honesty and integrity than sex. He felt deceived, especially because he said he repeatedly asked her before their marriage to be honest with him and reveal any important secrets.

If Ronald Askew believes total honesty is the foundation of good marriages, Fisher has a message for him: "Grow up."

"Since when is anyone truly honest with anyone?" Fisher said. "Did this man really want her to say: 'You're short, fat and you're terrible in bed'? Much of the world is amazed at what they see as brutal honesty in America. She was operating on an entirely different set of social values, which much of the world operates on—delicacy as opposed to brutal honesty."

Maria Cone,
Los Angeles Times

but also many of the messages you previously took for granted. Was last week's compliment really sincere? Was your joke really funny, or was the other person's laughter a put-on? Does the other person care about you as much as he or she claimed?

Research has shown that deception does, in fact, threaten relationships.[59] Not all lies are equally devastating, however. Feelings like dismay and betrayal are greatest when the relationship is most intense, the importance of the subject is high, and when there was previous suspicion that the other person wasn't being completely honest. Of these three factors, the importance of the information lied about proved to be the key factor in provoking a relational crisis. We may be able to cope with "misdemeanor" lying, but "felonies" are a grave threat.

An occasional white lie in an otherwise honest relationship doesn't pose much threat. Major deception, though—especially when it is part of a pattern of deceit—is likely to provoke a relational crisis. In fact, the discovery of major deception can lead to the end of the relationship. More than two-thirds of the subjects in one study reported that their relationship had ended since they discovered a lie. Furthermore, they attributed the breakup directly to the deception.

The lesson here is clear: Lying about major parts of your relationship can have the most grave consequences. If preserving a relationship is important, honesty—at least about important matters—really does appear to be the best policy.

EQUIVOCATING

Lying isn't the only alternative to self-disclosure. When faced with the choice between lying and telling an unpleasant truth, communicators can—and often do—equivocate. As Chapter Five explained, **equivocal language** has two or more equally plausible meanings. Sometimes people send equivocal messages without meaning to, resulting in confusion. "I'll meet you at the apartment," could refer to more than one place. But other times we are deliberately vague. For instance, when a friend asks what you think of an awful outfit, you could say "It's really unusual—one of a kind!" Likewise, if you are too angry to accept a friend's apology but don't want to appear petty, you might say "Don't mention it."

The value of equivocation becomes clear when you consider the alternatives. Consider the dilemma of what to say when you've been given an unwanted present—that ugly painting we mentioned before, for example—and the giver asks what you think of it. How can you respond? On one hand, you need to choose between telling the truth and lying. At the same time, you have a choice of whether to make your response clear or vague. Figure 8–12 displays these choices. After considering the alternatives, it's clear that the first option—an equivocal, true response—is far preferable to the other choices in several respects. First, it spares the receiver from embarrassment. For example, rather than flatly saying "No" to an unappealing invitation, it may be kinder to say "I have other plans"—even if those plans are to stay home and watch TV.

How does a business person provide a positive reference for an incompetent friend? Lehigh University professor Robert Thorton suggests that equivocation provides a middle way between the brutal truth and a misleading lie. A few examples:

For a lazy worker: "You will be lucky to get this person to work for you."

For someone with no talent: "I recommend this candidate with no qualifications."

For a candidate who should not be hired under any circumstances: "I can assure you that no person will be better for the job." or "Waste no time hiring this person."

Mixed Blessings

[Equivocations] are communications that do not communicate—full of reverberating hints, of meanings implied but not claimed. Like a reversible figure, a Nekker Cube, they change before one's eyes, saying something, then not saying it, then saying it again . . . arrows aimed to miss . . .

Janet Bavelas, Alex Black, Nicole Chovil, and Jennifer Mullett

Besides saving face for the recipient, honest equivocation can be less stressful for the sender than either telling the truth bluntly or lying. Because equivocation is often easier to take than the cold, hard truth, it spares the teller from feeling guilty. It's less taxing on the conscience to say, "I've never tasted anything like this" than to say "This meal tastes terrible," even though the latter comment is more precise. Few people *want* to lie, and equivocation provides an alternative to deceit.

A study by communication researcher Sandra Metts and her colleagues shows how equivocation can save face in difficult situations.[60] Several hundred college students were asked how they would turn down unwanted sexual overtures from a person whose feelings were important to them: either a close friend, a prospective date, or a dating partner. The majority of students chose a diplomatic reaction ("I just don't think I'm ready for this right now") as being more face-saving and comfortable than a direct statement like "I just don't feel sexually attracted to you." The diplomatic reaction seemed sufficiently clear to get the message across, but not so blunt as to embarrass or even humiliate the other person. (Interestingly, men said they

FIGURE 8–12
Dimensions of truthfulness and equivocation

Adapted from Bavelas, J.B., Black, A., Chovil, N. and Mullet, J. *Equivocal Communication*, Newbury Park, CA: Sage, 1990, p. 178.

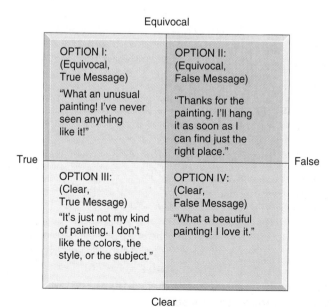

would be better able to handle a direct rejection more comfortably than women. The researchers suggest that one reason for the difference is that men stereotypically initiate sexual behaviors, and thus are more likely to expect rejection.)

Besides preventing embarrassment, equivocal language can also save the speaker from being caught lying. If a potential employer asks about your grades during an interview, you would be safe saying, "I had a B average last semester," even though your overall grade average is closer to C. The statement isn't a complete answer, but it is honest as far as it goes. As one team of researchers put it, "equivocation is neither a false message nor a clear truth, but rather an alternative used precisely when both of these are to be avoided."[61]

Given these advantages, it's not surprising that most people will usually choose to equivocate rather than tell a lie. In a series of experiments, subjects chose between telling a face-saving lie, the truth, and equivocating. Only 6 percent chose the lie and between 3 and 4 percent chose the hurtful truth. By contrast, over 90 percent chose the equivocal response.[62]

HINTING

Hints are more direct than equivocal statements. Whereas an equivocal message isn't necessarily aimed at changing others' behavior, a hint seeks to get a desired response from the other person. Some hints are designed to save the receiver from embarrassment:[63]

Direct statement

You're too overweight to be ordering dessert.
I'm too busy to continue with this conversation. I wish you
    would let me go.

Face-saving hint

These desserts are terribly overpriced.
 I know you're busy; I'd better let you go.

Other hints are less concerned with protecting the receiver than with saving the sender from embarrassment:

Direct statement

Please don't smoke here because it is bothering me.
I'd like to invite you out for lunch, but I don't want to risk a "no"
    answer to my invitation.

Hint

I'm pretty sure that smoking isn't permitted here.
Gee, it's almost lunchtime. Have you ever eaten at that new
    Italian restaurant around the corner?

The face-saving value of hints explains why communicators are more likely to be indirect than fully disclosing when they deliver a potentially embarrassing message.[64] The success of a hint depends on the other person's ability to pick up the unexpressed message. Your subtle remarks might go right over the head of an insensitive receiver . . . or one who chooses not to respond. If this happens, you may decide to be more direct. On the other hand, if the costs of a straightforward message seem too high, you can withdraw without risk.

THE ETHICS OF EVASION

It's easy to see why people choose hints, equivocations, and white lies instead of complete self-disclosure. These strategies provide a way to manage difficult situations that is easier than the alternatives for both the speaker and the receiver of the message. In this sense, successful liars, equivocators, and hinters can be said to possess a certain kind of communicative competence. On the other hand, there are certainly times when honesty is the right approach, even if it's painful. At times like these, evaders could be viewed as lacking the competence or the integrity to handle a situation most effectively.

Are hints, benign lies, and equivocations ethical alternatives to self-disclosure? Some of the examples in these pages suggest the answer is a qualified "yes." Many social scientists and philosophers agree. Some argue that the morality of a speaker's *motives* for lying ought to be judged, not the deceptive act itself.[65] Others ask whether the *effects* of a lie will be worth the deception. Ethicist Sissela Bok offers some circumstances in which deception may be justified: doing good, avoiding harm, and protecting a larger truth.[66] Perhaps the right questions to ask, then, are whether an indirect message is truly in the interests of the receiver, and whether this sort of evasion is the only effective way to behave. Bok suggests another way to check the justifiability of a lie: Imagine how others would respond if they knew what you were really thinking or feeling. Would they accept your reasons for not disclosing?

ETHICAL CHALLENGE

THE COURT OF SELF-DISCLOSURE

Recall three recent situations in which you have used each of the following evasive approaches: lying, equivocating, and hinting. Write an anonymous written description of each situation on a separate sheet of paper. Submit the cases to a panel of "judges" (most likely fellow students), who will evaluate the morality of this deception using the criteria of justifiable motives and desirable effects as described in the preceding paragraph.

✦ GUIDELINES FOR SELF-DISCLOSURE

By now it should be clear that deciding when and how much personal information to disclose is not a simple matter. The following guidelines can help you choose the level of self-disclosure that is appropriate in a given situation.

IS THE OTHER PERSON IMPORTANT TO YOU?   There are several ways in which someone might be important. Perhaps you have an ongoing relationship deep enough so that sharing significant parts of yourself justifies keeping your present level of togetherness intact. Or perhaps the person to whom you're considering disclosing is someone with whom you've previously related on a less personal level. But now you see a chance to grow closer, and disclosure may be the path toward developing that personal relationship.

IS THE RISK OF DISCLOSING REASONABLE?   Take a realistic look at the potential risks of self-disclosure. Even if the probable benefits are great, opening yourself up to almost certain rejection may be asking for trouble. For instance, it might be foolhardy to share your important feelings with someone you know is likely to betray your confidences or ridicule them. On the other hand, knowing that your partner is trustworthy and supportive makes the prospect of speaking out more reasonable.

Revealing personal thoughts and feelings can be especially risky on the job.[67] The politics of the workplace sometimes requires communicators to keep feelings to themselves in order to accomplish both personal and organizational goals. You might, for example, find the opinions of a boss or customer personally offensive but decide to bite your tongue rather than risk your job or lose goodwill for the company.

In anticipating risks, be sure that you are realistic. It's sometimes easy to indulge in catastrophic expectations and imagine all sorts of disastrous consequences when in fact such horrors are quite unlikely to occur.

ARE THE AMOUNT AND TYPE OF DISCLOSURE APPROPRIATE?   It is usually a mistake to share too much information too soon. Research shows that in most relationships the process of disclosure is gradual.[68] At first most of the information that is exchanged is relatively nonintimate. As the parties move into the intensifying, integrating, and bonding stages of the relationship, the rate of disclosure begins to grow.

As we've already seen, even in relationships in which disclosure is an important feature, the amount of personal information is relatively small when compared to nonintimate information. Most long-term relationships aren't characterized by a constant exchange of intimate details. Rather, they are a mixture of much everyday, nonintimate information and less frequent but more personal messages.

Besides being moderate in amount, self-disclosure should consist of positive information as well as negative details. Hearing nothing

"I'm a very sensual person. How about you, Mr. Gellerman?"

but a string of dismal confessions or complaints can be discouraging. In fact, people who disclose an excess of negative information are often considered "negatively adjusted."[69]

Finally, when considering the appropriateness of disclosure in any relationship, timing is also important. If the other person is tired, preoccupied, or in a bad mood it may be best to postpone an important conversation.

IS THE DISCLOSURE RELEVANT TO THE SITUATION AT HAND?   The kind of disclosure that is often a characteristic of highly personal relationships usually isn't appropriate in less personal settings. For instance, a study of classroom communication revealed that sharing all feelings—both positive and negative—and being completely honest resulted in less cohesiveness than a "relatively" honest climate in which pleasant but superficial relationships were the norm.[70]

Even in personal relationships—with close friends, family members, and so on—constant disclosure isn't a useful goal. The level of sharing in successful relationships rises and falls in cycles. You may go through a period of great disclosure and then spend another interval of relative non-disclosure. Even during a phase of high disclosure sharing *everything* about yourself isn't necessarily constructive. Usually the subject of appropriate self-disclosure involves the relationship rather than personal information. Furthermore, it is usually most constructive to focus your disclosure about the relationship on the "here and now" as opposed to "there and then." "How am I feeling now?" "How are we doing now?" These are appropriate topics for sharing personal thoughts and feelings. At times it's relevant to bring up the past, but only as it relates to what's going on in the present.

IS THE DISCLOSURE RECIPROCATED?   The amount of personal information you share will usually depend on how much the other person reveals. As a rule, disclosure is a two-way street. For example, couples are happiest when their levels of openness are roughly equal.[71]

There are few times when one-way disclosure is acceptable. Most of them involve formal, therapeutic relationships in which a client approaches a trained professional with the goal of resolving a problem. For instance, you wouldn't necessarily expect to hear about a physician's personal ailments during a visit to a medical office. Nonetheless, it's interesting to note that one frequently noted characteristic of effective psychotherapists, counselors, and teachers is a willingness to reveal their feelings about a relationship to their clients.

WILL THE EFFECT BE CONSTRUCTIVE?   Self-disclosure can be a vicious tool if it's not used carefully. Psychologists suggest that every person has a psychological "beltline." Below that beltline are areas about which the person is extremely sensitive. Bach says that jabbing at a "below-the-belt" area is a sure-fire way to disable another person, though usually at great cost to the relationship. It's important to consider the effects of your candor before opening up to others. Comments such as "I've always thought you were pretty unintelligent" or "Last year I made love to your best friend" *may* sometimes resolve old business and thus be constructive, but they also can be devastating—to the listener, to the relationship, and to your self-esteem.

IS THE SELF-DISCLOSURE CLEAR AND UNDERSTANDABLE?   When you are expressing yourself to others, it's important that you reveal yourself in a way that's intelligible. This means describing the sources of your message clearly. For instance, it's far better to describe another's behavior by saying, "When you don't answer my phone calls or drop by to visit anymore . . . " than to complain vaguely, "When you avoid me . . . "

SKILL BUILDER

APPROPRIATE SELF-DISCLOSURE

Use the guidelines on pages 357–359 to develop one scenario where you *might* reveal a self-disclosing message. Create a message of this type, and use the information in this chapter to discuss the risks and benefits of sharing this message.

✦ SUMMARY

Intimacy comes in several forms: physical, intellectual, emotional, and shared activities. As important as intimacy is to relationships, so is distance. Intimacy is not essential to all relationships, and even in relationships where it is important, it is not important all the time. Intimacy and distance exist together in a dialectical tension—as opposing forces in a constant battle for balance. Whether in a growing relationship, a stable one, or a deteriorating one, intimacy and distance form a cyclical pattern where first one and then the other is most important.

Gender and culture exert a strong influence on both the amount of intimacy in a relationship and how that intimacy is communicated. A female intimacy style is characterized by self-disclosure, and a male intimacy style is characterized by shared activities. These differences exist within larger cultural differences. Each culture has rules that govern intimate communication, from touching in public to the disclosure of personal information. Also, each culture defines the extent to which any relationship should be formal and distant or close and intimate.

An important determinant of intimacy, although not the only determinant, is self-disclosure. Self-disclosure consists of honest, revealing messages about the self that are intentionally directed toward others. Disclosing communication contains information that is generally unavailable via other sources. Revealing personal information does not guarantee that this communication will be perceived by others as disclosing. A number of factors govern whether a communicator will be judged as being a high- or low-level discloser.

The social penetration model describes two dimensions of self-disclosure: breadth and depth. Disclosure of feelings is usually more revealing than disclosure of opinions, and dis-

closure of opinions is usually more revealing than disclosure of facts. Clichés are the least revealing.

The Johari Window model is a useful way to illustrate self-disclosure. A window representing a single person can illustrate the amount of information that individual reveals to others, hides, is blind to, and is unaware of. Windows representing two communicators reveal how differing levels of disclosure can affect the level of intimacy in a relationship.

Communicators disclose personal information for a variety of reasons: catharsis, self-clarification, self-validation, reciprocal obligations, impression formation, relationship maintenance and enhancement, social control, and manipulation.

The percentage of messages that are self-disclosing is relatively low. Three alternatives to revealing personal facts, feelings, and opinions are lying, equivocating, and hinting. Unmalicious "white lies" serve a variety of functions: saving face for the sender or receiver, avoiding tension or conflict, guiding social interaction, managing relationships, and gaining power. When discovered by the recipient, lies have the potential to provoke a relational crisis, especially if the content of the information lied about is significant. Equivocal messages are an attractive alternative to lying and direct honesty. They allow a communicator to be honest without being blunt and causing undesirable reaction. Hints, more direct than equivocal statements, are used primarily to avoid embarrassment. Hints are risky in that they depend on the other person's ability to pick up unexpressed messages. Lies, equivocations, and hints may be ethical alternatives to self-disclosure; however, whether they are depends on the speaker's motives and the effects of the deception.

✛ KEY TERMS

avoiding	equivocal language	lie
bonding	exchange theory	self-disclosure
breadth	experimenting	social penetration
circumscribing	initiating	stagnating
clichés	integrating	terminating
depth	intensifying	uncertainty reduction
dialectical tension	intimacy	
differentiating	Johari Window	

✛ MORE RESOURCES ON INTIMACY AND DISTANCE

READINGS

Aronson, Eliot. *The Social Animal*, seventh edition. New York: Freeman, 1992.

Chapter 7 offers a thorough and clearly written survey of the factors influencing interpersonal attraction.

Berscheid, Ellen, and Elaine Walster. *Interpersonal Attraction*, second edition. Reading, Mass.: Addison-Wesley, 1978.

A readable discussion of the theories of attraction introduced in this chapter, plus a look at that special relationship, love.

Chovil, Nicole. "Equivocation as an Interactional Event." In *The Dark Side of Interpersonal Communication*. William R. Cupach and Brian H. Spitzberg, eds. Hillsdale, N.J.: Erlbaum, 1994.

This chapter describes how equivocal communication can be a form of "strategic ambiguity" that greases the wheels of social interaction. Chovil outlines the types of equivocal messages and identifies situations that elicit them.

Derlega, Valerian J., Sandra Metts, Sandra Petronio, and Stephen T. Margulis. *Self-Disclosure*. Newbury Park, Calif.: Sage, 1993.

This useful book examines the link between self-disclosure and the opposing needs for intimacy and privacy. A separate chapter explores the role of gender in self-disclosure, showing how men and women reveal personal information differently in both same-sex and opposite-sex relationships.

Jaska, James, and Michael S. Pritchard. *Communication Ethics: Methods of Analysis*, second edition. Belmont, Calif.: Wadsworth, 1994.

It's easy to say that "honesty is the best policy," but candor sometimes poses ethical dilemmas. Is it best to tell the truth when doing so violates a promise of confidentiality? Is self-disclosure wise when it will hurt another person deeply? Jaska and Pritchard don't always provide answers to questions like these, but raising the issues provides food for thought.

Kasson, John F. *Rudeness and Civility*, New York: Hill and Wang, 1990.

A look at notions of social behavior in various places and times. The historical perspective in this book shows that our notions of intimacy are not universal.

Knapp, Mark L. *Interpersonal Communication and Human Relationships*, second edition. Boston: Allyn and Bacon, 1992.

Knapp provides a thorough explanation of his theory of relational stages. An excellent source for readers interested in learning more about the rise and fall of interpersonal relationships.

Lewis, Michael, and Carolyn Saarni, eds. *Lying and Deception in Everyday Life*. New York: Guilford, 1993.

The authors move away from the idea that lying is inherently immoral and show how deceptive mes-

sages serve a variety of social goals. The text distinguishes what might be called "ethical" from "unethical" lies, showing how the former serve socially approved goals.

Miller, Gerald R., and James B. Stiff. *Deceptive Communication*. Newbury Park, Calif.: Sage, 1993.

This brief book surveys the extensive research on deceptive messages, showing their persuasiveness in everyday communication. Separate chapters explore such topics as the characteristics of deceptive behavior and the accuracy of humans as lie detectors.

Rubin, Lilian. *Just Friends: The Role of Friendship in Our Lives*. New York: Harper & Row, 1985.

An examination of the ambiguous yet vital relationship we call friendship. Based on interviews with three hundred men and women, this book explores the many varieties of friendship: casual versus "best friends," same- and opposite-gender friendships, marriage and friendship, and friendship and kinship.

FILMS

DIMENSIONS OF INTIMACY

Diner (1982) Rated R

This story takes place in the late 1950s, but update a few of the details and it could—and almost certainly does—take place today. A group of guys have been out of high school for a year or two. Billy (Timothy Daly) has gone away to college. Boogie (Mickey Rourke) is working his way through school while holding down a job. Shrevie (Daniel Stern) has married his high school sweetheart, Beth (Ellen Barkin). Eddie (Steve Gutenberg) is engaged, but isn't quite sure why he is getting married. Fenwick (Kevin Bacon) is probably the smartest of the group, but he is drowning the unhappiness of his life in booze.

Viewed from one perspective, the film looks like an indictment of the lack of intimacy in contemporary society. The guys have been friends for years, but they never express their obvious caring for one another. Their relationships with women seem distant at best: Shrevie confesses that marriage has taken the fun out of sex, and the strongest emotion he seems to feel toward his wife is anger when she forgets to put his records back on the shelf in alphabetical order. Boogie tries to pay back his gambling debts by seducing women while his friends watch in hiding. Eddie states that he will marry his fiancee only if she passes a football trivia test. This movie hardly seems like a textbook example of interpersonal communication.

A closer viewing of the film shows some strong examples of close relationships, however. Fenwick swallows his pride and asks his sanctimonious brother for money to save Boogie from a beating by the small-time hoods who have loaned him money. Boogie confesses his seductive strategy to Beth, when he could have gotten away with his plan and paid off his debt. Under director Barry Levinson's guidance, the buddies from the diner behave in ways that make their affection—even their love—for one another clear. This story is a clear illustration of traditionally male approaches to intimacy discussed on pages 320–321 of this chapter. The friends may not talk about their feelings toward one another, but through shared activities and the exchange of favors, they show they care. They know, and we know too.

INTERPERSONAL ATTRACTION

Stand by Me (1986) Rated R

Friendships can be improbable affairs. People who might seem to have little to do with one another form bonds that create good times and make the bad ones more bearable. *Stand by Me* is Rob Reiner's ode to friendship. Set in the 1950s, it chronicles the two-day adventure of four friends during the summer before they enter junior high school. The story is set in rural Oregon, where the boys track down the rumor that a dead body lies somewhere in the woods. Their quest—and their lives in general—is complicated by a variety of forces. Some of these forces are external, such as suspicious, critical, and indifferent parents and the high school bullies who want to find the body first. Personal and relational challenges also complicate the boys' journey. Gordie (Will Wheaton) suffers from low self-esteem due to parents who constantly compare him unfavorably to his dead brother; Chris (River Phoenix) and Teddy (Corey Feldman) have been labeled as the town losers. Vern (Jerry O'Connell) is the archetypal bumbling fat kid, eager for the approval of his more self-assured peers.

Despite their differences and their personal and relational problems, the boys are friends. Their bonds grow from many of the forces outlined on these pages, including the proximity of small-town life, a mix of similar interests and experiences, the benefits of complementary personalities, their reciprocal disclosures, and exchanges of support. The boys' friendship does not continue once their lives change, but the memories of its strength and value endure. *Stand by Me* provides a compelling and instructive model of relational attraction.

RELATIONAL DEVELOPMENT AND DETERIORATION

Betrayal (1983) Rated R

Most people would love to know the outcome of a relationship before it begins so they could decide if it is worth the investment. *Betrayal*, a film adaptation of Harold Pinter's play, allows viewers to watch a relationship through a crystal ball. The movie's opening scene depicts the end of an affair between Emma (Patricia Hoge) and Jerry (Jeremy Irons); each succeeding scene moves backward in time. Thus, the final scene of the movie shows the beginning of Emma and Jerry's romantic involvement.

In terms of relational stages, their affair is relatively sequential and predictable. They already know each other well before the affair begins, for Emma's husband Robert (Ben Kingsley) is Jerry's best friend. In a moment of drunkenness at a party, Emma and Jerry experiment with the idea of an affair. The rela-

tionship intensifies and soon they become an integrated couple through regular clandestine meetings. The bond becomes semi-official when they rent a flat for their weekly rendezvous.

As the affair's novelty wears off and Jerry and Emma feel the strain of hiding the relationship from their spouses, deterioration sets in. Certain topics become taboo and they begin keeping secrets from each other. The movie vividly portrays the pain of circumscribing, stagnation, and avoidance, as Jerry and Emma experience a chill where there used to be fire. The movie's first scene shows them meeting together two years after they have terminated their affair, and their communication is stilted and awkward. Although the story is difficult to watch at times, it faithfully chronicles the development and deterioration of a romantic relationship.

CHAPTER 02

Improving Communication Climates

ersonal relationships are a lot like the weather. Some are fair and warm, while others are stormy and cold; some are polluted, and others healthy. Some relationships have stable climates, while others change dramatically—calm one moment and turbulent the next. You can't measure the interpersonal climate by looking at a thermometer or glancing at the sky, but it's there nonetheless. Every relationship has a feeling, a pervasive mood that colors the interactions of the participants.

Although we can't change the external weather, we *can* act in ways that improve an interpersonal climate. This chapter will explain the forces that make some relationships happy and comfortable and others unpleasant. You will learn what kinds of behavior contribute to defensiveness and hostility, and what kinds lead to more positive feelings. After reading these pages you will have a better idea of the climate in each of your important relationships . . . and even more important, how to improve it.

✤ COMMUNICATION CLIMATE: THE KEY TO POSITIVE RELATIONSHIPS

The term **communication climate** refers to the emotional tone of a relationship. A climate doesn't involve specific activities as much as the way people feel about each other as they carry out those activities. Consider two interpersonal communication classes, for example. Both meet for the same length of time and follow the same syllabus. It's easy to imagine how one of these classes might be a friendly, comfortable place to learn, whereas the other could be cold and tense— even hostile. The same principle holds in other contexts. The role of climate in families and friendships is obvious. So is the impact of climate in the workplace. Have you ever held a job where backbiting, criticism, and suspicion were the norm? Or have you been lucky enough to work where the atmosphere was positive, encouraging, and supportive? If you've experienced both, you know what a difference climate makes. Research has demonstrated that employees have a higher level of commitment at jobs in which they experience a positive communication climate.[1] Studies also show that performance and job satisfaction increase when the communication climate is positive.[2] Whether it's the workplace, the classroom, or the home, people look for and stay in communication climates that affirm and support them.

Like their meteorological counterparts, communication climates are shared by everyone involved. It's rare to find one person describing a relationship as open and positive while another characterizes it as cold and hostile. Also, just like the weather, communication climates can change over time. A relationship can be overcast at one time and sunny at another. Carrying the analogy to its conclusion, we need to acknowledge that communication climate forecasting is not a perfect science. Unlike the weather, however, people can change the communication climates in their relationships. In this chapter we will explore ways to make your communication climates as satisfying as possible. We will begin by describing how communication climates develop. Next, we will explain how and why communicators respond defensively in certain climates. Finally—and most important—we will discuss what can be done to create positive climates and transform negative ones.

CONFIRMING AND DISCONFIRMING COMMUNICATION

What makes a communication climate positive or negative? In large part, the answer is surprisingly simple. The tone of a relationship is shaped by the degree to which the people believe themselves to be valued by one another.

Social scientists use the term **confirming communication** to describe messages that convey valuing, and **disconfirming communication** to define those that show a lack of regard. It's obvious that confirming messages are more desirable than disconfirming ones. But what characteristics distinguish them? Actually, it's an oversimplification to talk about one type of confirming message. In truth, confirming communication occurs on three increasingly positive levels.[3]

- *Recognition* The most fundamental act of confirmation is to recognize the other person. Recognition seems easy and obvious, and yet there are many times when we do not respond to others on this basic level. Failure to write or visit a friend is a common example. So is failure to return a phone message. Avoiding eye contact and not approaching someone you know on campus at a party or on the street sends a negative message. Of course, this lack of recognition may simply be an oversight. You might not notice your friend, or the pressures of work and school might prevent you from staying in touch. Nonetheless, if the other person *perceives* you as avoiding contact, the message has the effect of being disconfirming.

- *Acknowledgment* Acknowledging the ideas and feelings of others is a stronger form of confirmation. Listening is probably the most common form of acknowledgment. Of course, counterfeit listening—ambushing, stage-hogging, pseudolistening, and so on—have the opposite effect of acknowledgment. More active acknowledgment includes asking questions, paraphrasing, and reflecting. As you read in Chapter Seven, reflecting the speaker's thoughts and feelings can be a powerful way to offer support when others have problems.

- *Endorsement* Whereas acknowledging means you are interested in another's ideas, endorsement means that you agree with them. It's easy to see why endorsement is the strongest type of confirming message, since it communicates the highest form of valuing. The most obvious form of endorsement is agreeing. Fortunately, it isn't necessary to agree completely with another person in order to

Of all the Ten Commandments, "Thou shalt not murder" always seemed to me the one I would have to worry least about, until I got old enough to see that there are many different kinds of death, not all of them physical. There are murders as subtle as a turned eye. Dante was inspired to instill Satan in ice, cold indifference being so common a form of evil.

Anne Truitt,
Daybook

put me in your human eye
come taste
the bitter tears
that I cry
touch me
with your human hand
hear me with your ear
but notice me
damn you
notice me
I'm here.

Ric Masten

endorse her or his message. You can probably find something in the message that you endorse. "I can see why you were so angry," you might reply to a friend, even if you don't approve of his outburst. Of course, outright praise is a strong form of endorsement, and one you can use surprisingly often once you look for opportunities to compliment others.

In contrast to confirming messages, disconfirming communication shows a lack of regard for the other person, either by disputing or ignoring some important part of that person's message.[4] Disagreement can certainly be disconfirming, especially if it goes beyond disputing the other person's ideas and attacks the speaker personally. It may be tough to hear someone say, "I don't think that's a good idea," but a personal attack like "You're crazy" is even more insulting.

Not all disagreements are disconfirming, especially when compared to a total lack of acknowledgment. Most experts agree that it is psychologically healthier to have someone disagree with you than ignore you.[8] At its worst, a brutal disagreeing message can so devastate another person that the benefits of recognition and acknowledgment are lost. But in more constructive forms, disagreement includes two confirming components: recognition and acknowledgment. Communication researchers have demonstrated that constructive disagreements can lead to such benefits as enhanced self-concept[9], communicative competence,[10] and positive climate in the workplace.[11] The key to maintaining a positive climate while arguing is the way you present your ideas. It is crucial to attack issues, not people. In addition, a sound argument is better received when it's delivered in a supportive, affirming manner.[12] The types of supportive messages outlined on pages 379–385 in this chapter show how it is possible to argue in a respectful, constructive way.

DRAWING BY MANKOFF. © 1990 *THE NEW YORKER MAGAZINE*, INC.

Communication Transcript

DISCONFIRMING MESSAGES

Disconfirming messages convey a lack of respect or appreciation. Like their confirming counterparts, these messages can shape the climate of an entire relationship.

Verbal Abuse The most obvious type of disconfirming response is **verbal abuse:** communication that appears to be meant to cause psychological pain to another person.[5] In one survey of over 6,000 nationally representative families, about three-quarters of the husbands and wives reported being the target of verbally abusive messages over the most recent year.[6] Some abuse is overt, but at other times it can be disguised in malicious humor or sarcasm:

> "Come here, fatty."
> "I might not be perfect, but at least I'm not a loser like you."

Where verbal abuse exists in a relationship, it is seldom an isolated event.

Complaining Simple **complaining** may be less intense than verbal abuse, but it can still send a powerful disconfirming message.[7] Complaints may be about specific behavior in personal relationships, on the job, in school, or elsewhere:

> "The only thing you want to do on weekends is watch TV."
> "This work is full of mistakes. You'll have to do it over."
> "You're late again?"

More abstract complaints can be even more disconfirming, because they suggest that the flaw extends beyond one incident:

> I wish you would be more friendly."
> "Why can't you clean up after yourself?"
> "You need to have a more positive attitude."

Impervious Responses Ignoring the other person's attempt to communicate describes the **impervious response.** Refusing to answer another person in a face-to-face conversation is the most obvious kind of impervious response, though not the most common. Failing to return a phone call or write back in answer to a letter are more common impervious responses. So is not responding to a smile or a wave.

Interrupting Beginning to speak before the other person has finished can show a lack of concern about what the other person has to say. The occasional **interrupting response** is not likely to be taken as a disconfirmation, but repeatedly cutting in on a speaker can be both discouraging and irritating.

Irrelevant Responses A comment unrelated to what the other person has just said is an **irrelevant response.**

A   What a day! I thought it would never end. First the car overheated and I had to call a tow truck, and then the computer broke down at work.

B   Listen, we have to talk about a present for Ann's birthday. The party is on Saturday, and I only have tomorrow to shop for it.

A   I'm really beat. Could we talk about it in a few minutes? I've never seen a day like this one.

B   I just can't figure out what would suit Ann. She's got everything . . .

Tangential Responses Conversational "take aways" are called **tangential responses.** Instead of ignoring the speaker's remarks completely, the other party uses them as a starting point for a shift to a different topic.

A   I'd like to know for sure whether you want to go skiing during vacation. If we don't decide whether to go soon, it'll be impossible to get reservations anywhere.

B   Yeah. And if I don't pass my botany class, I won't be in the mood to go anywhere. Could you give me some help with this homework? . . .

Impersonal Responses Impersonal responses are loaded with clichés and other statements that never truly respond to the speaker.

A   I've been having some personal problems lately, and I'd like to take off work early a couple of afternoons to clear them up.

B   Ah, yes. We all have personal problems. It seems to be a sign of the times.

Ambiguous Responses Ambiguous responses contain messages with more than one meaning, leaving the other party unsure of the responder's position.

(continued on next page)

Communication Transcript *continued*

A I've been having some personal problems lately, and I'd like to take off work early a couple of afternoons to clear them up.

B Ah, yes. We all have personal problems. It seems to be a sign of the times.

Ambiguous Responses Ambiguous responses contain messages with more than one meaning, leaving the other party unsure of the responder's position.

A I'd like to get together with you soon. How about Tuesday?

B Uh, maybe so.

A Well, how about it. Can we talk Tuesday?

B Oh, probably. See you later.

Incongruous Responses The **incongruous response** contains two messages that seem to deny or contradict each other. Often at least one of these messages is nonverbal.

A Darling, I love you.

B I love you too. (giggles)

The worst sin towards our fellow creatures is not to hate them, but to be indifferent to them; that's the essence of inhumanity.

George Bernard Shaw

Being ignored can be more disconfirming than being dismissed or attacked. The list of disconfirming responses on pages 369–370 shows how impervious, interrupting, irrelevant, tangential, impersonal, ambiguous, and incongruous responses can show lack of respect for a communicator's importance.

It's important to note that disconfirming messages, like virtually every other kind of communication, are a matter of perception. Communicators are likely to downplay the significance of a potentially hurtful message that they consider to be unintentional.[13] On the other hand, even messages that aren't intended to devalue the other person can be interpreted as disconfirming. Your failure to return a phone call or respond to the letter of an out-of-town friend might simply be the result of a busy schedule; but if the other person views the lack of contact as a sign that you don't value the relationship, the effect can be powerful.

HOW COMMUNICATION CLIMATES DEVELOP

As soon as two people start to communicate, a relational climate begins to develop. If the messages are confirming, the climate is likely to be a positive one. If they disconfirm one another, the relationship is likely to be hostile, cold, or defensive.

Verbal messages certainly contribute to the tone of a relationship, but many climate-shaping messages are nonverbal. The very act of approaching others is confirming, whereas avoiding them can be disconfirming. Smiles or frowns, the presence or absence of eye contact, tone of voice, the use of personal space . . . all these and other cues send messages about how the parties feel toward one another.

Once a climate is formed, it can take on a life of its own and grow in a self-perpetuating **spiral:** a reciprocating communication pattern in which each person's message reinforces the other's.[14] In positive spirals, one partner's confirming message leads to a similar response from the other person. This positive reaction leads the first person to be even more reinforcing. Negative spirals are just as powerful, though they leave the partners feeling worse about themselves and each other. Research shows how spirals operate in relationships to reinforce the principle that "what goes around, comes around." In one study of married couples, each spouse's response in conflict situations was similar to the other's statement.[15] Conciliatory statements (for example, support, accepting responsibilities, agreeing) were likely to be followed by conciliatory responses. Confrontive acts (such as criticism, hostile questions, and faultfinding) were likely to trigger an aggressive response. The same pattern held for other kinds of messages: Avoidance begat avoidance, analysis evoked analysis, and so on.

Escalatory conflict spirals are the most visible way that disconfirming messages reinforce one another.[16] One attack leads to another until a skirmish escalates into a full-fledged battle:

A: (*mildly irritated*) Where were you? I thought we agreed to meet here a half-hour ago.

B: (*defensively*) I'm sorry. I got hung up at the library. I don't have as much free time as you do, you know.

A: I wasn't *blaming* you, so don't get so touchy. I do resent what you just said, though. I'm plenty busy. And I've got lots of better things to do than wait around for you!

B: Who's getting touchy? I just made a simple comment. You've sure been defensive lately. What's the matter with you?

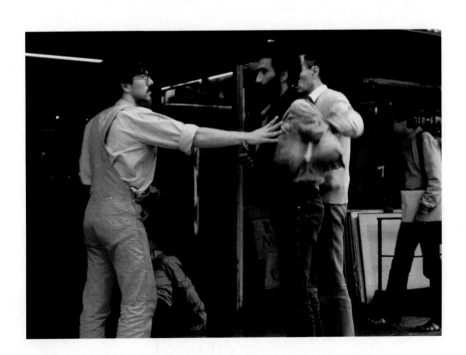

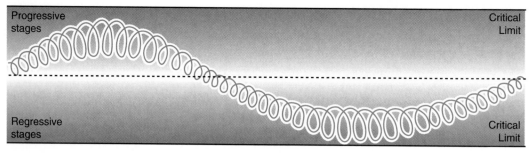

FIGURE 9–1
Progressive and regressive spiral phases of a marital dyad

Although they are less obvious, **de-escalatory conflict spirals** can also be destructive.[17] Rather than fighting, the parties slowly lessen their dependence on one another, withdraw, and become less invested in the relationship.

Spirals—whether positive or negative—rarely go on indefinitely. As Figure 9–1 shows, most relationships pass through cycles of progression and regression. If the spiral is negative, partners may find the exchange growing so unpleasant that they switch from negative to positive messages without discussing the matter. In other cases they may engage in metacommunication. "Hold on," one might say. "This is getting us nowhere." In some cases, however, partners pass the "point of no return," leading to the breakup of a relationship. Even positive spirals have their limit: Even the best relationships go through periods of conflict and withdrawal, although a combination of time and communication skills can eventually bring the partners back into greater harmony.

 INVITATION TO INSIGHT

EVALUATING COMMUNICATION CLIMATES

You can probably recognize the communication climate in each of your relationships without much analysis. But answering the following questions will help explain *why* these climates exist. Following these steps may also suggest how to improve negative climates.

1. Identify the communication climate of an important interpersonal relationship. Using weather metaphors (sunny, gloomy, calm) may help.

2. List the confirming or disconfirming communication that created and now maintains this climate. Be sure to identify both verbal and nonverbal messages.

3. Describe what you can do either to maintain the existing climate (if positive) or to change it (if negative). Again, list both verbal and nonverbal behaviors.

❖ DEFENSIVENESS: CAUSES AND REMEDIES

It is a curious psycho-logical fact that the man who seems to be "egotistic" is not suffering from too much ego, but from too little.

Sydney J. Harris

Probably no type of communication pollutes an interpersonal climate more often than defensive spirals. One verbal attack leads to another, and soon the dispute mushrooms out of control, leaving an aftermath of hurt and bitterness that is difficult—sometimes even impossible—to repair.

The word **defensiveness** suggests protecting oneself from attack, but what kind of attack? Surely, few if any of the times you become defensive involve a physical threat. If you're not threatened by bodily injury, what *are* you guarding against? To answer this question we need to talk more about the notions of the presenting self and face introduced in Chapter Two.

Recall that a person's face consists of the physical traits, personality characteristics, attitudes, aptitudes, and all the other parts of the image he or she wants to present to the world. Actually, it is a mistake to talk about a single face: We try to project different selves to different people. You might, for instance, try to impress a potential employer with your seriousness but want your friends to see you as a joker. Of course, not all parts of your presenting self are equally significant. Letting others know that you are right-handed or a Gemini is probably less important to you than convincing them you are good-looking or loyal.

When others are willing to accept and acknowledge important parts of our presenting image, there is no need to feel defensive. On the other hand, when others confront us with **face-threatening acts**—messages that seem to challenge the image we want to project—we are likely to resist their messages. Defensiveness, then, is the process of protecting our presenting self, our face.

You can understand how defensiveness operates by imagining what might happen if an important part of your presenting self were attacked. Suppose, for instance, that an instructor criticized you for making a stupid mistake. Or consider how you would feel if a friend called you self-centered or your boss labeled you as lazy. You would probably feel threatened if these attacks were untrue. But notice that you might very well react defensively even if you knew deep inside that the criticism was justified. For instance, you have probably responded defensively at times when you *did* make a mistake, act selfishly, or cut corners on your work. In fact, we often feel most defensive when criticism is right on target.[18]

One reason for such defensiveness has to do with our need for approval. In response to the question "Why am I afraid to tell you who I am?" author John Powell quotes one actual response: "Because if I tell you who I am, you may not like who I am, and that is all I have."[19] So one reason we wear defensive masks is to appear to be the kind of person who will gain the approval of others.

Responding defensively to unpleasant but accurate criticism not only involves fooling others but also ourselves. We want to believe the act we're putting on, since it's uncomfortable to admit that we are

♟ *I seem to get the most defensive when I think something I have done is "bad." The judgment as to what is bad is a judgment of mine as well as others around me. It cuts the most when someone else's judgment of me agrees with my own bad impression of myself.*

John T. Wood

not the person we would like to be. When faced with a situation where the truth might hurt, we are tempted to convince ourselves that we do fit the idealized picture we have constructed.

TYPES OF DEFENSIVE REACTIONS

When a part of your presenting self is attacked by others and you aren't willing to accept their judgment, you are faced with what psychologists call **cognitive dissonance**—an inconsistency between two conflicting pieces of information, attitudes, or behavior.[20] Dissonance is an uncomfortable condition, and communicators strive to resolve it by seeking consistency. One way to eliminate the dissonance, of course, is to accept the critic's judgment and revise your presenting self accordingly. You could agree that you were stupid or mistaken, for example. Sometimes, however, you aren't willing to accept attacks. The accusations of your critic may be false. And even if they are true, you may be unwilling to admit their accuracy. It isn't pleasant to admit that you were lazy, unfair, or foolish. There are three broad ways to resolve dissonance without agreeing with a critic. Each of them is characterized by **defense mechanisms:** psychological devices that resolve dissonance by maintaining a positive presenting image.

ATTACKING THE CRITIC   Counterattacking follows the old maxim that the best defense is a good offense. Attacking defensive maneuvers can take several forms.

- *Verbal aggression.* Sometimes the recipient uses **verbal aggression** to assault the critic directly. "Where do you get off calling me sloppy?" you might storm to a roommate. "You're the one who leaves globs of toothpaste in the sink and dirty clothes all over the bedroom!" This sort of response shifts the blame onto the critic, without acknowledging that the original judgment might be true. Other attacks on the critic are completely off the subject: "You're in no position to complain about my sloppiness. At least I pay my share of the bills on time." Again, this response resolves the dissonance without ever addressing the validity of the criticism.
- *Sarcasm.* Disguising the attack in the barbed, humorous message in **sarcasm** is a less direct form of aggression. "You think I ought to study more? Thanks for taking a break from watching soap operas and eating junk food to run my life." Sarcastic responses might score high on wit and quick thinking, but their hostile, disconfirming nature usually leads to a counterattack and a mutually destructive defensive spiral.

DISTORTING CRITICAL INFORMATION   A second way of defending a perceived self under attack is to somehow distort the information in a manner that leaves the presenting self intact—at least in the eyes of the defender. There are a number of ways to distort dissonant information.

- *Rationalization.* **Rationalization** is the invention of logical but untrue explanations of undesirable behavior. "I would help you out, but I really have to study," you might say as a convenient way to avoid an unpleasant chore. "I'm not overeating," you might protest to another critic who you secretly admit is on target. "I have a busy day ahead, and I need to keep my strength up." (See Table 9–1 for other examples.)

- *Compensation.* Those using **compensation** emphasize a strength in one area to cover up a weakness in another. A guilty parent might keep up the façade of being conscientious by protesting, "I may not be around much, but I give those kids the best things money can buy!" Likewise, you might try to convince yourself and others that you are a good friend by compensating: "Sorry I forgot your birthday. Let me give you a hand with that job." There's nothing wrong with most acts of compensation in themselves. The harm comes when they are used not sincerely but to maintain a fictitious presenting image.

- *Regression.* Another way to avoid facing attack is to play helpless, claiming you *can't* do something when in truth you *don't want* to do it. "I'd like to have a relationship with you, but I just can't: I'm not ready." "I wish I could do the job better, but I just can't: I just don't understand it." The test for **regression** is to substitute the

There is something I don't know that I am supposed to know.
I don't know what it is I don't know, and yet am supposed to know,
and I feel I look stupid if I seem both not to know it and not know what it is I don't know.
Therefore I pretend I know it. This is nerve-wracking since I don't know what I must pretend to know.
Therefore I pretend to know everything!

R.D. Laing,
Knots

TABLE 9 – 1   **Rationalization Reader for Students**

SITUATION	WHAT TO SAY
When the course is the lecture type:	We never get a chance to say anything.
When the course is the discussion type:	The professor just sits there. We don't know how to teach the course.
When all aspects of the course are covered in class:	All she does is follow the text.
When you're responsible for covering part of the course outside class:	She never covers half the things we're tested on.
When you're given objective tests:	They don't allow for any individuality in us.
When you're given essay tests:	They're too vague. We never know what's expected.
When the instructor gives no tests:	It isn't fair! She can't tell how much we really know.
When you have a lot of quizzes instead of a midterm and final:	We need major exams. Quizzes don't cover enough to really tell anything.
When you have only two exams for the whole course:	Too much rides on each one. You can just have a bad day.

word *won't* for *can't.* In many cases it becomes clear that "It's not my fault" is a fiction.

AVOIDING DISSONANT INFORMATION   A third way to protect a threatened presenting image is to avoid information altogether. Avoidance can take several forms.

- *Physical avoidance.* Steering clear of people who attack a presenting self is an obvious way to avoid dissonance. Sometimes **physical avoidance** may be wise. There's little profit in being battered by hostile or abusive criticism. In other cases, however, the relationship may be important enough and the criticism valid enough that avoiding the situation only makes matters worse.
- *Repression.* Sometimes we mentally block out dissonant information. You might, for instance, know that you ought to discuss a problem with a friend, boss, or instructor, yet you put the idea out of your mind whenever it arises. It's even possible to repress a problem in the face of a critic. Changing the subject, acting as if you don't understand, and even pretending you don't hear the criticism all fall into the category of **repression.**
- *Apathy.* Another avoidance response, **apathy,** is to acknowledge unpleasant information but pretend you don't care about it. You might for instance, sit calmly through a friend's criticism and act as if it didn't bother you. Similarly, you might respond to the loss of a job by acting indifferent: "Who cares? It was a dumb job anyhow."
- *Displacement.* **Displacement** occurs when we vent aggressive or hostile feelings against people or objects that are seen as less dangerous than the person or persons who threatened us originally. You may be mad at your boss, but rather than risk getting fired, you could displace your aggression by yelling at the people you live with. Displacement almost always lets us preserve (at least to ourselves) the image that we're *potent*—that we're in control and can't be pushed around by forces beyond our control. The very act of displacing proves this a lie, of course—but one the displacer fails to recognize.

INVITATION TO INSIGHT

DEFENSE MECHANISM INVENTORY

List the three defense mechanisms you use most often, and describe three recent examples of each. You can arrive at your list both by thinking about your own behavior and by asking others to share their impressions of you.

Conclude your inventory by describing

1. The people with whom you become defensive most often.
2. The parts of your presenting self you frequently defend.
3. The usual consequences of using defense mechanisms.
4. Any more satisfying ways you could act in the future.

I AM A ROCK

A winter's day
In a deep and dark December
I am alone
Gazing from my window
To the streets below
On a freshly fallen silent
      shroud of snow
I am a rock
I am an island.

I built walls
A fortress deep and mighty
That none may penetrate
I have no need of friendship
Friendship causes pain
Its laughter and its loving I
      disdain
I am a rock
I am an island.

Don't talk of love
Well, I've heard the word
      before
It's sleeping in my memory
I won't disturb the slumber
Of feelings that have died
If I'd never loved I never
      would have cried
I am a rock
I am an island.

I have my books
And my poetry to protect me.
I am shielded in armor
Hiding in my room
Safe within my womb
I touch no one and no one
      touches me
I am a rock
I am an island

And a rock feels no pain
And an island never cries.

Communication Transcript

A CHILD'S GARDEN OF DEFENSE MECHANISMS

Verbal Aggression

I was with my boyfriend a few months ago when this man ran a red light and smashed into the side of our van. It was definitely his fault—there were cars stopped in the lane next to him.

Even though this guy must have known he was guilty, he jumped out of his car and began yelling at us. He called us "dirty punks" and "bums." He let out all that verbal aggression just to cover up the truth—that he was wrong.

Rationalization

A guy I know broke up with his girlfriend not too long ago, and the way he handled the thing really shows how rationalization can hurt communication. The reason he gave her for splitting up was that he'd be going away to Europe soon and he didn't want to break off suddenly when he left. But the truth was that he was just tired of her. She knew this, and I think his rationalization hurt her way more than if he'd been honest. I know he was only fooling himself because he wants to think he's a great guy who is thinking only of her welfare!

Compensation

The other night I was at a party when the conversation turned to politics. I'm really turned off by that whole subject even though I know it's important. So when somebody brought up the election, I tried to change the subject to motorcycles, which I know a lot about. I do this a lot. When there's something I don't understand or don't like, I try to change the conversation to an area where I'm an authority.

Regression

I use regression at home when I don't want to do chores. If a job sounds unpleasant I claim I "can't" do it: I "can't" prune the fruit trees the right way, strip off the old paint, wax the car, and so on. This way I get other members of my family to help without admitting I'm lazy. It probably doesn't fool them—and now that I'm aware of it, this kind of regression won't fool me either.

Repression

My family is especially good at repressing our feelings about a serious problem. My brother is turning into an alcoholic, and I'm worried that it's going to hurt him and the family seriously soon. Despite the concern everyone feels, when we get together we pretend nothing's wrong. I think we hope that by acting like a happy, trouble-free family we'll become one.

Apathy

After learning about defense mechanisms I discovered that one of my "favorites" is apathy. When I'm criticized by my family, friends, or professors I pretend I don't care. I really *do* care a great deal, but it's hard to admit that I'm wrong. I guess being wrong isn't part of my presenting image. After thinking about it, I see that acting apathetic doesn't impress others, and it keeps me from changing for the better.

Displacement

Yesterday at work I used the defense mechanism of displacement. My supervisor had given me a bunch of static about a problem that was really his fault. He's an unrealistic old S.O.B. to begin with, and there's no use arguing with him. So I guess because I was so mad, when one of the guys on my crew asked me if he could take off a little early that afternoon, I chewed him out for being a lazy so-and-so. But all it was was my anger at the boss being displaced. I was really sorry and apologized later, but it'll take a few days for the guy to let the chip melt off his shoulder.

PREVENTING DEFENSIVENESS IN OTHERS

By now you understand how easily communicators become defensive when their presenting image is threatened. You probably recognize that the best chances for creating a favorable response come with messages that honor the other person's face by supporting his or her presenting self.[21] These facts might leave you caught in an apparent bind, asking yourself how to send a face-honoring message when you have a genuine gripe with someone.

The solution to this dilemma lies in the two-dimensional nature of communication. On a content level you can express dissatisfaction with the other person, but on a relational level you can be saying—explicitly or nonverbally—that you value him or her. The possibility of handling potentially delicate issues in ways that improve your relationships may seem overwhelming, but the influential work of researcher Jack Gibb offers some useful tools for controlling defensiveness.[22] After observing groups for several years, Gibb was able to isolate six types of defense-arousing communication and six contrasting behaviors that seemed to reduce the level of threat and defensiveness by conveying face-honoring relational messages of respect. The **Gibb categories** are listed in Table 9–2, and summarized in the following pages.

EVALUATION VS. DESCRIPTION   The first type of defense-arousing behavior Gibb noted was **evaluative communication.** Most people become irritated at judgmental statements, which they are likely to interpret as indicating a lack of regard. One form of evaluation is "you" language, described in Chapter Five.

Unlike evaluative "you" language, **descriptive communication** focuses on the *speaker's* thoughts and feelings instead of judging the other person. Descriptive messages often are expressed in "I" language, which tends to provoke less defensiveness than "you" statements.[23] Contrast the following evaluative "you" claims with their descriptive "I" counterparts:

Evaluation: "You don't know what you're talking about!"

Description: "I don't understand how you came up with that idea."

Evaluation: "This place is a mess!"

T A B L E   9 – 2   The Gibb Categories of Defensive and Supportive Behaviors

DEFENSIVE BEHAVIORS	SUPPORTIVE BEHAVIORS
1. evaluation	1. description
2. control	2. problem orientation
3. strategy	3. spontaneity
4. neutrality	4. empathy
5. superiority	5. equality
6. certainty	6. provisionalism

In interpersonal relationships, I believe first person singular is most appropriate because it places responsibility clearly.

If I say to another person, "I do not like what you did," then no contradiction is possible. No one can correct me because my perception and what I have decided to think about is mine alone. The other person may, however, suggest that I received only a portion of the information, or that I received it unclearly for one reason or another. In such a case, the meaning of the message may be tentative until it can be negotiated. It also is legitimate for me to perceive the message quite differently from the way the other person perceives it.

On the other hand, if I say "You have made me angry," then you may very well contradict me by responding with something such as "No I didn't." In fact, I am eliciting a defensiveness and also inviting "you" to attempt a control of me by your helplessness, suffering, or anger.

Only I am responsible for my behavior. Only I can change what I do. However, when I change my behavior, I may give the other person in the relationship the opportunity to evaluate his behavior and perhaps modify it.

John Narciso and David Burkett,
Declare Yourself

Description: "When you don't clean up, I have to either do it or live with your mess. That's why I'm mad!"

Evaluation: "You acted like a fool last night!"

Description: "When you told those off-color jokes, I got really embarrassed."

Note how each of the descriptive statements focuses on the speaker's thoughts and feelings without judging the other person. Despite its value, descriptive language isn't the only element necessary for success. Its effectiveness depends in part on when, where, and how the statement is delivered. You can imagine how each of the preceding descriptive statements would go over if said in front of a room full of bystanders or in a whining tone of voice. Even the best timing and delivery of a descriptive message won't guarantee success. Some people will react defensively to anything you say or do. Nonetheless, it's easy to see that describing how the other person's behavior affects you is likely to produce better results than judgmentally attacking the individual.

CONTROL VS. PROBLEM ORIENTATION   A second defense-provoking message involves some attempt to control another. **Controlling communication** occurs when a sender seems to be imposing a solution on the receiver with little regard for the receiver's needs or interests. The object of control can range from where to eat dinner or what TV show to watch to whether to remain in a relationship or how to spend a large sum of money. Whatever the situation, people who act in controlling ways create a defensive climate. None of us likes to feel that our ideas are worthless and that nothing we say will change other people's determination to have their way—yet this is precisely the attitude a controller communicates. Whether done with words, gestures, tone of voice, or through some other channel; whether control is accomplished through status, insistence on obscure or irrelevant rules, or physical power, the controller generates hostility wherever he or she goes. The unspoken message such behavior communicates is "I know what's best for you, and if you do as I say, we'll get along."

In contrast, in **problem orientation** communicators focus on finding a solution that satisfies both their needs and those of the others involved. The goal here isn't to "win" at the expense of your partner but to work out some arrangement in which everybody feels like a winner. (Chapter Ten has a great deal to say about "win–win" problem solving as a way to find problem-oriented solutions.)

STRATEGY VS. SPONTANEITY   Gibb uses the word **strategy** to characterize defense-arousing messages in which speakers hide their ulterior motives. The terms *dishonesty* and *manipulation* capture the essence of strategy. Even if the intentions that motivate strategic communication are honorable, the victim of deception who discovers an attempt to deceive is likely to feel offended at being played for a naive sucker.

Spontaneity is the behavior that contrasts with strategy. Spontaneity simply means expressing yourself honestly. Despite the misleading label Gibb chose for this kind of behavior, spontaneous communication needn't be blurted out as soon as an idea comes to you. You might want to plan the wording of your message carefully so that you can express yourself clearly. The important thing is to be honest. Often spontaneity won't get what you want, but in the long run it's usually better to be candid and perhaps miss out on some small goal than to say all the right things and be a fraud. More than once we've heard people say, "I didn't like what he said, but at least I know he was being honest."

Although it sounds paradoxical at first, spontaneity can be a strategy, too. Sometimes you'll see people using honesty in a calculating way, being just frank enough to win someone's trust or sympathy. This "leveling" is probably the most defense-arousing strategy of all because once we've learned someone is using frankness as a manipulation, there's almost no chance we'll ever trust that person again.

You may be getting the idea that using supportive behaviors such as description, problem orientation, empathy, and so on, is a good way to manipulate others. Before going any farther, we want to say loudly and clearly that if you ever act supportively without being sincere in what you're saying, you've misunderstood the idea behind this chapter, and you're running a risk of causing even more defensiveness than before. None of the ideas we present in this book can go into a "bag of tricks" that can be used to control others: If you ever find yourself using them in this way, beware!

ETHICAL CHALLENGE

SPONTANEITY AND SUPPORT

Gibb argues that spontaneous rather than strategic communication reduces defensiveness. In some situations, however, a strategic approach may hold the promise of a better climate than a completely honest message. Consider such situations as these:

1. You don't find your partner very attractive. He or she asks, "What's the matter?"

2. You intend to quit your job because you hate your boss, but you don't want to offend him or her. How do you explain the reasons for your departure?

3. You are tutoring a high school student in reading or math. The student is sincere and hard working, but is perhaps the most dull-witted person you have ever met. What do you say when the teenager asks, "How am I doing?"

Describe at least one situation from your experience where complete honesty increased another person's defensiveness. Discuss whether candor or some degree of strategy might have been the best approach in this situation. How can you reconcile your approach with Gibb's arguments in favor of spontaneity?

Looking at Diversity

POLICE WORK AND FACEWORK

In addition to his regular duties as a police officer in Santa Barbara, California, Lorenzo Duarte works with local schoolchildren and hosts a weekly call-in radio program for the city's Spanish-speaking residents. Duarte spent most of his childhood in California's agricultural regions, where his Mexican-born parents lived and worked. During his five years in the U.S. Air Force, he earned several awards, both as a weightlifter and for his work in security.

Saving face is a big part of a police officer's job. It's easy to understand why people feel threatened when they see a flashing red light, a badge, gun, baton, and handcuffs. This is true for law-abiding citizens, but it's especially true when people know they've done something wrong. In situations like this your most important tools as a police officer are your mind and communication skills. If you can make people feel less threatened, you can get them to cooperate without using force.

I've found that the best way to get cooperation is to treat everybody—and I really mean everybody—with respect. This might seem hard to do with some "bad guys," but it is possible. Let me give you an example. A while back we arrested a man we were sure

had been stealing from some of the poorest people in our town. It would have been easy to treat the guy like scum, but that wouldn't have helped us get a confession, which was what we wanted. When he told us what we knew were a bunch of lies, we laid out his options without being critical or judgmental. We told him that the courts would be investigating his story, and that he held his own destiny in his hands. He could do himself a favor and tell the truth or he could lie and take the consequences later. Not only did he confess, but he identified other burglars and took us to the place where the stolen property was kept. Because we were honest and respectful with him, we got four criminal convictions and put the stolen goods back in the hands of their owners. I'm sure that if we had disrespected this guy, he wouldn't have cooperated with us.

This story shows that there are several parts to being respectful. The obvious one is being polite: no name calling or scorn. Another part is giving people a sense of control over their lives. We didn't demand that this suspect confess; we laid out his options and then let him choose what would happen next. Letting people choose how they want an encounter to wind up usually works better than threatening them. Another part of respect is honesty, even with troublemakers. People may not always like

police officers, but they'll cooperate more if they know we're telling the truth. The last way to save face is by listening. Cutting somebody off is disrespectful. If you hear them out, even if they're obviously lying or jabbering, they're more likely to give you what you want.

Most of being respectful is just common sense: treating others the way you would like to be treated. Sometimes, though, knowing the customs or rules of a particular culture can help. For example, if I'm going to investigate a complaint in a home where the people were raised in a Hispanic culture, it's important to approach the man of the house—the husband or father. Questioning the wife or children first would be an insult. I would be making the man lose face by suggesting he wasn't the authority figure. This might not seem fair, especially if the man is the focus of a complaint; but I can still get the guy to cooperate more if I treat him the way he'd like to be treated. This is a small price to pay to solve a problem.

I'm not pretending that you can always be nice as a police officer. Sometimes you're forced to get rough. But it is always best to start by being polite and respectful. You can escalate if you have to. If you start an encounter by being aggressive, the other person is likely to get defensive. Once this happens, it's hard for everybody to back off.

NEUTRALITY VS. EMPATHY   Gibb used the term **neutrality** to describe a fourth behavior that arouses defensiveness. Probably a better descriptive word would be *indifference*. A neutral attitude is disconfirming because it communicates a lack of concern for the welfare of another and implies that the other person isn't very important to you. This perceived indifference is likely to promote defensiveness because people do not like to think of themselves as worthless, and they'll protect a self-concept that pictures themselves as worthwhile.

The poor effects of neutrality become apparent when you consider the hostility that most people have for the large, impersonal organizations with which they have to deal: "They think of me as a number instead of a person"; "I felt as if I were being handled by computers and not human beings." These two common statements reflect reactions to being handled in an indifferent way. Gibb has found that **empathy** helps rid communication of the quality of indifference. When people show that they care for the feelings of another, there's little chance that the person's self-concept will be threatened. Empathy means accepting another's feelings, putting yourself in another's place. This doesn't mean you need to agree with that person. By simply letting someone know about your care and respect, you'll be acting in a supportive way. Gibb noted the importance of nonverbal messages in communicating empathy. He found that facial and bodily expressions of concern are often more important to the receiver than the words used.

SUPERIORITY VS. EQUALITY   A fifth behavior creating a defensive climate involves **superiority.** How many interpersonal relationships have you dropped because you couldn't stand the superiority that the other person projected? An individual who communicates superiority arouses feelings of inadequacy in the recipients. We're not particular about

> *The need to be right—the sign of a vulgar mind.*
>
> Albert Camus

*"What do you mean 'Your guess is as good as mine?'
My guess is a hell of a lot better than your guess!"*

We do not need confirmation for qualities of which we are certain, but we will be extremely touchy when false claims are questioned.

Karen Horney

the type of superiority presented to us; we just become defensive. Money, power, intellectual ability, physical appearance, and athletic prowess are all areas our culture stresses. Consequently, we often feel a need to express our superiority along these lines.

Individuals who act superior communicate that they don't want to relate on equal terms with others in the relationship. Furthermore, people like this seem to imply that they don't want feedback or need help because it would be coming from someone "inferior." The listener is put on guard because the senders are likely to attempt to reduce the receiver's worth, power, or status to maintain or advance their own superiority.

Perhaps you've had professors who continually reminded their class of their superior intellectual ability and position. Remember how delighted you were when you or a classmate caught one of these superior types in a mistake? Why do you suppose that was so satisfying? Some might argue that this is a good strategy to keep students awake, but in reality much of the students' effort is then directed to defending self-worth rather than pursuing the objectives of the course.

When we detect people communicating superiority, we usually react defensively. We "turn them off," justify ourselves, or argue with them in our minds. Sometimes we choose to change the subject verbally or even walk away. Of course, there is always the counterattack, which includes an attempt to belittle the senders of the superiority message. We'll go to great lengths "to cut them down to size." All these defensive reactions to projected superiority are destructive to an interpersonal climate.

Many times in our lives we are in a relationship with individuals who possess talents greater than ours. But is it necessary for these people to project superiority? Your own experiences will tell you that it isn't. Gibb has found ample evidence that many who have superior skills and talents are capable of projecting feelings of **equality** rather than superiority. Such people communicate that although they may have greater talent in certain areas, they see others as having just as much worth as human beings.

CERTAINTY VS. PROVISIONALISM   Have you ever run into people who are positive they're right, who know that theirs is the only or proper way of doing something, who insist that they have all the facts and need no additional information? If you have, you've met individuals who project the defense-arousing behavior Gibb calls **certainty.**

How do you react when you're the target of such certainty? Do you suddenly find your energy directed to proving the dogmatic individual wrong? If you do, you're reacting normally, if not very constructively.

Communicators who regard their own opinions with certainty while disregarding the ideas of others demonstrate a rather clear lack of regard for the thoughts others hold to be important. It's likely the receiver will take the certainty as a personal affront, and react defensively.

In contrast to dogmatic communication is **provisionalism,** in which people may have strong opinions but are willing to acknowledge that they don't have a corner on the truth and will change their stand if another position seems more reasonable.

There is no guarantee that using Gibb's supportive, confirming approach to communication will build a positive climate. The other person may simply not be receptive. But the chances for a constructive relationship will be greatest when communication consists of the kind of constructive approach described here. Besides boosting the odds of getting a positive response from others, supportive communication can leave you feeling better in a variety of ways: more in control of your relationships, more comfortable, and more positive toward others.

INVITATION TO INSIGHT

DEFENSIVENESS FEEDBACK

1. Approach an important person in your life, and request some help in learning more about yourself. Inform the other person that your discussion will probably take at least an hour, so make sure both of you are prepared to invest the necessary amount of time.

2. Begin by explaining all twelve of the Gibb behaviors to your partner. Be sure to give enough examples so that each category is clearly understood.

3. When your explanation is complete and you've answered all your partner's questions, ask him or her to tell you which of the Gibb categories *you* use. Seek specific examples so that you are certain to understand the feedback fully. (Since you are requesting an evaluation, be prepared for a little defensiveness on your own part at this point.) Inform your partner that you are interested in discovering both the defense-arousing and the supportive behaviors you use and that you are sincerely interested in receiving a candid answer. (Note: If you don't want to hear the truth from your partner, don't try this exercise.)

4. As your partner speaks, record the categories he or she lists in sufficient detail for both of you to be sure that you have understood the comments.

5. When you have finished your list, show it to your partner. Listen to that person's reactions, and make any corrections that are necessary to reflect an accurate understanding of the comments. When your list is accurate, have your partner sign it to indicate that you have understood it clearly.

6. In a concluding statement note
   a. how you felt as your partner was describing you.
   b. whether you agree with the evaluation.
   c. what effect your use of the various Gibb categories has on your relationship with your partner.

BLONDIE

RESPONDING NONDEFENSIVELY TO CRITICISM

The world would be a happier place if everyone communicated supportively. But how can you respond nondefensively when others use evaluation, control, superiority, and all the other attacking behaviors Gibb identified? Despite your best intentions, it's difficult to be reasonable when you're faced with a torrent of criticism. Being attacked is hard enough when the critic is clearly being unfair, but it's often even more threatening when the judgments are on target. Despite the accuracy of your critic, the tendency is either to counterattack aggressively with a barrage of verbal aggression or to withdraw nonassertively.

Because neither of these responses is likely to resolve a dispute, we need alternative ways of behaving. There are two such methods. Despite their apparent simplicity, they have proved to be among the most valuable skills many communicators have learned.[24]

SEEK MORE INFORMATION   The response of seeking more information makes good sense when you realize that it's foolish to respond to a critical attack until you understand what the other person has said. Even comments that on first consideration appear to be totally unjustified or foolish often prove to contain at least a grain of truth and sometimes much more.

Many readers object to the idea of asking for details when they are criticized. Their resistance grows from confusing the act of *listening open-mindedly* to a speaker's comments with *accepting* them. Once you realize that you can listen to, understand, and even acknowledge the most hostile comments without necessarily accepting them, it becomes much easier to hear another person out. If you disagree with a speaker's objections, you will be in a much better position to explain yourself once you understand the criticism. On the other hand, after carefully listening to the other's remarks, you might just see that they are valid, in which case you have learned some valuable information about yourself. In either case, you have everything to gain and nothing to lose by paying attention to the critic.

Of course, after one has spent years of instinctively resisting criticism, learning to listen to the other person will take some practice. To make matters clearer, here are several ways in which you can seek additional information from your critics.

Ask for specifics   Often the vague attack of a critic is virtually useless even if you sincerely want to change. Abstract accusations such as "You're being unfair" or "You never help out" can be difficult to understand. In such cases it is a good idea to request more specific information from the sender. "What do I *do* that's unfair?" is an important question to ask before you can judge whether the accusation is correct. "When haven't I helped out?" you might ask before agreeing with or disputing the accusation.

If you already solicit specifics by using questions and are still accused of reacting defensively, the problem may be in the *way* you ask. Your tone of voice and facial expression, posture, or other non-verbal clues can give the same words radically different connotations. For example, think of how you could use the words "Exactly what are you talking about?" to communicate either a genuine desire to know or your belief that the speaker is crazy. It's important to request specific information only when you genuinely want to learn more from the speaker, for asking under any other circumstances will only make matters worse.

Love your enemies, for they tell you your faults.

Benjamin Franklin

Guess about specifics   On some occasions even your sincere and well-phrased requests for specific details won't meet with success. Sometimes your critics won't be able to define precisely the behavior they find offensive. In these instances, you'll hear such comments as "I can't tell you exactly what's wrong with your sense of humor—all I can say is that I don't like it." In other cases, your critics may know the exact behaviors they don't like, but for some reason they seem to get a perverse satisfaction out of making you struggle to figure it out. At times like this, you hear such comments as, "Well, if you don't know what you did to hurt my feelings, I'm certainly not going to tell you!"

Needless to say, failing to learn the details of another's criticism when you genuinely want to know can be frustrating. In instances like these, you can often learn more clearly what is bothering your critic by *guessing* at the specifics of a complaint. In a sense you become both detective and suspect, the goal being to figure out exactly what "crime" you have committed. Like the technique of asking for specifics, guessing must be done with goodwill if it's to produce satisfying results. You need to convey to the critic that for both your sakes you're truly interested in finding out what is the matter. Once you have communicated this intention, the emotional climate generally becomes more comfortable because, in effect, both you and the critic are seeking the same goal.

Here are some typical questions you might hear from someone guessing about the details of another's criticism:

"So you object to the language I used in writing the paper. Was my language too formal?"

"OK, I understand that you think the outfit looks funny. What is it that's so bad? Is it the color? Does it have something to do with the fit? The fabric?"

"When you say that I'm not doing my share around the house, do you mean that I haven't been helping enough with the cleaning?"

Paraphrase the speaker's ideas   Another strategy is to draw out confused or reluctant speakers by paraphrasing their thoughts and feelings and using the active listening skills described in Chapter Seven. Paraphrasing is especially good in helping others solve their problems; and since people generally criticize you because your behavior creates some problem for them, the method is especially appropriate at such times.

One advantage of paraphrasing is that you don't have to guess about the specifics of your behavior that might be offensive. By clarifying or amplifying what you understand critics to be saying, you'll learn more about their objections. A brief dialogue between a disgruntled customer and an especially talented store manager using paraphrasing might sound like this:

Customer: The way you people run this store is disgusting! I just want to tell you that I'll never shop here again.

Manager: (*reflecting the customer's feeling*) It seems that you're quite upset. Can you tell me your problem?

Customer: It isn't *my* problem; it's the problem your salespeople have. They seem to think it's a great inconvenience to help a customer find anything around here.

Manager: So you didn't get enough help locating the items you were looking for, is that it?

Customer: Help? I spent twenty minutes looking around in here before I even talked to a clerk. All I can say is that it's a hell of a way to run a store.

Manager: So what you're saying is that the clerks seemed to be ignoring the customers?

Customer: No. They were all busy with other people. It just seems to me that you ought to have enough help around to handle the crowds that come in at this hour.

Manager: I understand now. What frustrated you the most was the fact that we didn't have enough staff to serve you promptly.

Customer: That's right. I have no complaint with the service I get once I'm waited on, and I've always thought you had a good selection here. It's just that I'm too busy to wait so long for help.

Manager: Well, I'm glad you brought this to my attention. We certainly don't want loyal customers going away mad. I'll try to see that it doesn't happen again.

This conversation illustrates two advantages of paraphrasing. First, the critic often reduces the intensity of the attack once he or she realizes that the complaint is being heard. Often criticism grows from the frustration of unmet needs—which in this case was partly a lack of attention. As soon as the manager genuinely demonstrated interest in the customer's plight, the customer began to feel better and was able to leave the store relatively calm. Of course this sort of active listening won't always mollify your critic, but even when it doesn't, there's still another benefit that makes the technique worthwhile. In the sample conversation, for instance, the manager learned some valuable information by taking time to understand the customer. The manager discovered that there were certain times when the number of employees was insufficient to help the crowd of shoppers and also that the delays at these times seriously annoyed at least some shoppers, thus threatening a loss in business. This knowledge is certainly important, and by reacting defensively to the customer's complaint, the manager would not have learned from it. As you read earlier, even apparently outlandish criticism often contains at least a grain of truth, and thus a person who is genuinely interested in improving would be wise to hear it out.

Ask what the critic wants Sometimes your critic's demand will be obvious.

"Turn down that music!"

"I wish you'd remember to tell me about phone messages."

"Would you clean up your dirty dishes *now!*"

In other cases, however, you'll need to do some investigating to find out what the critic wants from you:

Alex: I can't believe you invited all those people over without asking me first!

Barb: Are you saying you want me to cancel the party?

Alex: No, I just wish you'd ask me before you make plans.

Cynthia: You're so critical! It sounds like you don't like *anything* about this paper.

Donna: But you asked for my opinion. What do you expect me to do when you ask?

Cynthia: I want to know what's wrong, but I don't *just* want to hear criticisms. If you think there's anything good about my work, I wish you'd tell me that too.

This last example illustrates the importance of accompanying your questions with the right nonverbal behavior. It's easy to imagine two ways Donna could have responded to "What do you expect me to do when you ask?" One would show a genuine desire to clarify what Cynthia wanted, while the other would have been clearly hostile and defensive. As with all the styles in this section, your responses to criticism have to be sincere to work.

Ask about the consequences of your behavior As a rule, people complain about your actions only when some need of theirs is not being met. One way to respond to this kind of criticism is to find out exactly what troublesome consequences your behavior has for them. You'll often find that actions that seem perfectly legitimate to you cause some difficulty for your critic; once you have understood this, comments that previously sounded foolish take on a new meaning.

Neighbor A: You say that I ought to have my cat neutered. Why is that important to you?

Neighbor B: Because at night he picks fights with my cat, and I'm tired of paying the vet's bills.

Worker A: Why do you care whether I'm late to work?

Worker B: Because when the boss asks, I feel obligated to make up some story so you won't get in trouble, and I don't like to lie.

Husband: Why does it bother you when I lose money at poker? You know I never gamble more than I can afford.

Wife: It's not the cash itself. It's that when you lose, you're in a grumpy mood for two or three days, and that's no fun for me.

Ask what else is wrong It might seem crazy to invite more criticism, but sometimes asking about other complaints can uncover the real problem:

Raul: Are you mad at me?

Tina: No, why are you asking?

Raul: Because the whole time we were at the picnic you hardly spent any time talking to me. In fact, it seemed like whenever I came over to where you were, you went off somewhere else.

Tina: Is anything else wrong?

Raul: Well, I've been wondering lately if you're tired of me.

This example shows that asking if anything else bothers your critic isn't just an exercise in masochism. If you can keep your defensiveness in check, probing further can lead the conversation to issues that are the source of the critic's real dissatisfaction.

Sometimes soliciting more information from a critic isn't enough. What do you do, for instance, when you fully understand the other person's objections and still feel a defensive response on the tip of your tongue? You know that if you try to protect yourself, you'll wind up in an argument; on the other hand, you simply can't accept what the other person is saying about you. The solution to such a dilemma is outrageously simple and is discussed in the following section.

AGREE WITH THE CRITIC But, you protest, how can you honestly agree with comments you don't believe are true? The following pages will answer this question by showing that there's virtually no situation in which you can't honestly accept the other person's point of view and still maintain your position. To see how this can be so, you need to realize that there are two different types of agreement, one of which you can use in almost any situation.

Agree with the truth This is the easiest type of agreement to understand, though not always to practice. You agree with the truth when another person's criticism is factually correct:

"You're right, I am angry."

"I suppose I *was* being defensive."

"Now that you mention it, I did get pretty sarcastic."

Agreeing with the fact seems quite sensible when you realize that certain matters are indisputable. If you agree to be somewhere at 4:00 and don't show up until 5:00, you *are* late, no matter how good your explanation for tardiness. If you've broken a borrowed object, run out of gas, or failed to finish a job you started, there's no point in denying it. In the same way, if you're honest, you will have to agree with many interpretations of your behavior even when they're not flattering. You do get angry, act foolishly, fail to listen, and behave inconsiderately. Once you rid yourself of the myth of perfection, it's much easier to acknowledge these truths.

But if it's so obvious that the descriptions others give of your behaviors are often accurate, why is it so difficult to accept them without being defensive? The answer to this question lies in a confusion between agreeing with the *facts* and accepting the *judgment* that so often accompanies them. Most critics don't merely describe the action that offends them; they also evaluate it, and it's this evaluation that we resist:

"It's silly to be angry."

"You have no reason for being defensive."

"You were wrong to be so sarcastic."

It's judgments like these that we resent. By realizing that you can agree with—and even learn from—the descriptive part of many criticisms and still not accept the accompanying evaluations, you'll often have a response that is both honest and nondefensive.

Of course, in order to reduce defensiveness, your agreements with the facts must be honest ones admitted without malice. It's humiliating to accept descriptions that aren't accurate, and maliciously pretending to agree with these only leads to trouble. You can imagine how unproductive the conversation given earlier would have been if the manager had spoken the same words in a sarcastic tone. Only agree with the facts when you can do so sincerely. Though this won't always be possible, you'll be surprised at how often you can use this simple response.

Agree with the critic's perception   Research shows that the relational climate improves when communicators admit their flaws.[25] But how can you confess when there seems to be no basis whatsoever for agreeing with your critic? You've listened carefully and asked questions to make sure you understand the objections, but the more you listen, the more positive you are that the critic is totally out of line. Even in

Placing the blame is a bad habit, but taking the blame is a sure builder of character.

O. A. Battista

PEANUTS

these cases there's a way of agreeing—this time not with the critics' conclusions but with their right to see things their way.

A: I don't believe you've been all the places you were just describing. You're probably just making all this up to impress us.

B: Well, I can see how you might think that. I've known people who lie to get approval.

C: I want to let you know right from the start that I was against hiring you for the job. I think you got it because you're a woman.

D: I can understand why you'd believe that with all the antidiscrimination laws on the books. I hope that after I've been here for a while, you'll change your mind.

E: I don't think you're being totally honest about your reason for wanting to stay home. You say that it's because you have a headache, but I think you're avoiding Mary and Walt.

F: I can see why that would make sense to you because Mary and I got into an argument the last time we were together. All I can say is that I do have a headache.

Responses such as these tell critics that you're acknowledging the reasonableness of their perception even though you don't choose to accept it yourself or change your behavior. This coping style is a valuable one, for it lets you avoid the debate over who is right and who is wrong, which can turn an exchange of ideas into an argument.

SKILL BUILDER

COPING WITH CRITICISM

Take turns practicing nondefensive responses with a partner:

1. Choose one of the following criticisms and brief your partner on how it might be directed at you:
   a. You're so selfish sometimes. You only think of yourself.
   b. Don't be so touchy!
   c. You say you understand me, but you don't really.
   d. I wish you'd do your share around here.
   e. You're so critical!

2. As your partner criticizes you, answer with the appropriate response from the preceding pages. As you do so, try to adopt an attitude of genuinely wanting to understand the criticism and finding parts you can sincerely agree with.

3. Ask your partner to evaluate your response. Does it follow the forms described in the previous pages? Does it sound sincere?

4. Replay the same scene, trying to improve your response.

Communication Transcript

RESPONDING NONDEFENSIVELY TO CRITICISM

Defending yourself—even when you're right—isn't always the best approach. This dialogue shows the importance of self-control and thinking before responding when you are being criticized. The employee realizes that arguing won't change his boss's mind, and so he decides to reply as honestly as he can without becoming defensive.

Boss How'd things go while I was out?

Employee Pretty well, except for one thing. Mr. Macintosh—he said you knew him—came in and wanted to buy about $200 worth of stuff. He wanted me to charge him wholesale, and I asked him for his tax resale number, just like you told me. He said he didn't have it, and so I told him he'd have to pay retail. He got pretty mad.

Boss He's a good customer. I hope you gave him the discount.

Employee *(beginning to sound defensive)* Well, I didn't. You told me last week that the law said we *had* to charge full price and sales tax unless the customer had a resale number.

Boss Oh my gosh! Didn't Macintosh tell you he had a number?

Employee *(becoming more defensive)* He did, but he didn't have it with him. I didn't want to get you mad at me for breaking the law.

Boss *(barely concealing his exasperation)* Well, customers don't always have their resale numbers

memorized. Macintosh has been coming here for years, and we just fill in his number on the records later.

Employee *(deciding to respond nondefensively instead of getting into an argument he knows he can't win)* I can see why it looks like I gave Mr. Macintosh a hard time. You don't ask him for the number, and I insisted on having it. *(agrees with the boss's perception)*

Boss Yes! There's a lot of competition in this business, and we have to keep our customers happy—especially the good ones—or we'll lose them. Macintosh drives across town to do business with us. There are places right near him. If we jerk him around he'll go there, and we'll lose a good customer.

Employee That's true. *(agrees with the fact that it is important to keep customers happy)* And I want to know how to treat customers right. But I'm confused about how to handle people who want a discount and don't have resale numbers. What *should* I do? *(asks what the boss wants)*

Boss Well, you need to be a little flexible with good customers.

Employee How should I do that? *(asks for specifics)*

Boss Well, it's OK to trust people who are regulars.

Employee So I don't need to ask regular customers for their resale numbers. I should look them up later? *(paraphrases to clarify boss's*

ambiguous directions to "trust" regular customers)

Boss That's right. You've got to use your head in business!

Employee *(ignores the indirect accusation about not "using his head," recognizing that there's no point in defending himself)* OK, so when regular customers come in, I won't even ask them for their resale numbers . . . right? *(paraphrases again, to be sure he has the message correct. The employee has no desire to get criticized again about this matter)*

Boss No, go ahead and ask for the number. If they have it, we won't have to look it up later. But if they don't have the number, just say OK and give them the discount.

Employee Got it. I only have one question: How can I know who the regular customers are? Should I take their word for it? *(asks for specifics)*

Boss Well, you'll get to know most of them after you've been here a while. But it's OK to trust them until then. If they say they're regulars, just take their word for it. You've got to trust people *sometimes,* you know!

Employee *(ignores the fact that the boss originally told him not to trust people, but to insist on getting their number. Decides instead to agree with the boss)* I can see how important it is to trust good customers.

Boss Right.

Employee Thanks for clearing up how to handle the resale numbers.

(continued on next page)

Communication Transcript continued ✤

Is there anything else I ought to know so things will run smoothly when you're not in the store? *(asks if anything else is wrong)*

Boss   I don't think so. *(patronizingly)* Don't get discouraged; you'll catch on. It took me twenty years to build this busi-

ness. Stick with it and some day you could be running a place like this.

Employee   *(trying to agree with his boss without sounding sarcastic)* I guess I could.

The employee's refusal to act defensively turned what might have been a scolding into a dis-

cussion about how to handle a business challenge in the future. The employee might not like the boss's patronizing attitude and contradictory directions, but his communication skill kept the communication climate positive—probably the best possible outcome for this situation.

✤ SUMMARY

Every relationship has a communication climate. Positive climates are characterized by confirming messages, which make it clear that the parties value one another. Communication in negative climates is usually disconfirming. In one way or another, messages in disconfirming relationships convey indifference or hostility. Communication climates develop early in a relationship, both from verbal and nonverbal messages. Once created, reciprocal messages create either positive or negative spirals in which either the frequency and intensity of positive or negative messages is likely to grow.

Defensive spirals are among the most destructive types of communication. Most defensiveness occurs when people try to protect key parts of a presenting self-image that they believe is under attack. Defensive communicators respond by attacking their critic, distorting critical information, or avoiding critical messages. Using the supportive behaviors defined by Jack Gibb when expressing potentially threatening messages can reduce the likelihood of triggering defensive reactions in others.

When faced with criticism by others, it is possible to respond nondefensively by attempting to understand the criticism, and by either agreeing with the facts or with the critic's perception.

✛ KEY TERMS

ambiguous response
apathy
certainty
cognitive dissonance
communication climate
compensation
complaining
confirming communication
controlling communication
de-escalatory conflict spiral
defense mechanism
defensiveness
descriptive communication
disconfirming communication
displacement

empathy
equality
escalatory conflict spiral
evaluative communication
face-threatening act
Gibb categories
impersonal response
impervious response
incongruous response
interrupting response
irrelevant response
neutrality
physical avoidance

problem orientation
provisionalism
rationalization
regression
repression
sarcasm
spiral
spontaneity
strategy
superiority
tangential response
verbal abuse
verbal aggression

✛ MORE RESOURCES ON COMMUNICATION CLIMATE

READINGS

Beck, Charles E., and Elizabeth Beck. "The Manager's Open Door and the Communication Climate." *Business Horizons* 29 (January–February 1986): 15–19.

Some managers pay lip service to creating an open, positive communication climate but fail to act in ways that follow through on their claims. This article applies Gibb's categories of defensive and supportive communication to the workplace, showing what it takes to create a genuinely supportive environment.

Cupach, William R., and Sandra Metts. *Facework.* Newbury Park, Calif.: Sage, 1994.

The authors describe the importance of maintaining face, revealing how communicators manage their own face and that of others when dealing with everyday challenges including embarrassing situations and critical messages. Separate chapters describe facework in escalating, ongoing, and de-escalating relationships.

Knapp, Mark L., and Anita L. Vangelisti. *Interpersonal Communication and Human Relationships,* second edition. Boston: Allyn and Bacon, 1992.

Knapp and Vangelisti provide a thorough, readable survey of the rise and fall of interpersonal relationships. Part VI, "Toward More Effective Communication," is especially informative about what kinds of behavior are judged to be positive.

Lyons, Gracie. *Constructive Criticism: A Handbook.* Berkeley, Calif.: Wingbow Press, 1988.

Despite the author's obvious political biases, this brief, practical book offers specific suggestions to help communicators give and receive criticism in a supportive, nondefensive way. The guidelines reinforce many of the skills introduced in this chapter and elsewhere in Looking Out/Looking In: *using specific language, describing feelings, stating your wants clearly, paraphrasing, and empathizing.*

Vangelisti, Anita L. "Messages that Hurt." In *The Dark Side of Interpersonal Communication,* William R. Cupach and Brian H. Spitzberg, eds. Hillsdale, N.J.: Erlbaum, 1994.

Vangelisti reports on research about hurtful messages. This chapter describes the types of messages that experimental subjects report as hurtful, as well as outlines the personal and relational factors that make some messages more painful than others. The material is a useful supplement to the information on communication climate in this chapter of Looking Out/Looking In.

Wells, Theodora. *Keeping Your Cool Under Fire: Communicating Non-Defensively.* New York: McGraw-Hill, 1980.

This is a lengthy but readable treatment of defensiveness. In addition to amplifying the material in this chapter, Wells discusses defensiveness in organizations and relates the subject to some of the principles of emotions you read about in Chapter Four of this book.

FILMS

POSITIVE AND NEGATIVE SPIRALS
Tin Men (1987) Rated R, and *When Harry Met Sally* (1989) Rated R

"Tin men" are con artists who sell aluminum siding when they are not hanging around a diner or nightclub bragging about the customers they have defrauded. This story revolves around two tin men, BB (Richard Dreyfus) and Tilley (Danny DeVito), whose cars collide just as BB is driving his brand-new Caddy out of the showroom. The incident sets off an escalating feud between the men. This film provides a 109-minute example of an escalatory spiral. The feud between BB and Tilley quicky moves beyond a crumpled fender into a matter of honor. The real issue at stake is saving face, and the extremes to which the combatants go are amusing for viewers who have never experienced the same sort of struggle. But for those who have seen their own lives distorted and damaged by defensive spirals, the laughs will be mingled with regret.

When Harry Met Sally also illustrates a defensive spiral, but this film shows that destructive communication patterns can be reversed. Harry (Billy Crystal) and Sally (Meg Ryan) meet just after graduating from college as they share a cross-country car ride to New York. She sizes him up as an oversexed boor, and he views her as an uptight prig. The negative spiral begins immediately: One aggressive comment leads to another, and by the time the trip is over they are glad to be rid of one another.

Harry and Sally continue running into one another in the following years. The climate between them continues to be stormy, until they drop their guards and begin talking about the pain of failed romances. A friendship develops as the tone of their communication changes: Neutrality is replaced by empathy, strategy by spontaneity, and superiority by equality. By the time the film ends, Harry and Sally have developed a relationship that would have been hard to predict from their first chilly encounter.

RELATIONAL CLIMATES
The Waterdance (1992) Rated R

Joel Garcia (Eric Stoltz) is a novelist who has just become a paraplegic. He is recovering in a ward with similarly injured people, ranging from angry motorcyclist Bloss (William Forsythe) to upbeat but troubled Raymond (Wesley Snipes). The biggest concern for most of the patients is whether they will be valued by their friends, family, lovers, and society. Raymond's worst fears come to pass—his wife divorces him. Joel is worried that his girlfriend, Anna (Helen Hunt), will leave him as well. Bloss is surrounded by his mother and biker friends, but he too feels devalued in a society that prizes mobility.

The climate that develops among the three main characters centers around Bloss's interactions with Raymond and Joel. Due to his prejudices, Bloss initially looks down on Raymond and treats him with contempt. Joel, on the other hand, comes across as educated, aloof, and all too composed—which also aggravates Bloss. At the beginning of the story, the climate between the patients is chilly. It changes when Bloss begins to recognize that he is neither superior to Raymond nor inferior to Joel. He empathizes with Raymond during times of pain and challenges Joel when he thinks Joel is avoiding reality. The three link arms in support of each other, fighting against a system in which they all feel disconfirmed. The movie is explicit and at times painful, but so is the topic it explores.

In another place and time, Bloss, Raymond, and Joel might have had little to do with one another. Their shared circumstances put them on equal ground, forcing them to confront their prejudices and leading them to create a confirming communication climate.

CHAPTER 10

Managing Interpersonal Conflicts

or most people, conflict has about the same appeal as a trip to the dentist. A quick look at the thesaurus offers a clue about the distasteful nature of conflict. Synonyms for the term include *battle, brawl, clash, competition, discord, disharmony, duel, fight, strife, struggle, trouble,* and *violence.* Even the metaphors we use to describe our conflicts show that we view conflict as something to be avoided.[1] We often talk about conflict as a kind of war: "He shot down my arguments." "Okay, fire away." "Don't try to defend yourself!" Another metaphor suggests conflict is explosive: "Don't blow up!" "I needed to let off steam." "You've got a short fuse." Sometimes conflict seems like a kind of trial, in which one party accuses another: "Come on, admit you're guilty." "Stop accusing me!" "Just listen to my case." Language that suggests conflict is a mess is also common: "Let's not open this can of worms." "That's a sticky situation." "Don't make such a stink!" Even the metaphor of a game implies that one side has to defeat the other: "That was out of bounds." "You're not playing fair." "I give up; you win!"

Despite images like these, the truth is that conflicts *can* be constructive. With the right set of communication skills, conflict can be less like a struggle and more like a kind of dance in which partners work together to create something that would be impossible without their cooperation. You may have to persuade the other person to become your partner, and you may be clumsy at first; but with enough practice and goodwill, you can work together instead of at cross-purposes.

The attitude you bring to your conflicts can make a tremendous difference between success and failure. One study revealed that college students in close romantic relationships who believed that conflicts are destructive were most likely to neglect or quit the relationship and less likely to seek a solution than couples who had less negative attitudes.[2] Of course, attitudes alone won't always guarantee satisfying solutions to conflicts. The kinds of skills you will learn in this chapter can help well-intentioned partners handle their disagreements constructively. But without the right attitude, all the skills in the world will be little help.

There are no magic tricks to resolve all the conflicts in your life. On the other hand, there are ways to manage these conflicts constructively. If you follow these methods you may find that your relationships are actually stronger and more satisfying than before.

❖ THE NATURE OF CONFLICT

Before focusing on how to solve interpersonal problems constructively, we need to take a brief look at the nature of conflict. What is it? Why is it an inevitable part of life? How can it be beneficial?

CONFLICT DEFINED

Before reading farther, make a list of the interpersonal conflicts in your life. They probably involve many different people, revolve around very different subjects, and take many different forms. Some become loud, angry arguments. Others may be expressed in calm, rational discussions. Still others might simmer along most of the time with brief but bitter flareups.

Whatever form they may take, all interpersonal conflicts share certain characteristics. Joyce Hocker and William Wilmot provide a thorough definition when they define **conflict** as *an expressed struggle between at least two interdependent parties who perceive incompatible goals, scarce rewards, and interference from the other party in achieving their goals.*[3] A closer look at the key parts of this definition will help you recognize how conflict operates in your life.

EXPRESSED STRUGGLE   A conflict can exist only when both parties are aware of a disagreement. For instance, you may be upset for months because a neighbor's loud stereo keeps you awake at night, but no conflict exists between the two of you until the neighbor learns of your problem. Of course, the expressed struggle doesn't have to be verbal. You can show your displeasure with somebody without saying a word. A dirty look, the silent treatment, or avoiding the other person are all ways of expressing yourself. One way or another, both parties must know that a problem exists before they're in conflict.

PERCEIVED INCOMPATIBLE GOALS   All conflicts look as if one party's gain would be another's loss. For instance, consider the neighbor whose stereo keeps you awake at night. Doesn't somebody have to lose? If the neighbor turns down the noise, she loses the enjoyment of hearing the music at full volume; but if the neighbor keeps the volume up, you're still awake and unhappy.

The goals in this situation really aren't completely incompatible—there are solutions that allow both parties to get what they want. For instance, you could achieve peace and quiet by closing your windows or getting the neighbor to close hers. You might use a pair of earplugs, or perhaps the neighbor could get a set of earphones, allowing the music to be played at full volume without bothering anyone. If any of these solutions prove workable, the conflict disappears.

Unfortunately, people often fail to see mutually satisfying answers to their problems. As long as they *perceive* their goals to be mutually exclusive, a conflict exists.

PERCEIVED SCARCE REWARDS   Conflicts also exist when people believe there isn't enough of something to go around. The most obvious example of a scarce resource is money—a cause of many conflicts. If a worker asks for a raise in pay and the boss would rather keep the money or use it to expand the business, the two parties are in conflict.

*We struggled together,
knowing. We prattled, pre-
tended, fought bitterly,
laughed, wept over sad books
or old movies, nagged, supported, gave, took, demanded, forgave, resented—hating
the ugliness of each other, yet
cherishing that which we
were. . . . Will I ever find
someone to battle with as we
battled, love as we loved,
share with as we shared,
challenge as we challenged,
forgive as we forgave? You
used to say that I saved up
all of my feelings so that I
could spew forth when I got
home. The anger I experi-
enced in school I could not
vent there. How many times
have I heard you chuckle as
you remembered the day I
would come home from
school and share with you all
of the feelings I had kept in.
"If anyone had been listening
they would have thought you
were punishing me, striking
out at me. I always survived
and you always knew that I
would still be with you when
you were through." There
was an honesty about our
relationship that may never
exist again.*

Vian Catrell

Time is another scarce commodity. As authors and family men, both of us constantly face struggles about how to use the limited time we have at home. Should we work on this book? Visit with our wives? Play with our children? Enjoy the luxury of being alone? With only twenty-four hours in a day, we're bound to wind up in conflicts with our families, editors, students, and friends—all of whom want more of our time than we have to give.

INTERDEPENDENCE However antagonistic they might feel, the parties in conflict are usually dependent on each other. The welfare and satisfaction of one depends on the actions of another. If not, then even in the face of scarce resources and incompatible goals there would be no need for conflict. Interdependence exists between conflicting nations, social groups, organizations, friends, and lovers. In each case, if the two parties didn't need each other to solve the problem, they would go their separate ways. In fact, many conflicts go unresolved because the parties fail to understand their interdependence. One of the first steps toward resolving a conflict is to take the attitude that "we're all in this together."

INTERFERENCE FROM THE OTHER PARTY No matter how much one person's position may differ from another's, a full-fledged conflict won't occur until the participants act in ways that prevent one another from reaching their goals. For example, you might let some friends know that you object to their driving after drinking too much alcohol, but the conflict will escalate if you act in ways that prevent them from getting behind the wheel. Likewise, a parent–child dispute about what clothing and music are appropriate will blossom into a conflict when the parents try to impose their position on the youngster.

CONFLICT IS NATURAL

Every relationship of any depth at all has conflict.[4] No matter how close, how understanding, how compatible you are, there will be times when your ideas or actions or needs or goals won't match those of others around you. You like rock music, but your companion prefers Beethoven; you want to date other people, but your partner wants to keep the relationship exclusive; you think a paper you've done is fine, but your instructor wants it changed; you like to sleep late on Sunday mornings, but your housemate likes to play the stereo—loudly! There's no end to the number and kinds of disagreements possible. College students who have kept diaries of their relationships report that they take part in about seven arguments per week. Most have argued with the other person before, often about the same topic.[5] When you consider that not all conflicts result in open arguments, this figure suggests that conflict is a fact of life for everyone.

And just as conflict is a fact of life, so are the feelings that go along with it—hurt, anger, frustration, resentment, disappointment. Because these feelings are usually unpleasant, there is a temptation to avoid them or pretend they don't exist. But as sure as conflicts are bound to arise, so are the emotions that go with them.

At first this might seem depressing. If problems are inevitable in even the best relationships, does this mean that you're doomed to relive the same arguments, the same hurt feelings, over and over? Fortunately, the answer to this question is a definite "no." Even though conflict is a part of a meaningful relationship, you can change the way you deal with it.

CONFLICT CAN BE BENEFICIAL

Since it is impossible to *avoid* conflicts, the challenge is to handle them well when they do arise. Effective communication during conflicts can actually keep good relationships strong. People who use the constructive skills described in this chapter are more satisfied with their relationships[6] and with the outcomes of their conflicts.[7]

Perhaps the best evidence of how constructive conflict skills can benefit a relationship focuses on communication between husbands and wives. Over twenty years of research shows that both happy and unhappy marriages have conflicts, but that they manage conflict in very different ways.[8] One nine-year study revealed that unhappy couples argued in ways that we have cataloged in this book as destructive.[9] They were more concerned with defending themselves than

Not everything that is faced can be changed, but nothing can be changed until it is faced.

James Baldwin

Are there genuinely nice, sweet people in this world? Yes, absolutely yes, and they get angry as often as you and I. They must— otherwise they would be full of vindictive feelings and slush, which would prevent genuine sweetness.

Theodore Isaac Rubin

with being problem-oriented; they failed to listen carefully to one another, had little or no empathy for their partners, used evaluative "you" language, and ignored one another's nonverbal relational messages.

Many satisfied couples think and communicate differently when they disagree. They view disagreements as healthy and recognize that conflicts need to be faced.[10] Although they may argue vigorously, they use skills like perception checking to find out what the other person is thinking, and they let one another know that they understand the other side of the dispute.[11] They are willing to admit their mistakes, both contributing to a harmonious relationship and helping to solve the problem at hand.

In the following pages, we will review communication skills that can make conflicts constructive, and we will introduce still more methods you can use to resolve the inevitable conflicts you face. Before doing so, however, we need to examine how individuals behave when faced with a dispute.

✚ PERSONAL CONFLICT STYLES

There are five ways in which people can act when their needs aren't met (see Table 10–1). Each approach has very different characteristics, as we can show by describing a common problem. At one time or another almost everyone has been bothered by a neighbor's barking dog. You know the story: Every passing car, distant siren, pedestrian, and falling leaf seem to set off a fit of barking that makes you unable to sleep, socialize, or study. In a description of the possible ways of handling this kind of situation, the differences between nonassertive, directly aggressive, passive aggressive, indirect, and assertive behavior should become clear.

NONASSERTIVE BEHAVIOR

Nonassertion is the inability or unwillingness to express thoughts or feelings in a conflict. Sometimes nonassertion comes from a lack of confidence. In other cases, people lack the awareness or skill to use a more direct means of expression. Sometimes people know how to communicate in a straightforward way but choose to behave nonassertively.

Nonassertion is a surprisingly common way of dealing with conflicts. One study revealed that dating partners do not express roughly 40 percent of their relational grievances to one another.[12] Another survey examined the conflict level of husbands and wives in "nondistressed" marriages. Over a five-day period, spouses reported that their partner engaged in an average of thirteen behaviors that were "displeasurable" to them, but that they had only *one* confrontation during the same period.[13]

Nonassertion can take a variety of forms. One is **avoidance**— either physical (steering clear of a friend after having an argument), or conversational (changing the topic, joking, or denying that a problem exists). People who avoid conflicts usually believe it's easier to put up with the status quo than to face the problem head-on and try to solve it. **Accommodation** is another type of nonassertive response. Accommodators deal with conflict by giving in, putting the other's needs ahead of their own.

Faced with the annoyance of a barking dog next door, a nonassertive person might try to ignore the noise by closing the windows and turning up the radio. Other nonassertive responses would be to deny that the problem even exists, or to hope that it would go away. None of these alternatives sounds very appealing. They probably would lead the nonassertive communicator to grow more and more angry at the neighbor, making a friendly relationship difficult. Nonassertion also can lead to a loss of self-respect: It's hard to respect yourself when you can't even cope with an everyday irritation.[17]

Nonassertion isn't always a bad idea. You might choose to keep quiet or give in if the risk of speaking up is too great: getting fired from a job you can't afford to lose, being humiliated in public, or even risking physical harm. You might also avoid a conflict if the relationship it involves isn't worth the effort. Even in close relationships, though, nonassertion has its logic. If the issue is temporary or minor,

T A B L E 1 0 – 1 Individual Styles of Conflict

	NONASSERTIVE	DIRECTLY AGGRESSIVE	PASSIVE AGGRESSIVE	INDIRECT	ASSERTIVE
APPROACH TO OTHERS	I'm not OK, you're OK.	I'm OK, you're not OK.	I'm OK, you're not OK. (But I'll let you think you are.)	I'm OK, you're not OK or I'm not OK, you're OK.	I'm OK, you're OK.
DECISION MAKING	Lets others choose.	Chooses for others. They know it.	Chooses for others. They don't know it.	Chooses for others. They don't know it.	Chooses for self
SELF-SUFFICIENCY	Low	High or low	Looks high, but usually low	High or low	Usually high
BEHAVIOR IN PROBLEM SITUATIONS	Flees; gives in	Outright attack	Concealed attack	Strategic, oblique	Direct confrontation
RESPONSE OF OTHERS	Disrespect, guilt, anger, or frustration	Hurt, defensiveness, humiliation	Confusion, frustration, feelings of manipulation	Unknowing compliance or resistance	Mutual respect
SUCCESS PATTERN	Succeeds by luck or charity of others	Feels compelled to beat out others	Wins by manipulation	Gains unwitting compliance of others	Attempts "win–win" solutions

Adapted with permission from Stanlee Phelps and Nancy Austin, *The Assertive Woman.* San Luis Obispo, CA: Impact, 1975, p. 11: and Gerald Piaget, American Orthopsychiatric Association, 1975. Further reproduction prohibited.

© 1963 Reprinted by permission of UFS, Inc.

you might let it pass. It might even make sense to keep your thoughts to yourself and give in if the issue is more important to the other person than it is to you. These reasons help explain why the communication of many happily married couples is characterized by "selectively ignoring" the other person's minor flaws.[15] This doesn't mean that a key to successful relationships is avoiding *all* conflicts. Instead, it suggests that it's smart to save energy for the truly important ones.

Like avoidance, accommodation can also be appropriate, especially in cases in which the other person's needs may be more important than yours. For instance, if a friend wants to have a serious talk and you feel playful, you'd most likely honor her request, particularly if that person is facing some kind of crisis and wants your help. In most cases, however, nonassertive accommodators fail to assert themselves either because they don't value themselves sufficiently, or because they don't know how to ask for what they want.

DIRECT AGGRESSION

In contrast to nonassertion, **direct aggression** occurs when a communicator expresses a criticism or demand that threatens the face of the person at whom it is directed. Communication researcher Dominic Infante identified several types of direct aggression: character attacks, competence attacks, physical appearance attacks, maledictions (wishing the other ill fortune), teasing, ridicule, threats, swearing, and nonverbal emblems.[16]

Direct aggression can have a severe impact on the target. Recipients can feel embarrassed, inadequate, humiliated, hopeless, desperate, or depressed. There is a significant connection between verbal aggression and physical aggression,[17] but even if the attacks never lead to blows, the psychological effects can be devastating. Aggressive behavior can punish the attacker as well as the victim. Medical researchers have found that newly married couples whose disagreements were marked by sarcasm, interruptions, and criticism suffered a drop in the effectiveness of their immune systems.[18]

Verbal aggression can affect the relationship as well as the individuals involved. One aggressive remark can lead to an equally combative reaction, starting a destructive spiral that can expand beyond the original dispute and damage the entire relationship. This fact explains why verbally abusive couples report significantly less relational satisfaction than do partners who communicate about their conflicts in other ways.[19] Even among well-adjusted couples, negative communication is more likely to be reciprocated than positive—and once hostility is expressed, it usually escalates.[20]

You could handle the dog problem with direct aggression by abusively confronting your neighbors, calling them names and threatening to call the dogcatcher the next time you see their hound running loose. If the town in which you live has a leash law, you would be within your legal rights to do so and thus you would gain your goal of bringing peace and quiet to the neighborhood. Unfortunately, your direct aggression would have other, less productive consequences. Your neighbors and you would probably cease to be on speaking terms, and you could expect a complaint from them the first time you violated even the most inconsequential of city ordinances. If you live in the neighborhood for any time at all, this state of hostilities isn't very appealing. This example shows why research confirms what common sense suggests: Unlike other conflict styles, direct aggression is judged incompetent by virtually everyone who encounters it.[21]

PASSIVE AGGRESSION

Passive aggression occurs when a communicator expresses hostility in an obscure way. In several of his works, psychologist George Bach terms this behavior "crazymaking."[22] **Crazymaking** occurs when people have feelings of resentment, anger, or rage that they are unable or unwilling to express directly. Instead of keeping these feelings to themselves, the crazymakers send these aggressive messages in subtle, indirect ways, thus maintaining the front of kindness. This amiable façade eventually crumbles, however, leaving the crazymaker's victim confused and angry at having been fooled. The targets of the crazymaker can either react with aggressive behavior of their own or retreat to nurse their hurt feelings. In either case passive aggression seldom has anything but harmful effects on a relationship.

You could respond to your neighbors and their dog in several crazymaking, passive-aggressive ways. One strategy would be to complain anonymously to the city pound and then, after the dog has been hauled away, express your sympathy. Or you could complain to everyone else in the neighborhood, hoping that their hostility would force the offending neighbors to quiet the dog or face being social outcasts.

There are a number of shortcomings to this sort of approach, each of which illustrates the risks of passive aggression. First, there is the chance that the crazymaking won't work: The neighbors might simply miss the point of your veiled attacks and continue to ignore the barking. On the other hand, they might get your message clearly, but either because of your lack of sincerity or out of sheer stubbornness, they might simply refuse to do anything about it. In either case, it's likely that in this and other instances passive aggression won't satisfy your unmet need.

Crazymakers: Passive-Aggressive Communication

George Bach, a leading authority on conflict and communication, explains that there are two types of aggression—clean fighting and dirty fighting. Either because they can't or won't express their feelings openly and constructively, dirty fighters sometimes resort to "crazymaking" techniques to vent their resentments. Instead of openly and caringly expressing their emotions, crazymakers (often unconsciously) use a variety of indirect tricks to get at their opponent. Because these "sneak attacks" don't usually get to the root of the problem and because of their power to create a great deal of hurt, crazymakers can damage relationships.

The Avoider

Avoiders refuse to fight. When a conflict arises, they leave, fall asleep, pretend to be busy at work, or keep from facing the problem in some other way. This behavior makes it very difficult for their partners to express feelings of anger, hurt, and so on, because the avoiders won't fight back. Arguing with an avoider is like trying to box with a person who won't even show up for a match.

The Pseudoaccommodator

Pseudoaccommodators refuse to face up to a conflict either by giving in or by pretending that there's nothing at all wrong. This drives their partner, who definitely feels there's a problem, crazy and causes feelings of guilt and resentment toward the accommodator.

The Guiltmaker

Instead of saying straight out that they don't want or approve of something, the guiltmakers try to make their partners feel responsible for causing pain. A guiltmaker's favorite line is "It's OK; don't worry about me . . . " accompanied by a big sigh.

The Subject Changer

Really a type of avoider, subject changers escape facing up to aggression by shifting the conversation whenever it approaches an area of conflict. Because of their tactics, subject changers and their partners never have the chance to explore their problem and do something about it.

The Distracter

Rather than come out and express their feelings about the object of their dissatisfaction, distracters attack other parts of their partner's life. Thus, they never have to share what's really on their minds and can avoid dealing with painful parts of their relationships.

The Mind Reader

Instead of allowing their partners to express feelings honestly, mind readers go into character analysis, explaining what the other person really means or what's wrong with the other person. By behaving this way mind readers refuse to handle their own feelings and leave no room for their partners to express themselves.

The Trapper

Trappers play an especially dirty trick by setting up a desired behavior for their partners and then when it's met, attacking the very thing they requested. An example of this technique is for the trapper to say, "Let's be totally honest with each other," and then attack the partner's self-disclosure.

The Crisis Tickler

Crisis ticklers almost bring what's bothering them to the surface, but never quite come out and express themselves. Instead of admitting concern about the finances, they innocently ask, "Gee, how much did that cost?" dropping a rather obvious hint but never really dealing with the crisis.

The Gunnysacker

These people don't respond immediately when angry. Instead, they put their resentment into a gunnysack, which after a while begins to bulge with both large and small gripes. Then, when the sack is about to burst, the gunnysacker pours out all the pent-up aggressions on the overwhelmed and unsuspecting victim.

The Trivial Tyrannizer

Instead of honestly sharing their resentments, trivial tyrannizers do things they know will get their part-ners' goat—leaving dirty dishes in the sink, clipping fingernails in bed, belching out loud, turning up the television too loud, and so on.

The Beltliner

Everyone has a psychological "beltline," and below it are subjects too sensitive to be approached without damaging the relationship. Beltlines may have to do with physical characteristics, intelligence, past behavior, or deeply ingrained personality traits a person is trying to overcome. In an attempt to "get even" or hurt their partners, beltliners will use intimate knowledge to hit below the belt, where they know it will hurt.

The Joker

Because they are afraid to face conflicts squarely, the jokers kid around when their partners want to be serious, thus blocking the expression of important feelings.

The Blamer

Blamers are more interested in finding fault than in solving a conflict. Needless to say, they usually don't blame themselves. Blaming behavior almost never solves a conflict and is an almost sure-fire way to make receivers defensive.

The Contract Tyrannizer

Contract tyrannizers will not allow their relationships to change from the way they once were. Whatever the agreements the partners had for roles and responsibilities at one time, they'll remain unchanged. "It's your job to . . . feed the baby, wash the dishes, discipline the kids. . . . "

The Kitchen Sink Fighter

These people are so named because in an argument they bring up things that are totally off the subject ("everything but the kitchen sink"): the way another person behaved last New Year's Eve, the unbalanced checkbook, bad breath—anything.

The Withholder

Instead of expressing their anger honestly and directly, the withholders punish their partners by keeping back something—courtesy, affection, good cooking, humor, sex. As you can imagine, this is likely to build up even greater resentments in the relationship.

The Benedict Arnold

These characters get back at their partners by sabotage, by failing to defend them from attackers, and even by encouraging ridicule or disregard from outside the relationship.

I was angry with my friend.
I told my wrath, my wrath did end.
I was angry with my foe:
I told it not, my wrath did grow.
And I watered it in fears,
Night and morning with my tears;
And I sunned it with smiles,
And with soft deceitful wiles.
And it grew both day and night,
Till it bore an apple bright;
And my foe beheld it shine,
And he knew that it was mine,
And into my garden stole
When the night had veiled the pole:
In the morning glad I see
My foe outstretched beneath the tree.

William Blake

Even when passive aggression proves successful in the short run, a second shortcoming lies in its consequences over the longer range. You might manage to intimidate your neighbors into shutting up their mutt, for instance, but in winning the battle you could lose what would become a war. As a means of revenge, they could wage their own campaign of crazymaking by such tactics as badmouthing your sloppy gardening to other neighbors or phoning in false complaints about your loud parties. It's obvious that feuds such as this one are counterproductive and outweigh the apparent advantages of passive aggression.

INDIRECT COMMUNICATION

The clearest communication is not necessarily the best approach. **Indirect communication** conveys a message in a roundabout manner, in order to save face for the recipient. Although indirect communication lacks the clarity of an aggressive or assertive message, it involves more initiative than nonassertion. It also has none of the hostility of passive-aggressive crazymaking. The goal is to get what you want without arousing the hostility of the other person. Consider the case of the annoying dog. One indirect approach would be to strike up a friendly conversation with the owners and ask if anything you are doing is too noisy for them, hoping they would get the hint.

Because it saves face for the other party, indirect communication is often kinder than blunt honesty. If your guests are staying too long, it's probably kinder to yawn and hint about your big day tomorrow than to bluntly ask them to leave. Likewise, if you're not interested in going out with someone who has asked you for a date, it may be more compassionate to claim that you're busy than to say "I'm not interested in seeing you."

At other times we communicate indirectly in order to protect ourselves. You might, for example, test the waters by hinting instead of directly asking the boss for a raise, or by letting your partner know indirectly that you could use some affection instead of asking outright. At times like these, an oblique approach may get the message across while softening the blow of a negative response.

The advantages of self-protection and saving face for others help explain why indirect communication is the most common way people make requests.[23] The risk of an indirect message, of course, is that the other party will misunderstand you or fail to get the message at all. There are also times when the importance of an idea is so great that hinting lacks the necessary punch. When clarity and directness are your goals, an assertive approach is in order.

ASSERTION

Assertion occurs when a message expresses the speaker's needs, thoughts, and feelings clearly and directly without judging or dictating to others. Most assertive messages follow the format described later in this chapter on pages 413–420.

An assertive course of action in the case of the barking dog would be to wait a few days to make sure the noise is not just a fluke. If the barking

...ER...UH... i DON'T SUPPOSE YOU'D LiKE TO ENROLL iN AN ASSERTiVENESS TRAiNiNG CLASS ...WOULD YOU ?

continues, you could introduce yourself to your neighbors and explain your problem. You could tell them that although they might not notice it, the dog often plays in the street and keeps barking at passing cars. You could tell them why this behavior bothers you. It keeps you awake at night and makes it hard for you to do your work. You could point out that you don't want to be a grouch and call the pound. Rather than behaving in these ways, you could tell them that you've come to see what kind of solution you can find that will satisfy both of you. This approach may not work, and you might then have to decide whether it is more important to avoid bad feelings or to have peace and quiet. But the chances for a happy ending are best with this assertive approach. And no matter what happens, you can keep your self-respect by behaving directly and honestly.

 INVITATION TO INSIGHT

YOUR CONFLICT STYLE

1. Think back over your recent history and recall five conflicts you've had. The more current they are, the better, and they should be ones that occurred with people who are important to you, people with whom your relationship matters.

2. Turn an 8½-by-11 sheet of paper horizontally and copy the following chart. To give yourself plenty of room you might extend your chart onto a second page.

I	II	III
The Conflict	**How I Managed It**	**The Results**
(Describe whom it was with, what it was about.)	(What did you say? How did you act?)	(How did you feel? How did the others involved feel? Are you happy with the results?)

3. For each of the conflicts, fill in the appropriate spaces on your chart.

4. Based on what you've written here, answer the following questions:
   a. Are you happy with the way you've handled your conflicts? Do you come away from them feeling better or worse than before?
   b. Have your conflicts made your relationships stronger or weaker?
   c. Do you recognize any patterns in your conflict style? For example, do you hold your angry feelings inside? Are you sarcastic? Do you lose your temper easily?
   d. If you could, would you like to change the way you deal with your conflicts?

WHICH STYLE IS BEST?

After reading this far, you might think that assertive communication is clearly superior to other styles. It allows you to express yourself honestly and seems to have the greatest chance of success. Actually, it's an oversimplification to say that any communication style is always best. A competent, successful communicator will choose the most effective style for a given situation.

How can you decide which style will be most effective? There are several factors to consider.

1. *The Situation.* When someone else clearly has more power than you, nonassertion may be the best approach. If the boss tells you to fill that order *"now!"* it may be smart to do it without comment. The more assertive response ("When you use that tone of voice, I feel defensive . . . ") might be more clear, but it also could cost you your job. Likewise, there are some situations when an aggressive message is most appropriate. Even the most mild-mannered parents will testify that sooner or later yelling seems to be the only way to get a child to respond: "I've told you three times not to bother the cat. Now *stop it,* or you'll be sorry!"

2. *The Receiver.* Although assertiveness has the best chance of success with most people, some receivers respond better to other approaches. One businessman illustrated this point when he described how his normally even-tempered boss used shouting in a phone conversation with a particularly difficult person:

> I've never heard him so angry. He was enraged. His face was red, and the veins were bulging on his neck. I tried to get his attention to calm him down, but he waved me away impatiently. As soon as the call was over, he turned to me and smiled. "There," he said. "That ought to do it." If I were the guy he'd been shouting at, let me tell you, that would have done it, too. But it was all a put on.[24]

3. *Your Goals.* When you want to solve a problem, assertiveness may seem like the best approach, but there are other reasons for communicating in a conflict. The other person might not like you as much when you assert your rights as when you keep quiet, so if the goal is to maintain harmony, nonassertion may be the best course.[25] The problem might not be worth the potential conflict. In other cases, your overriding concern may be to calm down an enraged or upset person. Tolerating an outburst from your crotchety and sick neighbor, for example, is probably better than standing up for yourself and triggering a stroke. Likewise, you might choose to sit quietly through the nagging of a family member rather than ruin Thanksgiving dinner. In still other cases, your moral principles might compel an aggressive statement even though it might not get you what you originally sought: "I've had enough of your racist jokes. I've tried to explain why they're so offensive, but you obviously haven't listened. I'm leaving!"

✦ ASSERTION WITHOUT AGGRESSION: THE CLEAR MESSAGE FORMAT

Knowing *when* to behave assertively isn't the same as knowing *how* to assert yourself. The next few pages will describe a method for communicating assertively. It works for a variety of messages: your hopes, problems, complaints, and appreciations.[26] Besides giving you a way to express yourself directly, this clear message format also makes it easy for others to understand you. Finally, since assertive messages are phrased in the kind of descriptive "I" language you learned in Chapter Five, they are less likely than aggressive attacks to cause a defensive reaction that will start a needless fight or shut down discussion altogether.

A complete assertive message has five parts. We'll examine each of these parts one by one and then discuss how to combine them in your everyday communication.

BEHAVIOR   A **behavioral description** describes the raw material to which you react. A behavioral description should be *objective,* describing an event without interpreting it.

Two examples of behavioral descriptions might look like this.

Example 1
"One week ago John promised me that he would ask my permission before smoking in the same room with me. Just a moment ago he lit up a cigarette without asking for my OK."

Example 2
"Chris has acted differently over the last week. I can't remember her laughing once since the holiday weekend. She hasn't dropped by my place like she usually does, hasn't suggested we play tennis, and hasn't returned my phone calls."

Notice that in both cases the descriptive statements record only data that are available through the senses. The observer has not attached any meaning. The value of describing the problem without using emotive language was demonstrated by a study examining conflicts between couples. The study revealed that satisfied partners tend to offer behavioral complaints ("You always throw your socks on the floor"), while unsatisfied couples make more complaints aimed at personal characteristics ("You're a slob").[27] Other research confirmed the fact that personal complaints are more likely to result in an escalated conflict episode.[28] The reason should be obvious—complaints about personal characteristics attack a more fundamental part of the presenting self. Talking about socks deals with a habit that can be changed; calling someone a slob is a character assault that is unlikely to be forgotten when the conflict is over.

INTERPRETATION   *Interpretation* is the process of attaching meaning to behavior. The important thing to realize about interpretations is that they are *subjective.* That is, there is more than one interpretation that we can attach to any behavior. For example, look at these two different interpretations of each of the preceding descriptions:

Example 1
Interpretation A "John must have forgotten about our agreement that he wouldn't smoke without asking me first. I'm sure he's too considerate to go back on his word on something he knows I feel strongly about."

Interpretation B "John is a rude, inconsiderate person. After promising not to smoke around me without asking, he's just deliberately done so. This shows that he only cares about himself. In fact, I bet he's deliberately doing this to drive me crazy!"

Example 2
Interpretation A "Something must be bothering Chris. It's probably her family. She'll probably just feel worse if I keep pestering her."

Interpretation B "Chris is probably mad at me. It's probably because I kidded her about losing so often at tennis. I'd better leave her alone until she cools off."

These examples show that interpretations are based on more than simple sense data. They grow out of many factors, including

- *Your past experience* "John has always (never) kept his promises in the past" or "When I'm preoccupied with personal problems I draw away from my friends."
- *Your assumptions* "An unkept promise is a sign of uncaring (forgetfulness)" or "Lack of communication with friends is a sign that something is wrong."
- *Your expectations* "John probably wants (doesn't want) to fight" or "I thought the family visit (or kidding about tennis) would upset her."
- *Your knowledge* "Long-time, habitual cigarette smokers aren't even aware of lighting up" or "I know Chris's dad has been sick lately."
- *Your current mood* "I feel good about John and about life in general" or "I've been awfully sarcastic lately. I went too far when I kidded Chris about her tennis game."

Once you become aware of the difference between observable behavior and interpretation, some of the reasons for communication breakdowns become clear. Many problems occur when a sender fails to describe the behavior on which an interpretation is based. For instance, imagine the difference between hearing a friend say

"You are a tightwad!" *(no behavioral description)*

and explaining

"When you never offer to pay me back for the coffee and snacks I often buy you, I think you're a tightwad." *(behavior plus interpretation)*

The first speaker's failure to specify behavior would probably confuse the receiver, who has no way of knowing what prompted the sender's remarks. This failure to describe behavior also reduces any chance that the receiver will change the offensive behavior, which, after all, is unknown to that person.

Just as important as specifying behavior is the need to label an interpretation as such behavior instead of presenting it as a matter of fact. Consider the difference between saying

"It's obvious that if you cared for me you'd write more often." *(interpretation presented as fact)*

and

"When I didn't get a letter or even a postcard from you, I thought that you didn't care for me." *(interpretation made clear)*

As you learned in Chapter Five, your comments are much less likely to arouse defensiveness in others when you present them using "I" language.

A third important rule is to avoid making statements that appear to describe behavior but are in fact interpretations. For instance, don't mistake these kinds of statements as objective descriptions:

"I see you're tired." (*Tired* is an interpretation. Your behavioral description might have been "I see your eyes closing and your head nodding.")

"I see you're in a hurry." (*Hurry* is an interpretation. The behavioral description could have been "I see you gathering up your books and looking at the clock.")

"I can tell that you're hungry." (*Hungry* is an interpretation. The behavior you heard was the sound of your friend's stomach growling.)

"You look anxious to get started." (*Anxious* is an interpretation. What could the behavior be in this case? The short time it took your friend to answer the doorbell? The outside clothing in which the person was already dressed?)

There's nothing wrong with making these interpretations. In fact, this is a necessary step because only by interpreting behavior do we arrive at a meaning. However, we often make inaccurate interpretations, and when we don't separate behavior from our interpretations, we fool ourselves into believing that our interpretations are reality—that is, what we *think* is what exists.

SKILL BUILDER
BEHAVIORS AND INTERPRETATIONS

1. Tell two other group members several interpretations you have recently made about other people in your life. For each interpretation, describe the behavior on which you based your remarks.

2. With your partners' help, consider some alternate interpretations of the behavior that might be as plausible as your original one.

3. After considering the alternate interpretations, decide
   a. which one was most reasonable.
   b. how you might share that interpretation (along with the behavior) with the other person involved in a tentative, nondogmatic way.

FEELING Reporting behavior and sharing your interpretations are important, but *feeling statements* add a new dimension to a message. For example, consider the difference between saying

"When you kiss me and nibble on my ear while we're watching television [*behavior*], I think you probably want to make love [*interpretation*], and *I feel excited.*"

and

"When you kiss me and nibble on my ear while we're watching television, I think you probably want to make love, and *I feel disgusted.*"

Notice how the expression of different feelings can change the meaning of another message.

"When you laugh at me [*behavior*], I think you find my comments foolish [*interpretation*], and *I feel embarrassed.*"

"When you laugh at me, I think you find my comments foolish, and *I feel angry.*"

No doubt you can supply other examples in which different feelings can radically affect a speaker's meaning. Recognizing this, we find it logical to say that we should identify our feelings in our conversations with others. Yet if we pay attention to the everyday acts of communication, we see that no such disclosure occurs.

It's important to recognize that some statements *seem* as if they're expressing feelings but are really interpretations or statements of intention. For instance, it's not accurate to say "I feel like leaving" (really an intention) or "I feel you're wrong" (an interpretation). Statements like these obscure the true expression of feelings.

What prevents people from sharing their feelings? Certainly one cause is that making such statements can bring on a great deal of anxiety. It's often frightening to come right out and say, "I'm angry," "I feel embarrassed," or "I love you," and often we aren't willing to take the risks that come with such clear-cut assertions.

A second reason why people fail to express their feelings clearly is simply because they don't recognize them. We aren't always aware that we're angry, confused, impatient, or sad. Asking yourself, "How do I feel?" can often uncover important information that needs to be communicated to your partner.

SKILL BUILDER

NAME THE FEELING

Add a feeling you would be likely to have to each of the following messages:

1. I felt _____ when I found out you didn't invite me on the camping trip. You said you thought I wouldn't want to go, but I have a hard time accepting that.

2. I felt _____ when you offered to help me move. I know how busy you are.

3. When you tell me you still want to be a friend but you want to "lighten up a little," I get the idea you're tired of me and I feel _____ .

4. You told me you wanted my honest opinion about your paintings, and then when I tell you what I think, you say I don't understand them. I'm _____ .

How would the impact of each message be different if it didn't include a feeling statement?

CONSEQUENCE   A **consequence statement** explains what happens as a result of the behavior you have described, your interpretation, the ensuing feeling, or all three. There are three types of consequences:

■ *What happens to you, the speaker*
"When I didn't get the phone message yesterday [*behavior*], I didn't know that my doctor's appointment was delayed and I would end up sitting in the office for an hour when I could have been studying or working [*consequences*]. It seems to me that you don't care enough about how busy I am to even write a simple note [*interpretation*], and that's why I'm so mad [*feeling*]."
"I appreciate [*feeling*] the help you've given me on my term paper [*behavior*]. It tells me you think I'm on the right track [*interpretation*], and this gives me a boost to keep working on the idea [*consequences*]."

■ *What happens to the person you're addressing*
"When you have four or five drinks at a party after I've warned you to slow down [*behavior*], you start to act strange: You make crude jokes that offend everybody, and on the way home you drive poorly [*consequences*]. For instance, last night you almost hit a phone pole while you were backing out of the driveway [*more behavior*]. I don't think you realize how differently you act [*interpretation*], and I'm worried [*feeling*] about what will happen if you don't drink less."

■ *What happens to others*
"You probably don't know because you couldn't hear her cry [*interpretation*], but when you rehearse your lines for the play without closing the doors [*behavior*], the baby can't sleep [*consequence*]. I'm especially concerned [*feeling*] about her because she's had a cold lately."
"I thought you'd want to know [*interpretation*] that when you kid Bob about his height [*behavior*], he gets embarrassed [*feeling*] and usually quiets down or leaves [*consequences*]."

Consequence statements are valuable for two reasons. First, they help you understand more clearly why you are bothered or pleased by another's behavior. Just as important, telling others about the consequences of their actions can clarify for them the results of their behavior. As with interpretations, we often think others *should* be aware of consequences without being told; but the fact is that they often aren't. By explicitly stating consequences, you can be sure that you or your message leaves nothing to the listener's imagination.

When you are stating consequences, it's important simply to describe what happens without moralizing. For instance, it's one thing to say, "When you didn't call to say you'd be late, I stayed up worrying," and another to rant on "How can I ever trust you? You're going to drive me crazy!" Remember, it's perfectly legitimate to express your thoughts and feelings, but it's important to label them as such. And when you want to request change from someone, you can use intention statements, which we'll now describe.

It's easy to confuse some interpretation, feeling, or intention statements with consequences. For example, you might say, "As a consequence of your turning down my invitation [*behavior*], I got the idea [*interpretation*] you're mad at me. I'm worried [*feeling*], and I want to know what you're thinking [*intention*]." To say that these are not consequences as we're using the term is more than semantic hairsplitting. Confusing interpretations, feelings, and intentions with consequences might prevent you from mentioning the true consequence—what has happened as a result of this event. In our example, a real consequence statement might be "... and that's why I've been so quiet lately." As you'll read on page 420, sometimes a consequence is combined with another message element. The important point to remember is that you somehow need to explain the consequences of an incident if the other person is to understand your concern completely.

INTENTION **Intention statements** are the final element of the assertive format. They can communicate three kinds of messages:

■ *Where you stand on an issue*
"When you call us 'girls' after I've told you we want to be called 'women' [*behavior*], I get the idea you don't appreciate how important the difference is to us [*interpretation*] and how demeaning it feels [*feeling*]. Now I'm in an awkward spot: Either I have to keep bringing the subject up, or else drop it and feel bad [*consequence*]. I want you to know how much this bothers me [*intention*]."
"I'm really grateful [*feeling*] to you for speaking up for me in front of the boss yesterday [*behavior*]. That must have taken a lot of courage [*interpretation*]. Knowing that you're behind me gives me a lot of confidence [*consequence*], and I want you to know how much I appreciate your support [*intention*].

■ *Requests of others*
"When I didn't hear from you last night [*behavior*], I thought you were mad at me [*interpretation*]. I've been thinking about it ever since [*consequence*], and I'm still worried [*feeling*]. I'd like to know whether you are angry [*intention*]."
"I really enjoyed [*feeling*] your visit [*behavior*], and I'm glad you had a good time, too [*interpretation*]. I hope you'll come again [*intention*]."

■ *Descriptions of how you plan to act in the future*
"I've asked you to repay the twenty-five dollars I loaned you three times now [*behavior*]. I'm getting the idea that you've been avoiding me [*interpretation*], and I'm pretty angry about it [*feeling*]. I want you to know that unless we clear this up now, you shouldn't expect me ever to loan you anything again [*intention*]."
"I'm glad [*feeling*] you liked [*interpretation*] the paper I wrote. I'm thinking about taking your advanced writing class next term [*intention*]."

Why is it so important to make your intentions clear? Because failing to do so often makes it hard for others to know what you want from them or how to act. Consider how confusing the following statements are because they lack a clear statement of intention.

"Wow! A frozen Snickers. I haven't had one of those in years." (Does the speaker want a bite or is she just making an innocent remark?)

"Thanks for the invitation, but I really should study Saturday night." (Does the speaker want to be asked out again, or is she indirectly suggesting that she doesn't ever want to go out with you?)

"To tell you the truth, I was asleep when you came by, but I should have been up anyway." (Is the speaker saying that it's OK to come by in the future, or is he hinting that he doesn't appreciate unannounced visitors?)

You can see from these examples that it's often hard to make a clear interpretation of another person's ideas without a direct statement of intention. Notice how much more direct statements become when the speakers make their position clear.

"Wow! A frozen Snickers. I haven't had one of those in years. *If I hadn't already eaten, I'd sure ask for a bite.*"

"Thanks for the invitation, but I really should study Saturday night. *I hope you'll ask me again soon.*"

"To tell you the truth, I was asleep when you came by, but I should have been up anyway. *Maybe the next time you should phone before dropping in so I'll be sure to be awake.*"

As in the preceding cases, we are often motivated by one single intention. Sometimes, however, we act from a combination of intentions, which may even be in conflict with each other. When this happens, our conflicting wants often make it difficult for us to reach decisions.

"I want to be truthful with you, but I don't want to violate my friend's privacy."

"I want to continue to enjoy your friendship and company, but I don't want to get too attached right now."

"I want to have time to study and get good grades, but I also want to have a job with some money coming in."

Although revealing your conflicting intentions is guaranteed to clear up confusion, sometimes an outright statement, such as the preceding, can help you come to a decision. Even when you remain mixed up, expressing your contrary wants has the benefit of letting others know where you stand.

USING THE CLEAR MESSAGE FORMAT   Before you try to deliver messages by using the behavior-interpretation-feeling-consequences-intention format, there are a few points to remember.

1. *The elements may be delivered in mixed order.* As the examples on the preceding pages show, it's sometimes best to begin by stating your feelings. In other cases, you can start by sharing your intentions or interpretations or by describing consequences.

2. *Word the message to suit your personal style.* Instead of saying "I interpret your behavior to mean . . . " you might choose to say "I think . . . " or "It seems to me . . . " or perhaps "I get the idea. . . ." In the same way, you can express your intentions by saying "I hope you'll understand (or do) . . . " or perhaps "I wish you would. . . ." The words you choose should sound authentic in order to reinforce the genuineness of your statement.

3. *When appropriate, combine two elements in a single phrase.* The statement " . . . and ever since then I've been wanting to talk to

you" expresses both a consequence and an intention. In the same way, saying " . . . and after you said that, I felt confused" expresses a consequence and a feeling. Whether you combine elements or state them separately, the important point is to be sure that each one is present in your statement.

4. *Take your time delivering the message.* It isn't always possible to deliver messages such as the ones here all at one time, wrapped up in neat paragraphs. It will often be necessary to repeat or restate one part many times before your receiver truly understands what you're saying. As you've already read, there are many types of psychological and physical noise that make it difficult for us to understand each other. In communication, as in many other activities, patience and persistence are essential.

Now try your hand at combining all these elements in this exercise.

SKILL BUILDER

PUTTING YOUR MESSAGE TOGETHER

1. Join with two other class members. Each person in turn should share a message he or she might want to send to another person, being sure to include behavior, interpretation, feeling, consequence, and intention statements in the remarks.

2. The others in the group should help the speaker by offering feedback about how the remarks could be made clearer if there is any question about the meaning.

3. Once the speaker has composed a satisfactory message he or she should practice actually delivering it by having another group member play the role of the intended receiver. Continue this practice until the speaker is confident that he or she can deliver the message effectively.

4. Repeat this process until each group member has had a chance to practice delivering a message.

✣ CONFLICT IN RELATIONAL SYSTEMS

So far we have focused on individual conflict styles. Even though the style you choose in a conflict is important, your approach isn't the only factor that will determine how a conflict unfolds. In reality, conflict is *relational:* Its character usually is determined by the way the parties interact with one another.[29] You might, for example, be determined to handle a conflict with your neighbor assertively, only to be driven to aggression by his uncooperative nature . . . or even to nonassertion by his physical threats. Likewise, you might plan to hint to a professor that you are bothered by her apparent indifference, but wind up discussing the matter in an open, assertive way in reaction to her constructive response. Examples like these suggest that conflict isn't just a matter of individual choice. Rather, it depends on how the partners interact.

When two or more people are in a long-term relationship they develop their own **relational conflict style**—a pattern of managing disagreements that repeats itself over time. The mutual influence that parties have on one another is so powerful that it can overcome our disposition to handle conflicts in the manner that comes most easily to one or the other.[30] As we will soon see, some relational conflict styles are constructive, while others can make life miserable and threaten relationships.

COMPLEMENTARY, SYMMETRICAL, AND PARALLEL STYLES

Partners in interpersonal relationships—and impersonal ones, too— can use one of three styles introduced in Chapter One to manage their conflicts. In relationships with a **complementary conflict style** the partners use different but mutually reinforcing behaviors. In a **symmetrical conflict style,** both parties use the same tactics. Some relationships are characterized by a **parallel conflict style,** which shifts between complementary and symmetrical patterns from one issue to another. Table 10–2 illustrates how the same conflict can unfold in very different ways, depending on whether the partners' communication is symmetrical or complementary. A parallel style would alternate between these two forms, depending on the situation.

Research shows that a complementary "fight-flight" style is common in many unhappy marriages. One partner—most commonly the wife—addresses the conflict directly, while the other—usually the husband—withdraws.[31] It's easy to see how this pattern can lead to a cycle of increasing hostility and isolation, since each partner punctuates the conflict differently, blaming the other for making matters worse. "I withdraw because she's so critical," a husband might say. The wife wouldn't organize the sequence in the same way, however. "I criticize because he withdraws" would be her perception.

Complementary styles aren't the only ones that can lead to problems. Some distressed marriages suffer from destructively symmetrical communication. If both partners treat one another with matching hostility, one threat and insult leads to another in an escalatory spiral. If the partners both withdraw from one another instead of facing their problems, a de-escalatory spiral results, in which the satisfaction and vitality ebb from the relationship, leaving it a shell of its former self.

As Table 10–2 shows, both complementary and symmetrical behavior can produce "good" results as well as "bad" ones. If the complementary behaviors are positive, then a positive spiral results

T A B L E 1 0 – 2 Complementary and Symmetrical Conflict Styles

SITUATION	COMPLEMENTARY STYLES	SYMMETRICAL STYLES
Example 1: Wife upset because husband is spending little time at home.	Wife complains; husband withdraws, spending even less time at home.	Wife complains. Husband responds angrily and defensively.
Example 2: Female employee offended when boss calls her "sweetie."	Employee objects to boss, explaining her reasons for being offended. Boss apologizes for his unintentional insult.	Employee turns the tables by calling boss "cutie." Boss gets the hint and stops using the term.
Example 3: Parents uncomfortable about teenager's new friends.	Parents express concerns. Child dismisses them, saying "There's nothing to worry about."	Teen expresses concern that parents are being too protective.

and the conflict stands a good chance of being resolved. This is the case in example 2 in Table 10–2, where the boss is open to hearing the employee's concerns, listening willingly as the employee talks. Here, a complementary talk–listen pattern works well.

Symmetrical styles can also be beneficial, as another look at the boss–employee example shows. Many women have found that giving insensitive men a taste of their own sexist medicine is an effective way to end harassment without provoking an argument. The clearest example of constructive symmetry occurs when both parties communicate assertively, listening to one another's concerns and working together to resolve them. The potential for this sort of solution occurs in example 3, in the parent–teenager conflict. With enough mutual respect and careful listening, both the parents and their teenager can understand one another's concerns, and very possibly find a way to give both parties what they want.

INTIMATE AND AGGRESSIVE STYLES

Another way to look at conflict styles is to examine the interaction between intimacy and aggression. The following scheme was originally used to describe communication between couples, but it also works well for other types of relationships.

■ *Nonintimate–Aggressive* These partners fight, but are unsuccessful at satisfying important content and relational goals. In some relationships aggression is expressed directly: "Forget it. I'm not going to another stupid party with your friends. All they do is gossip and eat." In other relationships, indirect aggression is the norm: *(Sarcastically* "Sure I'd *love* to go to another party with your friends." Neither of these approaches is satisfying, since there are few rewards to justify the costs of the unpleasantness.

■ *Nonintimate–Nonaggressive* The parties avoid conflicts—and one another—instead of facing issues head-on: "You won't be coming home for the holidays? Oh well, I guess that's okay. . . . " Relationships of this sort can be quite stable, but because this pattern of communication doesn't confront and resolve problems, the vitality and satisfaction can decline over time.

■ *Intimate–Aggressive* This pattern combines aggression and intimacy in a manner that might seem upsetting to outsiders, but which can work well in some relationships. Lovers may fight like cats and dogs, but then make up just as intensely. Co-workers might argue about how to get the job done, but cherish their association.

■ *Intimate–Nonaggressive* This sort of relationship has a low amount of attacking or blaming. Partners may confront one another directly or indirectly, but one way or another they manage to prevent issues from interfering with their relationship.

The pattern partners choose may reveal a great deal about the kind of relationship they have chosen. Communication researcher

Mary Ann Fitzpatrick identified three types of couples: separates, independents, and traditionals.[32] Further research revealed that partners in each type of relationship approached conflict in a different manner.[33] Separates and independents tended to avoid conflict. Traditionals, by contrast, spent the most time focusing on their interaction. They also felt most secure about their relationships. They expressed negative emotions frequently, but also sought and revealed a large amount of personal information. Satisfied traditional couples fit the intimate–nonaggressive pattern, communicating more positive and less negative information than independents.

Information like this suggests that there's no single "best" relational conflict style. Some families or couples may fight intensely but love one another just as strongly. Others might handle issues more rationally and calmly. Even a nonintimate–nonaggressive style can work well when there's no desire to have an interpersonal relationship. You might, for example, be willing to accommodate the demands of an eccentric professor for a semester, since rolling with the punches gets you the education you are seeking without provoking a confrontation that could be upsetting and costly.

INVITATION TO INSIGHT

UNDERSTANDING CONFLICT STYLES

You can gain a clearer idea of how conflict styles differ by completing the following exercise.

1. Join a partner and choose one of the following conflicts to work on for this exercise. If you prefer, you may substitute a different conflict of your own.
   Roommates disagree about the noise level in their apartment.
   Parents want their college sophomore son or daughter to stay home for the winter vacation. The son or daughter wants to travel with friends.
   One person in a couple wants to spend free time socializing with friends. The other wants to stay at home together.

2. Role-play the conflict four times, reflecting each of the following styles:
   Nonintimate–aggressive   Intimate–aggressive
   Nonintimate–nonaggressive   Intimate–nonaggressive

3. After experiencing each of these styles, determine which of them characterizes the way conflict is managed in one of your interpersonal relationships. Are you satisfied with this approach? If not, describe what style would be more appropriate.

CONFLICT RITUALS

When people have been in a relationship for some time, their communication often develops into **conflict rituals**—unacknowledged but very real repeating patterns of interlocking behavior.[34] Consider a few common rituals:

cathy®

by Cathy Guisewite

SOME COUPLES DEAL WITH EVERY ISSUE THE SECOND IT COMES UP.

THAT HURT ME, DON.

LET'S TALK ABOUT IT, PAM.

SOME COUPLES LET LITTLE PROBLEMS ACCUMULATE UNTIL THEY MERIT A BIG DISCUSSION.

SOME THINGS ARE BOTHERING ME, KAREN.

WE'LL WORK THROUGH THEM TOGETHER, JOE.

SOME COUPLES NEVER ACTUALLY DEAL WITH THE INDIVIDUAL ISSUES, PREFERRING TO LET THEM KEEP HEAPING UP UNTIL THE FULL RANGE OF EMOTION CAN BE EXPRESSED.

THE "BURNING-THE-IN-BASKET" APPROACH TO PROBLEM-SOLVING.

YOU MAKE ME SICK!!!

PBLLLTTT!!!

■ A young child interrupts her parents, demanding to be included in their conversation. At first the parents tell the child to wait, but she whines and cries until the parents find it easier to listen than to ignore the fussing.

■ A couple fights. One partner leaves. The other accepts the blame for the problem and begs forgiveness. The first partner returns, and a happy reunion takes place. Soon they fight again.

■ One friend is unhappy with the other. He or she withdraws until the other asks what's wrong. "Nothing," the first replies. The questioning persists until the problem is finally out in the open. The friends then resolve the issue and continue happily until the next problem arises, when the pattern repeats itself.

There's nothing inherently wrong with the interaction in many rituals. Consider the examples above. In the first, the little girl's whining may be the only way she can get the parents' attention. In the second, both partners might use the fighting as a way to blow off steam, and both might find that the joy of a reunion is worth the grief of the separation. The third ritual might work well when one friend is more assertive than the other.

Rituals can cause problems, though, when they become the *only* way relational partners handle their conflicts. As you learned in Chapter One, competent communicators have a large repertoire of behaviors, and they are able to choose the most effective response for a given situation. Relying on one ritual pattern to handle all conflicts is no more effective than using a screwdriver to handle every home repair or putting the same seasoning on every dish you cook: What works in one situation isn't likely to succeed in many others. Conflict rituals may be familiar and comfortable, but they aren't the best way to resolve the variety of conflicts that are part of any relationship.

INVITATION TO INSIGHT

YOUR CONFLICT RITUALS

Describe two conflict rituals in one of your important relationships. One of your examples should consist of a positive ritual and the other of one that generates unsatisfying results. For each example, explain

1. A subject that is likely to trigger the conflict (e.g., money, leisure time, affection).

2. The behavior of one partner that initiates the ritual.

3. The series of responses by both partners that follow the initiating event.

4. How the ritual ends.

Based on your description, explain an alternative to the unsatisfying ritual and describe how you might be able to change the way you manage the conflict in a more satisfying way.

✤ VARIABLES IN CONFLICT STYLES

By now you can see that every relational system is unique. The communication patterns in one family, business, or classroom are likely to be very different from any other. But along with the differences that arise in individual relationships, there are two powerful variables that affect the way people manage conflict: gender and culture. We will now take a brief look at each of these factors and see how they affect how conflict is managed.

GENDER

Men and women often approach conflicts differently. Even in childhood, males are more likely to be aggressive, demanding, and competitive, while females are more cooperative. Studies of children from preschool to early adolescence have shown that boys try to get their way by ordering one another around: "Lie down." "Get off my steps." "Gimme your arm." By contrast, girls are more likely to make proposals for action, beginning with the word "Let's": "Let's go find some." "Let's ask her, 'Do you have any bottles?'" "Let's move *these* out *first*."[35] Whereas boys tell each other what role to take in pretend play ("Come on, be a doctor"), girls more commonly ask each other what role they want ("Will you be the patient for a few minutes?") or make a joint proposal ("We can both be doctors"). Furthermore, boys often make demands without offering an explanation ("Look, man. I want the wire cutters right now"). By contrast, girls often give reasons for their suggestions ("We gotta *clean* 'em first . . . cause they got germs").

Differences like these often persist into adulthood. One survey of college students revealed that men and women viewed conflicts in contrasting ways.[36] Regardless of their cultural background, female students described men as being concerned with power and more interested in content than relational issues. Phrases used to describe male conflict styles included: "The most important thing to males in conflict is their egos." "Men don't worry about feelings." "Men are more direct." By contrast, women were described as being more concerned with maintaining the relationship during a conflict. Phrases used to describe female conflict styles included: "Women are better listeners." "Women try to solve problems without controlling the other person." "Females are more concerned with others' feelings."

These differences don't mean that men with attitudes like these are incapable of forming good relationships. Instead, their notions of what makes a good relationship are different. For some men, friendship and aggression aren't mutually exclusive. In fact, many strong male relationships are built around competition—at work or in athletics, for example. Women can be competitive too, but they also are more likely to use logical reasoning and bargaining than aggression.[37] When men communicate with women, they become less aggressive and more cooperative than they are in all-male groups.

Most theorists suggest that the primary reason for differences in conflict style is socialization.[38] Some social scientists have proposed a "threshold of assertiveness" may exist for people, especially women, allowing them to behave in an assertive way up to a point, but no further. Since women have been typically perceived as more compliant and cooperative, they may have seen themselves as reaching this threshold sooner than men, at which time they back off. Being less assertive may not feel right to women who justifiably think that they shouldn't be held to a different standard than men. Nonetheless, this is one case where gender equity doesn't produce the best results: Both women and men appear less tolerant of assertive behavior when it comes from a woman than from a man.[39]

Since men have been expected to be more assertive, they find it more comfortable and rewarding to persist in seeking their needs. As gender-role stereotyping becomes less common, it is likely that the differences between male and female conflict styles will become smaller.

CULTURE

The way in which people manage conflict varies tremendously depending on their cultural background. The straight-talking, assertive approach that characterizes many North Americans is not the universal norm.[40]

Perhaps the most important cultural factor in shaping attitudes toward conflict is an orientation toward individualism or collectivism.[41] In individualistic cultures like the United States, the goals, rights, and needs of each person are considered important, and most people would agree that it is an individual's right to stand up for himself or herself. By contrast, collectivist cultures (more common in

Latin America and Asia) consider the concerns of the group to be more important than those of any individual. In these cultures, the kind of assertive behavior that might seem perfectly appropriate to a North American would seem rude and insensitive.

Another factor that distinguishes the assertiveness that is so valued by North Americans and northern Europeans from other cultures is the difference between high- and low-context cultural styles.[42] Recall from our discussion in Chapter Six that low-context cultures like the United States place a premium on being direct and literal. By contrast, high-context cultures like Japan value self-restraint and avoid confrontation. Communicators in these cultures derive meaning from a variety of unspoken rules such as the context, social conventions, and hints. Preserving and honoring the face of the other person is a prime goal, and communicators go to great lengths to avoid any communication that might risk embarrassing a conversational partner. For this reason, what seems like "beating around the bush" to an American would be polite to an Asian. In Japan, for example, even a simple request like "close the door" would be too straightforward.[43] A more indirect statement such as "It is somewhat cold today" would be more appropriate. To take a more important example, Japanese are reluctant to say "no" to a request. A more likely answer would be "let me think about it for a while," which anyone familiar with Japanese culture would recognize as a refusal. When indirect communication is a cultural norm, it is unreasonable to expect more straightforward approaches to succeed. When people from different cultures face a conflict, their habitual communication patterns may not mesh smoothly. The challenge faced by an American husband and his Taiwanese wife illustrates this sort of problem:

Looking at Diversity

JAPANESE AND AMERICAN CONFLICT STYLES

Norie Kobayashi and Kentaro Ebiko both grew up in Japan. They came to the United States three years ago, and met while in college. They have been dating for seven months. Norie plans to become a nurse, and Kentaro hopes to begin a business career in the United States and later return to Japan.

Question: According to researchers, there are considerable differences between the way conflicts are dealt with in the U.S. and Japan. Do you agree?

Kentaro: Definitely. In the U.S.A. being direct and expressive is very important. In Japan, just the opposite is true. You almost never talk about conflicts there, at least not openly.

Question: If people don't talk about conflicts, how do they resolve them?

Kentaro: Sometimes they don't. In Japan the tradition is not to show your emotions. Outside appearances are very important. If you're upset, you still act as if everything is OK. So there are lots of times when you might be disappointed or angry with somebody and they would never know it.

Question: Do conflicts ever get expressed?

Kentaro: They aren't discussed openly, assertively very often. But in Japan a lot more is communicated nonverbally. If you guess that the other person is unhappy from the way they act, you might try to change to please them. But even then you wouldn't necessarily talk about the conflict directly.

Question: Would you say that the Japanese are better readers of nonverbal cues than Americans?

Kentaro: I do think they're more aware of nonverbal messages. But there are times when someone will misunderstand a nonverbal message. You might think a friend or a person at work is upset and try to change to make them happy, when they really weren't upset at all. But since nobody talks about their problems, these misunderstandings happen.

Question: Norie, does Kentaro hide his feelings very well?

Norie: No! He's more American than I am in this way. He will tell me how he's feeling sometimes. And even when he doesn't say anything, it's very easy to tell how he's feeling by his nonverbal communication.

Question: Do you appreciate his expressiveness?

Norie: Well, sometimes it makes me uncomfortable. I guess I appreciate it, but I'm still not used to communicating so directly. Kentaro's

open communication is also hard for some of our Japanese friends to understand. We have a group of Japanese students at our church, and when Kentaro shows his feelings, they get very concerned since they're not used to seeing a Japanese man showing his emotions.

Question: Norie, it sounds like you're less comfortable facing conflicts than Kentaro.

Norie: That's right. I think it's partly my Japanese upbringing and partly just my personality, but I don't like to confront people. For example, I was having a hard time studying and sleeping because one of my housemates would wash her clothes late at night. I wanted her to stop, but I would never have talked to her directly. I asked my housemother to take care of the problem. Asking a third party is very common in Japan. She did, and now things are fine. Confronting my housemate directly might have caused a fight, and that would have been very unpleasant.

Question: Do you think Japanese culture is becoming more direct and assertive, like the American style of handling conflicts?

Kentaro: Maybe a little bit. But the traditions of not showing emotion and of being direct are so strong that I don't think Japan will be very much like the U.S.A., at least not for a very long time.

The husband would typically try to confront his wife verbally and directly (as is typical in the United States), leading her to either become violently defensive or withdraw completely from the discussion. She, on the other hand, would attempt to indicate her displeasure by changes in mood and eye contact (typical of Chinese culture) that were either not noticed (or uninterpretable) by her husband. Thus, neither "his way" nor "her way" was working and they could not see any realistic way to "compromise."[44]

It isn't necessary to look at Asia to encounter cultural differences in conflict. Americans visiting Greece, for example, often think they are witnessing an argument when they are overhearing a friendly conversation.[45] A comparative study of American and Italian nursery-school children showed that one of the Italian children's favorite pastimes was a kind of heated debating that Italians call *discussione*, but which Americans would regard as arguing. Likewise, research has shown that the conversations of working-class Jewish speakers of Eastern European origin used arguments as a means of being sociable.

Within the United States, the ethnic background of communicators also plays a role in their ideas about conflict. When a group of African-American, Mexican-American, and Anglo-American college students was asked about their views regarding conflict, some important differences emerged.[46] For example, Anglo-Americans seem more willing to accept conflict as a natural part of relationships, while Mexican-Americans describe the short- and long-term dangers of disagreeing. Anglos' willingness to experience conflicts may be part of their individualistic, low-context communication style of speaking directly and avoiding uncertainty. It's not surprising that people from more collective, high-context cultures which emphasize harmony among people with close relationships tend to handle conflicts in less direct ways. With differences like these, it's easy to imagine how two friends, lovers, or fellow workers from different cultural backgrounds might have trouble finding a conflict style that is comfortable for them both.

✚ METHODS OF CONFLICT RESOLUTION

No matter what the relational style, gender, or culture of the participants, every conflict is a struggle to have one's goals met. Sometimes that struggle succeeds, and in other cases it fails. In the remainder of this chapter we'll look at various approaches to resolving conflicts and see which ones are most promising.

When faced with a disagreement, the parties have three choices:

- They can accept the status quo: "I don't like some of your friends, and you aren't crazy about mine, but there isn't much we can do about it. I suppose we'll just have to live with them."
- They can use coercion—physical, social, or economic—to impose a settlement: "Either we spend the vacation backpacking or I'm staying home."

Sometimes it's worse to win a fight than to lose.

Billie Holiday

■ They can reach an agreement by negotiating. **Negotiation** occurs when two or more parties discuss specific proposals in order to find a mutually acceptable agreement. Negotiation isn't foolproof: When poorly handled, it can leave a problem still unsolved or even worse than before. On the other hand, skillful negotiating can produce solutions that improve the situation for both parties.

WIN–LOSE

In **win–lose problem solving,** one party gets what he or she wants, whereas the other comes up short. People resort to this method of resolving disputes when they perceive a situation as being an "either–or" one: Either I get what I want or you get your way. The most clear-cut examples of win–lose situations are certain games such as baseball or poker, in which the rules require a winner and a loser. Some interpersonal issues seem to fit into this win–lose framework: two co-workers seeking a promotion to the same job, or a couple who disagree on how to spend their limited money.

Power is the distinguishing characteristic in win–lose problem solving, for it is necessary to defeat an opponent to get what one wants. The most obvious kind of power is physical. Some parents threaten their children with warnings such as "Stop misbehaving or I'll send you to your room." Adults who use physical power to deal with each other usually aren't so blunt, but the legal system is the implied threat: "Follow the rules or we'll lock you up."

Real or implied force isn't the only kind of power used in conflicts. People who rely on authority of many types engage in win–lose methods without ever threatening physical coercion. In most jobs, supervisors have the authority to assign working hours, job promotions, and desirable or undesirable tasks, and, of course, to fire an unsatisfactory employee. Teachers can use the power of grades to coerce students to act in desired ways.

Intellectual or mental power can also be a tool for conquering an opponent. Everyone is familiar with stories of how a seemingly weak hero defeats a stronger enemy through cleverness, showing that brains are more important than brawn. In a less admirable way, passive–aggressive crazymakers can defeat their partners by inducing guilt, avoiding issues, withholding desired behaviors, pseudo-accommodating, and so on.

Even the usually admired democratic principle of majority rule is a win–lose method of resolving conflicts. However fair it may be, with this system one group gets its way and another is unsatisfied.

There are some circumstances in which the win–lose method may be necessary, as when there are truly scarce resources and only one party can achieve satisfaction. For instance, if two suitors want to marry the same person, only one can succeed. And to return to an earlier example, it's often true that only one applicant can be hired for a job. But don't be too willing to assume that your conflicts are necessarily win–lose: As you'll soon read, many situations that seem to require a loser can be resolved to everyone's satisfaction. There is a second kind of situation when win–lose is the best method. Even when cooperation is possible, if the other person insists on trying to defeat you, the most logical response might be to defend yourself by fighting back.

A final and much less frequent justification for trying to defeat another person occurs when the other party is clearly behaving in a wrong manner and where defeating that person is the only way to stop the wrongful behavior. Few people would deny the importance of restraining a person who is deliberately harming others, even if the aggressor's freedom is sacrificed in the process. The danger of forcing wrongdoers to behave themselves is the wide difference in opinion between people about who is wrong and who is right. Given this difference, it would seem only justifiable in the most extreme circumstances to coerce others into behaving as we think they should.

LOSE–LOSE

In **lose–lose problem solving,** neither side is satisfied with the outcome. Although the name of this approach is so discouraging that it's hard to imagine how anyone could willingly use it, in truth lose–lose is a fairly common way to handle conflicts. In many instances the parties will both strive to be winners, but as a result of the struggle, both wind up losers. On the international scene many wars illustrate

THE FAR SIDE   By GARY LARSON

"OK, crybaby! You want the last soda?
Well, let me GET IT READY FOR YOU!"

this sad point. A nation that gains military victory at the cost of thousands of lives, large amounts of resources, and a damaged national consciousness hasn't truly won much. On an interpersonal level the same principle holds. Most of us have seen battles of pride in which both parties strike out and both suffer.

COMPROMISE

Unlike lose–lose outcomes, a **compromise** gives both parties at least some of what they wanted, though both sacrifice part of their goals. People usually settle for compromises when it seems that partial satisfaction is the best they can hope for. Although a compromise may be better than losing everything, this approach hardly seems to deserve the positive image it has with some people. In his valuable book on conflict resolution, Albert Filley makes an interesting observation about our attitudes toward this method.[47] Why is it, he asks, that if someone says, "I will compromise my values," we view the action unfavorably, yet we talk admiringly about parties in a conflict who compromise to reach a solution? Although compromises may be the best obtainable result in some conflicts, it's important to realize that both people in a dispute can often work together to find much better solutions. In such cases "compromise" is a negative word.

Most of us are surrounded by the results of bad compromises. Consider a common example, the conflict between one person's desire to smoke cigarettes and another's need for clean air. The win–lose outcomes on this issue are obvious: Either the smoker abstains or the nonsmoker gets polluted lungs—neither very satisfying. But a compromise in which the smoker gets to enjoy only a rare cigarette or must retreat outdoors and in which the nonsmoker still must inhale some fumes or feel like an ogre is hardly better. Both sides have lost a considerable amount of both comfort and goodwill. Of course, the costs involved in other compromises are even greater. For example, if a divorced couple compromise on child care by haggling over custody and then grudgingly agree to split the time with their children, it's hard to say that anybody has won.

Some compromises do leave both parties satisfied. You and the seller might settle on a price for a used car that is between what the seller was asking and what you wanted to pay. Although neither of you got everything you wanted, the outcome would still leave both of you satisfied. Likewise, you and your companion might agree to see a film that is the second choice for both of you in order to spend an evening together. As long as everyone is satisfied with an outcome, compromise can be an effective way to resolve conflicts.

WIN–WIN

In **win–win problem solving** the goal is to find a solution that satisfies the needs of everyone involved. Not only do the parties avoid trying to win at the other's expense, but they also believe that by working together it is possible to find a solution that goes beyond a mere compromise and allows all parties to reach their goals. Consider a few examples:

Gordon was a stamp collector; his wife, Elaine, loved to raise and show championship beagles. Their income didn't leave enough money for both to practice their hobbies, and splitting the cash they did have wouldn't have left enough for either. *Solution:* Put all the first year's money into the puppies, and then after they were grown, use the income from their litters and show prizes to pay for Gordon's stamps.

Mac loved to spend his evenings talking to people all over the world on his ham radio set, but his wife, Marilyn, felt cheated out of the few hours of each day they could spend together. *Solution:* Three or four nights each week Mac stayed up late and talked on his radio after spending the evening with Marilyn. On the following mornings she drove him to work instead of having him take the bus, which allowed him to sleep later.

Wendy and Kathy were roommates who had different studying habits. Wendy liked to do her work in the evenings, which left her days free for other things, but Kathy felt that nighttime was party time. *Solution:* Monday through Wednesday evenings Wendy studied at her boyfriend's place while Kathy did anything she wanted. Thursday and Sunday Kathy agreed to keep things quiet around the house.

When we think about cooperation at all, we tend to associate the concept with fuzzy-minded idealism or, at best, to see it as workable only in a very small number of situations. This may result from confusing cooperation with altruism. It is not at all true that competition is more successful because it relies on the tendency to "look out for number one" while cooperation assumes that we primarily want to help each other. Structural cooperation defies the usual egoism/altruism dichotomy. It sets things up so that by helping you I am helping myself at the same time. Even if my motive initially may have been selfish, our fates now are linked. We sink or swim together. Cooperation is a shrewd and highly successful strategy.

Alfie Kohn

TABLE 10–3   Choosing the Most Appropriate Method of Conflict

Consider deferring to the other person:

When you discover you are wrong
When the issue is more important to the other person than it is to you
To let others learn by making their own mistakes
When the long-term cost of winning may not be worth short-term gains

Consider compromising:

When there is not enough time to seek a win–win outcome
When the issue is not important enough to negotiate at length
When the other person is not willing to seek a win–win outcome

Consider competing:

When the issue is important and the other person will take advantage of your noncompetitive approach

Consider cooperating:

When the issue is too important for a compromise
When a long-term relationship between you and the other person is important
When the other person is willing to cooperate

I will not play at tug o'war.
I'd rather play at hug o'war,
Where everyone hugs
Instead of tugs,
Where everyone giggles
And rolls on the rug,
Where everyone kisses,
And everyone grins,
And everyone cuddles,
And everyone wins.

Shel Silverstein

The point here isn't that these solutions are the correct ones for everybody with similar problems: The win–win approach doesn't work that way. Different people might have found other solutions that suited them better. The win–win method gives you an *approach*—a way of creatively finding just the right answer for your unique problem. By using it you can tailor-make a way of resolving your conflicts that everyone can live with comfortably.

You should understand that the win–win approach doesn't call for compromises in which the participants give up something they really want or need. Sometimes a compromise is the only alternative, but in the method we're talking about you find a solution that satisfies everyone—one in which nobody had to lose.

Although a win–win approach sounds ideal, it is not always possible, or even appropriate. Table 10–3 lists some factors to consider when deciding which approach to take when facing a conflict. There will certainly be times when compromising is the most sensible approach. You will even encounter instances when pushing for your own solution is reasonable. Even more surprisingly, you will probably discover that there are times when it makes sense to willingly accept the loser's role.

A POSITIVE DEVELOPMENT IN THE PHILOSOPHY OF DIVORCE
LAWYER BELIEVES HIS ROLE SHOULD BE A PEACEMAKER

ositive divorce. Marital dissolution that is not the equivalent of emotional Pac-Man. Steered by attorneys who refuse to use the legal system to hobble, harass or otherwise obliterate the other side.

Divorce lawyers who see themselves not as adversaries but . . . peacemakers. And then expect a client not just to survive a breakup but to be in better shape because of it.

Are we dreaming?

As farfetched as all that may appear to some, such situations are increasingly the result of California divorce proceedings.

One law practice where such outcomes can virtually be counted on is that of Michael Kelly, a Santa Monica–based attorney and problem judge who has become something of a crusader on the subject. After creating positive marital dissolutions for the last six of his 15 years in law, Kelly has been lecturing on this alternative for about a year and a half.

As Kelly sees it, the legal system itself—the time-honored adversary system—is better designed to produce a confrontation than a mutually acceptable termination of a marriage. He defines the adversary proceedings as a struggle in which "each side puts out their version of the facts as strongly as possible and tries to destroy and eliminate the other side's version of the same story. And supposedly, somewhere within that wreckage, the truth is going to come out."

Precise Process

To avoid the demolition, Kelly has created a precise, step-by-step process that has resulted in about 80% of his clients settling their divorce disputes completely out of court and the remaining 20% with some litigation but no full trials. (His last complete trial occurred about 10 years ago.)

Predictably, however, a frequent reaction to the suggestion of positive divorce (with attorneys involved) often sounds something like this: "Great, honey, if we get divorced, you get this guy to represent you and I'll get the toughest rat in town."

"We hear that all the time," Kelly responds. "What that's saying is, 'I'm gonna get a bigger stick and beat you to death for leaving me.' I cannot, obviously, and will not stand idly by with a complete peace branch if I am dealing with one of the lawyers who simply litigates a case, period, no matter what happens. This is not a process that can be done unilaterally. It requires cooperation and intention (to settle rather than litigate). I cannot produce that result when the other party will not do it."

But Kelly does exercise considerable control of his clients and has been known to fire them for demanding that he "get" spouses. And he provides clients the same freedom to waltz out by signing a substitution of attorney agreement.

"Very often spouses forget that the person who's on the other side of litigation is the person they've been living with and sleeping with for the last 5 or 10 or 15 years and to the extent that you hurt that person, very often you mortally wound your own self," Kelly says. "You cannot have an emotional experience with somebody for that long and then damage that person or cheat that person as the last thing you do to them and ultimately be satisfied with that or feel good about it. People forget they're holding the other end of the stick of dynamite that they're trying to hand their spouse. What they will get out of that is a big bill and no satisfaction."

Both Sides Pay

"Clients sometimes have the mistaken notion that the other guy's going to pay for it. Well, in the rare instance that the husband is very wealthy and the wife has no income and they've been married 20 years, the husband may be made to pay it all. But more and more, judges are ordering the house sold and both sides are made to pay a share of the legal fees."

(continued)

(continued from page 437)

Kelly further notes that while people are consumed with anger and vengeance, they may also find it tricky to be productive in their work and impossible to create a fulfilling new relationship while they're "stuck" in the old one.

Lloyd Zeiderman, a business manager for entertainers, concurs. He refers many of his clients to Kelly for divorce representation. "My experience has been that a divorcing person in an extended litigation can probably lose 50% of his or her income during that year, in addition to the other costs of divorce. They're preoccupied with antagonism.

"I use Mike in every case that I can that does not include a belligerent opposition," Zeiderman says. "He has a method where he comes up with settlements that are fair to both sides without the antagonism most attorneys are known for. With the high-income, high-net-worth clients I represent, there is a tendency by the opposing attorneys to generate tremendously high legal fees that cause both parties an unnecessary cost. Mike's methods seem to create a very compassionate situation for the husband, wife and children."

Useless Confrontation

Reasons Kelly, "If you start out your conversation with another lawyer saying, 'What can we do to handle this problem between our clients?' as opposed to 'My client just told me your client (cheated) him or was a liar,' you start steering him toward a mutually acceptable termination as opposed to a useless confrontation."

Beyond that, Kelly works to isolate the matters both sides agree on and shuffle them out of the way so that areas of disagreement may (a) appear minimal by comparison and (b) be examined without the added confusion of the other matters. Through all this friendliness, Kelly insists that he invites opposing lawyers to meet him with no less than the same vigor, concentration and thoroughness they apply to other proceedings. He favors speed but cautions that haste can create its own set of difficulties.

Sometimes, though, all that still doesn't work. Kelly admits to having arrived at the end of seemingly flawless settlements only to find a land mine exploding in the form of one final item, say an antique dining table both parties want. His solution is to encourage his client to just give it up, let it go and get the whole odious event over with.

Clients' Gratitude

The benefits of this approach are evident not only in the percentage of cases Kelly settles but also in gratitude from his clients for ongoing ease in relationships with their ex-wives or ex-husbands.

Hollywood talent consultant Ashley Rothschild, for instance, retained Kelly to represent her in what looked to be a bitter custody battle for her son. She had lost custody of another son to her first husband, and after the breakup of her second marriage, both spouses were prepared to fight for full custody of their son.

"When my husband said, 'I want full custody,' I said, 'Over my dead body. I'll use every trick I can to get you,'" Rothschild recalls. "We would hang up screaming on the phone just to get each other. I was going to use every bit of ammunition that I could to get my child."

Kelly convinced her that joint custody might be more appropriate for all parties, especially the son.

"It's thanks to Michael Kelly's commitment that divorce doesn't have to be ugly, that my husband and I are friends now," Rothschild said.

There is no way to know precisely how typical the Rothschild case is of Kelly's practice. But one observer who's repeatedly watched Kelly operate suggests it may be a regular occurrence.

"I'm speaking only for myself, not for the court, but I'm favorably impressed," says commissioner John Alexander of the Los Angeles Superior Court, Santa Monica District.

"Is that a good idea? Of course it is," Alexander says. "A contested dissolution is an expensive thing and it's hard on the emotions. Kelly looks to me like the kind of person who would resign from the case rather than present an unreasonable demand. He's his own man. He won't let a client ask for the moon, the sun and the whole solar system."

Even opposing counsel have been impressed with Kelly's approach. One attorney, John Dunne, found his divorce methodology so "refreshing" that he invited Kelly and his partner, Michael Cogan, to move into his luxurious suite of offices overlooking the Pacific Ocean in Santa Monica (which they did).

"Kelly's an unusual lawyer," Dunne says. "His approach was so novel. He writes me this letter and wants to come over and sit down and brings all the facts and all the information that normally takes us a year to get and we settled a substantial case in, I think, four weeks. I'm always surprised when I get something like that from a lawyer. Usually it's something you get from a parish priest."

Beth Ann Krier,
Los Angeles Times

❖ WIN–WIN COMMUNICATION SKILLS

Win–win problem solving is clearly superior to the win–lose and lose–lose approaches. Why, then, is it so rarely used? There are three reasons. The first is lack of awareness. Some people are so used to competition that they mistakenly think winning requires them to defeat their "opponent."

Even when they know better, another reason prevents many people from seeking win–win solutions. Conflicts are often emotional affairs, in which people react combatively without stopping to think of better alternatives. Because this kind of emotional reflex prevents constructive solutions, it's often necessary to stop yourself from speaking out aggressively in a conflict and starting an escalating spiral of defensiveness. The time-honored advice of "counting to ten" applies here. Once you've thought about the matter, you'll be able to *act* constructively instead of *reacting* in a way that's likely to produce a lose–lose outcome.

A third reason win–win solutions are rare is that they require the other person's cooperation. It's difficult to negotiate constructively with someone who insists on trying to defeat you. In this case, use your best persuasive skills to explain that by working together you can find a solution that satisfies both of you.

In spite of these challenges, it is definitely possible to become better at resolving conflicts. In the following pages we will outline a method to increase your chances of being able to handle your conflicts in a win–win manner. As you read the following steps, try to imagine yourself applying them to a problem that's bothering you now.

> ❖ *Our marriage used to suffer from arguments that were too short. Now we argue long enough to find out what the argument is about.*
>
> Hugh Prather,
> *Notes to Myself*

STEP 1—IDENTIFY YOUR PROBLEM AND UNMET NEEDS

Before you speak out, it's important to realize that the problem that is causing conflict is yours. Whether you want to return an unsatisfactory piece of merchandise, complain to noisy neighbors because your sleep is being disturbed, or request a change in working conditions from your employer, the problem is yours. Why? Because in each case *you* are the person who "owns" the problem—the one who is dissatisfied. You are the one who has paid for the defective article; the merchant who sold it to you has the use of your good money. You are the one who is losing sleep as a result of your neighbors' activities; they are content to go on as before. You are the one who is unhappy with your working conditions, not your boss.*

Realizing that the problem is yours will make a big difference when the time comes to approach your partner. Instead of feeling and

---

*Of course, others involved in the conflict may have problems of their own. For instance, the shopkeeper, the noisy neighbors, and your boss may all be bothered by your requests. But the fact remains that the reason you are speaking up about these matters is because *you* are dissatisfied. Thus, the problem is at least initially yours.

acting in an evaluative way, you'll be more likely to state your problem in a descriptive way, which will not only be more accurate but also reduce the chance of a defensive reaction.

Once you realize that the problem is yours, the next step is to identify the unmet needs that make you dissatisfied. For instance, in the barking dog incident, your need may be to get some sleep or to study without interruptions. In the case of a friend who teases you in public, your need would probably be to avoid embarrassment.

Sometimes the task of identifying your needs isn't as simple as it first seems. Behind the apparent content of an issue is often a relational need. Consider these examples:

A friend hasn't returned some money you loaned long ago. Your apparent need in this situation might be to get the cash back. But a little thought will probably show that this isn't the only, or even the main, thing you want. Even if you were rolling in money, you'd probably want the loan repaid because of your most important need: *to avoid feeling victimized by your friend's taking advantage of you.*

Someone you care about who lives in a distant city has failed to respond to several letters. Your apparent need may be to get answers to the questions you've written about, but it's likely that there's another, more fundamental need: *the reassurance that you're still important enough to deserve a response.*

As you'll soon see, the ability to identify your real needs plays a key role in solving interpersonal problems. For now, the point to remember is that before you voice your problem to your partner, you ought to be clear about which of your needs aren't being met.

STEP 2—MAKE A DATE

Destructive fights often start because the initiator confronts a partner who isn't ready. There are many times when a person isn't in the right frame of mind to face a conflict, perhaps owing to fatigue, being in too much of a hurry to take the necessary time, being upset over another problem, or not feeling well. At times like these it's unfair to "jump" a person without notice and expect to get full attention for your problem. If you do persist, you'll probably have an ugly fight on your hands.

After you have a clear idea of the problem, approach your partner with a request to try to solve it. For example, "Something's been bothering me. Can we talk about it?" If the answer is "yes," you're ready to go further. If it isn't the right time to confront your partner, find a time that's agreeable to both of you.

STEP 3—DESCRIBE YOUR PROBLEM AND NEEDS

Your partner can't possibly meet your needs without knowing why you're upset and what you want. Therefore, it's up to you to describe your problem as specifically as possible. The best way to deliver a complete, accurate message is to use the assertive behavior-interpretation-feeling-consequence-intention format. Notice how well this approach works in the following examples:

Example 1
"I have a problem. It's about your leaving dirty clothes around the house after I've told you how much it bothers me [*behavior*]. It's a problem because I have to run around like crazy and pick things up whenever guests come, which is no fun at all [*consequence*]. I'm starting to think that either you're not paying attention to my requests or you're trying to drive me crazy [*thoughts*], and either way I'm getting more and more resentful [*feeling*]. I'd like to find some way to have a neat place without my having to be a maid or a nag."

Example 2
"I have a problem. When you drop by without calling ahead and I'm studying [*behavior*], I don't know whether to visit or ask you to leave [*thought*]. Either way, I get uncomfortable [*feeling*], and it seems like whatever I do, I lose: Either I have to put you off or get behind in my work [*consequences*]. I'd like to find a way to get my studying done and still socialize with you [*intention*]."

Example 3
"Something is bothering me. When you tell me you love me and yet spend almost all your free time with your other friends [*behavior*], I wonder whether you mean it [*thought*]. I get insecure [*feeling*], and then I start acting moody [*consequence*]. I need some way of finding out for sure how you feel about me [*intention*]."

STEP 4—CONSIDER YOUR PARTNER'S POINT OF VIEW

After stating your problem and describing what you need, it's important to make sure your partner has understood what you've said. As you can remember from the discussion of listening in Chapter Seven, there's a good chance—especially in a stressful conflict—that your words will be misinterpreted.

It's usually unrealistic to insist that your partner paraphrase your statement, and fortunately there are more tactful and subtle ways to make sure you've been understood. For instance, you might try saying, "I'm not sure I expressed myself very well just now—maybe you should tell what you heard me say so I can be sure I got it right." In any case, be absolutely sure that your partner understands your whole message before going any further. Legitimate agreements are tough enough, but there's no point in getting upset about a conflict that doesn't even exist.

Once you have made your position clear, it's time to find out what your partner needs to feel satisfied about this issue. There are two reasons why it's important to discover your partner's needs. First, it's fair. The other person has just as much right as you to feel satisfied, and if you expect help in meeting your needs, it's reasonable that you behave in the same way. But in addition to decency, there's another, practical reason for concerning yourself with what the other person wants. Just as an unhappy partner will make it hard for you to

A quarrel between friends, when made up, adds a new tie to friendship, as experience shows that the callosity formed round a broken bone makes it stronger than before.

St. Francis De Sales

become satisfied, a happy one will be more likely to cooperate in letting you reach your goals. Thus, it's in your own self-interest to discover and meet your partner's needs.

You can learn about your partner's needs simply by asking about them: "Now I've told you what I want and why. Tell me what you need to feel OK about this." Once your partner begins to talk, your job is to use the listening skills discussed earlier in this book to make sure you understand.

STEP 5—NEGOTIATE A SOLUTION

Now that you and your partner understand each other's needs, the goal becomes finding a way to meet them. This is done by developing as many potential solutions as possible and then evaluating them to decide which one best meets everyone's needs. Probably the best description of the win–win approach has been written by Thomas Gordon in his book *Parent Effectiveness Training.*[48] The following steps are a modification of this approach.

1. *Identify and define the conflict.* We've discussed identifying and defining the conflict in the preceding pages. It consists of discovering each person's problem and needs, setting the stage for meeting all of them.
2. *Generate a number of possible solutions.* In this step, the partners work together to think of as many means as possible to reach their stated ends. The key word here is *quantity:* It's important to generate as many ideas as you can think of without worrying about which ones are good or bad. Write down every thought that comes up, no matter how unworkable: Sometimes a far-fetched idea will lead to a more workable one.
3. *Evaluate the alternative solutions.* This is the time to talk about which solutions will work and which ones won't. It's important for all parties to be honest about their willingness to accept an idea. If a solution is going to work, everyone involved has to support it.
4. *Decide on the best solution.* Now that you've looked at all the alternatives, pick the one that looks best to everyone. It's important to be sure everybody understands the solution and is willing to try it out. Remember that your decision doesn't have to be final, but it should look potentially successful.

STEP 6—FOLLOW UP THE SOLUTION

You can't be sure the solution will work until you try it. After you've tested it for a while, it's a good idea to set aside some time to talk over its progress. You may find that you need to make some changes or even rethink the whole problem. The idea is to keep on top of the problem, to keep using creativity to solve it.

As you think about applying this method, it is important to keep two points in mind. First, realize the importance of following every step. Each one is essential to the success of your encounter, and skipping one or more can lead to misunderstandings that might cause the

conversation to degenerate into a negative spiral. After you have practiced the method a number of times and are familiar with it, this type
of problem solving will become almost second nature. You will then
be able to approach your conflicts without following this step-by-step
approach. But for the time being try to be patient and trust the value
of the pattern.

A second point to realize is that this method is not likely to flow
smoothly from one step to another in real life. You can expect and
prepare for a certain amount of resistance from the other person. As
Figure 10–1 shows, when a step doesn't meet with success, simply
move back and repeat the preceding ones as necessary.

Win–win solutions aren't always possible. There will be times

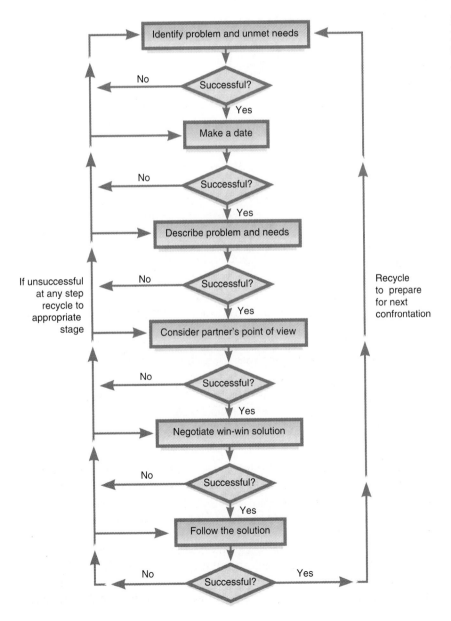

FIGURE 10–1
Flow chart of the win–win
negotiation process
Adapted from Rory Remer and Paul de
Mesquita. "Teaching and Learning Skills
of Interpersonal Confrontation" in *Inti-
mates in Conflict: A Communication
Perspective*, D.D. Cahn, ed., Hillsdale,
N.J.: Lawrence Erlbaum, 1990, p. 227.

© Bruce Eric Kaplan from The Cartoon Bank

when even the best-intentioned people simply won't be able to find a way of meeting all their needs. In cases like this, the process of negotiation has to include some compromises. But even then the preceding steps haven't been wasted. The genuine desire to learn what the other person wants and to try to satisfy those desires will build a climate of goodwill that can help you find the best solution to the present problem and also improve your relationship in the future.

SKILL BUILDER

WIN–WIN SOLUTIONS AND YOU

1. Make a list of the situations in your life in which a conflict of needs is creating tension between you and someone else.

2. Analyze what you're doing at present to resolve such conflicts, and describe whether your behavior is meeting with any success.

3. Pick at least one of the problems you just listed and, with the other people involved, try to develop a win–win solution by following the steps listed in the preceding pages.

4. After working through steps 1 to 5, disclose the results of your conference to the class. After you've had time to test your solution, report the progress you've made and discuss the follow-up conference described in step 6.

Communication Transcript

WIN–WIN PROBLEM SOLVING

It is 7:15 A.M. on a typical school day. Chris enters the kitchen and finds the sink full of dirty dishes. It was her roommate Terry's turn to do them. She sighs in disgust and begins to clean up, slamming pots and pans.

Terry   Can't you be a little more quiet? I don't have a class till 10:00 and I want to catch up on sleep.

Chris   *(Expressing her aggression indirectly in a sarcastic tone of voice)* Sorry to bother you. I was cleaning up last night's dinner dishes.

Terry   *(Misses the message)* Well, I wish you'd do it a little more quietly. I was up late studying last night, and I'm beat.

Chris   *(Decides to communicate her irritation more directly, if aggressively)* Well, if you'd done the dishes last night, I wouldn't have had to wash them now.

Terry   *(Finally realizes that Chris is mad at her, responds defensively)* I was going to do them when I got up. I've got two midterms this week and I was studying until midnight last night. What's more important, grades or a spotless kitchen?

Chris   *(Perpetuating the growing defensive spiral)* I've got classes too, you know. But that doesn't mean we have to live like pigs!

Terry   *(Angrily)* Forget it. If it's such a big deal, I'll never leave another dirty dish!

Chris and Terry avoid one another as they get ready for school. During the day Chris realizes that attacking Terry will only make matters worse. She decides on a more constructive approach that evening.

Chris   That wasn't much fun this morning. Want to talk about it?

Terry   I suppose so. But I'm going out to study with Kim and Alisa in a few minutes.

Chris   *(Realizing that it's important to talk at a good time)* If you have to leave soon, let's not get into it now. How about talking when you get back?

Terry   OK, if I'm not too tired.

Chris   Or we could talk tomorrow before class.

Terry   OK.

Later that evening Terry and Chris continue their conversation.

Chris   *(Defines the issue as her problem by using the assertive Clear Message format)* I hated to start the day with a fight. But I also hate having to do the dishes when it's not my turn *(behavior).* It doesn't seem fair for me to do my job and yours *(interpretation),* and that's why I got so mad *(feeling)* and nagged at you *(consequence).*

Terry   But I was studying! You know how much I have to do. It's not like I was partying.

Chris   *(Avoids attacking Terry by sincerely agreeing with the facts*

and explaining further why she was upset) I know. It wasn't just doing the dishes that got me upset. It seems like there have been a lot of times when I've done your jobs and mine too.

Terry   *(Defensively)* Like when?

Chris   *(Gives specific descriptions of Terry's behavior)* Well, this was the third time this week that I've done the dishes when it's your turn, and I can think of a couple of times lately when I've had to clean up your stuff before people came over.

Terry   I don't see why it's such a big deal. If you just leave the stuff there, I'll clean it up.

Chris   *(Still trying to explain herself, she continues to use "I" language.)* I know you would. I guess it's harder for me to put up with a messy place than it is for you.

Terry   Yeah. If you'd just relax, living together would be a lot easier!

Chris   *(Resenting Terry's judgmental accusation that the problem is all hers)* Hey, wait a second! Don't blame the whole thing on me. It's just that we have different standards. It looks to you like I'm too hung up on keeping the place clean . . .

Terry   Right.

Chris   . . . and if we do it your way, then I'd be giving up. I'd have to either live with the place messier than I like it or clean

(continued on next page)

Communication Transcript continued

everything up myself. Then I'd get mad at you and things would be pretty tense around here. *(Describes the unpleasant consequences of not solving the problem in a mutually satisfactory way)*

Terry I suppose so.

Chris We need to figure out how to take care of the apartment in a way that we can both live with. *(Describes the broad outline of a win–win solution)*

Terry Yeah.

Chris So what could we do?

Terry *(Sounding resigned)* Look, from now on I'll just do the dishes right away. It isn't worth arguing about.

Chris Sure it is. If you're sore, the apartment may be clean but it won't be worth it.

Terry *(Skeptically)* OK; what do you suggest?

Chris Well, I'm not sure. You don't want the pressure of having to clean up right away, and I don't want to have to do my jobs and yours too. Right?

Terry Yeah. *(Still sounding skeptical)* So what are we going to do—hire a housekeeper to clean up?

Chris *(Refusing to let Terry sidetrack the discussion)* That would be great if we could afford it. How about using paper plates? That would make cleaning up from meals easier.

Terry Yeah, but there would still be pots and pans.

Chris Well, it's not a perfect fix, but it might help a little. *(Goes on to suggest other ideas)* How about cooking meals that don't take a lot of work to clean up—maybe more salads and less fried stuff that sticks to pans. That would be a better diet, too.

Terry Yeah. I do hate to scrub crusty frying pans. But that doesn't do anything about your wanting the living room picked up all the time, and I bet I still wouldn't keep the kitchen as clean as you like it. Keeping the place super clean just isn't as big a deal to me as it is for you.

Chris That's true, and I *don't* want to have to nag you! *(Clarifies the end she's seeking)* You know, it's not really cleaning up that bothers me. It's doing more than my share of work. I wonder if there's a way I could be responsible for keeping the kitchen clean and picking up if you could do something else to keep the workload even.

Terry Are you serious? I'd *love* to get out of doing the dishes! You mean you'd do them . . . and keep the place picked up . . . if I did something else?

Chris As long as the work was equal and you really did your jobs without me having to remind you.

Terry What kind of work would you want me to do?

Chris How about cleaning up the bathroom?

Terry Forget it. That's worse than doing the dishes.

Chris OK. How about cooking?

Terry That might work, but then we'd have to eat together all the time. It's nice to do our own cooking when we want to. It's more flexible that way.

Chris OK. But what about shopping? I hate the time it takes, and you don't mind it that much, do you?

Terry You mean shop for groceries? You'd trade that for cleaning the kitchen?

Chris Sure. And picking up the living room. It takes an hour each time we shop and we make two trips every week. Doing the dishes would be much quicker.

Terry All right!

The plan didn't work perfectly: At first Terry put off marketing until all the food was gone, and Chris took advantage by asking Terry to run other errands during her shopping trips. But their arrangement proved much more successful than the old situation. The apartment was cleaner and the workload more even, which satisfied Chris. Terry was less the object of Chris's nagging and she had no kitchen chores, which made her happier. Just as important, the relationship between Chris and Terry was more comfortable—thanks to win–win problem solving.

✜ CONSTRUCTIVE CONFLICT: QUESTIONS AND ANSWERS

After learning about win–win negotiating, people often express doubts about how well it can work. "It sounds like a good idea," they say, "but. . . . " Three questions arise more than any others, and they deserve an answer.

ISN'T THE WIN–WIN APPROACH TOO GOOD TO BE TRUE?

Research shows that seeking mutual benefit is not only desirable—it works. In fact, the win–win approach produces better results than a win–lose negotiating style.

In a series of experiments, Robert Axelrod presented subjects with a bargaining situation called "prisoner's dilemma," in which they could choose either to cooperate or betray a confederate.[49] There are three types of outcome in prisoner's dilemma: One partner can win big by betraying a confederate, both can win by cooperating, or both can lose by betraying one another.

Although cynics might assume that the most effective strategy is to betray a partner (a win–lose approach), Axelrod demonstrated that cooperation is actually the best hard-nosed choice. He staged a tournament in which participants played against a computer that was programmed to represent several negotiating strategies. The winning strategy was one called "Tit-for-Tat." It starts out by cooperating and continues to cooperate until the other party betrays it. After that, the program always does what the other player did on the previous move. It never punishes an opponent more than once for a betrayal, and it will always cooperate if the other player does.

A win–win Tit-for-Tat strategy succeeds for several reasons.[50] First, it isn't a patsy. It responds quickly to betrayal, discouraging others from taking unfair advantage. At the same time, it is quick to forgive. It doesn't hold a grudge: As soon as the other party cooperates, it does too. Finally, it isn't too sneaky. By making its behavior obvious and predictable, Tit-for-Tat creates an atmosphere of trust.

There are certainly some conflicts that can't be resolved with win–win outcomes. Only one suitor can marry the prince or princess, and only one person can be hired for the advertised job. Furthermore, it's impossible to reach a win–win solution when your partner refuses to cooperate. Most of the time, however, good intentions and creative thinking can lead to outcomes that satisfy everyone's needs.

ISN'T THE WIN–WIN APPROACH TOO ELABORATE?

The win–win approach described in the preceding pages is detailed and highly structured. In everyday life you may rarely use every step: Sometimes the problem at hand won't justify the effort, and other times you and your partner might not need to be so deliberate to take care of the issue. Nonetheless, while learning to use the method try to follow all the steps carefully. Once you have become familiar and skillful at using them all, you will be able to use whichever ones prove necessary in a given situation. For important issues, you are likely to find that every step of the win–win approach is important. If this process seems time-consuming, just consider the time and energy that will likely be required if you *don't* resolve the issue at hand.

ISN'T WIN–WIN NEGOTIATING *TOO* RATIONAL?

Frustrated readers often complain that the win–win approach is so sensible that only a saint could use it successfully. "Sometimes I'm so angry that I don't care about being supportive or empathetic or anything else," they say. "I just want to blow my top!"

When you feel like this, it's almost impossible to be rational. At times like these probably the most therapeutic thing to do is get your feelings off your chest in what George Bach calls a "Vesuvius"—an uncontrolled, spontaneous explosion. A Vesuvius can be a terrific way of blowing off steam, and, after you do so, it's often much easier to figure out a rational solution to your problem.

So we encourage you to have a Vesuvius, with the following qualifications: Be sure your partner understands what you're doing and realizes that whatever you say doesn't call for a response. Your partner should let you rant and rave for as long as you want without getting defensive or "tying in." Then when your eruption subsides, you can take steps to work through whatever still troubles you.

IS IT POSSIBLE TO CHANGE OTHERS?

Readers often agree that win–win problem solving would be terrific—if everyone had read *Looking Out/Looking In* and understood the method. "How can I get the other person to cooperate?" the question goes.

Though you won't always be able to gain your partner's cooperation, a good job of selling can do the trick most of the time. The key lies in showing that it's in the other person's self-interest to work together: "Look, if we can't settle this, we'll both feel miserable. But if we can find an answer, think how much better off we'll be." Notice that this sort of explanation projects both the favorable consequences of cooperating and the costs of competing.

You can also boost the odds of getting your partner's cooperation by modeling the communication skills described in this book. You've read that defense-arousing behavior is reciprocal, but so is supportive communication. If you can listen sincerely, avoid evaluative attacks, and empathize with your partner's concerns, for example, there's a good chance you'll get the same kind of behavior in return. And even if your cooperative attitude doesn't succeed, you'll gain self-respect from knowing that at least you behaved honorably and constructively.

❖ SUMMARY

Conflict is a fact of life in every interpersonal relationship. The way in which conflicts are handled plays a major role in the quality of a relationship. When managed constructively, they can lead to stronger and more satisfying interaction; but when they are handled poorly, relationships will suffer.

There are four ways a person can behave when faced with a conflict. A nonassertive approach avoids the conflict altogether. A directly aggressive approach attacks the other party, while a passive-aggressive approach expresses hostility obliquely. An indirect style hints about the nature of a problem, while an assertive approach confronts the issue directly, but without attacking the other party. A complete assertive message describes the behavior in question, at least one interpretation, the speaker's feelings, the consequences of the situation, and the speaker's intentions in making the statement.

The way a conflict is handled is not always the choice of a single person, since the parties influence one another as they develop a relational conflict style. This style may be complementary, symmetrical, or parallel; it can involve a combination of intimate and aggressive elements; and it can include constructive or destructive rituals. Besides being shaped by the relationship, a conflict style is also influenced by a person's gender and cultural background.

There are three outcomes to conflicts: win–lose, lose–lose, and win–win. A win–lose approach often disintegrates into a lose–lose outcome in which all the parties suffer. Win–win solutions are often possible, if the parties possess the proper attitude and skills.

❖ KEY TERMS

accommodation
assertion
avoidance
behavioral description
complementary conflict style
compromise
conflict
conflict ritual

consequence statement
crazymaking
direct aggression
indirect communication
intention statement
lose–lose problem solving
negotiation

nonassertion
parallel conflict style
passive aggression
relational conflict style
symmetrical conflict style
win–lose problem solving
win–win problem solving

❖ MORE RESOURCES IN CONFLICT MANAGEMENT

READINGS

Axelrod, Robert. *The Evolution of Cooperation.* New York: Basic Books, 1984.

A detailed study of how cooperation is possible in a world run by self-interest. Axelrod is a political scientist, but his work also applies to interpersonal conflicts. Especially useful are chapters on "How to Promote Cooperation," "The Social *Structure of Cooperation," and "The Robustness of Reciprocity."*

Fisher, Roger, and Scott Brown. *Getting Together: Building a Relationship That Gets to Yes.* Boston: Houghton Mifflin, 1988.

This outstanding book offers specific guidelines for managing conflicts constructively. The authors focus on ways to improve the ability to solve such problems as sorting out relational issues from content-related disputes, balancing emotion and reason, and learning how to be trustworthy without being naive.

Fisher, Roger, and Scott Brown. *Getting to Yes: Negotiating Agreement Without Giving In.* Boston: Houghton Mifflin, 1981.

This is perhaps the best of the expanding collection of books on the subject of negotiating. Fisher and Brown show that you needn't choose between being an aggressive, demanding negotiator and a pushover. Their discussion of principled negotiation shows how to seek win–win solutions whenever possible and what to do when you face a partner who seems interested only in winning at your expense.

Hocker, Joyce L., and William W. Wilmot. *Interpersonal Conflict.* third edition. Dubuque, Iowa: W.C. Brown, 1991.

A thorough survey of the nature of interpersonal conflict and how it can be resolved. This is an ideal second step for readers who want to explore the subject in further detail.

Kohn, Alfie. *No Contest: The Case Against Competition.* Boston: Houghton Mifflin, 1986.

Kohn offers extensive evidence suggesting competition is inherently destructive, both in society at large and in personal relationships. He goes on to demonstrate how cooperation can make people happier, more productive, and secure.

Spitzberg, Brian H., Daniel J. Canary, and William R. Cupach. "A Competence-based Approach to the Study of Interpersonal Conflict." In *Conflict in Personal Relationships,* edited by D.D. Cahn, Hillsdale, N.J.: Erlbaum, 1994.

This chapter applies the principles of communicative competence to conflict management. It reinforces the notion of competence introduced in Chapter One of Looking Out/Looking In: *No single approach will work in every situation. In discussing the relative merits of assertive and more passive approaches, the chapter captures the challenges faced by communicators who strive to meet their personal goals while maintaining positive relationships.*

FILMS

LETTING GO OF AGGRESSION

On Golden Pond (1981) Rated PG

Eighty-year-old Norman Thayer, Jr. (Henry Fonda) is the textbook example of a curmudgeon. He grouses, complains, and tries to control every situation with a mixture of bravado and sarcasm. His loving wife, Ethel (Katharine Hepburn), takes Norman's sour disposition in stride, but their daughter, Chelsea (Jane Fonda), has always reacted to his criticism with a hostility that masks her pain at not receiving the affection she desperately wants. Norman begins to soften his tone after learning some important truths about parenting from part of a summer spent with Billy Ray, the young son of Chelsea's fiancé, and from an assertive message delivered by Billy's dad (Dabney Coleman).

As Norman softens his aggression, Chelsea can begin to lower her defenses too. A relationship that was a model of reciprocal hostility begins to move slowly and cautiously toward a more respectful one. Norman may never be able to express his love and his fears directly and assertively, but by moving away from a sarcastic, aggressive style he reaches out to his daughter before it is too late.

PORTRAIT OF LOSE–LOSE CONFLICT

The War of the Roses (1989) Rated R

The War of the Roses was billed as a black comedy, but there is little to laugh about in this grim film. Oliver and Barbara Rose (Michael Douglas and Kathleen Turner) play a couple whose "perfect marriage" falls apart when they encounter their respective mid-life crises. Their decision to divorce is not nearly as depressing as their escalating hostility: Oliver and Barbara would rather die than sacrifice either their egos or their possessions.

The Roses' battles soon escalate to the point of absurdity, but anyone who has seen the self-defeating lengths to which some people will go in a dysfunctional conflict will find the film's theme sadly familiar. A civil divorce is hardly the goal to which any couple aspires, but after viewing the mutual destruction that arises from situations like the Roses', couples who can handle their breakup decently seem as deserving of admiration as sympathy.

Endnotes

References for Chapter 1

1. J.B. Ross and M.M. McLaughlin, eds, *A Portable Medieval Reader* (New York: Viking, 1949).
2. S. Schachter, *The Psychology of Affiliation* (Stanford, Calif.: Stanford University Press, 1959), pp. 9–10.
3. VPI, *Wisconsin State Journal*, Sept. 7, 1978.
4. E.B. McDaniel with J. Johnson, *Scars and Stripes* (Philadelphia: A.J. Holman, 1975), p. 40.
5. Three articles in *The Journal of the American Medical Association* 267 (January 22/29, 1992) discuss the link between psychosocial influences and coronary heart disease: R.B. Case, A.J. Moss, N. Case, M. McDermott, and S. Eberly, "Living Alone After Myocardial Infarction" (pp. 515–519); R.B. Williams, J.C. Barefoot, R.M. Califf, T.L. Haney, W.B. Saunders, D.B. Pryon, M.A. Hlatky, I.C. Siegler, and D.B. Mark, "Prognostic Importance of Social and Economic Resources among Medically Treated Patients with Angiographically Documented Coronary Artery Disease" (pp. 520–524); and R. Ruberman, "Psychosocial Influences on Mortality of Patients with Coronary Heart Disease" (pp. 559–560).
6. R. Narem, "Try a Little TLC," research reported in *Science* 80: 1 (1980): 15.
7. J. Lynch, *The Broken Heart: The Medical Consequences of Loneliness* (New York: Basic Books, 1977), pp. 239–242.
8. Ibid.
9. E.A. Liljefors and R.H. Rahe, "Psychosocial Characteristics of Subjects with Myocardial Infarction in Stockholm," in *Life Stress Illness*, E.K. Gunderson and R.H. Rahe, eds. (Springfield, Ill.: Charles C Thomas, 1974), pp. 90–104.
10. W.D. Rees and S.G. Lutkins, "Mortality of Bereavement," *British Medical Journal* 4 (1967): 13.
11. R. Shattuck, *The Forbidden Experiment: The Story of the Wild Boy of Aveyron* (New York: Farrar, Straus & Giroux, 1980), p. 37.
12. A.M. Nicotera, "Where Have We Been, Where Are We, and Where Do We Go?" in *Interpersonal Communication in Friend and Mate Relationships*, A.M. Nicotera and associates, (Albany: State University of New York Press, 1993).
13. R.B. Rubin, E.M. Perse, and C.A. Barbato, "Conceptualization and Measurement of Interpersonal Communication Motives," *Human Communication Research* 14 (1988): 602–628.
14. W. Goldschmidt, *The Human Career: The Self in the Symbolic World* (Cambridge, Mass.: Basil Blackman, 1990).
15. J. Flanigan, "For All of Us, the Future of Labor Lies in Learning," *Los Angeles Times*, Sept. 5, 1993, p. D5.
16. R.M. Kanter, "The New Managerial Work," *Harvard Business Review* 66 (November–December 1989): 85–92.
17. A.H. Maslow, *Toward a Psychology of Being* (New York: Van Nostrand Reinhold, 1968).
18. C.E. Shannon and W. Weaver, *The Mathematical Theory of Communication* (Urbana, Ill.: University of Illinois Press, 1949).
19. J.B. Walther, "Impression Development in Computer-Mediated Interaction." *Western Journal of Communication* 57 (1993); 391–398 and J.B. Walther and J.K. Burgoon, "Relational Communication in Computer-Mediated Interaction." *Human Communication Research* 19 (1992): 50–88.
20. D. Kirkpatrick, "Here Comes the Payoff from PCs." *Fortune* (March 23, 1992): 93–102.
21. D. Tannen, "Gender Gap in Cyberspace." *Newsweek* (May 16, 1994): 52–53.
22. The issue of intentionality has been a matter of debate by communication theorists. For a sample of the arguments on both sides, see M.T. Motley, "On Whether One Can(not) Communicate: An Examination via Traditional Communication Postulates," *Western Journal of Speech Communication* 54 (1990): I–20; J.B. Bavelas, "Behaving and CommuniJcating: A Reply to Motley," *Western Journal of Speech Communication* 54 (1990): 593–602; and J. Stewart, "A Postmodern Look at Traditional Communication Postulates," *Western Journal of Speech Communication* 55 (1991): 354–379.
23. K.R. Colbert, "The Effects of Debate Participation on Argumentativeness and Verbal Aggression," *Communication Education* 42 (1993): 206–214.
24. E.M. Rogers and D.L. Kincaid, *Communication Networks: Toward a New Paradigm for Research* (New York: Free Press, 1981), pp. 43–48, 63–66.
25. S. Duck, "Relationships as Unfinished Business: Out of the Frying Pan and into the 1990s," *Journal of Social and Personal Relationships* 7 (1990): 5. See also J.N. Capella, "The Biological Origins of Automated Patterns of Human Interaction," *Communication Theory* 1 (1991): 4–35.
26. K.J. Gergen, *The Saturated Self: Dilemmas of Identity in Contemporary Life* (New York: Basic Books, 1991), p. 158.
27. M. Dainton and L. Stafford, "The Dark Side of 'Normal' Family Interaction," in *The Dark Side of Interpersonal Communication*, B.H. Spitzberg and W.R. Cupach, eds. (Hillsdale, N.J.: Erlbaum, 1993).
28. For a detailed rationale of the position argued in this section, see G.H. Stamp and M.L. Knapp, "The Construct of Intent in Interpersonal Communication," *Quarterly Journal of Speech* 76 (1990): 282–299.
29. For a thorough discussion of communication difficulties, see N. Coupland, H. Giles, and J.M. Wiemann, eds., *"Miscommunication" and Problematic Talk* (Newbury Park, Calif.: Sage, 1991).
30. Adapted from J. McCroskey and L. Wheeless, *Introduction to Human Communication* (Boston: Allyn and Bacon, 1976), pp. 3–10.
31. Ibid., p. 5. See also D.H. Cloven and M.E. Roloff, "Sense-Making Activities and Interpersonal Conflict: Communicative Cures for the Mulling Blues," *Western Journal of Speech Communication* 55 (1991): 134–158.
32. See, for example, G.R. Miller and M. Steinberg, *Between People: A New Analysis of Interpersonal Communication* (Chicago: SRA, 1975), and J. Stewart and C. Logan, *Together: Communicating Interpersonally*, 4th ed. (New York: McGraw-Hill, 1993).
33. M. Buber, *I and Thou*, trans. W. Kaufmann (New York: Scribner, 1970).
34. For a detailed discussion of the difference between interpersonal and impersonal communication, see J. Stewart, "Interpersonal Communication: Contact Between Persons" in *Bridges Not Walls: A Book About Interpersonal Communication*, 6th ed., J. Stewart, ed., (New York: McGraw-Hill, 1995), pp. 15–34.
35. For further discussion of the characteristics of impersonal and interpersonal communication, see Arthur P. Bochner, "The Functions of Human Communication in Interpersonal Bonding," in *Handbook of Rhetorical and Communication Theory*, C.C. Arnold and J.W. Bowers, eds. (Boston: Allyn and Bacon, 1984), p. 550; S. Trenholm and A. Jensen, *Interpersonal Communication*, 2nd ed. (Belmont, Calif.: Wadsworth, 1992), pp. 27–33; J. Stewart and G. D'Angelo, *Together: Communicating Interpersonally*, 3d ed. (New York: Random House, 1988), p. 5.
36. See P. Watzlawick, J.H. Beavin, and D.D. Jackson, *Pragmat-*

ics of Human Communication (New York: Norton, 1967), and W.J. Lederer and D.D. Jackson, *The Mirages of Marriage* (New York: Norton, 1968).

37. D. Tannen, *That's Not What I Meant! How Conversational Style Makes or Breaks Your Relations with Others* (New York: Morrow, 1986), p. 190.

38. T.S. Lim and J.W. Bowers, "Facework: Solidarity, Approbation, and Tact," *Human Communication Research* 17 (1991): 415–450.

39. M.T. Palmer, "Controlling Conversations: Turns, Topics, and Interpersonal Control," *Communication Monographs* 56 (1989): 1–18.

40. Watzlawick, Beavin, and Jackson, op. cit.

41. For a summary of the three types of symmetry, see W. Wilmot, *Dyadic Communication* (New York: Random House, 1987), pp. 132–134.

42. For a thorough review of this topic, see B.H. Spitzberg and W.R. Cupach, *Handbook of Interpersonal Competence Research* (New York: Springer-Verlag, 1989).

43. M. Fitzpatrick, *Between Husbands and Wives: Communication in Marriage* (Newbury Park, Calif.: Sage, 1989).

44. B.H. Spitzberg, "An Examination of Trait Measures of Interpersonal Competence," *Communication Reports* 4 (1991): 22–29.

45. See Y.Y. Kim, "Intercultural Communication Competence: A Systems-Theoretic View," in *Cross-Cultural Interpersonal Communication*, S. Ting-Toomey and F. Korzenny, eds. (Newbury Park, Calif.: Sage, 1991).

46. See, for example, L.A. Baxter, "The Social Side of Personal Relationships: A Dialectical Perspective," in *Social Context and Relationship*, S.W. Duck, ed., Newbury Park, Calif.: Sage 1993; W.K. Rawlins, *Friendship Matters: Communication, Dialectics, and the Life Course* (New York: Aldine de Gruyter, 1992); H. Spitzberg, "The Dark Side of (In)Competence," in B. Spitzberg and W.R. Cupach, eds., *The Dark Side of Interpersonal Communication*, op. cit.

47. J.M. Wiemann and P.M. Backlund, "Current Theory and Research in Communication Competence," *Review of Educational Research* 50 (1980): 185–199. See also M.V. Redmond, "The Relationship Between Perceived Communication Competence and Perceived Empathy," *Communication Monographs* 52 (December 1985): 377–382, and M.V. Redmond, "The Functions of Empathy (Decentering) in Human Relations," *Human Relations* 42 (1989): 593–605.

48. D.B. Wackman, S. Miller, and E.W. Nunnally, *Student Workbook: Increasing Awareness and Communication Skills* (Minneapolis: Interpersonal Communication Programs, 1976), p. 6.

49. See, for example, R. Martin, "Relational Cognition Complexity and Relational Communication in Personal Relationships," *Communication Monographs* 59 (1992): 150–163; D.W. Stacks and M.A. Murphy, "Conversational Sensitivity: Further Validation and Extension," *Communication Reports* 6 (1993); 18–24; and A.L. Vangelisti, and S.M. Draughton, "The Nature and Correlates of Conversational Sensitivity," *Human Communication Research* 14 (1987): 167–202.

50. Research summarized in D.E. Hamachek, *Encounters with the Self*, 2d ed. (Fort Worth, Tex. : Holt, Rinehart and Winston, 1987), p. 8.

51. Adapted from the work of R.P. Hart as reported by M.L. Knapp in *Interpersonal Communication and Human Relationships* (Boston: Allyn and Bacon, 1984), pp. 342–344. See also R.P. Hart and D.M. Burks, "Rhetorical Sensitivity and Social Interaction," *Speech Monographs* 39 (1972): 75–91;

and R.P. Hart, R.E. Carlson, and W.F. Eadie, "Attitudes Toward Communication and the Assessment of Rhetorical Sensitivity," *Communication Monographs* 47 (1980), 1–22.

References for Chapter 2

1. For a discussion of how the self-concept develops, see D. Hamachek, *Encounters with the Self*, 3rd ed. (Fort Worth, Tex. : Holt, Rinehart and Winston, 1992), pp. 5–8.

2. C.H. Cooley, *Human Nature and the Social Order* (New York: Scribner's, 1912).

3. J.B. Miller, "Learning from Early Relationship Experience," in *Learning About Relationships*, S. Duck, ed. (Newbury Park, Calif.: Sage, 1993).

4. G.J. McCall, "The Self-Concept and Interpersonal Communication," in M.E. Roloff and G.R. Miller, eds., *Interpersonal Processes: New Directions in Communication Research* (Newbury Park, Calif.: Sage, 1987).

5. J.D. Brown, N.J. Novick, K.A. Lord, and J.M. Richards, "When Gulliver Travels: Social Context, Psychological Closeness, and Self-Appraisals," *Journal of Personality and Social Psychology* 62 (1992): 717–734.

6. P.N. Myers and F.A. Biocca, "The Elastic Body Image: The Effect of Television Advertising and Programming on Body Image Distortions in Young Women," *Journal of Communication* 42 (1992): 108–134.

7. J.D. Brown and T.A. Mankowski, "Self-Esteem, Mood, and Self-Evaluation: Changes in Mood and the Way You See You," *Journal of Personality and Social Psychology* 64 (1993): 421–430.

8. M.A. Gara, R.L. Woolfolk, B.D. Cohen, R.B. Goldston, "Perception of Self and Other in Major Depression," *Journal of Abnormal Psychology* 102 (1993): 93–100.

9. B. Bower, "Truth Aches: People Who View Themselves Poorly May Seek the 'Truth' and Find Despair," *Science News* (August 15, 1992): 110–111; and W.B. Swann, R.M. Wenzlaff, D.S. Krull, and B.W. Pelham, "Allure of Negative Feedback: Self-Verification Strivings among Depressed Persons," *Journal of Abnormal Psychology* 101 (1992): 293–306.

10. L.C. Miller, L.L. Cooke, J. Tsang, and F. Morgan, "Should I Brag? Nature and Impact of Positive and Boastful Disclosures for Women and Men," *Human Communication Research* 18 (1992): 364–399.

11. H. Giles and P. Johnson, "'Ethnolinguistic Identity Theory': A Social Psychological Approach to Language Maintenance," *International Journal of Sociology of Language* 68 (1987): 69–99.

12. S.P. Banks, "Achieving 'Unmarkedness' in Organizational Discourse: A Praxis Perspective on Ethnolinguistic Identity," *Journal of Language and Social Psychology* 6 (1982): 171–190.

13. J. Servaes, "Cultural Identity and Modes of Communication," in *Communication Yearbook 12*, J.A. Anderson, ed. (Newbury Park, Calif.: Sage, 1989), p. 396.

14. A. Bharti, "The Self in Hindu Thought and Action," in *Culture and Self: Asian and Western Perspectives* (New York: Tavistock, 1985).

15. W.B. Gudykunst and S. Ting-Toomey, *Culture and Interpersonal Communication* (Newbury Park, Calif.: Sage, 1988).

16. L.A. Samovar and R.E. Porter, *Communication between Cultures* (Belmont, Calif.: Wadsworth, 1991), p. 91.

17. D. Klopf, "Cross-Cultural Apprehension Research: A Summary of Pacific Basin Studies," in *Avoiding Communication: Shyness, Reticence, and Communication*

Apprehension, J. Daly and J. McCroskey, eds. (Beverly Hills, Calif.: Sage, 1984).

18. S. Ting-Toomey, "A Face-Negotiation Theory," in *Theory in Interpersonal Communication,* Y. Kim and W. Gudykunst, eds. (Newbury Park, Calif.: Sage, 1988).

19. J. Kolligan, Jr., "Perceived Fraudulence as a Dimension of Perceived Incompetence," in R.J. Sternberg and J. Kolligen, Jr., eds. *Competence Considered* (New Haven, Conn.: Yale University Press, 1990).

20. R. Rosenthal and L. Jacobson, *Pygmalion in the Classroom* (New York: Holt, Rinehart and Winston, 1968).

21. Ibid., pp. 5–6.

22. E. Goffman, *The Presentation of Self in Everyday Life* (Garden City, N.Y.: Doubleday, 1959) and *Relations in Public* (New York: Basic Books, 1971).

23. V. Brightman, A. Segal, P. Werther, and J. Steiner, "Ethological Study of Facial Expression in Response to Taste Stimuli," *Journal of Dental Research* 54 (1975): 141.

24. N. Chovil, "Social Determinants of Facial Displays," *Journal of Nonverbal Behavior* 15 (1991): 141–154.

25. M.R. Leary and R.M. Kowalski, "Impression Management: A Literature Review and Two-Component Model," *Psychological Bulletin* 107 (1990): 34–47.

26. M. Snyder, *Public Appearances, Private Realities: The Psychology of Self-Monitoring* (New York: W.H. Freeman, 1987).

27. The following discussion is based on material in Hamachek, *Encounters with the Self,* 3rd ed., pp. 24–26.

28. L.M. Coleman and B.M. DePaulo, "Uncovering the Human Spirit: Moving beyond Disability and 'Missed' Communications," in *"Miscommunication" and Problematic Talk,* N. Coupland, H. Giles, and J.M. Wiemann, eds. (Newbury Park, Calif.: Sage, 1991), pp. 61–84.

29. J.W. Vander Zanden, *Social Psychology,* 3rd ed. (New York: Random House, 1984), pp. 235–237.

References for Chapter 3

1. The graphic demonstrations of factors influencing perception in this and the following paragraph are borrowed from Dennis Coon's *Introduction to Psychology,* 6th ed. (St. Paul, Minn.: West, 1992).

2. G.W. Allport, *The Nature of Prejudice* (New York: Doubleday Anchor, 1958), p. 185.

3. M. Hewstone and R. Brown, "Contact Is Not Enough," in M. Hewstone and R. Brown, eds., *Contact and Conflict in Intergroup Encounters* (Oxford, U.K.: Basil Blackwell, 1986), p. 29. See also H. Giles, N. Coupland, J. Coupland, A. Williams, and J. Nussbaum, "Intergenerational Talk and Communication with Older People," *International Journal of Aging and Human Development* 33 (1992): 251–297.

4. P. Watzlawick, J. Beavin, and D.D. Jackson, *Pragmatics of Human Communication* (New York: Norton, 1967), p. 65.

5. See T.N. Bradbury and F.D. Fincham, "Attributions in Marriage: Review and Critique," *Psychological Bulletin* 107 (1990): 3–33; and V. Manusov, "An Application of Attribution Principles to Nonverbal Behavior in Romantic Dyads," *Communication Monographs* 57 (1990): 104–118.

6. V. Manusov, "It Depends on Your Perspective: Effects of Stance and Beliefs about Intent on Person Perception," *Western Journal of Communication* 57 (1993): 27–41.

7. T. Adler, "Enter Romance, Exit Objectivity," *APA Monitor* (June 1992): 18.

8. For a detailed description of how the senses affect perception, see N. Ackerman, *A Natural History of the Senses* (New York: Random House, 1990).

9. J. Piaget, *The Origins of Intelligence in Children* (New York: International Universities Press, 1952).

10. C. Cooper and C. McConville, "Interpreting Mood Scores: Clinical Implications of Individual Differences in Mood Variability," *British Journal of Medical Psychology* 63 (1990): 215–225. See also J. Mendlewicz and H.M. van Praag, eds., *Biological Rhythms and Behavior* (New York: Karger, 1983).

11. E. Ramey, "Men's Cycles," *Ms.* 1 (Spring 1972): 10–14.

12. J.W. Bagby, "A Cross-Cultural Study of Perceptual Predominance in Binocular Rivalry," *Journal of Abnormal and Social Psychology* 54 (1957): 331–334.

13. R. Armao, "Worst Blunders; Firms Laugh through Tears," *American Business* (January 1981): 11.

14. R. Harrison, "Nonverbal Behavior: An Approach to Human Communication," in *Approaches to Human Communication,* R. Budd and B. Ruben, eds. (New York: Spartan Books, 1972).

15. E.T. Hall, *The Hidden Dimension* (New York: Doubleday Anchor, 1969), p. 160.

16. H. Giles, N. Coupland, and J.M. Wiemann, "Talk Is Cheap . . . But 'My Word Is My Bond': Beliefs about Talk," in *Sociolinguistics Today: International Perspectives,* K. Bolton and H. Kwok, eds. (London: Routledge & Kegan Paul, 1992).

17. J. Horn, "Conversation Breakdowns: As Different as Black and White," *Psychology Today* 8 (May 1974): 30.

18. P. Andersen, M. Lustig, and J. Anderson, "Changes in Latitude, Changes in Attitude: The Relationship Between Climate, Latitude, and Interpersonal Communication Predispositions," paper presented at the annual convention of the Speech Communication Association, Boston, 1987; and P. Andersen, M. Lustig, and J. Andersen, "Regional Patterns of Communication in the United States: Empirical Tests," paper presented at the annual convention of the Speech Communication Association, New Orleans, 1988.

19. See S.A. Rathus, *Psychology,* 5th ed. (Fort Worth, Tex. : Harcourt Brace Jovanovich, 1993), pp. 640–643; and C. Wade and C. Tavris, *Psychology* (New York: Harper & Row, 1987), pp. 488–490.

20. S.L. Bem, "Androgyny and Gender Schema Theory: A Conceptual and Empirical Integration," in *Nebraska Symposium on Motivation: Psychology and Gender,* T.B. Sonderegger, ed. (Lincoln: University of Nebraska Press, 1985).

21. P.G. Zimbardo, C. Haney, and W.C. Banks, "A Pirandellian Prison," *New York Times Magazine,* April 8, 1973.

22. See, for example, P. Baron, "Self-Esteem, Ingratiation, and Evaluation of Unknown Others," *Journal of Personality and Social Psychology* (1974): 104–109.

23. D.E. Hamachek, *Encounters with Others: Interpersonal Relationships and You* (New York: Holt, Rinehart and Winston, 1982), p. 3.

24. D. Hamachek, *Encounters with the Self,* 3d ed. (Fort Worth, Tex. : Harcourt Brace Jovanovich, 1992).

25. For a review of these perceptual biases, see Hamachek, *Encounters with the Self.* See also Bradbury and Fincham, op. cit.

26. B. Sypher and H.E. Sypher, "Seeing Ourselves as Others See Us," *Communication Research* 11 (January 1984): 97–115.

27. Reported by D. Myers, "The Inflated Self," *Psychology Today* 14 (May 1980): 16.

28. J.B. Stiff, J.P. Dillard, L. Somera, H. Kim, and C. Sleight, "Empathy, Communication, and Prosocial Behavior," *Communication Monographs* 55 (1988): 198–213.

29. R. Lennon and N. Eisenberg, "Gender and Age Differences in Empathy and Sympathy," in *Empathy and Its Development,* N. Eisenberg and J. Strayer, eds. (Cambridge, U.K.: Cambridge University Press, 1987).

30. T. Adler, "Look at Duration, Depth in Research on Emotion," *APA Monitor* (October 1990): 10.
31. N.D. Feshbach, "Parental Empathy and Child Adjustment/Maladjustment," in Eisenberg and Strayer, op. cit.
32. Paul Reps, "Pillow Education in Rural Japan," in *Square Sun, Square Moon* (New York: Tuttle, 1967).

References for Chapter 4

1. P. Ekman, R.W. Levenson, and W.V. Friesen, "Autonomic Nervous System Activity Distinguishes among Emotions," *Science* 221 (September 16, 1983): 1208–1210.
2. S. Valins, "Cognitive Effects of False Heart-Rate Feedback," *Journal of Personality and Social Psychology* 4 (1966): 400–408.
3. P. Zimbardo, *Shyness: What It Is, What to Do about It* (Reading, Mass.: Addison-Wesley, 1977), p. 53.
4. Ibid., p. 54.
5. R. Plutchik, "A Language for the Emotions," *Psychology Today* 14 (February 1980): 68–78. For a more detailed explanation, see R. Plutchik, *Emotion: A Psychoevolutionary Synthesis* (New York: Harper & Row, 1980).
6. C.R. Bush, J.P. Bush, and J. Jennings, "Effects of Jealousy Threats on Relationship Perceptions and Emotions," *Journal of Social and Personal Relationships* 5 (1988): 285–303.
7. M. Mikulincer and J. Segal, "A Multidimensional Analysis of the Experience of Loneliness," *Journal of Social and Personal Relationships* 7 (1990): 209–230.
8. Plutchik, "A Language for the Emotions."
9. W.B. Gudykunst and Y.K. Young, *Communicating with Strangers* (New York: McGraw-Hill, 1992), pp. 173–174.
10. S. Ting-Toomey, "Intimacy Expressions in Three Cultures: France, Japan, and the United States," *International Journal of Intercultural Relations* 15 (1991): 29–46.
11. Ibid., p. 176. See also C. Gallois, "The Language and Communication of Emotion: Universal, Interpersonal, or Intergroup?" *American Behavioral Scientist* 36 (1993): 309–338.
12. H.C. Triandis, *Culture and Social Behavior* (New York: McGraw-Hill, 1994), p. 169. See also F.M. Moghaddam, D.M. Taylor, and S.C. Wright, *Social Psychology in Cross-Cultural Perspective* (New York: Freeman, 1993).
13. L.R. Brody and J.A. Hall, *Gender and Emotion*, in *Handbook of Emotions*, M. Lewis and J.M. Haviland, eds. (New York: Guilford, 1993), pp. 451–452.
14. J. Hall, "Gender Effects in Decoding Nonverbal Cues," *Psychological Bulletin* 85 (1978): 845–857.
15. S.E. Snodgrass, "Women's Intuition: The Effect of Subordinate Role on Interpersonal Sensitivity," *Journal of Personality and Social Psychology* 49 (1985): 146–155.
16. S.B. Shimanoff, "Commonly Named Emotions in Everyday Conversations," *Perceptual and Motor Skills* 58 (1984): 514. See also J.M. Gottmann, "Emotional Responsiveness in Marital Conversations," *Journal of Communication* 32 (1982): 108–120.
17. S.B. Shimanoff, "Degree of Emotional Expressiveness as a Function of Face-Needs, Gender, and Interpersonal Relationship," *Communication Reports* 1 (1988): 43–53.
18. C.A. Stearns and P. Stearns, *Anger: The Struggle for Emotional Control in America's History* (Chicago: University of Chicago Press, 1986).
19. S.B. Shimanoff, "Rules Governing the Verbal Expression of Emotions Between Married Couples," *Western Journal of Speech Communication* 49 (1985): 149–165.
20. S. Duck, "Social Emotions: Showing Our Feelings about Other People," in *Human Relationships* (Newbury Park, Calif.: Sage, 1992). See also S.B. Shimanoff, "Expressing Emotions in Words: Verbal Patterns of Interaction," *Journal of Communication* 35 (1985): 16–31.

21. L.B. Rosenfeld, "Self-Disclosure and Avoidance: Why Am I Afraid to Tell You Who I Am?" *Communication Monographs* 46 (1979): 63–74.
22. S.A. McCornack and T.R. Levine, "When Lovers Become Leery: The Relationship between Suspicion and Accuracy in Detecting Deception," *Communication Monographs* 57 (1990): 219–230.
23. M. Booth-Butterfield and M.R.Trotta, "Attributinal Patterns for Expressions of Love." *Communication Reports* 7 (1994): 119–129.
24. J.A. Bargh, "Automatic Information Processing: Implications for Communication and Affect," in *Communication, Social Cognition, and Affect*, H.E. Sypher and E.T. Higgins, eds. (Hillsdale, N.J.: Erlbaum, 1988).
25. S. Metts and W.R. Cupach, "The Influence of Relationship Beliefs and Problem-Solving Relationships on Satisfaction in Romantic Relationships," *Human Communication Research* 17 (1990): 170–185.
26. A. Meichenbaum, *Cognitive Behavior Modification* (New York: Plenum, 1977).

References for Chapter 5

1. O. Sacks, *Seeing Voices: A Journey Into the World of the Deaf* (Berkeley: University of California Press, 1989), p. 17.
2. S.I. Hayakawa, *Language in Thought and Action* (New York: Harcourt Brace Jovanovich, 1964), p. 27.
3. M.L. Hecht, M.J. Collier, and S.A. Ribeau, *African American Communication: Ethnic Identity and Cultural Interpretation* (Newbury Park, Calif.: Sage, 1993), pp. 84–89.
4. E. K. E. Graham, M. Papa, and G.P. Brooks, "Functions of Humor in Conversation: Conceptualization and Measurement," *Western Journal of Communication* 56 (1992): 161–183.
5. W.B. Pearce and V. Cronen, *Communication, Action, and Meaning* (New York: Praeger, 1980). See also V. Cronen, V. Chen, and W.B. Pearce, "Coordinated Management of Meaning: A Critical Theory," in *Theories in Intercultural Communication*, Y.Y. Kim and W.B. Gudy-kunst, eds. (Newbury Park, Calif.: Sage, 1988).
6. M.G. Marcus, "The Power of a Name," *Psychology Today* 9 (October 1976): 75–77, 106.
7. A. Mehrabian, "Interrelationshps among Name Desirability, Name Uniqueness, Emotion Characteristics Connoted by Names, and Temperament," *Journal of Applied Social Psychology* 22 (1992): 1797–1808.
8. K.M. Steele and L.E. Smithwick, "First Names and First Impressions: A Fragile Relationship," *Sex Roles* 21 (1989): 517–523.
9. K. Foss and B. Edson, "What's in a Name? Accounts of Married Women's Name Choices," *Western Journal of Speech Communication* 53 (1989): 356–373.
10. K.L. Dion, "What's in a Title? The Ms. Stereotype and Images of Women's Titles of Address," *Psychology of Women Quarterly* 11 (1987): 21–36.
11. See, for example, R.K. Aune and Toshiyuki Kikuchi, "Effects of Language Intensity Similarity of Perceptions of Credibility, Relational Attributions, and Persuasion," *Journal of Language and Social Psychology* 12 (1993): 224–238.
12. H. Giles, J. Coupland, and N. Coupland, eds., *Contexts of Accommodation: Developments in Applied Sociolinguistics* (Cambridge: Cambridge University Press, 1991).
13. M. Weiner and A. Mehrabian, *A Language Within Language: Immediacy, a Channel in Verbal Communication* (New York: Appleton-Century-Crofts, 1968).
14. J.J. Bradac, J.M. Wiemann, and K. Schaefer, "The Language of Control in Interpersonal Communication," in *Strategic*

Interpersonal Communication, J.A. Daly and J.M. Wiemann, eds. (Hillsdale, N.J.: Erlbaum, 1994), pp. 102–104. See also S.H. Ng and J.J. Bradac, *Power in Language: Verbal Communication and Social Influence* (Newbury Park, Calif.: Sage 1993), p. 27.

15. L.A. Hosman, "The Evaluative Consequences of Hedges, Hesitations, and Intensifiers: Powerful and Powerless Speech Styles," *Human Communication Research* 15 (1989): 383–406.

16. J. Bradac and A. Mulac, "Attributional Consequences of Powerful and Powerless Speech Styles in a Crisis-Intervention Context," *Journal of Language and Social Psychology* 3 (1984): 1–19.

17. J.J. Bradac, "The Language of Lovers, Flovers [sic], and Friends: Communicating in Social and Personal Relationships," *Journal of Language and Social Psychology* 2 (1983): 141–162.

18. D. Geddes, "Sex Roles in Management: The Impact of Varying Power of Speech Style on Union Members' Perception of Satisfaction and Effectiveness," *Journal of Psychology* 126 (1992): 589–607.

19. E.M. Eisenberg, "Ambiguity as Strategy in Organizational Communication," *Communication Monographs* 51 (1984): 227–242; and E.M. Eisenberg and M.G. Witten, "Reconsidering Openness in Organizational Communication," *Academy of Management Review* 12 (1987): 418–426.

20. Reprinted in *Newsweek,* March 7, 1994, 54, and *Time,* October 11, 1993, 24.

21. See, for example, G.F. Will, "Sex Amidst Semicolons," *Newsweek,* October 4, 1993.

22. J.K. Alberts, "An Analysis of Couples' Conversational Complaints," *Communication Monographs* 55 (1988): 184–197.

23. T. Wallsten, "Measuring the Vague Meanings of Probability Terms," *Journal of Experimental Psychology* 115 (1986): 348–365.

24. E.S. Kubany, D.C. Richard, G.B. Bauer, and M.Y. Muraoka, "Impact of Assertive and Accusatory Communication of Distress and Anger: A Verbal Component Analysis," *Aggressive Behavior* 18 (1992): 337–347.

25. T. Gordon, *P.E.T.: Parent Effectiveness Training* (New York: Wyden, 1970), p. 145.

26. R. Raskin and R. Shaw, "Narcissism and the Use of Personal Pronouns," *Journal of Personality* 56 (1988): 393–404; and A.L. Vangelisti, M.L. Knapp, and J.A. Daly, "Conversational Narcissism," *Communication Monographs* 57 (1990): 251–274.

27. A.S. Dreyer, C.A. Dreyer, and J.E. Davis, "Individuality and Mutuality in the Language of Families of Field-Dependent and Field-Independent Children," *Journal of Genetic Psychology* 148 (1987): 105–117.

28. R.F. Proctor and J.R. Wilcox, "An Exploratory Analysis of Responses to Owned Messages in Interpersonal Communication," *ETC: A Review of General Semantics* 50 (1993): 201–220; and Vangelisti et al., *Conversational Narcissism,* op. cit.

29. S.L. Kirkland, J. Greenberg, and T. Pyszczynski, "Further Evidence of the Deleterious Effects of Overheard Derogatory Ethnic Labels: Derogation beyond the Target," *Personality and Social Psychology Bulletin* 12 (1987): 216–227.

30. See, for example, A. Haas and M.A. Sherman, "Conversational Topic as a Function of Role and Gender," *Psychological Reports* 51 (1982): 453–454; A. Haas and M.A. Sherman, "Reported Topics of Conversation among Same-Sex Adults," *Communication Quarterly* 30 (1982): 332–342.

31. J.T. Wood, *Gendered Lives: Communication, Gender, and Culture* (Belmont, Calif.: Wadsworth, 1994), p. 141.

32. M.A. Sherman and A. Haas, "Man to Man, Woman to Woman," *Psychology Today* 17 (June 1984): 72–73.

33. Haas and Sherman, "Conversational Topic as a Function of Role and Gender."

34. Research summarized by D. Tannen, *You Just Don't Understand: Women and Men in Conversation* (New York: Morrow, 1990).

35. J. Sachs, "Young Children's Language Use in Pretend Play," in *Language, Gender, and Sex in Comparative Perspective,* S.U. Philips, S. Steele, and C. Tanz, eds. (Cambridge: Cambridge University Press, 1987).

36. For a summary of research on differences between male and female conversational behavior, see H. Giles and R.L. Street, Jr., "Communication Characteristics and Behavior," in *Handbook of Interpersonal Communication,* M.L. Knapp and G.R. Miller, eds. (Beverly Hills, Calif.: Sage, 1985), pp. 205–261; and A. Kohn, "Girl Talk, Guy Talk," *Psychology Today* 22 (February 1988): 65–66.

37. V. deKlerk, "Expletives: Men Only?" *Communication Monographs* 58 (1991): 156–169.

38. A.J. Mulac, J.M. Wiemann, S.J. Widenmann, and T.W. Gibson, "Male/Female Language Differences and Effects in Same-Sex and Mixed-Sex Dyads: The Gender-Linked Language Effect," *Communication Monographs* 55 (1988): 315–335.

39. L.L. Carli, "Gender, Language, and Influence," *Journal of Personality and Social Psychology* 59 (1990): 941–951.

40. C.J. Zahn, "The Bases for Differing Evaluations of Male and Female Speech: Evidence from Ratings of Transcribed Conversation," *Communication Monographs* 56 (1989): 59–74.

41. D.S. Geddes, "Cross-Disciplinary Dialogue on the Effects of Gender Stereotypical Speech Style in a Management Setting." Paper presented at the Annual Meeting of the Eastern Communication Association, Baltimore, Md., April 1988.

42. For a thorough discussion of the challenges involved in translation from one language to another, see L.A. Samovar and R.E. Porter, *Communication between Cultures* (Dubuque, Iowa: W.C. Brown, 1991), pp. 165–169.

43. The examples in this paragraph are taken from D. Ricks, *Big Business Blunders: Mistakes in International Marketing* (Homewood, Ill.: Dow Jones-Irwin, 1983), p. 41.

44. N. Sugimoto, "'Excuse me' and 'I'm sorry': Apologetic Behaviors of Americans and Japanese." Paper presented at the Conference on Communication in Japan and the United States, California State University, Fullerton, California: March 1991.

45. A summary of how verbal style varies across cultures can be found in Chapter 5 of W.B. Gudykunst and S. Ting-Toomey, *Culture and Interpersonal Communication* (Newbury Park, Calif.: Sage, 1988).

46. E. Hall, *Beyond Culture* (New York: Doubleday, 1959).

47. M. Morris, *Saying and Meaning in Puerto Rico: Some Problems in the Ethnology of Discourse* (Oxford: Pergamon, 1981).

48. A. Almaney and A. Alwan, *Communicating with the Arabs* (Prospect Heights, Ill.: Waveland, 1982).

49. K. Basso, "To Give Up on Words: Silence in Western Apache Culture," *Southern Journal of Anthropology* 26 (1970): 213–230.

50. J. Yum, "The Practice of Uye-ri in Interpersonal Relationships in Korea," in *Communication Theory from Eastern and Western Perspectives,* D. Kincaid, ed. (New York: Academic Press, 1987).

51. L. Martin and G. Pullum, *The Great Eskimo Vocabulary Hoax* (Chicago: University of Chicago Press, 1991).

52. H. Giles and A. Franklyn-Stokes, "Communicator Characteristics," in *Handbook of International and Intercultural Communication,* M.K. Asante and W.B. Gudykunst, eds. (Newbury Park, Calif.: Sage, 1989).

53. L. Sinclair, "A Word in Your Ear," in *Ways of Mankind* (Boston: Beacon Press, 1954).

54. B. Whorf, "The Relation of Habitual Thought and Behavior to Language," in *Language, Thought, and Reality*, J.B. Carrol, ed. (Cambridge, Mass.: MIT Press, 1956).

55. H. Hoijer, quoted in T. Seinfatt, "Linguistic Relativity: Toward a Broader View," in *Language, Communication, and Culture: Current Directions*, S. Ting-Toomey and F. Korzenny, eds. (Newbury Park, Calif.: Sage, 1989).

56. H. Rheingold, *They Have a Word for It* (Los Angeles, Calif.: Jeremy P. Tarcher, 1988).

57. D.A. Prentice, "Do Language Reforms Change Our Ways of Thinking?" *Journal of Language and Social Psychology* 13 (1994): 3–19.

58. "Most Blacks Prefer 'Black' to 'African American,'" *Society* 28 May/June 1991: 2–3.

59. M. Hecht and S. Ribeau, "Sociocultural Roots of Ethnic Identity," *Journal of Black Studies* 21 (1991): 501–513.

References for Chapter 6

1. Research summarized by J.K Burgoon, "Nonverbal Signals," in *Handbook of Interpersonal Communication*, M.L. Knapp and G.R. Miller, eds. (Newbury Park, Calif.: Sage, 1994), p. 235.

2. Not all communication theorists agree with the claim that all nonverbal behavior has communicative value. For a contrasting opinion, see Burgoon, "Nonverbal Signals," pp. 229–232.

3. F. Manusov, "Perceiving Nonverbal Messages: Effects of Immediacy and Encoded Intent on Receiver Judgments," *Western Journal of Speech Communication* 55 (Summer 1991): 235–253.

4. R. Birdwhistell, *Kinesics and Context* (Philadelphia: University of Pennsylvania Press, 1970), Chapter 9.

5. P. Ekman, W.V. Friesen, and J. Baer, "The International Language of Gestures," *Psychology Today* 18 (May 1984): 64–69.

6. E. Hall, *The Hidden Dimension* (Garden City, N.Y.: Anchor Books, 1969).

7. A.M. Warnecke, R.D. Masters, and G. Kempter, "The Roots of Nationalism: Nonverbal Behavior and Xenophobia," *Ethnology and Sociobiology* 13 (1992): 267–282.

8. Hall, *The Hidden Dimension*.

9. D.L. Rubin, "'Nobody Play By the Rule He Know': Ethnic Interference in Classroom Questioning Events," in *Interethnic Communication: Recent Research*, Y.Y. Kim, ed. (Newbury Park, Calif.: Sage, 1986).

10. S. Weitz, ed., *Nonverbal Communication: Readings with Commentary* (New York: Oxford University Press, 1974).

11. J. Eibl-Eibesfeldt, "Universals and Cultural Differences in Facial Expressions of Emotions," *Nebraska Symposium on Motivation*, J. Cole, ed. (Lincoln, Neb.: University of Nebraska Press, 1972).

12. M. Booth-Butterfield and F. Jordan, "'Act Like Us': Communication Adaptation among Racially Homogeneous and Heterogeneous Groups." Paper presented at the Speech Communication Association meeting, New Orleans, 1988.

13. See S.W. Smith, "Perceptual Processing of Nonverbal Relational Messages," in *The Cognitive Bases of Interpersonal Communication*, D.E. Hewes, ed. (Hillsdale, N.J.: Erlbaum, 1994).

14. M.T. Motley, "Facial Affect and Verbal Context in Conversation: Facial Expression as Interjection," *Human Communication Research* 20 (1993): 3–40.

15. M. Moore, "Nonverbal Courtship Patterns in Women: Context and Consequences," *Ethology and Sociobiology* 6 (1985): 237–247.

16. P. Ekman and W.V. Friesen, "The Repertoire of Nonverbal Behavior: Categories, Origins, Usage, and Coding," *Semiotica* 1 (1969): 49–98.

17. See, for example, K. Drummond and R. Hopper, "Acknowledgment Tokens in Series," *Communication Reports* 6 (1993): 47–53; and H.M. Rosenfeld, "Conversational Control Functions of Nonverbal Behavior," in *Nonverbal Behavior and Communication*, 2d ed., A.W. Siegman and S. Feldstein, eds. (Hillsdale, N.J.: Erlbaum, 1987).

18. J. Hale and J.B. Stiff, "Nonverbal Primacy in Veracity Judgments," *Communication Reports* 3 (1990): 75–83; and J.B. Stiff, J.L. Hale, R. Garlick, and R.G. Rogan, "Effect of Cue Incongruence and Social Normative Influences on Individual Judgments of Honesty and Deceit," *Southern Speech Communication Journal* 55 (1990): 206–229.

19. J.K. Burgoon, T. Birk, and M. Pfau, "Nonverbal Behaviors, Persuasion, and Credibility," *Human Communication Research* 17 (1990): 140–169.

20. See, for example, B.M. DePaulo, "Detecting Deception Modality Effects," in *Review of Personality and Social Psychology*, Vol. 1, L. Wheeler, ed. (Beverly Hills, Calif.: 1980), and J. Greene, D. O'Hair, M. Cody, and C. Yen, "Planning and Control of Behavior During Deception," *Human Communication Research* 11 (1985): 335–364.

21. P. Kalbfleisch, "Deceit, Distrust, and Social Milieu: Applications of Deception Research in a Troubled World," *Journal of Applied Communication Research* (1992): 308–334.

22. D.B. Buller, J. Comstock, R.K. Aune, and K.D. Stryzewski, "The Effect of Probing on Deceivers and Truthtellers," *Journal of Nonverbal Behavior* 13 (1989): 155–170. See also D.B. Buller, K.D. Strzyzewski, and J. Comstock, "Interpersonal Deception: I. Deceivers' Reactions to Receivers' Suspicions and Probing," *Communication Monographs* 58 (1991): 1–24.

23. D.A. Lieberman, T.G. Rigo, and R.F. Campain, "Age-Related Differences in Nonverbal Decoding Ability," *Communication Quarterly* 36 (1988): 290–297.

24. S.A. McCornack and M.R. Parks, "What Women Know that Men Don't: Sex Differences in Determining the Truth Behind Deceptive Messages," *Journal of Social and Personal Relationships* 7 (1990): 107–118.

25. M.A. deTurck, "Training Observers to Detect Spontaneous Deception: Effects of Gender," *Communication Reports* 4 (1991): 81–89.

26. D. Druckmann, R. Rozelle, and J. Baxter, *Nonverbal Communication: Survey, Theory, and Research* (Beverly Hills, Calif.: Sage, 1982), p. 52.

27. M. Motley and C. Camden, "Facial Expression of Emotion: A Comparison of Posed Versus Spontaneous Expressions in an Interpersonal Communication Setting," *Western Journal of Speech Communication* 52 (1988): 1–22.

28. M.L. Knapp and J. Hall, *Nonverbal Communication in Human Interaction*, 3rd ed. (Fort. Worth, Tex.: Harcourt Brace Jovanovich, 1992), pp. 466–477.

29. J.A. Hall, "Gender, Gender Roles, and Nonverbal Communication Skills," in *Skill in Nonverbal Communication: Individual Differences*, R. Rosenthal, ed. (Cambridge, Mass.: Oelgeschlager, Gunn, and Hain, 1979), pp. 32–67.

30. Summarized in Burgoon, "Nonverbal Signals."

31. A. Mehrabian, *Silent Messages*, 2d ed. (Belmont, Calif.: Wadsworth, 1981), pp. 47–48, 61–62.

32. M.B. Myers, D. Templer, and R. Brown, "Coping Ability of Women Who Become Victims of Rape," *Journal of Consulting and Clinical Psychology* 52 (1984): 73–78. See also C. Rubenstein, "Body Language That Speaks to Muggers," *Psychology Today* 20 (August 1980): 20; and J. Meer, "Profile of a Victim," *Psychology Today* 24 (May 1984): 76.

33. A.E. Scheflen, "Quasi-Courting Behavior in Psychotherapy," *Psychiatry* 228 (1965): 245–257.

34. P. Ekman, *Telling Lies, Clues to Deceit in the Marketplace, Politics, and Marriage* (New York: Norton, 1985), pp. 109–110.
35. P. Ekman and W.V. Friesen, "Nonverbal Behavior and Psychopathology," in *The Psychology of Depression: Contemporary Theory and Research,* R.J. Friedman and M.N. Katz, eds. (Washington, D.C.: J. Winston, 1974).
36. Ekman, *Telling Lies,* p. 107.
37. P. Ekman and W.V. Friesen, *Unmasking the Face: A Guide to Recognizing Emotions from Facial Clues* (Englewood Cliffs, N.J.: Prentice-Hall, 1975).
38. Ibid., p. 150.
39. E.H. Hess and J.M. Polt, "Pupil Size as Related to Interest Value of Visual Stimuli," *Science* 132 (1960): 349–350.
40. E.T. Hall, *The Silent Language* (New York: Fawcett, 1959).
41. For a summary, see Knapp and Hall, op. cit., pp. 344–346.
42. A. Mehrabian and M. Wiener, "Decoding of Inconsistent Communications," *Journal of Personality and Social Psychology* 6 (1967): 109–114; also, A. Mehrabian and S. Ferris, "Interference of Attitudes from Nonverbal Communication in Two Channels," *Journal of Consulting Psychology* 31 (1967): 248–252.
43. D. Buller and K. Aune, "The Effects of Speech Rate Similarity on Compliance: Application of Communication Accommodation Theory," *Western Journal of Communication* 56 (1992): 37–53. See also D. Buller, B.A. LePoire, K. Aune, and S.V. Eloy, "Social Perceptions as Mediators of the Effect of Speech Rate Similarity on Compliance," *Human Communication Research* 19 (1992): 286–311; "The Effects of Vocalics and Nonverbal Sensitivity on Compliance: A Speech Accommodation Theory Explanation," *Human Communication Research* 14 (1988): 301–332.
44. Ekman, *Telling Lies,* p. 93.
45. P.A. Anderson, "Nonverbal Communication in the Small Group," in *Small Group Communication: A Reader,* 4th ed., R.S. Cathcart and L.A. Samovar, eds. (Dubuque, Iowa: W.C. Brown, 1984).
46. C.E. Kimble and S.D. Seidel, "Vocal Signs of Confidence," *Journal of Nonverbal Behavior* 15 (1991): 99–105.
47. M. Zuckerman and R.E. Driver, "What Sounds Beautiful Is Good: The Vocal Attractiveness Stereotype," *Journal of Nonverbal Behavior* 13 (1989): 67–82.
48. S.H. Ng and J.J. Bradac, *Power in Language: Verbal Communication and Social Influence* (Newbury Park, Calif.: Sage, 1993), p. 40.
49. H. Giles, K. Henwood, N. Coupland, J. Harriman, and J. Coupland, "Language Attitudes and Cognitive Mediation," *Human Communication Research* 18 (1992): 500–527.
50. R. Heslin and T. Alper, "Touch: A Bonding Gesture," in *Nonverbal Interaction,* J.M. Wiemann and R.P. Harrison, eds. (Beverly Hills, Calif.: Sage, 1983), pp. 47–75.
51. Ibid.
52. A.L. Darling, "Talking about Sex in the Classroom: What Can We Learn from the William Kennedy Smith Trial?" Paper presented at the Speech Communication Association meeting, Chicago, 1992.
53. S. Thayer, "Close Encounters," *Psychology Today* 22 (March 1988): 31–36.
54. J. Burgoon, J. Walther, and E. Baesler, "Interpretations, Evaluations, and Consequences of Interpersonal Touch," *Human Communication Research* 19 (1992): 237–263.
55. C.R. Kleinke, "Compliance to Requests Made by Gazing and Touching Experimenters in Field Settings," *Journal of Experimental Social Psychology* 13 (1977): 218–223.
56. F.N. Willis and H.K. Hamm, "The Use of Interpersonal Touch in Securing Compliance," *Journal of Nonverbal Behavior* 5 (1980): 49–55.
57. A.H. Crusco and C.G. Wetzel, "The Midas Touch: Effects of Interpersonal Touch on Restaurant Tipping," *Personality and Social Psychology Bulletin* 10 (1984): 512–517.
58. H. Bakwin, "Emotional Deprivation in Infants," *Journal of Pediatrics* 35 (1949): 512–521.
59. T. Adler, "Congressional Staffers Witness Miracle of Touch," *APA Monitor* (February 1993): 12–13.
60. M.S. Driscoll, D.L. Newman, and J.M. Seal, "The Effect of Touch on the Perception of Counselors," *Counselor Education and Supervision* 27 (1988): 344–354; and J.M. Wilson, "The Value of Touch in Psychotherapy," *American Journal of Orthopsychiatry* 52 (1982): 65–72.
61. V.J. Derlega, R.J. Lewis, S. Harrison, B.A. Winstead, and R. Costanza, "Gender Differences in the Initiation and Attribution of Tactile Intimacy," *Journal of Nonverbal Behavior* 13 (1989): 83–96.
62. D.K. Fromme, W.E. Jaynes, D.K. Taylor, E.G. Hanold, J. Daniell, J.R. Rountree, and M. Fromme, "Nonverbal Behavior and Attitudes Toward Touch," *Journal of Nonverbal Behavior* 13 (1989): 3–14.
63. For a summary, see Knapp and Hall, *Nonverbal Communication in Human Interaction,* pp. 93–132.
64. V. Ritts, M.L. Patterson, and M.E. Tubbs, "Expectations, Impressions, and Judgments of Physically Attractive Students: A Review," *Review of Educational Research* 62 (1992): 413–426.
65. W. Thourlby, *You Are What You Wear* (New York: New American Library, 1978), p. 1.
66. L. Bickman, "The Social Power of a Uniform," *Journal of Applied Social Psychology* 4 (1974): 47–61.
67. S.G. Lawrence and M. Watson, "Getting Others to Help: The Effectiveness of Professional Uniforms in Charitable Fund Raising," *Journal of Applied Communication Research* 19 (1991): 170–185.
68. J.H. Fortenberry, J. Maclean, P. Morris, and M. O'Connell, "Mode of Dress as a Perceptual Cue to Deference," *The Journal of Social Psychology* 104 (1978).
69. L. Bickman, "Social Roles and Uniforms: Clothes Make the Person," *Psychology Today* 7 (April 1974): 48–51.
70. M. Lefkowitz, R.R. Blake, and J.S. Mouton, "Status of Actors in Pedestrian Violation of Traffic Signals," *Journal of Abnormal and Social Psychology* 51 (1955): 704–706.
71. L.E. Temple and K.R. Loewen, "Perceptions of Power: First Impressions of a Woman Wearing a Jacket," *Perceptual and Motor Skills* 76 (1993): 339–348.
72. T.F. Hoult, "Experimental Measurement of Clothing as a Factor in Some Social Ratings of Selected American Men," *American Sociological Review* 19 (1954): 326–327.
73. Hall, *The Hidden Dimension.*
74. M. Hackman and K. Walker, "Instructional Communication in the Televised Classroom: The Effects of System Design and Teacher Immediacy," *Communication Education* 39 (1990): 196–206. See also J.C. McCroskey and V.P. Richmond, "Increasing Teacher Influence through Immediacy," in *Power in the Classroom: Communication, Control, and Concern,* V.P. Richmond and J.C. McCroskey, eds. (Hillsdale, N.J.: Erlbaum, 1992).
75. C. Conlee, J. Olvera, and N. Vagim, "The Relationships among Physician Nonverbal Immediacy and Measures of Patient Satisfaction with Physician Care," *Communication Reports* 6 (1993): 25–33.
76. E. Sadalla, "Identity and Symbolism in Housing," *Environment and Behavior* 19 (1987): 569–587.
77. A. Maslow and N. Mintz, "Effects of Aesthetic Surroundings: Initial Effects of Those Aesthetic Surroundings upon Perceiving 'Energy' and 'Well-Being' in Faces," *Journal of Psychology* 41 (1956): 247–254.

78. R. Levine, "The Pace of Life across Cultures," in *The Social Psychology of Time*, J.E. McGrath, ed., (Newbury Park, Calif.: Sage, 1988).

79. R. Levine and E. Wolff, "Social Time: The Heartbeat of Culture," *Psychology Today* 19 (March 1985): 28–35.

References for Chapter 7

1. L. Barker, R. Edwards, C. Gaines, K. Gladney, and R. Holley, "An Investigation of Proportional Time Spent in Various Communication Activities by College Students," *Journal of Applied Communication Research* 8 (1981): 101–109.

2. Research summarized in A.D. Wolvin and C.G. Coakley, "A Survey of the Status of Listening Training in Some Fortune 500 Corporations," *Communication Education* 40 (1991): 152–164.

3. A.L. Vangelisti, "Couples' Communication Problems: The Counselor's Perspective," *Journal of Applied Communication Research* 22 (1994): 106–126.

4. A.D. Wolvin, "Meeting the Communication Needs of the Adult Learners," *Communication Education* 33 (1984): 267–271.

5. B.D. Sypher, R.N. Bostrom, and J.H. Seibert, "Listening Communication Abilities and Success at Work," *Journal of Business Communication* 26 (1989): 293–303.

6. M.H. Lewis and N.L. Reinsch, Jr., "Listening in Organizational Environments," *Journal of Business Communication* 23 (1988): 49–67.

7. B.A. Pisher, *Interpersonal Communication: The Pragmatics of Human Relationships* (New York: Random House, 1987), p. 390.

8. A.L. Vangelisti, M.L. Knapp, and J.A. Daly, "Conversational Narcissism," *Communication Monographs* 57 (1990): 251–274.

9. K.B. McComb and F.M. Jablin, "Verbal Correlates of Interviewer Empathic Listening and Employment Interview Outcomes," *Communication Monographs* 51 (1984): 367.

10. A. Mulac, J.M. Wiemann, S.J. Widenmann, and T.W. Gibson, "Male/Female Language Differences and Effects in Same-Sex and Mixed-Sex Dyads: The Gender-Linked Language Effect," *Communication Monographs* 55 (1988): 315–335.

11. A. Wolvin and C.G. Coakley, *Listening*, 3rd ed. (Dubuque, Iowa: W.C. Brown, 1988), p. 208.

12. R. Nichols, "Listening Is a Ten-Part Skill," *Nation's Business* 75 (September 1987): 40.

13. J. Brownell, "Perceptions of Effective Listeners: A Management Study," *Journal of Business Communication* 27 (1990): 401–415.

14. N. Spinks and B. Wells, "Improving Listening Power: The Payoff," *Bulletin of the Association for Business Communication* 54 (1991): 75–77.

15. R. Remer and P. DeMesquita, "Teaching and Learning the Skills of Interpersonal Confrontation," in *Intimates in Conflict: A Communication Perspective*, D. Cahn, ed. (Norwood, N.J.: Erlbaum, 1991), p. 242.

16. B. Burleson and W. Samter, "Cognitive Complexity, Communication Skills, and Friendship." Paper presented at the Seventh International Congress on Personal Construct Psychology, Memphis, Tenn., August 1987.

17. See, for example, J. Ekenrode, "Impact of Chronic and Acute Stressors on Daily Reports of Mood," *Journal of Personality and Social Psychology* 46 (1984): 907–918; A.D. Kanner, J.C. Coyne, C. Schaefer, and R.S. Lazarus, "Comparison of Two Modes of Stress Measurement: Daily Hassles and Uplifts versus Major Life Events," *Journal of Behavioral Medicine* 4 (1981): 1–39; A. DeLongis, J.C. Coyne, G. Dakof, S. Polkman, and R.S. Lazarus, "Relation of Daily Hassles, Uplifts, and Major Life Events to Health Status," *Health Psychology* 1 (1982): 119–136.

18. C.J. Notarius and L.R. Herrick, "Listener Response Strategies to a Distressed Other," *Journal of Social and Personal Relationships* 5 (1988): 97–108.

19. W. Samter, B.R. Burleson, and L.B. Murphy, "Comforting Conversations: The Effects of Strategy Type of Evaluations of Messages and Message Producers," *Southern Speech Communication Journal* 52 (1987): 263–284.

20. M. Davidowitz and R.D. Myrick, "Responding to the Bereaved: An Analysis of 'Helping' Statements," *Death Education* 8 (1984): 1–10.

21. Adapted from B.R. Burleson, "Comforting Messages: Features, Functions, and Outcomes," in *Strategic Interpersonal Communication*, J.A. Daly and J.M. Wiemann, eds. (Hillsdale, N.J.: Erlbaum, 1994), p. 140.

22. Research summarized in J. Pearson, *Communication in the Family* (New York: Harper & Row, 1989), pp. 272–275.

23. See J. Bruneau, "Empathy and Listening: A Conceptual Review and Theoretical Directions," *Journal of the International Listening Association* 3 (1989): 1–20; and K.N. Cissna and R. Anderson, "The Contributions of Carl R. Rogers to a Philosophical Praxis of Dialogue," *Western Journal of Speech Communication* 54 (1990): 137–147.

24. C.R. Rogers, "Reflection of Feelings," *Personal-Centered Review* 1 (1986): 375–377.

25. L.A. Hosman, "The Evaluational Consequences of Topic Reciprocity and Self-Disclosure Reciprocity," *Communication Monographs* 54 (1987): 420–435.

26. See, for example, R. Silver and C. Wortman "Coping with Undesirable Life Events," in *Human Helplessness: Theory and Applications*, J. Garber and M. Seligman, eds. (New York: Academic Press, 1981), pp. 279–340; and C.R. Young, D.E. Giles, and M.C. Plantz, "Natural Networks: Help-Giving and Help-Seeking in Two Rural Communities," *American Journal of Community Psychology* 10 (1982): 457–469.

27. See research cited in B. Burleson, "Comforting Communication: Does It Really Matter?" Paper presented at the annual convention of the Western Speech Communication Association, San Diego, 1988; and in B. Burleson, "Comforting Messages: Their Significance and Effects," in *Communicating Strategically: Strategies in Interpersonal Communication*, J.A. Daly and J.M. Wiemann, eds. (Hillside, N.J.: Erlbaum, 1990).

References for Chapter 8

1. C.E. Crowther and G. Stone, *Intimacy: Strategies for Successful Relationships* (Santa Barbara, Calif.: Capra Press, 1986), p. 13.

2. L.M. Register and T.B. Henley, "The Phenomenology of Intimacy," *Journal of Social and Personal Relationships* 9 (1992): 467–481.

3. D. Morris, *Intimate Behavior* (New York: Bantam, 1973), p. 7.

4. L.A. Baxter, "A Dialogic Approach to Relationship Maintenance," in *Communication and Relational Maintenance*, D. Canary and L. Stafford, eds. (San Diego: Academic Press, 1994).

5. E.M. Eisenberg, "Jamming: Transcendence through Organizing," *Communication Research* 17 (1990): 139–164.

6. See, for example, R. Bellah, W.M. Madsen, A. Sullivan, and S.M. Tipton, *Habits of the Heart: Individualism and Commitment in American Life* (Berkeley: University of California Press, 1985); R. Sennett, *The Fall of Public Man: On the Social Psychology of Capitalism* (New York: Random House, 1974); and S. Trenholm and A. Jensen, "The Guarded Self: Toward a Social History of Interpersonal Styles." Paper pre-

sented at the Speech Communication Association meeting, San Juan, Puerto Rico, 1990.

7. Sennett, *The Fall of Public Man*, p. 264.

8. C.A. VanLear, "Testing a Cyclical Model of Communicative Openness in Relationship Development," *Communication Monographs* 58 (1991): 337–361.

9. Baxter, "A Dialogic Approach to Relationship Maintenance."

10. L.A. Baxter, "The Social Side of Personal Relationships: A Dialectical Perspective," in *Social Context and Relationships*, S. Duck, ed. (Newbury Park, Calif.: Sage, 1993).

11. D. Julien and H.J. Markman, "Social Support and Social Networks as Determinants of Individual and Marital Outcomes," *Journal of Social and Personal Relationships* 8 (1991): 549–568.

12. Morris, *Intimate Behavior*, pp. 21–29.

13. J.T. Wood and C.C. Inman, "In a Different Mode: Masculine Styles of Communicating Closeness," *Applied Communication Research* 21 (1993): 279–295.

14. See, for example, K. Dindia and M. Allen, "Sex Differences in Self-Disclosure: A Meta-Analysis," *Psychological Bulletin* 112 (1992): 106–124; D. Ivy, and P. Backlund, *Exploring GenderSpeak* (New York: McGraw-Hill, 1994), p. 219; and J.C. Pearson, L.H. Turner, and W. Todd-Mancillas, *Gender and Communication*, 2d ed. (Dubuque, Iowa: W.C. Brown, 1991), pp. 170–171.

15. S. Swain, "Covert Intimacy in Men's Friendships: Closeness in Men's Friendships," in *Gender in Intimate Relationships: A Microstructural Approach*, B.J. Risman and P. Schwartz, eds. (Belmont, Calif.: Wadsworth, 1989).

16. C.K. Reissman, *Divorce Talk: Women and Men Make Sense of Personal Relationships* (New Brunswick: Rutgers University Press, 1990).

17. J. Adamopoulos, "The Emergence of Interpersonal Behavior: Diachronic and Cross-Cultural Processes in the Evolution of Intimacy," in *Cross-Cultural Interpersonal Communication*, S. Ting-Toomey and F. Korzenny, eds. (Newbury Park, Calif.: Sage, 1991). See also G. Fontaine, "Cultural Diversity in Intimate Intercultural Relationships," in *Intimates in Conflict: A Communication Perspective*, D.D. Cahn, ed. (Hillsdale, N.J.: Erlbaum, 1990).

18. J. Adamopoulos and R.N. Bontempo, "Diachronic Universals in Interpersonal Structures," *Journal of Cross-Cultural Psychology* 17 (1986): 169–189.

19. M. Argyle and M. Henderson, "The Rules of Relationships," in *Understanding Personal Relationships*, S. Duck and D. Perlman, eds. (Beverly Hills, Calif.: Sage, 1985).

20. W.B. Gudykunst and S. Ting-Toomey, *Culture and Interpersonal Communication* (Newbury Park, Calif.: Sage, 1988), pp. 197–198.

21. C.W. Franklin, "'Hey Home—Yo Bro:' Friendship Among Black Men," in *Men's Friendships*, P.M. Nardi, ed. (Newbury Park, Calif.: Sage, 1992).

22. H.C. Triandis, *Culture and Social Behavior* (New York: McGraw-Hill, 1994), p. 230.

23. K. Lewin, *Principles of Topological Psychology* (New York: McGraw-Hill, 1936).

24. See, for example, B.R. Burleson and W.H. Denton, "A New Look at Similarity and Attraction in Marriage: Similarities in Social-Cognitive and Communication Skills as Predictors of Attraction and Satisfaction," *Communication Monographs* 59 (1992): 268–287; and B.R. Burleson, W. Samter, and A.E. Lucchetti, "Similarity in Communication Values as a Predictor of Friendship Choices: Studies of Friends and Best Friends," *Southern Communication Journal* 57 (1992): 260–276.

25. M.L. Knapp and A.L. Vangelisti, *Interpersonal Communication and Human Relationships*, 2d ed. (Boston: Allyn and Bacon, 1992), pp. 32–56.

26. D.J. Canary and L. Stafford, eds., *Communication and Rela-tional Maintenance* (San Diego: Academic Press, 1994).

27. For a discussion of relational development in nonintimate relationships, see A. Jensen and S. Trenholm, "Beyond Intimacy: An Alternative Trajectories Model of Relationship Development." Paper presented at The Speech Communication Association annual meeting, New Orleans, 1988.

28. C.R. Berger, "Communicating under Uncertainty," in M.E. Roloff and G.R. Miller, eds., *Interpersonal Processes: New Directions in Communication Research* (Newbury Park, Calif.: Sage, 1987). See also C.R. Berger, and R.J. Calabrese, "Some Explorations in Initial Interaction and Beyond: Toward a Developmental Theory of Interpersonal Communication," *Human Communication Research* 1 (1975): 99–112.

29. Knapp and Vangelisti, *Interpersonal Communication and Human Relationships*, p. 37.

30. W.B. Gudykunst and S. Ting-Toomey, *Culture and Interpersonal Communication* (Newbury Park, Calif.: Sage, 1988), p. 193.

31. W. Douglas, "Uncertainty, Information-seeking, and Liking during Initial Interaction," *Western Journal of Speech Communication* 54 (1990): 66–81.

32. J.H. Tolhuizen, "Communication Strategies for Intensifying Dating Relationships: Identification, Use and Structure," *Journal of Social and Personal Relationships* 6 (1989): 413–434.

33. R.A. Bell and N.L. Buerkel-Rothfuss, "(S)he Loves Me, S(he) Loves Me Not: Predictors of Relational Information-Seeking in Courtship and Beyond," *Communication Quarterly* 38 (1990): 64–82.

34. L.A. Baxter, "Symbols of Relationship Identity in Relationship Culture," *Journal of Social and Personal Relationships* 4 (1987): 261–280.

35. R.A. Bell and J.G. Healey, "Idiomatic Communication and Interpersonal Solidarity in Friends' Relational Cultures," *Human Communication Research* 18 (1992): 307–335.

36. M. Roloff, C.A. Janiszewski, M.A. McGrath, C.S. Burns, and L.A. Manrai, "Acquiring Resources from Intimates: When Obligation Substitutes for Persuasion," *Human Communication Research* 14 (1988): 364–396.

37. J.K. Burgoon, R. Parrott, B.A. LePoire, D.L. Kelley, J.B. Walther, and D. Perry, "Maintaining and Restoring Privacy through Different Types of Relationships," *Journal of Social and Personal Relationships* 6 (1989): 131–158.

38. J.A. Courtright, F.E. Miller, L.E. Rogers, and D. Bagarozzi, "Interaction Dynamics of Relational Negotiation: Reconciliation versus Termination of Distressed Relationships," *Western Journal of Speech Communication* 54 (1990): 429–453.

39. S. Metts, W.R. Cupach, and R.A. Bejllovec, "'I Love You Too Much to Ever Start Liking You': Redefining Romantic Relationships," *Journal of Social and Personal Relationships* 6 (1989): 259–274.

40. R.L. Conville, *Relational Transitions: The Evolution of Personal Relationships* (New York: Praeger, 1991), p. 80.

41. L.A. Baxter, "Dialectical Contradictions in Relationship Development," *Journal of Social and Personal Relationships* 7 (1990): 69–88. See also D. Goldsmith, "A Dialectic Perspective on the Expression of Autonomy and Connection in Romantic Relationships," *Western Journal of Speech Communication* 54 (1990): 537–556.

42. I. Altman and D.A. Taylor, *Social Penetration: The Development of Interpersonal Relationships* (New York: Holt, Rinehart and Winston, 1973). See also D.A. Taylor and I. Altman, "Communication in Interpersonal Relationships: Social Penetration Processes," in *Interpersonal Processes: New Directions in Communication Research*, M.E. Roloff and G.R. Miller, eds. (Newbury Park, Calif.: Sage, 1987).

43. J. Luft, *Of Human Interaction* (Palo Alto, Calif.: Natural Press, 1969).

44. J.C. Pearson, *Communication in the Family,* 2d ed. (New York: HarperCollins, 1993), pp. 292–296.

45. K. Dindia, M.A. Fitzpatrick, and D.A. Kenny, "Self-Disclosure in Spouse and Stranger Interaction: A Social Relations Analysis." Paper presented at the annual meeting of The International Communication Association, New Orleans, 1988; and S.W. Duck and D.E. Miell, "Charting the Development of Personal Relationships," in *Studying Interpersonal Interaction,* R. Gilmour and S.W. Duck, eds. (N.J. 1991), pp. 133–144.

46. S. Duck, "Some Evident Truths about Conversations in Everyday Relationships: All Communications Are Not Created Equal," *Human Communication Research* 18 (1991): 228–267.

47. Adapted from V.J. Derlega and J. Grezlak, "Appropriateness of Self-Disclosure," in *Self-Disclosure,* G.J. Chelune, ed. (San Francisco: Jossey-Bass, 1979).

48. See V.J. Derlega and A.L. Chaikin, *Sharing Intimacy: What We Reveal to Others and Why* (Englewood Cliffs, N.J.: Prentice-Hall, 1975).

49. H.L. Wintrob, "Self-Disclosure as a Marketable Commodity," *Journal of Social Behavior and Personality* 2 (1987): 77–88.

50. E. Aronson, *The Social Animal,* 4th ed. (New York: W.H. Freeman, 1984), p. 316.

51. F.D. Fincham and T.N. Bradbury, "The Impact of Attributions in Marriage: An Individual Difference Analysis," *Journal of Social and Personal Relationships* 6 (1989): 69–85.

52. V.G. Downs, "Grandparents and Grandchildren: The Relationship between Self-Disclosure and Solidarity in an Intergenerational Relationship," *Communication Research Reports* 5 (1988): 173–179.

53. L.B. Rosenfeld and W.L. Kendrick, "Choosing to Be Open: Subjective Reasons for Self-Disclosing," *Western Journal of Speech Communication* 48 (Fall 1984): 326–343.

54. J.A. Jaksa and M. Pritchard, *Communication Ethics: Methods of Analysis,* 2d ed. (Belmont, Calif.: Wadsworth, 1993), pp. 65–66.

55. D. O'Hair and M.J. Cody, "Interpersonal Deception: The Dark Side of Interpersonal Communication?" in *The Dark Side of Interpersonal Communication,* B.H. Spitzberg and W.R. Cupach, eds. (Hillsdale, N.J.: Erlbaum, 1993).

56. R.E. Turner, C. Edgely, and G. Olmstead, "Information Control in Conversation: Honesty Is Not Always the Best Policy," *Kansas Journal of Sociology* 11 (1975): 69–89.

57. J. Bavelas, "Situations That Lead to Disqualification," *Human Communication Research* 9 (1983): 130–145.

58. D. Hample, "Purposes and Effects of Lying," *Southern Speech Communication Journal* 46 (1980): 33–47.

59. S.A. McCornack and T.R. Levine, "When Lies Are Uncovered: Emotional and Relational Outcomes of Discovered Deception," *Communication Monographs* 57 (1990): 119–138.

60. S. Metts, W.R. Cupach, and T.T. Imahori, "Perceptions of Sexual Compliance-Resisting Messages in Three Types of Cross-Sex Relationships," *Western Journal of Communication* 56 (1992): 1–17.

61. J.B. Bavelas, A. Black, N. Chovil, and J. Mullett, *Equivocal Communication* (Newbury Park, Calif.: Sage, 1990), p. 171.

62. Ibid.

63. M.T. Motley, "Mindfulness in Solving Communicators' Dilemmas," *Communication Monographs* 59 (1992): 306–314.

64. S.B. Shimanoff, "Degree of Emotional Expressiveness as a Function of Face-Needs, Gender, and Interpersonal Relationship," *Communication Reports* 1 (1988): 43–53.

65. D.B. Buller and J.K. Burgoon, "Deception," in *Communicating Strategically: Strategies in Interpersonal Communication* (Hillsdale, N.J.: Erlbaum, 1994).

66. S. Bok, *Lying: Moral Choice in Public and Private Life* (New York: Pantheon, 1978).

67. E.M. Eisenberg and M.G. Witten, "Reconsidering Openness in Organizational Communication," *Academy of Management Review* 12 (1987): 418–428.

68. T.E. Runge and R.L. Archer, "Reactions to the Disclosure of Public and Private Self-Information," *Social Psychology Quarterly* 44 (December 1981): 357–362.

69. C.L. Kleinke, "Effects of Personal Evaluations," in *Self-Disclosure* (San Francisco: Jossey-Bass, 1979).

70. L.B. Rosenfeld and J.R. Gilbert, "The Measurement of Cohesion and Its Relationship to Dimensions of Self-Disclosure in Classroom Settings," *Small Group Behavior* 20 (1989): 291–301.

71. L.B. Rosenfeld and G.I. Bowen, "Marital Disclosure and Marital Satisfaction: Direct-Effect versus Interaction-Effect Models," *Western Journal of Speech Communication* 55 (1991): 69–84.

References for Chapter 9

1. R. Guzley, "Organizational Climate and Communication Climate: Predictors of Commitment to the Organization," *Management Communication Quarterly* 5 (1992): 379–402.

2. D. Pincus, "Communication Satisfaction, Job Satisfaction, and Job Performance," *Human Communication Research* 12 (1986): 395–419.

3. K. Cissna and E. Seiberg, "Patterns of Interactional Confirmation and Disconfirmation," in *Rigor and Imagination: Essays from the Legacy of Gregory Bateson,* C. Wilder-Mott and J.H. Weakland, eds. (New York: Praeger, 1981), pp. 253–287.

4. E. Seiberg, "Confirming and Disconfirming Communication in an Organizational Setting," in *Communication in Organizations,* J. Owen, P. Page, and G. Zimmerman, eds. (St. Paul, Minn.: West, 1976), pp. 129–149.

5. D.A. Infante, B.L. Riddle, C.L. Horvath, and S.A. Tumlin, "Verbal Aggressiveness: Messages and Reasons," *Communication Quarterly* 40 (1992): 116–126.

6. M. Straus, S. Sweet, and Y.M. Vissing, "Verbal Aggression against Spouses and Children in a Nationally Representative Sample of American Families." Paper presented at the annual meeting of The Speech Communication Association, San Francisco, 1989.

7. J.K. Alberts, "A Descriptive Taxonomy of Couples' Complaint Interactions," *Southern Speech Communication Journal* 54 (1989): 125–143.

8. See, for example, A. Holte and L. Wichstrom, "Disconfirmatory Feedback in Families of Schizophrenics," *Scandinavian Journal of Psychology* 31 (1990): 198–211.

9. A.S. Rancer, R.L. Kosberg, and R.A. Baukus, "Beliefs about Arguing as Predictors of Trait Argumentativeness: Implications for Training in Argument and Conflict Management," *Communication Education* 41 (1992): 375–387.

10. E.O. Onyekwere, R.B. Rubin, and D.A. Infante, "Interpersonal Perception and Communication Satisfaction as a Function of Argumentativeness and Ego-Involvement," *Communication Quarterly* 39 (1991): 35–47.

11. Infante et al., "Verbal Aggressiveness."

12. D.A. Infante and W.I. Gorden, "Argumentativeness and Affirming Communicator Style as Predictors of Satisfaction/Dissatisfaction with Subordinates," *Communication Quarterly* 37 (1989): 81–90.

13. A.L. Vangelisti, "Messages that Hurt," in *The Dark Side of Interpersonal Communication,* W.R. Cupach and B.H. Spitzberg, eds. (Hillsdale, N.J.: Erlbaum, 1994).

14. W.W. Wilmot, *Dyadic Communication* (New York: Random House, 1987), pp. 149–158.

15. C. Burggraf and A.L. Sillars, "A Critical Examination of Sex Differences in Marital Communication," *Communication*

Monographs 54 (1987): 276–294. See also D.A. Newton and J.K. Burgoon, "The Use and Consequences of Verbal Strategies during Interpersonal Disagreements," *Human Communication Research* 16 (1990): 477–518.

16. J.L. Hocker and W.W. Wilmot, *Interpersonal Conflict*, 3rd ed. (Dubuque, Iowa: W.C. Brown, 1991), p. 34.

17. Ibid., p. 36.

18. G.H. Stamp, A.L. Vangelisti, and J.A. Daly, "The Creation of Defensiveness in Social Interaction," *Communication Quarterly* 40 (1992): 177–190.

19. J. Powell, *Why Am I Afraid to Tell You Who I Am?* (Chicago: Argus Communications, 1969), p. 12.

20. L. Festinger, *A Theory of Cognitive Dissonance* (Stanford, Calif.: Stanford University Press, 1957).

21. A.M. Nicotera, *Interpersonal Communication in Friend and Mate Relationships* (Albany: State University of New York, 1993).

22. J. Gibb, "Defensive Communication," *Journal of Communication* 11 (September 1961): 141–148. See also W.F. Eadie, "Defensive Communication Revisited: A Critical Examination of Gibb's Theory," *Southern Speech Communication Journal* 47 (1982): 163–177.

23. R.F. Proctor and J.R. Wilcox, "An Exploratory Analysis of Responses to Owned Messages in Interpersonal Communication," *ETC: A Review of General Semantics* 50 (1993): 201–220.

24. Adapted from M. Smith, *When I Say No, I Feel Guilty* (New York: Dial Press, 1975), pp. 93–110.

25. Stamp et al., *Creation of Defensiveness*.

References for Chapter 10

1. J.L. Hocker and W.W. Wilmot, *Interpersonal Conflict*, 3rd ed. (Dubuque, Iowa: W.C. Brown, 1991), pp. 21–30.

2. S. Metts and W. Cupach, "The Influence of Relationship Beliefs and Problem-Solving Responses on Satisfaction in Romantic Relationships," *Human Communication Research* 17 (1990): 170–185.

3. Hocker and Wilmot, *Interpersonal Conflict*, pp. 11–20.

4. For a summary of research detailing the prevalence of conflict in relationships, see D.H. Cloven and M.E. Roloff, "Sense-Making Activities and Interpersonal Conflict: Communicative Cures for the Mulling Blues," *Western Journal of Speech Communication* 55 (1991): 134–158.

5. W.L. Benoit and P.J. Benoit, "Everyday Argument Practices of Naive Social Actors," in *Argument and Critical Practices*, J. Wenzel, ed. (Annandale, Va.: Speech Communication Association, 1987).

6. J.M. Gottman, "Emotional Responsiveness in Marital Conversations," *Journal of Communication* 32 (1982): 108–120. See also W.R. Cupach, "Communication Satisfaction and Interpersonal Solidarity as Outcomes of Conflict Message Strategy Use." Paper presented at The International Communication Association Conference, Boston, May 1982.

7. P. Koren, K. Carlton, and D. Shaw, "Marital Conflict: Relations among Behaviors, Outcomes, and Distress," *Journal of Consulting and Clinical Psychology* 48 (1980): 460–468.

8. Hocker and Wilmot, *Interpersonal Conflict*, p. 37.

9. J.M. Gottman, *Marital Interaction: Experimental Investigations* (New York: Academic Press, 1979). See also D.A. Infante, S.A. Myers, and R.A. Buerkel, "Argument and Verbal Aggression in Constructive and Destructive Family and Organizational Disagreements," *Western Journal of Communication* 58 (1994): 73–84.

10. S.E. Crohan, "Marital Happiness and Spousal Consensus on Beliefs about Marital Conflict: A Longitudinal Investigation," *Journal of Science and Personal Relationships* 9 (1992): 89–102.

11. D.J. Canary, H. Weger, Jr., and L. Stafford, "Couples' Argu-

ment Sequences and Their Associations with Relational Characteristics," *Western Journal of Speech Communication* 55 (1991): 159–179.

12. M.E. Roloff and D.H. Cloven, "The Chilling Effect in Interpersonal Relationships: The Reluctance to Speak One's Mind," in *Intimates in Conflict: A Communication Perspective*, D.D. Cahn, ed. (Hillsdale, N.J.: Erlbaum, 1990).

13. G.R. Birchler, R.L. Weiss, and J.P. Vincent, "Multimethod Analysis of Social Reinforcement Exchange between Maritally Distressed and Nondistressed Spouse and Stranger Dyads," *Journal of Personality and Social Psychology* 31 (1975): 349–360.

14. For a detailed discussion of the drawbacks of nonassertion, see Roloff and Cloven, "The Chilling Effect in Interpersonal Relationships."

15. D.D. Cahn, *Conflict in Intimate Relationships* (New York: Guilford, 1992), p. 100.

16. D.A. Infante, "Aggressiveness," in *Personality and Interpersonal Communication*, J.C. McCroskey and J.A. Daly, eds. (Newbury Park, Calif.: Sage, 1987).

17. D.A. Infante, T.A. Chandler, and J.E. Rudd, "Test of an Argumentative Skill Deficiency Model of Interspousal Violence," *Communication Monographs* 56 (1989): 163–177.

18. "Marital Tiffs Spark Immune Swoon," *Science News*, September 4, 1993, p. 153.

19. T.C. Sabourin, D.A. Infante, and J.E. Rudd, "Verbal Aggression in Marriages: A Comparison of Violent, Distressed but Nonviolent, and Nondistressed Couples," *Human Communication Research* 20 (1993): 245–267.

20. Cahn, *Conflict in Intimate Relationships*, pp. 29–30.

21. B.H. Spitzberg, D.J. Canary, and W.R. Cupach, "A Competence-based Approach to the Study of Interpersonal Conflict," in *Conflict in Personal Relationships*, D.D. Cahn, ed. (Hillsdale, N.J.: Erlbaum, 1994), p. 191.

22. See, for example, G. Bach, *Aggression Lab: The Fair Fight Manual* (Dubuque, Iowa: Kendall-Hunt, 1971), pp. 193–200.

23. J. Jordan and M.E. Roloff, "Acquiring Assistance from Others: The Effect of Indirect Requests and Relational Intimacy on Verbal Compliance," *Human Communication Research* 16 (1990): 519–555.

24. C. Tavris, "Anger Defused," *Psychology Today* 16 (November 1982): 34.

25. Spitzberg, Canary, and Cupach, "A Competence-based Approach," p. 190.

26. Adapted from S. Miller, E.W. Nunnally, and D.B. Wackman, *Alive and Aware: How to Improve Your Relationships through Better Communication* (Minneapolis, Minn.: International Communication Programs, 1975). See also R. Remer and P. deMesquita, "Teaching and Learning the Skills of Interpersonal Confrontation," in Cahn, *Intimates in Conflict*.

27. J.K. Alberts, "An Analysis of Couples' Conversational Complaints," *Communication Monographs* 55 (1988): 184–197.

28. J.K. Alberts and G. Driscoll, "Containment versus Escalation: The Trajectory of Couples' Conversational Complaints," *Western Journal of Communication* 56 (1992): 394–412.

29. Hocker and Wilmot, *Interpersonal Conflict*; M.L. Knapp, L.L. Putnam, and L.J. Davis, "Measuring Interpersonal Conflict in Organizations: Where Do We Go from Here?" *Management Communication Quarterly* 1 (1988): 414–429.

30. C.S. Burggraf and A.L. Sillars, "A Critical Examination of Sex Differences in Marital Communication," *Communication Monographs* 53 (1987): 276–294.

31. J.M. Gottman and L.J. Krokoff, "Marital Interaction and Satisfaction: A Longitudinal View," *Journal of Consulting and Clinical Psychology* 67 (1989): 47–52; G.R. Pike and A.L.

Sillars, "Reciprocity of Marital Communication," *Journal of Social and Personal Relationships* 2 (1985): 303–324.

32. M.A. Fitzpatrick, "A Typological Approach to Communication in Relationships," in *Communication Yearbook 1*, B. Rubin, ed. (New Brunswick, N.J.: Transaction Books, 1977).

33. M.A. Fitzpatrick, J. Fey, C. Segrin, and J.L. Schiff, "Internal Working Models of Relationships and Marital Communication," *Journal of Language and Social Psychology* 12 (1993): 103–131. See also M.A. Fitzpatrick, S. Fallis, and L. Vance, "Multifunctional Coding of Conflict Resolution Strategies in Marital Dyads," *Family Relations* 21 (1982): 61–70.

34. Hocker and Wilmot, *Interpersonal Conflict*, p. 142.

35. Research summarized by D. Tannen in *You Just Don't Understand: Women and Men in Conversation* (New York: William Morrow, 1989), pp. 152–157, 162–165.

36. M.J. Collier, "Conflict Competence within African, Mexican, and Anglo-American Friendships," in *Cross-Cultural Interpersonal Communication*, S. Ting-Toomey and F. Korzenny, eds. (Newbury Park, Calif.: Sage, 1991).

37. See M.J. Papa and E.J. Natalle, "Gender, Strategy Selection, and Discussion Satisfaction in Interpersonal Conflict," *Western Journal of Speech Communication* 52 (1989): 260–272.

38. See, for example, J.C. Pearson, *Gender and Communication*, 2d ed. (Dubuque, Iowa: W.C. Brown, 1991), pp. 183–184.

39. Spitzberg, Canary, and Cupach, "A Competence-based Approach," p. 190.

40. For a more detailed discussion of culture, conflict, and context, see W.B. Gudykunst and S. Ting-Toomey, *Culture and Interpersonal Communication* (Newbury Park, Calif.: Sage, 1988), pp. 153–160.

41. S. Ting-Toomey, "Managing Conflict in Intimate Intercultural Relationships," in *Conflict in Personal Relationships*, D.D. Cahn, ed. (Hillsdale, N.J.: Erlbaum, 1994).

42. See, for example, S. Ting-Toomey, "Rhetorical Sensitivity Style in Three Cultures: France, Japan, and the United States," *Central States Speech Journal* 39 (1988): 28–36.

43. K. Okabe, "Indirect Speech Acts of the Japanese," in *Communication Theory: Eastern and Western Perspectives*, L. Kincaid, ed. (San Diego: Academic Press, 1987), pp. 127–136.

44. G. Fontaine, "Cultural Diversity in Intimate Intercultural Relationships," in Cahn, *Intimates in Conflict*.

45. The following research is summarized in Tannen, *You Just Don't Understand*, p. 160.

46. Collier, "Conflict Competence."

47. A.C. Filley, *Interpersonal Conflict Resolution* (Glenview, Ill.: Scott, Foresman, 1975), p. 23.

48. T. Gordon, *Parent Effectiveness Training* (New York: Wyden, 1970), pp. 236–264.

49. R. Axelrod, *The Evolution of Cooperation* (New York: Basic Books, 1984).

50. M. Kinsley, "It Pays to Be Nice," *Science* 222 (1984): 162.

Glossary

Abstraction ladder   A range of more to less abstract terms describing an event or object.

Accenting   Nonverbal behaviors that emphasize part of a verbal message.

Accommodation   A nonassertive response style in which the communicator submits to a situation rather than attempt to have his or her needs met.

Active listening   Restating a speaker's thoughts and feelings in the listener's own words.

Advising response   A helping response in which the receiver offers suggestions about how the speaker should deal with a problem.

Affection   The social need to care for others and to be cared for by them.

Affinity   The degree to which persons like or appreciate one another.

Ambiguous response   A disconfirming response with more than one meaning, leaving the other party unsure of the responder's position.

Ambushing   A style in which the receiver listens carefully in order to gather information to use in an attack on the speaker.

Analyzing statement   A helping style in which the listener offers an interpretation of a speaker's message.

Androgynous   Possessing both masculine and feminine traits.

Apathy   A defense mechanism in which a person avoids admitting emotional pain by pretending not to care about an event.

Assertion   A direct expression of the sender's needs, thoughts, or feelings, delivered in a way that does not attack the receiver's dignity.

Attending   The process of filtering out some messages and focusing on others.

Attribution   The process of attaching meaning to behavior.

Avoidance   A nonassertive response style in which the communicator is unwilling to confront a situation in which his or her needs are not being met.

Avoiding   A stage of relational development immediately prior to terminating in which the parties minimize contact with one another.

Back   The region in which behavior will not be perceived by an audience. *See* Front.

Behavior   Observable actions that can be interpreted as communicative messages.

Behavioral description   An account that refers only to observable phenomena.

Body orientation   Type of nonverbal communication characterized by the degree to which we face forward or away from someone.

Bonding   A stage of relational development in which the parties make symbolic public gestures to show that their relationship exists.

Breadth   First dimension of self-disclosure involving the range of subjects being discussed.

"But" statements   Statements in which the word "but" cancels out the expression that preceded it.

Certainty   Attitude behind messages that dogmatically imply that the speaker's position is correct and that the other person's ideas are not worth considering. Likely to generate a defensive response.

Channel   The medium through which a message passes from sender to receiver.

Chronemics   The study of how humans use and structure time.

Circumscribing   A stage of relational development in which partners begin to reduce the scope of their contact and commitment to one another.

Cliché   A ritualized, stock statement delivered in response to a social situation.

Cognitive complexity   The ability to construct a variety of frameworks for viewing an issue.

Cognitive conservatism   The tendency to seek and attend to information that conforms to an existing self-concept.

Cognitive dissonance   An inconsistency between two conflicting pieces of information, attitudes, or behaviors. Communicators strive to reduce dissonance, often through defense mechanisms that maintain an idealized presenting image.

Communication   A continuous, irreversible, transactive process involving communicators who occupy different but overlapping environments and are simultaneously senders and receivers of messages, many of which are distorted by physical and psychological noise.

Communication climate   The emotional tone of a relationship between two or more individuals.

Communication competence   The ability to accomplish one's personal goals in a manner that maintains a relationship on terms that are acceptable to all parties.

Compensation   A defense mechanism in which a person stresses a strength in one area to camouflage a shortcoming in some other area.

Competitive symmetry   A relational condition in which both parties strive to gain control.

Complaining   A disconfirming response that implicitly or explicitly attributes responsibility for the speaker's displeasure to another party.

Complementary communication   Communication in which one partner consistently occupies a powerful position, while the other responds in a subservient manner.

Complementary conflict style   A relational conflict style in which partners use different but mutually reinforcing behaviors.

Complementary relationship   One in which the distribution of power is unequal, with one party occupying a "one-up" and the other a "one-down" position.

Complementing   Nonverbal behavior that reinforces a verbal message.

Compromise   An approach to conflict resolution in which both parties attain at least part of what they wanted through self-sacrifice.

Confirming communication   A message that expresses caring or respect for another person.

Conflict   An expressed struggle between at least two inter-dependent parties who perceive incompatible goals, scarce rewards, and interference from the other party in achieving their goals.

Conflict ritual   An unacknowledged repeating pattern of interlocking behavior used by participants in a conflict.

Congruency   The matching of verbal and nonverbal mes-sages sent by a communicator.

Connotation   The emotional associations of a term.

Consequence statement   An explanation of the results that follow from either the behavior of the person to whom the message is addressed or from the speaker's interpreta-tion of the addressee's behavior. Consequence statements can describe what happens to the speaker, the addressee, or others.

Content message   A message that communicates informa-tion about the subject being discussed. *See also* Relational message.

Contradicting   Nonverbal behavior that is inconsistent with a verbal message.

Control   The social need to influence others.

Controlling communication   Messages in which the sender tries to impose some sort of outcome on the receiver, usually resulting in a defensive reaction.

Convergence   The process of adapting one's speech style to match that of others with whom the communicator wants to identify. *See also* Divergence.

Conversational control   The power to determine who speaks in a conversation.

Counterfeit questions   Questions that disguise the speaker's true motives, which do not include a genuine desire to understand the other person. *See* Sincere questions.

Crazymaking   *See* Passive aggression.

Debilitative emotions   Emotions that prevent a person from functioning effectively.

Deception cues   Nonverbal behaviors that signal the untruthfulness of a verbal message.

Decision control   The power to influence which person in a relationship decides what activities will take place.

Decoding   The process in which a receiver attaches mean-ing to a message. Synonymous with *Interpreting*.

De-escalatory conflict spiral   A communication spiral in which the parties slowly lessen their dependence on one another, withdraw, and become less invested in the relation-ship.

Defense mechanism   A psychological device used to maintain a presenting self-image that an individual believes is threatened.

Defensive listening   A response style in which the receiver perceives a speaker's comments as an attack.

Defensiveness   The attempt to protect a presenting image a person believes is being attacked.

Denotation   The objective, emotion-free meaning of a term. *See also* Connotation.

Depth   A dimension of self-disclosure involving a shift from relatively nonrevealing messages to more personal ones.

Descriptive communication   Messages that describe the speaker's position without evaluating others. Synonymous with "I" language.

Desired self   The person we would like to be. It may be identical to or different from the perceived and presenting selves.

Dialectical tension   The state that exists when two oppos-ing or incompatible forces exist simultaneously.

Differentiating   A stage of relational development in which the parties re-establish their individual identities after having bonded together.

Direct aggression   A criticism or demand that threatens the face of the person at whom it is directed.

Disconfirming communication   A message that expresses a lack of caring or respect for another person.

Disfluency   A nonlinguistic verbalization, for example, um, er, ah.

Displacement   A defense mechanism in which a person vents hostile or aggressive feelings on a target that cannot strike back, instead of on the true target.

Divergence   Speaking mannerisms that emphasize a com-municator's differences from others. *See also* Convergence.

Double message   Contradiction between a verbal message and one or more nonverbal cues.

Dyad   Two individuals communicating. The interaction may or may not be interpersonal in nature.

Emblems   Deliberate nonverbal behaviors with precise meanings, known to virtually all members of a cultural group.

Emotive language   Language that conveys the sender's atti-tude rather than simply offer an objective description.

Empathy   The ability to project oneself into another per-son's point of view, so as to experience the other's thoughts and feelings.

Encoding   The process of putting thoughts into symbols, most commonly words.

Ends   The ultimate goal a person is seeking. Ends are often confused with means, resulting in unproductive con-flicts. *See also* Means.

Environment   The field of experiences that leads a person to make sense of another's behavior. Environments consist of physical characteristics, personal experiences, relational history, and cultural background.

Equality   A type of supportive communication described by Gibb, suggesting that the sender regards the receiver as worthy of respect.

Equivocal language   Ambiguous language that has two or more equally plausible meanings.

Escalatory conflict spiral   A communication spiral in which one attack leads to another until the initial skir-mish escalates into a full-fledged battle.

Euphemisms   Pleasant terms substituted for blunt ones in order to soften the impact of unpleasant information.

Evaluative communication   Messages in which the sender judges the receiver in some way, usually resulting in a defensive response.

Exchange theory   A socioeconomic theory of relational development that suggests people seek relationships in which the rewards they receive from others are greater than or equal to the costs they encounter.

Experimenting   An early stage in relational development, consisting of a search for common ground. If the experimentation is successful, the relationship will progress to intensifying. If not, it may go no further.

External noise   Factors outside the receiver that interfere with the accurate reception of a message.

Face   The socially approved identity that a communicator tries to present. *See also* Impression management.

Face-threatening act   Behavior by another that is perceived as attacking an individual's presenting image, or face.

Facework   Verbal and nonverbal behavior designed to create and maintain a communicator's face and the face of others.

Facilitative emotions   Emotions that contribute to effective functioning.

Factual statement   A statement based on direct observation of sense data.

Fallacy of approval   The irrational belief that it is vital to win the approval of virtually every person a communicator deals with.

Fallacy of catastrophic expectations   The irrational belief that the worst possible outcome will probably occur.

Fallacy of causation   The irrational belief that emotions are caused by others and not by the person who has them.

Fallacy of helplessness   The irrational belief that satisfaction in life is determined by forces beyond one's control.

Fallacy of overgeneralization   Irrational beliefs in which (1) conclusions (usually negative) are based on limited evidence or (2) communicators exaggerate their shortcomings.

Fallacy of perfection   The irrational belief that a worthwhile communicator should be able to handle every situation with complete confidence and skill.

Fallacy of shoulds   The irrational belief that people should behave in the most desirable way.

Feedback   The discernible response of a receiver to a sender's message.

Feeling statement   An expression of the sender's emotions that results from interpretation of sense data.

Front   Publicly visible behavior. *See also* Back, Face.

Gestures   Motions of the body, usually hands or arms, that have communicative value.

Gibb categories   Six sets of contrasting styles of verbal and nonverbal behavior. Each set describes a communication style that is likely to arouse defensiveness and a contrasting style that is likely to prevent or reduce it. Developed by Jack Gibb.

Hearing   The physiological dimension of listening.

High-context cultures   Cultures that avoid direct use of language, relying on the context of a message to convey meaning.

"I" language   A statement that describes the speaker's reaction to another person's behavior without making judgments about its worth. *See also* "You" language.

Ideal self   The person each wishes to be. *See also* Perceived self and Presenting self.

Illustrators   Nonverbal behaviors that accompany and support verbal messages.

Impersonal communication   Behavior that treats others as objects rather than individuals. *See* Interpersonal communication.

Impersonal response   A disconfirming response that is superficial or trite.

Impervious response   A disconfirming response that ignores another person's attempt to communicate.

Impression management   Strategies used by communicators to influence the way others view them.

Inclusion   The social need to feel a sense of belonging in some relationship with others.

Incongruous response   A disconfirming response in which two messages, one of which is usually nonverbal, contradict one another.

Indirect communication   An oblique way of expressing wants or needs in order to save face for the recipient.

Influence   *See* Control.

Initiating   The first stage in relational development, in which the parties express interest in one another.

Insensitive listening   Failure to recognize the thoughts or feelings that are not directly expressed by a speaker; instead, accepting the speaker's words at face value.

Insulated listening   A style in which the receiver ignores undesirable information.

Instrumental goals   Goals aimed at getting others to behave in desired ways.

Integrating   A stage of relational development in which the parties begin to take on a single identity.

Intensifying   A stage of relational development following integrating, in which the parties move toward integration by increasing the amount of contact and the breadth and depth of self-disclosure.

Intention statement   A description of where the speaker stands on an issue, what he or she wants, or how he or she plans to act in the future.

Interaction constructs   Perceptual schema that categorize people according to their social behavior.

Interactive communication model   A characterization of communication as a two-way event in which sender and receiver exchange messages in response to one another.

Interpersonal communication   Communication in which the parties consider one another as unique individuals rather than as objects. It is characterized by minimal use of stereotyped labels; unique, idiosyncratic social rules; and a high degree of information exchange.

Interpersonal relationship   An association in which the parties meet each other's social needs to a greater or lesser degree.

Interpretation   The process of attaching meaning to sense data; synonymous with *Decoding*.

Interrupting response   A disconfirming response in which one communicator interrupts another.

Intimacy   A state of personal sharing arising from physical, intellectual, and/or emotional contact.

Intimate distance   One of Hall's four distance zones, ranging from skin contact to eighteen inches.

Irrelevant response   A disconfirming response in which one communicator's comments bear no relationship to the previous speaker's ideas.

"It" statements   Statements that replace the personal pronoun "I" with the less immediate word "it," often reducing the speaker's acceptance of responsibility for the statement.

Johari Window   A model that describes the relationship between self-disclosure and self-awareness.

Judging response   A reaction in which the receiver evaluates the sender's message either favorably or unfavorably.

Kinesics   The study of body position and motion.

Leakage   Nonverbal behaviors that reveal information a communicator does not disclose verbally.

Lie   A deliberate attempt to hide or misrepresent the truth.

Linear communication model   A characterization of communication as a one-way event in which a message flows from sender to receiver.

Linguistic determinism   The theory that a culture's world view is unavoidably shaped and reflected by the language its members speak.

Linguistic relativism   A more moderate form of linguistic determinism which argues that language exerts a strong influence on the perceptions of the people who speak it.

Listening   Process that consists of hearing, attending, understanding, responding, and remembering an aural message.

Lose–lose problem solving   An approach to conflict resolution in which neither side achieves its goals. Sometimes lose–lose outcomes result from both parties seeking a win–lose victory over one another. In other cases, the parties settle for a lose–lose outcome (for example, compromise) because they cannot find any better alternative.

Low-context cultures   Cultures that use language primarily to express thoughts, feelings, and ideas as clearly and logically as possible.

Manipulators   Movements in which one part of the body grooms, massages, rubs, holds, fidgets, pinches, picks, or otherwise manipulates another part.

Means   Ways of achieving one's ends. There are usually several means to an end. Unproductive conflicts often occur when people argue over a limited number of means rather than focus on finding the best ones to achieve their ends.

Membership constructs   Perceptual schema that categorize people according to the groups to which they belong.

Message   Information sent from a sender to a receiver.

Metacommunication   Messages (usually relational) that refer to other messages: communication about communication.

Microexpressions   Brief facial expressions.

Mixed emotions   Emotions that are combinations of primary emotions. Some mixed emotions can be expressed in single words (that is, *awe, remorse*), whereas others require more than one term (that is, *embarrassed and angry, relieved and grateful*).

Negotiation   A process in which two or more parties discuss specific proposals in order to find a mutually acceptable agreement.

Neutrality   A defense-arousing behavior described by Gibb in which the sender expresses indifference toward a receiver.

Neutralized symmetry   A relational condition in which the balance of control shifts between the partners according to the issue at hand.

Noise   External, physiological, and psychological distractions that interfere with the accurate transmission and reception of a message.

Nonassertion   The inability to express one's thoughts or feelings when necessary. Nonassertion may be due to a lack of confidence or communication skill or both.

Nonverbal communication   Messages expressed by other than linguistic means.

One-way communication   Communication in which a receiver provides no feedback to a sender.

Operational definition   A definition that refers to observable referents rather than using other words with no apparent concrete meanings.

Organization   The stage in the perception process that involves arranging data in a meaningful way.

Paralanguage   Nonlinguistic means of vocal expression: rate, pitch, tone, and so on.

Parallel conflict style   A relational conflict style in which the approach of the partners varies from one situation to another.

Parallel relationship   One in which the balance of power shifts from one party to the other, according to the situation.

Paraphrasing   Restating a speaker's thoughts and feelings in the listener's own words.

Passive aggression   An indirect expression of aggression, delivered in a way that allows the sender to maintain a façade of kindness.

Passive listening   *See* One-way communication.

Perceived self   The person we believe ourselves to be in moments of candor. It may be identical with or different from the presenting and ideal self.

Perception checking   A three-part method for verifying the accuracy of interpretations, including a description of the sense data, two possible interpretations, and a request for confirmation of the interpretations.

Perceptual schema   Cognitive frameworks that allow individuals to organize perceptual data that they have selected from the environment.

Personal distance   One of Hall's four distance zones, ranging from eighteen inches to four feet.

Personality   A relatively consistent set of traits exhibited by a person across a variety of situations.

Phonological rules   Linguistic rules that govern how sounds are combined to form words.

Physical avoidance   A defense mechanism whereby the person steers clear of people who attack a presenting self to avoid dissonance.

Physical constructs   Perceptual schema that categorize people according to their appearance.

Physiological noise   Biological factors in the receiver that interfere with accurate reception of a message.

Pillow method   A method for understanding an issue from several perspectives rather than with an egocentric "I'm right and you're wrong" attitude.

Posture   The way in which individuals carry themselves—erect, slumping, and so on.

Powerless speech mechanisms   Ways of speaking that may reduce perceptions of a communicator's power.

Pragmatic rules   Linguistic rules that help communicators understand how messages may be used and interpreted in a given context.

Presenting self   The image a person presents to others. It may be identical with or different from the perceived and ideal self.

Primary emotions   Basic emotions. Some researchers have identified eight primary emotions: joy, acceptance, fear, surprise, sadness, disgust, anger, and anticipation.

Problem orientation   A supportive style of communication described by Gibb in which the communicators focus on working together to solve their problems instead of trying to impose their own solutions on one another.

Prompting   Using silences and brief statements of encouragement to draw out a speaker.

Proprioceptive stimuli   Sensations activated by movement of internal tissues (for example, upset stomach, pounding heart).

Provisionalism   A supportive style of communication described by Gibb in which the sender expresses a willingness to consider the other person's position.

Proxemics   The study of how people and animals use space.

Pseudolistening   An imitation of true listening in which the receiver's mind is elsewhere.

Psychological constructs   Perceptual schema that categorize people according to their apparent personalities.

Psychological noise   Forces within a communicator that interfere with the ability to express or understand a message accurately.

Public distance   One of Hall's four distance zones, extending outward from twelve feet.

Punctuation   The process of determining the causal order of events.

Questioning response   A style of helping in which the receiver seeks additional information from the sender. Some questioning responses are really disguised advice.

Rationalization   A defense mechanism in which logical but untrue explanations maintain an unrealistic desired or presenting self-image.

Receiver   One who notices and attends to a message.

Reference groups   Groups against which we compare ourselves, thereby influencing our self-concept and self-esteem.

Reflected appraisal   The theory that a person's self-concept matches the way the person believes others regard him or her.

Regression   A defense mechanism in which a person avoids assuming responsibility by pretending that he or she is unable to do something instead of admitting to being simply unwilling.

Regulating   One function of nonverbal communication, in which nonverbal cues control the flow of verbal communication among individuals.

Relational conflict style   A pattern of managing disagreements that repeats itself over time in a relationship.

Relational message   A message that expresses the social relationship between two or more individuals.

Relationship   *See* Interpersonal relationship.

Relative words   Words that gain their meaning by comparison.

Remembering   Ability to recall information.

Repeating   Nonverbal behaviors that duplicate the content of a verbal message.

Repression   A defense mechanism in which a person avoids facing an unpleasant situation or fact by denying its existence.

Respect   The social need to be held in esteem by others.

Responding   Giving observable feedback to the speaker.

Role constructs   Perceptual schema that categorize people according to their social position.

Sapir–Whorf hypothesis   Theory of linguistic determinism in which language is determined by a culture's perceived reality.

Sarcasm   A potential defensive reaction in which an individual redirects a perceived threat to his or her presenting self by attacking the critic with contemptuous, often ironical remarks.

Selection   The first stage in the perception process in which some data are chosen to attend to and others to ignore.

Selective listening   A listening style in which the receiver responds only to messages that interest him or her.

Self-actualization   One of Maslow's five needs; the desire to reach one's maximum potential.

Self-concept   The relatively stable set of perceptions each individual holds of himself or herself.

Self-disclosure   The process of deliberately revealing information about oneself that is significant and that would not normally be known by others.

Self-esteem   The degree of regard a person holds for himself or herself.

Self-fulfilling prophecy   A prediction or expectation of an event that makes the outcome more likely to occur than would otherwise have been the case.

Self-monitoring   The process of attending to one's behavior and using these observations to shape the way one behaves.

Self-serving bias   The tendency to interpret and explain information in a way that casts the perceiver in the most favorable manner.

Self-talk   The nonvocal process of thinking. On some level, self-talk occurs as a person interprets another's behavior.

Semantic rules   Rules that govern the meaning of language, as opposed to its structure. *See also* Syntactic rules.

Sender   The creator of a message.

Sex role   The social orientation that governs behavior, rather than the biological gender.

Significant other   A person whose opinion is important enough to affect one's self-concept strongly.

Sincere questions   Questions that are aimed at soliciting information that enable the asker to understand the other person. *See* Counterfeit questions.

Social comparison   Evaluation of oneself in terms of or by comparison to others.

Social distance   One of Hall's distance zones, ranging from four to twelve feet.

Social penetration   A model that describes relationships in terms of their breadth and depth.

Spiral   A reciprocal communication pattern in which each person's message reinforces the other's. *See also* De-escalatory conflict spiral, Escalatory conflict spiral.

Spontaneity   A supportive communication behavior described by Gibb in which the sender expresses a message without any attempt to manipulate the receiver.

Stage-hogging   A listening style in which the receiver is more concerned with making his or her own point than in understanding the speaker.

Stagnating   A stage of relational development characterized by declining enthusiasm and standardized forms of behavior.

Static evaluation   The tendency to view people or relationships as unchanging.

Stereotyping   Categorizing individuals according to a set of characteristics assumed to belong to all members of a group.

Strategy   A defense-arousing style of communication described by Gibb in which the sender tries to manipulate or deceive a receiver.

Submissive symmetry   A relational condition in which both parties strive to shift control to the other person.

Substituting   Nonverbal behavior that takes the place of a verbal message.

Superiority   A defense-arousing style of communication described by Gibb in which the sender states or implies that the receiver is not worthy of respect.

Supportive responses   Responses that demonstrate solidarity with a speaker's situation.

Symmetrical communication   Communication in which the power is distributed evenly between the parties.

Symmetrical conflict style   A relational conflict style in which both partners use the same tactics.

Symmetrical relationship   A relationship in which the partners seek an equal amount of control.

Sympathy   Compassion for another's situation. *See also* Empathy.

Syntactic rules   Rules that govern the ways symbols can be arranged, as opposed to the meanings of those symbols. *See also* Semantic rules.

Tangential response   A disconfirming response that uses the speaker's remark as a starting point for a shift to a new topic.

Terminating   The concluding stage of relational development, characterized by the acknowledgement of one or both parties that the relationship is over.

Territory   A stationary area claimed by an individual.

Transactional communication model   A characterization of communication as the simultaneous sending and receiving of messages in an ongoing, irreversible process.

Two-way communication   An exchange of information in which the receiver deliberately provides feedback to a sender.

Uncertainty reduction   The process of getting to know others by gaining more information about them.

Understanding   Occurs when sense is made of a message.

Verbal abuse   A disconfirming response intended to cause psychological pain to another.

Verbal aggression   A defense mechanism in which a person avoids facing unpleasant information by verbally attacking the confronting source.

"We" statement   Statement that implies that the issue is the concern and responsibility of both the speaker and receiver of a message. *See also* "I" language and "You" language.

Whorf–Sapir hypothesis   The theory that the structure of a language shapes the world view of its users.

Win–lose problem solving   An approach to conflict resolution in which one party reaches its goal at the expense of the other.

Win–win problem solving   An approach to conflict resolution in which the parties work together to satisfy all their goals.

"You" language   A statement that expresses or implies a judgment of the other person. *See also* Evaluative communication, "I" language.

Photo Credits

Literary Credits

PREFACE   xiii Peanuts by Schultz © 1970. Reprint by permission of UFS, Inc.

CHAPTER 1   4 "The Silencing" © 1973 by Newsweek, Inc. All rights reserved. Reprinted by permission. 9 Table: "National Preferences in Business and Communication Education," by D. B. Curtis, J. L. Winsor, and R. D. Stephens, Communication Education 38 (1989): 6–14 25 Excerpt: From The Accidental Tourist by Anne Tyler. © 1985 by Anne Tyler Modarressi. Reprinted by permission Alfred A. Knopf, Inc. 26 Drawing by Mike Ewers. Reprinted by permission. 29 Excerpt pp.32–33 from That's Not What I Meant by Deborah Tannen. © 1986 by Deborah Tannen. By permission of William Morrow and Company, Inc. 39 Calvin and Hobbs by Watterson: © 1994 by Watterson. Dist. Universal Press Syndicate. Reprinted with permission. All rights reserved.

CHAPTER 2   50 Poem "Premier Artist" by Lenni S. Goldstein. Used by permission of the poet. 53 Ziggy by Tom Wilson. © 1986 Universal Press Syndicate. Reprinted by permission. All rights reserved. 54 & 55 "Cipher in the Snow" by Jean Mizer from Today's Education, 11–1964. Used by permission of Jean Todhunter Mizer and Today's Education. 56 Drawing by Schoenbaum: © 1990 The New Yorker Magazine, Inc. 65 CATHY by Guisewite: © 1994 Reprinted by permission Universal Press Syndicate. All rights reserved. 67 Excerpt: From Crazy Talk, Stupid Talk by Neil Postman © 1976. Used courtesy of Neil Postman. 69 Drawing by Gahan Wilson: © Gahan Wilson. Reprinted by permission. 72 Drawing by Dana Fradon, © 1983 The New Yorker Magazine, Inc. 75 Self-Monitoring Inventory from "The Many Me's of the Self-Monitor" by Mark Snyder. Published in Psychology Today 1983. Reprinted courtesy Mark Snyder. 77 & 78 Excerpt: From Person to Person by Barry Stevens. © 1967 Real People Press. Reprinted courtesy of publisher.

CHAPTER 3   88 Drawing by Escher. © 1995 M. C. Escher/Condon Art-Baarn-Holland. All rights reserved. 90 Cathy by Cathy Guisewite; © 1986. Reprinted by permission Universal Press Syndicate. All rights reserved. 94 Farcus by Walsglass/Coulthart; © 1993 Farcus Cartoons. Dist. by Universal Press Syndicate. Reprinted with permission. All rights reserved. 97 Excerpt: From Crazy Talk, Stupid Talk by Neil Postman; © 1976. Used courtesy of Neil Postman. 99 Excerpt: From "Trying on Old Age" by Holly Hall. Reprinted with permission from Psychology Today Magazine. © 1988 (Sussex Publishers, Inc.)

100 Sally Forth by Greg Howard; © 1982. Reprinted with special permission of North American Syndicate, Inc. 101 Excerpt: From That's Not What I Meant by Deborah Tannen. © 1986 by Deborah Tannen. Reprinted by permission of William Mor-row & Company, Inc. 102 Excerpt: By David Suzuki from Breaking Through: A Canadian Literary Mosaic edited by John Borovilos. © 1990 Prentice Hall. Used courtesy of David Suzuki. 107 Drawing by John Jonik. Published in Psychology Today 1984. Reprinted by permission of the John Jonik. 109 & 110 Article: "Field Experiment: Preparation for the Changing Police Role" by Fred Ferguson. Used courtesy of the author. 113 Drawing by Lorenz. Reprinted with the permission from the Saturday Evening Post. 118 Excerpt: From Siblings Without Rivalry by Adele Faber and Elaine Mazlish. © 1987 by W.W. Norton and Company, Inc. All rights reserved. Reprinted by permission. 119 Calvin and Hobbs by Watterson. © 1994 by Watterson. Dist. by Universal Press Syndicate. Reprinted with permission. All rights reserved.

CHAPTER 4   135 Drawing by Weber. © 1981 The New Yorker Magazine, Inc. 151 Drawing by R. Guindon © 1990. Used courtesy of Richard Guindon. 159 Drawing by Steve Delmonte. © 1990 by Steve Delmonte. Used by permission.

CHAPTER 5   172 Calvin and Hobbs by Watterson; © 1992 by Watterson. Dist. Universal Press Syndicate. Reprinted with permission. All rights reserved. 175 Article: "Penn Debates the Meaning of Water Buffalo" by David G. Savage. © 1993 Los Angeles Times. Reprinted by permission. 176 Table: Adapted from W. B. Pearce and V. Cronen, Communication, Action, and Meaning. © 1980 Preager Publishers. 179 & 180 Article: "The Great Mokusatsu Mistake" by William Coughlin. © 1953 by Harper's Magazine. All rights reserved. Reproduced from the March issue by special permission. 185 Excerpt: From That's Not What I Meant by Deborah Tannen. © 1986 by Deborah Tannen. By permission of William Morrow and Company, Inc. 186 Drawing by Schochet published in The Wall Street Journal. Permission by Cartoon Features Syndicate. 187 Excerpt: From Conversation and Communication by J. A. M. Meerloo. Reprinted by permission of International Universities Press, Inc. © 1952 by International Universities Press. 189 Cathy by Cathy Guisewite. © 1983 Universal Press Syndicate. All rights reserved. Reprinted by permission. 195 Article: "The Husbands in My Life" by Mary Graham

Index

MICROSOFT® *CINEMANIA*® '95

Harcourt Interactive is pleased to offer to users of *Looking Out, Looking In*, the best-selling Microsoft *Cinemania '95* at great savings! As entertaining as the movies it presents, Microsoft *Cinemania '95* is your personal guide to the world's films — complete with reviews, video and audio clips, biographies, and cinema insight. Covering films from the past 80 years of moviemaking — from famous masterpieces to infamous duds — *Cinemania '95* includes more than 19,000 reviews by such renowned critics as Roger Ebert, Leonard Maltin, and Pauline Kael. But Cinemania is much more than a collection of reviews. You can also access photo portraits, motion picture stills, dialog clips, tracks of film music, and more than 20 video scenes. *Cinemania '95* will even tell you about ratings and Academy Award winners and nominees. So no matter what you're interested in finding out, it's here.

Many professors and students analyze interpersonal communication by analyzing situations set up in movies. This CD ROM software can help you locate the movies that will illustrate the interpersonal concepts you want to analyze.

30% OFF RETAIL!

Harcourt Interactive is offering this software to students at a greatly reduced price. Compare our price with your local computer store!

If you wish to order this outstanding CD ROM software, please complete the attached order form and mail it to the address listed below or call 1-800-782-4479 and mention reference number 32363.

Please send me the following CD-ROM and charge my credit card $34.95 plus applicable tax and shipping.

Indicate Credit Card ( ) AMEX ( ) MasterCard ( ) VISA

Indicate your preference:

Credit card number _____

( ) Macintosh (ISBN 0-15-503559-2)

Name as shown on card _____

( ) Windows (ISBN 0-15-503558-4)

Expiration date _____

Your signature _____

Shipping information (allow 3-4 weeks for delivery)

Name _____

Address _____ Apt. # _____

City _____ State _____.

Zip Code _____ Phone (_____) _____

Please mail this form to:

Harcourt Interactive
Harcourt Brace College Publishers
Reference #32363
Order Fulfillment Department
6277 Sea Harbor Drive
Orlando, FL 32887